Mike Meyers'

CompTIA A+® Guide: PC Technician

(Exams 220-602, 220-603, & 220-604)

Mike Meyers

New York   Chicago   San Francisco
Lisbon   London   Madrid   Mexico City   Milan
New Delhi   San Juan   Seoul   Singapore   Sydney   Toronto

The McGraw·Hill Companies

Cataloging-in-Publication Data is on file with the Library of Congress

Sponsoring Editor
TIMOTHY GREEN

Editorial Supervisor
PATTY MON

Project Editor
LAURA STONE

Acquisitions Coordinator
JENNIFER HOUSH

Technical Editor
ED JENNINGS

Copy Editors
LAURA STONE, LISA THEOBALD,
LEEANN PICKRELL, ANDY CARROLL

Proofreaders
ANDREA FOX, PAUL TYLER

Indexer
JACK LEWIS

Production Supervisor
JAMES KUSSOW

Composition
INTERNATIONAL TYPESETTING AND
COMPOSITION

Illustration
INTERNATIONAL TYPESETTING AND
COMPOSITION

Art Director, Cover
JEFF WEEKS

Cover Designer
JEFF WEEKS

Cover Photograph
KEN DAVIES/MASTERFILE

Mike Meyers' CompTIA A+® Guide: PC Technician (Exams 220-602, 220-603, & 220-604)

1234567890 QPD QPD 01987

ISBN-13: Book P/N 978-0-07-226359-6
and CD P/N 978-0-07-226360-2
of set 978-0-07-226358-9

ISBN-10: Book P/N 0-07-226359-8
and CD P/N 0-07-226360-1
of set 0-07-226358-X

■ About the Author

Mike Meyers, lovingly called the "AlphaGeek" by those who know him, is the industry's leading authority on CompTIA A+ certification. He is the president and co-founder of Total Seminars, LLC, a provider of PC and network repair seminars, books, videos, and courseware for thousands of organizations throughout the world. Mike has been involved in the computer and network repair industry since 1977 as a technician, instructor, author, consultant, and speaker. Author of numerous popular PC books and videos, including the best-selling *CompTIA A+ Certification All-in-One Exam Guide,* Mike is also the series editor for the highly successful Mike Meyers' Certification Passport series, the Mike Meyers' Computer Skills series, and the Mike Meyers' Guide to series, all published by McGraw-Hill/Osborne.

■ About the Contributors

A number of people contributed to the development of *Mike Meyers' A+ Guide to Managing and Troubleshooting PCs.*

Scott Jernigan wields a mighty red pen as Editor in Chief for Total Seminars. With a Master of Arts degree in Medieval History, Scott feels as much at home in the musty archives of London as he does in the warm CRT glow of Total Seminars' Houston headquarters. After fleeing a purely academic life, he dove headfirst into IT, working as an instructor, editor, and writer. Scott has edited and contributed to more than a dozen books on computer literacy, hardware, operating systems, networking, and certification. His latest book is *Computer Literacy – Your Ticket to IC³ Certification* (2006). Scott co-authored the best-selling *A+ Certification All-in-One Exam Guide,* 5th edition, and the *A+ Guide to Managing and Troubleshooting PCs* (both with Mike Meyers). He has taught computer classes all over the United States, including stints at the United Nations in New York and the FBI Academy in Quantico.

Alec Fehl (BM, Music Production and Engineering, and MCSE, A+, NT-CIP, ACE, ACI certified) has been a technical trainer, computer consultant, and Web application developer since 1999. After graduating from the prestigious Berklee College of Music in Boston, he set off for Los Angeles with the promise of becoming a rock star. After ten years gigging in Los Angeles, teaching middle-school math, and auditioning for the Red Hot Chili Peppers (he didn't get the gig), he moved to Asheville, North Carolina with his wife Jacqui, where he teaches computer classes at Asheville-Buncombe Technical Community College and WCI/SofTrain Technology Training Center. Alec is author or coauthor of several titles covering Microsoft Office 2007, Microsoft Vista, Web design and HTML, and Internet systems and applications.

Darril Gibson has been a technical trainer for over eight years, specializing in delivering leading-edge technical training. He has developed several video training courses for Keystone Learning on topics such as A+, MCSE 2003, and Exchange 2003. He has taught as an adjunct instructor at several colleges and universities. Darril is currently working on a key government contract providing extensive training on a wide array of technologies to Air Force personnel in support of a major Network Operations Support Center. He holds almost 20 current certifications including A+, Network+, MCT, MCSE, MCSD, and MCITP.

Technical Editor

Ed Jennings has 25+ years experience in information technology. His career has been spent with such leading firms as Digital Equipment Corporation and Microsoft Corporation. Ed is CompTIA A+, Network+, and Certified Technical Trainer+ certified. Ed is also a Microsoft Certified Systems Engineer (MCSE). He has published several planning and design services for a national services company and is a certified courseware designer. He has published and delivered several online courses. Ed is currently employed as a technical instructor in the computer information technology program at Branford Hall Career Institute (www.branfordhall.com), a division of Premier Education Group (www.premiereducationgroup.com).

Peer Reviewers

Thank you to the reviewers, past and present, who contributed insightful reviews, criticisms, and helpful suggestions that continue to shape this textbook.

■ Acknowledgments

Scott Jernigan, my Editor-in-Chief, Counter-Strike Foe, Master Bard, and *Bon Vivant*, was the glue that made this product happen. There's not a word or picture I put into this book that he hasn't molded and polished into perfection.

My acquisitions editor, Tim Green, did a fabulous job keeping me motivated and excited about this project. Tim, you're the poster child for "Californians who can actually get along with loud, obnoxious Texans." Let's do another one!

My in-house Graphics Guru and Brother Tech, Michael Smyer, took every bizarre illustration idea I could toss at him and came back with exactly what I needed. To top it off, his outstanding photographs appear on nearly every page in this book. Great job, Michael!

Cindy Clayton's title might be "Editor" but it should be "Go to Gal," as she was always there for any job we needed to get done.

Cary Dier and Brian Schwarz came in at the 11th hour to save our bacon with copy edits and technical editing. Thanks, guys!

On the McGraw-Hill side, their crew worked with the diligence of worker bees and the patience of saints to put this book together.

Laura Stone did it all this time, a true pleasure to work with as project editor, copy editor, and frequent long-distance companion during many late nights. Your words of encouragement and praise—and laughter at my bad jokes—helped me finish this book with sanity and a smile. I could not have asked for a better editor, Laura. Thanks!

Jenni Housh offered a quiet voice and helpful spirit as acquisitions coordinator. I enjoyed our Monday meetings and am looking forward to the next project.

My technical editor, Ed Jennings, kept a close eye on me throughout the book and made great suggestions and corrections. Thanks for the excellent work!

To the copy editors, page proofers, and layout folks—Lisa Theobald, LeeAnn Pickrell, Andy Carroll, Andrea Fox, Paul Tyler, and the folks at ITC—thank you! You did a marvelous job.

■ To my wonderful daughter, Emily—even though you're far away, you're always in my thoughts. I love you.
—Mike Meyers

■ CompTIA Authorized Quality Curriculum

The logo of the CompTIA Authorized Quality Curriculum (CAQC) program and the status of this or other training material as "Authorized" under the CompTIA Authorized Quality Curriculum program signifies that, in CompTIA's opinion, such training material covers the content of CompTIA's related certification exam.

The contents of this training material were created for the CompTIA A+ exams covering CompTIA certification objectives that were current as of November 2006.

CompTIA has not reviewed or approved the accuracy of the contents of this training material and specifically disclaims any warranties of merchantability or fitness for a particular purpose. CompTIA makes no guarantee concerning the success of persons using any such "Authorized" or other training material in order to prepare for any CompTIA certification exam.

How to Become CompTIA Certified:

This training material can help you prepare for and pass a related CompTIA certification exam or exams. In order to achieve CompTIA certification, you must register for and pass a CompTIA certification exam or exams.

To become CompTIA certified, you must:

1. Select a certification exam provider. For more information, please visit http://www.comptia.org/certification/general_information/exam_locations.aspx

2. Register for and schedule a time to take the CompTIA certification exam(s) at a convenient location.

3. Read and sign the Candidate Agreement, which will be presented at the time of the exam(s). The text of the Candidate Agreement can be found at http://www.comptia.org/certification/general_information/candidate_agreement.aspx

4. Take and pass the CompTIA certification exam(s).

For more information about CompTIA's certifications, such as its industry acceptance, benefits or program news, please visit www.comptia.org/certification.

CompTIA is a not-for-profit information technology (IT) trade association. CompTIA's certifications are designed by subject matter experts from across the IT industry. Each CompTIA certification is vendor-neutral, covers multiple technologies, and requires demonstration of skills and knowledge widely sought after by the IT industry.

To contact CompTIA with any questions or comments, please call (1) (630) 678 8300 or e-mail questions@comptia.org.

About This Book

■ Important Technology Skills

Information technology (IT) offers many career paths, leading to occupations in such fields as PC repair, network administration, telecommunications, Web development, graphic design, and desktop support. To become competent in any IT field, *however, you need certain basic computer skills. Mike Meyers' A+ Guide builds a foundation for success in the IT field by introducing you to fundamental technology concepts and giving you essential computer skills.*

Cross Check
questions develop reasoning skills: ask, compare, contrast, and explain.

Tech Tip sidebars provide inside information from experienced IT professionals.

Try This! exercises apply core skills in a new setting.

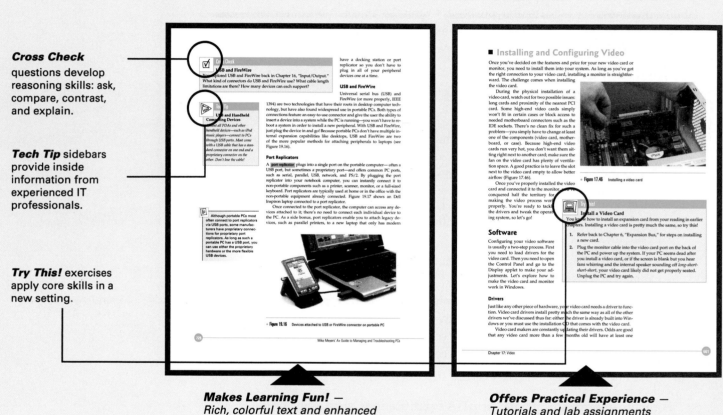

Makes Learning Fun! —
Rich, colorful text and enhanced illustrations bring technical subjects to life.

Offers Practical Experience —
Tutorials and lab assignments develop essential hands-on skills and put concepts in real-world contexts.

Proven Learning Method Keeps You on Track

Mike Meyers' A+ Guide is structured to give you comprehensive knowledge of computer skills and technologies. The textbook's active learning methodology guides you beyond mere recall and, through thought-provoking activities, labs, and sidebars, helps you develop critical-thinking, diagnostic, and communication skills.

Effective Learning Tools

This pedagogically rich book is designed to make learning easy and enjoyable and to help you develop the skills and critical-thinking abilities that will enable you to adapt to different job situations and troubleshoot problems.

Mike Meyers' proven ability to explain concepts in a clear, direct, even humorous way makes these books interesting, motivational, and fun.

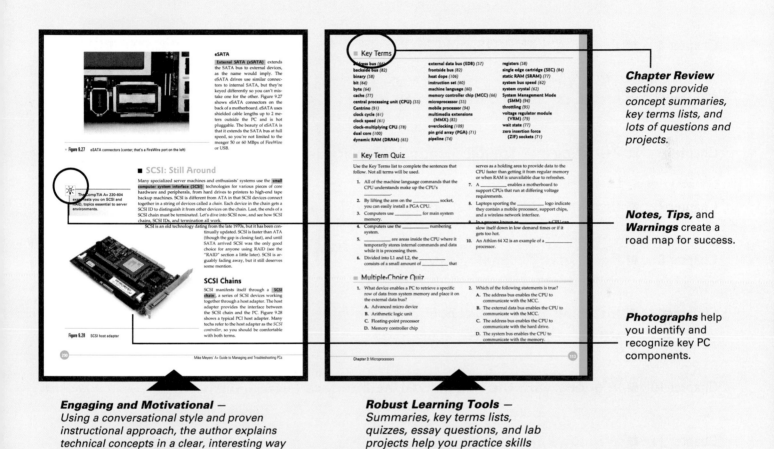

Chapter Review sections provide concept summaries, key terms lists, and lots of questions and projects.

Notes, Tips, and **Warnings** create a road map for success.

Photographs help you identify and recognize key PC components.

Engaging and Motivational —
Using a conversational style and proven instructional approach, the author explains technical concepts in a clear, interesting way using real-world examples.

Robust Learning Tools —
Summaries, key terms lists, quizzes, essay questions, and lab projects help you practice skills and measure progress.

Each chapter includes...

- **Learning objectives** that set measurable goals for chapter-by-chapter progress

- Plenty of **photographs** and **illustrations** that provide clear, up-close pictures of the technology, making difficult concepts easy to visualize and understand

- **Try This!**, **Cross Check**, and **Tech Tip** sidebars that encourage you to practice and apply concepts in real-world settings

- **Notes, Tips,** and **Warnings** that guide you through difficult areas

- **Highlighted Key Terms, Key Terms lists, and Chapter Summaries** that provide you with an easy way to review important concepts and vocabulary

- **Challenging end-of-chapter tests** that include vocabulary-building exercises, multiple-choice questions, essay questions, and on-the-job lab projects

CONTENTS AT A GLANCE

CONTENTS

PREFACE

I started writing computer books for the simple reason that no one wrote the kind of books I wanted to read. The books were either too simple (Chapter 1, "Using Your Mouse") or too complex (Chapter 1, "TTL Logic and Transistors"), and none of them provided a motivation for me to learn the information. I believed that there were geeky readers just like me who wanted to know *why* they needed to know the information in a computer book.

Good books motivate readers to learn what they are reading. For example, if a book discusses binary arithmetic but doesn't explain why I need to learn it, that's not a good book. Tell me that understanding binary makes it easier to understand how a CPU works or why a megabyte is different from a million bytes—then I get excited, no matter how geeky the topic. If I don't have a good motivation to do something, then I'm simply not going to do it (which explains why I haven't jumped out of an airplane!).

In this book, I teach you why you need to understand the technology that runs almost every modern business. You'll learn to build and fix computers, exploring every nook and cranny, and master the art of the PC tech. In the process, you'll gain the knowledge you need to pass the CompTIA A+ 220-602, 220-603, and 220-604 exams.

Enjoy, my fellow geek.

—Mike Meyers

Getting to Know
the A+ Exams

"It does not matter how slowly you go, so long as you do not stop."
—CONFUCIUS

In this chapter, you will learn how to

■ **Explain the importance of gaining skill in managing and troubleshooting PCs**

■ **Explain the importance of CompTIA A+ certification**

■ **Describe how to become a CompTIA A+ Certified Technician**

Computers have taken over the world, or at least many professions. Everywhere you turn, a quick dig beneath the surface sawdust of construction, the grease of auto mechanics, and the hum of medical technology reveals one or more personal computers (PCs) working away, doing essential jobs. Because the PC evolved from novelty item to essential science tool to everyday object in a short period of time, there's a huge demand for a workforce that can build, maintain, troubleshoot, and repair PCs.

■ The Importance of Skill in Managing and Troubleshooting PCs

The people who work with computers—the **information technology (IT)** workforce—do such varied jobs as design hardware, write computer programs that enable you to do specific jobs on the PC, and create small and large groupings of computers— **networks** —that enable people to share computer resources. IT people built the Internet, one of the most phenomenal inventions of the 20th century. IT people maintain the millions of computers that make up the Internet. Computer technicians, or **PC techs** as those of us in the field call each other, make up the core of the IT workforce. Without the techs, none of the other stuff works. Getting workers with skill in building, maintaining, troubleshooting, and fixing PCs is essential for success for every modern business.

In the early days of the personal computer, anyone who used a PC had to have skills as a PC tech. The PC was new, buggy, and prone to problems. You didn't want to rely on others to fix your PC when the inevitable problems arose. Today's PCs are much more robust and have fewer problems, but they're also much more complex machines. Today's IT industry, therefore, needs specialized workers who know how to make the machines run well.

The Concept of Certifications

Every profession requires specialized skills. For the most part, if you want to *get* or *keep* a job that requires those specialized skills, you need some type of **certification** or license. If you want a job fixing automobiles, for example, you get the *Automotive Service Excellence (ASE)* certification. If you want to perform companies' financial audits, you get your *Certified Public Accountant (CPA)* certification.

Nearly every profession has some criteria that you must meet to show your competence and ability to perform at a certain level. While the way this works varies widely from one profession to another, all

---

Try This!

Six Degrees of Personal Computers

As a fun exercise, divide up your class or your study partners and try this. One side comes up with a profession that seemingly doesn't use or depend on personal computers. The other side then, within six steps, tries to knock that argument down. Here's an example.

Side A: Poets don't need computers.

Side B: Sure, the poet could handwrite his or her poetry, but eventually would want the poems typewritten, thus a computer.

Side A counters: The poet could use an old-fashioned typewriter.

Side B: Okay, then to submit the poem for publication, the poet would have to use the mail—the mail is sorted electronically by computers.

Side A counters: The poet could hand-deliver the typed manuscript.

Side B: To get into print, the poem would have to be made electronically, whether by someone at the publisher's typing it in or even using a scanner to get it into electronic form.

Side A: Arghh!!!

You get the idea? Have fun and let your imagination run the game. By the end of a few minutes, you'll probably be convinced that computers are indeed everywhere and involved in just about every aspect of modern life.

---

of them will at some point make you take an exam or series of exams. Passing these exams proves that you have the necessary skills to work at a certain level in your profession, whether you're an aspiring plumber, teacher, barber, or lawyer.

If you successfully pass these exams, the organization that administers those exams grants you certification. You receive some piece of paper or pin or membership card that you can show to potential clients or employers. This certification gives those clients or employers a level of confidence that you can do what you say you can do. Without this certification, either you will not find suitable work in that profession or no one will trust you to do the work.

■ The Importance of CompTIA A+ Certification

Although microcomputers were introduced in the late 1970s, for many years PC technicians did not have a universally recognized way to show clients or employers that they know what to do under the hood of a personal computer. Sure, there were vendor-specific certifications, but the only way to get them was to get a job at an authorized warranty or repair facility first, and then get the certification. Not that there's anything wrong with vendor-specific training; it's just that no one manufacturer has taken enough market share to make IBM training, for example, something that works for any job. (Then there is always that little detail of getting the job first before you can get certified!)

The software/networking side of our business has not suffered from the same lack of certifications. Due to the dominance of certain companies at one time or another (for example, Microsoft and Novell), the vendor-specific certifications have provided a great way to get and keep a job. For example, Microsoft's *Microsoft Certified Systems Engineer (MCSE)*, Novell's *Certified Novell Engineer (CNE)*, and Cisco's *Cisco Certified Internetwork Expert (CCIE)* have opened the doors for many.

But what about the person who runs around all day repairing printers, repartitioning hard drives, upgrading device drivers, and building systems? What about the PC hobbyists who want to get paid for their skills? What about the folks who, because they had the audacity to show that they knew the difference between CMOS and a command prompt, find themselves with a new title like "PC Support Technician" or "Electronic Services Specialist"? On the other hand, how about the worst title of them all: "The Person Who Doesn't Get a Nickel Extra but Who Fixes the Computers"? CompTIA A+ certification fills that need.

What Is CompTIA A+ Certification?

CompTIA A+ certification is an industry-wide, vendor-neutral certification program developed and sponsored by the **Computing Technology Industry Association (CompTIA)**. The CompTIA A+ certification shows that you have a basic competence in supporting microcomputers. You achieve this certification by taking two computer-based, multiple-choice examinations. The tests cover what technicians should know after nine months of full-time PC support experience. CompTIA A+ certification enjoys wide recognition throughout the computer industry. To date, more than 600,000 technicians have become CompTIA A+ certified, making it the most popular of all IT certifications.

Who Is CompTIA?

CompTIA is a nonprofit, industry trade association based in Oakbrook Terrace, Illinois. It consists of over 20,000 members in 102 countries. You'll find CompTIA offices in such diverse locales as Amsterdam, Dubai, Johannesburg, Tokyo, and São Paulo.

CompTIA provides a forum for people in these industries to network (as in meeting people), represents the interests of its members to the government, and provides certifications for many different aspects of the computer industry. CompTIA sponsors A+, Network+, i-Net+, Security+, and other certifications. CompTIA works hard to watch the IT industry and constantly looks to provide new certifications to meet the ongoing demand from its membership. Check out the CompTIA Web site at www.comptia.org for details on the other certifications that you can obtain from CompTIA.

Virtually every company of consequence in the IT industry is a member of CompTIA. Here are a few of the biggies:

Adobe Systems	AMD	Best Buy	Brother International
Canon	Cisco Systems	CompUSA	Fujitsu
Gateway	Hewlett-Packard	IBM	Intel
Kyocera	McAfee	Microsoft	NCR
Novell	Panasonic	Sharp Electronics	Siemens
Symantec	Toshiba	Total Seminars, LLC (that's my company)	Plus many thousands more!

CompTIA began offering CompTIA A+ certification back in 1993. When it first debuted, the IT industry largely ignored CompTIA A+ certification. Since that initial stutter, however, the CompTIA A+ certification has grown to become the de facto requirement for entrance into the PC industry. Many companies require CompTIA A+ certification for all of their PC support technicians, and the CompTIA A+ certification is widely recognized both in the United States and internationally. Additionally, many other certifications recognize CompTIA A+ certification and use it as credit toward their certifications.

The Path to Other Certifications

Most IT companies—big and small—see CompTIA A+ certification as the entry point to IT. From CompTIA A+, you have a number of certification options, depending on whether you want to focus more on hardware and operating systems, or move into network administration (although these aren't mutually exclusive goals). The following three certifications are worth serious consideration:

- CompTIA Network+ certification
- Microsoft Certified Professional certifications
- Cisco certifications

CompTIA Network+ Certification

If you haven't already taken the CompTIA Network+ certification exam, make it your next certification. Just as CompTIA A+ certification shows you have solid competency as a PC technician, **CompTIA Network+ certification** demonstrates your skills as a network technician, including understanding of network hardware, installation, and troubleshooting. CompTIA's Network+ certification is a natural step for continuing toward your Microsoft, Novell, or Cisco certifications. Take the CompTIA Network+: it's your obvious next certification!

Microsoft Certified Professional Certifications

Microsoft operating systems control a huge portion of all installed networks, and those networks need qualified support people to make them run. Microsoft's series of certifications for networking professionals are a natural next step after the CompTIA certifications. They offer a whole slew of tracks and exams, but you should first pursue the **Microsoft Certified Professional (MCP)**. The MCP is the easiest Microsoft certification to get, as it only requires you to pass one of many different exams—and all of these exams count towards more advanced Microsoft certifications.

When it comes to advanced certifications, Microsoft's ever-popular Microsoft Certified Systems Engineer (MCSE) certification holds a lot of clout in the job market. The MCSE consists of seven exams: six core exams covering three study areas—client operating system, networking system, and design—and one elective. You can find more details on Microsoft's training Web site at www.microsoft.com/learning/mcp/default.asp.

Cisco Certifications

Let's face it, Cisco routers pretty much run the Internet and most intranets in the world. A *router* is a networking device that controls and directs the flow of information over networks, such as e-mail messages, Web browsing, and so on. Cisco provides three levels of certification for folks who want to show their skills at handling Cisco products. Nearly everyone interested in Cisco certification starts with the **Cisco Certified Network Associate (CCNA)**. The CCNA can be yours for the price of only one completed exam, after which you can happily slap the word Cisco on your resume! After your CCNA, you should consider the Cisco Certified Networking Professional (CCNP) certification. See the Cisco certification Web site here for more details: www.cisco.com/web/learning/le3/learning_career_certifications_and_learning_paths_home.html.

■ How Do I Become CompTIA A+ Certified?

You become CompTIA A+ certified, in the simplest sense, by taking and passing two computer-based, multiple-choice exams. No prerequisites are required for taking the CompTIA A+ certification exams. There is no required training course, and there are no training materials to buy. You *do* have to pay a testing fee for each of the two exams. You pay your testing fees, go to a local testing center, and take the tests. You immediately know whether you have passed or failed. By passing both exams, you become a **CompTIA A+ Certified Service Technician** . There are no requirements for professional experience. You do not have to go through an authorized training center. There are no annual dues. There are no continuing education requirements. You pass; you're in. That's it. Now for the details.

The Basic Exam Structure

CompTIA offers three tracks to CompTIA A+ certification: a primary (referred to as the IT Technician track) and two secondary (Help Desk and Depot Technician tracks). All three tracks require you to take two exams, the first of which is called the **CompTIA A+ Essentials** .

The Essentials exam concentrates on understanding terminology and technology, how to do fundamental tasks such as upgrading RAM, and basic Windows operating system support.

To follow the primary track, you would also take the **CompTIA A+ 220-602** exam, called the "602" or "IT Technician exam." The IT Technician exam builds on the Essentials exam, concentrating on advanced configuration and troubleshooting, including using the command line to accomplish tech tasks. This exam also includes network and Internet configuration questions.

To attain CompTIA A+ certification on one of the two secondary tracks, you would take Essentials and follow with either the **CompTIA A+ 220-603** exam (Help Desk Technician) or the **CompTIA A+ 220-604** exam (Depot Technician). Both exams test on a subset of the information covered in the IT Technician exam, but go more in depth on some subjects and have less coverage on other subjects. Nearly a third of all questions on the Help Desk Technician exam ask about managing, configuring, and troubleshooting operating systems, for example, whereas only one in five questions on the IT Technician exam hits that subject.

All of the exams are extremely practical, with little or no interest in theory. All questions are multiple choice or "click on the right part of the picture" questions. The following is an example of the type of question you will see on the exams:

A dot-matrix printer is printing blank pages. Which item should you check first?

    A. Printer drivers

    B. Platen

    C. Print head

    D. Ribbon

The correct answer is D, the ribbon. You can make an argument for any of the others, but common sense (and skill as a PC technician) tells you to check the simplest possibility first.

The 2006 tests use a regular test format, in which you answer a set number of questions and are scored based on how many correct answers you get,

Tech Tip

The Big Change in CompTIA A+ Certification

In June of 2006, CompTIA announced the most comprehensive changes to the CompTIA A+ certification exams. Up to this point, the CompTIA A+ certification consisted of two exams very different from what we now use. CompTIA gave these two exams a number of different official names over the years, but regardless of the name they boiled down to what we called the "hardware" exam and the "operating system" exam. That split always seemed forced because you can't have a functional computer without both hardware and operating systems working together to get things done.

In keeping with the idea of a PC as a single system instead of the PC as two separate entities—a pile of hardware and a pile of software—CompTIA reshaped the exams into a basic, conceptual exam followed by a more in-depth configuration/ maintenance/repair exam, for which you have three choices. This book will get you through the 220-602 IT Technician exam.

Tech Tip

Adaptive Exams

Even though the current CompTIA A+ certification exams use a regular, multiple-choice exam format, CompTIA has in the past used an adaptive format. It's worth your time to make sure you know the difference between the two types of exams. The main difference between a regular exam and an adaptive exam is that on an adaptive exam, each question is assigned a difficulty level (for example, easy, medium, or difficult). When you answer a medium question correctly, the exam adapts and asks you a harder question. If you miss one, the exam adapts and asks an easier question. There is a maximum number of questions the test will offer you, but not a set number of questions against which you are scored, like you'd find on a regular exam. To get a passing score on an adaptive exam, you need to answer enough difficult-level questions to prove your mastery of the material. Adaptive exams need far fewer questions than regular exams before the test ends, usually less than half the number of questions. Another big difference is that you cannot go back and check previous questions within adaptive exams, so make sure you have the answer you want before you move on to the next question!

rather than the adaptive format used in recent years. These exams will have no more than 100 questions each.

Be aware that CompTIA may add new questions to the exams at any time to keep the content fresh. The subject matter covered by the exams won't change, but new questions may be added periodically at random intervals. This policy puts stronger emphasis on understanding concepts and having solid PC-tech knowledge rather than trying to memorize specific questions and answers that may have been on the tests in the past. Going forward, no book or Web resource will have all the "right answers" because those answers will constantly change. Luckily for you, however, this book does not just teach you what steps to follow in a particular case, but how to be a knowledgeable tech who understands *why* you're doing those steps, so that when you encounter a new problem (or test question), you can work out the answer. Not only will this help you pass the exams, you'll be a better PC tech!

To keep up to date, we monitor the CompTIA A+ exams for new content and update the special Tech Files section of the Total Seminars Web site (www.totalsem.com) with new articles covering subjects we believe may appear on future versions of the exams.

IT Technician (Exam 220-602)

The CompTIA A+ 220-602 exam covers the same eight domains, although they're weighted differently and emphasize different aspects of the tasks involved. Table 1.1 lists the domains and percentages.

The IT Technician exam covers the same hardware and software as Essentials, but with much more focus on determining the appropriate technology for a situation—running diagnostics, and troubleshooting—rather than identification of hardware or operating system utilities. The exam tests your knowledge of computer components and programs so you can make informed recommendations to customers. You need to understand how all the technology should work, know the proper steps to figure out why something doesn't work, and then fix it.

The first domain, "Personal Computer Components," provides a stark example of the difference in focus between the exams. Essentials talks about

Table 1.1	Exam 220-602 Domains and Percentages	
Domain		**Percentage**
1.0 Personal Computer Components		18%
2.0 Laptop and Portable Devices		9%
3.0 Operating Systems		20%
4.0 Printers and Scanners		14%
5.0 Networks		11%
6.0 Security		8%
7.0 Safety and Environmental Issues		5%
8.0 Communication and Professionalism		15%

identifying names, purposes, and characteristics of various devices. The IT Technician exam, in contrast, goes into more depth: "Add, remove, and configure personal computer components, *including selection and installation of appropriate components.*" [Emphasis mine.]

"Laptops and Portable Devices" gives another great example. Domain 2.1 is the same for both exams, "Identify fundamental principles of using laptops and portable devices." Digging a little deeper into the domains shows the differences. Essentials: "Identify names, purposes, and characteristics of laptop-specific [devices such as] peripherals, expansion slots, [and] communication devices." IT Technician: "Identify appropriate applications for laptop-specific communication connections such as Bluetooth, infrared, cellular WAN, and Ethernet." The former has you identify the technology; the latter requires you to understand it in detail.

The two exams differ greatly in the "Operating Systems" domain. Essentials tests you on standard installation, configuration, and diagnostic tools, for example, but the IT Technician exam goes much deeper. You need to understand intimately how to use the command line to manage the operating systems. You're expected to know all sorts of disk structures and run all the major disk management tools. Finally, the IT Technician exam grills you on operating system recovery tools and techniques, so you can help customers get back up and running quickly.

Help Desk Technician (Exam 220-603)

The CompTIA A+ 220-603 exam emphasizes skills you need to succeed as a help desk technician, remotely helping people who run into problems on their PCs. As such, you'll be tested a lot more intensely on operating system questions than you would be on the IT Technician exam. In fact, almost a third of the questions cover OS diagnostic and troubleshooting problems. Perhaps even more interesting is the coverage of "Communication and Professionalism." *One out of every five questions* is about the proper way to talk with people, working to get the most information and being polite and kind when speaking to angry and upset people. Table 1.2 lists the domains and percentages.

Although the Help Desk exam removes mention of portable computers, the percentages on the "Security" and "Safety and Environmental Issues" domains go up a lot (from 8% and 5% to 15% for both). You've got to know these topics very well to succeed on this exam.

The IT Technician exam puts a lot of emphasis on the last domain, "Communication and Professionalism." At 15% of the exam, expect many questions about ethics, proper behavior in the work place, ways to communicate with customers to get the most information in troubleshooting situations, and more.

Table 1.2	Exam 220-603 Domains and Percentages
Domain	**Percentage**
1.0 Personal Computer Components	15%
2.0 Operating Systems	29%
3.0 Printers and Scanners	10%
4.0 Networks	11%
5.0 Security	15%
6.0 Communication and Professionalism	20%

A fundamental difference between the IT Technician and Help Desk Technician exams is that the former covers installing devices in detail, whereas the latter emphasizes troubleshooting even more. Of the two, the Help Desk Technician exam is clearly the more difficult. You should go that route only if your employer insists upon it!

Depot Technician (Exam 220-604)

The CompTIA A+ 220-604 exam is targeted at folks who work behind the scenes fixing computers. These are the techs who don't interact with customers much, so the emphasis on this exam is hardware, hardware, and even more hardware. If you can't build, maintain, troubleshoot, and repair any personal computer—desktop and portable—on the planet, this path is not for you! Table 1.3 lists the domains and percentages.

A quick glance at the domain percentages tells the tale. Almost half of all questions are on installing, configuring, optimizing, and upgrading PCs. Although operating systems as a domain has been removed, you definitely need to know a lot about them to install, configure, and troubleshoot devices. "Laptop and Portable Devices" and "Printers and Scanners" domains leap up to 40% of the exam questions. You'll be grilled on fixing portables and printers! Because the exam assumes you'll be in a lab environment rather than in an office space, security is de-emphasized. The presumed lack of communication between tech and customer caused the "Communication and Professionalism" objective to go completely away.

Help! Which Exam Should I Take?

With three different tracks to becoming a CompTIA A+ Certified Technician, the inevitable question revolves around choosing the proper track. *The bottom line is that unless you have an employer specifically telling you otherwise, do the primary track.* Take Essentials and follow that with the 220-602 IT Technician exam. This is by far the more common track and the one the vast majority of employers will want to see on your résumé! When you complete a track, your test results will show which track you chose.

If you choose the primary IT Technician track, potential employers will know they're getting a properly well-rounded tech who can be thrown into pretty much any IT situation and handle it well. The Help Desk and Depot Technician tracks target very specific jobs, so unless that job is yours, completing one of these tracks—and not doing the IT Technician track—limits your employment opportunities.

Table 1.3	Exam 220-604 Domains and Percentages
Domain	**Percentage**
1.0 Personal Computer Components	45%
2.0 Laptop and Portable Devices	20%
3.0 Printers and Scanners	20%
4.0 Security	5%
5.0 Safety and Environmental Issues	10%

A glance at the competencies for the three Technician exams (602, 603, and 604) might suggest that it would be easier to take 603 or 604 because they have fewer domains than 602, but that assumption could prove very painful indeed. The Help Desk and Depot Technician exams test you on the same material as the IT Technician exam, but emphasize different aspects or different ways to tackle personal computer issues.

Help! What Chapters Cover the Help Desk and Depot Technician Exams?

The *Mike Meyers' A+ Guide to Managing and Troubleshooting PCs* teaches you what you need to know to become a great tech, first and foremost. It just so happens that by learning how to become a great tech, you learn enough to pass the CompTIA A+ certification exams. Because the book focuses on tech and not exclusively on certification, the sections covered under the IT Technician banner in each chapter pertain to all three advanced exams: 220-602, 220-603, and 220-604.

To pass the 603 or 604 exams, focus more time on chapters weighted more heavily in the CompTIA domains for those exams. Table 1.4 shows the full eight domains for Essentials and IT Technician exams, with a series of check marks that tell you where to focus for which exam. The key is pretty straightforward. One check means around 10% on the domains. Two checks means ~20%, three checks ~30%, and so on.

How Do I Take the Exams?

Two companies, **Prometric** and **Pearson/VUE**, administer the actual CompTIA A+ testing. There are thousands of Prometric and Pearson/VUE testing centers across the United States and Canada, and the rest of the world.

Table 1.4	Where to Focus Your Study Time			
Domain	**Essentials**	**220-602**	**220-603**	**220-604**
Personal Computer Components	✓✓	✓✓	✓✓	✓✓✓✓
Laptop and Portable Devices	✓	✓	✓✓✓	✓✓
Operating Systems	✓✓	✓✓	✓	
Printers and Scanners	✓	✓	✓	✓✓
Networks	✓	✓	✓	
Security	✓	✓	✓✓	✓
Safety and Environmental Issues	✓	✓		✓
Communication and Professionalism	✓	✓✓	✓✓	

You may take the exams at any testing center. Both Prometric and Pearson/VUE offer complete listings online of all available testing centers. You can select the closest training center and schedule your exams right from the comfort of your favorite Web browser:

www.prometric.com
www.vue.com

Alternatively, in the United States and Canada, call Prometric at 800-776-4276 or Pearson/VUE at 877-551-PLUS (7587) to schedule the exams and to locate the nearest testing center. International customers can find a list of Prometric and Pearson/VUE international contact numbers for various regions of the world on CompTIA's Web site at www.comptia.org by selecting the Find Your Test Center link on the CompTIA A+ certification page.

You must pay for the exam when you call to schedule. Be prepared to sit on hold for a while. Have your Social Security number (or international equivalent) and a credit card ready when you call. Both Prometric and Pearson/VUE will be glad to invoice you, but you won't be able to take the exam until they receive full payment.

If you have special needs, both Prometric and Pearson/VUE will accommodate you, although this may limit your selection of testing locations.

How Much Does the Exam Cost?

The cost of the exam depends on whether you work for a CompTIA member or not. At this writing, the cost for non-CompTIA members is $158 (U.S.) for each exam. International prices vary, but you can check the CompTIA Web site for international pricing. Of course, the prices are subject to change without notice, so always check the CompTIA Web site for current pricing!

Very few people pay full price for the exam. Virtually every organization that provides CompTIA A+ training and testing also offers discount **vouchers** . You buy a discount voucher and then use the voucher number instead of a credit card when you schedule the exam. Vouchers are sold per exam, so you'll need two vouchers for the two CompTIA A+ exams. **Total Seminars** is one place to get discount vouchers. You can call Total Seminars at 800-446-6004 or 281-922-4166, or get vouchers via the Web site: www.totalsem.com. No one should ever pay full price for CompTIA A+ exams!

How to Pass the CompTIA A+ Exams

The single most important thing to remember about the CompTIA A+ certification exams is that CompTIA designed the exams to test the knowledge of a technician with only nine months' experience—so keep it simple! The exams aren't interested in your ability to overclock CAS timings in CMOS or whether you can explain the exact difference between the Intel 975X Express and the NVIDIA nForce590 SLI chipsets. Don't bother with a lot of theory—think in terms of practical knowledge. Read the book, do whatever works for you to memorize the key concepts and procedures, take the practice exams on the CD in the back of the book, review any topics you miss, and you should pass with no problem.

Some of you may be in or just out of school, so studying for exams is nothing novel. But if it's been a while since you've had to study for and take an exam, or if you think maybe you could use some tips, you may find the next section valuable. It lays out a proven strategy for preparing to take and pass the CompTIA A+ exams. Try it. It works.

Those of you who just want more knowledge in managing and troubleshooting PCs can follow the same strategy as certification-seekers. Think in practical terms and work with the PC as you go through each chapter.

Obligate Yourself

The very first step you should take is to schedule yourself for the exams. Have you ever heard the old adage, "heat and pressure make diamonds"? Well, if you don't give yourself a little "heat," you'll end up procrastinating and delay taking the exams, possibly forever! Do yourself a favor. Using the information below, determine how much time you'll need to study for the exams, and then call Prometric or VUE and schedule them accordingly. Knowing the exams are coming up makes it much easier to turn off the television and crack open the book! You can schedule an exam as little as a few weeks in advance, but if you schedule an exam and can't take it at the scheduled time, you must reschedule at least a day in advance or you'll lose your money.

Set Aside the Right Amount of Study Time

After helping thousands of techs get their CompTIA A+ certification, we at Total Seminars have developed a pretty good feel for the amount of study time needed to pass the CompTIA A+ certification exams. Table 1.5 provides an estimate to help you plan how much study time you must commit to the CompTIA A+ certification exams. Keep in mind that these are averages. If you're not a great student or if you're a little on the nervous side, add 10 percent; if you're a fast learner or have a good bit of computer experience, you may want to reduce the figures.

To use the table, just circle the values that are most accurate for you and add them up to get your estimated total hours of study time.

To that value, add hours based on the number of months of direct, professional experience you have had supporting PCs, as shown in Table 1.6.

A total neophyte usually needs around 200 hours of study time. An experienced tech shouldn't need more than 40 hours.

Total hours for you to study: _____.

A Strategy for Study

Now that you have a feel for how long it's going to take, it's time to develop a study strategy. I'd like to suggest a strategy that has worked for others who've come before you, whether they were experienced techs or total newbies. This book is designed to accommodate the different study agendas of these two different groups of students. The first group is experienced techs who already have strong PC experience, but need to be sure they're ready to be tested on the specific subjects covered by the CompTIA A+ exams. The second group is those with little or no background in the computer field. These techs can benefit from a more detailed understanding of the history and concepts that underlie modern PC technology, to help them remember the specific subject matter information they must know for the exams.

Table 1.5	Analyzing Skill Levels			
		Amount of Experience		
Tech Task	**None**	**Once or Twice**	**Every Now and Then**	**Quite a Bit**
Installing an adapter card	12	10	8	4
Installing hard drives	12	10	8	2
Installing modems and NICs	8	6	6	3
Connecting a computer to the Internet	8	6	4	2
Installing printers and scanners	4	3	2	1
Installing RAM	8	6	4	2
Installing CPUs	8	7	5	3
Fixing printers	6	5	4	3
Fixing boot problems	8	7	7	5
Fixing portable computers	8	6	4	2
Building complete systems	12	10	8	6
Using the command line	8	8	6	4
Installing/optimizing Windows	10	8	6	4
Using Windows 2000	6	6	4	2
Using Windows XP	6	6	4	2
Configuring NTFS permissions	6	4	3	2
Configuring a wireless network	6	5	3	2
Configuring a software firewall	6	4	2	1
Installing a sound card	2	2	1	0
Using OS diagnostic tools	8	8	6	4
Using a Volt-Ohm Meter	4	3	2	1

I'll use the shorthand terms Old Techs and New Techs for these two groups. If you're not sure which group you fall into, pick a few chapters and go through some end-of-chapter questions. If you score less than 70%, go the New Tech route.

Table 1.6	Adding Up Your Study Time
Months of Direct, Professional Experience...	**To Your Study Time...**
0	Add 50
Up to 6	Add 30
6 to 12	Add 10
Over 12	Add 0

I have broken most of the chapters into three distinct parts:

- **Essentials Review**   A very quick review of topics from the 601 exam that you should know.

- **IT Technician**   Topics that clearly fit under the CompTIA A+ IT Technician exam domains.

- **Beyond A+**   More advanced issues that probably will not be on the CompTIA A+ exams—yet.

The beginning of each of these areas is clearly marked with a large banner that looks like this:

Not all chapters will have all three sections!

Essentials Review

Those of you who fall into the Old Tech group may want to proceed straight to the IT Technician area in each chapter. After reading that section, jump immediately to the questions at the end of the chapter. The end-of-chapter questions concentrate on information in the IT Technician section. If you run into problems, read the Essentials Review section in that chapter. Note that you may need to skip back to previous chapters to get the review information you need for later chapters.

After going through every chapter as described, Old Techs can move directly to testing their knowledge using the free practice exams on the CD-ROM that accompanies the book. Once you start scoring in the 85 to 90 percent range, you're ready to take the exams!

If you're a New Tech or if you're an Old Tech who wants the full learning experience this book can offer, start by reading the book, *the whole book,* as though you were reading a novel, from page one to the end without skipping around. Because so many computer terms and concepts build on each other, skipping around greatly increases the odds you will become confused and end up closing the book and firing up your favorite PC game. Not that I have anything against PC games, but unfortunately that skill is *not* useful for the CompTIA A+ exams!

Your goal on this first read is to understand concepts, the *whys* behind the *hows*. It is very helpful to have a PC nearby as you read so you can stop and inspect the PC to see a piece of hardware or how a particular concept manifests in the real world. As you read about floppy drives, for example, inspect the cables. Do they look like the ones in the book? Is there a variation? Why? It is imperative that you understand why you are doing something, not just how to do it on one particular system under one specific set of conditions. Neither the exams nor real life as a PC tech works that way!

If you're reading this book as part of a managing and troubleshooting PCs class, rather than a certification-prep course, then I highly recommend going the New Tech route, even if you have a decent amount of experience. The book contains a lot of details that can trip you up if you focus only on the test-specific sections of the chapters. Plus, your program might stress historical and conceptual knowledge as well as practical, hands-on skills.

The CompTIA A+ certification exams assume that you have basic user skills. The exams really try to trick you with questions on processes that you may do every day and not really think about. Here's a classic: "In order to move a file from the C:\WINDOWS folder to the A:\ drive using Windows Explorer, what key must you hold down while dragging the file?" If you can answer that without going to your keyboard and trying a few likely keys, you're better than most techs! In the real world, you can try a few wrong answers before you hit on the right one, but for the exams, you have to *know* it! Whether Old Tech or New Tech, make sure you are proficient at user-level Windows skills, including the following:

- Recognizing all the components of the standard Windows desktop (Start Menu, System Tray, etc.)

- Manipulating windows—resizing, moving, and so on

- Creating, deleting, renaming, moving, and copying files and folders within Windows

- Understanding file extensions and their relationship with program associations

- Using common keyboard shortcuts/hotkeys

Any PC technician who has been around a while will tell you that one of the great secrets in the computer business is that there's almost never anything completely new in the world of computer technology. Faster, cleverer, smaller, wider—absolutely—but the underlying technology, the core of what makes your PC and its various peripheral devices operate, has changed remarkably little since PCs came into widespread use a few decades ago.

After you've completed the first read-through, go through the book again, this time in textbook mode. If you're an Old Tech, this is where you start your studying. Try to cover one chapter at a sitting. Concentrate on the IT Technician sections. Get a highlighter and mark the phrases and sentences that bring out major points. Be sure you understand how the pictures and illustrations relate to the concepts being discussed.

Try This!

Windows Vista

Microsoft's Windows Vista operating system debuted in January 2007, and although CompTIA won't immediately put it on the CompTIA A+ certification exams, every tech will need to know it. Do yourself and your customers a favor and work with Windows Vista as soon as you can *after* you finish getting CompTIA A+ certified, even if it means using a school computer or making a lot of trips to computer stores.

I suggest waiting only because you'll want to keep the details of how to do things in Windows 2000 and Windows XP as fresh as possible before you take the exams. If you're studying simply to gain knowledge and are not worried about getting certified, then jump right in!

Once you have access to a Windows Vista computer, skim through this book and ask yourself these questions. What's different about setting up drives? What about installation? What diagnostic and troubleshooting tools does Vista offer that you can't find or that differ significantly from tools in Windows 2000 or Windows XP?

Once you feel you have a good grasp of the material in the book, you can check your knowledge using the practice exams included on the CD-ROM in the back of the book. These can be taken in Practice mode or Final mode. In Practice mode, you can use the Assistance window to get a helpful hint for the current questions, find the chapter that covers the question using the Reference feature, check your answer for the question, and see an explanation of the correct answer. In Final mode, you answer all the questions and are given an exam score at the end, just like the real thing.

Both modes show you an overall grade, expressed as a percentage, as well as a breakdown of how well you did on each exam domain. The Review Questions feature lets you see what questions you missed and what the correct answers are. Use these results to guide further studying. Continue reviewing the topics you miss and taking additional exams until you are consistently scoring in the 85% to 95% range. When you get there, you are ready to pass the CompTIA A+ certification exams!

If you have any problems, any questions, or if you just want to argue about something, feel free to send an e-mail to the author—michaelm@totalsem.com, or to the editor—scottj@totalsem.com.

For any other information you might need, contact CompTIA directly at their Web site: www.comptia.org.

> ### Tech Tip
>
> **Study Strategies**
>
> *Perhaps it's been a while since you had to study for a test. Or perhaps it hasn't, but you've done your best since then to block the whole experience from your mind! Either way, savvy test-takers know there are certain techniques that make studying for tests more efficient and effective.*
>
> *Here's a trick used by students in law and medical schools who have to memorize reams of information: write it down. The act of writing something down (not typing, **writing**) in and of itself helps you to remember it, even if you never look at what you wrote again. Try taking separate notes on the material and recreating diagrams by hand to help solidify the information in your mind.*
>
> *Another oldie but goodie: make yourself flash cards with questions and answers on topics you find difficult. A third trick: take your notes to bed and read them just before you go to sleep. Many people find they really do learn while they sleep!*

Chapter 1 Review

■ Chapter Summary

After reading this chapter and completing the exercises, you should understand the following about the CompTIA A+ exams.

The Importance of Skill in Managing and Troubleshooting PCs

■ The IT workforce designs, builds, and maintains computers, computer programs, and networks, the basic information tools of the early 21st century. PC techs take care of personal computers, so they represent an essential component in that workforce. As PCs become more complex, the IT workforce needs specialized PC techs.

■ Certifications prove to employers that you have the necessary skill to work in your chosen field. If you want a job fixing automobiles, for example, you get the *Automotive Service Excellence (ASE)* certification. To get certified, you take and successfully pass exams. Then the organization that administers those exams grants you certification. This is particularly important for IT workers.

The Importance of CompTIA A+ Certification

■ In the early days of the personal computer, you could get vendor-specific certifications such as "IBM Technician," but nothing general for PC techs. Worse, you often had to have a job at that company to get the vendor-specific certification.

■ CompTIA A+ certification is an industry-wide, vendor-neutral certification program that shows that you have a basic competence in supporting microcomputers. You achieve this certification by taking two computer-based, multiple-choice examinations. The tests cover what technicians should know after nine months of full-time PC support experience. CompTIA A+ certification enjoys wide recognition throughout the computer industry.

■ CompTIA is a nonprofit, industry trade association based in Oakbrook Terrace, Illinois. It consists of over 20,000 members in 102 countries. CompTIA provides a forum for people in these industries to network, represents the interests of its members to the government, and provides certifications for many different aspects of the computer industry. CompTIA sponsors A+, Network+, i-Net+, Security+, and other certifications.

■ The CompTIA A+ certification is the de facto entry point to IT. From CompTIA A+, you have a number of certification options, depending on whether you want to focus more on hardware and operating systems, or move into network administration. You can get CompTIA Network+ certification, for example, or go on to get Microsoft or Cisco certified. CompTIA Network+ certification is the most obvious certification to get after becoming CompTIA A+ certified.

How to Become CompTIA A+ Certified

■ You become CompTIA A+ certified, in the simplest sense, by taking and passing two computer-based, multiple-choice exams. No prerequisites are required for taking the CompTIA A+ certification exams. There is no required training course, and there are no training materials to buy. You *do* have to pay a testing fee for each of the two exams.

■ CompTIA offers three tracks to CompTIA A+ certification, a primary (referred to as the IT Technician track) and two secondary (Help Desk and Depot Technician tracks). All three tracks require you to take two exams, the first of which is called the CompTIA A+ Essentials. The Essentials exam concentrates on understanding terminology and technology, how to do fundamental tasks such as upgrading RAM, and basic Windows operating system support. The IT Technician exam builds on the Essentials exam, concentrating on advanced configuration and troubleshooting.

■ To attain CompTIA A+ certification on one of the two secondary tracks, you would take Essentials and follow with either the CompTIA 220-603 exam (Help Desk Technician) or the CompTIA 220-604 exam (Depot Technician). Both exams test on a subset of the information covered in the IT Technician exam, but go more in depth on some subjects and have less coverage on other subjects.

- All of the exams are extremely practical, with little or no interest in theory. All questions are multiple choice or "click on the right part of the picture" questions. CompTIA may add new questions to the exams at any time to keep the content fresh, although the subject matter covered by the exams won't change.

- Of the three tracks to becoming a CompTIA A+ Certified Technician, most techs take the Essentials plus 220-602, IT Technician. Take one of the secondary tracks only if an employer specifically requires it.

- Two companies, Prometric and Pearson/VUE, administer the actual CompTIA A+ testing. You can schedule exam time and location via the Web site for either company, www.prometric.com or www.vue.com. Check CompTIA's Web site for international links.

- To achieve success with the CompTIA A+ certification exams, think in terms of practical knowledge. Read the book. Work through the problems. Work with computers. Take the practice exams. You should obligate yourself by scheduling your exams. This keeps you focused on study.

Key Terms

certification *(1)*

Cisco Certified Network Associate (CCNA) *(4)*

CompTIA A+ 220-602 (IT Technician) *(5)*

CompTIA A+ 220-603 (Help Desk Technician) *(5)*

CompTIA A+ 220-604 (Depot Technician) *(5)*

CompTIA A+ certification *(2)*

CompTIA A+ Certified Service Technician *(5)*

CompTIA A+ Essentials *(5)*

CompTIA Network+ certification *(4)*

Computing Technology Industry Association (CompTIA) *(2)*

information technology (IT) *(1)*

Microsoft Certified Professional (MCP) *(4)*

network *(1)*

PC tech *(1)*

Pearson/VUE *(9)*

Prometric *(9)*

Total Seminars *(10)*

vouchers *(10)*

Key Term Quiz

Use the Key Terms list to complete the sentences that follow. Not all terms will be used.

1. You can use a(n) _____ when you schedule your exam to save some money.

2. Of the three advanced exams, the _____ is considered the primary path to CompTIA A+ certification.

3. Of the three advanced exams, the _____ is targeted at folks who work behind the scenes fixing computers, rather than on the floor interacting with customers.

4. A person desiring to work in Windows-based networking should pursue _____ certification after completing his or her CompTIA certifications.

5. You can find the latest information about the CompTIA A+ certification exams at the Web site of the _____.

Multiple-Choice Quiz

1. Which of the following exams focuses most heavily on testing your skills working on laptops and portable devices?
   A. CompTIA A+ Essentials
   B. CompTIA A+ 220-602
   C. CompTIA A+ 220-603
   D. CompTIA A+ 220-604

2. Which of the following exams focuses most heavily on testing your skills interacting with customers?
   A. CompTIA A+ Essentials
   B. CompTIA A+ 220-602
   C. CompTIA A+ 220-603
   D. CompTIA A+ 220-604

3. Which of the following exams focuses on determining the appropriate technology for a situation, running diagnostics, and troubleshooting?

   A. CompTIA A+ Essentials

   B. CompTIA A+ 220-602

   C. CompTIA A+ 220-603

   D. CompTIA A+ 220-604

4. What sort of question would you be least likely to see on a CompTIA A+ 220-604 exam? (Select the best answer.)

   A. Personal computer components

   B. Operating systems

   C. Laptops and portable devices

   D. Communication and professionalism

5. Who should take a secondary path to CompTIA A+ certification through Essentials and 220-604?

   A. The majority of CompTIA A+ candidates should go the 220-604 (Depot Technician) path.

   B. CompTIA A+ candidates who are required to take the 220-604 (Depot Technician) path by an employer.

   C. No one—the 220-604 (Depot Technician) path is not good.

   D. Everyone—all techs should take all three CompTIA A+ paths.

Essay Quiz

1. Describe the differences among the four A+ certification exams. Which one is required? Which of the others do you plan to take? Why?

Lab Projects

① If you have access to the Internet, browse to the Prometric Web site and find out the cost of the 220-601 certification exam and the location of the nearest testing center. Do the same from the Pearson/VUE Web site. Is the cost the same? Are the locations the same?

Installing and Troubleshooting CPUs

*"I have a theory about the human mind. A **brain** is a lot like a **computer**. It will only take so many facts, and then it will go on overload and blow up."*
—ERMA BOMBECK

The 602 exam's coverage of CPUs is one of the very few areas that differ from the A+ exam's rule of Identify/Understand in the Essentials exam and Install/Troubleshoot in the 602. You will find plenty of CPU install questions in the 602, as well as a few advanced CPU concepts. This chapter addresses the more advanced concepts as well as CPU cooling and troubleshooting.

In this chapter, you will learn how to

- **Install and upgrade CPUs**
- **Understand and implement CPU cooling**
- **Troubleshoot CPUs**

Essentials Review

You'll find this chapter far more interesting if you are aware of CPU topics covered in the A+ Essentials exam. Before beginning this chapter, make sure you can

- Identify the major components of a CPU, including registers, pipelines, address bus, frontside bus, backside bus, and CPU cache
- Distinguish between 32-bit and 64-bit processing
- Explain specialized CPU functions such as power management and graphic support
- Define the role of the system crystal and how it relates to CPU speed including core speed and multipliers
- Name and explain the major types of CPUs from the Pentium III and early Athlon to the Intel Core and Athlon XP
- Recognize the function and variety of CPU packages and their associated sockets, including the old slotted packages
- Explain the concepts of hyperthreading and multicore CPUs

IT Technician

■ Installing CPUs

Installing or replacing a CPU is a remarkably straightforward process. You take off the fan and heat sink assembly, remove the CPU, put a new CPU in, and snap the fan and heat sink assembly back on. The trick to installing or replacing a CPU begins with two important questions. Do you need to replace your CPU? What CPU can you put in the computer?

Why Replace a CPU?

The CPU is the brain of your system, so it seems a natural assumption that taking out an old, slow CPU and replacing it with some new, fast CPU would make your computer run faster. No doubt it will, but before you do you need to consider a few issues, such as cost, cooling, and performance.

Cost

If you have an older CPU, there's a better than average chance that a faster version of your CPU is no longer available for retail purchase. In that case, replacing your CPU with a new one would require you to replace the motherboard and probably the RAM too. This is doable, but does it make sense cost-wise? How much would this upgrade compare to a whole new system?

Cooling

Faster CPUs run hotter than slower ones. If you get a new CPU, you will almost certainly need a new fan to dissipate the heat generated by the more powerful processor. In addition, you may discover your case fans are not sufficient, causing the CPU to overheat and making the system lock up. Adding improved cooling can be done, but it might require a new case.

Performance

A faster CPU will make your computer run faster, but by how much? The results are often disappointing. As you go through this book, you will discover many other areas where upgrading might make a much stronger impact on your system's performance.

Determining the Right CPU

So you go through all the decision-making and decide to go for a new CPU. Perhaps you're building a brand-new system or maybe you're ready to go for that CPU upgrade. The single most important bit of documentation is called the motherboard book (Figure 2.1). Every computer should come with this important book, which contains all the details about what CPUs you can use as well as any special considerations for installing a CPU. Usually in the first few pages, the motherboard book will tell you exactly which CPUs your system can handle (as shown in Figure 2.2).

If you don't have a motherboard book, call the place where you got the PC and ask for it. If they don't have it, get online and find it—I'll show you where to look in later chapters.

● **Figure 2.1** Sample motherboard books

Your first concern is the socket. You can't install an Athlon 64 X2 into a Pentium D's Socket 775—it won't fit! If your motherboard book lists the CPU you want to install, you're ready to start shopping.

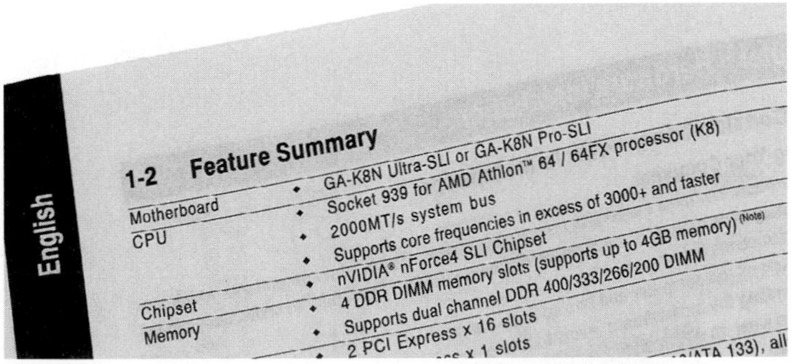

● **Figure 2.2** Allowed CPUs

Buying a CPU

Buying a CPU is a tricky game because most stores will not accept returns unless the CPU is bad. If you're not careful, you could get stuck with a useless CPU. Here are a few tricks.

CPUs come packaged two ways, as **retail-boxed CPUs** or OEM CPUs. Retail-boxed CPUs have two advantages. First, they are the genuine article. There are a surprising number of illegal CPUs on the market. Second, they come with a fan that is rated to work with that CPU.

Most stores have an installation deal and will install a new CPU for very cheap. I will take advantage of this sometimes, even though it may mean I don't have my PC for a few days. Why does your humble author, the Alpha Geek, have others do work he can do himself? Well, that way I'm not out of luck if there is a problem! Heck, I can change my own oil in my car, but I let others do that, too!

If you buy an OEM CPU, you will need the right fan. See "The Art of Cooling" section later in this chapter.

Preparing to Install

Once you're comfortable that your new CPU will work with your motherboard, get back to that motherboard book and see if there are any tiny jumpers or switches that you must adjust for your CPU. These jumpers might adjust the motherboard speed, the multiplier, or the voltage. Take your time, read the motherboard book, and set those jumpers or switches properly. Locate the fan power connector, usually called the CPU fan, as shown in Figure 2.3.

Most CPUs use some form of mounting bracket for the CPU fan. Some of these brackets require mounting underneath the motherboard, which means removing the motherboard from the system case.

If you're removing an old CPU, you'll need to take off the old fan. Removing CPU fans scares me more than any other physical act I do on a PC. Many (not all) CPU fans use a metal clamp on both sides of the socket. These clamps usually require you to pry them off to remove them using a flat-head

Many motherboards have no jumpers or switches.

Before attempting to do anything inside the system unit, make sure you have adequate ESD protection. Make sure the power is off and the system is unplugged.

• **Figure 2.3**   Fan connection

● **Figure 2.4** Removing an old fan

screwdriver (Figure 2.4). You need a lot of force—usually far more than you think you should use, so take your time and pry that old fan off!

Inserting a PGA-Type CPU

Inserting and removing **pin grid array (PGA)** CPUs is a relatively simple process; just *don't touch the pins* or you might destroy the CPU. Figure 2.5 shows a technician installing a Sempron into a Socket 754. Note the pins on the CPU only fit in one orientation. These *orientation markers* are designed to help you align the CPU correctly. Although the orientation marks make it very difficult to install a CPU improperly, incorrectly installing your CPU will almost certainly destroy the CPU or the motherboard, or both!

To install, lift the **zero insertion force (ZIF) socket** arm or open the metal cover, align the CPU, and it should drop right in (Figure 2.6). If it doesn't, verify your alignment and check for bent pins on the CPU. If you encounter a slightly bent pin, try a mechanical pencil that takes thick (0.9mm) lead. Take the lead out of the mechanical pencil, slide the pencil tip over the bent pin, and straighten it out. Be careful! A broken CPU pin ruins the CPU. Make sure the CPU is all the way in (no visible pins) and then snap down the arm or drop over the metal cover.

Now it's time for the fan! Before inserting the fan, you need to add a small amount of thermal compound (also called **heat dope**). Many fans come with thermal compound already on them; the thermal compound on these pre-doped fans is covered by a small square of tape—take it off before you snap down the fan. If you need to put thermal compound

● **Figure 2.5** Orienting the CPU

● **Figure 2.6**   CPU inserted

● **Figure 2.7**   Applying thermal compound

on from a tube (see Figure 2.7), know that it only takes a tiny amount of this compound! Spread it on as thinly, completely, and evenly as you can. Unlike so many other things in life, you *can* have too much thermal compound!

Securing fans makes even the most jaded PC technician a little nervous (Figure 2.8). In most cases, you must apply a fairly strong amount of force to snap the fan into place—far more than you might think. Also, make certain that the fan you install works with your CPU package.

Testing Your New CPU

The next step is to turn on the PC and see if the system boots up. If life were perfect, every CPU installation would end right here as you watch the system happily boot up. Unfortunately, the reality is that sometimes nothing happens when you press the On button. Here's what to do if this happens.

First, make sure the system has power—we'll be going through lots of power issues throughout the book. Second, make sure the CPU is firmly pressed down into the socket. Get your head down and look at the mounted CPU from the side—do you see any of the CPU's wires showing? Does the CPU look level in its mount? If not, reinstall the CPU. If the system still does not boot, double-check any jumper settings—it's very easy to mess them up.

As the computer starts, make sure the CPU fan is spinning within a few seconds. If it doesn't spin up instantly, that's okay, but it must start within about 30 seconds at the least.

● **Figure 2.8**   Installing the fan

The Art of Cooling

There once was a time long ago when CPUs didn't need any type of cooling device. You just snapped in the CPU and it worked.

Well, those days are gone. Long gone. If you're installing a modern CPU, you will have to cool it. Fortunately, you have choices.

- **OEM Fans** OEM fans are included with a retail-boxed CPU. OEM CPUs, on the other hand, don't normally come bundled with fans. Crazy, isn't it? OEM fans have one big advantage: you know absolutely that they will work with your CPU.

- **Specialized Fans** Lots of companies sell third-party fans for different CPUs. These usually exceed the OEM fans in the amount of heat they dissipate. These fans invariably come with eye-catching designs to look really cool inside your system—some are even lighted! (See Figure 2.9.)

The last choice is the most impressive of all— **liquid cooling** ! That's right, you can put a little liquid cooling system right inside your PC case! Liquid cooling works by running some liquid—usually water—through a metal block that sits on top of your CPU, absorbing heat. The liquid gets heated by the block, runs out of the block and into something that cools the liquid, and the liquid is then pumped through the block again. Any liquid cooling system consists of three main parts:

- A hollow metal block that sits on the CPU

- A pump to move the liquid around

- Some device to cool the liquid

And, of course, you need plenty of hosing to hook them all together! Figure 2.10 shows a typical liquid-cooled CPU.

A number of companies sell these liquid-cooling systems. Although they look really impressive and certainly cool your CPU, the reality is that unless you're overclocking or want a quiet system, a good fan will more than suffice.

● **Figure 2.9** Cool retail fan

● **Figure 2.10** Liquid-cooled CPU

Whether you have a silent or noisy cooling system for your CPU, always remember to keep everything clean. Once a month or so, take a can of compressed air and clean dust off the fan or radiator. CPUs are very susceptible to heat; a poorly working fan can create all sorts of problems, such as system lockups, spontaneous reboots, and more.

Beyond A+

Overclocking

For the CPU to work, it must have the motherboard speed, multiplier, and voltage set properly. In most modern systems, the motherboard uses the CPUID functions to set these options automatically. Some motherboards enable you to adjust these settings manually by moving a jumper, changing a CMOS setting, or with software; many enthusiasts deliberately change these settings to enhance performance.

Starting way back in the days of the Intel 80486 CPU, people intentionally ran their systems at clock speeds higher than the CPU was rated, a process called **overclocking**, and they worked. Well, *sometimes* the systems worked, and sometimes they didn't. Intel and AMD have a reason for marking a CPU at a particular clock speed—that's the highest speed they guarantee will work.

Before I say anything else, I must warn you that intentional overclocking of a CPU immediately voids any warranty. Overclocking has been known to destroy CPUs. Overclocking might make your system unstable and prone to lockups and reboots. I neither applaud nor decry the practice of overclocking. My goal here is simply to inform you of the practice. You make your own decisions.

CPU makers dislike overclocking. Why would you pay more for a faster processor when you can take a cheaper, slower CPU and just make it run faster? To that end, CPU makers, especially Intel, have gone to great lengths to discourage the practice. For example, both AMD and Intel now make all their CPUs with locked multipliers and special overspeed electronics to deter the practice.

I don't think Intel or AMD really care too much what *end users* do with their CPUs. You own it; you take the risks. A number of criminals, however, learned to make a good business of remarking CPUs with higher than rated speeds and selling them as legitimate CPUs. These counterfeit CPUs have created a nightmare where unsuspecting retailers and end users have been given overclocked CPUs. When they run into trouble, they innocently ask for warranty support, only to discover that their CPU is counterfeit and the warranty is void.

If you want to know exactly what type of CPU you're running, download a copy of the very popular and free CPU-Z utility from www.cpuid.com. CPU-Z gives you every piece of information you'll ever want to know about your CPU (Figure 2.11).

Most people make a couple of adjustments to overclock successfully. First, through jumpers, CMOS settings, or software configuration, increase the bus speed for the system. Second, you often have to increase the voltage going into the CPU by just a little to provide stability. You do that by changing a jumper or CMOS setting.

Overriding the defaults can completely lock up your system, to the point where even removing and reinstalling the CPU doesn't bring the motherboard back to life. (There's also a slight risk of toasting the processor, although all modern processors have circuitry that shuts them down quickly before they overheat.) Most motherboards have a jumper setting called *CMOS clear* (Figure 2.12) that makes the CMOS go back to default settings. Before you try overclocking on a modern system, find the CMOS clear jumper and make sure you know how to use it! Hint: Look in the motherboard manual.

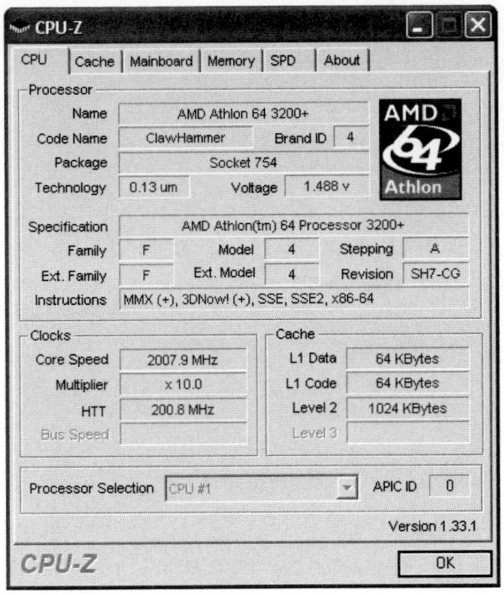

● **Figure 2.11** CPU-Z in action

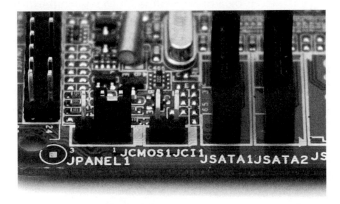

● **Figure 2.12** CMOS clear jumper

Chapter 2: Installing and Troubleshooting CPUs

Chapter 2 Review

Chapter Summary

After reading this chapter and completing the exercises, you should understand the following about installing and troubleshooting CPUs.

Installing CPUs

- Before upgrading your CPU, consider the implications on your whole system, because an upgraded CPU may require an updated motherboard and RAM.

- Consult your motherboard documentation to see what CPUs are compatible with your system. Not all CPUs are compatible with all motherboards.

- Cooling is critical. Make sure you have a fan rated to work with your CPU.

- Never touch the pins on the underside of a CPU, as this can permanently damage the processor.

- A PGA CPU fits only one way in the ZIF socket. Don't force it. If you find the CPU will not seat properly, take a second look at the orientation markers and verify the CPU is in the correct direction. Check the pins on the underside to make sure none are bent.

- There should be a small amount of heat sink compound between the CPU and heat sink/fan assembly. If your fan came with the compound already applied, be sure to remove the protective tape covering the compound before attaching the fan to the CPU. If you are using your own heat dope from a tube, spread it thinly and evenly.

CPU Cooling

- OEM fans are included with a retail-boxed CPU. Specialty fans, sold by third-party vendors, typically exceed the OEM fans in performance.

- Liquid cooling involves running liquid through a metal block on top of the CPU. In addition to the metal block, liquid cooling systems include a pump to move the liquid, a device to cool the liquid, and a hose to distribute the liquid.

Key Terms

heat dope *(23)*

liquid cooling *(25)*

OEM fan *(25)*

overclocking *(26)*

pin grid array (PGA) *(23)*

retail-boxed CPU *(22)*

specialized fan *(25)*

zero insertion force (ZIF) sockets *(23)*

Key Term Quiz

Use the Key Terms list to complete the sentences that follow. Not all terms will be used.

1. A(n) _____ comes with a fan rated to work with the CPU.

2. The pins on a CPU are arranged in a(n) _____.

3. A thin layer of _____ sits between the CPU and fan.

4. A(n) _____ usually outperforms the fan that comes with a CPU.

5. If you are overclocking or if the fan that came with your CPU is too loud, consider a(n) _____ system.

■ Multiple-Choice Quiz

1. Which of the following statements is true?

    A. If you have an AMD-compatible motherboard, you can install a Celeron processor.

    B. Replacing the CPU may not be the upgrade that is most cost effective or that has the strongest impact on your system's performance.

    C. As the size of the address bus increases, the amount of RAM the CPU can use decreases.

    D. You can upgrade your CPU if you make sure that a new CPU will fit into the socket or slot on your motherboard.

2. What steps do you need to take to install an Athlon 64 X2 CPU into an LGA775 motherboard?

    A. Lift the ZIF socket arm; place the CPU according to the orientation markings; snap on the heatsink and fan assembly.

    B. Lift the ZIF socket arm; place the CPU according to the orientation markings; add a dash of heat dope; snap on the heatsink and fan assembly.

    C. Lift the ZIF socket arm; place the CPU according to the orientation markings; snap on the heatsink and fan assembly; plug in the fan.

    D. Take all the steps you want to take because it's not going to work.

3. What are the differences between a retail-boxed CPU and an OEM CPU? (Choose two.)

    A. Retail-boxed CPUs are always genuine, whereas an OEM CPU may be counterfeit.

    B. OEM CPUs are always genuine, whereas a retail-boxed CPU may be counterfeit.

    C. Retail-boxed CPUs come with a fan rated for the CPU, whereas OEM CPUs do not come with a fan.

    D. OEM CPUs come with a fan rated for the CPU, whereas retail-boxed CPUs do not come with a fan.

4. Which statement about installing CPUs is true?

    A. You must always adjust the motherboard jumpers for your specific CPU.

    B. You must always adjust the jumpers on the CPU to work with your motherboard and chipset.

C. CPUs that carry the ESDx logo have electrostatic discharge protection built in and therefore do not require the use of an antistatic wrist strap during installation.

    D. The CPU fan must be plugged into the motherboard's fan power connector for it to work.

5. What is the best way to straighten out a bent CPU pin?

    A. Use thin needle-nose pliers with a rubber grip to gently pry the pin back into position.

    B. Use an empty mechanical pencil and slide it over the bent pin; then gently straighten it.

    C. Use your fingernails to massage the bent pin into position.

    D. There is no reason to straighten a bent pin. Once a pin is bent, the CPU must be replaced.

6. Which statement about heat dope is true?

    A. You must use a thin layer for it to be effective.

    B. You should use a fairly large amount to ensure the maximum amount of heat is dissipated.

    C. You may apply it directly to the CPU's pins for extra cooling.

    D. Heat dope spray can be applied more evenly than heat dope gel and is therefore recommended.

7. Elana purchased an OEM CPU and two sticks of RAM from an online retailer. Upon delivery, she noticed there was no CPU fan in the shipment. What should Elana do?

    A. Elana should contact the online retailer, as their shipping department made an obvious mistake by not shipping the fan.

    B. Elana should contact the CPU manufacturer, as all CPUs are warranted/guaranteed by the manufacturer—not the reseller.

    C. Elana should do nothing, as OEM CPUs do not require fans.

    D. Elana should purchase a fan rated for her CPU separately, as OEM CPUs do not come with fans.

8. What problems can be caused by a poorly working CPU fan? (Choose all that apply.)

    A. System lockups

    B. Random reboots

C. Flickering monitor

D. Printer jams

9. What advantage do liquid cooling systems offer over fans?

A. Liquid cooling systems are less expensive than fans.

B. Liquid cooling systems are quieter than fans.

C. Liquid cooling systems improve monitor output, as they do not emit the electromagnetic interference that fans do.

D. Liquid cooling systems eliminate the need to dust out the inside of the system case.

10. What changes are typically made to overclocked systems?

A. The system bus speed is increased and the CPU voltage is decreased.

B. The system bus speed is increased and the CPU voltage is increased.

C. The system bus speed is decreased and the CPU voltage is decreased.

D. The system bus speed is decreased and the CPU voltage is increased.

■ Essay Quiz

1. It is important that the CPU stays cool. A number of different technical advances have been made in the design of CPUs along with various devices made to keep the CPU from overheating. Discuss at least two cooling features or cooling options.

2. Explain overclocking and list several pros and cons of overclocking.

Lab Projects

• Lab Project 2.1

Imagine that you are going to buy components to build your own computer. What processor will you use? Typically, the latest and greatest CPU is a lot more expensive than recent models. Intel processors usually cost more than comparable AMD processors. Check CPU features and prices in newspapers or magazines or on the Internet at a site like www.newegg.com. Decide what CPU you want to use for your computer. Write a paragraph explaining why you selected it and how much you will spend for the CPU.

• Lab Project 2.2

If your school hardware lab has motherboards and processors for hands-on labs, practice removing and installing PGA processors on the motherboards. Take note of how the mechanical arm on a ZIF socket works. Answer the following about your experience:

■ How do you know in which direction to place the CPU?

■ How does the mechanical arm lift up? Does it lift straight up or is there a lip it must clear?

■ What effect does lifting the arm have on the socket?

■ How does the ZIF socket hold the CPU in place?

Installing and Troubleshooting RAM

chapter
3

"Many complain of their memory, few of their judgment."

—Benjamin Franklin

Installing RAM is easy to do and very forgiving of mistakes, making it the most common upgrade for PCs. Although the physical act of snapping in RAM is simple, there are a number of tricks to ensure the RAM you buy works when you do put it in a machine. This chapter covers what you need to know about choosing the right type of RAM, installing RAM in a PC, and troubleshooting the few RAM-specific issues that may occur.

In this chapter, you will learn how to

- **Determine memory requirements for a system**
- **Install and upgrade RAM**
- **Perform basic RAM troubleshooting**

Essentials Review

You'll find this chapter far more interesting if you are aware of RAM topics covered in the A+ Essentials exam. Before beginning this chapter, make sure you can

- Describe the different types of DRAM, particularly new types such as RDRAM, DDR, and DDR2
- Recognize the different types of RAM packaging (sticks) and how these relate to different types of RAM
- Explain the different types of RAM speed ratings
- Determine RAM type simply by looking at the speed rating for a particular stick of RAM
- Explain parity and ECC RAM, including when and how these types of RAM are used
- Define double-sided and single-sided RAM, including what determines if a system can use double-sided RAM

IT Technician

■ Working with RAM

Whenever someone comes up to me and asks what single hardware upgrade they can do to improve their system performance, I always tell them the same thing—add more RAM. Adding more RAM can improve overall system performance, processing speed, and stability—if you get it right. Botching the job can cause dramatic system instability, such as frequent, random crashes and reboots. Every tech needs to know how to install and upgrade system RAM of all types.

To get the desired results from a RAM upgrade, you must first determine if insufficient RAM is the cause of system problems. Second, you need to pick the proper RAM for the system. Finally, you must use good installation practices. Always store RAM sticks in anti-static packaging whenever they're not in use, and use strict ESD handling procedures. Like many other pieces of the PC, RAM is *very* sensitive to ESD and other technician abuse (Figure 3.1)!

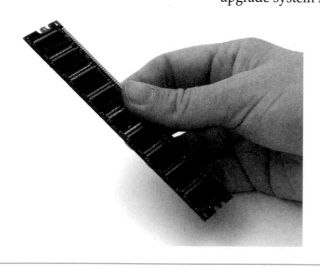

● **Figure 3.1**   Don't do this! Grabbing the contacts is a *bad thing*.

Do You Need RAM?

Two symptoms point to the need for more RAM in a PC: general system sluggishness and excessive hard drive accessing. If programs take forever to load and running programs seem to stall and move more slowly than you would like, the problem could stem from insufficient RAM. A friend with a new Windows XP Professional system complained that her PC seemed snappy when she first got it, but takes a long time to do the things she wants to do with it, such as photograph retouching in Adobe Photoshop and document layout for a print zine she produces. Her system had only 256 MB of RAM, sufficient to run Windows XP Professional, but woefully insufficient for her tasks—she kept maxing out the RAM and thus the system slowed to a crawl. I replaced her stick with a pair of 1-GB sticks and suddenly she had the powerhouse workstation she desired.

Try This!

Checking the Page File

How much of your hard drive does Windows use for a page file? Does the level change dramatically when you open typical applications, such as Microsoft Word, Solitaire, and Paint Shop Pro? The answers to these questions can give a tech a quick estimation about RAM usage and possibly RAM needs for a particular system, so try this.

Windows 2000/XP gives you a very easy way to glance at your page file usage through the Task Manager. To access the Task Manager, press CTRL-ALT-DEL simultaneously once. Click the Performance tab. The second box on the left, titled PF Usage, displays the amount of hard drive the page file is currently using.

1. How big is the page file when you have no applications open?
2. How much does it change when you open applications?

Excessive hard drive activity when you move between programs points to a need for more RAM. Every Windows PC has the capability to make a portion of your hard drive look like RAM in case you run out of real RAM. This is called the **page file** or *swap file*. If you fill your RAM up with programs, your PC will automatically start loading some programs into the page file. You can't see this process taking place just by looking at the screen—these swaps are done in the background. But you will notice the hard drive access LED going crazy as Windows rushes to move programs between RAM and the page file in a process called **disk thrashing**. Windows uses the page file all the time, but excessive disk thrashing suggests that you need more RAM.

You can diagnose excessive disk thrashing through simply observing the hard drive access LED flashing, or through various third-party tools. I like FreeMeter (www.tiler.com/freemeter/). It's been around for quite a while, runs on all versions of Windows, and is easy to use (Figure 3.2). Notice on the FreeMeter screenshot that some amount of the page file is being used. That's perfectly normal.

System RAM Recommendations

Microsoft sets the minimum RAM requirements listed for the various Windows operating systems very low to get the maximum number of users to upgrade or convert, and that's fine. A Windows XP Professional machine will run on 64 MB of RAM. Just don't ask it to do any serious computing, like run Doom III! Here are my recommendations for system RAM.

Operating System	Microsoft Minimum	Solid Performance	Power User
Windows 2000	32 MB	256 MB	512 MB
Windows XP	64 MB	512 MB	1 GB
Windows Vista	512 MB	1 GB	2 GB

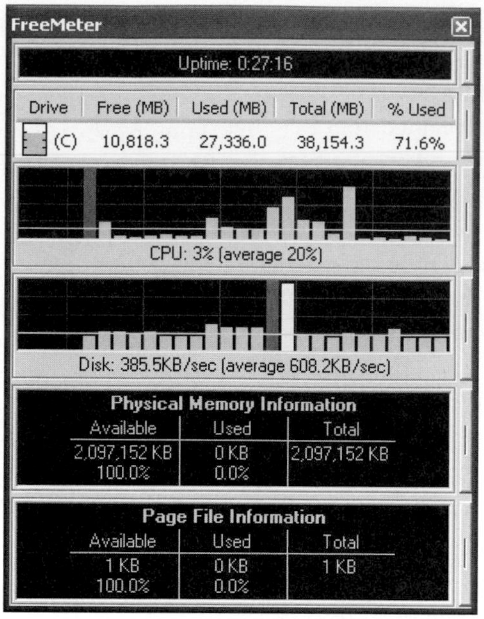

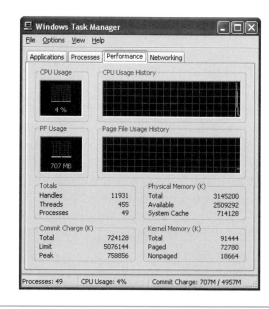

Figure 3.2   FreeMeter

Determining Current RAM Capacity

Before you go get RAM, you obviously need to know how much RAM you currently have in your PC. Every version of Windows works the same way. Just select the Properties for My Computer to see how much RAM is in your system (Figure 3.3). If you have a newer keyboard, you can access the screen with the WINDOWS-PAUSE/BREAK keystroke combination. Windows 2000 and XP come with the handy Performance tab under the Task Manager (as shown in Figure 3.4).

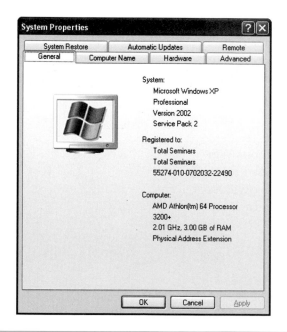

Figure 3.3   Mike has a lot of RAM!

Figure 3.4   Performance tab on the Windows XP Task Manager

Getting the Right RAM

To do the perfect RAM upgrade, determine the optimum capacity of RAM to install and then get the right RAM for the motherboard. Your first two stops toward these goals are the inside of the case and your motherboard manual. Open the case to see how many sticks of RAM you have installed currently and how many free slots you have open. Check the motherboard book to determine the total capacity of RAM the system can handle and what specific technology works with your system. You can't put DDR SDRAM into a system that can only handle SDR SDRAM, after all, and it won't do you much good to install a pair of 512-MB DIMMs when your system tops out at 784 MB! Figure 3.5 shows the RAM limits for my Gigabyte motherboard.

Mix and Match at Your Peril

All motherboards can handle different capacities of RAM. If you have three slots, you may put a 512-MB stick in one and a 1-GB stick in the other with a high chance of success. To ensure maximum stability in a system, however, shoot for as close as you can get to uniformity of RAM. Choose RAM sticks that match in technology, capacity, and speed. Even on motherboards that offer slots for radically different RAM types, I recommend uniformity.

Dual Channel Memory Configuration

The GA-K8N Ultra-SLI/GA-K8N Pro-SLI supports the Dual Channel Technology. When the Dual Channel Technology is activated, the bandwidth of memory bus will be double the original one.

Due to CPU limitation, if you want to operate the Dual Channel Technology, please follow the guidelines below for Dual Channel memory configuration.
1. Dual Channel mode will not be enabled if only one DDR memory module is installed.
2. To enable Dual Channel mode with 2 memory modules (it is recommended to use memory modules of identical brand, size, chips, and speed), you must install them into DIMM sockets of the same color.
3. To enable Dual Channel mode with 4 memory modules, it is recommended to use memory modules of identical brand, size, chips, and speed.

The following is a Dual Channel Memory configuration table: (DS: Double Side, SS: Single Side)

	DDR1	DDR2	DDR3	DDR4
2 memory modules	DS/SS	DS/SS	X	X
	X	X	DS/SS	DS/SS
4 memory modules	DS/SS	DS/SS	DS/SS	DS/SS

NOTE: If two memory modules are to be used to achieve Dual Channel mode, we recommend installing them in DDR1 and DDR2 DIMM sockets.

CAUTION: All of the memory configurations below will cause system unable to boot. (DS: Double Side, SS: Single Side)

	DDR1	DDR2	DDR3	DDR4
1 memory module	X	DS/SS	X	X
	X	X	X	DS/SS
2 memory modules	X	DS/SS	DS/SS	X
	DS/SS	X	X	DS/SS
	X	DS/SS	X	DS/SS
3 memory modules	DS/SS	DS/SS	DS/SS	X
	X	DS/SS	DS/SS	DS/SS
	DS/SS	X	DS/SS	DS/SS
	DS/SS	DS/SS	X	DS/SS

- **Figure 3.5** The motherboard book shows how much RAM that Athlon 64 can handle.

Mixing Speeds

With so many different DRAM speeds available, you may often find yourself tempted to mix speeds of DRAM in the same system. Although in many situations you can get away with mixing speeds on a system, the safest, easiest rule to follow is to use the speed of DRAM specified in the motherboard book, and make sure that every piece of DRAM runs at that speed. In a worst-case scenario, mixing DRAM speeds can cause the system to lock up every few seconds or every few minutes. You might also get some data corruption. Mixing speeds sometimes works fine, but don't do your income tax on a machine with mixed DRAM speeds until the system has proven to be stable for a few days. The important thing to note here is that you won't break anything, other than possibly data, by experimenting.

Okay, I have mentioned enough disclaimers. Modern motherboards provide some flexibility regarding RAM speeds and mixing. First, you can use RAM that is faster than what the motherboard specifies. For example, if the system needs PC3200 DDR2 SDRAM, you may put in PC4200 DDR2 SDRAM and it should work fine. Faster DRAM is not going to make the system run any faster, however, so don't look for any system improvement.

Second, you can sometimes get away with putting one speed of DRAM in one bank and another speed in another bank, as long as all the speeds are as fast or faster than the speed specified by the motherboard. Don't bother trying to put different-speed DRAMs in the same bank with a motherboard that uses dual-channel DDR. Yes, it works once in a while, but it's too chancy. I avoid it.

Installing DIMMs and RIMMs

Installing DRAM is so easy that it's one of the very few jobs I recommend to non-techie folks. First, attach an anti-static wrist strap or touch some bare metal on the power supply to ground yourself and avoid ESD. Then swing the side tabs on the RAM slots down from the upright position. Pick up a stick of RAM—don't touch those contacts! A good hard push down is usually all you need to ensure a solid connection. Make sure that the DIMM snaps into position to show it is completely seated. You will also notice that the two side tabs will move in to reflect a tight connection (Figure 3.6).

SPD

Your motherboard should detect and automatically set up any DIMM or RIMM you install, assuming you have the right RAM for the system. RAM makers add a handy chip to modern sticks called the serial presence detect (SPD) chip (Figure 3.7). The SPD stores all the information about your DRAM, including size, speed, ECC or non-ECC, registered or unregistered, and a number of other more technical bits of information.

● **Figure 3.6**   Inserting a DIMM

When a PC boots, it queries the SPD so that the MCC knows how much RAM is on the stick, how fast it runs, and other information. Any program can query the SPD. Take a look at Figure 3.8 with the results of the popular **CPU-Z** program showing RAM information from the SPD.

All new systems count on the SPD to set the RAM timings properly for your system when it boots. If you add a RAM stick with a bad SPD, you'll get a POST error message and the system will not boot. You can't fix a broken SPD; you just buy a new stick of RAM.

The RAM Count

After installing the new RAM, turn on the PC and watch the boot process closely. If you installed the RAM correctly, the RAM count on the PC will reflect the new value. If the RAM value stays the same, you probably have installed the RAM in a slot the motherboard doesn't want you to use (for example, if you need to use a particular slot first) or the RAM is not properly installed. If the computer does not boot and you've got a blank screen, you probably have not installed all the RAM sticks correctly. Usually, a good second look is all you need to determine the problem (Figures 3.9 and 3.10). Reseat or reinstall the RAM stick and try again.

RAM counts are confusing because RAM uses megabytes and gigabytes as opposed to millions and billions. Here are some examples of how different systems would show 256 MB of RAM:

268435456 (exactly 256 × 1 MB)
256M (some PCs try to make it easy for you)
262,144 (number of KB)

You should know how much RAM you're trying to install and use some common sense. If you've got 512 MB and you add another 512-MB stick, you need a number that looks like one gigabyte. If after you add the second stick, you see a RAM count of 524582912—that sure looks like 512 MB, not the one gigabyte!

Installing SO-DIMMs in Laptops

It wasn't that long ago that adding RAM to a laptop was either impossible or required you to send the system back to the manufacturer. For years, every laptop maker had custom-made, proprietary

• **Figure 3.7**   SPD chip on stick

• **Figure 3.8**   CPU-Z showing RAM information

```
Award Modular BIOS v6.00PG, An Energy Star Ally
Copyright (C) 1984-2005, Award Software, Inc.

GA-K8NP F13

Processor : AMD Athlon(tm) 64 Processor 3200+
<CPUID:0000F4A Patch ID:003A>
Memory Testing : 1048576K OK
CPU clock frequency : 200 Mhz

Detecting IDE drives ...
```

• **Figure 3.9**   Hey, where's the rest of my RAM?!

```
Award Modular BIOS v6.00PG, An Energy Star Ally
Copyright (C) 1984-2005, Award Software, Inc.

GA-K8NP F13

Processor : AMD Athlon(tm) 64 Processor 3200+
<CPUID:0000F4A Patch ID:003A>
Memory Testing : 3145728K OK
CPU clock frequency : 200 Mhz

Detecting IDE drives ...
```

• **Figure 3.10**   RAM count after proper insertion of DIMMs

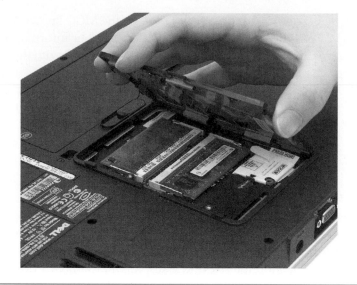

● **Figure 3.11**   A RAM access panel on a laptop

● **Figure 3.12**   Snapping in an SO-DIMM

RAM packages that were difficult to handle and stagger-ingly expensive. The wide acceptance of SO-DIMMs over the last few years has virtually erased these problems. All laptops now provide relatively convenient access to their SO-DIMMs, enabling easy replacement or addition of RAM.

Access to RAM usually requires removing a panel or lifting up the keyboard—the procedure varies among laptop manufacturers. Figure 3.11 shows a typical laptop RAM access panel. You can slide the panel off to reveal the SO-DIMMs. SO-DIMMs usually insert exactly like the old SIMMs—slide the pins into position and snap the SO-DIMM down into the retaining clips (Figure 3.12).

Before doing any work on a laptop, turn the system off, disconnect it from the AC wall socket, and remove all batteries. Use an anti-static wrist strap because laptops are far more susceptible to ESD than desktop PCs.

■ Troubleshooting RAM

"Memory" errors show up in a variety of ways on modern systems, including parity errors, ECC error messages, system lockups, page faults, and other error screens in Windows. These errors can indicate bad RAM, but often point to something completely unrelated to RAM. This is especially true with intermit-tent problems. The challenge for techs is to recognize these errors and then de-termine which part of the system caused the memory error.

You can get two radically different types of parity errors: real and phantom. Real parity errors are simply errors that the MCC detects from the parity or ECC chips (if you have them). The operating system then reports the problem in an error message, such as "Parity error at *xxxx:xxxxxxxx*," where *xxxx:xxxxxxxx* is a hexadecimal value (a string of numbers and letters, like A5F2:004EEAB9). If you get an error like this, write down the value. A real parity/ECC error will show up at the same place in memory each time, and almost always indicates that you have a bad RAM stick.

Phantom parity errors show up on systems that don't have parity or ECC memory. If Windows generates parity errors with different addresses, you most likely do *not* have a problem with RAM. These phantom errors can occur for a variety of reasons, including software problems, heat or dust, solar flares, fluctuations in the Force … you get the idea.

System lockups and page faults (they often go hand in hand) in Windows can indicate a problem with RAM. A system lockup is when the computer stops functioning. A **page fault** is a milder error that can be caused by memory issues, but not necessarily system RAM problems. Certainly page faults *look* like RAM issues because Windows generates frightening error messages filled with long strings of hexadecimal digits, such as "KRNL386 caused a page fault at 03F2:25A003BC." (See Figure 3.13.) Just because the error message contains a memory address, however, does not mean that you have a problem with your RAM. Write down the address. If it repeats in later error messages, you probably have a bad RAM stick. If Windows displays different memory locations, you need to look elsewhere for the culprit.

Every once in a while, something potentially catastrophic happens within the PC, some little electron hits the big red panic button, and the

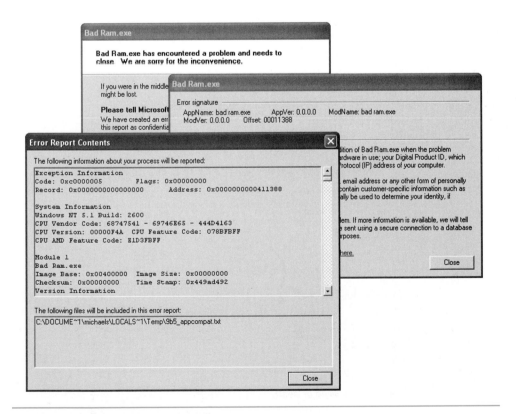

• **Figure 3.13**　Windows error message

Chapter 3: Installing and Troubleshooting RAM

operating system has to shut down certain functions running in order to save data. This panic button inside the PC is called a **non-maskable interrupt (NMI)**, more simply defined as an interruption the CPU cannot ignore. An NMI manifests to the user as what techs lovingly call the **Blue Screen of Death (BSoD)**—a bright blue screen with a scary-sounding error message on it (Figure 3.14).

Bad RAM sometimes triggers an NMI, although often the culprit lies with buggy programming or clashing code. The BSoD varies according to the operating system, and it would require a much lengthier tome than this one to cover all the variations. Suffice it to say that RAM *could* be the problem when that delightful blue screen appears.

Finally, **intermittent memory errors** can come from a variety of sources, including a dying power supply, electrical interference, buggy applications, buggy hardware, and so on. These errors show up as lockups, general protection faults, page faults, and parity errors, but never have the same address or happen with the same applications. Try the power supply first with non-application-specific intermittent errors of any sort.

> A *general protection fault (GPF)* is an error that can cause an application to crash. Often they're caused by programs stepping on each other's toes. Chapter 11 goes into more detail on Windows errors.

Testing RAM

Once you discover that you may have a RAM problem, you have a couple of options. First, several companies manufacture hardware RAM testing devices, but unless you have a lot of disposable income, they're probably priced way too high for the average tech (US$1500 and higher). Second, you can use the method I use—*replace and pray*. Open the system case and replace each stick, one at a time, with a known good replacement stick.

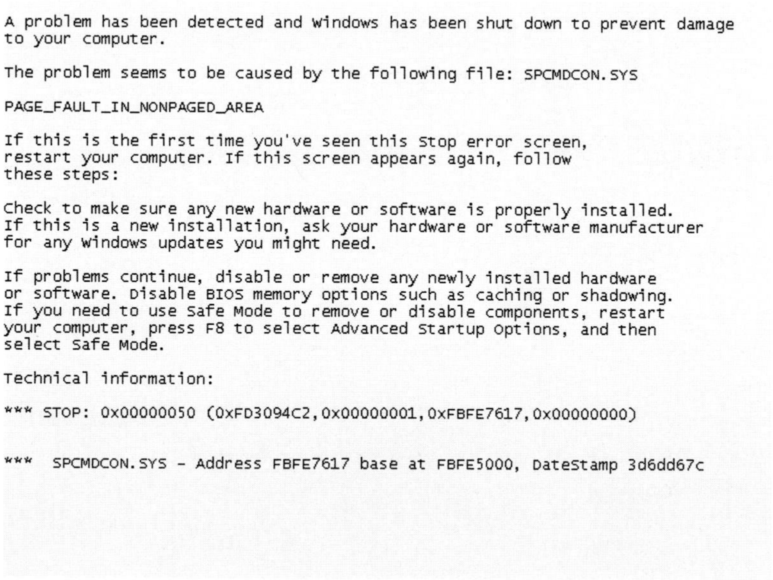

```
A problem has been detected and windows has been shut down to prevent damage
to your computer.

The problem seems to be caused by the following file: SPCMDCON.SYS

PAGE_FAULT_IN_NONPAGED_AREA

If this is the first time you've seen this Stop error screen,
restart your computer. If this screen appears again, follow
these steps:

Check to make sure any new hardware or software is properly installed.
If this is a new installation, ask your hardware or software manufacturer
for any windows updates you might need.

If problems continue, disable or remove any newly installed hardware
or software. Disable BIOS memory options such as caching or shadowing.
If you need to use Safe Mode to remove or disable components, restart
your computer, press F8 to select Advanced Startup Options, and then
select Safe Mode.

Technical information:

*** STOP: 0x00000050 (0xFD3094C2,0x00000001,0xFBFE7617,0x00000000)


***   SPCMDCON.SYS - Address FBFE7617 base at FBFE5000, DateStamp 3d6dd67c
```

• **Figure 3.14** Blue Screen of Death

```
       Memtest86+ v1.65     : Pass 11% ####
Athlon 64 (0.09) 2009 MHz   : Test 12% ####
L1 Cache:  128K 16468MB/s    : Test #4  [Moving inversions, random pattern]
L2 Cache:  512K 16468MB/s    : Testing:  108K -  256M  256M
Memory  :  256M 11224MB/s    : Pattern:  94a989c0
Chipset : Intel i440BX

  WallTime   Cached  RsvdMem    MemMap    Cache   ECC   Test   Pass   Errors  ECC Errs
 ---------  -------  -------   --------  ------  ----  -----  -----  -------  --------
   0:00:05    256M     216K   e820-Std     on    off    Std      0        0

 (ESC)Reboot  (c)configuration  (SP)scroll_lock  (CR)scroll_unlock
```

- **Figure 3.15**   Memtest86 in action

(You have one of those lying around, don't you?) This method, although potentially time-consuming, certainly works. With PC prices as low as they are now, you could simply replace the whole system for less than the price of a dedicated RAM tester.

Third, you could run a software-based tester on the RAM. Because you have to load a software tester into the memory it's about to scan, there's always a small chance that simply starting the software RAM tester might cause an error. Still, you can find some pretty good free ones out there. My favorite is the venerable **Memtest86** written by Mr. Chris Brady (www.memtest86.com). Memtest86 will exhaustively check your RAM and report bad RAM when it finds it (Figure 3.15).

Beyond A+

The Next Generations

Computer games have done more for advances in PC hardware than anything else. Have you ever seen a late-generation game such as Half-Life 2 or Far Cry? These games require powerful video cards, and every video card comes with DRAM. To make these beautiful games, the video card's DRAM needs to be incredibly fast. Video card makers adopted many DRAM technologies such as DDR even before they were popular as system RAM on PCs. If you want to see where DRAM is going, check out video cards (Figure 3.16).

Two advancements to DDR2 originally found only in video cards will show up as primary system memory within a year of this writing: DDR3 and DDR4. DDR3 uses even less power than DDR2 and doubles again the speed of the DRAM's I/O. DDR4 chips push the speed even higher than DDR3!

Go to Chapter 12 for a more detailed description of video memory.

Tech Tip

Serial Connections

Serial connections run ones and zeroes through a single wire, as opposed to parallel connections that use many wires. With only one wire to worry about, manufacturers can heavily shield serial connections and make them run blazingly fast. You'll see the shift from parallel to serial in many aspects of the modern PC.

Half-Life 2—these beautiful graphics are possible because of fast DRAM (and other technology improvements).

DDR3 and DDR4 will almost certainly appear in the upcoming **fully buffered DIMMs (FB-DIMMs)** . FB-DIMMs are registered— but with a twist. They replace the 64-bit-wide DIMM data connection with a staggeringly fast serial connection, expected to reach as much as 4.8 GBps! That should be fast enough to keep our PCs happy for the next few years!

Chapter 3 Review

■ Chapter Summary

After reading this chapter and completing the exercises, you should understand the following about installing and troubleshooting RAM.

Working with RAM

- Disk thrashing is constant hard drive activity symptomatic of insufficient RAM. It occurs when Windows repeatedly uses up all available RAM space and has to move data not immediately needed out of the RAM into a temporary file on the hard drive called a swap file or page file, and then swap the data back into RAM when it is needed by the program. You can monitor the size of your swap file in the Task Manager.

- You must know what type of RAM (such as regular SDRAM, DDR RAM, or DDR2 RAM) your motherboard accepts before you purchase a RAM upgrade. You also need to know the maximum amount of RAM your motherboard supports and the maximum supported per slot.

- Though not required, it is good practice to make sure all sticks of RAM in any system are as close to identical as possible. It will lessen the chance of problems and incompatibility if your RAM modules match in technology, capacity, speed, and manufacturer.

- The serial presence detect (SPD) chip on modern DIMMs automatically supplies all the information about the RAM to the system, such as the size, speed, ECC or non-ECC, registered or unregistered, and other details.

- Installing SO-DIMMs in a laptop requires the removal of a panel on the underside of the laptop or removing the keyboard to find the RAM slots. The SO-DIMM slides into the slot and snaps down into position. Unplug the laptop and remove the battery before attempting a RAM upgrade, and protect the RAM from ESD by wearing an anti-static wristband.

Troubleshooting RAM

- Symptoms of bad RAM include parity errors, system lockups, page faults, and other error screens in Windows. However, other failing components can cause similar problems. Bad RAM usually results in error screens displaying messages such as "Parity error at $xxxx:xxxxxxxx$" where $xxxx:xxxxxxxx$ is a hexadecimal value such as A5F2:004EEAB9. A real parity error will show up in the same place in memory each time—if that hexadecimal code is always the same, you probably have bad RAM.

- Page faults result in error screens such as "KRNL386 caused a page fault at 03F2:25A003BC." The process that caused the page fault (in this case, KRNL386) may change, but if the hexadecimal address is the same across numerous error screens, you probably have bad RAM.

- A non-maskable interrupt (NMI) results in a Blue Screen of Death (BSoD). Although BSoDs are often blamed on bad RAM, they are more often caused by buggy application program code.

- If you suspect you have bad RAM and you don't have a hardware RAM testing device, swap one of the sticks in your system with a known-good stick. If the system works, you've found the bad stick. If the system still has errors, replace the stick you removed and swap a different stick for the known-good stick. Another option is to use a software RAM tester like Memtest86.

■ Key Terms

Blue Screen of Death (BSoD) *(40)*	**intermittent memory error** *(40)*	**page file** *(33)*
CPU-Z *(37)*	**Memtest86** *(41)*	**serial presence detect (SPD)**
disk thrashing *(33)*	**non-maskable interrupt**	**chip** *(36)*
fully buffered DIMM	**(NMI)** *(40)*	
(FB-DIMM) *(42)*	**page fault** *(39)*	

■ Key Term Quiz

Use the Key Terms list to complete the sentences that follow. Not all terms will be used.

1. If the LED for your hard drive stays on most of the time, your computer is suffering from _____, a sure sign you need to add more memory.

2. Modern systems automatically detect new RAM by polling the module's _____.

3. If a PC's RAM is full, it will load some programs into the _____.

4. A(n) _____ is a mild error, but does not necessarily indicate a problem with RAM.

5. The CPU cannot ignore a(n) _____, which results in a _____.

6. A new memory technology called a(n) _____ uses a very fast serial connection rather than the typical 64-bit-wide DIMM connection.

7. If you think your RAM might be bad, running the popular _____ is a good way to test RAM.

8. A bad power supply often causes a(n) _____.

9. _____ is a great program to run for detailed information about your installed RAM.

■ Multiple-Choice Quiz

1. If you upgrade your memory but notice that the RAM count does not reflect the additional memory, what should you do?

   A. Remove the RAM and try to reinstall it.

   B. Restart the computer.

   C. Return the memory because it's probably bad.

   D. Go to Setup and configure the memory to reflect the new amount.

2. What does a non-maskable interrupt cause the CPU to produce?

   A. The Blue Screen of Death

   B. A parity error

   C. Excessive heat

   D. An incorrect memory count

3. If you are running Windows 2000 or Windows XP, you can use all of the following methods to find out how much RAM is installed in your computer *except* _____.

   A. From the Control Panel, select System and then the Hardware tab.

   B. Use the Performance tab under the Task Manager.

   C. Select Properties from My Computer.

   D. With a newer keyboard, press the WINDOWS-PAUSE/BREAK keystroke combination.

4. What happens if you mix RAM sticks of different speeds?

   A. Your computer will work fine as long as it uses dual-channel architecture.

   B. Your computer may slow down.

   C. Your computer will work fine if all the memory sticks are slower than the speed of the motherboard.

   D. Your computer may lock up every few seconds or provide corrupted data.

5. What is true about a double-sided DIMM?

   A. It has memory chips on the front and back.

   B. It can be installed forward or backwards.

   C. It is twice as fast as a single-sided DIMM.

   D. It has half the capacity of a quad-sided DIMM.

6. Not enough RAM in your system can cause which of the following symptoms?

   A. Disk thrashing

   B. BSoD

   C. Data loss

   D. Excessive heat

7. What is the minimum requirement for RAM in Windows XP?

   A. 64 MB

   B. 128 MB

   C. 192 MB

   D. 256 MB

8. What is the purpose of the serial presence detect chip?

   A. It corrects parity errors.

   B. It stores all the information about your DRAM, including size, speed, and other more technical bits of information.

   C. It reports if it is serial RAM or parallel RAM to the CPU.

   D. It detects serial devices, such as USB, and provides these devices with direct access to RAM.

9. In what types of systems are SO-DIMMs typically used?

   A. High-end servers

   B. Average desktops

   C. Laptops

   D. Business workstations

10. Why should you never hold a stick of RAM by the contacts?

    A. RAM sticks can store an electrical charge that can shock you if you touch the contacts.

    B. The contacts are extremely brittle and can easily snap off if touched.

    C. The contacts are coated with a protective chemical that is harmful to human skin.

    D. Ram sticks are sensitive to ESD.

11. How can you check the size of your page file in Windows 2000/XP?

    A. Right-click My Computer, choose Properties, and look on the General tab.

    B. Double-click the System applet in the Control Panel and then look on the General tab.

    C. Right-click My Computer, choose Manage, and then select Device Manager. Finally, expand the System tree.

    D. Press CONTROL-ALT-DELETE to display Task Manager and then look at the Performance tab.

12. How can you upgrade your system from using regular SDRAM to DDR RAM?

    A. You can't. You must purchase a new motherboard that supports DDR RAM.

    B. Purchase an SDRAM-to-DDR adapter.

    C. Install a DDR expansion card into any available PCI slot.

    D. Use external DDR RAM.

13. Harold suspects a bad stick of RAM in his home computer. How would you recommend he test it?

    A. Purchase a hardware RAM testing device, which is within the budget of most home users.

    B. Replace the suspected bad RAM with a stick of known good RAM.

    C. RAM is so expensive, it is best that he just replace the entire system.

    D. Use the Windows RAMTest administrative tool.

■ Essay Quiz

1. Your cousin James recently bought a new AMD computer with 128 MB of RAM and Windows XP operating system. He's complaining about how slow his new computer is, especially when he's working with his graphics applications. How can you convince him that he needs more memory?

2. Now that you've convinced your cousin James that he needs more memory for his new PC, how will you explain what kind he should buy and how he should install it? You may assume that he has the motherboard book and that his computer has a 233-MHz system bus and can support double data rate RAM.

3. Your computer is acting funny. Sometimes you get an error message on the screen. Other times data seems to be corrupted. Sometimes the computer just locks up. You suspect that it may be bad memory. How can you find out whether a memory problem or something else is causing your trouble?

Lab Projects

• Lab Project 3.1

Grab your personal PC or a lab PC at your school and determine the manufacturer and model of the motherboard. Armed with that information, use the Internet or motherboard manual to find out the following:

1. How much total RAM does the system support?
2. What type of RAM does the system support?
3. What is the maximum capacity supported per bank?

• Lab Project 3.2

If your computer lab has hardware for hands-on activities, practice removing and installing desktop RAM and laptop RAM. Pay attention to the force required to release the side clips when removing RAM and the downward force required to snap a DIMM in place. Once you've installed a stick, boot the computer to verify the RAM is recognized. Answer the following about your experience with one of the systems:

1. What type of RAM does your motherboard use?
2. What color(s) are the RAM slots?
3. How many RAM slots are there?
4. Is it possible to install a stick of RAM backwards or upside-down? Why or why not?
5. How many sticks of RAM are installed? How many slots are filled? How many banks are filled?

Working with BIOS and CMOS

chapter

4

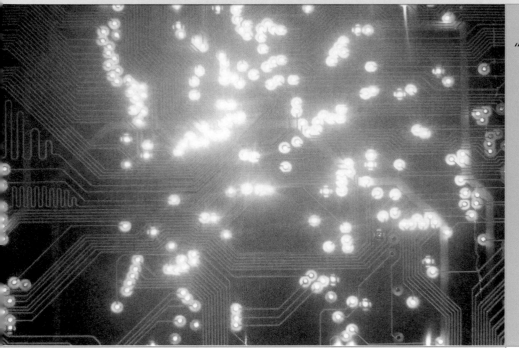

"It is impossible to design a system so perfect that no one needs to be good."

—T. S. Eliot

The CMOS setup program is used to configure your PC's most critical hardware, but what happens when critical hardware isn't working properly? For example, how do you know if your keyboard has become unplugged or your hard drive has suddenly died? That's what you'll learn in this chapter. Here you'll be introduced to the testing part of BIOS—the power-on self test (POST). You'll learn how the POST informs you of problems and how to deal with those problems as they arrive. This chapter also covers how to maintain your BIOS/CMOS by working with the onboard CMOS battery. You'll even learn how to update your BIOS to accept newer hardware and operating systems.

In this chapter, you will learn how to

- **Recognize and use the power-on self test**

- **Troubleshoot CMOS**

- **Update BIOS**

Essentials Review

You'll find this chapter far more interesting if you are aware of BIOS and CMOS topics covered in the A+ Essentials exam. Before beginning this chapter, make sure you can

- Explain the concept of BIOS and why it exists on your PC
- Discuss the relationship of BIOS to CMOS
- List the dominant makers of BIOS/CMOS setup programs
- Explain why Flash ROM technology is important to the BIOS industry
- Discuss when and how the CMOS setup is accessed and contrast scenarios when you would want to access CMOS versus when you would not
- Give examples of the options available in a typical CMOS
- Explain why every hardware device on your computer needs programming and discuss the many ways that this programming is provided

IT Technician

■ Power-On Self Test (POST)

BIOS isn't the only program on your system ROM. When the computer is turned on or reset, it initiates a special program, also stored on the system ROM chip, called the **power-on self test (POST)**. The POST program checks out the system every time the computer boots. To perform this check, the POST sends out a command that says to all the devices, "Check yourselves out!" All the standard devices in the computer then run their own internal diagnostic—the POST doesn't specify what they must check. The quality of the diagnostic is up to the people who made that particular device.

Let's consider the POST for a moment. Suppose some device—let's say it's the keyboard controller chip—runs its diagnostic and determines that it is not working properly. What can the POST do about it? Only one thing really: Tell the human in front of the PC! So how does the computer tell the human? PCs convey POST information to you in two ways: beep codes and text error codes.

Before and During the Video Test: The Beep Codes

The computer tests the most basic parts of the computer first, up to and including the video card. In early PCs, you'd hear a series of beeps—called **beep codes**—if anything went wrong. By using beep codes before and during the video test, the computer could communicate with you. (If a POST

You'll find lots of online documentation about beep codes, but it's usually badly outdated!

error occurs before the video is available, obviously the error must manifest itself as beeps because nothing can display on the screen.) The meaning of the beep code you'd hear varied among different BIOS manufacturers. You could find the beep codes for a specific motherboard in its motherboard manual.

Most modern PCs have only a single beep code, which is for bad or missing video—one long beep followed by three short beeps.

You'll hear three other beep sequences on most PCs (although they're not officially beep codes). At the end of a successful POST, the PC will produce one or two short beeps, simply to inform you that all is well. Most systems make a rather strange noise when the RAM is missing or very seriously damaged. Unlike traditional beep codes, this code repeats until you shut off the system. Finally, your speaker might make beeps for reasons that aren't POST or boot related. One of the more common is a series of short beeps after the system's been running for a while. That's a CPU alarm telling you the CPU is approaching its high heat limit.

Tech Tip

Talking BIOS

Some newer motherboards can also talk to you if there is a problem during POST. To use this feature, all that is normally required is to plug a pair of speakers or headphones into the onboard sound card.

Text Errors

After the video has tested okay, any POST errors will display on the screen as a **text error**. If you get a text error, the problem is usually, but not always, self-explanatory (Figure 4.1). Text errors are far more useful than beep codes because you can simply read the screen to determine the bad device.

```
PhoenixBIOS 4.0 release 6.0
Copyright 1985-2000 Phoenix Technologies Ltd.
All Rights Reserved

CPU = Pentium III  500MHz
640K System RAM Passed
47M Extended RAM Passed
USB upper limit segment address:  EEFE
Mouse initialized

HDD Controller Failure
Press <F1> to resume
```

● **Figure 4.1**   Text error messages

POST Cards

Beep codes and text error codes, although helpful, can sometimes be misleading. Worse than that, an inoperative device can sometimes disrupt the POST, forcing the machine into an endless loop. This causes the PC to act dead—no beeps and nothing on the screen. In this case, you need a device, called a **POST card**, to monitor the POST and identify which piece of hardware is causing the trouble.

POST cards are simple cards that snap into an expansion slot on your system. A small, two-character light-emitting diode (LED) readout on the card indicates what device the POST is currently testing (Figure 4.2). The documentation that comes with the POST card tells you what the codes mean. BIOS makers also provide this information on their Web sites. Manufacturers make POST cards for all types of desktop PCs. POST cards work with any BIOS, but you need to know the type of BIOS you have in order to interpret the readout properly.

I usually only pull out a POST card when the usual POST errors fail to appear. When a computer provides a beep or text error code that doesn't make sense, or if your machine keeps locking up, some device has stalled the POST. Because the POST card will tell you which device is being tested, the frozen system will

● **Figure 4.2**   POST card in action

stay at that point in the POST, and the error will stay on the POST card's readout.

Many companies sell POST cards today, with prices ranging from the affordable to the outrageous. Spend the absolute least amount of money you can. The more expensive cards add bells and whistles that you do not need, such as diagnostic software and voltmeters.

Using a POST card is straightforward. Simply power down the PC, install the POST card in any unused slot, and turn the PC back on. As you watch the POST display, notice the different hexadecimal readouts and refer to them as the POST progresses. Notice how quickly they change. If you get an "FF" or "00," that means the POST is over and everything passed—time to check the operating system. If a device stalls the POST, however, the POST card will display an error code. That's the problem device! Good technicians often memorize a dozen or more different POST codes because it's much faster than looking them up in a book.

So you got a beep code, a text error code, or a POST error. Now what do you do with that knowledge? Remember that a POST error does not fix the computer; it only tells you where to look. You then have to know how to deal with that bad or improperly configured component. If you use a POST card, for example, and it hangs at the "Initializing Floppy Drive" test, you'd better know how to work on a floppy drive!

Sometimes the POST card returns a bizarre or confusing error code. What device do you point at when you get a "CMOS shutdown register read/write error" beep code from an older system? First of all, read the error carefully. Let's say on that same system you got an "8042—gate A20 failure" beep code. What will you do? Assuming you know (and you should!) that the "8042" refers to the keyboard, a quick peek at the keyboard and its connection would be a good first step. Beyond that specific example, here is a good general rule: If you don't know what the error means or the bad part isn't replaceable, replace the motherboard. Clearly, you will stumble across exceptions to this rule, but more often than not, the rule stands.

The Boot Process

All PCs need a process to begin their operations. Once you feed power to the PC, the tight interrelation of hardware, **firmware** (programming stored on chips), and software (programming stored on mass storage) enables the PC to start itself, to "pull itself up by the bootstraps" or boot itself.

When you first power on a PC, the power supply circuitry tests for proper voltage and then sends a signal down a special wire called the **power good wire** to awaken the CPU. In every Intel and clone CPU, the moment the power good wire wakes up the CPU, the CPU immediately sends a built-in memory address via its address bus. This special address is the same on every Intel and clone CPU, from the oldest 8086 to the most recent microprocessor. This address is the first line of the POST program on the system ROM! That's how the system starts the POST.

After the POST has finished, there must be a way for the computer to find the programs on the hard drive to start the operating system. The POST passes control to the last BIOS function: the bootstrap loader. The **bootstrap loader** is little more than a few dozen lines of BIOS code tacked to the end of the POST program. Its job is to find the operating system. The bootstrap loader reads CMOS information to tell it where to look first for an operating system. Your PC's CMOS setup utility has an option that you configure to tell the bootstrap loader which devices to check for an operating system and in which order (Figure 4.3).

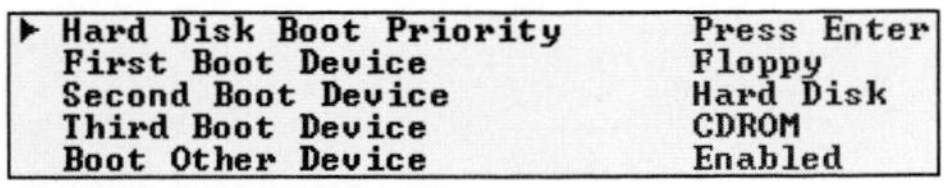

```
▶ Hard Disk Boot Priority      Press Enter
  First Boot Device             Floppy
  Second Boot Device            Hard Disk
  Third Boot Device             CDROM
  Boot Other Device             Enabled
```

● **Figure 4.3**   CMOS boot order

Almost all storage devices—floppy disks, hard disks, CDs, DVDs, and even USB thumb drives—can be configured to boot an operating system by setting aside a specific location called the *boot sector*. If the device is bootable, its boot sector will contain special programming designed to tell the system where to locate the operating system. Any device with a functional operating system is called a **bootable disk** or a **system disk**. If the bootstrap loader locates a good boot sector, it passes control to the operating system and removes itself from memory. If it doesn't, it will go to the next device in the boot order you set in the CMOS setup utility. Boot order is an important tool for techs because it enables you to load in special bootable devices so you can run utilities to maintain PCs without using the primary operating system.

■ Care and Feeding of BIOS and CMOS

BIOS and CMOS are areas in your PC that you don't go to very often. BIOS itself is invisible. The only real clue you have that it even exists is the POST. The CMOS setup utility, on the other hand, is very visible if you start it. Most CMOS setup utilities today work acceptably well without ever being touched. You're an aspiring tech, however, and all self-respecting techs start up the CMOS setup utility and make changes. That's when most CMOS setup utility problems take place.

If you mess with the CMOS setup utility, remember to make only as many changes at one time as you can remember. Document the original settings and the changes on a piece of paper. That way, you can put things back if necessary. Don't make changes unless you know what they mean! It's easy to screw up a computer fairly seriously by playing with CMOS settings you don't understand.

Losing CMOS Settings

Your CMOS needs a continuous trickle charge to retain its data. Motherboards use some type of battery, usually a coin battery like those used in wrist watches, to give the CMOS the charge it needs when the computer is turned off (Figure 4.4). This battery also keeps track of the date and time when the PC is turned off.

If the battery runs out of charge, you lose all of your CMOS information. If some mishap suddenly erases the information on the CMOS chip, the computer might not boot up or you'll get nasty-looking errors at boot. Any PC made after 2002 will boot to factory defaults if the CMOS clears, so the

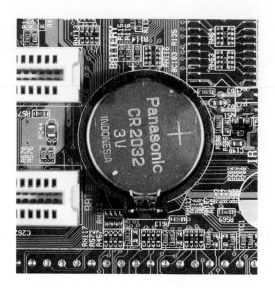

chances of not booting are slim—but you'll still get errors at boot. Here are a few examples of errors that point to lost CMOS information:

- CMOS configuration mismatch
- CMOS date/time not set
- No boot device available
- CMOS battery state low

Here are some of the more common reasons for losing CMOS data:

- Pulling and inserting cards
- Touching the motherboard
- Dropping something on the motherboard
- Dirt on the motherboard
- Faulty power supplies
- Electrical surges
- Chip creep

Most of these items should be fairly self-explanatory, but chip creep might be a new term for some of you. As PCs run, the components inside get warm. When a PC is turned off, the components cool off. This cycling of hot and cold causes the chips to expand and contract in their mounts. While the chip designers account for this, in some extreme cases this thermal expansion and contraction will cause a chip to work out of its mount and cause a failure called **chip creep**. Chip creep was a common problem in the earlier days of PCs, but after more than a quarter century of experience, the PC industry has done a pretty good job of designing mounts that will hold all your chips in place dependably.

If you encounter any of these errors, or if the clock in Windows resets itself to January 1st every time you reboot the system, the battery on the motherboard is losing its charge and needs to be replaced. To replace it, use a screwdriver to pry the battery's catch gently back. The battery should pop up for easy removal. Before you install the new battery, double-check that it has the same voltage and amperage as the old battery. To retain your CMOS settings while replacing the battery, simply leave your PC plugged into an AC outlet. The 5-volt soft power on all modern motherboards will provide enough electricity to keep the CMOS charged and the data secure. Of course, I know you're going to be *extremely* careful about ESD while prying up the battery from a live system!

Clearing CMOS

All techs invariably do things in CMOS they want to undo, but sometimes simply making a change in CMOS prevents you from getting back to the CMOS setup utility to make the change back. A great example is when someone sets a CMOS password and then forgets the password. If you ever run into a system with an unknown CMOS password, you'll need to erase the CMOS and then reset everything. All motherboards have a **clear CMOS jumper** somewhere on the motherboard (Figure 4.5). Check your motherboard book for the correct location.

To clear the CMOS, turn off the PC. Then locate one of those tiny little plastic pieces (officially called a *shunt*) and place it over the two jumper wires for a moment. Next, restart the PC and immediately go into CMOS and restore the settings you need.

Flashing ROM

Flash ROM chips can be reprogrammed to update their contents. With flash ROM, when you need to update your system BIOS to add support for a new technology, you can simply run a small command-line program, combined with an update file, and voilà, you've got a new, updated BIOS! Different

• **Figure 4.5**   Clear CMOS jumper

BIOS makers use slightly different processes for **flashing the BIOS**, but in general you must boot from a floppy diskette and then run the relevant updating command from the A:\> prompt. This example shows how simple it can be:

```
A:\> aw athxpt2.bin
```

Some motherboard makers even provide Windows-based flash ROM update utilities that will check the Internet for updates and download them for you to install (Figure 4.6). Most of these utilities will also enable you to back up your current BIOS so you can return to it if the updated version causes trouble. Without a good backup, you could end up throwing away your motherboard if a flash BIOS update goes wrong, so you should always make one! Finally, don't update your BIOS unless you have some compelling reason to do so. As the old saying goes, "If it ain't broke, don't fix it!"

• **Figure 4.6**   ROM updating program for an ASUS motherboard

Chapter 4 Review

■ Chapter Summary

After reading this chapter and completing the exercises, you should understand the following about working with BIOS and CMOS.

Power-On Self Test (POST)

- In addition to the BIOS routines and the CMOS setup program, the system ROM also includes a special program called the power-on self test (POST) that is executed every time the computer boots. POST first has basic devices up to and including video run self-diagnostic. If a device detects an error, the computer alerts you with a series of beeps. Different ROM manufacturers have used different beep codes, but your motherboard book should explain them (particularly in older systems). After the basic devices, POST tells the rest of the devices to run tests and displays a text error message on the screen if anything is wrong. Some manufacturers use numeric error codes or combine numeric and text messages.

- The computer may beep in two situations that are not related to POST beep codes. If the computer beeps constantly until you shut it off, it means that RAM is missing or damaged. If the computer beeps after it is booted, it is probably a warning that the system is overheating.

- If the computer appears dead with no beeps or screen response, you can place a POST card in an expansion slot to diagnose the problem using the LED readout on the card. The documentation that comes with the POST card will explain the LED codes for your particular BIOS.

- A beep code, text error message, or POST error may identify a problem, but it does not fix it. After you know which device is causing the problem, you should check the connection for the troublesome device and replace it if possible. If you cannot remove the bad part or if you cannot interpret the error message, you may need to replace the motherboard.

- The last job of the BIOS is to start the boot process. The CPU is the first component that wakes up. It checks the *power good* wire of the power supply to see that it has sufficient voltage to begin the booting process. If so, the CPU issues a memory address that executes the first line of the POST program. After POST has finished, it passes control to the bootstrap loader function on the system BIOS. This program looks for an operating system, checking the floppy drive, hard drives, or other bootable devices to find the boot sector that identifies the location of the operating system. When the BIOS finds a bootable or system disk or device that has a functional operating system, it passes control to that disk or device.

Care and Feeding of BIOS/CMOS

- A constant trickle of electricity is provided to CMOS via the motherboard battery. A dead battery results in the loss of all CMOS data and the computer's date and time information. Old PCs may not even boot with a dead motherboard battery and cleared CMOS data, but PCs made after 2002 will boot to factory defaults.

- Turning a PC on and off results in a cycle of heating and cooling. This causes components to contract and expand and possibly creep out of their sockets. Modern systems feature well-designed mounts that hold the chips better, so chip creep is rare on newer systems.

- To replace a motherboard battery, gently pry back the battery socket's catch with a screwdriver until you can remove the old battery. Double-check the replacement battery for the proper voltage and amperage, and make sure to pay attention to whether the positive or negative side goes up or down. You can retain your current CMOS data while changing the battery by leaving the PC plugged into an AC wall outlet (being extremely careful to avoid ESD).

- To clear all CMOS data, including any CMOS passwords, locate the clear CMOS jumper on the motherboard. Typically, you turn off the PC, reposition the jumper shunt, and reboot. However, it's always a good idea to consult the motherboard manual for the procedure for your system.

- You can update your ROM BIOS by booting with a floppy disk and running a small command-line program combined with an update file, both of which are usually free downloads from the motherboard manufacturer's Web site.

Some manufacturers also offer an update utility that can run from within the Window GUI. BIOS updates should be performed when there is a true need to do so, not just because there is an update available.

Key Terms

beep codes *(48)*

bootable disk *(51)*

bootstrap loader *(51)*

chip creep *(52)*

clear CMOS jumper *(53)*

firmware *(50)*

flashing the BIOS *(54)*

POST card *(49)*

power good wire *(50)*

power-on self test (POST) *(48)*

system disk *(51)*

text error *(49)*

Key Term Quiz

Use the Key Terms list to complete the sentences that follow. Not all terms will be used.

1. If the computer appears dead with no beeps or screen responses, you can insert a(n) _____ in an expansion slot to diagnose what is wrong.

2. When the computer starts, it runs a program on the system BIOS called _____ that checks the hardware.

3. If a disk contains the operating system files necessary to start the computer, it is called a _____ or _____.

4. Audible tones that indicate system problems at boot time are called _____.

5. The _____ has the single job of finding the operating system during startup.

6. Software stored on ROM chips is known as _____.

7. When a computer turns on, voltage on the _____ wakes up the CPU.

8. During the POST, your PC will use a _____ to indicate any problems once the video has tested okay.

9. To erase the CMOS, you usually need to short the _____.

10. The process of updating your BIOS is called _____.

11. The process whereby integrated circuits tend to work themselves loose due to heat and vibration is called _____.

Multiple-Choice Quiz

1. When you try to boot the computer, you get the error message "Non-system disk or disk error." What is the most likely cause of this error message?
   A. You left a non-bootable disk in the floppy drive.
   B. The CMOS battery has gone dead.
   C. Your hard drive has crashed.
   D. The registry has become corrupted.

2. What is the correct boot sequence for a PC?
   A. CPU, POST, power good, boot loader, operating system
   B. POST, power good, CPU, boot loader, operating system
   C. Power good, boot loader, CPU, POST, operating system
   D. Power good, CPU, POST, boot loader, operating system

3. Which of the following is the first to "wake up" when you turn on a PC?

   A. The CPU

   B. The setup program

   C. The POST

   D. The CMOS chip

4. Which of the following will result in a POST beep code message?

   A. The system is overheating.

   B. The video card is not seated properly.

   C. The keyboard is unplugged.

   D. The hard drive has crashed.

5. After a sudden power outage, Morgan's PC rebooted, but nothing appeared on the screen. The PC just beeps at him, over and over and over. What's most likely the problem?

   A. The power outage toasted his RAM.

   B. The power outage toasted his video card.

   C. The power outage toasted his hard drive.

   D. The power outage toasted his CPU.

6. Mohinder finds that a disgruntled former employee decided to sabotage her computer when she left by putting a password in CMOS that stops the computer from booting. What can Mohinder do to solve this problem?

   A. Mohinder should boot the computer holding the left SHIFT key. This will clear the CMOS information.

   B. Mohinder should try various combinations of the former employee's name. The vast majority of people use their name or initials for CMOS passwords.

   C. Mohinder should find the CMOS clear jumper on the motherboard. Then he can boot the computer with a shunt on the jumper to clear the CMOS information.

   D. Mohinder should find a replacement motherboard. Unless he knows the CMOS password, there's nothing he can do.

7. Jill boots up an older Pentium III system that has been the cause of several user complaints at the office. The system powers up and starts to run through POST, but then stops. The screen displays a "CMOS configuration mismatch" error. Of the following list, what is the most likely cause of this error?

   A. Dying CMOS battery

   B. Bad CPU

   C. Bad RAM

   D. Corrupt system BIOS

8. Carthic boots up his computer and, after a brief pause, it produces two short beeps. What is wrong with his system?

   A. The hard drive has failed.

   B. The monitor is unplugged.

   C. The keyboard is unplugged.

   D. Nothing is wrong. Two short beeps indicate a successful POST.

9. Evangelina boots her computer, but nothing happens. It appears totally dead. What would be the most effective method for troubleshooting this problem?

   A. Replace the motherboard

   B. Flash the BIOS

   C. Install a POST card

   D. Reinstall the operating system

10. Which devices can be used to boot a computer?

    A. Floppy disk

    B. CD

    C. USB thumb drive

    D. All of the above

11. What is true about flashing system ROM?

    A. You should update your BIOS whenever a new version is released.

    B. You should only upgrade your BIOS when there is a compelling reason to do so.

    C. If a flash update fails, you can reboot and begin the process over again.

    D. You should back up your BIOS before flashing with the Windows BIOSBack administrative utility.

1. You've been hired as a tutor for Tom, a fellow student in your hardware class. He's having a difficult time understanding the role that the system BIOS plays in booting the computer. How will you explain this process to him? Be sure to explain in order the step-by-step process that the BIOS goes through from the time you turn on the computer until it relinquishes control to the operating system. Make sure Tom understands why you may get an error message if you left a diskette in the floppy drive.

2. Why do some POST error messages manifest themselves as beep codes while others display as text messages? What should you do if you get a POST error message?

3. What symptoms will your computer show if the CMOS battery is dying or dead? What happens to the information stored in CMOS when you replace the battery? What must you do if a built-in battery goes dead?

Lab Projects

• Lab Project 4.1

Use the motherboard book (if you have one or can download one) or check the Web site of your BIOS manufacturer to identify what each of the following POST error messages means:

- A numeric message of 301
- One long beep followed by three short beeps
- A numeric message of 601
- HDD controller failure

Installing Internal Devices

"Insert Tab A into Slot B."

—Common installation instructions

- **Install and upgrade internal devices**
- **Install and configure device drivers**
- **Troubleshoot expansion cards**

Many devices take advantage of your external connections to work with your PC, but there are still plenty of devices that you need to install *inside* your PC via expansion slots. No external device can match the raw speed of an internal device running in a modern expansion slot. This chapter covers the steps required to successfully install an internal device and what to do if there's a problem.

Essentials Review

You'll find this chapter far more interesting if you are aware of expansion bus topics covered in the A+ Essentials exam. Before beginning this chapter, make sure you can

- Explain why expansion buses exist
- Name the most common types of expansion buses used in PCs, up to and including PCIe
- Explain the role of system resources and list and describe the four types
- Discuss the function of LPT and COM ports and name the common system resources they use

IT Technician

■ Installing Expansion Cards

Installing an expansion card successfully—another one of those bread-and-butter tasks for the PC tech—requires at least four steps. First, you need to know that the card works with your system and your operating system. Second, you have to insert the card in an expansion slot properly and without damaging that card or the motherboard. Third, you need to provide drivers for the operating system—that's *proper* drivers for the *specific* OS. Fourth, you should always verify that the card functions properly before you walk away from the PC.

Step 1: Knowledge

Learn about the device you plan to install—preferably before you purchase it! Does the device work with your system and operating system? Does it have drivers for your operating system? If you use Windows, the answer to these questions is almost always "yes." If you use an old operating system like Windows 98 or a less common operating system such as Linux, these questions become critical. A lot of older, pre-XP hardware simply won't work with Windows XP at all. Check the device's documentation and check the device manufacturer's Web site to verify that you have the correct drivers. While you're checking, make sure that you have the latest version of the driver; most devices get driver updates more often than the weather changes in Texas.

For Windows systems, your best resource for this knowledge is the Windows Marketplace . This used to be called the Hardware Compatibility List (HCL) , and you'll still hear lots of people refer to it as such. You can check out the Web site (http://testedproducts.windowsmarketplace.com) to see if your product is listed, but most people just look on the box of the device in question (Figure 5.1)—all Windows-certified devices will proudly display that they work with Windows.

Tech Tip

Installation Order

Some manufacturers insist on a different order for device installation than the traditional one listed here. The most common variation requires you to install the drivers and support software for an expansion card before you insert the card. Failure to follow the manufacturer's directions with such a card can lead to hours of frustration while you uninstall the card and reinstall the drivers, sometimes manually removing some drivers and software from the system. The bottom line? Read the instructions that come with a particular card! I'll provide more specific examples of problem devices in later chapters.

Windows Marketplace is also a great resource to check whether a particular software program works with your version of Windows.

Step 2: Physical Installation

To install an expansion card successfully, you need to take steps to avoid damaging the card, the motherboard, or both. This means knowing how to handle a card and avoiding electrostatic discharge (ESD) or any other electrical issue. You also need to place the card firmly and completely into an available expansion slot.

Optimally, a card should always be in one of two places: in a computer or in an anti-static bag. When inserting or removing a card, be careful to hold the card only by its edges. Do not hold the card by the slot connectors or touch any components on the board (Figure 5.2).

Use an anti-static wrist strap if possible, properly attached to the PC. If you don't have a wrist strap, you can use the tech way of avoiding ESD by touching the power supply after you remove the expansion card from its anti-static bag. This puts you, the card, and the PC at the same electrical potential and thus minimizes the risk of ESD.

Modern systems have a trickle of voltage on the motherboard at all times when the computer is plugged into a power outlet. Chapter 7, "Installing and Troubleshooting Power Supplies," covers power for the PC and how to deal with it in detail, but here's the short version: *Always unplug the PC before inserting an expansion card!* Failure to do so can destroy the card, the motherboard, or both. It's not worth the risk!

Never insert or remove a card at an extreme angle. This may damage the card. A slight angle is acceptable and even necessary when removing a card. Always screw the card to the case with a connection screw. This keeps the card from slipping out and potentially shorting against other cards.

• **Figure 5.1**   Works with Windows!

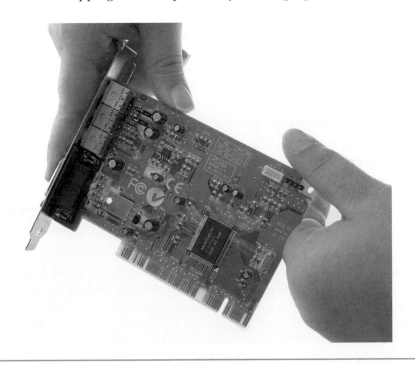

• **Figure 5.2**   Where to handle a card

• **Figure 5.3** Always screw down all cards.

Also, many cards use the screw connection to ground the card to the case (Figure 5.3).

Many technicians have been told to clean the slot connectors if a particular card is not working. This is almost never necessary after a card is installed, and if done improperly, can cause damage. You should clean slot connectors only if you have a card that's been on the shelf for a while and the contacts are obviously dull. *Never use a pencil eraser for this purpose.* Pencil erasers can leave behind bits of residue that wedge between the card and slot, preventing contact and causing the card to fail. Grab a can of contact cleaning solution and use it instead. Contact cleaning solution is designed exactly for this purpose, will clean the contact nicely, and won't leave any residue. You can find contact cleaning solution at any electronics store.

A fully inserted expansion card will sit flush against the back of the PC case—assuming the motherboard is mounted properly, of course— with no gap between the mounting bracket on the card and the screw hole on the case. If the card is properly seated, no contacts will be exposed above the slot. Figure 5.4 shows a properly seated (meaning fitted snugly in the slot) expansion card.

• **Figure 5.4** Properly seated expansion card; note the tight fit between case and mounting bracket and the evenness of the card in the slot

Step 3: Device Drivers

You know from the Essentials course that all devices, whether built into the motherboard or added along the way, require BIOS. For almost all expansion cards, that BIOS comes in the form of **device drivers**—software support programs—loaded from a CD-ROM disc provided by the card manufacturer.

Installing device drivers is fairly straightforward. You should use the correct drivers—kind of obvious, but you'd be surprised how many techs mess this up—and, if you're upgrading, you might have to unload current drivers before loading new drivers. Finally, if you have a problem, you may need to uninstall the drivers you just loaded or, with Windows XP, roll back to earlier, more stable drivers.

Getting the Correct Drivers

To be sure you have the best possible driver you can get for your device, you should always check the manufacturer's Web site. The drivers that

Cross Check

BIOS

Although most devices bring their own BIOS in the form of device drivers, that's not always the case as you know from the Essentials course. See if you can answer these questions. What other way can a device bring BIOS to a system not originally built anticipating its installation? What about devices that are common and necessary, like the keyboard? How do they bring their own BIOS to a system? Or do they?

come with a device may work well, but odds are good that you'll find a newer and better driver on the Web site. How do you know that the drivers on the Web site are newer? First, take the easy route: look on the CD. Often the version is printed right on the CD itself. If it's not printed there, you're going to have to load the CD in your CD-ROM drive and poke around. Many driver discs have an AutoRun screen that advertises the version. If there's nothing on the pop-up screen, look for a Readme file (Figure 5.5).

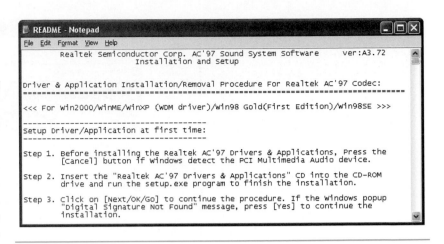

● **Figure 5.5**   Part of a Readme file showing the driver version

Driver or Device?

In almost all cases, you should install the device driver after you install the device. Without the device installed, the driver installation will not see the device and will give an error screen. The only exceptions to this rule are USB and FireWire devices—with these you should always install the driver first!

Removing the Old Drivers

Some cards—and this is especially true with video cards—require you to remove old drivers of the same type before you install the new device. To do this, you must first locate the driver in Device Manager. Right-click the device driver you want to uninstall and select Uninstall (Figure 5.6). Many devices, especially ones that come with a lot of applications, will have an uninstall option in the Add/Remove Programs (Windows 2000) or Add or Remove Programs (Windows XP) applet in the Control Panel (Figure 5.7).

● **Figure 5.6**   Uninstalling a device

Unsigned Drivers

Microsoft wants your computer to work, it really does, and the company provides an excellent and rigorous testing program for hardware manufacturers called the Microsoft Windows Logo Program. Developers initially use software to test their devices and, when they're ready, submit the device to the Windows Hardware Quality Labs (WHQL) for further testing. Hardware and drivers that survive the WHQL and other processes get to wear the Designed for Windows logo. The drivers get a digital signature that says Microsoft tested and found all was well.

Not all driver makers go through the rather involved process of the WHQL and other steps in the Windows Logo Program, so their software does not get a digital signature from Microsoft. When Windows runs into such a driver, it brings up a scary-looking screen (Figure 5.8) that says you're about to install an unsigned driver.

The fact that a company refuses to use the Windows Logo Program doesn't mean that its drivers are bad—it simply means that they haven't gone through Microsoft's exhaustive quality-assurance certification procedure.

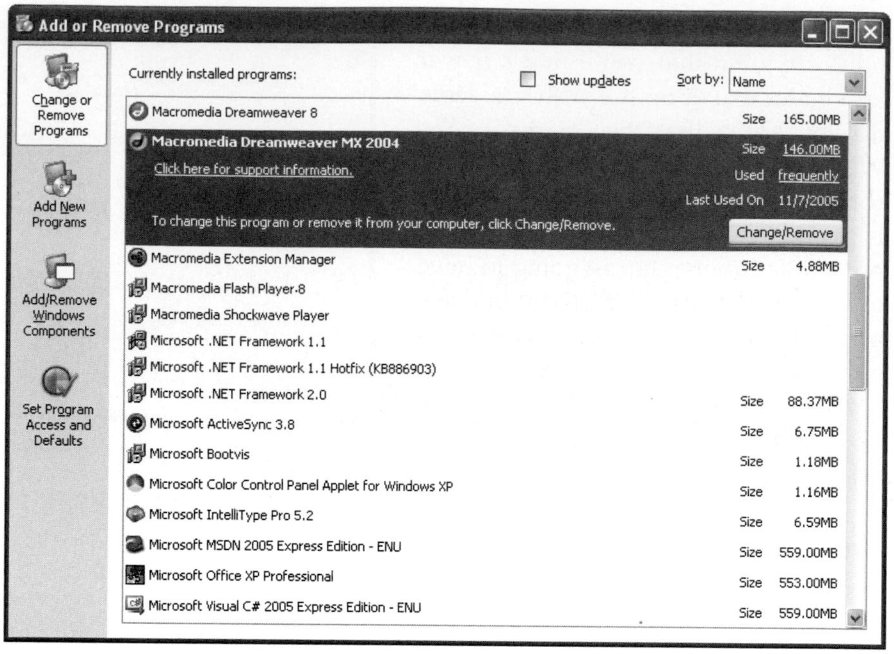

Figure 5.7 The Change/Remove option in Add or Remove Programs

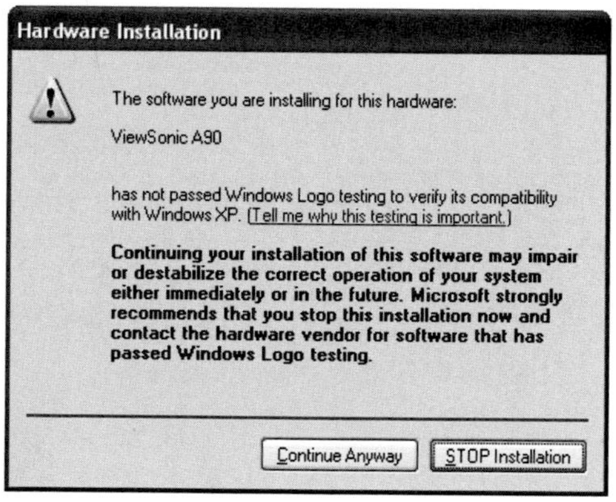

Figure 5.8 Unsigned driver warning

If I run into this, I usually check the driver's version to make sure I'm not installing something outdated, and then I just take my chances and install it. (I've yet to encounter a problem with an unsigned driver that I haven't also seen with Designed for Windows drivers.)

Installing the New Driver

You've got two ways to install a new driver: using the installation CD directly or using the Add Hardware Wizard in the Control Panel. Most experienced techs prefer to run from the installation CD. Most devices come with extra programs. My motherboard comes with a number of handy applications for monitoring temperature and overclocking. The **Add Hardware Wizard** does not install anything but the drivers. Granted, some techs find this a blessing because they don't want all the extra junk that sometimes comes with a device, but most installation discs give clear options to enable you to pick and choose what you want to install (Figure 5.9).

The other reason to use installation CDs instead of the Add Hardware Wizard stems from the fact that many expansion cards are actually many devices in one, and each device needs its own drivers. Sound cards often come with joystick ports, for example, and video cards often have built-in TV tuners. The Add Hardware Wizard will install all the devices, but the installation CD brings them to your attention. Go for the CD program first and save the Add Hardware Wizard for problems, as you'll see in the next section.

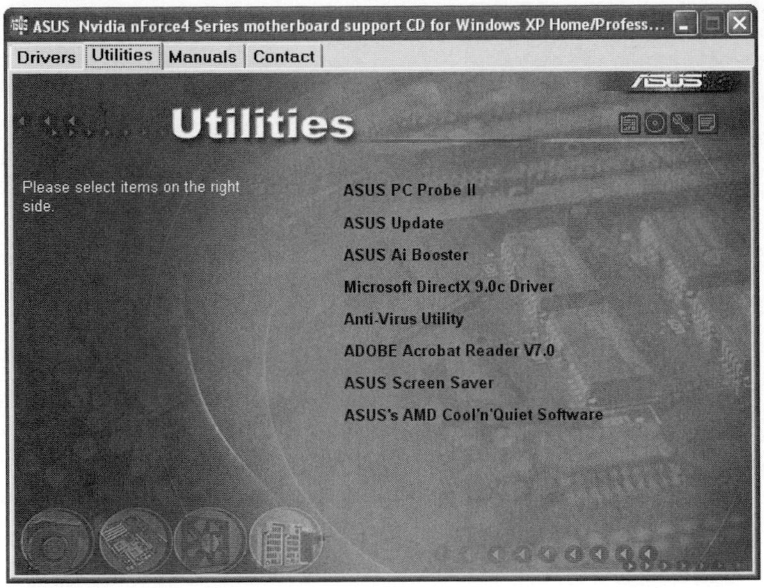

Figure 5.9 Installation menu

Driver Rollback

Windows XP offers the nifty **driver rollback** feature for rolling back to previous drivers after an installation or driver upgrade. If you decide to live on the edge and install beta drivers for your video card, for example, and your system becomes frightfully unstable, you can back up to the drivers that worked before. (Not that I've ever had to use that feature, of course!) To access the rollback feature, simply open Device Manager and access the properties for the device you want to adjust. On the Driver tab (Figure 5.10), you'll find the Roll Back Driver button.

Figure 5.10 Driver rollback feature

Tech Tip

Permissions

To install drivers in a Windows computer, you need to have the proper permission. I'm not talking about asking somebody if you're allowed to install the device! Permissions are granted in Windows to enable people to perform certain tasks, such as adding a printer to a computer or installing software, or to stop people from being able to do such tasks. Specifically, you need administrative *permissions to install drivers.*

Tech Tip

Beta Drivers

Many PC enthusiasts try to squeeze every bit of performance out of their PC components, much like auto enthusiasts tinker with engine tunings to get a little extra horsepower out of their engines. Expansion card manufacturers love enthusiasts, who often act as free testers for their unpolished drivers, known as beta drivers. *Beta drivers are fine for the most part, but they can sometimes cause amazing system instability—never a good thing! If you use beta drivers, make sure you know how to uninstall or roll back to previous drivers.*

Chapter 5: Installing Internal Devices

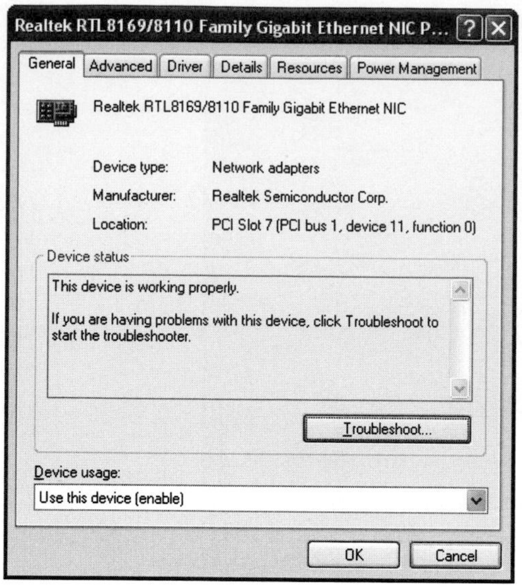

• **Figure 5.11**   Device Manager shows the device working properly.

Step 4: Verify

As a last step in the installation process, inspect the results of the installation and verify that the device works properly. Immediately after installing, you should open Device Manager and verify that Windows sees the device (Figure 5.11). Assuming that Device Manager shows the device working properly, your next check is to put the device to work by making it do whatever it is supposed to do. If you installed a printer, print something; if you installed a scanner, scan something. If it works, you're done!

■ Troubleshooting Expansion Cards

A properly installed expansion card rarely makes trouble—it's the botched installations that produce headaches. Chances are high that you'll have to troubleshoot an expansion card installation at some point, usually from an installation that you botched personally.

The first sign of an improperly installed card usually shows up the moment you first try to get that card to do whatever it's supposed to do and it doesn't do it. When this happens, your primary troubleshooting process is a reinstallation—after checking in with Device Manager.

Other chapters in this book cover specific hardware troubleshooting—sound cards in Chapter 13, for example, and video cards in Chapter 12. Use this section as your general methodology to decide what to look for and how to deal with the problem.

Device Manager

Device Manager provides the first diagnostic and troubleshooting tool in Windows. After you install a new device, Device Manager gives you many clues if something has gone wrong.

Occasionally, Device Manager may not even show the new device. If that happens, verify that you inserted the device properly and, if needed, that the device has power. Run the Add/Remove Hardware Wizard and see if Windows recognizes the device. If Device Manager doesn't recognize the device at this point, you have one of two problems: either the device is physically damaged and you must replace it, or the device is an onboard device, not a card, and is turned off in CMOS.

It's rare that Device Manager completely fails to see a device. More commonly, device problems manifest themselves in Device Manager via error icons—a black "!" or a red "X" or a blue "i."

- A black "!" on a yellow circle indicates that a device is missing, that Windows does not recognize a device, or that there's a device driver problem. A device may still work even while producing this error.

- A red "X" indicates a disabled device (Figure 5.12). This usually points to a device that's been manually turned off, or a damaged device. A device producing this error will not work.

- A blue "i" on a white field indicates a device on which someone has configured the system resources manually. This only occurs on non-ACPI systems. This symbol merely provides information and does not indicate an error with the device.

The "!" symbol is the most common error symbol and usually the easiest to fix. First, double-check the device's connections. Second, try reinstalling the driver with the Update Driver button. To get to the Update Driver button, right-click the desired device in Device Manager and select Properties. In the Properties dialog box, select the Driver tab. On the Driver tab, click the Update Driver button (Figure 5.13).

A red "X" error strikes fear into most technicians. If you get one, first check that the device isn't disabled. Right-click on the device and select Enable. If that doesn't work (it often will not), try rolling back the driver (if you updated the driver) or uninstalling (if it's a new install). Shut the system down and make triple-sure you have the card physically installed. Then redo the entire driver installation procedure, making sure you have the most current driver for that device. If none of these procedures works, return the card—it's almost certainly bad.

As you look at the errors in Device Manager, you'll notice error codes for the device that does not work properly. Windows has about 20 error codes, but the fixes still boil down to the same methods just shown. If you really want to frustrate yourself, try the Troubleshooter. It starts most fixes the same way—by reinstalling the device driver.

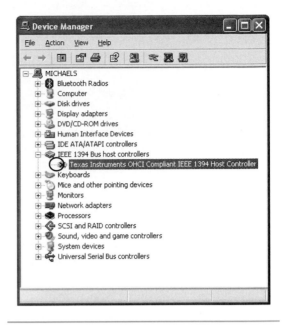

● **Figure 5.12**   An "X" in Device Manager, indicating a problem with the selected device

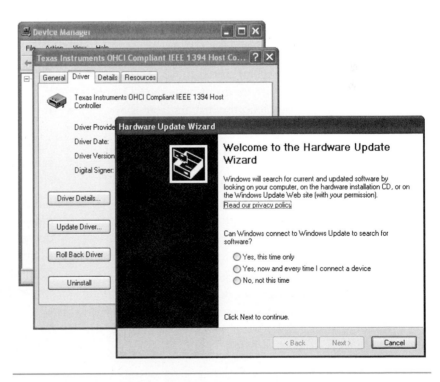

● **Figure 5.13**   Updating the driver

Chapter 5 Review

■ Chapter Summary

After reading this chapter and completing the exercises, you should understand the following about installing internal devices.

Installing Expansion Cards

■ There are four basic steps to follow when installing an expansion card: determine that the card is compatible with your system, physically install the card, install the drivers, and verify that the card works.

■ Determine that the card is compatible with your system. Many older cards do not work with Windows XP, and not every card works with older versions of Windows or other operating systems (such as Linux or Macintosh). Read the box before you buy, consult the device manufacturer's Web site, and if Windows is your operating system, consult the Windows Marketplace (formerly the Hardware Compatibility List).

■ Physically install the card without damaging it or other system components. Keep the card in its anti-static bag until you are ready to install it. Power off and unplug the computer. Wear an anti-static wrist strap or use an alternative method of dissipating static electricity.

■ Install the correct drivers, which should come on a CD with the device. If you don't have the CD, you may be able to download the drivers from the manufacturer's Web site.

■ Some manufacturers use the Microsoft Windows Logo Program to verify and digitally sign their drivers. This means their drivers have been verified by Microsoft to work properly. Other manufacturers skip the certification process and produce unsigned drivers that in most cases work just fine.

■ Sometimes driver updates go bad and you find the new driver just doesn't work. With Windows XP, you can roll back to the previous version driver by double-clicking the device in Device Manager, clicking the Driver tab, and then clicking the Roll Back Driver button.

■ Always verify that your newly installed device works. Immediately after installation, open Device Manager and verify that no error icons are displayed. Next, check the physical device. Finally, test the device's functionality.

Troubleshooting Expansion Cards

■ If you find a device is not working as expected, your first step is to check Device Manager. If the device is not listed in Device Manager, verify that you inserted it correctly and it has power. You can also try the Add Hardware Wizard to see if Windows recognizes the device.

■ A good tech is familiar with Device Manager's trouble icons. A black "!" on a yellow circle indicates that the device is missing, the device is not recognized, or there is a problem with the driver. A device may still work even when displaying this icon. A red "X" indicates a disabled device and usually means the device has been turned off or is damaged. A device with a red "X" will not work. A blue "i" on a white circle indicates that system resources have been configured manually. This icon is informational and does not imply any error.

■ If you encounter the "!" icon, verify the device's connections. Next, try to reinstall the driver by right-clicking the device in Device Manager and selecting Properties. Click the Driver tab and then click the Update Driver button.

■ If a device displays the red "X" icon, right-click the device in Device Manager and select Enable. If that doesn't work, try rolling back or uninstalling the driver. Shut down the system, verify the device's connections, and repeat the installation procedure. If the device still doesn't work, it is likely the device is either bad or not compatible with your operating system. Return the card to the place of purchase.

Key Terms

Add Hardware Wizard *(64)*
Designed for Windows logo *(63)*
device driver *(62)*
Device Manager *(66)*
driver rollback *(65)*

Hardware Compatibility List (HCL) *(60)*
Microsoft Windows Logo Program *(63)*
unsigned driver *(63)*

Windows Hardware Quality Labs (WHQL) *(63)*
Windows Marketplace *(60)*

Key Term Quiz

Use the Key Terms list to complete the sentences that follow. Not all terms will be used.

1. A device driver that has not been approved by the Microsoft Windows Logo Program will be reported as a(n) _____.

2. Most expansion cards require the installation of a(n) _____ before they will work.

3. To see if your hardware is officially supported by Windows, consult the _____.

4. Manufacturers who want their device drivers approved by Microsoft must submit their drivers to the _____ for testing.

5. Hardware and device drivers that have officially been approved by the Microsoft Windows Logo Program are allowed to carry the _____.

6. A device or driver that has not participated in the _____ may still work perfectly well, even if the operating system reports it as being unsigned.

7. The _____ has been replaced by the Windows Marketplace.

8. If a driver upgrade results in an unstable system, use the _____ feature to return to the previous driver.

9. Use _____ for diagnosing and troubleshooting devices and drivers in Windows.

10. To install only device drivers, without any additional software that may be on the installation CD, use the _____.

Multiple-Choice Quiz

1. Which of the following is the testing part of the Windows Logo Program?
   A. ACL
   B. HCL
   C. WHQL
   D. WKRP

2. What should you do *before* installing an expansion card? (Select two.)
   A. Attach an anti-static wrist strap
   B. Install the drivers
   C. Plug the PC into a grounded outlet
   D. Unplug the PC

3. In a Windows XP workstation, Steven updated the drivers for a NIC that worked, but he thought could be faster. Almost immediately, he discovered that the new drivers not only didn't speed up the NIC, but also made it start dropping data! What is his best option?
   A. Download the driver pack from Microsoft
   B. Reinstall the networking software
   C. Remove the NIC
   D. Use the driver rollback feature to return to the previous drivers

4. What does a red "X" next to a device in Device Manager indicate?
   A. A compatible driver has been installed that may not provide all the functions for the device.
   B. The device is missing or Windows cannot recognize it.
   C. The system resources have been assigned manually.
   D. The device has been disabled because it is damaged or has a system resource conflict.

5. Lloyd receives a message indicating the driver he is installing for a new expansion card is an unsigned driver. How should he proceed?

   A. Return the device to the store because it is defective

   B. Continue with the installation anyway

   C. Click the *Check the Web for a New Driver* button in the dialog box

   D. Contact the WHQL and request a signed driver

6. What is the most effective method for protecting an expansion card from ESD?

   A. Wear an anti-static wrist strap during installation

   B. Touch the expansion card after removing it from its anti-static bag

   C. Leave the computer plugged in as you install the expansion card

   D. Hold the expansion card by the slot connectors to provide additional grounding

7. Which statement is true about an expansion card's slot connectors?

   A. You should use a pencil eraser to clean an expansion card's slot connectors.

   B. You should use special contact cleaning solution to clean an expansion card's slot connectors.

   C. You should always see a little bit of an expansion card's slot connectors sticking out of the expansion slot as the slot connectors are a little taller than the slot itself.

   D. The slot connector is the best place to hold an expansion card.

8. Ricardo installed an updated network card driver and now cannot connect to the Internet. What should he do?

   A. Download the latest driver from the manufacturer's Web site

   B. Start Device Manager, select the Properties for his network card, and click the Driver Roll Back button on the General tab

   C. Start Device Manager, select the Properties for his network card, and click the Driver Roll Back button on the Driver tab

   D. Purchase a new network card as his is obviously faulty

9. What is the best way to get updated drivers for any device?

   A. Perform an update through the Windows Update Web site

   B. Download drivers from the device manufacturer's Web site

   C. Install the driver from the device's installation disk

   D. E-mail the device manufacturer's tech support

10. What types of expansion cards usually require you to uninstall old drivers before installing newer drivers?

    A. Network interface cards

    B. Sound cards

    C. Video cards

    D. Modems

11. What is true about unsigned drivers?

    A. They failed the WHQL's tests.

    B. It's usually fine to install them.

    C. They always function properly.

    D. You should never install them.

12. What benefit does an installation CD offer that the Add Hardware Wizard does not?

    A. Ability to install additional software that shipped with the device

    B. Ability to specify the driver you want to install

    C. Supports plug and play

    D. Enables the driver rollback feature in Device Manager

13. Where can you go to verify that a device works with your version of Windows?

    A. The WHQL

    B. The Windows Marketplace

    C. The HAL

    D. The Microsoft TechNet network

14. What is the safest way to install an expansion card?

    A. Power off the PC but leave it plugged into the wall to provide a ground.

    B. Expansion cards are hot-swappable, so there is no need to power off a modern PC when installing an expansion card.

C. Hold the expansion card firmly by the contacts so as not to touch any of the circuitry on the card.

D. Unplug the PC from the wall and use an anti-static wrist strap.

15. Jolie says you must always install the device driver before physically installing the expansion card. Geni says you must first physically install the expansion card and then install the device driver. Who is correct?

A. Jolie is correct. Device drivers must always be installed first so they can detect the new expansion card.

B. Geni is correct. The physical hardware must be installed prior to software device drivers.

C. Neither one is correct as it varies from product to product.

D. Neither one is correct as modern expansion cards install their own drivers.

■ Essay Quiz

1. Your friend Alan just called. He bought a new sound card for his computer and tried to install it. It's not working. What should he do now? Using the methodology for card installation that you learned in this chapter, explain the steps that he should follow to determine whether he installed the card wrong or the card itself is faulty.

2. Device Manager is the main tool for determining if devices have been installed and configured correctly. Write a quick user manual to help a new technician determine how to use Device Manager for the Windows operating system you use. Include how to access Device Manager and which buttons/tabs to use to see if devices are installed correctly. Also include how to use Device Manager to update and uninstall drivers.

3. You've been tasked by your manager to teach some new techs the ropes. Write a short essay on how to get and install updated drivers for the computer systems at your office, the Acme Architecture Design and Bicycle shop. Feel free to discuss the types of cards in the various computers and any special issues for installation. Wrap up with a brief discussion on what to do if the updated driver is not good.

Lab Projects

• Lab Project 5.1

Open your computer case and determine the kind of expansion slots available on your motherboard. How many of each kind are available? What cards are installed in the slots? Now examine the back and front of the computer case to see what ports are available. What devices do you have plugged into the ports?

chapter 6

Installing and Troubleshooting Motherboards

"A clear conscience is a sure card."

—John Lyly, circa 1579

In this chapter, you will learn how to

- **Install and upgrade motherboards**
- **Understand and implement CPU cooling**
- **Troubleshoot motherboards**

In the world of PC hardware, nothing compares to the complexity of installing a motherboard in terms of the number of screws to unscrew and parts to remove. In this chapter, you'll learn how to choose the proper motherboard for a system and install it.

Essentials Review

You'll find this chapter far more interesting if you are aware of motherboard concepts covered in the A+ Essentials exam. Before beginning this chapter, make sure you can

- Explain the benefits of using form factors for motherboards
- Define a "riser card"
- List the major form factors and the features and benefits of each
- Describe the function of the chipset
- Recognize the types of ports that are commonly used on motherboards

■ Upgrading and Installing Motherboards

To most techs, the concept of adding or replacing a motherboard can be extremely intimidating. It really shouldn't be; motherboard installation is a common and necessary part of PC repair. It is inexpensive and easy, although it can sometimes be a little tedious and messy due to the large number of parts involved. This section covers the process of installation and replacement and will show you some of the tricks that make this necessary process easy to handle.

IT Technician

Choosing the Motherboard and Case

Choosing a motherboard and case can prove quite a challenge for any tech, whether newly minted or a seasoned veteran. You first have to figure out the type of motherboard you want, such as AMD- or Intel-based. Then you need to think about the **form factor**, which determines the physical size of the motherboard as well as the general location of components and ports. Third, how rich in features is the motherboard and how tough is it to configure? You've got to read the motherboard manual to find out! Finally, you need to select the case that matches your space needs, budget, and form factor. Let's look at each step in a little more detail.

First, determine what motherboard you need. What CPU are you using? Will the motherboard work with that CPU? Because most of us buy the CPU and the motherboard at the same time, make the seller guarantee that the CPU will work with the motherboard. If you can, choose a motherboard that works with much higher speeds than the CPU you can afford; that way you can upgrade later. How much RAM do you intend to install? Are extra RAM sockets available for future upgrades?

Being able to select and install a motherboard appropriate for a client or customer is something every CompTIA A+ technician should know. This is particularly important if you're studying for the CompTIA A+ 220-604 Depot Technician exam, but less so for those working toward the CompTIA A+ 220-603 Help Desk Technician exam.

Building a Recommendation

Family, friends, and potential clients often solicit the advice of a tech when they're thinking about upgrading their PC. This solicitation puts you on the spot to make not just any old recommendation, but one that works with the needs and budget of the potential upgrader. To do this successfully, you need to manage expectations and ask the right questions, so Try This!

1. What does the upgrader want to do that compels him or her to upgrade? Write it down! Some of the common motivations for upgrading are to play that hot new game or to take advantage of new technology. What's the minimum system needed to run tomorrow's action games? What do you need to make multimedia sing? Does the motherboard need to have FireWire and high-speed USB built in to accommodate digital video and better printers?

2. How much of the current system does the upgrader want to save? Upgrading a motherboard can very quickly turn into a complete system rebuild. How old is the case? If it's an AT case, you pretty much need to look at a full computer replacement, but if it's a generic ATX case, you can usually save that much. On the other hand, if you want to use front-mounted USB and FireWire ports, then you'll want a new case as well. You'll most likely want to replace the CPU, so your first decision is AMD vs. Intel. The former gives you more bang for the buck, but the latter offers peace of mind for non-techs. What about RAM? Do you stick with the SDRAM or DDR SDRAM currently in the PC and go for a lower-end board that supports the older technology, or buy a board that uses DDR2? Do you go for a motherboard that supports AGP—and thus keep the current video card—or go for a PCI Express board that will require a new video card as well?

3. Once you've gathered information on motivation and assessed the current PC of the upgrader, it's time to get down to business: field trip time! This is a great excuse to get to the computer store and check out the latest motherboards and gadgets. Don't forget to jot down notes and prices while you're there! By the end of the field trip, you should have the information to give the upgrader an honest assessment of what an upgrade will entail, at least in monetary terms. Be honest—in other words, don't just tell the upgrader what you think he or she wants to hear—and you won't get in trouble!

A number of excellent motherboard manufacturers are available today. Some of the more popular brands are Abit, Asus, Biostar, DFI, Gigabyte, Intel, MSI, and Shuttle. Your supplier may also have some lesser-known but perfectly acceptable brands of motherboards. As long as the supplier has an easy return policy, it's perfectly fine to try one of these.

Second, make sure you're getting a form factor that works with your case. Don't try to put a regular ATX motherboard into a microATX case!

Third, all motherboards come with a technical manual, better known as the **motherboard book** (Figure 6.1). You must have this book! This book is your primary source for all of the critical information about the motherboard. If you set up CPU or RAM timings incorrectly in CMOS, for example, and you have a dead PC, where would you find the CMOS clear jumper? Where do you plug in the speaker? Even if you let someone else install the motherboard, insist on the motherboard book; you will need it.

Fourth, pick your case carefully. Cases come in six basic sizes: slimline, desktop, mini-tower, mid-tower, tower, and cube. Slimline and desktop models generally sit on the desk, beneath the monitor. The various tower cases usually occupy a bit of floor space next to the desk. The mini-tower and mid-tower cases are the most popular choices. Make sure you get a case that will fit your motherboard—many microATX and all FlexATX cases are too small for a regular ATX motherboard. Cube cases generally require a specific motherboard, so be prepared to buy both pieces at once. A quick test fit before you buy saves a lot of return trips to the supplier.

Cases come with many different options, but three more common options point to a better case. One option is a **removable face** (Figure 6.2)—many cheaper cases will screw the face into the metal frame using wood screws. A removable face makes disassembly much easier by offering movable tabs that hold the face in place rather than screws.

Another option is a detachable motherboard mount. Clearly, the motherboard will have to be attached to the case in some fashion. In better cases, this is handled by a removable tray or plate called a **motherboard mount**

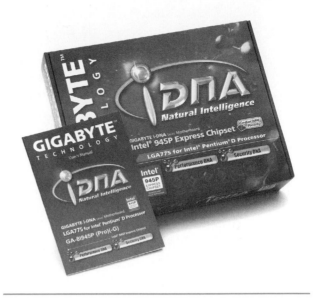

• **Figure 6.1**   Motherboard box and book

Tech Tip

Replacement Motherboard Books

If you have a motherboard with no manual, you can usually find a copy of the manual in Adobe Acrobat (.pdf) format online at the manufacturer's Web site. It's a good idea to grab and print a copy to keep with the motherboard. I often tape a copy (either hard copy or burned onto a CD) of the manual inside the case where I installed the motherboard. Just don't cover any vents!

• **Figure 6.2**   Removable face

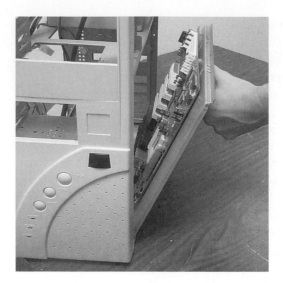

• **Figure 6.3**   Motherboard tray

(Figure 6.3). This enables you to attach the motherboard to the case separately, saving you from the chore of sticking your arms into the case to turn screws.

The third option, front-mounted ports for USB, FireWire, and headphones, can make using a PC much easier. Better cases offer these ports, although you can also get add-on components that fit into the increasingly useless floppy drive bay to bring added front connectivity to the PC. Figure 6.4 shows a case with both types of front connectors.

Power supplies often come with the case. Watch out for "really good deal" cases because that invariably points to a cheap or missing power supply. You also need to verify that the power supply has sufficient wattage.

Installing the Motherboard

If you're replacing a motherboard, first remove the old motherboard. Begin by removing all the cards. Also remove anything else that might impede removal or installation of the motherboard, such as hard or floppy drives. Keep track of your screws—the best idea is to return the screws to their mounting holes temporarily, at least until you can reinstall the parts. Sometimes even the power supply has to be removed temporarily to enable access to the motherboard. Document the position of the little wires for the speaker, power switch, and reset button in case you need to reinstall them.

Unscrew the motherboard. *It will not simply lift out.* The motherboard mounts to the case via small connectors called **standouts** that slide into keyed slots or screw into the bottom of the case (Figure 6.5). Screws then go into the standouts to hold the motherboard in place. Be sure to place the standouts properly before installing the new motherboard.

When you insert the new motherboard, do not assume that you will put the screws and standouts in the same place as they were in your old motherboard. When it comes to the placement of screws and standouts, only one rule applies:

• **Figure 6.4**   Case with both front-mounted ports and an add-on flash memory card reader

⚠ Watch out for ESD here! Remember that it's very easy to damage or destroy a CPU and RAM with a little electrostatic discharge. It's also fairly easy to damage the motherboard with ESD. Wear your anti-static wrist strap!

● **Figure 6.5**   Standout in a case, ready for the motherboard

anywhere it fits. Do not be afraid to be a little tough here! Installing motherboards can be a wiggling, twisting, knuckle-scraping process.

Once you get the motherboard mounted in the case with the CPU and RAM properly installed, it's time to insert the power connections and test it. A POST card, which can be inserted in an available expansion slot to display any POST errors, can be helpful with the system test because you won't have to add the speaker, a video card, monitor, and keyboard to verify that the system is booting. If you have a POST card, start the system and watch to see if the POST takes place—you should see a number of POST codes before the POST stops. If you don't have a POST card, install a keyboard, speaker, video card, and monitor. Boot the system and see if the BIOS information shows up on the screen. If it does, you're probably okay. If it doesn't, it's time to refer to the motherboard book to see where a mistake was made.

Wires, Wires, Wires

The last, and often the most frustrating, part of motherboard installation is connecting the LEDs, buttons, and front-mounted ports on the front of the box. These usually include the following:

- Soft power
- Reset button
- Speaker
- Hard drive activity LED
- Power LED
- USB
- FireWire
- Sound

Tech Tip

Before the Case

A lot of techs install the CPU, CPU fan, and RAM into the motherboard before installing the motherboard into the case. This helps in several ways, especially with a new system. First, you want to make certain that the CPU and RAM work well with the motherboard and with each other—without that, you have no hope of setting up a stable system. Second, installing these components first prevents the phenomenon of flexing the motherboard. Some cases don't provide quite enough support for the motherboard, and pushing in RAM can make the board bend. Third, attaching a CPU fan can be a bear of a task, one that's considerably easier to do on a table top than within the confines of a case. Finally, on motherboards that require you to set jumpers or switches, it's much easier to read the tiny information stenciled on the PCB before you add the shadows from the case! If necessary, set any jumpers and switches for the specific CPU according to information from the motherboard manual.

⚠️ Pay attention to the location of the standouts if you're swapping a motherboard. If you leave a screw-type standout beneath a spot on the motherboard where you can't add a screw and then apply power to the motherboard, you run the risk of shorting the motherboard.

• **Figure 6.6**   Motherboard wire connections labeled on the motherboard

• **Figure 6.7**   Sample of case wires

These wires have specific pin connections to the motherboard. Although you can refer to the motherboard book for their location, usually a quick inspection of the motherboard will suffice for an experienced tech (Figure 6.6).

A few rules need to be followed when installing these wires. First, the lights are LEDs, not light bulbs—they have a positive and negative side. If they don't work one way, turn the connector around and try the other. Second, when in doubt, guess. Incorrect installation only results in the device not working; it won't damage the computer. Refer to the motherboard book for the correct installation. The third and last rule is that with the exception of the soft power switch on an ATX system, you do not need any of these wires for the computer to run! Many techs often simply ignore these wires, although this would not be something I'd do to any system but my own!

No hard-and-fast rule exists for determining the function of each wire. Often the function of each wire is printed on the connector (Figure 6.7). If not, track each wire to the LED or switch to determine its function.

■ Troubleshooting Motherboards

Motherboards fail. Not often, but motherboards and motherboard components can die from many causes: time, dust, cat hair, or simply slight manufacturing defects made worse by the millions of amps of current sluicing through the motherboard traces. Installing cards, electrostatic discharge, flexing the motherboard one time too many when swapping out RAM or drives—any of these factors can cause a motherboard to fail. The motherboard is a hard-working, often abused component of the PC! Unfortunately for the common tech, troubleshooting a motherboard problem can be very difficult and time-consuming. This chapter concludes with a look at symptoms of a failing motherboard, techniques for troubleshooting, and the options you have when you discover a motherboard problem.

If you're studying for the CompTIA A+ 220-604 Depot Tech exam, pay particular attention to the techniques for troubleshooting motherboards.

Symptoms

Motherboard failures commonly fall into three types: catastrophic, component, and ethereal. With a **catastrophic failure**, the PC just won't boot. This sort of problem happens with brand-new systems due to manufacturing defects—often called a **burn-in failure**—and to any system that gets a shock of electrostatic discharge. Burn-in failure is uncommon, but usually happens in the first 30 days of use. Swap out the motherboard for a replacement and you should be fine. If you accidentally zap your motherboard when inserting a card or moving wires around, be chagrined. Change your daring ways and wear an anti-static wrist strap!

Component failure happens rarely, but appears as flaky connections between a device and motherboard, or as intermittent problems. A hard drive plugged into a faulty controller on the motherboard, for example, might show up in CMOS autodetect, but be inaccessible in Windows. A serial controller that worked fine for months until a big storm took out the external modem hooked to it, but doesn't work anymore, even with a replacement modem, is another example.

The most difficult of the three types of symptoms to diagnose are those I call *ethereal* symptoms. Stuff just doesn't work all the time. The PC reboots itself. You get blue screens of death in the midst of heavy computing, like right before you smack the villain and rescue the damsel. What can cause such symptoms? If you answered any of the following, you win the prize:

- Faulty component
- Buggy device driver
- Buggy application software
- Slight corruption of the operating system
- Power supply problems

Err…you get the picture.

What a nightmare scenario to troubleshoot! The Way of the Tech knows paths through such perils, though, so let's turn to troubleshooting techniques now.

Techniques

To troubleshoot a potential motherboard failure requires time, patience, and organization. Some problems will certainly be quicker to solve than others. If the hard drive doesn't work as expected, as in the example above, check the settings on the drive. Try a different drive. Try the same drive with a different motherboard to verify that it's a good drive. Like every other troubleshooting technique, all you try to do with motherboard testing is to isolate the problem by eliminating potential factors.

This three-part system—check, replace, verify good component—works for the simpler and the more complicated motherboard problems. You can even apply the same technique to ethereal-type problems that might be anything, but you should add one more verb: *document.* Take notes on the individual components tested so you don't repeat efforts or waste time. Plus, this can lead to the establishment of patterns. Being able to re-create a system crash by performing certain actions in a specific order can often lead you to the root of the problem. Document your actions. Motherboard testing is time-consuming enough without adding inefficiency!

Options

Once you determine that the motherboard has problems, you have several options for fixing the three types of failures. If you have a catastrophic failure, you must replace the motherboard. Even if it works somewhat, don't mess around. The motherboard should provide bedrock stability for the system. If it's even remotely buggy or problematic, get rid of it!

If you have a component failure, you can often replace the component with an add-on card that will be as good as or better than the failed device. Promise Technology, for example, makes fine hard drive controller cards that can replace one or both hard drive controllers on the motherboard (Figure 6.8).

If your component failure is more a technology issue rather than physical damage, then you can try upgrading the BIOS on the motherboard.

⚠️ If you've lost components due to ESD or a power surge, then you would most likely be better off replacing the motherboard. The damage you *can't* see can definitely sneak up to bite you and create system instability.

Tech Tip

Limits of BIOS Upgrades

Flashing the BIOS for a motherboard can fix a lot of system stability problems and provide better implementation of built-in technology. What it cannot do for your system is improve the hardware. If AMD comes out with a new, improved, lower-voltage Athlon 64, for example, and your motherboard cannot scale down the voltage properly, then you cannot use that CPU—even if it fits in your motherboard's Socket AM2. No amount of BIOS flashing can change the hardware built into your motherboard.

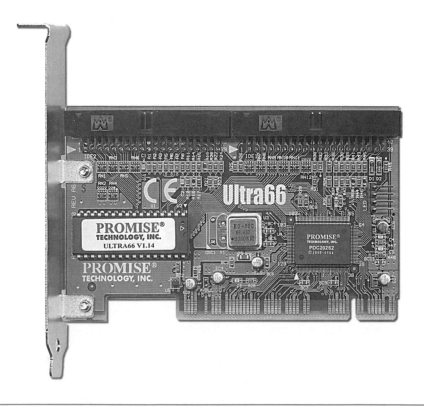

• **Figure 6.8**   Promise Technology PCI hard drive controller card

Every motherboard comes with a small set of code that enables the CPU to communicate properly with the devices built into the motherboard. You can quite readily upgrade this programming by **flashing the BIOS**: running a small command-line program to write new BIOS in the flash ROM chip. Figure 6.9 shows a couple of typical flash ROMs. Refer back to Chapter 4 for the details on flashing.

Finally, if you have an ethereal, ghost-in-the-machine type of problem that you have finally determined to be motherboard related, you have only a couple of options for fixing the problem. You can flash the BIOS in a desperate attempt to correct whatever it is, which sometimes does work and is less expensive than the other option. Or, you can replace the motherboard.

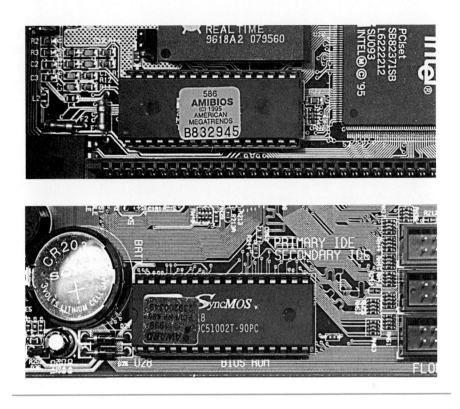

• **Figure 6.9**   AMI and Award flash ROM chips

Beyond A+

Shuttle Form Factor

In the early 2000s, Shuttle started making a very interesting line of tiny cube-shaped PCs called XPCs that became an overnight sensation and continue to be popular today (Figure 6.10). These boxes use a tiny, proprietary

Tech Tip

Small Form Factor

Many companies followed Shuttle's lead and started making cube or cube-like small cases. You'll hear these cases commonly referred to as small form factor (SFF), *but there's no industry-wide standard. Some SFF cases accommodate microATX and FlexATX motherboards.*

• **Figure 6.10**   Shuttle XPC *(photo courtesy of Shuttle Computer Group, Inc.)*

form factor motherboard, called *Shuttle Form Factor,* installed in a proprietary case with a proprietary power supply. Originally, these systems were sold *barebones,* meaning they came with only a motherboard, case, and power supply. You had to supply a CPU, RAM, video card, keyboard, mouse, and monitor. Shuttle now produces a full line of computers.

Mini-ITX

Watch out for all the pretty colors on today's motherboards! To catch the consumer's eye, a lot of motherboard manufacturers have started making wildly colorful motherboard components. There is no universally accepted standard for connection colors on the inside of a motherboard.

If you really want to get small, check out Mini-ITX (Figure 6.11). Developed by VIA Technologies in 2001, Mini-ITX has a maximum size of only 17 centimeters by 17 centimeters! These tiny systems only use the VIA C3 family of CPUs, so if you want to get really picky, Mini-ITX is a proprietary computer system, not really a form factor. Mini-ITX also has its own tiny power supply standard. The low power requirements don't require a fan on some systems. The VIA C3 CPUs aren't as powerful as the latest offerings from Intel and AMD, but they're great for specialized jobs such as home theater systems or manufacturing.

• **Figure 6.11**　Mini-ITX motherboard

Chapter 6 Review

■ Chapter Summary

After reading this chapter and completing the exercises, you should understand the following about installing and troubleshooting motherboards.

Upgrading and Installing Motherboards

- Not all motherboards fit in all cases. If you upgrade a motherboard, make sure the new motherboard fits in the existing case. If you purchase a new motherboard and a new case, make sure you purchase a case that supports the form factor of your motherboard.

- Determine the CPU you or your client wants before purchasing a motherboard. Not all CPUs are supported by, or even fit in, all motherboards. Make sure your motherboard supports your CPU and, if possible, purchase a motherboard that supports higher speeds than your CPU in case you want to upgrade the processor at a later time.

- To replace a motherboard, first remove all the expansion cards from the old motherboard. Document the position of all the little wires before removing them. Unscrew the motherboard and remove it from the case.

- Before installing a new motherboard in the case, attach the CPU, heat sink/fan, and RAM. Check the standouts in the case—you might have to add or remove a few to accommodate the new motherboard. Once installed, boot the system and make sure there are no POST errors and the BIOS information appears on the screen. Then install any expansion cards.

- Cases come with a series of little wires that connect to LEDs on the front of the case. These wires need to be plugged in to the motherboard for the LEDs to function. LEDs have a positive and a negative side, so the wires must be connected the right way or the LEDs will not work. If you find the LEDs are not working, turn the connector around to reverse the positive/negative connection. Getting it wrong will not damage your system—it will only cause the LEDs not to light up.

Troubleshooting Motherboards

- Motherboards and motherboard components can die for many reasons including time, dust, pet hair, manufacturing defects, ESD, or physical damage. Motherboard failures usually fall into one of three main categories: catastrophic, component, or ethereal.

- Catastrophic failure is typically caused by manufacturing defects (burn-in failure) or ESD. Burn-in failures are uncommon and usually manifest within the first 30 days of use. In the case of a catastrophic failure, replace the motherboard.

- Component failure appears as a flaky connection between a device and the motherboard or as intermittent problems. In the case of a component failure, replace the failed component with an expansion card or peripheral device. Sometimes a BIOS upgrade can fix component failures.

- Ethereal failure is the most difficult to diagnose. Symptoms vary from the PC rebooting itself to blue screens of death and can be caused by a faulty component, buggy device driver, buggy application software, operating system corruption, or power supply problems.

- Use three steps to troubleshoot problems: check, replace, and verify. For example, first check the settings of the problem device. If the device still fails, replace the device. If the device continues to malfunction, try the device with a different motherboard. Remember to document your troubleshooting steps. Not only will it help you to become an efficient troubleshooter, but it can lead to the establishment of patterns. Being able to re-create a system crash by performing certain actions in a specific order can often lead you to the root of the problem.

■ Key Terms

burn-in failure *(79)*
catastrophic failure *(79)*
component failure *(79)*
flashing the BIOS *(81)*

form factor *(73)*
motherboard book *(75)*
motherboard mount *(75)*
POST card *(77)*

removable face *(75)*
standouts *(76)*

■ Key Term Quiz

Use the Key Terms list to complete the sentences that follow. Not all terms will be used.

1. The _____ is your primary source for all of the critical information about the motherboard.

2. The motherboard mounts to the case via small connectors called _____ that slide into keyed slots or screw into the bottom of the case.

3. A system that has suffered a(n) _____ will simply not boot.

4. When a single device, connection, or component exhibits intermittent problems, _____ is the likely cause.

5. Manufacturing defects may result in a(n) _____.

6. High-quality cases provide a removable _____ to which you can more easily attach the motherboard.

7. Sometimes you can upgrade a motherboard's technology by _____.

8. The _____ determines the physical size of the motherboard.

9. A(n) _____ makes disassembly of a case much easier.

10. A(n) _____ enables you to identify POST errors without having to connect a monitor or speaker.

■ Multiple-Choice Quiz

1. In a routine check of a system newly built by her latest intern, Sarah discovers that everything works except the hard drive and power LEDs on the front of the case. What could be the problem? (Select two.)

   A. The intern forgot to connect the LED leads to the motherboard.

   B. The intern reversed the LED leads to the motherboard.

   C. There is no power to the motherboard.

   D. There is no activity on the hard drive.

2. Robert installed a new motherboard, CPU, and RAM into his old case. After he attached the power correctly and pressed the power button, not only did the system not boot up, but he could smell ozone and realized the motherboard had shorted out. What could have been the cause?

   A. Robert installed an ATX motherboard into a BTX case.

   B. Robert installed a BTX motherboard into an ATX case.

   C. Robert used an AT power supply on an ATX motherboard.

   D. Robert left a standout in the wrong place under the motherboard.

3. Martin bought a new motherboard to replace his older ATX motherboard. As he left the shop, the tech on duty called after him, "Check your standouts!" What could the tech have meant?

   A. Standouts are the connectors on the motherboard for the front panel buttons, like the on/off switch and reset button.

   B. Standouts are the metal edges on some cases that aren't rolled.

   C. Standouts are the metal connectors that attach the motherboard to the case.

   D. Standouts are the dongles that enable a motherboard to support more than four USB ports.

4. Amanda bought a new system that, right in the middle of an important presentation, gave her a blue screen of death. Now her system won't boot at all, not even to CMOS. After extensive troubleshooting, she determined that the motherboard was at fault and replaced it. Now the system runs fine. What was the most likely cause of the problem?

    A. Burn-in failure

    B. Electrostatic discharge

    C. Component failure

    D. Power supply failure

5. Solon has a very buggy computer that keeps locking up at odd moments and rebooting spontaneously. He suspects the motherboard. How should he test it?

    A. Check settings and verify good components.

    B. Verify good components and document all testing.

    C. Replace the motherboard first to see if the problems disappear.

    D. Check settings, verify good components, replace components, and document all testing.

6. As tech support for a computer shop, you receive a call from an irate customer insisting that you sent him the wrong motherboard because it won't fit in his old case. Which of the following questions might enable you to determine the problem? Select the best answer.

    A. Could you describe the location of the connectors on the back of the motherboard?

    B. Could you describe the location of the standouts on the case?

    C. What kind of CPU are you using?

    D. What type of RAM are you using?

7. What should you avoid when purchasing a new case?

    A. Removable faceplate

    B. Front-mounted USB ports

    C. A good deal with an included power supply

    D. Detachable motherboard mount

8. What is the correct order of steps for installing a motherboard?

    A. Secure the motherboard to the case, install RAM and CPU, configure jumpers

    B. Install the CPU, secure the motherboard to the case, install RAM

    C. Configure jumpers, secure the motherboard to the case, install RAM and CPU

    D. Install RAM and CPU, configure jumpers, secure the motherboard to the case

9. How can you test a new motherboard without a keyboard or monitor?

    A. Use a POST card

    B. If the power supply fan spins, the motherboard is good

    C. Use a multimeter

    D. You cannot test a motherboard without a keyboard and monitor

10. What damage can be done by incorrectly attaching the LED wires to a motherboard?

    A. You can destroy the motherboard

    B. Data corruption on the hard drive

    C. Loss of CMOS data

    D. No damage, the LEDs simply will not work

■ Essay Quiz

1. Prepare a PowerPoint presentation or write a paper that would help your classmates select and replace a bad motherboard. Be sure to walk through all the necessary steps.

2. Your neighbors Dora and Jim just learned that you're studying computer hardware. They feel that their computer is slightly out of date.

They want to upgrade the processor, but not the motherboard. Prepare a list of at least five questions that you should ask them before you know what CPU they can choose or whether it is feasible to upgrade their system.

Lab Projects

• Lab Project 6.1

You know now how important the motherboard chipset is in determining the kind of CPU and RAM that can be installed in the computer. You also know that motherboards that may look similar may have very different features and prices. Imagine that you are going to build a new computer by ordering the components. Price is not a problem, so you will want to select the best and most powerful components. On the Internet, search such sites as www.intel.com or www.amd.com along with sites such as www .newegg.com to select a motherboard and a particular chipset. Then select a compatible CPU and RAM. Explain where you found the information about the components, what brands/models you selected, and how much each will cost.

Now imagine that your budget will not allow you to buy these components at this time. In fact, you've decided that you can afford only 75 percent of the cost of these components. What will you do to save money? Will you change the motherboard and the chipset or will you use a less powerful CPU with a smaller amount of RAM? Consider what you can upgrade at a later time when you have more available cash. Again, search the Internet and select components that would be satisfactory but are not the latest and the greatest. Be sure that the CPU and RAM you select are indeed compatible with your motherboard and chipset. What did you select and how much will it cost you?

Installing and Troubleshooting Power Supplies

"We believe that electricity exists, because the electric company keeps sending us bills for it, but we cannot figure out how it travels inside wires."

—Dave Barry

Power supplies are the least appreciated and most misunderstood part of a PC. It's far too easy for someone building a PC to concentrate on CPU, RAM, and motherboard, only to choose a bad power supply simply because it's inexpensive. In this chapter, you will learn about the many options and pitfalls in PC power supplies and know how to choose the right one for your system.

In this chapter, you will learn how to

- **Install and upgrade power supplies**
- **Understand and implement system cooling**
- **Troubleshoot power supplies**

Essentials Review

You'll find this chapter far more interesting if you are aware of PC power concepts covered in the A+ Essentials exam. Before beginning this chapter, make sure you can

- Define voltage, amperage, wattage, and resistance
- Explain the concept of current and differentiate between AC and DC current
- Define the type of power used in the United States and show an example of power standards used in other countries
- Use a multimeter to test an AC outlet
- Explain the different devices used to protect PCs from electrical surges and spikes and determine the appropriate device for a given situation
- Define the different PC power supply standards and their features
- Show the different types of connectors used on PC power supplies and their uses

IT Technician

■ Installing, Maintaining, and Troubleshooting Power Supplies

Installing, maintaining, and troubleshooting power supplies take a little less math than selecting the proper power supply for a system but remain essential skills for any tech. Installing takes but a moment, and maintaining is almost as simple, but troubleshooting can cause headaches. Let's take a look.

Installing

The typical power supply, also known as the **power supply unit (PSU)**, connects to the PC with four standard computer screws, mounted in the back of the case (Figure 7.1). Unscrew the four screws and the power supply lifts out easily (Figure 7.2). Insert a new power supply that fits the case and attach it using the same four screws.

Handling ATX power supplies requires special consideration. Understand that an

● **Figure 7.1** Mounting screws for power supply

ATX power supply *never turns off*. As long as that power supply stays connected to a power outlet, the power supply will continue to supply 5 volts to the motherboard. Always unplug an ATX system before you do any work! For years, techs bickered about the merits of leaving a PC plugged in or unplugged while you serviced it. ATX settled this issue forever. Many ATX power supplies provide a real on/off switch on the back of the PSU (see Figure 7.3). If you really need the system shut down with no power to the motherboard, use this switch.

When working on an ATX system, you may find using the power button inconvenient because you're not using a case or you haven't bothered to plug the power button's leads into the motherboard. That means there is no power button! One trick you can use when in that situation is to use a set of car keys or a screwdriver to contact the two wires to start and stop the system (see Figure 7.4).

Your first task after acquiring a new power supply is simply making sure it works. Insert the motherboard power connectors before starting the system. If you have video cards with power connectors, plug them in, too. Other connectors such as hard drives can wait until you've got one successful boot—or if you're cocky, just plug everything in!

Cooling

Heat and computers are not the best of friends. Cooling is therefore a vital consideration when building a computer. Electricity equals heat. Computers, being electrical devices, generate heat as they

• **Figure 7.2**   Removing power supply from system unit

• **Figure 7.3**   On/off switch for an ATX system

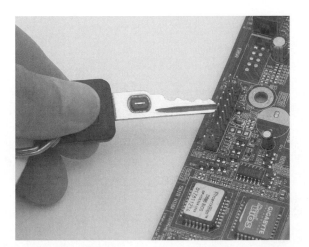

• **Figure 7.4**   Shorting the soft on/off jumpers

● **Figure 7.5**   Power supply fan

● **Figure 7.6**   Three-wire fan sensor connector

operate, and too much can seriously damage a computer's internal components.

The **power supply fan** (Figure 7.5) provides the basic cooling for the PC. It not only cools the voltage regulator circuits *within* the power supply, but it also provides a constant flow of outside air throughout the interior of the computer case. A dead power supply fan can rapidly cause tremendous problems, even equipment failure. If you ever turn on a computer and it boots just fine, but you notice that it seems unusually quiet, check to see if the power supply fan has died. If it has, quickly turn off the PC and replace the power supply.

Some power supplies come with a built-in sensor to help regulate the airflow. If the system gets too hot, the power supply fan spins faster. The 3-pin, 3-wire fan sensor connector plugs into the motherboard directly (Figure 7.6).

Case fans (Figure 7.7) are large, square fans that snap into special brackets on the case or screw directly to the case, providing extra cooling for key components. Most cases come with a case fan, and no modern computer should really be without one or two.

The single biggest issue related to case fans is where to plug them in. Most case fans come with standard **Molex connectors** (the large, 4-pin connectors that power IDE hard drives and CD/DVD drives), which are easy to plug in, but other case fans come with special three-pronged power connectors that need to connect to the motherboard. You can get adapters to plug three-pronged connectors into Molex connectors or Molex connectors into three-pronged connectors.

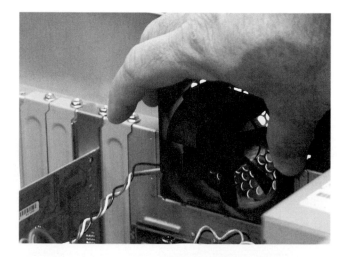

● **Figure 7.7**   Case fan

Mike Meyers' CompTIA A+ Guide: PC Technician (Exams 220-602, 220-603, & 220-604)

Maintaining Airflow

A computer is a closed system and computer cases help the fans keep things cool: everything is inside a box. Although many tech types like to run their systems with the side panel of the case open for easy access to the components, in the end they are cheating themselves. Why? A closed case enables the fans to create airflow. This **airflow** substantially cools off interior components. When the side of the case is open, you ruin the airflow of the system, and you lose a lot of cooling efficiency.

An important point to remember when implementing good airflow inside your computer case is that hot air rises. Warm air always rises above cold air, and you can use this principle to your advantage in keeping your computer cool.

In the typical layout of case fans for a computer case, an intake fan is located near the bottom of the front bezel of the case. This fan draws cool air in from outside the case and blows it over the components inside the case. Near the top and rear of the case (usually near the power supply), you'll usually find an exhaust fan. This fan works the opposite of the intake fan: it takes the warm air from inside the case and sends it to the outside.

Another important part of maintaining proper airflow inside the case is ensuring that all empty expansion bays are covered by **slot covers** (Figure 7.8). To maintain good airflow inside your case, you shouldn't provide too many opportunities for air to escape. Slot covers not only assist in maintaining a steady airflow; they help keep dust and smoke out of your case.

Missing slot covers can cause the PC to overheat!

Reducing Fan Noise

Fans generate noise. In an effort to ensure proper cooling, many techs put several high-speed fans into a case, making the PC sound like a jet engine. You can reduce fan noise by getting manually adjustable-speed fans, larger fans, or specialty "quiet" fans. Many motherboards enable you to control fans through software.

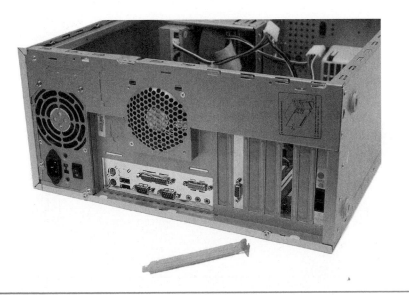

• **Figure 7.8** Slot covers

Manually adjustable fans have a little knob you can turn to speed up or slow down the fan (Figure 7.9). This kind of fan can reduce some of the noise, but you run the risk of slowing down the fan too much and thus letting the interior of the case heat up. A better solution is to get quieter fans.

Larger fans that spin slower are another way to reduce noise while maintaining good airflow. Fans sizes are measured in millimeters (mm) or centimeters (cm). Traditionally, the industry used 80-mm power supply and cooling fans, but today you'll find 100-mm, 120-mm, and even larger fans in power supplies and cases.

Many companies manufacture and sell higher-end, low-noise fans. The fans have better bearings than the run-of-the-mill fans, so they cost a little more, but they're definitely worth it. They market these fans as "quiet" or "silencer," or other similar adjectives. If you run into a PC that sounds like a jet, try swapping out the case fans for a low-decibel fan from Papst, Panasonic, or Cooler Master. Just check the decibel rating to decide which one to get. Lower, of course, is better.

Because the temperature inside a PC changes depending on the load put on the PC, the best solution for noise reduction combines a good set of fans with temperature sensors to speed up or slow down the fans automatically. A PC at rest will use less than half of the power of a PC running a video-intensive computer game and therefore makes a lot less heat. Virtually all modern systems support three fans through three **3-pin fan connectors** on the motherboard. The CPU fan uses one of these connectors, but the other two are for system fans or the power supply fan.

Most CMOS setup utilities provide a little control over fans plugged into the motherboard. Figure 7.10 shows a typical CMOS setting for the fans. Note that there's no way to tell the fans when to come on or off—only when to set off an alarm when they reach a certain temperature.

Software is the best way to control your fans. Some motherboards come with system monitoring software that enables you to set the temperature at which you want the fans to come on and off. If no program came with your

• **Figure 7.9** Manual fan adjustment device

motherboard and the manufacturer's Web site doesn't offer one for download, try the popular freeware SpeedFan utility (Figure 7.11), written by Alfredo Milani Comparetti, that monitors voltages, fan speeds, and temperatures in computers with hardware monitor chips. SpeedFan can even access S.M.A.R.T. information for hard disks that support this feature and shows hard disk temperatures too, if supported. You can find SpeedFan at www.almico.com/speedfan.php.

Even if you don't want to mess with your fans, always make a point to turn on your temperature alarms in CMOS. If the system gets too hot, an alarm will warn you. There's no way to know if a fan dies other than to have an alarm.

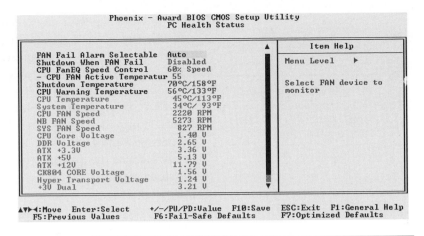

• **Figure 7.10**   CMOS fan options

> ⚠️ SpeedFan is a powerful tool that does far more than work with fans. Don't tweak any settings that you don't understand!

When Power Supplies Die

Power supplies fail in two ways: sudden death and slowly over time. When they die suddenly, the computer will not start and the fan in the power supply will not turn. In this case, verify that electricity is getting to the power supply before you do anything! Avoid the embarrassment of trying to repair a power supply when the only problem is a bad outlet or an extension cord that is not plugged in. Assuming that the system has electricity, the best way to verify that a power supply is working or not working is to check the voltages coming out of the power supply with a multimeter (see Figure 7.12).

Do not panic if your power supply puts out slightly more or less voltage than its nominal value. The voltages supplied by most PC power supplies can safely vary by as much as ±10 percent of their stated values. This means that the 12-volt line can vary from roughly

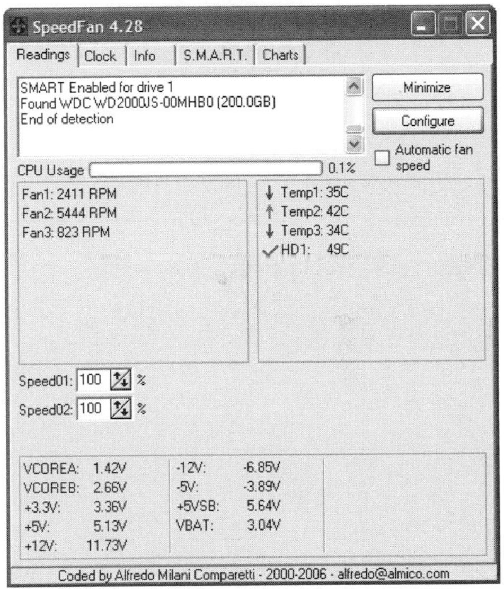

• **Figure 7.11**   SpeedFan

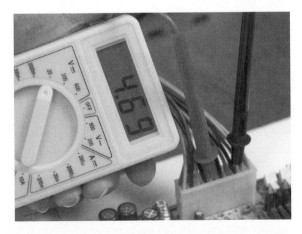

• **Figure 7.12**   Testing one of the 5-volt DC connections

10.5 to 12.9 volts without exceeding the tolerance of the various systems in the PC. The 5.0- and 3.3-volt lines offer similar tolerances.

Be sure to test every connection on the power supply—that means every connection on your main power as well as every Molex and mini. Because all voltages are between –20 and +20 VDC, simply set the voltmeter to the 20-V DC setting for everything. If the power supply fails to provide power, throw it into the recycling bin and get a new one—even if you're a component expert and a whiz with a soldering iron. Don't waste your or your company's time; the price of new power supplies makes replacement the obvious way to go.

> Many CMOS utilities and software programs monitor voltage, saving you the hassle of using a multimeter.

• **Figure 7.13**   ATX power supply tester

No Motherboard

Power supplies will not start unless they're connected to a motherboard, so what do you do if you don't have a motherboard you trust to test? First, try an . Many companies make these devices. Look for one that supports both 20- and 24-pin motherboard connectors as well as all of the other connectors on your motherboard. Figure 7.13 shows a power supply tester.

Switches

Broken power switches form an occasional source of problems for power supplies that fail to start. The power switch is behind the on/off button on every PC. It is usually secured to the front cover or inside front frame on your PC, making it a rather challenging part to access. To test, try shorting the soft power jumpers as described earlier. A key or screwdriver will do the trick.

When Power Supplies Die Slowly

If all power supplies died suddenly, this would be a much shorter chapter. Unfortunately, the majority of PC problems occur when power supplies die slowly over time. This means that one of the internal electronics of the power supply has begun to fail. The failures are *always* intermittent and tend to cause some of the most difficult to diagnose problems in PC repair. The secret to discovering that a power supply is dying lies in one word: intermittent. Whenever you experience intermittent problems, your first guess should be that the power supply is bad. Here are some other clues you may hear from users:

- "Whenever I start my computer in the morning, it starts to boot, and then locks up. If I press CTRL-ALT-DEL two or three times, then it will boot up fine."

- "Sometimes when I start my PC, I get an error code. If I reboot it goes away. Sometimes I get different errors."

- "My computer will run fine for an hour or so. Then it locks up, sometimes once or twice an hour."

Sometimes something bad happens and sometimes it does not. That's the clue for replacing the power supply. And don't bother with the voltmeter; the voltages will show up within tolerances, but only *once in a while* they will spike and sag (far more quickly than your voltmeter can measure) and cause these intermittent errors. When in doubt, change the power supply. Power supplies break in computers more often than any other part of the PC except the floppy disk drives. You might choose to keep power supplies on hand for swapping and testing.

Fuses and Fire

Inside every power supply resides a simple fuse. If your power supply simply pops and stops working, you might be tempted to go inside the power supply and check the fuse. This is not a good idea. First off, the capacitors in most power supplies carry high voltage charges that can hurt a lot if you touch them. Second, fuses blow for a reason. If a power supply is malfunctioning inside, you want that fuse to blow, because the alternative is much less desirable.

Failure to respect the power of electricity will eventually result in the most catastrophic of all situations: a fire. Don't think it won't happen to you! Keep a fire extinguisher handy. Every PC workbench needs a fire extinguisher, but you need to make sure you have the right one. The fire prevention industry has divided fire extinguishers into three fire classes:

- **Class A** Ordinary free-burning combustible, such as wood or paper
- **Class B** Flammable liquids, such as gasoline, solvents, or paint
- **Class C** Live electrical equipment

As you might expect, you should only use a Class C fire extinguisher on your PC if it should catch fire. All fire extinguishers are required to have their type labeled prominently on them. Many fire extinguishers are multi-class in that they can handle more than one type of fire. The most common fire extinguisher is type ABC—it works on all common types of fires.

Beyond A+

Power supplies provide essential services for the PC, creating DC out of AC and cooling the system, but that utilitarian role does not stop the power supply from being an enthusiast's plaything. Plus, server and high-end workstations have somewhat different needs than more typical systems, so naturally they need a boost in power. Let's take a look Beyond A+ at these issues.

It Glows!

The enthusiast community has been modifying, or *modding,* their PCs for years, cutting holes in the cases, adding fans to make overclocking feasible, and slapping in glowing strips of neon and cold cathode tubes. The power

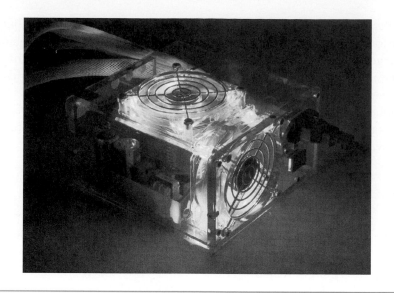

• **Figure 7.14**   See-through power supply that glows blue

supply escaped the scene for a while, but it's back. A quick visit to a good computer store off or online, such as Directron.com, reveals a line of power supplies that light up, sport a fancy color, or have more fans than some rock stars. Figure 7.14 shows a see-through PSU.

On the other hand, you also find super-quiet stealth power supplies (Figure 7.15), with single or double high-end fans that react to the temperature inside your PC—speeding up when necessary but running slowly and silently when not. One of these would make a perfect power supply for a home entertainment PC, because it would provide function without adding excessive decibels of noise.

Modular Power Supplies

It's getting more and more popular to make PCs that look good on both the inside and the outside. Unused power cables dangling around inside PCs

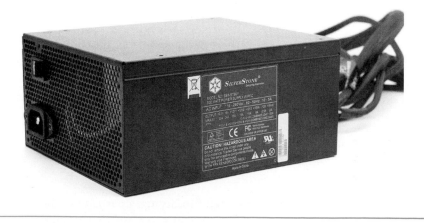

• **Figure 7.15**   High-end power supply

creates a not-so-pretty picture. To help out stylish people, manufacturers created power supplies with modular cables (Figure 7.16).

Modular cables are pretty cool, because you add only the lines you need for your system. On the other hand, some techs claim that modular cables hurt efficiency because the modular connectors add resistance to the lines. You make the choice: is a slight reduction in efficiency worth a pretty look?

Rail Power

When you start using more powerful CPUs and video cards, you can run into a problem I call "rail power." Every ATX12V power supply using multiple rails supplies only a certain amount of power, measured in amps (A), on each rail. The problem is with the 12-V rails. The ATX12V standard requires up to 18 A for each 12-V rail—more than enough for the majority of users, but not enough when you're using a powerful CPU and one or more PCIe video cards. If you've got a powerful system, get online and read the detailed specs for your power supply. Figure 7.17 shows sample power supply specs. Many power supply makers do not release detailed specs—avoid them!

Look for power supplies that offer about 16 to 18 A per rail. These will be big power supplies—400 W and up. Nothing less will support a big CPU and one or two PCIe video cards.

Watch out for power supplies that list their operating temperature at 25° C—about room temperature. A power supply that provides 500 W at 25° C will supply substantially less in warmer temperatures, and the inside of your PC is usually 15° C warmer than the outside air. Sadly, many power supply makers—even those who make good power supplies—fudge this fact.

● **Figure 7.16**   Modular cable power supply

NeoHE 550

FEATURES	
Switches	ATX Logic on-off Additional power rocker switch
Maximum Power	550W
Transient Response	+12V, +5Vand +3.3V independent output circuitry provides stable power and tighter cross regulation (+/- 3%)
P. G. Signal	100-500ms
Over Voltage Protection recycle AC to reset	+5V trip point < +6.5V +3.3V trip point < +4.1V +12V trip point < +14.3V
Special Connectors	ATX12V/EPS12V Compatible 4 + 4 pin +12V Molex Peripheral Floppy SATA PCI Express
Leakage Current	<3.5mA @ 115VAC

OUTPUT							
Output Voltage	+3.3V	+5V	+12V1	+12V2	+12V3	-12V	+5Vsb
Max. Load	24A	20A	18A	18A	18A	0.8A	2.5A
Min. Load	0.5A	0.3A	1A	1A	1A	0A	0A
Regulation	3%	3%	3%	3%	3%	6%	3%
Ripple & Noise(mV)	50	50	120	120	120	120	50
Available Power	79.2W	100W		504W		9.6W	12.5W
Total Power	550W continuous output @ 50C ambient temperature						

● **Figure 7.17**   Sample specs

Chapter 7 Review

Chapter Summary

After reading this chapter and completing the exercises, you should understand the following about installing and troubleshooting power supplies.

Install and Upgrade Power Supplies

- Power supplies connect to the PC case via four screws mounted in the rear of the case. Unscrew the four screws and the power supply will lift out. As ATX power supplies are always on, be sure to unplug it from the wall outlet before working on it.

Understand and Implement System Cooling

- Adequate cooling is important to prevent damage to the computer's internal components. The fan inside the power supply itself cools the voltage regulator circuits within the power supply and provides a constant flow of outside air throughout the interior of the computer case. If the fan is not working, turn the computer off before you experience equipment failure. Some power supplies regulate airflow by using a sensor, with a three-wire connector that plugs into the motherboard.

- To improve cooling, most cases come with a case fan. If the case does not have one, you should add one. Most case fans use standard Molex connectors, but some use a special three-pronged power connector that plugs directly into the motherboard. To enable the fans to create airflow, the case needs to be closed. If slot covers are left off empty expansion bays, it can cause the computer to overheat. Slot covers also help keep dust and smoke out of the case. Beware of "great deals" on cases that come with power supplies, as the included power supply is often substandard.

Troubleshoot Power Supplies

- Electrical problems range from irregular AC to dying or faulty power supplies. Power supplies may fail suddenly or slowly over time. After you make sure that the wall outlet is providing electricity, checking voltages from the power supply with a voltmeter is the best way to verify that the power supply is working or has failed. A power supply is functioning properly if the output voltages are within 10 percent over or under the expected voltage. Be sure to check all the connections on the power supply. If you determine that it is bad, the most economical solution is to throw it away and replace it with a new one.

- Power supplies will not start unless they are connected to a motherboard. If you need to test a power supply but don't have a motherboard, use an ATX tester.

- If one of the internal electrical components in the power supply begins to fail, the result is usually intermittent problems, making it difficult to diagnose. If you are experiencing intermittent problems, such as lockups or different error codes that disappear after rebooting, suspect the power supply. Unfortunately, the voltmeter is not good for diagnosing intermittent problems. Since power supply failures rank second behind floppy drive failures, it is a good idea to keep power supplies in stock for swapping and testing.

- Never open a power supply, even to check the fuse, because the unit contains capacitors that carry high voltage charges that can hurt you.

- Every PC workbench should have a Class C fire extinguisher handy in case of an electrical fire. Although some fire extinguishers are multi-class, handling all types of fire, use only a Class C fire extinguisher on your PC.

Key Terms

3-pin fan connector (92)	Class A fire extinguisher (95)	Molex connector (90)
airflow (91)	Class B fire extinguisher (95)	power supply fan (90)
ATX tester (94)	Class C fire extinguisher (95)	power supply unit (PSU) (88)
case fan (90)	manually adjustable fan (92)	slot covers (91)

Key Term Quiz

Use the Key Terms list to complete the sentences that follow. Not all terms will be used.

1. The _____ provides the basic cooling for the PC.

2. As long as an ATX _____ is plugged in, it supplies electricity to the motherboard.

3. A case fan usually gets power via a standard _____.

4. A(n) _____ is required for electrical fires.

5. Some fans connect to the motherboard via a(n) _____.

6. You can test a power supply with a small device known as a(n) _____.

7. To maintain airflow inside your case, make sure all _____ are covered.

8. _____ are large, square fans that attach directly to the computer case.

9. _____ have a knob that enables you to control the speed of the fan.

10. Leaving a case open prevents proper _____ and causes a loss of cooling efficiency.

Multiple-Choice Quiz

1. Which kind of fire extinguisher should you use for computer equipment?
   A. Class A
   B. Class B
   C. Class C
   D. Class D

2. Under what conditions should a PC technician work inside the power supply?
   A. Only when it is unplugged
   B. Only when the technician is wearing an anti-static wrist strap
   C. Anytime, because the power supply only has low-energy DC electricity that will not hurt the technician
   D. Never, because the power supply has capacitors that hold electrical charges that may harm the technician

3. What should you check first if a computer will not start and the fan in the power supply will not turn?
   A. Check the voltages coming out of the power supply.
   B. Check the motherboard power connector.
   C. Check the power coming into the power supply.
   D. Check the power switch.

4. Which of the following problems points to a dying power supply?
   A. Intermittent lockups at bootup
   B. A power supply fan that does not turn
   C. A multimeter reading of 11 V for the 12 V power line
   D. A computer that won't start by shorting the soft power jumpers

5. Which statement is true about ATX power supplies?
   A. They provide a constant flow of 12 V power to the motherboard.
   B. The power supply fan is powered through a Molex connector.
   C. They should be kept plugged into the wall outlet when working on the inside of a PC to provide a ground.
   D. They provide a constant flow of 5 V power to the motherboard.

6. Which statement is true about power supply fans?
   A. They draw cool air into the system.
   B. They snap into special brackets on the case to provide extra cooling for key components.
   C. They are easily replaced.
   D. They can be enabled or disabled through CMOS setup.

7. Barry claims that leaving the cover off a computer case keeps a system cool. Brian claims that leaving the cover on but the slot covers off provides cooling, much like opening a window in a hot house. Who is correct?

   A. Only Barry is correct.

   B. Only Brian is correct.

   C. Both Barry and Brian are correct.

   D. Neither Barry nor Brian is correct.

8. How can you effectively reduce fan noise?

   A. Replace the existing fans with larger fans.

   B. Replace the existing fans with specialty "quiet" fans.

   C. Replace the existing fans with manually adjustable-speed fans.

   D. All of these methods will reduce fan noise.

9. After testing his power supply with a multimeter, Ruben noticed the 12-volt line was outputting a mere 10.5 volts. What might be the problem?

   A. Ruben has his multimeter set incorrectly.

   B. The power supply is faulty and should be replaced.

   C. There is a problem with the alternating current from the power company.

   D. There is no problem. A variance of plus or minus 10 percent is normal.

10. Haylie heard a pop, and her power supply stopped working. What might be the problem, and how can she fix it?

   A. The fuse blew. She should open the power supply and replace the fuse.

   B. The fuse blew. She should replace the power supply.

   C. The fuse blew. She should flip the breaker switch on the back of the power supply.

   D. A fan blade cracked. She should replace the power supply.

Essay Quiz

1. As microprocessors have become more powerful and more devices have been invented for the computer, the wattage demands for the PC have gone up. So has the need for cooling. Discuss the cooling devices that come with today's PCs and what the user needs to know about keeping the PC cool.

2. Helene's computer worked fine last week. Although she has not changed anything since then, today her computer won't even boot. You suspect that the power supply died. You know that she does not have a multimeter. What will you tell her to check to confirm this opinion? If she does need to replace the power supply, how can she be sure that the new one will work with her PC?

Lab Projects

• Lab Project 7.1

Every technician needs a multimeter. Visit a local electronics store and look at its line of multimeters. (If a store is not nearby, you may use the Internet instead.) What features do the different multimeters offer? What kinds of measurements do they provide? Is the output from some in digital format and others in analog? Which output do you find easier to read? Is one kind more accurate than another? What price ranges are available for multimeters? Then, select the multimeter you would like to add to your toolkit. Why did you choose that model? Now, start saving your pennies so you can buy it!

Hard Drive Technologies

"It would appear that we have reached the limits of what it is possible to achieve with computer technology, although one should be careful with such statements, as they tend to sound pretty silly in five years."

—JOHN VON NEUMANN, 1949

O f all the hardware on a PC, none gets more attention—or gives more anguish—than the hard drive. There's a good reason for this: if the hard drive breaks, you lose data. As you probably know, when the data goes, you have to redo work or restore from backup—or worse. It's good to worry about the data, because the data runs the office, maintains the payrolls, and stores the e-mail. This level of concern is so strong that even the most neophyte PC users are exposed to terms such as *IDE, ATA,* and *controller*—even if they don't put the terms into practice!

This chapter focuses on how hard drives work, beginning with the internal layout and organization of the hard drive. You'll look at the different types of hard drives used today (PATA, SATA, and SCSI), how they interface with the PC, and how to install them properly into a system. The chapter covers how more than one drive may work with other drives to provide data safety and improve speed through a feature called RAID. Let's get started.

In this chapter, you will learn how to

- **Explain how hard drives work**
- **Identify and explain the ATA hard drive interfaces**
- **Identify and explain the SCSI hard drive interfaces**
- **Describe how to protect data with RAID**
- **Explain how to install drives**
- **Configure CMOS and install drivers**
- **Troubleshoot hard drive installation**

■ How Hard Drives Work

All hard drives are composed of individual disks, or *platters*, with read/write heads on actuator arms controlled by a servo motor—all contained in a sealed case that prevents contamination by outside air (see Figure 8.1).

☑ **Cross Check**

Implementing Hard Drives

In the Essentials book you covered the process of implementing a preinstalled drive. What are the two steps that must be performed on every installed hard drive so that the operating system can use the drive?

The aluminum platters are coated with a magnetic medium. Two tiny read/write heads service each platter, one to read the top and the other to read the bottom of the platter (see Figure 8.2).

The coating on the platters is phenomenally smooth! It has to be, as the read/write heads actually float on a cushion of air above the platters, which spin at speeds between 3500 and 10,000 rpm. The distance (flying height) between the heads and the disk surface is less than the thickness of a fingerprint. The closer the read/write heads are to the platter, the more densely the data packs onto the drive. These infinitesimal tolerances demand that the platters never be exposed to outside air. Even a tiny dust particle on a platter would act like a mountain in the way of the read/write heads and would cause catastrophic damage to the drive. To keep the air clean inside the drive, all hard drives use a tiny, heavily filtered aperture to keep the air pressure equalized between the interior and the exterior of the drive.

● **Figure 8.1**   Inside the hard drive

Data Encoding

Although the hard drive stores data in binary form, visualizing a magnetized spot representing a one and a non-magnetized spot representing a zero grossly oversimplifies the process. Hard drives store data in tiny magnetic

● **Figure 8.2**   Top and bottom read/write heads and armatures

● **Figure 8.3** Data is stored in tiny magnetic fields.

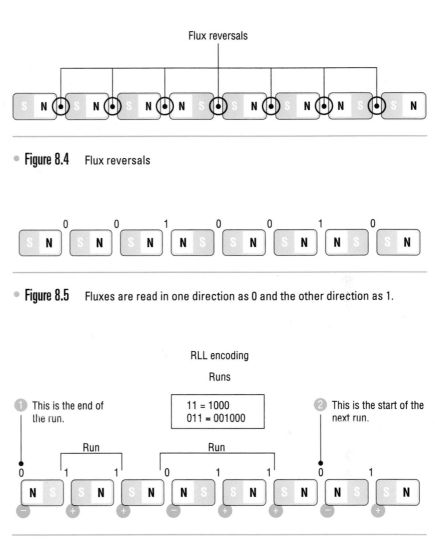

fields—think of them as tiny magnets that can be placed in either direction on the platter, as shown in Figure 8.3. Each tiny magnetic field, called a *flux*, can switch back and forth through a process called a *flux reversal* (see Figure 8.4). Electronic equipment can read and write flux reversals much faster and easier than it can magnetize or not magnetize a spot to store a one or a zero.

In early hard drives, as the read/write head moved over a spot, the direction of the flux reversal defined a one or a zero. As the read/write head passed from the left to right, it recognized fluxes in one direction as a zero and the other direction as a one (Figure 8.5). Hard drives read these flux reversals at a very high speed when accessing or writing data.

Today's hard drives use a more complex and efficient method to interpret flux reversals using special data encoding systems. Instead of reading individual fluxes, a modern hard drive reads groups of fluxes called *runs*. Starting around 1991, hard drives began using a data encoding system known as *run length limited (RLL)*. With RLL, any combination of ones and zeroes can be stored in a preset combination of about 15 different runs. The hard drive looks for these runs and reads them as a group, resulting in much faster and much more dense data. Whenever you see RLL, you also see two numbers: the minimum and the maximum run length, such as RLL 1,7 or RLL 2,7. Figure 8.6 shows two sequential RLL runs.

● **Figure 8.4**   Flux reversals

● **Figure 8.5**   Fluxes are read in one direction as 0 and the other direction as 1.

● **Figure 8.6**   Sequential RLL runs

Current drives use an extremely advanced method of RLL called **Partial Response Maximum Likelihood (PRML)** encoding. As hard drives pack more and more fluxes on the drive, the individual fluxes start to interact with each other, making it more and more difficult for the drive to verify where one flux stops and another starts. PRML uses powerful, intelligent circuitry to analyze each flux reversal and to make a "best guess" as to what type of flux reversal it just read. As a result, the maximum run length for PRML drives reaches up to around 16 to 20 fluxes, far more than the 7 or so on RLL drives. Longer run lengths enable the hard drive to use more complicated run combinations so that the hard drive can store a phenomenal amount of data. For example, a run of only 12 fluxes on a hard drive might equal a string of 30 or 40 ones and zeroes when handed to the system from the hard drive.

The size required by each magnetic flux on a hard drive has reduced considerably over the years, resulting in higher capacities. As fluxes become smaller, they begin to interfere with each other in weird ways. I have to say *weird* since to make sense of what's going on at this subatomic level (I told you these fluxes were small!) would require that you take a semester of quantum mechanics! Let's just say that laying fluxes flat against the platter has reached its limit. To get around this problem, hard drive makers recently began to make hard drives that store their flux reversals vertically (up and down) rather than longitudinally (forward and backward), enabling them to make hard drives in the 1 terabyte (1024 gigabyte) range. Manufacturers call this vertical storage method *perpendicular recording* (Figure 8.7).

For all this discussion and detail on data encoding, the day-to-day PC technician never deals with encoding. Sometimes, however, knowing what you don't need to know helps as much as knowing what you do need to know. Fortunately, data encoding is inherent to the hard drive and completely invisible to the system. You're never going to have to deal with data encoding, but you'll sure sound smart when talking to other PC techs if you know your RLL from your PRML!

Moving the Arms

The read/write heads move across the platter on the ends of *actuator arms*. In the entire history of hard drives, manufacturers have used only two technologies to move the arms: **stepper motor** and **voice coil**. Hard drives first used stepper motor technology, but today they've all moved to voice coil.

Stepper motor technology moved the arm in fixed increments or steps, but the technology had several limitations that doomed it. Because the interface between motor and actuator arm required minimal slippage to ensure precise and reproducible movements, the positioning of the arms became less precise over time. This physical deterioration caused data transfer errors. Additionally, heat deformation wreaked havoc with stepper motor drives. Just as valve clearances in automobile engines change with operating temperature, the positioning accuracy changed as the PC operated and various hard drive components got warmer. Although very small, these changes caused problems. Accessing the data written on a cold hard drive, for example, became difficult after the disk warmed. In addition, the read/write heads could damage the disk surface if not "parked" (set in a non-data area) when not in use, requiring techs to use special parking programs before transporting a stepper motor drive.

All hard drives made today employ a linear motor to move the actuator arms. The linear motor, more popularly called a voice coil motor, uses a permanent magnet surrounding a coil on the actuator arm. When an

Floppy disk drives still use stepper motors.

Traditional   Perpendicular

● **Figure 8.7**   Perpendicular versus traditional longitudinal recording

Mike Meyers' CompTIA A+ Guide: PC Technician (Exams 220-602, 220-603, & 220-604)

electrical current passes, the coil generates a magnetic field that moves the actuator arm. The direction of the actuator arm's movement depends on the polarity of the electrical current through the coil. Because the voice coil and the actuator arm never touch, no degradation in positional accuracy takes place over time. Voice coil drives automatically park the heads when the drive loses power, making the old stepper motor park programs obsolete.

Lacking the discrete "steps" of the stepper motor drive, a voice coil drive cannot accurately predict the movement of the heads across the disk. To make sure voice coil drives land exactly in the correct area, the drive reserves one side of one platter for navigational purposes. This area essentially "maps" the exact location of the data on the drive. The voice coil moves the read/write head to its best guess about the correct position on the hard drive. The read/write head then uses this map to fine-tune its true position and make any necessary adjustments.

Now that you have a basic understanding of how a drive physically stores data, let's turn to how the hard drive organizes that data so we can use that drive.

Geometry

Have you ever seen a cassette tape? If you look at the actual brown Mylar (a type of plastic) tape, nothing will tell you whether sound is recorded on that tape. Assuming the tape is not blank, however, you know *something* is on the tape. Cassettes store music in distinct magnetized lines. You could say that the physical placement of those lines of magnetism is the tape's "geometry."

Geometry also determines where a hard drive stores data. As with a cassette tape, if you opened up a hard drive, you would not see the geometry. But rest assured that the drive has geometry; in fact, every model of hard drive uses a different geometry. We describe the geometry for a particular hard drive with a set of numbers representing three values: heads, cylinders, and sectors per track.

Heads

The number of heads for a specific hard drive describes, rather logically, the number of read/write heads used by the drive to store data. Every platter requires two heads. If a hard drive has four platters, for example, it would need eight heads (see Figure 8.8).

Based on this description of heads, you would think that hard drives would always have an even number of heads, right? Wrong! Most hard drives reserve a head or two for their own use. Therefore, a hard drive can have either an even or an odd number of heads.

Cylinders

To visualize cylinders, imagine taking a soup can and opening both ends of the can. Wash off the label and clean out the inside. Now look at the shape of the can; it is a geometric shape called a cylinder. Now imagine taking that cylinder and sharpening one end so that it easily cuts through the hardest metal. Visualize placing the ex-soup can over the hard drive and pushing it down through the drive. The can cuts into one side and out the other of

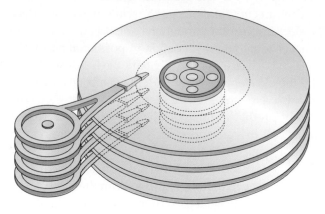

Four platters = Eight heads

• **Figure 8.8** Two heads per platter

each platter. Each circle transcribed by the can is where you store data on the drive, and is called a **track** (Figure 8.9).

Each side of each platter contains tens of thousands of tracks. Interestingly enough, the individual tracks themselves are not directly part of the drive geometry. Our interest lies only in the groups of tracks of the same diameter, going all of the way through the drive. Each group of tracks of the same diameter is called a **cylinder** (see Figure 8.10).

There's more than one cylinder! Go get yourself about a thousand more cans, each one a different diameter, and push them through the hard drive. A typical hard drive contains thousands of cylinders.

Sectors per Track

Now imagine cutting the hard drive like a birthday cake, slicing all the tracks into tens of thousands of small slivers. Each sliver is called a *sector*, and each sector stores 512 bytes of data (see Figure 8.11). Note that **sector**

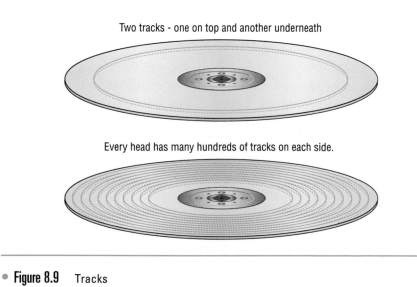

Two tracks - one on top and another underneath

Every head has many hundreds of tracks on each side.

• **Figure 8.9** Tracks

refs to the sliver when discussing geometry, but it refers to the specific spot on a single track within that sliver when discussing data capacity.

The sector is the universal "atom" of all hard drives. You can't divide data into anything smaller than a sector. Although sectors are important, the number of sectors is not a geometry. The geometry value is called  (sectors/track). The sectors/track value describes the number of sectors in each track (see Figure 8.12).

The Big Three

Cylinders, heads, and sectors/track combine to define the hard drive's geometry. In most cases, these three critical values are referred to as *CHS*. The importance of these three values lies in the fact that the PC's BIOS needs to know the drive's geometry to know how to talk to the drive. Back in the old days, a technician needed to enter these values into the CMOS setup program manually. Today, every hard drive stores the CHS information in the drive itself, in an electronic format that enables the BIOS to query the drive automatically to determine these values. You'll see more on this later in the chapter in the section called "Autodetection."

Two other values—write precompensation cylinder and landing zone—no longer have relevance in today's PCs; however, these terms still are tossed around and a few CMOS setup utilities still support them—another classic example of a technology appendix! Let's look at these two holdouts from another era so when you access CMOS, you won't say, "What the heck are these?"

Write Precompensation Cylinder

Older hard drives had a real problem with the fact that sectors toward the inside of the drives were much smaller than sectors toward the outside. To handle this, an older drive would spread data a little farther apart once it got to a particular cylinder. This cylinder was called the write precompensation

All tracks of the same diameter are called a cylinder.

Track

• **Figure 8.10**   Cylinder

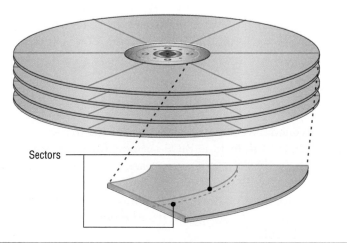

Sectors

• **Figure 8.11**   Sectors

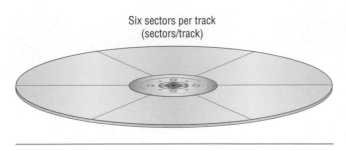

Six sectors per track
(sectors/track)

● **Figure 8.12**   Sectors per track

(write precomp) cylinder, and the PC had to know which cylinder began this wider data spacing. Hard drives no longer have this problem, making the write precomp setting obsolete.

Landing Zone

On older hard drives with stepper motors, the landing zone value designated an unused cylinder as a "parking place" for the read/write heads. As mentioned earlier, old stepper motor hard drives needed to have their read/write heads parked before being moved in order to avoid accidental damage. Today's voice coil drives park themselves whenever they're not accessing data, automatically placing the read/write heads on the landing zone. As a result, the BIOS no longer needs the landing zone geometry.

IT Technician

■ ATA—The King

Over the years, many interfaces existed for hard drives, with such names as ST-506 and ESDI. Don't worry about what these abbreviations stood for; neither the CompTIA A+ certification exams nor the computer world at large has an interest in these prehistoric interfaces. Starting around 1990, an interface called ATA appeared that now virtually monopolizes the hard drive market. ATA hard drives are often referred to as **integrated drive electronics (IDE)** drives. Only one other type of interface, the moderately popular small computer system interface (SCSI), has any relevance for hard drives. ATA drives come in two basic flavors. The older **parallel ATA (PATA)** drives send data in parallel, on a 40- or 80-wire data cable. PATA drives dominated the industry for more than a decade but are being replaced by **serial ATA (SATA)** drives that send data in serial, using only one wire for data transfers. The leap from PATA to SATA is only one of a large number of changes that have taken place over the years with ATA. To appreciate these changes, we'll run through the many ATA standards forwarded over the years.

ATA-1

When IBM unveiled the 80286-powered IBM PC AT in the early 1980s, it introduced the first PC to include BIOS support for hard drives. This BIOS supported up to two physical drives, and each drive could be up to 504 MB— far larger than the 5-MB and 10-MB drives of the time. Although having built-in support for hard drives certainly improved the power of the PC, at that time, installing, configuring, and troubleshooting hard drives could at best be called difficult.

To address these problems, Western Digital and Compaq developed a new hard drive interface and placed this specification before the *American*

Tech Tip

IDE

The term IDE (integrated drive electronics) refers to any hard drive with a built-in controller. All hard drives are technically IDE drives, although we only use the term IDE when discussing ATA drives.

Tech Tip

External Hard Drives

A quick trip to any major computer store will reveal a thriving trade in external hard drives. You used to be able to find external drives that connected to the slow parallel port, but external drives today connect to a FireWire, Hi-Speed USB 2.0, or eSATA port. All three interfaces offer high data transfer rates and hot-swap capability, making them ideal for transporting huge files such as digital video clips. Regardless of the external interface, however, inside the casing you'll find an ordinary PATA or SATA drive, just like those described in this chapter.

National Standards Institute (ANSI) committees, which in turn put out the *AT Attachment (ATA)* interface in March of 1989. The ATA interface specified a cable and a built-in controller on the drive itself. Most importantly, the ATA standard used the existing AT BIOS on a PC, which meant that you didn't have to replace the old system BIOS to make the drive work—a very important consideration for compatibility but one that would later haunt ATA drives. The official name for the standard, ATA, never made it into the common vernacular until recently, and then only as PATA to distinguish it from SATA drives.

The ANSI subcommittee directly responsible for the ATA standard is called Technical Committee T13. If you want to know what's happening with ATA, check out the T13 Web site: www.t13.org.

Early ATA Physical Connections

The first ATA drives connected to the computer with a **40-pin ribbon cable** that plugged into the drive and to a hard drive controller. The cable has a colored stripe down one side that denotes pin 1 and should connect to the drive's pin 1 and to the controller's pin 1. Figure 8.13 shows the "business end" of an early ATA drive, with the connectors for the ribbon cable and the power cable.

The controller is the support circuitry that acts as the intermediary between the hard drive and the external data bus. Electronically, the setup looks like Figure 8.14.

Wait a minute! If ATA drives are IDE (see the Tech Tip), they already have a built-in controller. Why do they then have to plug into a *controller* on the motherboard? Well, this is a great example of a term that's not used properly, but everyone (including the motherboard and hard drive makers) uses it this way. What we call the ATA controller is really no more than an interface providing a connection to the rest of the PC system. When your BIOS talks to the hard drive, it actually talks to the onboard circuitry on the drive, not the connection on the motherboard. But, even though the *real* controller resides on the hard drive, the 40-pin connection on the motherboard is called the controller. We have a lot of misnomers to live with in the ATA world!

The ATA-1 standard defined that no more than two drives attach to a single IDE connector on a single ribbon cable. Because up to two drives can attach to one connector via a single cable, you need to be able to identify each drive on the cable. The ATA standard identifies the two different drives as "master" and "slave." You set one drive as master and one as slave using tiny jumpers on the drives (Figure 8.15).

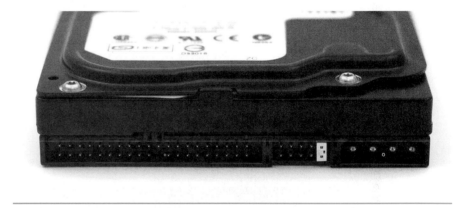

● **Figure 8.13**   Back of IDE drive showing 40-pin connector (left), jumpers (center), and power connector (right)

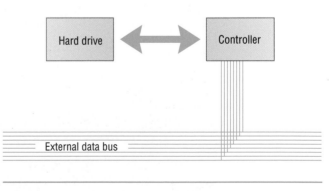

● **Figure 8.14**   Relation of drive, controller, and bus

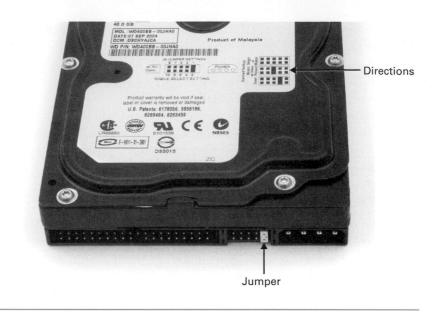

Directions

Jumper

• **Figure 8.15**   A typical hard drive with directions for setting a jumper

The controllers are on the motherboard and manifest themselves as two 40-pin male ports, as shown in Figure 8.16.

PIO and DMA Modes

If you're making a hard drive standard, you must define both the method and the speed at which the data's going to move. ATA-1 defined two different methods, the first using programmed I/O (PIO) addressing and the second using direct memory access (DMA) mode.

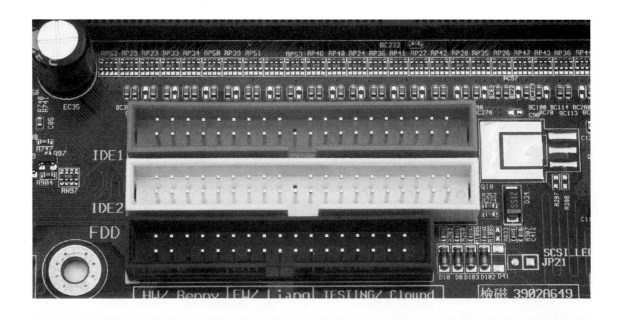

• **Figure 8.16**   IDE interfaces on a motherboard

PIO is nothing more than the traditional I/O addressing scheme, where the CPU talks directly to the hard drive via the BIOS to send and receive data. Three different PIO speeds called **PIO modes** were initially adopted:

- PIO mode 0: 3.3 MBps (megabytes per second)
- PIO mode 1: 5.2 MBps
- PIO mode 2: 8.3 MBps

DMA modes defined a method to enable the hard drives to talk to RAM directly using old-style DMA commands. (The ATA folks called this *single word DMA*.) This old-style DMA was slow, and the resulting three ATA single word DMA modes were also slow:

- Single word DMA mode 0: 2.1 MBps
- Single word DMA mode 1: 4.2 MBps
- Single word DMA mode 2: 8.3 MBps

When a computer booted up, the BIOS queried the hard drive to see what modes it could use and would then automatically adjust to the fastest mode.

ATA-2

In 1990, the industry adopted a series of improvements to the ATA standard called ATA-2. Many people called these new features **Enhanced IDE (EIDE)**. EIDE was really no more than a marketing term invented by Western Digital, but it caught on in common vernacular and is still used today, although its use is fading. Regular IDE drives quickly disappeared, and by 1995, EIDE drives dominated the PC world. Figure 8.17 shows a typical EIDE drive.

The terms *ATA, IDE,* and *EIDE* are used interchangeably.

● **Figure 8.17**   EIDE drive

ATA-2 was the most important ATA standard, as it included powerful new features such as higher capacities; support for non–hard drive storage devices; support for two more ATA devices, for a maximum of four; and substantially improved throughput.

Higher Capacity with LBA

IBM created the AT BIOS to support hard drives many years before IDE drives were invented, and every system had that BIOS. The developers of IDE made certain that the new drives would run from the same AT BIOS command set. With this capability, you could use the same CMOS and BIOS routines to talk to a much more advanced drive. Your motherboard or hard drive controller wouldn't become instantly obsolete when you installed a new hard drive.

Unfortunately, the BIOS routines for the original AT command set allowed a hard drive size of only up to 528 million bytes (or 504 MB—remember that a mega = 1,048,576, not 1,000,000). A drive could have no more than 1024 cylinders, 16 heads, and 63 sectors/track:

1024 cylinders × 16 heads × 63 sectors/track × 512 bytes/sector = 504 MB

For years, this was not a problem. But when hard drives began to approach the 504 MB barrier, it became clear that there needed to be a way of getting past 504 MB. The ATA-2 standard defined a way to get past this limit with **logical block addressing (LBA)**. With LBA, the hard drive lies to the computer about its geometry through an advanced type of sector translation. Let's take a moment to understand sector translation, and then come back to LBA.

Sector Translation Long before hard drives approached the 504 MB limit, the limits of 1024 cylinders, 16 heads, and 63 sectors/track gave hard drive makers fits. The big problem was the heads. Remember that every two heads means another platter, another physical disk that you have to squeeze into a hard drive. If you wanted a hard drive with the maximum number of 16 heads, you would need a hard drive with eight physical platters inside the drive! Nobody wanted that many platters: it made the drives too tall, it took more power to spin up the drive, and that many parts cost too much money (see Figure 8.18).

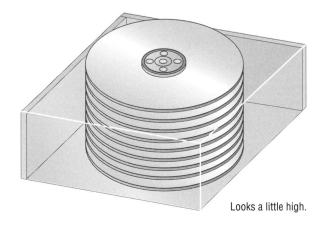

Looks a little high.

Manufacturers could readily produce a hard drive that had fewer heads and more cylinders, but the stupid 1024/16/63 limit got in the way. Plus, the traditional sector arrangement wasted a lot of useful space. Sectors toward the inside of the drive, for example, are much shorter than the sectors on the outside. The sectors on the outside don't need to be that long, but with the traditional geometry setup, hard drive makers had no choice. They could make a hard drive store a lot more information, however, if hard drives could be made with more sectors/track on the outside tracks (see Figure 8.19).

• **Figure 8.18**   Too many heads

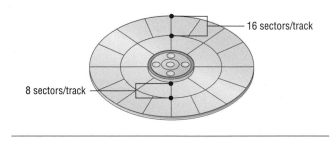

16 sectors/track

8 sectors/track

• **Figure 8.19**   Multiple sectors/track

Mike Meyers' CompTIA A+ Guide: PC Technician (Exams 220-602, 220-603, & 220-604)

The ATA specification was designed to have two geometries. The *physical geometry* defined the real layout of the CHS inside the drive. The *logical geometry* described what the drive told the CMOS. In other words, the IDE drive "lied" to the CMOS, thus side-stepping the artificial limits of the BIOS. When data was being transferred to and from the drive, the onboard circuitry of the drive translated the logical geometry into the physical geometry. This function was, and still is, called sector translation .

Let's look at a couple of hypothetical examples in action. First, pretend that Seagate came out with a new, cheap, fast hard drive called the ST108. To get the ST108 drive fast and cheap, however, Seagate had to use a rather strange geometry, shown in Table 8.1.

Notice that the cylinder number is greater than 1024. To overcome this problem, the IDE drive performs a sector translation that reports a geometry to the BIOS that is totally different from the true geometry of the drive. Table 8.2 shows the actual geometry and the "logical" geometry of our mythical ST108 drive. Notice that the logical geometry is now within the acceptable parameters of the BIOS limitations. Sector translation never changes the capacity of the drive; it changes only the geometry to stay within the BIOS limits.

Table 8.1	Seagate's ST108 Drive Geometry		
ST108 Physical		**BIOS Limits**	
Cylinders	2048	Cylinders	1024
Heads	2	Heads	16
Sectors/Track	52	Sectors/Track	63
Total Capacity	108 MB		

Table 8.2	Physical and Logical Geometry of the ST108 Drive		
Physical		**Logical**	
Cylinders	2048	Cylinders	512
Heads	2	Heads	8
Sectors/Track	52	Sectors/Track	52
Total Capacity	108 MB	Total Capacity	108 MB

Back to LBA   Now let's watch how the advanced sector translation of LBA provides support for hard drives greater than 504 MB. Let's use an old drive, the Western Digital WD2160, a 2.1-GB hard drive, as an example. This drive is no longer in production but its smaller CHS values make understanding LBA easier. Table 8.3 lists its physical and logical geometries.

Note that, even with sector translation, the number of heads is greater than the allowed 16! So here's where the magic of LBA comes in. The WD2160 is capable of LBA. Now assuming that the BIOS is also capable of LBA, here's what happens. When the computer boots up, the BIOS asks the drives if they can perform LBA. If they say yes, the BIOS and the drive work together to change the way they talk to each other. They can do this without conflicting with the original AT BIOS commands by taking advantage of unused commands to use up to 256 heads. LBA enables support for a

Table 8.3	Western Digital WD2160's Physical and Logical Geometries		
Physical		**Logical**	
Cylinders	16,384	Cylinders	1024
Heads	4	Heads	*64*
Sectors/Track	63	Sectors/Track	63
Total Capacity	2.1 GB	Total Capacity	2.1 GB

maximum of $1024 \times 256 \times 63 \times 512$ bytes = 8.4-GB hard drives. Back in 1990, 8.4 GB was hundreds of time larger than the drives used at the time. Don't worry, later ATA standards will get the BIOS up to today's huge drives!

Not Just Hard Drives Anymore: ATAPI

With the introduction of ATAPI, the ATA standards are often referred to as ATA/ATAPI instead of just ATA.

ATA-2 added an extension to the ATA specification, called **Advanced Technology Attachment Packet Interface (ATAPI)**, that enabled non–hard drive devices such as CD-ROM drives and tape backups to connect to the PC via the ATA controllers. ATAPI drives have the same 40-pin interface and master/slave jumpers as ATA hard drives. Figure 8.20 shows an ATAPI CD-RW drive attached to a motherboard. The key difference between hard drives and every other type of drive that attaches to the ATA controller is in how the drives get BIOS support. Hard drives get it through the system BIOS, whereas non–hard drives require the operating system to load a software driver.

• **Figure 8.20** ATAPI CD-RW drive attached to a motherboard via a standard, 40-pin ribbon cable

More Drives with ATA-2

ATA-2 added support for a second controller, raising the total number of supported drives from two to four. Each of the two controllers is equal in power and capability. Figure 8.21 is a close-up of a typical motherboard, showing the primary controller marked as *IDE1* and the secondary marked as *IDE2*.

Increased Speed

ATA-2 defined two new PIO modes and a new type of DMA called *multi-word DMA* that was a substantial improvement over the old DMA.

• **Figure 8.21** Primary and secondary controllers labeled on a motherboard

Technically, multi-word DMA was still the old-style DMA, but it worked in a much more efficient manner so it was much faster.

- PIO mode 3: 11.1 MBps
- PIO mode 4: 16.6 MBps
- Multi-word DMA mode 0: 4.2 MBps
- Multi-word DMA mode 1: 13.3 MBps
- Multi-word DMA mode 2: 16.6 MBps

ATA-3

ATA-3 came on quickly after ATA-2 and added one new feature called **Self-Monitoring, Analysis, and Reporting Technology (S.M.A.R.T.**, one of the few PC acronyms that requires the use of periods after each letter). S.M.A.R.T. helps predict when a hard drive is going to fail by monitoring the hard drive's mechanical components.

S.M.A.R.T. is a great idea and is popular in specialized server systems, but it's complex, imperfect, and hard to understand. As a result, only a few utilities can read the S.M.A.R.T. data on your hard drive. Your best sources are the hard drive manufacturers. Every hard drive maker has a free diagnostic tool (that usually works only for their drives) that will do a S.M.A.R.T. check along with other tests. Figure 8.22 shows Western Digital's Data Lifeguard Tool in action. Note that it says only whether the drive has passed or not. Figure 8.23 shows some S.M.A.R.T. information.

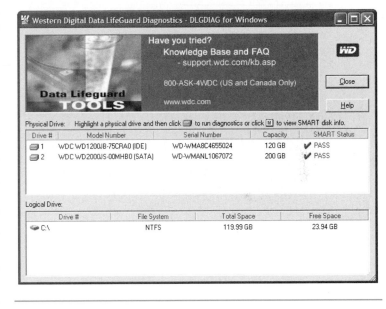

• **Figure 8.22** Data Lifeguard

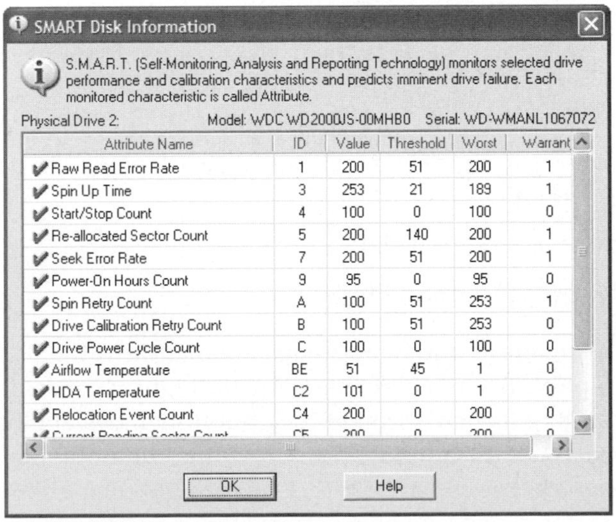

• **Figure 8.23** S.M.A.R.T. information

Although you can see the actual S.M.A.R.T. data, it's generally useless or indecipherable. It's best to trust the manufacturer's opinion and run the software provided.

ATA-4

Anyone who has opened a big database file on a hard drive appreciates that a faster hard drive is better. ATA-4 introduced a new DMA mode called Ultra DMA that is now the primary way a hard drive communicates with a PC. **Ultra DMA** uses DMA bus mastering to achieve far faster speeds than was possible with PIO or old-style DMA. ATA-4 defined three Ultra DMA modes:

- Ultra DMA mode 0: 16.7 MBps
- Ultra DMA mode 1: 25.0 MBps
- Ultra DMA mode 2: 33.3 MBps

Ultra DMA mode 2, the most popular of the ATA-4 DMA modes, is also called ATA/33.

INT13 Extensions

Here's an interesting factoid for you: The original ATA-1 standard allowed for hard drives up to 137 GB! It wasn't the ATA standard that caused the 504-MB size limit, it was the fact that the standard used the old AT BIOS and the BIOS, not the ATA standard, could support only 504 MB. LBA was a work-around that told the hard drive to lie to the BIOS to get it up to 8.4 GB. But eventually hard drives started edging close to the LBA limit and something had to be done. The T13 folks said, "This isn't *our* problem! It's the ancient BIOS problem. You BIOS makers need to fix the BIOS!" And they did.

In 1994, Phoenix Technologies (the BIOS manufacturer) came up with a new set of BIOS commands called **Interrupt 13 (INT13) extensions**. INT13 extensions broke the 8.4-GB barrier by completely ignoring the CHS values and instead feeding the LBA a stream of addressable sectors. A system with INT13 extensions can handle drives up to 137 GB. The entire PC industry quickly adopted INT13 extensions and every system made since 2000–2001 supports INT13 extensions.

ATA-5

Ultra DMA was such a huge hit that the ATA folks adopted two faster Ultra DMA modes with ATA-5:

- Ultra DMA mode 3: 44.4 MBps
- Ultra DMA mode 4: 66.6 MBps

Ultra DMA mode 4, the most popular of the ATA-5 DMA modes, is also called ATA/66.

Ultra DMA modes 4 and 5 ran so quickly that the ATA-5 standard defined a new type of ribbon cable of handling the higher speeds. This **80-wire cable** still has 40 pins on the connectors, but it includes another 40 wires in the cable that act as grounds to improve the cable's ability to handle high-speed signals. The 80-wire cable, just like the 40-pin ribbon cable, has a colored stripe down one side give you proper orientation for pin 1 on the controller and the hard drive. Previous versions of ATA didn't define where the different drives were plugged into the ribbon cable, but ATA-5 defined exactly where the controller, master, and slave drives connected, even defining colors to identify them. Take a look at the ATA/66 cable in Figure 8.24. The connector on the left is colored blue (which you could see if the photo was in color!)—that connector must be the one used to plug into the controller. The connector in the middle is grey—that's for the slave drive. The connector on the right is black—that's for the master drive. Any ATA/66 controller connections are colored blue to let you know it is an ATA/66 controller.

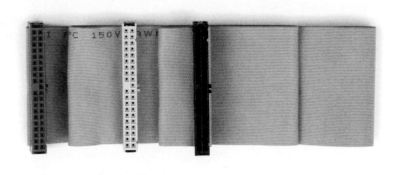

● **Figure 8.24**   ATA/66 cable

ATA/66 is backward compatible, so you may safely plug an earlier drive into an ATA/66 cable and controller. If you plug an ATA/66 drive into an older controller it will work—just not in ATA/66 mode. The only risky action is to use an ATA/66 controller and hard drive with a non-ATA/66 cable. Doing so will almost certainly cause nasty data losses!

ATA-6

Hard drive size exploded in the early 21st century and the seemingly impossible-to-fill 137-GB limit created by INT13 extensions became a barrier to fine computing more quickly than most people had anticipated. When drives started hitting the 120-GB mark, the T13 committee adopted an industry proposal pushed by Maxtor (a major hard drive maker) called *Big Drive* that increased the limit to more than 144 petabytes (approximately 144,000,000 GB). T13 also thankfully gave the new standard a less-silly name, calling it **ATA/ATAPI-6 or simply ATA-6**. Big Drive was basically just a 48-bit LBA, supplanting the older 24-bit addressing of LBA and INT13 extensions. Plus, the standard defined an enhanced block mode, enabling drives to transfer up to 65,536 sectors in one chunk, up from the measly 256 sectors of lesser drive technologies.

ATA-6 also introduced Ultra DMA mode 5, kicking the data transfer rate up to 100 MBps. Ultra DMA mode 5 is more commonly referred to as ATA/100, which requires the same 80-wire connectors as ATA/66.

ATA-7

ATA-7 brought two new innovations to the ATA world—one evolutionary and the other revolutionary. The evolutionary innovation came with the last of the parallel ATA Ultra DMA modes; the revolutionary was a new form of ATA called serial ATA (SATA).

ATA/133

ATA-7 introduced the fastest and probably least adopted of all the ATA speeds, Ultra DMA mode 6 (ATA/133). Even though it runs at a speed of 133 MBps, the fact that it came out with SATA kept many hard drive manufacturers away. ATA/133 uses the same cables as Ultra DMA 66 and 100.

While you won't find many ATA/133 hard drives, you will find plenty of ATA/133 controllers. There's a trend in the industry to color the controller connections on the hard drive red, although this is not part of the ATA-7 standard.

Serial ATA

The real story of ATA-7 is SATA. For all its longevity as the mass storage interface of choice for the PC, parallel ATA has problems. First, the flat ribbon cables impede airflow and can be a pain to insert properly. Second, the cables have a limited length, only 18 inches. Third, you can't hot-swap PATA drives. You have to shut down completely before installing or replacing a drive. Finally, the technology has simply reached the limits of what it can do in terms of throughput.

Serial ATA addresses these issues. SATA creates a point-to-point connection between the SATA device—hard disk, CD-ROM, CD-RW, DVD-ROM, DVD-RW, and so on—and the SATA controller. At a glance, SATA devices look identical to standard PATA devices. Take a closer look at the cable and power connectors, however, and you'll see significant differences (Figure 8.25).

Because SATA devices send data serially instead of in parallel, the SATA interface needs far fewer physical wires—seven instead of the eighty wires that is typical of PATA—resulting in much thinner cabling. This might not seem significant, but the benefit is that thinner cabling means better cable control and better airflow through the PC case, resulting in better cooling.

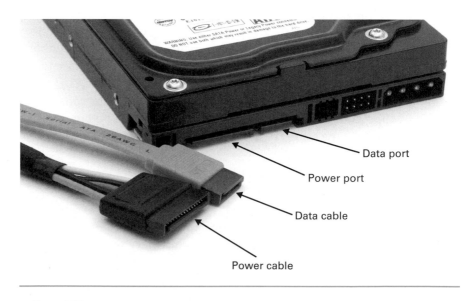

Data port

Power port

Data cable

Power cable

● **Figure 8.25**   SATA hard drive cables and connectors

Further, the maximum SATA device cable length is more than twice that of an IDE cable—about 40 inches (1 meter) instead of 18 inches. Again, this might not seem like a big deal, unless you've struggled to connect a PATA hard disk installed into the top bay of a full-tower case to an IDE connector located all the way at the bottom of the motherboard!

SATA does away with the entire master/slave concept. Each drive connects to one port, so no more daisy-chaining drives. Further, there's no maximum number of drives—many motherboards are now available that support up to eight SATA drives. Want more? Snap in a SATA host card and load 'em up!

The big news, however, is in data throughput. As the name implies, SATA devices transfer data in serial bursts instead of parallel, as PATA devices do. Typically, you might not think of serial devices as being faster than parallel, but in this case, that's exactly the case. A SATA device's single stream of data moves much faster than the multiple streams of data coming from a parallel IDE device—theoretically up to 30 times faster! SATA drives come in two common varieties, the 1.5Gb and the 3Gb, that have a maximum throughput of 150 MBps and 300 MBps, respectively.

SATA is backward compatible with current PATA standards and enables you to install a parallel ATA device, including a hard drive, optical drive, and other devices, to a serial ATA controller by using a **SATA bridge**. A SATA bridge manifests as a tiny card that you plug directly into the 40-pin connector on a PATA drive. As you can see in Figure 8.26, the controller chip on the bridge requires separate power; you plug a Molex connector into the PATA drive as normal. When you boot the system, the PATA drive shows up to the system as a SATA drive.

SATA's ease of use has made it the choice for desktop system storage, and its success is already showing in the fact that more than 90 percent of all hard drives sold today are SATA drives.

Tech Tip

SATA Names

Number-savvy readers might have noticed a discrepancy between the names and throughput of the two SATA drives. After all, 1.5 Gb per second throughput translates to 192 MB per second, a lot higher than the advertised speed of a "mere" 150 MBps. The same is true of the 3Gb/300 MBps drives. The encoding scheme used on SATA drives takes about 20 percent of the overhead for the drive, leaving 80 percent for pure bandwidth. The 3Gb drive created all kinds of problems, because the name of the committee working on the specifications was called the SATA II committee, and marketers picked up on the SATA II name. As a result, you'll find many brands called SATA II rather than 3Gb. The SATA committee now goes by the name SATA-IO.

• **Figure 8.26**   SATA bridge

● Figure 8.27   eSATA connectors (center; that's a FireWire port on the left)

eSATA

External SATA (eSATA) extends the SATA bus to external devices, as the name would imply. The eSATA drives use similar connectors to internal SATA, but they're keyed differently so you can't mistake one for the other. Figure 8.27 shows eSATA connectors on the back of a motherboard. eSATA uses shielded cable lengths up to 2 meters outside the PC and is hot pluggable. The beauty of eSATA is that it extends the SATA bus at full speed, so you're not limited to the meager 50 or 60 MBps of FireWire or USB.

■ SCSI: Still Around

The CompTIA A+ 220-604 exam tests you on SCSI and RAID, topics essential to server environments.

Many specialized server machines and enthusiasts' systems use the **small computer system interface (SCSI)** technologies for various pieces of core hardware and peripherals, from hard drives to printers to high-end tape backup machines. SCSI is different from ATA in that SCSI devices connect together in a string of devices called a *chain.* Each device in the chain gets a SCSI ID to distinguish it from other devices on the chain. Last, the ends of a SCSI chain must be terminated. Let's dive into SCSI now, and see how SCSI chains, SCSI IDs, and termination all work.

SCSI is an old technology dating from the late 1970s, but it has been continually updated. SCSI is faster than ATA (though the gap is closing fast), and until SATA arrived SCSI was the only good choice for anyone using RAID (see the "RAID" section a little later). SCSI is arguably fading away, but it still deserves some mention.

SCSI Chains

● Figure 8.28   SCSI host adapter

SCSI manifests itself through a **SCSI chain**, a series of SCSI devices working together through a host adapter. The host adapter provides the interface between the SCSI chain and the PC. Figure 8.28 shows a typical PCI host adapter. Many techs refer to the host adapter as the *SCSI controller,* so you should be comfortable with both terms.

All SCSI devices can be divided into two groups: internal and external. Internal SCSI devices are attached inside the PC and connect to the host adapter through the latter's internal connector. Figure 8.29 shows an internal SCSI device, in this case a CD-ROM drive. External devices hook to the external connector of the host adapter. Figure 8.30 is an example of an external SCSI device.

Internal SCSI devices connect to the host adapter with a 68-pin ribbon cable (Figure 8.31). This flat, flexible cable functions precisely like a PATA cable. Many external devices connect to the host adapter with a 50-pin high density (HD) connector. Figure 8.32 shows a host adapter external port. Higher end SCSI devices use a 68-pin high density (HD) connector.

• **Figure 8.29**   Internal SCSI CD-ROM

Multiple internal devices can be connected together simply by using a cable with enough connectors. Figure 8.33, for example, shows a cable that can take up to four SCSI devices, including the host adapter.

Assuming the SCSI host adapter has a standard external port (some controllers don't have external connections at all), plugging in an external SCSI device is as simple as running a cable from device to controller. The external SCSI connectors are D-shaped, so you can't plug them in backward. As an added bonus, some external SCSI devices have two ports, one to connect to the host adapter and a second to connect to another SCSI device. The process of connecting a device directly to another device is called *daisy-chaining*.

• **Figure 8.30**   Back of external SCSI device

• **Figure 8.31**   Typical 68-pin ribbon cable

• **Figure 8.32**   50-pin HD port on SCSI host adapter

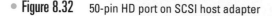

Old SCSI equipment allowed SCSI IDs from 0 to 7 only.

You can daisy-chain up to 15 devices to one host adapter. SCSI chains can be internal, external, or both (see Figure 8.34).

SCSI IDs

If you're going to connect a number of devices on the same SCSI chain, you must provide some way for the host adapter to tell one device from another. To differentiate devices, SCSI uses a unique identifier called the **SCSI ID** . The SCSI ID number can range from 0 to 15. SCSI IDs are similar to many other PC hardware settings in that a SCSI device can theoretically have any SCSI ID, as long as that ID is not already taken by another device connected to the same host adapter.

Some conventions should be followed when setting SCSI IDs. Typically, most people set the host adapter to 7 or 15, but you can change this setting. Note that there is no order for the use of SCSI IDs. It does not matter which device gets which number, and you can skip numbers. Restrictions on IDs apply only within a single chain. Two devices can have the same ID, in other words, as long as they are on different chains (Figure 8.35).

Every SCSI device has some method of setting its SCSI ID. The trick is to figure out how as you're holding the device in your hand. A SCSI device may use jumpers, dip switches, or even tiny dials; every new SCSI device is a new adventure as you try to determine how to set its SCSI ID.

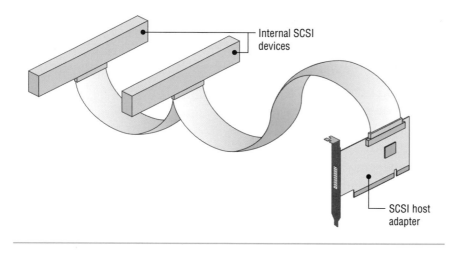

Internal SCSI devices

SCSI host adapter

• **Figure 8.33**   Internal SCSI chain with two devices

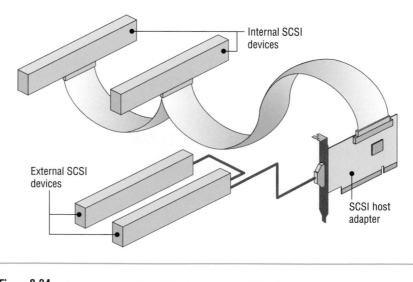

Internal SCSI devices

External SCSI devices

SCSI host adapter

• **Figure 8.34**   Internal and external devices on one SCSI chain

Termination

Whenever you send a signal down a wire, some of that signal reflects back up the wire, creating an echo and causing electronic chaos. SCSI chains use **termination** to prevent this problem. Termination simply means putting something on the ends of the wire to prevent this echo. Terminators are usually pull-down resistors and can manifest themselves in many different ways. Most of the devices within a PC have the appropriate termination built in. On other devices, including SCSI chains and some network cables, you have to set termination during installation.

The rule with SCSI is that you *must* terminate *only* the ends of the SCSI chain. You have to terminate the ends of the cable, which usually means that you need to terminate the two devices at the ends of the cable. Do *not* terminate devices that are not on the ends of the cable. Figure 8.36 shows some examples of where to terminate SCSI devices.

Because any SCSI device might be on the end of a chain, most manufacturers build SCSI devices that can self-terminate. Some devices will detect that they are on the end of the SCSI chain and will automatically terminate themselves. Most devices, however, require that you set a jumper or switch to enable termination (Figure 8.37).

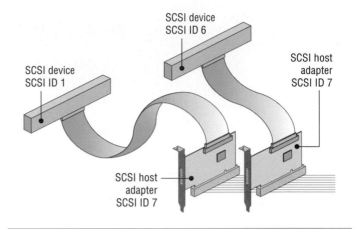

• **Figure 8.35**   IDs don't conflict between separate SCSI chains.

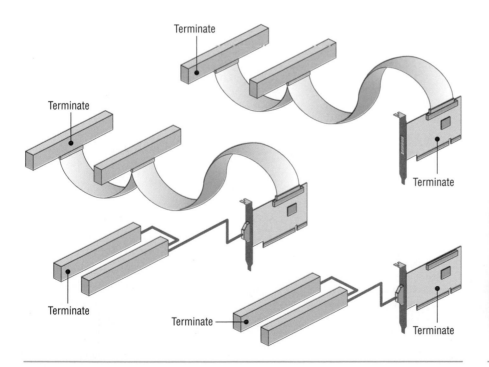

• **Figure 8.36**   Location of the terminated devices

• **Figure 8.37**   Setting termination

■ Protecting Data with RAID

Ask experienced techs, "What is the most expensive part of a PC?" and they'll all answer in the same way: "It's the data." You can replace any single part of your PC for a few hundred dollars at most, but if you lose critical data—well, let's just say I know of two small companies that went out of business just because they lost a hard drive full of data.

Data is king; data is your PC's *raison d'être*. Losing data is a bad thing, so you need some method to prevent data loss. Now, of course, you can do backups, but if a hard drive dies, you have to shut down the computer, reinstall a new hard drive, reinstall the operating system, and then restore the backup. There's nothing wrong with this as long as you can afford the time and cost of shutting down the system.

A better solution, though, would save your data if a hard drive died and enable you to continue working throughout the process. This is possible if you stop relying on a single hard drive and instead use two or more drives to store your data. Sounds good, but how do you do this? Well, first of all, you could install some fancy hard drive controller that reads and writes data to two hard drives simultaneously (Figure 8.38). The data on each drive would always be identical. One drive would be the primary drive and the other drive, called the *mirror* drive, would not be used unless the primary drive failed. This process of reading and writing data at the same time to two drives is called disk mirroring .

If you really want to make data safe, you can use two separate controllers for each drive. With two drives, each on a separate controller, the system will continue to operate, even if the primary drive's controller stops working. This super-drive mirroring technique is called disk duplexing (Figure 8.39). Disk duplexing is also much faster than disk mirroring because one controller does not write each piece of data twice.

Even though duplexing is faster than mirroring, they both are slower than the classic one drive, one controller setup. You can use multiple drives to increase your hard drive access speed. Disk striping (without parity) means spreading the data among multiple (at least two) drives. Disk striping by itself provides no redundancy. If you save a small Microsoft Word file, for example, the file is split into multiple pieces; half of the pieces go on one drive and half on the other (Figure 8.40).

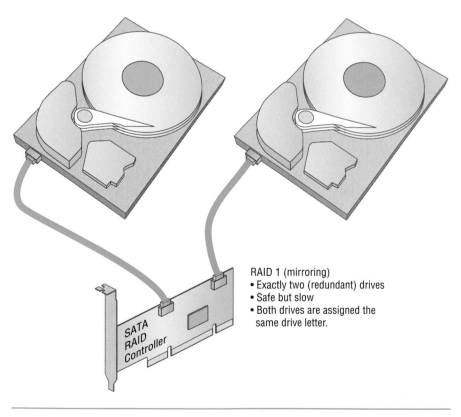

RAID 1 (mirroring)
• Exactly two (redundant) drives
• Safe but slow
• Both drives are assigned the same drive letter.

• **Figure 8.38** Mirrored drives

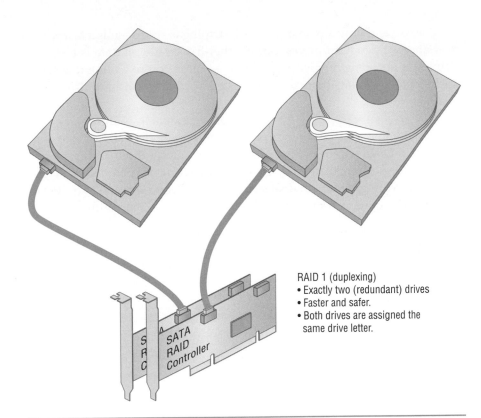

RAID 1 (duplexing)
• Exactly two (redundant) drives
• Faster and safer.
• Both drives are assigned the
  same drive letter.

• **Figure 8.39** Duplexing drives

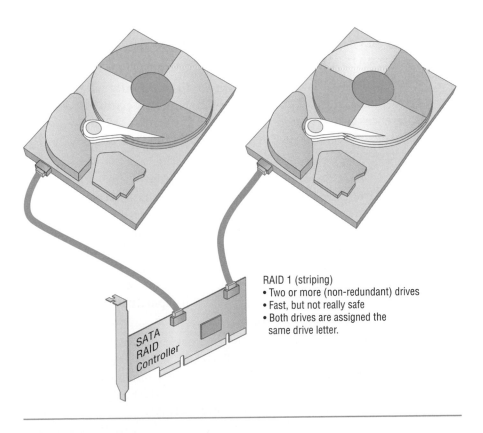

RAID 1 (striping)
• Two or more (non-redundant) drives
• Fast, but not really safe
• Both drives are assigned the
  same drive letter.

• **Figure 8.40** Disk striping

The one and only advantage of disk striping is speed—it is a fast way to read and write to hard drives. But if either drive fails, *all* data is lost. Disk striping is not something you should do—unless you're willing to increase the risk of losing data to increase the speed at which your hard drives save and restore data.

Disk striping with parity, in contrast, protects data by adding extra information, called *parity data,* that can be used to rebuild data should one of the drives fail. Disk striping with parity requires at least three drives, but it is common to use more than three. Disk striping with parity combines the best of disk mirroring and plain disk striping. It protects data and is quite fast. The majority of network servers use a type of disk striping with parity.

RAID

A couple of sharp guys in Berkeley back in the 1980s organized the many techniques for using multiple drives for data protection and increasing speeds as the **redundant array of independent (or inexpensive) disks (RAID)**. They outlined seven levels of RAID, numbered 0 through 6.

- **RAID 0—Disk Striping** Disk striping requires at least two drives. It does not provide redundancy to data. If any one drive fails, all data is lost.

- **RAID 1—Disk Mirroring/Duplexing** RAID 1 arrays require at least two hard drives, although they also work with any even number of drives. RAID 1 is the ultimate in safety, but you lose storage space since the data is duplicated—you need two 100-GB drives to store 100 GB of data.

- **RAID 2—Disk Striping with Multiple Parity Drives** RAID 2 was a weird RAID idea that never saw practical use. Unused, ignore it.

- **RAID 3 and 4—Disk Striping with Dedicated Parity** RAID 3 and 4 combined dedicated data drives with dedicated parity drives. The differences between the two are trivial. Unlike RAID 2, these versions did see some use in the real world but were quickly replaced by RAID 5.

- **RAID 5—Disk Striping with Distributed Parity** Instead of dedicated data and parity drives, RAID 5 distributes data and parity information evenly across all drives. This is the fastest way to provide data redundancy. RAID 5 is by far the most common RAID implementation and requires at least three drives. RAID 5 arrays effectively use one drive's worth of space for parity. If, for example, you have three 200-GB drives, your total storage capacity is 400 GB. If you have four 200-GB drives, your total capacity is 600 GB.

- **RAID 6—Disk Striping with Extra Parity** If you lose a hard drive in a RAID 5 array, your data is at great risk until you replace the bad hard drive and rebuild the array. RAID 6 is RAID 5 with extra parity information. RAID 6 needs at least five drives, but in exchange you can lose up to two drives at the same time. RAID 6 is gaining in popularity for those willing to use larger arrays.

 An *array* in the context of RAID refers to a collection of two or more hard drives.

Tech Tip

RAID Lingo

No tech worth her salt says things like, "We're implementing disk striping with parity." Use the RAID level. Say, "We're implementing RAID 5." It's more accurate and very impressive to the folks in the accounting department!

After these first RAID levels were defined, some manufacturers came up with ways to combine different RAIDs. For example, what if you took two pairs of striped drives and mirrored the pairs? You would get what is called RAID 0+1. Or what (read this carefully now) if you took two pairs of mirrored drives and striped the pairs? You then get what we call RAID 1+0 or what is often called RAID 10. Combinations of different types of single RAID are called *multiple RAID* solutions. Multiple RAID solutions, while enjoying some support in the real world, are quite rare when compared to single RAID solutions RAID 0, 1, and 5.

Implementing RAID

RAID levels describe different methods of providing data redundancy or enhancing the speed of data throughput to and from groups of hard drives. They do not say *how* to implement these methods. Literally thousands of different methods can be used to set up RAID. The method used depends largely on the desired level of RAID, the operating system used, and the thickness of your wallet.

The obvious starting place for RAID is to connect at least two hard drives in some fashion to create a RAID array. For many years, if you wanted to do RAID beyond RAID 0 and RAID 1, the only technology you could use was good-old SCSI. SCSI's chaining of multiple devices to a single controller made it a natural for RAID. SCSI drives make superb RAID arrays, but the high cost of SCSI drives and RAID-capable host adapters kept RAID away from all but the most critical systems—usually big file servers.

In the last few years, substantial leaps in ATA technology have made ATA a viable alternative to SCSI drive technology for RAID arrays. Specialized ATA RAID controller cards support ATA RAID arrays of up to 15 drives—plenty to support even the most complex RAID needs. In addition, the inherent hot-swap capabilities of serial ATA have virtually guaranteed that serial ATA will quickly take over the lower end of the RAID business.

You'll hear the term *nested RAID* used for multiple RAID solutions. The terms are synonymous.

There is actually a term for a storage system composed of multiple independent disks, rather than disks organized using RAID: *JBOD,* which stands for Just a Bunch of Disks (or Drives).

Try This!

Managing Heat with Multiple Drives

Adding three or more fast hard drives into a cramped PC case can be a recipe for disaster to the unwary tech. All those disks spinning constantly create a phenomenal amount of heat. Heat kills PCs! You've got to manage the heat inside a RAID-enabled system or risk losing your data, drives, and basic system stability. The easiest way to do this is to add fans, so Try This!

Open up your PC case and look for built-in places to mount fans. How many case fans do you have installed now? What size are they? What sizes can you use? (Most cases use 80 mm fans, but 60 and 120 mm fans are common as well.) Jot down the particulars of your system and take a trip to the local PC store to check out the fans.

Before you get all fan-happy and grab the biggest and baddest fans to throw in your case, don't forget to think about the added noise level. Try to get a compromise between keeping your case cool enough and not causing early deafness!

Personally, I think the price and performance of serial ATA mean SCSI's days are numbered.

Once you have a number of hard drives, the next question is whether to use hardware or software to control the array. Let's look at both options.

You can use Disk Management in Windows 2000 and Windows XP Professional to create RAID 1 and RAID 5 arrays, but you can use Disk Management only remotely on a server version of Windows (2000 Server or Server 2003). In other words, the capability is there, but Microsoft has limited the OS. If you want to use software RAID in Windows 2000 or XP (Home or Professional), you need to use a third-party tool to set it up.

Hardware versus Software

All RAID implementations break down into either hardware or software methods. Software is often used when price takes priority over performance. Hardware is used when you need speed along with data redundancy. Software RAID does not require special controllers—you can use the regular ATA controllers or SCSI host adapters to make a software RAID array. But you do need "smart" software. The most common software implementation of RAID is the built-in RAID software that comes with Windows 2000 Server and Windows Server 2003. The Disk Management program in these Windows Server versions can configure drives for RAID 0, 1, or 5, and it works with ATA or SCSI (Figure 8.41). Disk Management in Windows 2000 Professional and Windows XP Professional, in contrast, can only do RAID 0.

Windows Disk Management is not the only software RAID game in town. A number of third-party software programs can be used with Windows or other operating systems.

Software RAID means the operating system is in charge of all RAID functions. It works for small RAID solutions but tends to overwork your operating system easily, creating slowdowns. When you *really* need to keep going, when you need RAID that doesn't even let the users know a problem has occurred, hardware RAID is the answer.

Hardware RAID centers around an *intelligent* controller—either a SCSI host adapter or an ATA controller that handles all of the RAID functions (Figure 8.42). Unlike a regular ATA controller or SCSI host adapter, these controllers have chips that know how to "talk RAID."

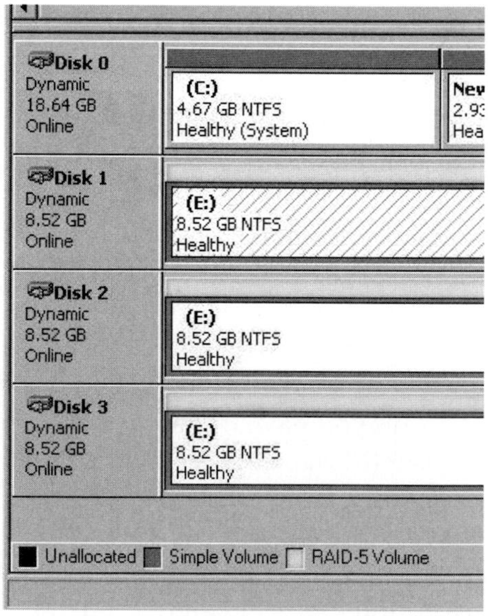

• **Figure 8.41**   Disk Management in Windows Server 2003

● **Figure 8.42**   Serial ATA RAID controller

Most RAID setups in the real world are hardware-based. Almost all of the many hardware RAID solutions provide *hot-swapping*—the ability to replace a bad drive without disturbing the operating system. Hot-swapping is common in hardware RAID.

Hardware-based RAID is invisible to the operating system and is configured in several ways, depending on the specific chips involved. Most RAID systems have a special configuration utility in Flash ROM that you access after CMOS but before the OS loads. Figure 8.43 shows a typical firmware program used to configure a hardware RAID solution.

Personal RAID

Due to drastic reductions in the cost of ATA RAID controller chips, in the last few years we've seen an explosion of ATA-based hardware RAID

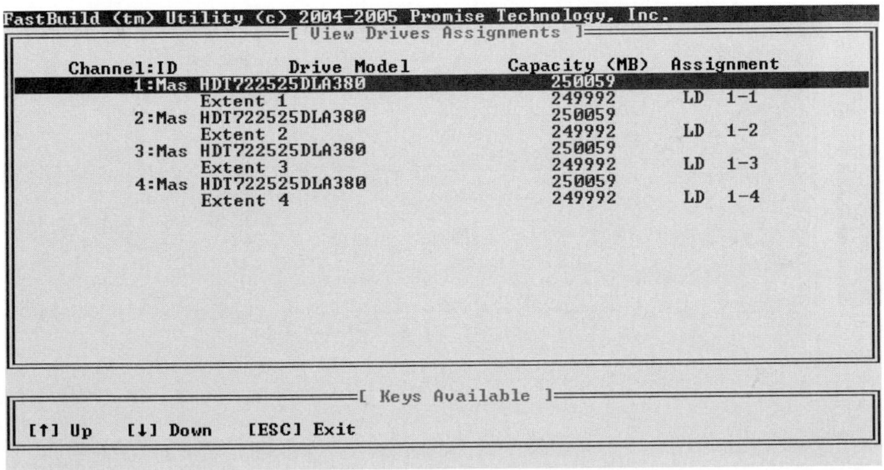

```
FastBuild (tm) Utility (c) 2004-2005 Promise Technology, Inc.
                        ═[ View Drives Assignments ]═
      Channel:ID          Drive Model        Capacity (MB)   Assignment
            1:Mas  HDT722525DLA380              250059
                   Extent 1                     249992         LD   1-1
            2:Mas  HDT722525DLA380              250059
                   Extent 2                     249992         LD   1-2
            3:Mas  HDT722525DLA380              250059
                   Extent 3                     249992         LD   1-3
            4:Mas  HDT722525DLA380              250059
                   Extent 4                     249992         LD   1-4




                        ═[ Keys Available ]═
   [↑] Up    [↓] Down    [ESC] Exit
```

● **Figure 8.43**   RAID configuration utility

RAID controllers aren't just for internal drives; some models can handle multiple eSATA drives configured using any of the different RAID levels. If you're feeling lucky, you can create a RAID array using both internal and external SATA drives.

solutions built into mainstream motherboards. While this "ATA RAID on the motherboard" began with parallel ATA, the introduction of serial ATA made motherboards with built-in RAID extremely common.

These personal RAID motherboards might be quite common, but they're not used too terribly often given that these RAID solutions usually provide only RAID 0 or RAID 1. If you want to use RAID, spend a few extra dollars and buy a RAID 5–capable controller.

The Future Is RAID

RAID has been with us for about 20 years, but until only recently it was the domain of big systems and deep pockets. During those 20 years, however, a number of factors have come together to make RAID a reality for both big servers and common desktop systems. Imagine a world where dirt-cheap RAID on every computer means no one ever again losing critical data. I get goose bumps just thinking about it!

■ Connecting Drives

Installing a drive is a fairly simple process if you take the time to make sure you've got the right drive for your system, configure the drive properly, and do a few quick tests to see if it's running properly. Since PATA, SATA, and SCSI have different cabling requirements, we'll look at each of these separately.

Choosing Your Drive

First, decide where you're going to put the drive. Look for an open ATA connection. Is it PATA or SATA? Is it a dedicated RAID controller? Many motherboards with built-in RAID controllers have a CMOS setting that enables you to turn the RAID on or off (Figure 8.44). Do you have the right controller for a SCSI drive?

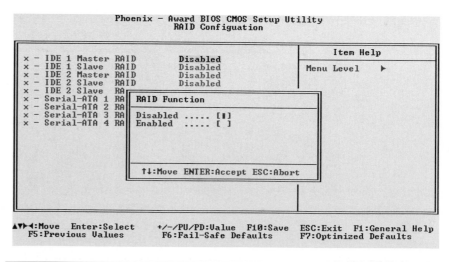

• **Figure 8.44**   Settings for RAID in CMOS

Second, make sure you have room for the drive in the case. Where will you place it? Do you have a spare power connector? Will the data and power cables reach the drive? A quick test fit is always a good idea.

Don't worry about PIO Modes and DMA—a new drive will support anything your controller wants to do.

Jumpers and Cabling on PATA Drives

If you have only one hard drive, set the drive's jumpers to master or standalone. If you have two drives, set one to master and the other to slave. See Figure 8.45 for a close-up of a PATA hard drive showing the jumpers.

At first glance, you might notice that the jumpers aren't actually labeled *master* and *slave*. So how do you know how to set them properly? The easiest way is to read the front of the drive; most drives have a diagram on the housing that explains how to set the jumpers properly. Figure 8.46 shows the front of one of these drives, so you can see how to set the drive to master or slave.

Hard drives may have other jumpers that may or may not concern you during installation. One common set of jumpers is used for diagnostics at the manufacturing plant or for special settings in other kinds of devices that use hard drives. Ignore them. They have no bearing in the PC world. Second, many drives provide a third setting, which is used if only one drive connects to a controller. Often, master and single drive are the same setting on the hard drive, although some hard drives require separate settings. Note that the name for the single drive setting varies among manufacturers. Some use Single; others use 1 Drive or Standalone.

Many current PATA hard drives use a jumper setting called *cable select*, rather than master or slave. As the name implies, the position on the cable determines which drive will be master or slave: master on the end, slave in the middle. For cable select to work properly with two drives, both drives must be set as cable select and the cable itself must be a special cable-select cable. If you see a ribbon cable with a pinhole through one wire, watch out! That's a cable-select cable.

If you don't see a label on the drive that tells you how to set the jumpers, you have several options. First, look for the drive maker's Web site. Every drive manufacturer lists its drive jumper settings on the Web, although it can take a while to find the information you want. Second, try phoning the hard drive maker directly. Unlike many other PC parts manufacturers, hard drive producers tend to stay in business for a long period of time and offer great technical support.

Hard drive cables have a colored stripe that corresponds to the number-one pin—called *pin 1*—on the connector. You need to make

• **Figure 8.45** Master/slave jumpers on a hard drive

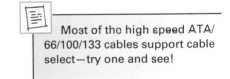

Most of the high speed ATA/ 66/100/133 cables support cable select—try one and see!

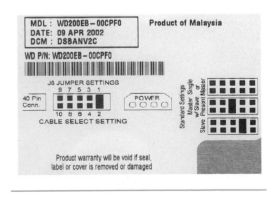

• **Figure 8.46** Drive label showing master/slave settings

certain that pin 1 on the controller is on the same wire as pin 1 on the hard drive. Failing to plug in the drive properly will also prevent the PC from recognizing the drive. If you incorrectly set the master/slave jumpers or cable to the hard drives, you won't break anything; it just won't work.

Finally, you need to plug a Molex connector from the power supply into the drive. All modern PATA drives use a Molex connector.

Cabling SATA Drives

Installing SATA hard drives is even easier than installing IDE devices due to the fact that there's no master, slave, or cable select configuration to mess with. In fact, there are no jumper settings to worry about at all, as SATA supports only a single device per controller channel. Simply connect the power and plug in the controller cable as shown in Figure 8.47—the OS automatically detects the drive and it's ready to go! The keying on SATA controller and power cables makes it impossible to install either incorrectly.

The biggest problem with SATA drives is that many motherboards come with four or more. Sure, the cabling is easy enough, but what do you do when it comes time to start the computer and the system is trying to find the right hard drive to boot up! That's where CMOS comes into play.

• **Figure 8.47**   Properly connected SATA cable

Connecting SCSI Drives

Connecting SCSI drives requires three things. You must use a controller that works with your drive. You need to set unique SCSI IDs on the controller and the drive. Finally, you need to connect the ribbon cable and power connections properly. With SCSI, you need to attach the data cable correctly. You can reverse a PATA cable, for example, and nothing happens except the drive doesn't work. If you reverse a SCSI cable, however, you can seriously damage the drive. Just as with PATA cables, pin 1 on the SCSI data cable must go to pin 1 on both the drive and the host adapter.

■ BIOS Support: Configuring CMOS and Installing Drivers

Every device in your PC needs BIOS support, and the hard drive controllers are no exception. Motherboards provide support for the ATA hard drive controllers via the system BIOS, but they require configuration in CMOS for the specific hard drives attached. SCSI drives require software drivers or firmware on the host adapter.

In the old days, you had to fire up CMOS and manually enter CHS information whenever you installed a new ATA drive to ensure the system saw the drive. Today, this process still takes place, but it's much more automated. Still, there's plenty to do in CMOS when you install a new hard drive.

CMOS settings for hard drives vary a lot among motherboards. The following information provides a generic look at the most common settings, but you'll need to look at your specific motherboard manual to understand all the options available.

Configuring Controllers

As a first step in configuring controllers, make certain they're enabled. It's easy to turn off controllers in CMOS, and many motherboards turn off secondary ATA controllers by default. Scan through your CMOS settings to locate the controller on/off options (see Figure 8.48 for typical settings). This is also the time to check whether your onboard RAID controllers work in both RAID and non-RAID settings.

Autodetection

If the controllers are enabled and the drive is properly connected, the drive should appear in CMOS through a process called *autodetection*. Autodetection is a powerful and handy feature, but it seems every CMOS has a different way to manifest it, and how it is manifested may affect how your computer decides which hard drive to try to boot when you start your PC.

One of your hard drives stores the operating system needed when you boot your computer, and your system needs a way to know where to look for this operating system. The traditional BIOS supported a maximum of only four ATA drives on two controllers, called the *primary controller* and the *secondary controller*. The BIOS looked for the master drive on the primary controller when the system booted up. If you used only one controller, you used the primary controller. The secondary controller was used for CD-ROMs, DVDs, or other non-bootable drives.

Older CMOS made this clear and easy, as shown in Figure 8.49. When you booted up, the CMOS would query the drives through autodetection, and whatever drives the CMOS saw would show up here. Some even older CMOS had a special menu option called Autodetect that you had to run to

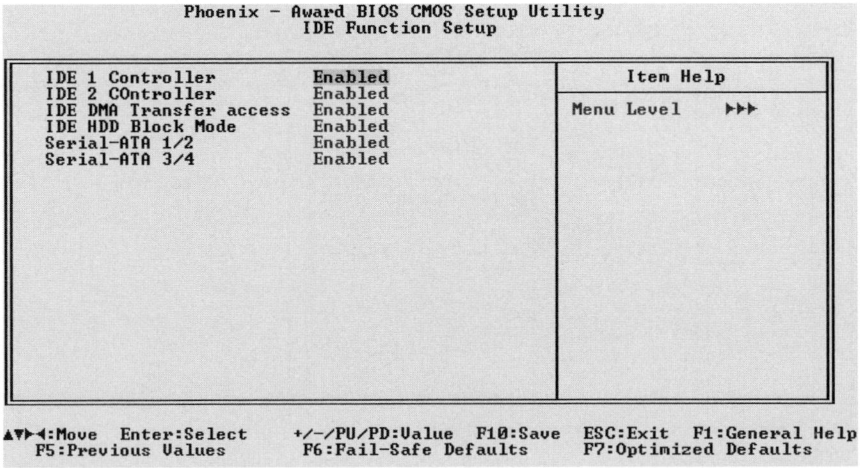

• **Figure 8.48**   Typical controller settings in CMOS

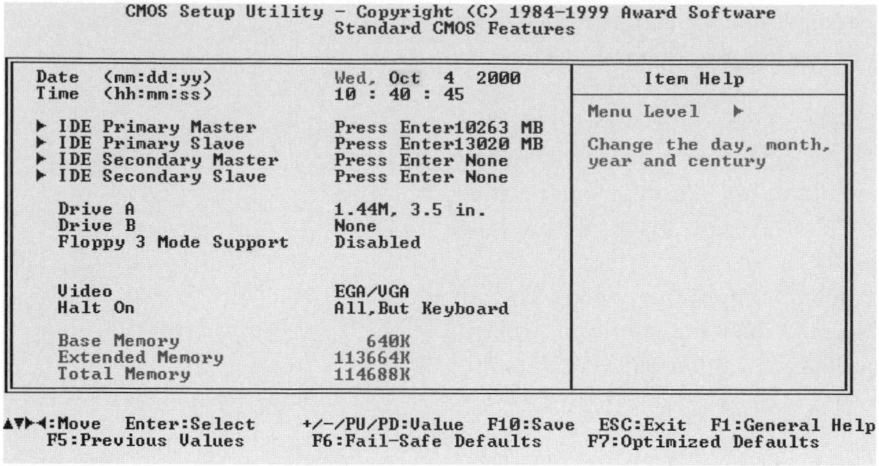

```
        CMOS Setup Utility - Copyright (C) 1984-1999 Award Software
                       Standard CMOS Features
    ┌──────────────────────────────────────────────┬──────────────────────┐
    │  Date   (mm:dd:yy)          Wed, Oct  4  2000 │      Item Help       │
    │  Time   (hh:mm:ss)          10 : 40 : 45      ├──────────────────────┤
    │                                               │  Menu Level    ▶     │
    │  ▶ IDE Primary Master       Press Enter10263 MB                      │
    │  ▶ IDE Primary Slave        Press Enter13020 MB Change the day, month,│
    │  ▶ IDE Secondary Master     Press Enter None  │  year and century    │
    │  ▶ IDE Secondary Slave      Press Enter None  │                      │
    │                                               │                      │
    │    Drive A                  1.44M, 3.5 in.    │                      │
    │    Drive B                  None              │                      │
    │    Floppy 3 Mode Support    Disabled          │                      │
    │                                               │                      │
    │    Video                    EGA/VGA           │                      │
    │    Halt On                  All,But Keyboard  │                      │
    │                                               │                      │
    │    Base Memory                     640K       │                      │
    │    Extended Memory              113664K       │                      │
    │    Total Memory                 114688K       │                      │
    └──────────────────────────────────────────────┴──────────────────────┘
    ▲▼▶◀:Move   Enter:Select    +/-/PU/PD:Value  F10:Save  ESC:Exit  F1:General Help
         F5:Previous Values       F6:Fail-Safe Defaults   F7:Optimized Defaults
```

● **Figure 8.49**   Old standard CMOS settings

see the drives in this screen. There are places for up to four devices—notice not all of them actually have a device.

The autodetection screen indicated that you installed a PATA drive correctly. If you installed a hard drive on the primary controller as master, but messed up the jumper and set it to slave, it would show up in the autodetection screen as the slave. If you had two drives and set them both to master, one drive or the other (or sometimes both) didn't appear, telling you that something was messed up in the physical installation. If you forgot to plug in the ribbon cable or the power, the drives wouldn't autodetect.

SATA messed up the autodetection happiness. There's no such thing as master, slave, or even primary and secondary controller in the SATA world. To get around this, motherboards with PATA and SATA today use a numbering system—and every motherboard uses its own numbering system! One common numbering method uses the term *channels* for each controller. The first boot device is channel 1, the second is channel 2, and so on. PATA channels may have a master and a slave, but a SATA channel has only a master, as SATA controllers support only one drive. So instead of names of drives, you see numbers. Take a look at Figure 8.50.

Whew! Lots of hard drives! This motherboard supports the traditional four PATA drives, but it also supports four SATA drives. Each controller is assigned a number—note that channel 1 and channel 2 have master/slave settings, and that's how you know channel 1 and 2 are the PATA drives. Channels 3 through 6 are SATA, even though the listing says *master*. (SATA's still somewhat new, and a CMOS using incorrect terms like *master* is common.)

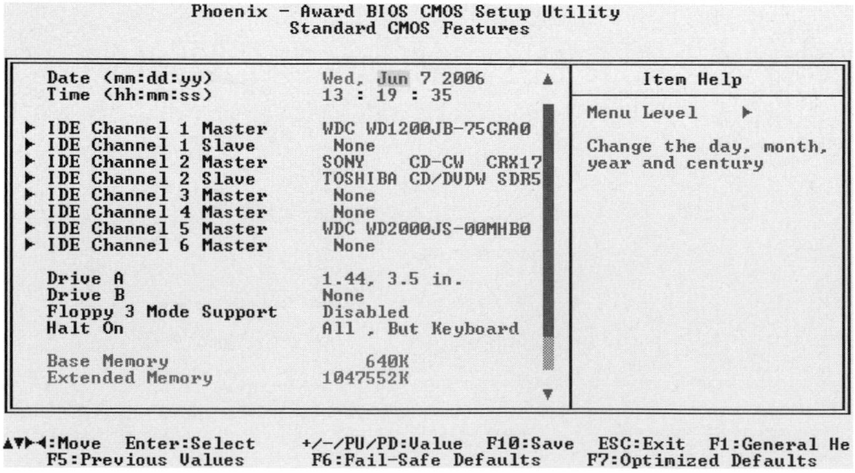

Boot Order

If you want your computer to run, it's going to need an operating system to boot. While the PCs of our forefathers (those of the 1980s and early 1990s) absolutely required you to put the operating system on the primary master, most BIOS makers by 1995 enabled you to put the OS on any of the four drives and then tell the system through CMOS which hard drive to boot. Additionally, you may need to boot from

```
              Phoenix - Award BIOS CMOS Setup Utility
                       Standard CMOS Features
    ┌──────────────────────────────────────────────────┬──────────────────┐
    │  Date (mm:dd:yy)           Wed, Jun 7 2006     ▲  │    Item Help     │
    │  Time (hh:mm:ss)           13 : 19 : 35           ├──────────────────┤
    │  ▶ IDE Channel 1 Master    WDC WD1200JB-75CRA0    │  Menu Level   ▶  │
    │  ▶ IDE Channel 1 Slave     None                   │                  │
    │  ▶ IDE Channel 2 Master    SONY   CD-CW  CRX17     │ Change the day, month,│
    │  ▶ IDE Channel 2 Slave     TOSHIBA CD/DVDW SDR5    │ year and century │
    │  ▶ IDE Channel 3 Master    None                   │                  │
    │  ▶ IDE Channel 4 Master    None                   │                  │
    │  ▶ IDE Channel 5 Master    WDC WD2000JS-00MHB0     │                  │
    │  ▶ IDE Channel 6 Master    None                   │                  │
    │                                                   │                  │
    │    Drive A                 1.44, 3.5 in.          │                  │
    │    Drive B                 None                   │                  │
    │    Floppy 3 Mode Support   Disabled               │                  │
    │    Halt On                 All , But Keyboard     │                  │
    │                                                   │                  │
    │    Base Memory                    640K            │                  │
    │    Extended Memory            1047552K         ▼  │                  │
    └──────────────────────────────────────────────────┴──────────────────┘
    ▲▼▶◀:Move   Enter:Select    +/-/PU/PD:Value  F10:Save  ESC:Exit  F1:General He
         F5:Previous Values       F6:Fail-Safe Defaults   F7:Optimized Defaults
```

● **Figure 8.50**   New standard CMOS features

a floppy, CD-ROM, or even a thumb drive at times. CMOS takes care of this by enabling you to set a *boot order*.

Figure 8.51 shows a typical boot order screen. It has a first, second, and third boot option. Many users like to boot first from floppy or CD-ROM, and then from a hard drive. This enables them to put in a bootable floppy or CD-ROM if they're having problems with the system. Of course, you can set it to boot first from your hard drive and then go into CMOS and change it when you need to—it's your choice.

Most modern CMOS lump the hard drive boot order onto a second screen. This screen works like an autodetect in that it shows only actual hard drives attached. This beats the heck out of guessing!

```
▶ Hard Disk Boot Priority    Press Enter
  First Boot Device          Floppy
  Second Boot Device         Hard Disk
  Third Boot Device          CDROM
  Boot Other Device          Enabled
```

• **Figure 8.51**   Boot order

Device Drivers

Devices that do not get BIOS via the system BIOS routines naturally require some other source for BIOS. For ATAPI devices and many SATA controllers, the source of choice is software device drivers, but both technologies have a couple of quirks you should know about.

Try This!

Working with CMOS

One of the best ways to get your mind around the different drive standards and capabilities is to run benchmarking software on the hard drive to get a baseline of its capabilities. Then, change CMOS settings to alter the performance of the drive and run the diagnostics again. Try this!

1. Get a reliable hard drive benchmarking program. I recommend HD Tach (www.simplisoftware.com) as reliable and rugged.

2. Run the software, and record the scores.

3. Change some or all of the following CMOS settings, and then run the benchmarking utility again: PIO mode, DMA mode, Block mode.

4. What were the effects of changing settings?

ATAPI Devices and BIOS

ATAPI drives plug into an ATA controller on the motherboard and follow the same conventions on cabling and jumpers used by PATA hard drives. In fact, all current CMOS setup utilities *seem* to autodetect CD-media ATAPI drives. If you go into CMOS after installing a CD-ROM drive as master on the secondary IDE controller, for example, the drive will show up just fine, as in Figure 8.52.

The reporting of installed CD-media drives in CMOS serves two purposes. First, it tells the technician that he or she has good connectivity on the ATAPI drive. Second, it shows that you have the option to boot to CD-media, such as a Windows XP disc. What it doesn't do, however, is provide true BIOS support for that drive! That has to come with a driver loaded at boot-up.

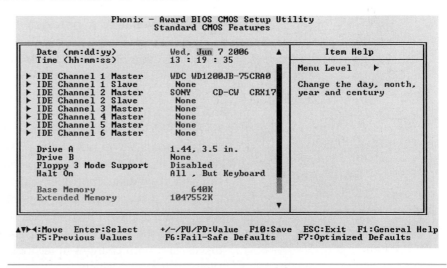

• **Figure 8.52**   CMOS screen showing a CD-ROM drive detected

■ Troubleshooting Hard Drive Installation

The CompTIA A+ 220-603 exam is interested in troubleshooting storage devices, but more from the software side than the physical installation angle.

The best friend a tech has when it comes to troubleshooting hard drive installation is the autodetection feature of the CMOS setup utility. When a drive doesn't work, the biggest question, especially during installation, is, "Did I plug it in correctly?" With autodetection, the answer is simple; if it doesn't see the drives, something is wrong with the hardware configuration. Either a device has physically failed or, more likely, you didn't give the hard drive power, plugged a cable in backwards, or messed up some other connectivity issue.

It takes four things to get a drive installed and recognized by the system: jumpers (PATA only), data cable, power, and CMOS setup recognizing the drive. If any of these steps is missed or messed up, you have a drive that simply doesn't exist according to the PC! To troubleshoot hard drives, simply work your way through each step to figure out what went wrong.

First, set the drive to master, slave, standalone, or cable select, depending on where you decide to install the drive. If a drive is alone on the cable, set it to master or standalone. With two drives, one must be master and the other slave. Alternatively, you can set both drives to cable select and use a cable-select cable.

Second, the data cable must be connected to both the drive and controller, Pin 1 to Pin 1. Reversing the data cable at one end is remarkably easy to do, especially with the rounded cables. They obviously don't have a big red stripe down the side to indicate the location of Pin 1! If you can't autodetect the drive, check the cabling.

Third, be sure to give the hard drive power. Most hard drives use a standard Molex connector. If you don't hear the whirring of the drive, make certain you plugged in a Molex from the power supply, rather than from another source such as an otherwise disconnected fan. You'd be surprised how often I've seen that!

Fourth, you need to provide BIOS for the controller and the drive. This can get tricky as the typical CMOS setup program has a lot of hard drive options. Plus, you have an added level of confusion with RAID settings and non-integrated controllers that require software drivers.

Once you've checked the physical connections, run through these issues in CMOS. Is the controller enabled? Is the storage technology—LBA, INT13, ATA/ATAPI-6—properly set up? Similarly, can the motherboard support the type of drive you're installing? If not, you have a couple of options. You can flash the BIOS with an upgraded BIOS from the manufacturer or you can get a hard drive controller that goes into an expansion slot.

Finally, make certain with non-integrated hard drive controllers, such as those that come with many SATA drives, that you've installed the proper drivers for the controller. Driver issues can crop up with new, very large drives, and with changes in technology. Always check the manufacturer's Web site for new drivers.

Spindle (or Rotational) Speed

Hard drives run at a set spindle speed, measured in *revolutions per minute* (RPM). Older drives run at the long-standard speed of 3600 RPM, but new drives are hitting 15,000 RPM! The faster the spindle speed, the faster the controller can store and retrieve data. Here are the common speeds: 4500, 5400, 7200, and 10,000 RPM.

Faster drives mean better system performance, but they can also cause the computer to overheat. This is especially true in tight cases, such as minitowers, and in cases containing many drives. Two 4500 RPM drives might run forever, snugly tucked together in your old case. But slap a hot new 10,000 RPM drive in that same case and watch your system start crashing right and left!

You can deal with these hotrod drives by adding drive bay fans between the drives or migrating to a more spacious case. Most enthusiasts end up doing both. Drive bay fans sit at the front of a bay and blow air across the drive. They range in price from $10 to $100 (U.S.) and can lower the temperature of your drives dramatically. Figure 8.53 shows a picture of a double-fan drive bay cooler.

Air flow in a case can make or break your system stability, especially when you add new drives that increase the ambient temperature. Hot systems get flaky and lock up at odd moments. Many things can impede the air flow—jumbled up ribbon cables, drives squished together in a tiny case, fans clogged by dust or animal hair, and so on.

Technicians need to be aware of the dangers when adding a new hard drive to an older system. Get into the habit of tying off ribbon cables, adding front fans to cases when systems lock up intermittently, and making sure the fan(s) run well. Finally, if a client wants a new drive and his system is a tiny minitower with only the power supply fan to cool it off, be gentle, but definitely steer him to one of the slower drives!

• **Figure 8.53**   Bay fans

Hybrid Hard Drives

Windows Vista supports hybrid hard drives (HHDs), drives that combine flash memory and spinning platters to provide fast and reliable storage. Samsung has drives with 128-MB and 256-MB flash cache, for example, that shave boot times in half and, because the platters don't have to spin all the time, add 20–30 minutes more of battery life for portable computers. Adding that much more run time with only a tiny price premium and no extra weight is the Holy Grail of portable computing!

Chapter 8 Review

■ Chapter Summary

After reading this chapter and completing the exercises, you should understand the following about hard drive technologies.

How Hard Drives Work

■ Hard drives contain aluminum platters coated with a magnetic medium and read/write heads that float on a cushion of air. Hard drives store data in a tiny magnetic field called a flux that defines a zero or a one. The switching back and forth of the field is called flux reversal. The incredible storage capacity of today's drives is due to Partial Response Maximum Likelihood (PRML) encoding that includes intelligent circuitry to analyze each flux reversal.

■ Two different technologies have been used to move read/write heads across the platters: stepper motors and voice coil. Very susceptible to physical deterioration and temperature changes, the now obsolete stepper motors moved the actuator arm in fixed increments or steps, often resulting in data transfer errors or the inability to access data on a cold drive. The heads had to be parked to a non-data area when not in use to prevent possible damage to the disk surface. Today's drives use a linear or voice coil motor consisting of a permanent magnet surrounding a coil on the actuator arm. Electrical current causes the coil to generate a magnetic field that moves the actuator arm and thus the read/write heads. Containing no data, one side of one platter is used as a map to position the heads directly over the data. Voice coil technology automatically parks the heads when the drive loses power.

■ Disk geometry for a particular hard drive consists of three primary values: heads, cylinders, and sectors per track. There are two read/write heads per platter. A hard drive can have either an even or an odd number of heads. A cylinder defines a group of tracks of the same diameter. Each track is sliced into tiny slivers called sectors, each of which stores 512 bytes of data. Disk geometry uses the number of sectors per track. Combining cylinders, heads, and sectors per track is referred to as CHS. Write precompensation and landing zone, two other geometric values, have no relevance in today's PCs, but most CMOS utilities still support them.

ATA—The King

■ Today's hard drives have either an ATA interface or a SCSI interface. ATA drives may be parallel ATA (PATA) or the newer serial ATA (SATA). A specification of the American National Standards Institute (ANSI), the AT Attachment (ATA) interface (commonly but incorrectly referred to as IDE) used a 40-pin ribbon cable, had a built-in controller, and did not require a low-level format. By 1995, EIDE was the dominant interface. Its features include higher capacities, support for non–hard drive storage devices, a four device maximum, and improved throughput. The terms ATA, IDE, and EIDE are used interchangeably to describe all PATA devices.

■ PATA drives use a 40-pin plug and a controller that connects them to the external data bus. Although the real controller is built into the hard drive itself, the 40-pin connector on the motherboard is called the controller. Most modern motherboards contain two PATA controllers, each capable of supporting up to two PATA devices. By looking at the motherboard itself or at the motherboard book, you can determine which is the primary controller and which is the secondary. If you are using only one controller, it should be the primary one.

■ The Advanced Technology Attachment Packet Interface (ATAPI) enables non–hard drive devices to use a PATA controller. ATAPI devices, such as CD-ROM drives, use the same 40-pin interface and follow the same rules of master, slave, and cable select jumper settings. Non–hard drives must get their BIOS from option RAM or a software driver.

■ Originally, IDE drives used the same BIOS command set introduced years earlier. Maximum values of 1024 cylinders, 16 heads, and 63 sectors per track limited an IDE drive's capacity to 528 million bytes (504 MB). Western Digital developed the LBA sector translation method to accommodate larger EIDE drives. LBA supports drives with up to 256 heads, for a storage capacity limit of 8.4 GB.

- As drive capacity neared the 8.4-GB maximum, Phoenix Technologies broke the limit by coming up with a new set of BIOS commands called Interrupt 13 extensions (INT13). Completely ignoring the CHS values, INT13 supports drives up to 137 GB by reporting a stream of "addressable sectors" to LBA.

- As drive capacity neared the 137-GB limit, the ANSI ATA committee adopted ATA/ATAPI-6, a new standard that increased the limit to more than 144 petabytes (144,000,000 GB). It uses a 48-bit addressing scheme and an enhanced block mode that transfers up to 65,536 sectors at a time.

- Newer hard drives use direct memory access (DMA) mode to send data directly to RAM, bypassing the CPU. Instead of using the slow DMA controller chip, today's DMA transfers use bus mastering to transfer 32 bits of data. Hard drives typically use one of the following modes: Ultra DMA mode 4 (ATA/66), Ultra DMA mode 5 (ATA/100), and Ultra DMA mode 6 (ATA/133). To use Ultra DMA, you must have a controller and an 80-wire ribbon cable. Some motherboards combine different speeds of ATA controllers, with the higher speed controller indicated with a bright color. The 80-wire ribbon cable indicates where the master and slave drives should be connected. High-end PATA devices can use lower end controllers, but they will operate at the slower speed.

- Serial ATA (SATA) devices look identical to standard PATA devices (except their data and power connectors), but their thinner seven-wire cables provide better airflow and may be up to a meter (39.4 inches) long. SATA does away with the entire master/slave concept. Each drive connects to one port, so no more daisy-chaining drives.

- SATA devices are hot-swappable, great for RAID technology. SATA transfers data in serial bursts, for up to 30 times the throughput of PATA. SATA drives come in two common varieties, the 1.5Gb and the 3Gb, that have a maximum throughput of 150 MBps and 300 MBps, respectively.

SCSI: Still Around

- All SCSI chains, which support either 8 or 16 devices including the controller, require proper termination to prevent signal echo. Additionally, each device on a chain requires a unique SCSI ID, which can be set by jumpers, switches, or dials.

- All SCSI devices can be divided into two groups: internal and external. Internal SCSI devices connect to the host adapter with a 68-pin ribbon cable. External devices connect to the host adapter with either a 50-pin HD connector or a 68-pin HD connector. SCSI enables you to daisy-chain devices together to form longer SCSI chains.

- Improper termination or incorrect SCSI ID settings are the two most common causes of SCSI devices not working. The key factor here is that you must terminate only the ends of the SCSI chain.

Protecting Data with RAID

- Drive mirroring writes data simultaneously to two hard drives, enabling the system to continue to work if one hard drive dies. A faster and even more effective technique is drive duplexing, which performs mirroring using separate controllers for each drive. A third way to create redundant data is disk striping with parity. This technique, requiring at least three drives, combines the redundancy of disk mirroring with the speed of disk striping. Although disk striping without parity works very fast, splitting the data across two drives means you'll lose *all* data if either drive fails.

- Numbered 0 through 6, there are seven official levels of RAID, but the most commonly used ones are RAID 0 (disk striping), RAID 1 (disk mirroring or duplexing), and RAID 5 (disk striping with distributed parity).

- RAID may be implemented through hardware or software methods. While software implementation is cheaper, hardware techniques provide better performance. Windows 2000 Server and Windows 2003 Server include built-in RAID software for RAID 0, RAID 1, and RAID 5 for either ATA or SCSI. Windows 2000 and XP Professional include Disk Management for RAID 0. RAID software solutions tend to overwork your operating system, resulting in slowdowns. Hardware RAID is invisible to the OS and is usually hot-swappable. A hardware ATA RAID controller usually requires CMOS configuration. Many motherboards include built-in ATA-based hardware RAID 0 and RAID 1 capabilities.

- SCSI drives were a natural for the multiple-disk RAID. Specialized ATA RAID controller cards support ATA RAID arrays of up to 15 drives. With its hot-swap capabilities, SATA may soon take over lower end RAID from SCSI.

Connecting Drives

- Older PATA drives use a 40-wire cable, while the newer Ultra DMA drives use an 80-wire cable. Either round or flat and containing no twists, each ribbon cable supports two drives. A diagram on the hard drive's housing shows how to set its jumpers to identify it as master, slave, standalone (on some drives), or cable select (cable position determines whether the drive will be master or slave). Two devices on one cable must both be set to cable select, and the cable itself must also be cable select, as indicated with a pinhole through one wire. Align the colored stripe on the cable with pin 1 on the controller and the drive. Use a Molex connector to provide power to the drive.

- SATA supports only a single device per controller channel, so there are no master, slave, or cable select jumpers. SATA controller and power cables are keyed to prevent incorrect insertion. You can connect a PATA device to a SATA motherboard controller by way of a SATA bridge.

BIOS Support: Configuring CMOS and Installing Drivers

- While system BIOS supports built-in PATA controllers, hard drives require configuration in CMOS. ATAPI devices require software drivers to provide BIOS support. Built-in SATA controllers on a motherboard also require software drivers, as does a SATA controller on a separate expansion card. All SATA devices get BIOS support from the SATA controller, but some drives require additional configuration; in particular, with RAID systems, you may also have to configure the controller Flash ROM settings for the specific drive(s) you install.

- When the hard drive type is set to "Auto," PATA devices can be queried directly by BIOS routines, resulting in the correct CMOS settings for up to four ATA devices. Autodetection made hard drive types obsolete. Because PATA drives have CHS values stored inside them, the BIOS routine, when set to "Auto," updates the CMOS each time the computer boots. An alternative is to run the autodetection option from the CMOS screen.

- Even if the autodetect feature indicates that an optical ATAPI drive has been installed, this merely shows that the drive is connected properly and has the option to function as a boot device. This autodetection does *not* provide true BIOS support. You must still install drivers to provide the BIOS. If the driver is installed in a graphical mode, you will be unable to access the drive if you boot to a command prompt–only environment.

- It takes four things to get a drive installed and recognized by the system: jumpers, data cable, power, and CMOS setup or providing BIOS. If any of these steps is missed or messed up, your drive simply doesn't exist according to the PC.

- If the autodetection feature of the CMOS utility does not detect a drive, it means it is installed incorrectly or the drive itself is bad. Check the master/slave jumper settings. Make sure that the ribbon cable aligns pin 1 with pin 1, and that the Molex connector is supplying power to the drive.

- Once you've checked the physical connections, run through these issues in CMOS. Is the controller enabled? Is the storage technology—LBA, Large, INT13, ATA/ATAPI-6—properly set up? What about the data transfer settings for PIO and DMA modes? Similarly, can the motherboard support the type of drive you're installing? If not, you can flash the BIOS or get a hard drive controller that goes into an expansion slot. Make certain with non-integrated hard drive controllers, such as those that come with many SATA drives, that you've installed the proper drivers for the controller. Always check the manufacturer's Web site for new drivers.

Troubleshooting Hard Drive Installation

- It takes four things to get a drive installed and recognized by the system: jumpers (PATA only), data cable, power, and CMOS setup recognizing the drive. If any of these steps is missed or messed up, you have a drive that simply doesn't exist according to the PC! To troubleshoot hard drives, simply work your way through each step to figure out what went wrong.

- Once you've checked the physical connections, run through these issues in CMOS. Is the controller enabled? Is the storage technology—LBA, INT13, ATA/ATAPI-6—properly set up? Similarly, can the motherboard support the type of drive you're installing? If not, you have a couple of options. You can flash the BIOS with an upgraded BIOS from the manufacturer or you can get a hard drive controller that goes into an expansion slot.

Key Terms

40-pin ribbon cable *(109)*	**geometry** *(105)*	**SCSI chain** *(120)*
80-wire cable *(116)*	**heads** *(105)*	**SCSI ID** *(122)*
Advanced Technology Attachment Packet Interface (ATAPI) *(114)*	**integrated drive electronics (IDE)** *(108)*	**sector** *(106)*
		sector translation *(113)*
ATA/133 *(118)*	**Interrupt 13 (INT13) extensions** *(116)*	**sectors per track** *(107)*
ATA/ATAPI-6 or simply ATA-6 *(117)*	**logical block addressing (LBA)** *(112)*	**Self-Monitoring, Analysis, and Reporting Technology (S.M.A.R.T.)** *(115)*
cylinder *(106)*	**PIO modes** *(111)*	
disk duplexing *(124)*	**parallel ATA (PATA)** *(108)*	**serial ATA (SATA)** *(108)*
disk mirroring *(124)*	**Partial Response Maximum Likelihood (PRML)** *(103)*	**small computer system interface (SCSI)** *(120)*
disk striping *(124)*		
disk striping with parity *(126)*	**redundant array of independent (or inexpensive) disks (RAID)** *(126)*	**stepper motor** *(104)*
DMA modes *(111)*		**termination** *(123)*
Enhanced IDE (EIDE) *(111)*		**track** *(106)*
External SATA (eSATA) *(120)*	**SATA bridge** *(119)*	**Ultra DMA** *(116)*
		voice coil *(104)*

Key Term Quiz

Use the Key Terms list to complete the sentences that follow. Not all terms will be used.

1. An ATA hard drive connects to the controller with a(n) _____ while an Ultra DMA drive uses a(n) _____.

2. A(n) _____ is composed of a group of tracks of the same diameter that the read/write heads can access without moving.

3. To install a parallel ATA device to a serial ATA controller, use a tiny card called a(n) _____.

4. LBA, developed by Western Digital, uses _____ to get around the limits of 1024 cylinders, 16 heads, and 63 sectors/track.

5. Seen in RAID 5, _____ uses at least three drives and combines the best features of disk mirroring and disk striping.

6. A(n) _____-compliant CD-ROM drive installs and cables just like an EIDE drive.

7. The ANSI ATA committee adopted the _____ standard, called "Big Drives" by Maxtor, that allows drives with more than 144 petabytes.

8. _____ drives transfer data at 133 MBps.

9. Drives that use _____ bypass the CPU and send data directly to memory.

10. _____ devices require termination at both ends of a chain.

Multiple-Choice Quiz

1. Which of the following is NOT used to compute storage capacity in CHS disk geometry?
   A. Sectors per track
   B. Tracks
   C. Heads
   D. Cylinders

2. Which level of RAID is disk striping with distributed parity?
   A. RAID 0
   B. RAID 1
   C. RAID 5
   D. RAID 6

3. Which of the following is the most efficient encoding method?
   A. Partial Response Maximum Likelihood (PRML)
   B. Frequency modulation (FM)
   C. Run length limited (RLL)
   D. Modified frequency modulation (MFM)

4. Counting both channels, what is the maximum number of drives/devices that EIDE can support?
   A. One
   B. Two
   C. Seven
   D. Four

5. Which of the following is NOT true about cable select?
   A. Both drives/devices should be set for cable select.
   B. It requires a special cable with a pinhole through one wire.
   C. The colored stripe on the ribbon cable should align with pin 1 on the controller and drive.
   D. Position of the drives on the cable does not matter.

6. If you install two IDE drives on the same cable, how will the computer differentiate them?
   A. The CMOS setup allows you to configure them.
   B. You must set jumpers to determine which drive functions as master and which functions as slave.
   C. You will set jumpers so each drive will have a unique ID number.
   D. The drives will be differentiated by whether you place them before or after the twist in the ribbon cable.

7. What was the maximum hard drive size allowed by BIOS routines for the original AT command set?
   A. 528 MB
   B. 1024 MB
   C. 504 MB
   D. 1028 MB

8. Which of the following terms does NOT describe parallel ATA devices?

A. IDE
B. EIDE
C. SCSI
D. ATA

9. Shelby wants to add a new 100-GB hard drive to her computer. Which of the following will allow her to do so?
   A. CHS
   B. LBA
   C. ECHS
   D. INT13

10. Which of the following techniques provides redundancy by using two disks and two controllers?
    A. Drive mirroring
    B. Drive duplexing
    C. Disk striping
    D. Disk striping with parity

11. How many wires does an Ultra DMA cable have?
    A. 24
    B. 34
    C. 40
    D. 80

12. Billy just installed a second hard drive, but the autodetection utility in CMOS does not detect it. Sara told him he probably had the jumpers set incorrectly or had forgotten to connect the Molex power connector. John told him his new hard drive is probably bad and he should return it. Is Sara or John probably correct?
    A. Sara is correct.
    B. John is correct.
    C. Neither is correct.
    D. Either John or Sara may be correct.

13. Which of the following is NOT an advantage of serial ATA (SATA)?
    A. It is hot-swappable.
    B. Thinner cables provide better airflow inside the case.
    C. SATA provides faster data throughput than PATA.
    D. SATA cable must be shorter than PATA cables.

14. Which of the following two CMOS configuration options are obsolete with today's hard drives?

    A. Cylinders and heads

    B. Heads and sectors

    C. Sectors and write precompensation

    D. Write precompensation and landing zone

15. What standard did the ANSI ATA committee adopt that increased disk storage capacity to more than 144 petabytes?

    A. ATA/ATAPI-6

    B. LBA

    C. INT13

    D. ECHS

■ Essay Quiz

1. Discuss at least three advantages of serial ATA over parallel ATA.

2. Compare and contrast hardware and software RAID implementation.

3. Your friend Blaine has a Pentium III computer with a 100-MHz bus. Currently, it has only a 20-GB ATA/100 hard drive and a CD-RW drive. Since he's interested in graphics, he knows he needs more storage capacity and wants to add a second hard drive. What advice will you give him about selecting a new hard drive?

4. Use www.google.com or a site such as www.newegg.com to compare one of the following pairs of hard drives to determine their features including storage capacity, interface, RPM, and cost:

    ■ Maxtor Model # 6Y120L0 and Maxtor Model # 6Y120M0

    ■ Western Digital Model # WD1200JB and Western Digital Model # WD1200JD

5. Hard drives include other features and characteristics not included in this chapter. Choose one of the following topics and use the Internet to define and explain it to the class.

    ■ Zone bit recording

    ■ "Pixie dust" hard drives

Lab Projects

● Lab Project 8.1

Access the CMOS setup for your computer and examine the settings that apply to your hard drive(s) and EIDE interface. In particular, look at the initial screen to see if it is set to autodetect the kind of hard drive. Is the mode set to LBA or something else? Now find the screen that includes the autodetect utility and run it. Does it offer different modes with different drive capacities? Try to find a screen that includes PIO modes and examine this setting. What other screens apply to the hard drive? When you finish, be sure to choose Quit without Saving.

● Lab Project 8.2

Visit your local computer store or use the Internet to discover what kinds of hard drives and hard drive interfaces are commonly offered with a new computer. Try to determine whether the motherboards offer only parallel ATA interfaces or if they offer serial ATA interfaces, either onboard or through an expansion card. If you were purchasing a new computer, would you select PATA or SATA? Why?

• Lab Project 8.3

Your supervisor has decided to implement RAID on the old company server machine, where everyone stores their work-related data. Come up with two competing RAID setups, one that maximizes security of data at the lowest cost possible, and the other that maximizes speed but retains some security. Cost is not a factor for the second RAID plan.

• Lab Project 8.4

If your lab has the equipment, install a second hard drive in your system. Install it on the same cable as the existing drive and jumper it as the slave. (You may need to jumper the existing drive as master.) Reboot, enter CMOS, and verify both drives are detected. Boot into your operating system and verify that both drives are accessible. (You may need to partition and format the second drive before it is actually usable.)

Installing and Troubleshooting Removable-Media Drives

"Never judge a book by its movie."

—J. W. EAGAN

Removable media has traditionally been the primary method to store and trade data and to install large applications for PCs. Although Internet installation now makes up a substantial part of the storage and trade business (many programs are easily downloaded right to a PC), removable media still has an important job in backups and—most important to techs like us—bootability. There's no PC ever made that isn't designed to boot from a floppy disk, optical disc, or even a USB thumb drive. Without a way for techs to boot an operating system, we'd never be able to install a copy of Windows on a shiny new system or run boot disk utilities to test and repair an ailing computer.

This chapter focuses on two types of removable-media drives: the old floppy drives and optical drives (CDs and DVDs). Here you will install CD-ROM and DVD drives. Then you will learn how to keep floppy and optical drives running smoothly.

In this chapter, you will learn how to

- **Install all types of optical drives**
- **Understand how optical drives work with applications**
- **Troubleshoot floppy drives**
- **Troubleshoot optical drives and media**

Essentials Review

You'll find this chapter far more interesting if you are aware of removable-media concepts covered in the A+ Essentials exam. Before beginning this chapter, make sure you can

- List the different sizes and capacities of floppy drives and disks
- Install and configure floppy drives
- Explain the different types of flash memory and their uses
- Explain the different CD and DVD formats and their uses
- List the capacities for all types of CD and DVD media

IT Technician

■ Installing Optical Drives

From ten feet away, CD-ROM, CD-R, CD-RW, DVD-RW, and DVD+RW drives look absolutely identical. Figure 9.1 shows a CD-ROM, CD-RW, and a DVD drive. Can you tell them apart just by a glance? In case you were wondering, the CD-RW is on the top, the CD-ROM is in the center, and the DVD is on the bottom. If you look closely at an optical drive, its function is normally either stamped on the front of the case or printed on a label somewhere less obvious (see Figure 9.2).

Connections

Most optical drives use PATA or SATA connections and support the ATAPI standard. (Other connections, such as SCSI and USB, are possible but less common.) ATAPI treats an optical drive exactly as though it were an ATA drive.

● **Figure 9.1** CD-ROM, CD-RW, and DVD

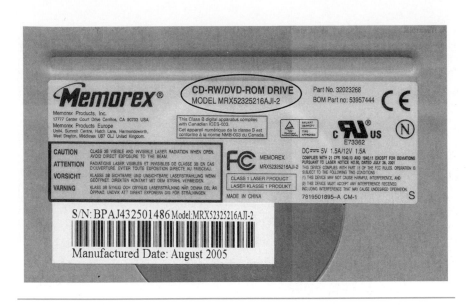

● **Figure 9.2**   Label on optical drive indicating its type and speeds

PATA optical drives have regular 40-pin IDE connectors and master/slave jumpers, just like IDE hard drives. SATA optical drives use standard SATA cables. You install them the same way you would install any ATA hard drive. Figure 9.3 shows a typical DVD installation using PATA. The DVD is configured as slave with a master hard drive on a system's primary IDE controller.

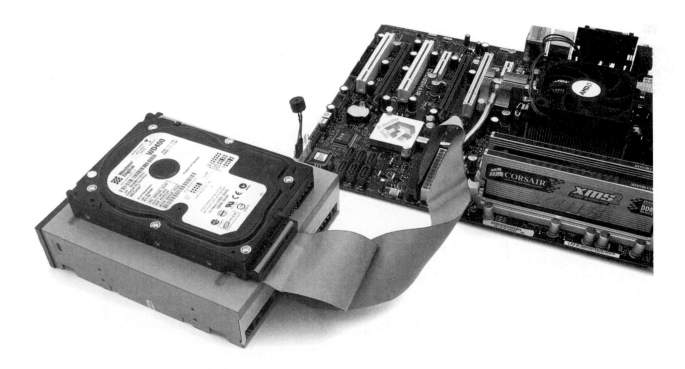

● **Figure 9.3**   Typical DVD installation

Chapter 9: Installing and Troubleshooting Removable-Media Drives

ATAPI drives require no CMOS changes as part of the install process. When the industry first introduced ATAPI drives, techs familiar with hard-drive installations swamped the CD-ROM makers' service departments asking how to set up the drives in CMOS. To reduce these calls, BIOS makers added a CD-ROM option in many CMOS setup utilities, just to give the techs something to do! You can find this option in many older CMOS setup utilities. This setting actually didn't do anything at all; it just kept users from bothering the CD-ROM makers with silly support calls. Modern motherboards report the actual model numbers of optical drives, giving a tech a degree of assurance that he or she configured and installed the drive correctly (Figure 9.4).

Device Manager

When you install a new CD-ROM into an existing system, the first question to ask is, "Does Windows recognize my CD-ROM?" You can determine this by opening the My Computer icon and verifying that a CD-ROM is present (see Figure 9.5). When you want to know more, go to Device Manager.

Device Manager contains most of the information about the CD-ROM. The General tab tells you about the current status of the CD-ROM, basically saying whether the device is working properly or not—rather less useful than actually trying the device. Other tabs, such as the Driver tab shown in Figure 9.6, provide other pertinent information about the drive.

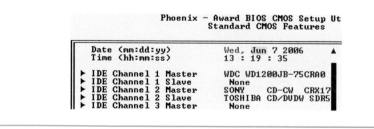

Phoenix – Award BIOS CMOS Setup Ut
Standard CMOS Features

```
Date (mm:dd:yy)         Wed, Jun 7 2006    ▲
Time (hh:mm:ss)         13 : 19 : 35

► IDE Channel 1 Master   WDC WD1200JB-75CRA0
► IDE Channel 1 Slave    None
► IDE Channel 2 Master   SONY    CD-CW  CRX17
► IDE Channel 2 Slave    TOSHIBA CD/DUDW SDR5
► IDE Channel 3 Master   None
```

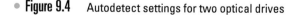

● **Figure 9.4**   Autodetect settings for two optical drives

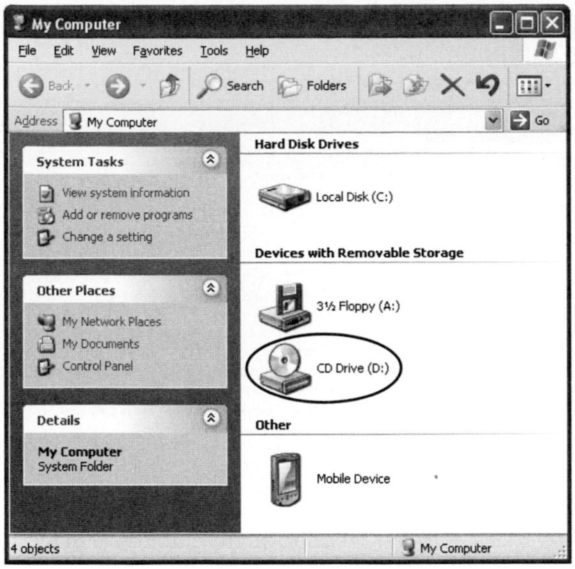

Figure 9.5 CD-ROM drive letter in My Computer

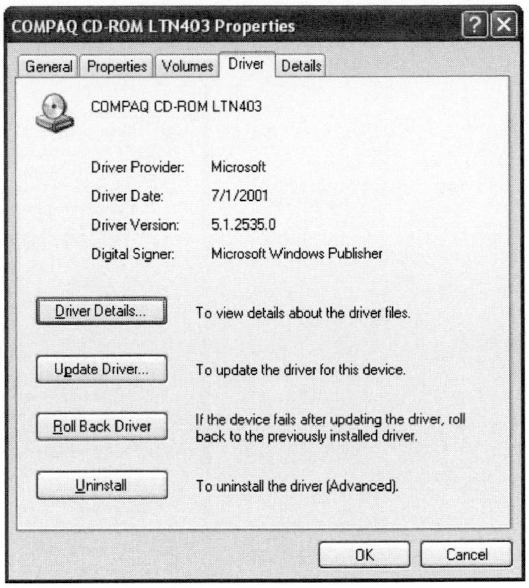

Figure 9.6 Driver tab in Device Manager

Auto Insert Notification

Another setting of note is the Auto Insert Notification option, often referred to as `AutoPlay` in Windows 2000/XP. This setting enables Windows to detect automatically the presence of audio or data CD-ROMs when they are placed in the drive.

Windows 2000 and Windows XP have very different ways of dealing with AutoPlay. In Windows 2000, if the CD is an audio disc, track 1 plays automatically. If the CD-ROM is a data disc, Windows searches the disc's root directory for a special text file called `AUTORUN.INF`.

Although handy, this option can sometimes be annoying and unproductive. Windows 2000 does not provide a simple method to turn off AutoPlay. The only way to turn it off is to edit the registry. You can use the `REGEDT32` version of the Registry Editor and do it directly. In REGEDT32, access this subkey:

HKEY_LOCAL_MACHINE\SYSTEM\CurrentControlSet\Services\Cdrom

Change Autorun 0×1 to 0×0.

Most techs will use `Group Policy` to make the change because it gives you much more control in multiple CD and DVD drive situations. With Group Policy, you can turn off AutoPlay on your CD-RW drive, for example, but leave it enabled for your DVD drive. Group Policy is a very powerful tool that goes well beyond CompTIA A+, so be careful with what you're about to do. To run Group Policy, go to Start | Run and type **gpedit.msc** in the Run dialog box. Click OK to open the MMC. To turn off AutoPlay, navigate down in the menu to the left as follows: Local Computer Policy | Computer Configuration | Administrative Templates. Select the System option and you'll see the *Turn off Autoplay* option in the Setting section on the right pane of the MMC (Figure 9.7).

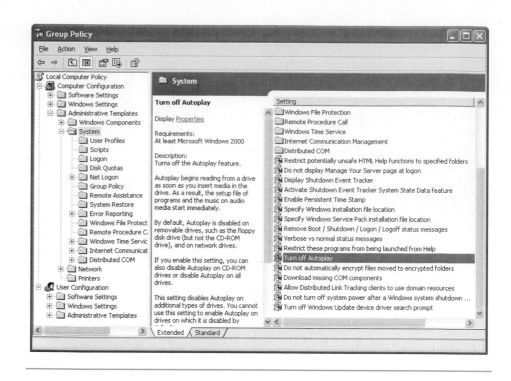

● **Figure 9.7**　Group Policy MMC with Turn off Autoplay selected

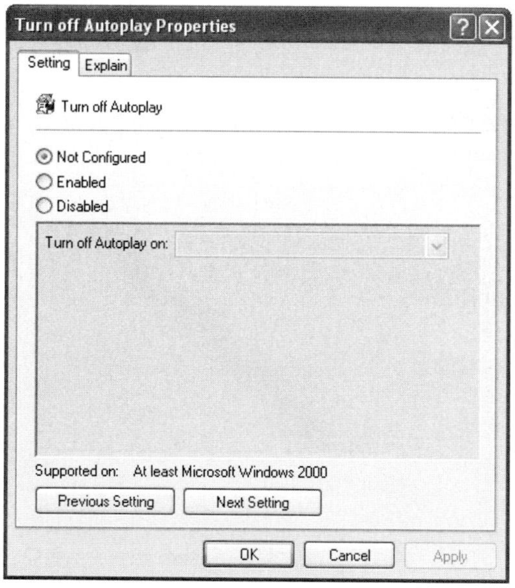

● **Figure 9.8**　Turn off Autoplay Properties dialog box

Double-click or right-click Turn off Autoplay to open the Properties. Note in Figure 9.8 that the default option is Not Configured, but you can enable or disable it here. The words are messy here, so make sure you know what you're doing. *Enabling* Turn off Autoplay gives you the option to stop an optical drive from automatically playing a disc. *Disabling* Turn off Autoplay prevents you or any other user from stopping any optical drive from automatically playing a disc. Got the distinction?

Windows XP provides a much more sophisticated and simpler approach to AutoPlay. By default, when you insert a CD- or DVD-media disc that doesn't have an AUTORUN.INF file, XP asks you what you want to do (Figure 9.9). You can change the default behavior simply by accessing the properties for a particular drive in My Computer and making your selection on the AutoPlay tab. Figure 9.10 shows some of the options for a typical Windows XP machine.

As a final note, Windows 2000 and XP enable you to change the drive letter for an optical drive, just like you can change the letter of a hard drive. You'll find that option in Disk Management (Figure 9.11).

Applications

A regular CD-ROM drive installation involves no applications. You install it, Windows sees it, and you're done. CD-R and CD-RW drives, in contrast, require applications to enable their burning features. DVD-media drives

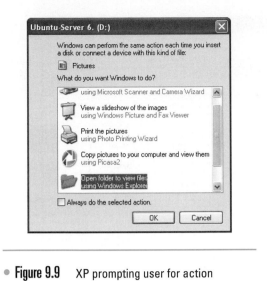

• **Figure 9.9** XP prompting user for action

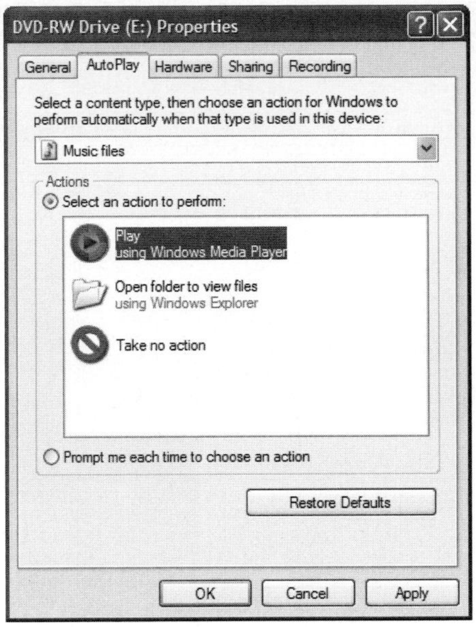

• **Figure 9.10** AutoPlay tab for a DVD-RW drive

need software to enable you to watch movies, burn DVDs, and so on. As of this writing, Nero Burning ROM (www.nero.com) and Roxio's Easy Media Creator (www.roxio.com) suites of programs share the reigns as the most popular CD-burning software programs. If you're looking for a free burner, try CDBurnerXP Pro, pictured in Figure 9.12 (www.cdburnerxp.se). Windows XP contains basic CD-burning capabilities built into the operating system. With XP, you can readily drag and drop files to your CD-R or CD-RW drive and move those files from

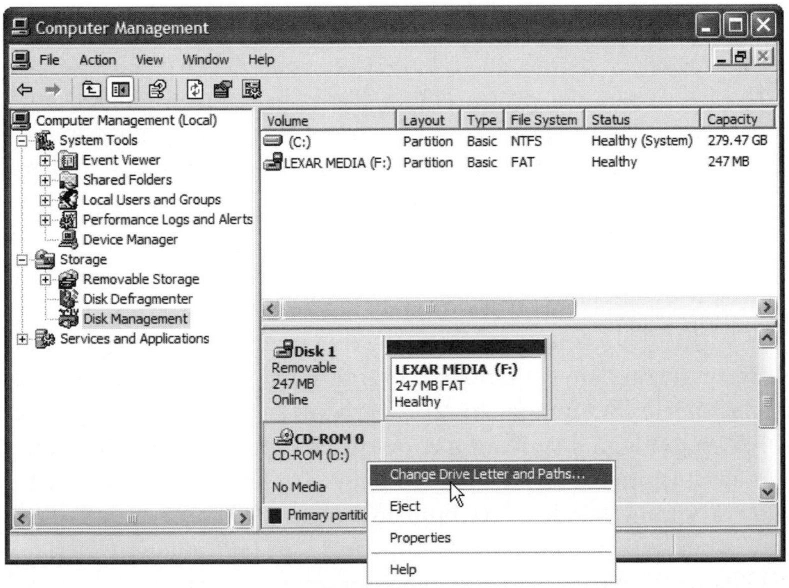

• **Figure 9.11** Change CD drive letter option in Disk Management

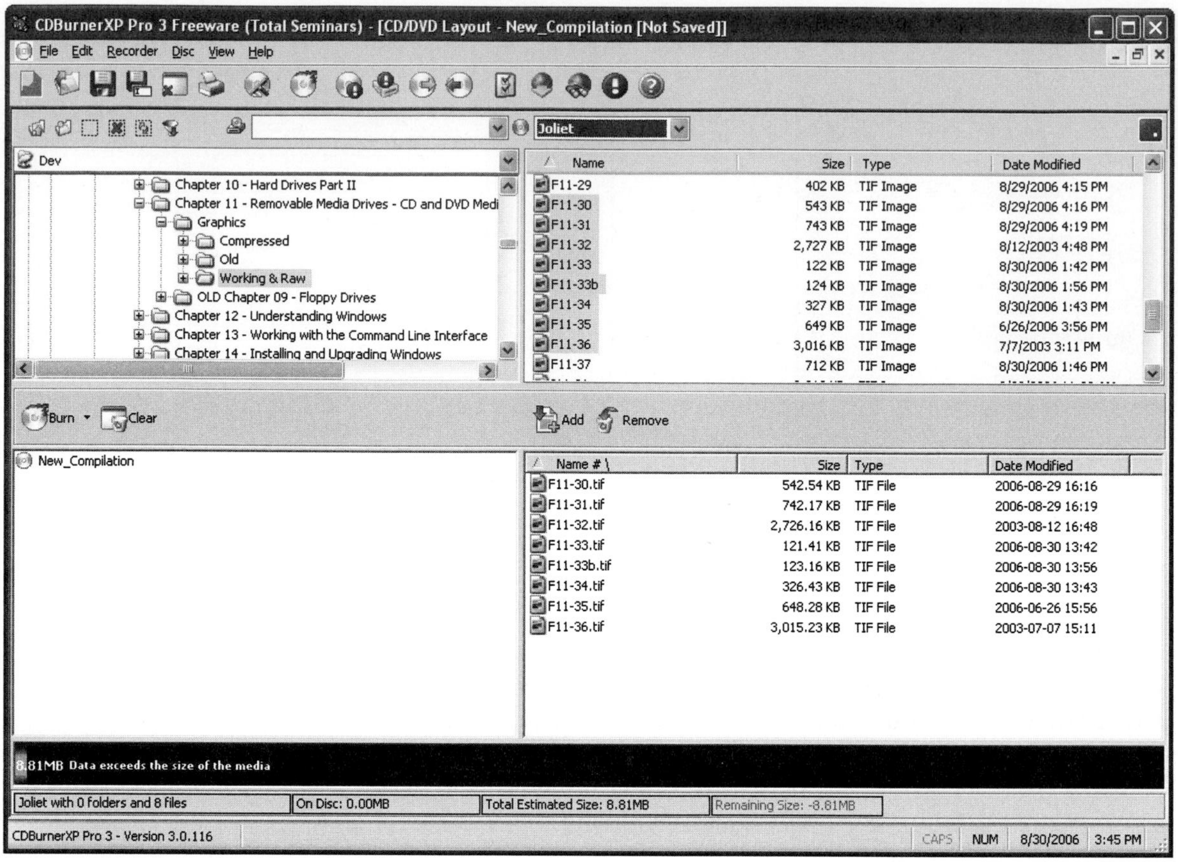

Figure 9.12   Typical third-party CD-burning program

PC to PC. Almost all optical drives will read the discs burned in an XP system.

Windows Media Player that comes free with Windows makes an excellent DVD-watching application, but for DVD burning you need to turn to a third-party tool. Nero and Roxio make excellent software that handles every DVD recordable standard (as well as CD-R and CD-RW) that your drive can use.

Ever wanted to make a perfect copy of a CD so that you can keep your original in a safe place? You can do so using a special file type called an ISO file. An **ISO file** is a complete copy—an ISO image as we say—of a CD. As you might imagine, they are huge files, but they are also very important to techs. Techs use ISO images to send each other copies of bootable utility CDs. For example, if you want a copy of the Ultimate Boot CD, you go to their Web site and download an ISO image. You then take your third-party burning program (Windows XP built-in burning software can't do this) and go through a special process called burning an ISO image. Learn how to burn ISO images with your burning program; you'll use it all the time!

Burning Digital Music Files to a CD

Almost all computers and many portable CD players now have the ability to play recordable CDs loaded with MP3 files. This enables you to mix songs from your music collection and fit a lot of songs on a disc (MP3s are smaller than CD-audio files). That's a great feature—but where do digital audio files come from and how do you put them on a CD?

You can create MP3s from your favorite CDs by using a *ripper*. A ripper is a piece of software that takes standard CD-audio files and compresses them, using specialized algorithms, into much smaller files while maintaining most of the audio qualities of the original file. One legal note, however—you should only make MP3s from CDs that you have purchased. Borrowing a CD from a friend and ripping MP3s from it is illegal! Likewise, downloading MP3s from unauthorized sources on the Internet is also illegal. You don't want to go to jail because you just had to listen to the latest, greatest single from your favorite artist, right?

Now that I've taken care of the legal disclaimer, get ready to rip your MP3s. You need three things—a recordable/rewritable optical drive, some CD authoring software, and of course, a blank disc. I recommend a CD-R. (Audio-only devices stand a much better chance of playing a CD-R successfully rather than a CD-RW.)

1. Confirm that you have a CD-R/RW drive installed in your computer. You don't have to have a drive like this in order to rip audio files *from* a CD, but you must have one in order to burn digital audio to a CD-R.

2. Launch your favorite CD authoring software. Popular titles in this category include Nero Burning ROM and Easy CD Creator.

3. Most CD authoring programs use a simple drag-and-drop interface, similar to the Windows Explorer interface. Browse to the location of the audio files and select them. Then drag them into the appropriate area—this is often called the *queue*.

4. After you've selected all the files you want to have on your CD, it's time to burn! The procedure for initiating the CD-burning sequence is different for each program. You should always make sure to *close* the CD after you've burned it. Most standalone CD players (even ones that play MP3s) won't play CD-Rs that haven't been closed.

Once you get all the configuration information keyed in, just sit back and watch the fireworks. Always be sure to use CD-media that is rated appropriately for your drive, for both speed and media type. In no time at all, you'll be listening to MP3s while jogging around the park!

■ Troubleshooting Removable Media

Floppy disk drives, flash memory, and optical drives are fairly robust devices that rarely require troubleshooting due to an actual hardware failure. Most problems with removable media stem from lack of knowledge, improper installation, abuse, and incorrect use of associated applications. There's no way to repair a truly broken flash memory—once a flash card dies, you replace it—so let's concentrate on troubleshooting floppy drives and CD- and DVD-media drives.

Floppy Drive Maintenance and Troubleshooting

No single component fails more often than the floppy drive. This is not really that surprising because floppy drives have more exposure to the outside environment than anything but the keyboard. Only a small door (or in the case of 5¼-inch drives, not even a door) divides the read/write heads from dust and grime. Floppy drives are also exposed to the threat of mechanical damage. Many folks destroy floppy drives by accidentally inserting inverted disks, paper clips, and other foreign objects. Life is tough for floppy drives!

In the face of this abuse, the key preventive maintenance performed on floppy drives is cleaning. You can find floppy drive **cleaning kits** at some electronics stores, or you can use a cotton swab and some denatured alcohol to scour gently inside the drive for dust and other particles.

Repairing Floppy Drives

When a floppy drive stops working, follow these steps to resolve the problem:

1. Check for a bad floppy disk.
2. Check for data errors on the disk.
3. Check the CMOS settings.
4. Blame the floppy controller.
5. Check the cable.
6. Replace the floppy drive.

First, Check the Floppy Disk

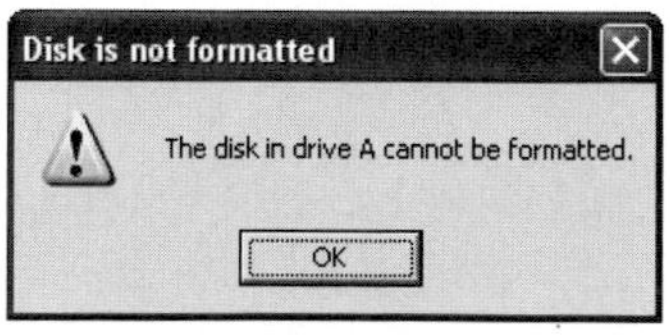

The vast majority of the time, when the floppy drive decides it won't read a floppy disk, the bad guy is the floppy disk, not the floppy drive. When the floppy drive refuses to read a floppy disk, you usually get an error like the one shown in Figure 9.13.

If you get this error, first try inserting another floppy disk. If a new disk from a fresh box won't work, don't insert another one from the same box. Find another disk, preferably from another box or one just lying around, to retest. If the floppy drive refuses to read two floppy disks, then suspect the floppy drive is the problem. Otherwise, blame the disk!

● **Figure 9.13**   Floppy disk read error

Second, Check for Data Errors on the Disk

If other floppy disks work in the drive, the floppy disk has a problem. If a floppy disk fails, you have three options. First, just throw it away. Second, reformat the floppy disk. The only downside to these two options is that you lose the data on the floppy disk, and sometimes that is not an acceptable option. Your third option is to run some sort of recovery/fixing software on the disk.

Floppy disks come preformatted from the manufacturer. We reformat floppies for one of two reasons: either as a handy way to completely erase a floppy disk or as a last-ditch effort to try to fix a bad floppy. To reformat a floppy disk in any version of Windows, go to My Computer and right-click the floppy icon. Select Format to see the dialog box shown in Figure 9.14.

Note that in Windows XP, although the first three settings appear to be pull-down menus, you don't actually get any format options besides the ones showing. In Windows 2000, the Capacity pull-down menu does let you format the floppy as an ancient 720 KB as well as a modern 1.44 MB type. The Format Type radio button group enables you to choose between Quick Format (just erases data), or Create an MS-DOS Startup Disk (don't format the floppy—save the data, just make it bootable). You can add a Volume Label, which simply enables you to place a small amount of text on the floppy to help describe the contents. Volume labels were quite popular in the DOS days but are almost never used today.

The third option (recovery software) may save the data—and possibly the disk! A bad floppy disk often holds data that you need. Don't panic! Unless the floppy disk has substantial physical damage—for example, your

Tech Tip

Check Inside the Drive

Sometimes pieces of a floppy disk—the metal shutter, for example, or the spring—can get jammed into the drive by users who keep trying to shove a disk into the drive. The user won't notice anything different except that the disk doesn't work and sometimes sticks in the drive. If you have any trouble inserting the floppy disk, take a flashlight and peer inside the drive to check for stray bits that don't belong!

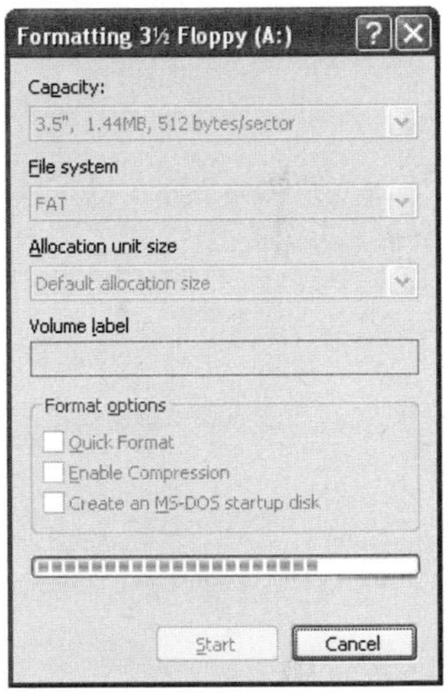

• **Figure 9.14** Formatting a floppy disk

Try This!

Creating a Windows 98 Startup Disk

If you have a computer system running Windows 98, you should have a startup disk you can boot from when your computer locks up and won't boot normally. Grab a blank floppy disk and try this:

1. Open the Control Panel from the Start menu. Double-click on the Add/Remove Programs icon to start that applet. Select the Startup Disk tab and click the Create Disk button.
2. Insert a floppy disk when prompted. Windows will create a bootable floppy by formatting the disk and adding certain key files that will enable Windows to boot from it. When the process is finished, remove the floppy and label it *Windows 98 Startup Disk.*
3. Restart the system with the Startup disk inserted. You should see a Windows startup screen with several boot options. Select Start Computer with CD-ROM support, and watch the boot process progress to the A:\> prompt. Remove the startup disk and reboot into Windows.

dog chewed on it for 20 minutes—certain utility programs can retrieve the data. The process for repairing floppy disks is identical to the process for repairing hard drives.

Third, Check the CMOS Settings

CMOS settings for floppy drives rarely cause problems. All BIOS makers default the CMOS settings for the A: drive to 3½-inch high density if the CMOS is accidentally erased. So although an erased CMOS might keep everything else on your computer from running, at least the floppy will still work (assuming you have a 3½-inch A: drive). The rare instances of a problem with CMOS can be dangerous because technicians rarely look there. Double-check the CMOS: A quick peek can save a lot of time!

Next, Blame the Floppy Controller

If the data cable or power plug is loose, the POST will flag with either "FDD Controller Failure" or "Drive Not Ready" errors. At this point, open the machine and verify the connections. If the connections are good, it's possible that your motherboard has a bad floppy drive controller. Checking the floppy drive controller requires two basic steps. First, turn off the onboard controller. To turn off the controller, go into CMOS and find the Onboard FDD Controller option (or something like that), shown in Figure 9.15, and disable it. Some motherboards don't give you the option to do this, in which case you need to disable the controller in Device Manager.

Second, go to the computer store (hooray!) and buy one of two items. On the off chance that the store has a PCI FDD controller card, pick it up. You can install it and plug in the floppy drive. If the drive then works, suspect the onboard controller. If the floppy drive still doesn't work, remove the card and re-enable the CMOS setting for the onboard controller.

Alternatively, you can get an external USB floppy drive (Figure 9.16). This won't give you a bootable floppy drive, but you can bypass the internal components altogether and access it in Windows. Figure 9.17 shows My Computer in a system with only a USB FDD installed. Note that the USB

```
            Phoenix - Award BIOS CMOS Setup Utility
                   Integrated Peripherals

 ▶ OnChip IDE/RAID Function     Press Enter          Item Help
   Init Display First           PCIe
   OnChip USB                   U1.1+2.0        Menu Level    ▶
    - USB Keyboard Support       Enabled
    - USB Mouse Support          Enabled
   OnChip Audio Controller      Auto
   OnChip LAN Controller        Auto
    - Onboard LAN Boot ROM       Disabled
   Onboard FDD Controller       Enabled
   Onboard Serial Port          3F8/IRQ4
   Onboard Parallel Port        Disabled
 x - Parallel Port Mode         SPP
 x - EPP Mode Select            EPP1.7
 x - Ecp Mode Use DMA           3



▲▼▶◀:Move  Enter:Select   +/-/PU/PD:Value  F10:Save   ESC:Exit  F1:General Help
   F5:Previous Values            F6:Fail-Safe Defaults  F7:Optimized Defaults
```

• **Figure 9.15**   Onboard FDD Controller option

● **Figure 9.16**   USB floppy disk drive

● **Figure 9.17**   My Computer showing the USB FDD as both D: and A:

device shows up as D:, but that you have the option of clicking on the A: drive as well. Clicking on either drive icon will access the same floppy disk.

Maybe It's the Cable ...

Your next investigation should focus on whether the cable is the culprit. The 34th wire on the floppy-drive cable is called the **drive change signal** (or disk change signal). When a floppy disk is inserted or removed, this wire is active. When Windows first reads a floppy disk, it keeps a copy of the directory in RAM and will not update that information unless the floppy drive detects a disk removal and activates the drive change signal. This keeps the system from constantly accessing the very slow floppy drive. Windows waits until it knows it needs to reread the disk. However, if the drive change signal disconnects because of a bent pin or bad cable, you will keep seeing the same directory, even if you change the disk! This problem almost always traces back to a bad floppy cable, so replace it and retry.

Connectivity plays a big (and sometimes embarrassing) role in floppy drive failure. One of the most common errors techs make installing floppy drives is reversing the ribbon cable on one or both ends. If you reverse it on *one end,* invariably the LED on the drive (the light) comes on the moment you turn on the system and *stays on.* Always check the light on the floppy drive when installing a new floppy! If you reverse the cable on *both ends,* the LED *will not come on at all*—most of the time. Usually, you will get an FDD error at POST, and the drive simply will not work. As mentioned earlier, newer systems key the floppy drive connector and ribbon cable to minimize this issue, but no rule requires the floppy drive manufacturers to abide by this standard! Always check the cable!

Last, Replace the Floppy Drive

At this point, if the floppy drive isn't working, the only recourse is to replace the drive. When you replace a bad drive, throw it away. Keeping a bad floppy drive is a study in frustration because almost all bad floppy drives aren't consistently bad—just sometimes bad. Technicians are often tempted to give a bad floppy drive one more chance. They install the drive, and it works! They're convinced they made a mistake and declare the drive good. If the drive is reinstalled somewhere else, however, it will soon die again. Throw it away.

Floppy drives fail more than any other part of a computer system. In any five PCs, at least one floppy drive will need to be replaced in a year. So keep floppy drives in stock. Purchase them in quantity, at least five at a time, so you'll receive a discount. Buying floppy drives one at a time is expensive and a waste of time.

Troubleshooting Optical Drives and Discs

Optical drives are extremely reliable and durable PC components. There are times, however, when a reliable and durable device decides to turn into an unreliable, non-durable pile of plastic and metal frustration. This section covers a few of the more common problems with optical drives and discs—installation issues, burning issues, and firmware updates—and how to fix them.

Installation Issues

The single biggest problem with optical drives, especially in a new installation, is the connection. Your first guess should be that the drive has not been properly installed in some way. A few of the common culprits are forgetting to plug in a power connector, inserting a cable backward, and misconfiguring jumpers/switches. Although you need to know the type of drive, the test for an improper physical connection is always the same: using BIOS to see whether the system can see the optical drive.

```
● Award Modular BIOS v6.00PG, An Energy Star Ally
■ Copyright (C) 1984-2003 Phonix Technologies, LTD


Main Processor : AMD Athlon(tm) 64 Processor 3200+
Memory Testing : 1048576K OK
CPU0 Memory Information: DDR 400 CL:3 ,1T Dual Channel, 128-bit

IDE Channel 1 Master : WDC WD1200JB-75CRA0 16.06V16
IDE Channel 1 Slave  : None
IDE Channel 2 Master : TOSHIBA CD=DVDW SDR5372V TV11
IDE Channel 2 Slave  : None
```

• **Figure 9.18**   BIOS recognizing an optical drive at boot

The way in which a BIOS detects an optical drive depends on the system. Most BIOS makers have created intelligent BIOS software that can see an installed optical drive. Figure 9.18 shows a modern Award Software, Inc., BIOS recognizing a CD-RW during startup.

If the device is detected in BIOS, Windows will recognize the drive and you'll see it in My Computer and Device Manager.

If the drive won't read a CD-R or CD-RW disc, first try a commercial CD-ROM disc that is in good condition. CD-R and CD-RW discs sometimes have compatibility issues with CD-ROM drives. The same goes for a DVD-RW or any other writable DVD disc in your DVD drive. As noted earlier, DVD drives have issues with media incompatibility. Also, no optical drive will read badly scratched discs.

If the drive still does not see a disc, try cleaning the drive. Most modern optical drives have built-in cleaning mechanisms, but from time to time, you need to use a commercial optical-drive cleaning kit (see Figure 9.19).

Optical drives are not cleaned too often, but the discs are. Although a number of fine optical disc cleaning kits are available, most discs can be cleaned quite well with nothing more than a damp soft cloth. Occasionally, a mild detergent can be added. Always wipe from the center of the optical disc to the edge—never clean a CD or DVD using a circular motion! A common old tech's tale about cleaning optical discs is that they can be washed in a dishwasher! Although this may seem laughable, the tale has become so common that it requires a serious response. This is *not true* for two reasons: First, the water in most dishwashers is too hot and can cause the discs to warp. Second, the water pushes the discs around, causing them to hit other objects and get scratched. Don't do it!

The final problem with optical drives—stuck discs—comes from *technician* error and is not actually the fault of the drives. I can't tell you the number of times I've pulled an optical drive out of a system to replace it, only to discover that I or my customer left an essential disc inside the now-powerless drive. Luckily, most optical drives have a small hole in the front, usually just below the drive opening, into which you can insert a wire—an unbent paper clip is the standard tool for this purpose—and push on an internal release lever that will eject the disc. Try it!

● **Figure 9.19**   Optical drive cleaning kit

Burning Issues

The tremendous growth of the CD-R and CD-RW industry—and to a lesser extent, the recordable DVD industry—has led to a substantial number of incompatibility issues between discs and drives. Some of these incompatibilities trace back to serious IO (Ignorant Operator) problems; people try to make these discs do jobs they aren't designed to do. Even when people read the manuals and jump through the proper hoops, real problems do arise, many of which you can easily solve with a few checks.

Know What It Can Do   Most mistakes take place at the point of purchase, when someone buys a drive without completely understanding its capabilities. Don't just assume that the device will do everything! Before I purchase a CD-RW drive, for example, I make it a point to get my hands on every technical document provided by the maker to verify exactly what capabilities the drive possesses. I make sure that the drive has a good reputation—just use any search engine and type in **review** and the model number of the drive to get several people's opinions.

Media Issues   The CD-R and CD-RW standards committees refused to mandate the types of materials used in the construction of discs. As a result, you see substantial quality differences among CD-R and CD-RW discs of different brands and sources (they are made in several different countries). As mentioned earlier, CD-R discs use organic inks as part of the burning process. Fellow techs love to talk about which color to use or which color gives the best results. Ignore them—the color itself means nothing. Instead, try a few different brands of CD-R discs when you first get your drive to determine what works best for you. If you have a particular reason for burning CDs, such as music recording, you may want to ask for opinions and recommendations among folks in online communities with the same focus. They're usually happy to share their hard-won knowledge about what's good.

In general, two items can affect media quality: speed and inks. Most CD-R and CD-RW media makers certify their CDs to work up to a certain speed multiplier. A media maker often has two product lines: a quality line guaranteed to work at a certain speed, and a generic line where you take your chances. As a rule, I buy both. I primarily use cheap discs, but I always stash five to ten good quality discs in case I run into a problem. Again, this will in large part depend on what you want them for—you may want to pull out the cheapies for temporary backups, but stick with the high-end discs for archiving musical performances.

All of the discussion above about CD-Rs and CD-RWs definitely holds true for recordable DVD discs and drives as well. Factor in the incompatibility of standards and you're looking at a fine mess. Do your homework before you buy or advise a client to buy a DVD-writable or -rewritable drive.

Buffer Underrun Every CD and DVD burner comes with onboard RAM, called *buffer RAM*—usually just called the buffer—that stores the incoming data from the recording source. **Buffer underrun**, the inability of the source device to keep the burner loaded with data, creates more *coasters*—that is, improperly burned and therefore useless CDs and DVDs—than any other single problem. Buffer underrun most often occurs when copying from CD-ROM to CD-R/RW or from DVD-ROM to DVD-writable of all stripes. Many factors contribute to buffer underrun, but two stand out as the most important. The first factor is buffer size. Make sure you purchase drives with large buffers, a minimum of 2 MB. Unlike with system RAM, you can't get a buffer upgrade. Second is multitasking. Most systems won't enable you to run any other programs while the burner is running.

One trick to reduce underrun is using an ISO. Unlike some CD and DVD media drives, *any* hard drive can keep up with a CD or DVD burner. Doing a bit-by-bit copy from disc to disc dramatically reduces the chance of a buffer underrun adding to your coaster collection.

All current CD-RW and DVD burners include the BURN-Proof technology developed by Sanyo, which has eliminated the underrun issue. These drives can literally turn off the burning process if the buffer runs out of information and automatically restart as soon as the buffer refills. I love this feature, as I can now burn CDs in the background and run other programs without fear of underrun. If you're buying a new CD-RW drive, make sure you get one that uses the BURN-Proof technology.

Firmware Updates

Almost all optical drives come with an upgradeable flash ROM chip. If your drive doesn't read a particular type of media, or if any other non-intermittent reading/writing problems develop, check the manufacturer's Web site to see if it offers a firmware upgrade. Almost every optical drive seems to get one or two firmware updates during its production cycle.

Conclusion

The world of removable media continues to change at a pretty hectic pace. Within the last couple of years, floppy drives have just about died out; thumb drives have become the rewritable media of choice for most users; high-definition optical drives and discs (HD DVD and Blu-ray Disc, see the "Beyond A+" section) have hit the store shelves, although they're both outrageously expensive as of this writing. Manufacturers keep inventing new and exciting technologies that seem to appear out of nowhere. A CompTIA A+ certified technician would be wise to keep removable media on his or her radar, well after taking and passing the CompTIA A+ exams!

Beyond A+

Color Books

The term *color books* is often used in the world of CD-media. Books are—well, books! In this case, they're the standards developed in the industry to describe various media. For example, the Red book describes the original audio CD format. If you have a lot of money—say, US$3000—you may purchase copies of these books, and yes, their covers really match the colors of the standards. You might hear a fellow computer support person using these terms. Instead of saying, "Does your CD-ROM read CD-RWs?" they will say, "Is that CD-ROM of yours Orange book?" Technical specifications also use these terms. I personally don't like the way many people refer to these book colors, but the terms are used enough that you should memorize the meanings of at least three book colors: Red, Yellow, and Orange. Table 9.1 shows a complete list of CD-media book colors.

Table 9.1	CD-Media Book Colors	
Application	**Book**	**Subtypes**
Audio CDs	Red book	N/A
Data CDs	Yellow book	Mode 1 Original Format Mode 2 Form 1 and Form 2
CD-I	Green book	N/A
Recordable CDs	Orange book	Part I CD-MO (Magneto-Optical) Part II CD-R, includes Photo-CD Part III CD-RW
Video CD	White book	N/A
CD Extra	Blue book	N/A

High-Definition Optical Drives

At the time of this writing, two optical standards are duking it out to see which will become the Next Great Thing™ in optical media: HD DVD and Blu-ray Disc. HD DVD (High-Density DVD) offered the initial salvo, coming out with 30-GB optical discs that could contain 8 hours of High-Definition video. Sweet! Blu-ray (no special meaning aside from using blue lasers rather than red lasers) responded with 50-GB discs, and the gloves were off. Right now it appears that HD DVD will be the eventual winner on the video front, but Blu-ray Disc might win on the data-storage front. Time will tell. For more information, check out the respective camps' Web sites:

www.thelookandsoundofperfect.com (I am not making this up!)

www.blu-raydisc.com

Chapter 9 Review

■ Chapter Summary

After reading this chapter and completing the exercises, you should understand the following about floppy disk drives and optical-media technology.

Install Optical Drives

■ All optical drives use PATA or SATA connections and support the ATAPI standard. PATA drives use a regular 40-pin IDE connector; SATA drives use a standard SATA connector. They are installed just as if you were installing any ATA hard drive. After installing a new optical drive, check My Computer or Device Manager to confirm that Windows sees the drive.

■ The Windows feature Auto Insert Notification (or AutoPlay) causes Windows to automatically begin an action when an optical disc is inserted in the drive. In Windows 2000, if an audio CD is inserted, track 1 plays automatically. If a data CD or DVD is inserted, AutoPlay scans the root of the disc for the AUTORUN.INF file and executes the commands in that file. In Windows 2000, the only way to disable AutoPlay was to manually edit the registry. Windows XP can be configured by accessing the AutoPlay tab in the drive's Properties window.

■ An ISO file is a complete copy of an entire CD or DVD disc. Windows 2000/XP can't burn an ISO back to disc, but third-party programs like Ahead Nero Burning ROM or Roxio Easy Media Creator can.

Troubleshoot Removable-Media Drives

■ No single component fails more often than a floppy disk drive. If your floppy drive stops working, try the following: check for a bad floppy disk, check for disk data errors, check CMOS settings, check the cables, and finally replace the floppy drive.

■ A bad or incorrectly attached floppy data cable can cause strange errors. The same directory may be displayed even after swapping disks, or the LED on the front of the drive may stay on. Check that the red stripe on the cable is aligned with pin 1 on the drive and the motherboard. If it is and the drive still malfunctions, replace the cable.

■ If your optical drive doesn't work, first check the installation. Specifically, look at the master/slave jumper settings, data cable, and power cable. If the drive is seen by Windows but can't read a particular disc, try a commercial disc. It's also possible your drive doesn't support your media type; for example, your DVD-R drive may not be able to read your DVD+RW disc. Clean the disc with a soft damp cloth, wiping from the center towards the edge. Never clean an optical disc in the dishwasher!

■ If an optical disc becomes stuck in a drive, or if the drive has no power and you need to eject the disc, use a paper clip. Straighten the paper clip and look for the small hole on the front of the drive. Insert the paper clip in the hole and push the internal release lever to eject the disc.

■ Not all media brands are created equally, and not all drives play nicely with all brands of media. Experiment and try different brands of media with your drive until you find one that works reliably.

■ A buffer underrun is caused by the source device failing to keep the recording device loaded with data. Buffer underruns are the leading cause of improperly burned, and therefore useless, CDs and DVDs. Purchase a drive with a large buffer—at least 2 MB. Some drives protect against buffer underrun with a technology called BURN-Proof. Purchase a BURN-Proof drive and your buffer underruns will be eliminated.

■ Most optical drives come with an upgradeable flash ROM chip. If your drive is suffering read/write problems, check the manufacturer's Web site for a firmware upgrade.

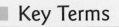

Key Terms

40-pin IDE connector *(147)*
AutoPlay *(149)*
AUTORUN.INF *(149)*
buffer underrun *(160)*

cleaning kit *(154)*
drive change signal *(157)*
Group Policy *(149)*
ISO file *(152)*

master/slave jumper *(147)*
REGEDT32 *(149)*

Key Term Quiz

Use the Key Terms list to complete the sentences that follow. Not all terms will be used.

1. Drives with BURN-Proof technology were designed to eliminate the problem of
    _____.

2. The 34th wire of a floppy drive cable, or _____, detects the removal of a floppy disk.

3. The _____ setting enables Windows to detect automatically the presence of audio or data CD-ROMs when they are placed in a drive.

4. A special text file named _____ determines what program or window is opened when a data CD is inserted.

5. A(n) _____ is a perfect copy of a CD stored as a single file.

6. A PATA CD drive has a ribbon cable with a regular _____, just like an IDE hard drive.

7. To disable the Auto Insert Notification in Windows 2000, use _____ to edit the registry.

8. When connecting a PATA optical drive and IDE hard drive to the same cable, be sure to properly set the _____ settings on both devices.

9. You can adjust the AutoPlay options for all drives in a system at once by using
    _____.

10. You can extend the life of your floppy or optical drives and media by purchasing a(n) _____, which comes with all the necessary items for preventive maintenance.

Multiple-Choice Quiz

1. You installed a floppy drive that you want to function as the A: drive, but your system won't boot to it. What is the most likely cause of this problem?

    A. You attached the drive to the middle connector on the cable.

    B. You attached the drive to the end connector on the cable.

    C. You forgot to configure the CMOS settings for drive A:.

    D. You forgot to configure the CMOS settings for a single floppy drive.

2. You just installed a floppy drive and you notice that the floppy drive LED stays on. What is most likely the problem?

    A. You attached the floppy drive to the wrong connector on the ribbon cable.

    B. You forgot to configure the floppy drive through the CMOS setup.

    C. You did not attach the colored stripe on the ribbon cable to pin 1 at the drive or at the controller.

    D. You forgot to attach the power cable to the floppy drive.

3. If the floppy disk you used last week will not work today in your floppy drive, what should you do first to determine if the problem is the drive or the disk?

    A. Try another disk in the drive or try the disk in another drive.

    B. Open the computer and check the ribbon cable.

C. Replace the floppy drive.

D. Check the CMOS settings.

4. When a CD is inserted, the AutoPlay feature of Windows looks for what file?

A. AUTOPLAY.INF

B. AUTORUN.INF

C. AUTORUN.INI

D. AUTORUN.EXE

5. A copy of a CD or DVD can be saved as what type of file?

A. ISO

B. ISO-9660

C. INF

D. CDDA

6. What settings in the CMOS setup must you change to install an optical drive?

A. Number of heads and cylinders the drive has

B. Whether the drive is installed on the primary or secondary IDE channel

C. Whether the jumpers on the drive are set to master or slave

D. None, because an optical drive is not configured through the CMOS setup

7. PATA optical drives use what type of data cable?

A. 25-pin ribbon cable

B. 34-pin ribbon cable

C. 40-pin ribbon cable

D. 50-pin ribbon cable

8. What is the recommended way to disable AutoPlay in Windows 2000?

A. Clear the AutoPlay option on the General tab of the drive's property sheet in Device Manager

B. Clear the AutoPlay option on the Hardware tab of the drive's property sheet in Device Manager

C. Right-click the drive in My Computer, select the Hardware tab, and clear the AutoPlay option

D. Edit the registry

9. What is the recommended way to disable AutoPlay in Windows XP?

A. Clear the AutoPlay option on the General tab of the drive's property sheet in Device Manager

B. Clear the AutoPlay option on the Hardware tab of the drive's property sheet in Device Manager

C. Right-click the drive in My Computer, select the AutoPlay tab, and select Take No Action

D. Edit the registry

10. What are two new competing DVD standards?

A. DVD+RW, DVD-RW

B. High-Density DVD, Blu-ray Disc

C. Red-laser DVD, Blue-laser DVD

D. HiDef DVD, Blu-Ray

▉ Essay Quiz

1. Your friend Jack's hard drive died last week, so he bought a new hard drive and installed it. Now he's trying to install Windows 2000, but his computer will not boot to the CD-ROM drive. He's called you for help. What does he need to do to get his computer to recognize and boot to the CD-ROM drive so he can install the OS?

2. You gave your friend Sandra a gift certificate to the local computer store for her birthday. She decided to buy an ATAPI CD-RW drive and does not know how to install it on her Windows XP computer that currently has only a single PATA hard drive. Guide her step-by-step through the installation process.

Lab Projects

• Lab Project 9.1

If your lab PC has a floppy disk drive, install a second floppy disk drive. How does your system determine which is drive A: and which is drive B:? Reverse the ribbon cable on the A: drive so the red stripe no longer aligns with pin 1. What happens when you boot the system back up? Can the drive read disks in this condition?

• Lab Project 9.2

Adding a second optical drive to a PC enables you to do some fun things, from making your own music CDs to watching movies. Assuming you want to install an ATAPI drive, you then need to face some issues. Which controller should you use, primary or secondary? Should both optical drives be on the same controller or on different controllers? Why?

Most techs would install a burner as secondary master and put a read-only drive on the primary as slave, but different drives require different considerations. If you don't plan to copy CD to CD, there's no reason the read-only CD shouldn't be secondary slave. The key is you have to experiment.

Install a second optical drive—preferably a burner—and run it through its paces. Copy files and burn discs to and from the optical and hard drives. Then change the configuration of your drives (such as having both optical drives on the same controller) and run through the testing process again. Do you notice any differences?

Working with the Command-Line Interface

"Keyboard. How quaint."

—SCOTTY, *STAR TREK IV: THE VOYAGE HOME*

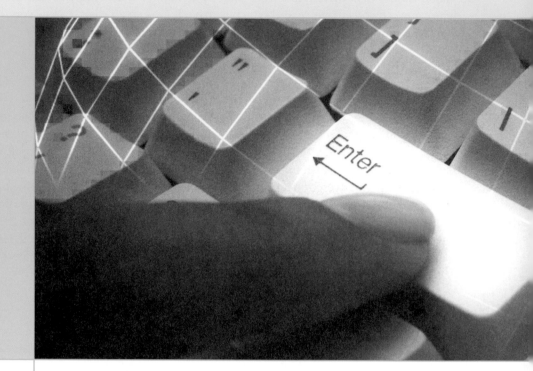

In this chapter, you will learn how to

- **Explain the operation of the command-line interface**
- **Execute fundamental commands from the command line**
- **Manipulate files and folders from the command line**

Whenever I teach a class of new techs and we get to the section on working with the command line, I'm invariably met with a chorus of moans and a barrage of questions and statements. "Why do we need to learn this old stuff?" "We're running Windows XP Professional, not Windows 3.1!" "Is this ritualistic hazing appropriate in an IT class?"

For techs who master the interface, the command line provides a powerful, quick, and elegant tool for working on a PC. If you want to go beyond baby-tech status, you'll need to learn that interface and understand how to make it work. You simply cannot work on all PCs without knowing the command line! It's not just me who thinks this way. The CompTIA A+ certification exams test you on a variety of command-line commands for doing everything from renaming a file to rebuilding a system file.

If you're interested in moving beyond Windows and into other operating systems such as Linux, you'll find that pretty much all of the serious work is done at a command prompt. Even the Mac OS, for years a purely graphical operating system, now supports a command prompt. Why is the command prompt so popular? Well, for three reasons: First, if you know what you're doing, you can get most jobs done more quickly typing a text command than clicking through a GUI. Second, a command-line interface doesn't take much operating system firepower, so it's the natural choice for jobs where you don't need or don't want (or can't get to, in the case of Linux) a full-blown GUI for your OS. Third, text commands take very little bandwidth when sent across the network to another system.

So, are you sold on the idea of the command prompt? Good! This chapter gives you a tour of the Windows command-line interface, explaining how it works and what's happening behind the scenes. You'll learn the concepts and master essential commands, and then you'll work with files and folders throughout your drives. The chapter wraps up with a brief section on encryption and file compression in the "Beyond A+" section. A good tactic for absorbing the material in this chapter is to try out each command or bit of information as it is presented. If you have some experience working with a command prompt, many of these commands should be familiar to you. If the command line is completely new to you, please take the red pill and join me as we step into the Matrix.

Operating systems existed long before PCs were invented. Ancient, massive computers called *mainframes* and *minicomputers* employed sophisticated operating systems. It wasn't until the late 1970s that IBM went looking for an OS for a new *microcomputer*—the official name for the PC—the company was developing, called the IBM Personal Computer, better known as the PC. After being rebuffed by a company called Digital Research, IBM went to a tiny company that had written a popular new version of the programming language called BASIC. They asked the company president if he could create an OS for the IBM PC. Although his company had never actually written an OS, he brazenly said, "Sure!" That man was Bill Gates, and the tiny company was Microsoft.

After shaking hands with IBM representatives, Bill Gates hurriedly began to search for an OS based on the Intel 8086 processor. He found a primitive OS called *Quick-and-Dirty Operating System (QDOS)*, which was written by a one-man shop, and he purchased it for a few thousand dollars. After several minor changes, Microsoft released it as MS-DOS (Microsoft Disk Operating System) version 1.1. Although primitive by today's standards, MS-DOS 1.1 could provide all the functions needed for an OS. Over the years, MS-DOS went through version after version until the last Microsoft version, MS-DOS 6.22, was released in 1994. Microsoft licensed MS-DOS to PC makers so they could add their own changes and then rename the program. IBM called its version PC-DOS.

DOS used a command-line interface. You typed a command at a prompt, and DOS responded to that command. When Microsoft introduced Windows 95 and Windows NT, many computer users and techs thought that the DOS interface would go away, but it turned out that techs not only continued to use the command line, they *needed it* to troubleshoot and fix problems! With Windows 2000, it seemed once again that the command line would die, but again, that just didn't turn out to be the case.

Finally recognizing the importance of the command-line interface, Microsoft beefed it up in Windows XP. The command line in Windows XP offers commands and options for using various commands that go well beyond anything seen in previous Microsoft operating systems. This chapter starts with some essential concepts of the command line and then turns to more specific commands.

IT Technician

■ Deciphering the Command-Line Interface

So how does a command-line interface work? It's a little like having an Instant Message conversation with your computer. The computer tells you it's ready to receive commands by displaying a specific set of characters called a **prompt**.

```
Computer: Want to play a game?
Mike: _
```

You type a command and press ENTER to send it.

```
Mike: What kind of game?
Computer: _
```

The PC goes off and executes the command, and when it's done it displays a new prompt, often along with some information about what it did.

```
Computer: A very fun game...
Mike: _
```

Once you get a new prompt, it means the computer is ready for your next instruction. You give the computer commands in the graphical user interface (GUI) of Windows as well, just in a different way, by clicking buttons and menu options with your mouse instead of typing on the keyboard. The results are basically the same: you tell the computer to do something and it responds.

When you type in a command from the command line, you cause the computer to respond. As an example, suppose you want to find out the contents of a particular folder. From the command line, you'd type a command (in this case **DIR**, but more on that in a minute), and the computer would respond by displaying a screen like the one in Figure 10.1.

In the GUI, you would open My Computer and click the C: drive icon to see the contents of that directory. The results might look like Figure 10.2, which at first glance isn't much like the command-line screen; however,

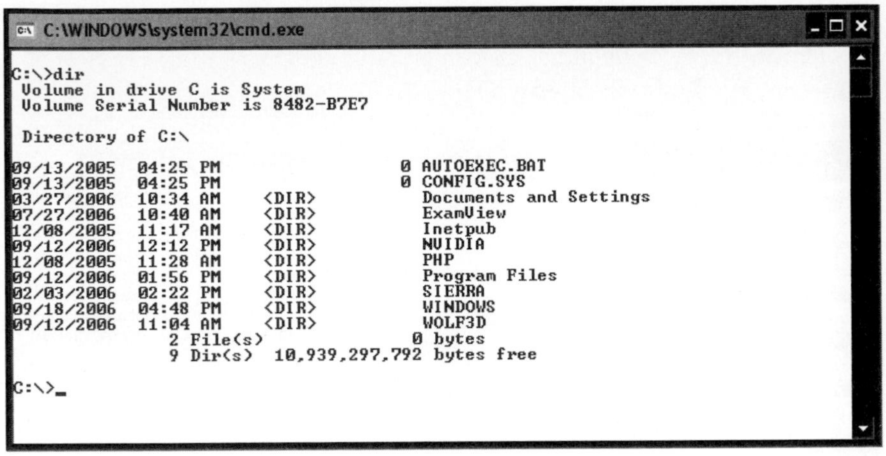

```
C:\WINDOWS\system32\cmd.exe

C:\>dir
 Volume in drive C is System
 Volume Serial Number is 8482-B7E7

 Directory of C:\

09/13/2005  04:25 PM                 0 AUTOEXEC.BAT
09/13/2005  04:25 PM                 0 CONFIG.SYS
03/27/2006  10:34 AM    <DIR>          Documents and Settings
07/27/2006  10:40 AM    <DIR>          ExamView
12/08/2005  11:17 AM    <DIR>          Inetpub
09/12/2006  12:12 PM    <DIR>          NVIDIA
12/08/2005  11:28 AM    <DIR>          PHP
09/12/2006  01:56 PM    <DIR>          Program Files
02/03/2006  02:22 PM    <DIR>          SIERRA
09/18/2006  04:48 PM    <DIR>          WINDOWS
09/12/2006  11:04 AM    <DIR>          WOLF3D
               2 File(s)              0 bytes
               9 Dir(s)  10,939,297,792 bytes free

C:\>_
```

● **Figure 10.1**   Contents of C: directory from the command line

simply by choosing a different view (Figure 10.3), you can make the results look quite a bit like the command-line version, albeit much prettier (Figure 10.4). The point here is that whichever interface you use, the information available to you is essentially the same.

Accessing the Command Line

Before you can use the command-line interface, you've got to open it. You can use various methods to do this, depending on the flavor of Windows

● **Figure 10.2**   Contents of C: in My Computer—Icon view

● **Figure 10.3**   Selecting Details view in My Computer

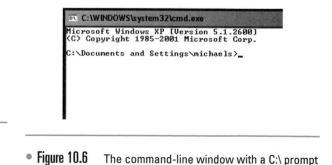

Name △	Size	Type	Date Modified
Documents and Settings		File Folder	3/27/2006 10:34 AM
ExamView		File Folder	7/27/2006 10:40 AM
Inetpub		File Folder	12/8/2005 11:17 AM
NVIDIA		File Folder	9/12/2006 12:12 PM
PHP		File Folder	12/8/2005 11:28 AM
Program Files		File Folder	9/12/2006 1:56 PM
SIERRA		File Folder	2/3/2006 2:22 PM
WINDOWS		File Folder	9/18/2006 4:48 PM
WOLF3D		File Folder	9/12/2006 11:04 AM

• **Figure 10.4**   Contents of C: in My Computer—Details view

that you might be using. Some methods are simpler than others—just make sure that you know at least one, or you'll never get off the starting line!

One easy way to access the command-line interface is by using the **Run dialog box**. Click the Start button, and then select Run. If you're using Windows 2000 or Windows XP, type **CMD** or **COMMAND** and press the ENTER key (Figure 10.5). A window will pop up on your screen with a black background and white text—this is the command-line interface. Alternatively, buried in the Start menu of *most* computers, under Programs | Accessories, is a link to the command-line interface. In Windows 2000 and XP, it's called Command Prompt. These links, just like the Run dialog box, pull up a nice command-line–interface window (Figure 10.6). To close the window, you can either click the Close

---

Try This!

Accessing the Command Line

This chapter will be much more fun if you follow along with your own command line, so try this! Using one of the methods outlined in this section, access a command prompt in Windows. Just remember that everything you do at the prompt can affect the functioning of your PC. So don't delete stuff if you don't know what it's for!

Run

Type the name of a program, folder, document, or Internet resource, and Windows will open it for you.

Open: cmd

OK   Cancel   Browse...

• **Figure 10.5**   Type CMD in the Run dialog box to open a command-line window.

C:\WINDOWS\system32\cmd.exe

```
Microsoft Windows XP [Version 5.1.2600]
(C) Copyright 1985-2001 Microsoft Corp.

C:\Documents and Settings\michaels>_
```

• **Figure 10.6**   The command-line window with a C:\ prompt

box, like on any other window, or simply type **EXIT** at any command prompt and press ENTER.

The Command Prompt

The command prompt is always *focused* on a specific folder. This is important because any commands you issue are performed *on the files in the folder* on which the prompt is focused. For example, if you see a prompt that looks like the line below you know that the focus is on the root directory of the C: drive:

```
C:\>
```

If you see a prompt that looks like Figure 10.7, you know that the focus is on the C:\Diploma\APLUS\ folder of the C: drive. The trick to using a command line is first to focus the prompt on the drive and folder where you want to work.

Filenames and File Formats

Windows manifests each program and piece of data as an individual file. Each file has a name, which is stored with the file on the drive. Windows inherits the idea of files from older operating systems—namely DOS—so a quick review of the old-style DOS filenames helps in understanding how Windows filenames work. Names are broken down into two parts: the filename and the extension. In true DOS, the filename could be no longer than eight characters, so you'll often see oddly named files on older systems. The extension, which is optional, could be up to three characters long in true DOS, and most computer programs and users continue to honor that old limit, even though it does not apply to modern PCs. No spaces or other illegal characters (/ \ [ ] | ÷ + = ; , * ?) could be used in the filename or extension. The filename and extension are separated by a period, or *dot*. This naming system was known as the 8.3 (eight-dot-three) naming system.

Here are some examples of acceptable true DOS filenames:

FRED.EXE	SYSTEM.INI	FILE1.DOC
DRIVER3.SYS	JANET	CODE33.H

Here are some unacceptable true DOS filenames:

4CHAREXT.EXEC	WAYTOOLONG.FIL	BAD÷CHAR.BAT	.NO

I mention the true DOS limitations for a simple reason: *backward compatibility*. All versions of Windows starting with *9x* did not suffer from the 8.3

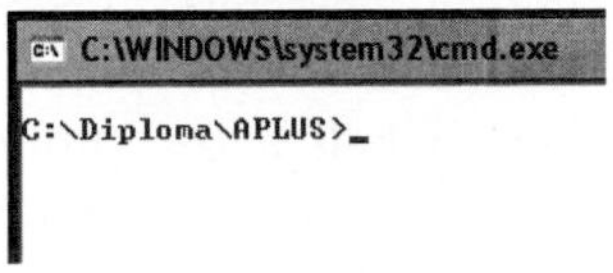

```
C:\WINDOWS\system32\cmd.exe

C:\Diploma\APLUS>_
```

• **Figure 10.7**   Command prompt indicating focus on the C:\Diploma\APLUS\ folder

filename limitation, instead supporting filenames of up to 255 characters (but still using the three-character extension) using a trick called long filenames (LFN). Windows systems using LFN retained complete backward compatibility by automatically creating two names for every file, an 8.3 filename and a long filename. Modern Windows using NTFS works almost exactly the same way as LFNs.

Whether you're running an ancient DOS system or the latest version of Windows Vista, the extension is very important, because the extension part of the filename tells the computer the type or function of the file. Program files use the extension .EXE (for executable) or .COM (for command). Anything that is not a program is some form of data to support a program. Different programs use different types of data files. The extension usually indicates which program uses that particular data file. For example, Microsoft Word uses the extension .DOC, while WordPerfect uses .WPD, and PowerPoint uses .PPT. Graphics file extensions, in contrast, often reflect the graphics standard used to render the image, such as .GIF for CompuServe's Graphics Interchange Format or .JPG for the JPEG (Joint Photographic Experts Group) format.

Changing the extension of a data file does not affect its contents, but without the proper extension, Windows won't know which program uses it. You can see this clearly in My Computer. Figure 10.8 shows a folder with two identical image files. The one on top shows the Photoshop icon, which is the program that Windows will use to open that file; the one on the bottom shows a generic icon, because I deleted the extension. Windows GUI doesn't show file extensions by default. Figure 10.9 shows the contents of that same folder from the command line.

All files are stored on the hard drive in binary format, but every program has its own way of reading and writing this binary data. Each unique method of binary organization is called a file *format*. One program cannot read another program's files unless it has the ability to convert the other program's format into its format. In the early days of DOS, no programs were capable of performing this type of conversion, yet people wanted to exchange files. They wanted some type of common format that any program could read. The answer was a special format called American Standard Code for Information Interchange (ASCII).

The ASCII standard defines 256, eight-bit characters. These characters include all the letters of the alphabet (uppercase and lowercase), numbers, punctuation, many foreign characters (such as accented letters for French and Spanish—é, ñ, ô—and other typical non-English characters), box-drawing characters, and a series of special characters for commands such as a carriage return, bell, and end of file (Figure 10.10). ASCII files, more commonly known as *text files*, store all data in ASCII format. The ASCII standard, however, is for more

• **Figure 10.8** What kind of file is the one on the lower right?

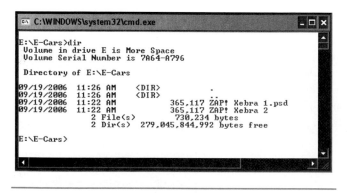

• **Figure 10.9** One file has no extension.

than just files. For example, the keyboard sends the letters of keys you press, in ASCII code, to the PC. Even the monitor outputs in ASCII when you are running DOS.

ASCII was the first universal file format. Virtually every type of program—word processors, spreadsheets, databases, presentation programs—can read and write text files. However, text files have severe limitations. A text file can't store important information such as shapes, colors, margins, or text attributes (bold, underline, font, and so on). Therefore, even though text files are fairly universal, they are also limited to the 256 ASCII characters.

000	(nul)	032	sp	064	@	096	`	128	Ç	160	á	192	└	224	α
001	☺ (soh)	033	!	065	A	097	a	129	ü	161	í	193	┴	225	ß
002	☻ (stx)	034	"	066	B	098	b	130	é	162	ó	194	┬	226	Γ
003	♥ (etx)	035	#	067	C	099	c	131	â	163	ú	195	├	227	π
004	♦ (eot)	036	$	068	D	100	d	132	ä	164	ñ	196	─	228	Σ
005	♣ (enq)	037	%	069	E	101	e	133	à	165	Ñ	197	┼	229	σ
006	♠ (ack)	038	&	070	F	102	f	134	å	166	ª	198	╞	230	µ
007	• (bel)	039	'	071	G	103	g	135	ç	167	º	199	╟	231	τ
008	◘ (bs)	040	(	072	H	104	h	136	ê	168	¿	200	╚	232	Φ
009	(tab)	041	)	073	I	105	i	137	ë	169	⌐	201	╔	233	Θ
010	(lf)	042	*	074	J	106	j	138	è	170	¬	202	╩	234	Ω
011	♂ (vt)	043	+	075	K	107	k	139	ï	171	½	203	╦	235	δ
012	♀ (np)	044	,	076	L	108	l	140	î	172	¼	204	╠	236	∞
013	(cr)	045	-	077	M	109	m	141	ì	173	¡	205	═	237	φ
014	♫ (so)	046	.	078	N	110	n	142	Ä	174	«	206	╬	238	ε
015	☼ (si)	047	/	079	O	111	o	143	Å	175	»	207	╧	239	∩
016	► (dle)	048	0	080	P	112	p	144	É	176	░	208	╨	240	≡
017	◄ (dc1)	049	1	081	Q	113	q	145	æ	177	▒	209	╤	241	±
018	↕ (dc2)	050	2	082	R	114	r	146	Æ	178	▓	210	╥	242	≥
019	‼ (dc3)	051	3	083	S	115	s	147	ô	179	│	211	╙	243	≤
020	¶ (dc4)	052	4	084	T	116	t	148	ö	180	┤	212	╘	244	⌠
021	§ (nak)	053	5	085	U	117	u	149	ò	181	╡	213	╒	245	⌡
022	▬ (syn)	054	6	086	V	118	v	150	û	182	╢	214	╓	246	÷
023	↨ (etb)	055	7	087	W	119	w	151	ù	183	╖	215	╫	247	≈
024	↑ (can)	056	8	088	X	120	x	152	ÿ	184	╕	216	╪	248	°
025	↓ (em)	057	9	089	Y	121	y	153	Ö	185	╣	217	┘	249	·
026	→ (eof)	058	:	090	Z	122	z	154	Ü	186	║	218	┌	250	·
027	← (esc)	059	;	091	[	123	{	155	¢	187	╗	219	█	251	√
028	∟ (fs)	060	<	092	\	124	|	156	£	188	╝	220	▄	252	ⁿ
029	↔ (gs)	061	=	093	]	125	}	157	¥	189	╜	221	▌	253	²
030	▲ (rs)	062	>	094	^	126	~	158	₧	190	╛	222	▐	254	■
031	▼ (us)	063	?	095	_	127	⌂	159	ƒ	191	┐	223	▀	255	

• Figure 10.10   ASCII characters

Even in the most basic text, you need to perform a number of actions beyond just printing simple characters. For example, how does the program reading the text file know when to start a new line? This is where the first 32 ASCII characters come into play. These first 32 characters are special commands (actually, some of them are both commands and characters). For example, the ASCII value 7 can be either a large dot or a command to play a note (bell) on the PC speaker. ASCII value 9 is a Tab. ASCII value 27 is an Escape.

ASCII worked well for years, but as computers became used worldwide, the industry began to run into a problem—there's a lot more than 256 characters used all over the world! Nobody could use Arabic, Greek, Hebrew, or even Braille! In 1991, the Unicode Consortium, an international standards group, introduced *Unicode*. Basic **Unicode** is a 16-bit code that covers every character for the most common languages plus a few thousand symbols. With Unicode you can make just about any character or symbol you might imagine—plus a few thousand more you'd never even think of. The first 256 Unicode characters are exactly the same as ASCII characters, making for easy backward compatibility.

Drives and Folders

When working from the command line, you need to be able to

Try This!

Make Some Unicode!

A lot of e-mail programs can use Unicode characters, as can Internet message boards such as my Tech Forums. You can use Unicode characters to accent your writing or simply to spell a person's name correctly—Martin *Acuña*—when you address him. Working with Unicode is fun, so try this!

1. Open a text editing program, such as Notepad in the Windows GUI.

2. Hold down the ALT key on your keyboard, and, referring to Figure 10.10, press numbers on your keyboard's number pad to enter special characters. For example, pressing ALT-164 should display an *ñ*, whereas ALT-168 will show a *¿*.

3. If you have access to the Internet, surf over to the Tech Forums (www.totalsem.com) and say howdy! Include some Unicode in your post, of course!

focus the prompt at the specific drive and folder that contains the files or programs with which you want to work. This can be a little more complicated than it seems, especially in Windows 2000 and Windows XP.

At boot, Windows assigns a drive letter (or name) to each hard drive partition and to each floppy or other disk drive. The first floppy drive is called A:, and the second, if installed, is called B:. Hard drives usually start with the letter C: and can continue to Z: if necessary. CD-media drives by default get the next available drive letter after the last hard drive. Windows 2000 and XP enable you to change the default lettering for drives, so you're likely to see all sorts of lettering schemes. On top of that, Windows 2000 and XP let you mount a hard drive as a volume in another drive.

Whatever the names of the drives, Windows uses a hierarchical directory tree to organize the contents of these drives. All files are put into groups Windows calls *folders*, although you'll often hear techs use the term *directory* rather than *folder*, a holdover from the true DOS days. Any file not in a folder *within* the tree—that is, any file in the folder at the root of the directory tree—is said to be in the root directory . A folder inside another folder is called a *subfolder*. Any folder can have multiple subfolders. Two or more files with the same name can exist in different folders on a PC, but two files in the same folder cannot have the same name. In the same way, no two subfolders under the same folder can have the same name, but two subfolders under different folders can have the same name.

When describing a drive, you use its letter and a colon. For example, the hard drive would be represented by C:. To describe the root directory, put a backslash (\) after the C:, as in C:\. To describe a particular directory, add the name of the directory. For example, if a PC had a directory in the root directory called TEST, it would be C:\TEST. Subdirectories in a directory are displayed by adding backslashes and names. If the TEST directory had a subdirectory called SYSTEM, it would be shown like this: C:\TEST\SYSTEM. This naming convention provides for a complete description of the location and name of any file. If the C:\TEST\SYSTEM directory included a file called TEST2.TXT, it would be C:\TEST\SYSTEM\TEST2.TXT.

The exact location of a file is called its path . The path for the TEST2.TXT file is C:\TEST\SYSTEM. Here are some examples of possible paths:

```
C:\PROGRAM FILES
C:\WINNT\system32\1025
F:\FRUSCH3\CLEAR
A:\REPORTS
D:\
```

Here are a few items to remember about folder names and filenames.

- Folders and files may have spaces in their names.
- The only disallowed characters are the following eleven: * " / \ [ ] : ; | = ,
- Files aren't required to have extensions, but Windows won't know the file type without an extension.
- Folder names may have extensions—but they are not commonly used.

Tech Tip

Directory Trees

It helps to visualize a directory tree as upside down, because in geek-speak, the trunk, or root directory, is spoken of as if it were "above" the folders that divide it, and those subfolders "below" root are spoken of as being "above" the other subfolders inside them. For example, "The file is in the Adobe folder under Program Files."

■ Mastering Fundamental Commands

It's time to try using the command line, but before you begin, a note of warning is in order: the command-line interface is picky and unforgiving. It will do what you *say*, not what you *mean*, so it always pays to double-check that those are one and the same before you press ENTER and commit the command. One careless keystroke can result in the loss of crucial data, with no warning and no going back. In this section, you'll explore the structure of commands and then play with four commands built into all versions of Microsoft's command-line interface: DIR, CD, MD, and RD.

Structure: Syntax and Switches

All commands in the Windows command-line interface use a similar structure and execute in the same way. You type the name of the command followed by the target of that command and any modifications of that command that you want to apply. You can call up a modification by using an extra letter or number, called a **switch** or *option,* which may follow either the command or the target, depending on the command. The proper way to write a command is called its **syntax**. The key with commands is that you can't spell anything incorrectly or use a \ when the syntax calls for a /. The command line is completely inflexible, so you have to learn the correct syntax for each command.

```
[command] [target (if any)] [switches]
```

or

```
[command] [switches] [target (if any)]
```

How do you know what switches are allowed? How do you know whether the switches come before or after the target? If you want to find out the syntax and switches used by a particular command, always type the command followed by a **/?** to get help.

DIR Command

The **DIR command** shows you the contents of the directory where the prompt is focused. DIR is used more often than any other command at the command prompt. When you open a command-line window in Windows XP, it opens focused on your user folder. You will know this because the prompt will look like this: `C:\Documents and Settings\username>`. By typing in **DIR** and then pressing the ENTER key (remember that you must always press ENTER to execute a command from the command line), you will see something like Figure 10.11.

If you are following along on a PC, remember that different computers contain different files and programs, so you will absolutely see something different from what's shown in Figure 10.11! If a lot of text scrolls quickly down the screen, try typing **DIR /P** (pause). Don't forget to press ENTER. The DIR /P command is a lifesaver when you're looking for something in a large directory.

> **Tech Tip**
>
> **Do You Need Spaces?**
>
> *Some commands give you the same result whether you include spaces or not. DIR/P and DIR /P, for example, provide the same output. Some commands, however, require spaces between the command and switches. In general, get into the habit of putting spaces between your command and switches and you won't run into problems.*

```
C:\WINDOWS\system32\cmd.exe

C:\Documents and Settings\michaels>dir
 Volume in drive C is System
 Volume Serial Number is 8482-B7E7

 Directory of C:\Documents and Settings\michaels

09/18/2006  02:11 PM    <DIR>          .
09/18/2006  02:11 PM    <DIR>          ..
07/18/2006  10:31 AM    <DIR>          .netbeans
04/05/2006  11:54 AM           305,719 AdobeFnt10.lst
09/15/2005  11:04 AM                 0 AdobeWeb.log
09/18/2006  03:56 PM    <DIR>          Desktop
08/07/2006  02:04 PM    <DIR>          Favorites
11/28/2005  10:10 AM    <DIR>          Jake2
09/12/2006  11:14 AM               600 PUTTY.RND
09/13/2005  11:14 AM    <DIR>          Start Menu
11/02/2005  10:48 AM    <DIR>          WINDOWS
               3 File(s)        306,319 bytes
               8 Dir(s)  10,937,204,736 bytes free

C:\Documents and Settings\michaels>_
```

Extra text typed after a command to modify its operation, such as the /W or /P after DIR, is called a *switch*. Almost all switches can be used simultaneously to modify a command. For example, try typing **DIR /W /P**.

• **Figure 10.11** DIR in a user's folder

When you type a simple DIR command, you will see that some of the entries look like this:

```
09/04/2008    05:51 PM                63,664 bambi.jpg
```

All of these entries are files. The DIR command lists the creation date, creation time, file size in bytes, filename, and extension. Any entries that look like this are folders:

```
12/31/2004   10:18 AM     <DIR>        WINDOWS
```

The DIR command lists the creation date, creation time, *<DIR>* to tell you it is a folder, and the folder name. If you ever see a listing with *<JUNCTION>* instead of *<DIR>*, you're looking at a hard drive partition that's been mounted as a folder instead of a drive letter:

```
08/06/2006   02:28 PM     <JUNCTION>    Other Drive
```

Now type the **DIR /W** command. Note that the DIR /W command shows only the filenames, but they are arranged in five columns across your screen. Finally, type **DIR /?** to see the screen shown in Figure 10.12, which lists all possible switches for the command.

Typing any command followed by a **/?** brings up a help screen for that particular command. Although these help screens can sometimes seem a little cryptic, they're useful when you're not too familiar with a command or you can't figure out how to get a command to do what you need. Even though I have almost every command memorized,

```
C:\WINDOWS\system32\cmd.exe

C:\Documents and Settings\michaels>dir /?
Displays a list of files and subdirectories in a directory.

DIR [drive:][path][filename] [/A[[:]attributes]] [/B] [/C] [/D] [/L] [/N]
  [/O[[:]sortorder]] [/P] [/Q] [/S] [/T[[:]timefield]] [/W] [/X] [/4]

  [drive:][path][filename]
              Specifies drive, directory, and/or files to list.

  /A          Displays files with specified attributes.
  attributes   D  Directories                R  Read-only files
               H  Hidden files               A  Files ready for archiving
               S  System files               -  Prefix meaning not
  /B          Uses bare format (no heading information or summary).
  /C          Display the thousand separator in file sizes.  This is the
              default.  Use /-C to disable display of separator.
  /D          Same as wide but files are list sorted by column.
  /L          Uses lowercase.
  /N          New long list format where filenames are on the far right.
  /O          List by files in sorted order.
  sortorder    N  By name (alphabetic)       S  By size (smallest first)
               E  By extension (alphabetic)  D  By date/time (oldest first)
               G  Group directories first    -  Prefix to reverse order
  /P          Pauses after each screenful of information.
Press any key to continue . . .
```

• **Figure 10.12** Typing DIR /? lists all possible switches for DIR command

I still refer to these help screens—you should use them as well. If you're really lost, type **HELP** at the command prompt for a list of commands you may type. Once you find one, type **HELP** and then the name of the command. For example, if you type **HELP DIR**, you'll see the screen shown in Figure 10.12.

Directories: The CD Command

The **CD (or CHDIR) command** enables you to change the focus of the command prompt to a different directory. To use the CD command, type **CD** followed by the name of the directory on which you want the prompt to focus. For example, to go to the C:\OBIWAN directory, you would type **CD\OBIWAN**, and then press ENTER. If the system has an OBIWAN directory, the prompt will change focus to that directory, and appear as C:\OBIWAN>. If no OBIWAN directory exists or if you accidentally typed something like **OBIWAM**, you get the error "The system cannot find the path specified." If only I had a dollar for every time I've seen those errors! I usually get them due to typing too fast. If you get this error, check what you typed and try again.

To return to the root directory, type **CD** and press ENTER. You can use the CD command to point DOS to any directory. For example, you could type CD\FRED\BACKUP\TEST from a C:\ prompt, and the prompt would change to C:\FRED\BACKUP\TEST\>—assuming, of course, that your system *has* a directory called C:\FRED\BACKUP\TEST.

Once the prompt has changed, type **DIR** again. You should see a different list of files and directories. Every directory holds different files and subdirectories, so when you point DOS to different directories, the DIR command will shows you different contents.

The CD command allows you to use a space instead of a backslash, a convenient shortcut. For example, you could go to the C:\WINDOWS directory from the root directory simply by typing **CD WINDOWS** at the C:\ prompt. You can use the **CD [space]** command to move one level at a time, like this:

```
C:\>CD FRED
C:\FRED\>CD BACKUP
C:\FRED\BACKUP>CD TEST
```

Or, you can jump multiple directory levels in one step, like this:

```
C:\>CD FRED\BACKUP\TEST
C:\FRED\BACKUP\TEST>
```

A final trick: if you want to go *up* a single directory level, you can type **CD** followed immediately by two periods. So, for example, if you're in the C:\FRED\BACKUP directory and you want to move up to the C:\FRED directory, you can simply type **CD..** and you'll be there:

```
C:\FRED\BACKUP>CD..
C:\FRED>
```

Take some time to move the DOS focus around the directories of your PC using the CD and DIR commands. Use DIR to find a directory, and then use CD to move the focus to that directory. Remember, CD\ will always get you back to the root directory.

Tech Tip

Errors Are Good!

Consider errors in general for a moment—not just command prompt errors like "Invalid directory," but any error, including Windows errors. Many new computer users freeze in horror when they see an error message. Do not fear error messages. Error messages are good! Love them. Worship them. They will save you.

Seriously, think how confusing it would be if the computer didn't tell you when you messed up! Error messages tell you what you did wrong so you can fix it. You absolutely cannot hurt your PC in any way by typing the DIR or CD command incorrectly. Take advantage of this knowledge and experiment. Intentionally make mistakes to familiarize yourself with the error messages. Have fun and learn from errors!

Moving Between Drives

The CD command is *not* used to move between drives. To get the prompt to point to another drive ("point" is command line geek-speak for "switch its focus"), just type the drive letter and a colon. If the prompt points at the C:\Sierra directory and you want to see what is on the floppy (A:) drive, just type **A:** and DOS will point to the floppy drive. You'll see the following on the screen:

```
C:\Sierra>A:
A:\>
```

To return to the C: drive, just type **C:** and you'll see the following:

```
A:\>C:
C:\Sierra>
```

Note that you return to the same directory you left. Just for fun, try typing in a drive letter that you know doesn't exist. I know that my system does not have a W: drive. If I type in a nonexistent drive on a Windows system, I get the following error:

```
The system cannot find the drive specified.
```

Try inserting a floppy disk and using the CD command to point at its drive. Do the same with a CD-media disc. Type **DIR** to see the contents of the floppy or CD-media. Type **CD** to move the focus to any folders on the floppy or CD-media. Now return focus to the C: drive.

Using the DIR, CD, and drive letter commands, you can access any folder on any storage device on your system. Make sure you can use these commands comfortably to navigate inside your computer.

Making Directories

Now that you have learned how to navigate in a command-prompt world, it's time to start making stuff, beginning with a new directory.

To make a directory, use the **MD (or MKDIR) command**. To create a directory called STEAM under the root directory C:, for example, first ensure that you are in the root directory by typing **CD**. You should see the prompt.

```
C:\>
```

Now that the prompt points to the root directory, type the following:

```
C:\>MD STEAM
```

Once you press ENTER, Windows will execute the command, but it won't volunteer any information about what it did. You must use the DIR command to see that you have, in fact, created a new directory. Note that the STEAM directory in this example is not listed last, as you might expect.

```
C:\>DIR
 Volume in Drive C is
 Volume Serial Number is 1734-3234
 Directory of C:\
```

```
07/12/2006   04:46 AM    <DIR>               Documents and Settings
06/04/2008   10:22 PM    <DIR>               STEAM
09/11/2006   11:32 AM    <DIR>               NVIDIA
08/06/2007   02:28 PM    <JUNCTION>          Other Drive
09/14/2006   11:11 AM    <DIR>               Program Files
09/12/2006   08:32 PM                    21 statusclient.log
07/31/2005   10:40 PM                   153 systemscandata.txt
03/13/2006   09:54 AM             1,111,040 t3h0
04/21/2006   04:19 PM    <DIR>               temp
07/12/2006   10:18 AM    <DIR>               WINDOWS
             3 file(s)            1,111,214 bytes
                         294,182,881,834   bytes free
```

What about uppercase and lowercase? Windows will support both but it always interprets all commands as uppercase. Use the MD command to make a folder called steam (note the lowercase) and see what happens. This also happens in the graphical Windows. Go to your desktop and try to make two folders, one called STEAM and the other called steam, and see what Windows tells you.

To create a FILES subdirectory in the STEAM directory, first use the CD\ command to point the prompt at the STEAM directory:

```
CD\STEAM
```

Then run the MD command to make the FILES directory:

```
MD FILES
```

Make sure that the prompt points to the directory in which you want to make the new subdirectory before you execute the MD command. When you're done, type **DIR** to see the new FILES subdirectory. Just for fun, try the process again and add a GAMES directory under the STEAM directory. Type **DIR** to verify success.

Removing Directories

Removing subdirectories works exactly like making them. First, get to the directory that contains the subdirectory you want to delete, and then execute the RD (or RMDIR) command. In this example, delete the FILES subdirectory in the C:\STEAM directory. First, get to where the FILES directory is located—C:\STEAM—by typing **CD\STEAM**. Then type **RD FILES**. If no response was received from Windows, you probably did it right! Type **DIR** to check that the FILES subdirectory is gone.

The plain RD command will not delete a directory in Windows if the directory contains files or subdirectories. If you want to delete a directory that contains files or subdirectories, you must first empty that directory using the DEL (for files) or RD (for subdirectories) command. You can use the RD command followed by the /S switch to delete a directory as well as all files and subdirectories. RD followed by the /S switch is handy but dangerous, because it's easy to delete more than you want. When deleting, always follow the maxim "check twice and delete once."

Now delete the STEAM and GAMES directories with RD followed by the /S switch. Because the STEAM directory is in the root directory, point to the root directory with CD\. Now execute the command **RD C:\STEAM /S**. In a rare display of mercy, Windows will respond with the following:

```
C:\>rd steam /s
steam, Are you sure (Y/N)?
```

Press the Y key and both C:\STEAM and C:\STEAM\GAMES will be eliminated.

Running a Program

To run a program from the command line, simply change the prompt focus to the folder where the program is located, type the name of the program, and then press the ENTER key on your keyboard. Try this safe example. Go to the C:\WINNT\System32 or C:\WINDOWS\System32—the exact name of

---

Try This!

Working with Directories

It's important for a PC tech to be comfortable creating and deleting directories. To get some practice, try this:

1. Create a new directory in the root directory using the make directory command (MD). Type **CD** to return to the root directory. At the command prompt, type the following:

   ```
   C:\>MD JEDI
   ```

2. As usual, the prompt tells you nothing—it just presents a fresh prompt. Do a DIR (that is, type the **DIR** command) to see your new directory. Windows will create the new directory wherever it is pointing when you issue the command, whether or not that's where you meant to put it. To demonstrate, point the prompt to your new directory using the CD command:

   ```
   C:\>CD JEDI
   ```

3. Now use the make directory command again to create a directory called YODA:

   ```
   C:\JEDI>MD YODA
   ```

   Do a DIR again, and you should see that your JEDI directory now contains a YODA directory.

4. Type **CD** to return to the root directory so you can delete your new directories using the remove directory command (RD):

   ```
   C:\>RD /S JEDI
   ```

   In another rare display of mercy, Windows responds with the following:

   ```
   jedi, Are you sure <Y/N>?
   ```

5. Press Y to eliminate both C:\JEDI and C:\JEDI\YODA.

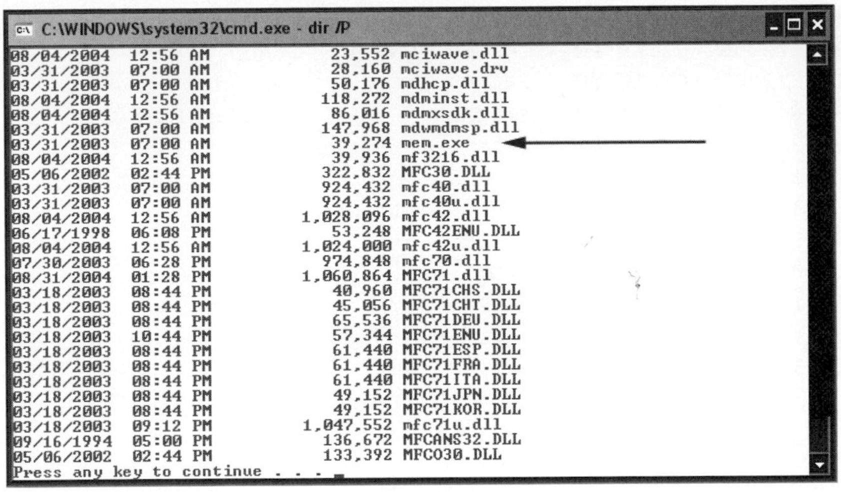

```
C:\WINDOWS\system32\cmd.exe - dir /P                                    _ □ ×
08/04/2004  12:56 AM              23,552 mciwave.dll
03/31/2003  07:00 AM              28,160 mciwave.drv
03/31/2003  07:00 AM              50,176 mdhcp.dll
08/04/2004  12:56 AM             118,272 mdminst.dll
08/04/2004  12:56 AM              86,016 mdmxsdk.dll
03/31/2003  07:00 AM             147,968 mdwmdmsp.dll
03/31/2003  07:00 AM              39,274 mem.exe        ←
08/04/2004  12:56 AM              39,936 mf3216.dll
05/06/2002  02:44 PM             322,832 MFC30.DLL
03/31/2003  07:00 AM             924,432 mfc40.dll
03/31/2003  07:00 AM             924,432 mfc40u.dll
08/04/2004  12:56 AM           1,028,096 mfc42.dll
06/17/1998  06:08 PM              53,248 MFC42ENU.DLL
08/04/2004  12:56 AM           1,024,000 mfc42u.dll
07/30/2003  06:28 PM             974,848 mfc70.dll
08/31/2003  01:28 PM           1,060,864 MFC71.dll
03/18/2003  08:44 PM              40,960 MFC71CHS.DLL
03/18/2003  08:44 PM              45,056 MFC71CHT.DLL
03/18/2003  08:44 PM              65,536 MFC71DEU.DLL
03/18/2003  10:44 PM              57,344 MFC71ENU.DLL
03/18/2003  08:44 PM              61,440 MFC71ESP.DLL
03/18/2003  08:44 PM              61,440 MFC71FRA.DLL
03/18/2003  08:44 PM              61,440 MFC71ITA.DLL
03/18/2003  08:44 PM              49,152 MFC71JPN.DLL
03/18/2003  08:44 PM              49,152 MFC71KOR.DLL
03/18/2003  09:12 PM           1,047,552 mfc71u.dll
09/16/1994  05:00 PM             136,672 MFCANS32.DLL
05/06/2002  02:44 PM             133,392 MFCO30.DLL
Press any key to continue . . .
```

• Figure 10.13   MEM.EXE displayed in the System32 folder

this folder varies by system. Type **DIR/P** to see the files one page at a time. You should see a file called MEM.EXE (Figure 10.13).

As mentioned earlier, all files with extensions .EXE and .COM are programs, so MEM.EXE is a program. To run the MEM.EXE program, just type the filename, in this case **MEM**, and press ENTER (Figure 10.14). Note that you do not have to type the .EXE extension, although you can. Congratulations! You have just run your first program from the command line!

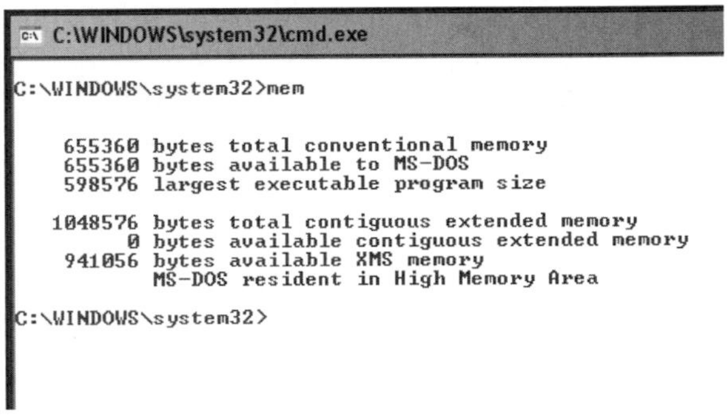

```
C:\WINDOWS\system32\cmd.exe

C:\WINDOWS\system32>mem

   655360 bytes total conventional memory
   655360 bytes available to MS-DOS
   598576 largest executable program size

  1048576 bytes total contiguous extended memory
        0 bytes available contiguous extended memory
   941056 bytes available XMS memory
          MS-DOS resident in High Memory Area

C:\WINDOWS\system32>
```

• Figure 10.14   Running MEM in Windows XP

Windows includes a lot of command-line tools for specific jobs such as starting and stopping services, viewing computers on a network, converting hard drive file systems, and more. The book discusses these task-specific tools in the chapters that reflect their task. I couldn't resist throwing in two of the more interesting tools, COMPACT and CIPHER, in the Beyond A+ section of this chapter.

■ Working with Files

This section deals with basic file manipulation. You will learn how to look at, copy, move, rename, and delete files. You'll look at the ins and outs of batch files. The examples in this section are based on a C: root directory with the following files and directories:

```
C:\>dir
 Volume in drive C has no label.
 Volume Serial Number is 4C62-1572

 Directory of C:\

05/26/2006  11:37 PM                      0 AILog.txt
05/29/2006  05:33 PM                  5,776 aoedoppl.txt
05/29/2006  05:33 PM                  2,238 aoeWVlog.txt
07/12/2006  10:38 AM    <DIR>                books
07/15/2005  02:45 PM                  1,708 CtDrvStp.log
07/12/2006  04:46 AM    <DIR>                Documents and Settings
06/04/2006  10:22 PM    <DIR>                Impressions Games
```

```
09/11/2005    11:32 AM    <DIR>              NVIDIA
08/06/2006    02:28 PM    <JUNCTION>         Other Drive
01/03/2005    01:12 PM    <DIR>              pers-drv
09/14/2006    11:11 AM    <DIR>              Program Files
09/12/2006    08:32 PM                   21  statusclient.log
07/31/2005    10:40 PM                  153  systemscandata.txt
03/13/2006    09:54 AM            1,111,040  t3h0
04/21/2006    04:19 PM    <DIR>              temp
01/10/2006    07:07 PM    <DIR>              WebCam
12/31/2004    10:18 AM    <DIR>              WINDOWS
09/14/2006    12:48 PM    <DIR>              WINNT
01/03/2005    09:06 AM    <DIR>              WUTemp
                7 File(s)        1,120,936 bytes
               12 Dir(s)    94,630,002,688 bytes free
```

Because you probably don't have a PC with these files and directories, follow the examples but use what's on your drive. In other words, create your own folders and copy files to them from various folders currently on your system.

Attributes

All files have four special values, or attributes, which determine how programs (like My Computer) treat the file in special situations. The first attribute is the hidden attribute. If a file is hidden, it will not be displayed when the DIR command is issued. Next is the read-only attribute. A read-only file cannot be modified or deleted. Third is the system attribute, which is used only for system files such as NTLDR and BOOT.INI. In reality, it does nothing more than provide an easy identifier for these files. Fourth is the archive attribute, which is used by backup software to identify files that have been changed since their last backup.

ATTRIB.EXE is an external command-line program that enables you to inspect and change file attributes. To inspect a file's attributes, type the ATTRIB command followed by the name of the file. To see the attributes of the file AILog.txt, type **ATTRIB AILOG.TXT**. The result is

```
A        AILog.txt
```

The letter *A* stands for archive, the only attribute of AILog.txt.

Go to the C:\ directory and type **ATTRIB** by itself. You'll see a result similar to the following:

```
C:\>attrib
A              C:\AILog.txt
A              C:\aoedoppl.txt
A              C:\aoeWVlog.txt
A     H        C:\AUTOEXEC.BAT
A     SH       C:\boot.ini
A     H        C:\CONFIG.SYS
A              C:\CtDrvStp.log
A     SH       C:\hiberfil.sys
A     SHR      C:\IO.SYS
```

```
A   SHR      C:\MSDOS.SYS
A   SHR      C:\NTDETECT.COM
A   SHR      C:\ntldr
A   SH       C:\pagefile.sys
A            C:\statusclient.log
A            C:\systemscandata.txt
A            C:\t3h0
```

The letter *R* means read-only, *H* is hidden, and *S* is system. Hey! There are some new files there! That's right, some were hidden. Don't panic if you see a number of files different from those just listed. No two C:\ directories are ever the same. In most cases, you'll see many more files than just these. Notice that important files, NTLDR and NTDETECT.COM, have the system, hidden, and read-only attributes set. Microsoft does this to protect them from accidental deletion.

The ATTRIB command is also used to change a file's attributes. To add an attribute to a file, type the attribute letter preceded by a plus sign (+) as an option, and then type the filename. To delete an attribute, use a minus sign (–). For example, to add the read-only attribute to the file AILog.txt, type this:

```
ATTRIB +R AILOG.TXT
```

To remove the archive attribute, type this:

```
ATTRIB -A AILOG.TXT
```

Multiple attributes can be added or removed in one command. Here's an example of removing three attributes from the NTDETECT.COM file:

```
ATTRIB -R -S -H NTDETECT.COM
```

You can also automatically apply ATTRIB to matching files in subdirectories by using the /s switch at the end of the statement. For example, if you had lots of files in your My Music folder that you wanted to hide, but they were neatly organized in many subdirectories, you could readily use ATTRIB to change all of them with a simple command. Change directories from the prompt until you're at the My Music folder and then type the following:

```
ATTRIB +H *.MP3 /S
```

When you press the ENTER key, all your music files in My Music and any My Music subdirectories will become hidden files.

Try This!

Working with Attributes

It's important for you to know that everything you do at the command line affects the same files at the GUI level, so Try This!

1. Go to My Computer and create a folder in the root directory of your C: drive called TEST.

2. Copy a couple of files into that folder and then right-click one to see its properties.

3. Open a command-line window and navigate to the C:\TEST folder. Type **DIR** to see that the contents match what you see in My Computer.

4. From the command line, change the attributes of one or both files. Make one a hidden file, for example, and the other read-only.

5. Now go back to My Computer and access the properties of each file. Any changes?

Wildcards

Visualize having 273 files in one directory. A few of these files have the extension .DOC, but most do not. You are looking only for files with the .DOC extension. Wouldn't it be nice to type the DIR command so that only the .DOC files come up? You can do this using wildcards.

A **wildcard** is one of two special characters, asterisk (*) and question mark (?), that can be used in place of all or part of a filename, often to enable a command-line command to act on more than one file at a time. Wildcards work with all command-line commands that take filenames. A great example is the DIR command. When you execute a plain DIR command, it finds and displays all the files and folders in the specified directory; however, you can also narrow its search by adding a filename. For example, if you type the command **DIR AILOG.TXT** while in your root (C:\) directory, you get the following result:

```
C:\>dir AILOG.TXT
 Volume in drive C has no label.
 Volume Serial Number is 4C62-1572
 Directory of C:\
05/26/2006  11:37 PM                     0 AILog.txt
              1 File(s)             0 bytes
              0 Dir(s)   94,630,195,200 bytes free
```

If you just want to confirm the presence of a particular file in a particular place, this is very convenient. But suppose you want to see all files with the extension .TXT. In that case, you use the * wildcard, like this: **DIR *.TXT**. A good way to think of the * wildcard is *"I don't care."* Replace the part of the filename that you don't care about with an asterisk (*). The result of DIR *.TXT would look like this:

```
 Volume in drive C has no label.
 Volume Serial Number is 4C62-1572

 Directory of C:\

05/26/2006  11:37 PM                     0 AILog.txt
05/29/2006  05:33 PM                 5,776 aoedoppl.txt
05/29/2006  05:33 PM                 2,238 aoeWVlog.txt
07/31/2005  10:40 PM                   153 systemscandata.txt
              4 File(s)         8,167 bytes
              0 Dir(s)   94,630,002,688 bytes free
```

Wildcards also substitute for parts of filenames. This DIR command will find every file that starts with the letter *a:*

```
C:\>dir a*.*
 Volume in drive C has no label.
 Volume Serial Number is 4C62-1572

 Directory of C:\

05/26/2006  11:37 PM                     0 AILog.txt
05/29/2006  05:33 PM                 5,776 aoedoppl.txt
05/29/2006  05:33 PM                 2,238 aoeWVlog.txt
              3 File(s)         8,014 bytes
              0 Dir(s)   94,629,675,008 bytes free
```

So far you've seen how to use wildcards only with the DIR command, but virtually every command that deals with files will take wildcards. Next, I'll show you the REN and DEL commands and how they use wildcards.

Renaming Files

To rename files, you use the **REN (or RENAME) command**, which seems pretty straightforward. To rename the file IMG033.jpg to park.jpg, type this and press the ENTER key:

```
ren img033.jpg park.jpg
```

"That's great," you might be thinking, "but what about using a more complex and descriptive filename, like Sunny day in the park.jpg?" Type what should work, like this:

```
ren img033.jpg Sunny day in the park.jpg
```

But you'll get an error message (Figure 10.15). Even the tried-and-true method of seeking help by typing the command followed by /? doesn't give you the answer.

You can use more complicated names by putting them in quotation marks. Figure 10.16 shows the same command that failed but now succeeds because of the quotation marks.

Deleting Files

To delete files, you use the **DEL (or ERASE) command**. DEL and ERASE are identical commands and can be used interchangeably. Deleting files is simple—maybe too simple. Windows' users enjoy the luxury of retrieving deleted files from the Recycle Bin on those "Oops, I didn't mean to delete that" occasions everyone encounters at one time or another. The command line, however, shows no such mercy to the careless user. It has no function equivalent to the Windows Recycle Bin. Once a file has been erased, it can be recovered only by using a special recovery utility such as Norton's UNERASE. Again, the rule here is to *check twice and delete once.*

```
C:\WINDOWS\system32\cmd.exe

E:\pictures>dir
 Volume in drive E is More Space
 Volume Serial Number is 7A64-A796

 Directory of E:\pictures

09/19/2006  01:07 PM    <DIR>          .
09/19/2006  01:07 PM    <DIR>          ..
09/19/2006  01:07 PM                 0 img033.jpg
               1 File(s)              0 bytes
               2 Dir(s)  279,048,781,824 bytes free

E:\pictures>Ren img033.jpg Sunny day in the park.jpg
The syntax of the command is incorrect.

E:\pictures>
```

● **Figure 10.15**   Rename failed me.

```
C:\WINDOWS\system32\cmd.exe

E:\pictures>Ren img033.jpg "Sunny day in the park.jpg"

E:\pictures>dir
 Volume in drive E is More Space
 Volume Serial Number is 7A64-A796

 Directory of E:\pictures

09/19/2006  01:08 PM    <DIR>          .
09/19/2006  01:08 PM    <DIR>          ..
09/19/2006  01:07 PM                 0 Sunny day in the park.jpg
               1 File(s)              0 bytes
               2 Dir(s)  279,048,781,824 bytes free

E:\pictures>
```

● **Figure 10.16**   Success at last

To delete a single file, type the **DEL** command followed by the name of the file to delete. To delete the file AILOG.TXT, for example, type this:

```
DEL AILOG.TXT
```

Although nothing will appear on the screen to confirm it, the file is now gone. To confirm that the AILOG.TXT file is no longer listed, use the DIR command.

As with the DIR command, you can use wildcards with the DEL and ERASE commands to delete multiple files. For example, to delete all files with the extension .TXT in a directory, you would type this:

```
DEL *.TXT
```

To delete all files with the filename CONFIG in a directory, type **DEL CONFIG.***. To delete all the files in a directory, you can use the popular *.* wildcard (often pronounced "star-dot-star"), like this:

```
DEL *.*
```

This is one of the few command-line commands that will elicit a response. Upon receiving the DEL *.* command, Windows will respond with "Are you sure? (Y/N)," to which you respond with a *Y* or *N*. Pressing Y will erase every file in the directory, so be careful when using *.*!

Don't confuse deleting *files* with deleting *directories*. DEL deletes files, but it will not remove directories. Use RD to delete directories.

Copying and Moving Files

The ability to copy and move files in a command line is crucial to all technicians. Due to its finicky nature and many options, the COPY command is also rather painful to learn, especially if you're used to dragging icons in Windows. The following tried-and-true, five-step process will make it easier, but the real secret is to get in front of a C:\ prompt and just copy and move files around until you're comfortable. Keep in mind that the only difference between copying and moving is whether the original is left behind (COPY) or not (MOVE). Once you've learned the **COPY command**, you've learned the **MOVE command**!

Mike's Five-Step COPY/MOVE Process

I've been teaching folks how to copy and move files for years using this handy process. Keep in mind that hundreds of variations on this process exist. As you become more confident with these commands, try doing a COPY /? or MOVE /? at any handy prompt to see the real power of these commands. But first, follow this process step-by-step:

1. Point the command prompt to the directory containing the files to be copied or moved.
2. Type **COPY** or **MOVE** and a space.
3. Type the *name(s)* of the file(s) to be copied/moved (with or without wildcards) and a space.
4. Type the *path* of the new location for the files.
5. Press ENTER.

Here's an example. The directory C:\STEAM contains the file README.TXT. Here's how to copy this file to the floppy drive (A:).

1. Type **CD\STEAM** to point command prompt to the STEAM directory.

   ```
   C:\>CD\STEAM
   ```

2. Type **COPY** and a space.

   ```
   C:\STEAM>COPY
   ```

3. Type **README.TXT** and a space.

   ```
   C:\STEAM>COPY README.TXT
   ```

4. Type **A:**.

   ```
   C:\STEAM>COPY README.TXT A:\
   ```

5. Press ENTER.

The entire command and response would look like this:

```
C:\STEAM>COPY README.TXT A:\
1 file(s) copied
```

If you point the command prompt to the A: drive and type **DIR**, the README.TXT file will be visible. Here's another example. Suppose 100 files are in the C:\DOCS directory, 30 of which have the .DOC extension, and suppose you want to move those files to the C:\STEAM directory. Follow these steps:

1. Type **CD\DOCS** to point the command prompt to the DOCS directory.

   ```
   C:\>CD\DOCS
   ```

2. Type **MOVE** and a space.

   ```
   C:\DOCS>MOVE
   ```

3. Type ***.DOC** and a space.

   ```
   C:\DOCS>MOVE *.DOC
   ```

4. Type **C:\STEAM**.

   ```
   C:\DOCS>MOVE *.DOC C:\STEAM
   ```

5. Press ENTER.

   ```
   C:\DOCS>MOVE *.DOC C:\STEAM
   30 file(s) copied
   ```

The power of the COPY/MOVE command makes it rather dangerous. The COPY/MOVE command not only lets you put a file in a new location, but it lets you change the name of the file at the same time. Suppose you want to copy a file called AUTOEXEC.BAT from your C:\ folder to a floppy disk, for example, but you want the name of the copy on the floppy disk to be AUTO1.BAT. You can do both things with one COPY command, like this:

```
COPY C:\AUTOEXEC.BAT A:\AUTO1.BAT
```

Not only does the AUTOEXEC.BAT file get copied to the floppy disk, but the copy also gets the new name AUTO1.BAT.

As another example, move all of the files with the extension .DOC from the C:\DOCS directory to the C:\BACK directory and simultaneously change the DOC extension to .SAV. Here is the command:

```
MOVE C:\DOCS\*.DOC C:\BACK\*.SAV
```

This says, "Move all files that have the extension .DOC from the directory C:\DOCS into the directory C:\BACK, and while you're at it, change their file extensions to .SAV." This is very handy, but very dangerous!

Say, for example, that I made one tiny typo. Here I typed a semicolon instead of a colon after the second C:

```
MOVE C:\DOCS\*.DOC C;\BACK\*.SAV
```

The command line understands the semicolon to mean "end of command" and therefore ignores both the semicolon and anything I type after it. As far as the command line is concerned, I typed this:

```
MOVE C:\DOCS\*.DOC C
```

This, unfortunately for me, means "take all the files with the extension .DOC in the directory C:\DOCS and copy them back into that same directory, but squish them all together into a single file called C." If I run this command, Windows gives me only one clue that something went wrong:

```
MOVE C:\DOCS\*.DOC C
1 file(s) copied
```

See "1 file(s) copied"? Feeling the chilly hand of fate slide down my spine, I do a DIR of the directory, and I now see a single file called C, where there used to be 30 files with the extension .DOC. All of my DOC files are gone, completely unrecoverable.

XCOPY

The standard COPY and MOVE commands can work only in one directory at a time, making them a poor choice for copying or moving files in multiple directories. To help with these multi-directory jobs, Microsoft added the XCOPY command. (Note that there is no XMOVE, only XCOPY.)

XCOPY works similar to COPY, but XCOPY has extra switches that give it the power to work with multiple directories. Here's how it works. Say I have a directory on my C: drive called \DATA. The \DATA directory has three subdirectories: \JAN, \FEB, and \MAR. All of these directories, including the \DATA directory, contain about 50 files. If I wanted to copy all of these files to my D: drive in one command, I would use XCOPY in the following manner:

```
XCOPY C:\DATA D:\DATA /S
```

Because XCOPY works on directories, you don't have to use filenames as you would in COPY, although XCOPY certainly accepts filenames and wildcards. The /S switch, the most commonly used of all the many switches that come with XCOPY, tells XCOPY to copy all subdirectories except for empty ones. The /E switch tells XCOPY to copy empty subdirectories. When you have a lot of copying to do over many directories, XCOPY is the tool to use.

Their power and utility make the DEL, COPY/MOVE, and XCOPY commands indispensable for a PC technician, but that same power and utility can cause disaster. Only a trained Jedi, with The Force as his ally...well, wrong book, but the principle remains: Beware of the quick and easy keystroke, for it may spell your doom. Think twice and execute the command once. The data you save may be yours!

Working with Batch Files

Batch files are nothing more than text files that store a series of commands, one command per line. The only thing that differentiates a batch file from any other text file is the .BAT extension. Take a look at Figure 10.17 and note the unique icon used for a batch file compared to the icon for a regular text file.

Readme   Batch

• **Figure 10.17** Text and batch file icons

You can create and edit batch files using any text editor program—good old Notepad is often the tool of choice. This is the command-line chapter, though, so it's time to dust off the ancient but still important Edit program—it comes with every version of Windows—and use it to create and edit batch files.

Edit

Get to a command prompt on any Windows system and use the CD\ command to get to the root directory (use C: to get to the C: drive if you're not on the C: drive by default). From there, type **EDIT** at the command prompt to see the Edit program's interface (Figure 10.18).

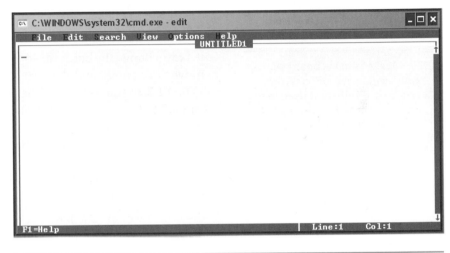

• **Figure 10.18** Edit interface

Now that you've started Edit, type in the two commands as shown in Figure 10.19. Make sure they look exactly the same as the lines in Figure 10.19.

Great! You have just made your first batch file! All you need to do now is save it with some name—the name doesn't matter, but this example uses FIRST as the filename. It is imperative, however, that you use the extension .BAT. Even though you could probably figure this out on your own later, do it now. Hold down the ALT key to activate the menu. Press the F (File) key. Then press S (Save). Type in the name **first.bat** as shown in Figure 10.20. Press ENTER and the file is now saved.

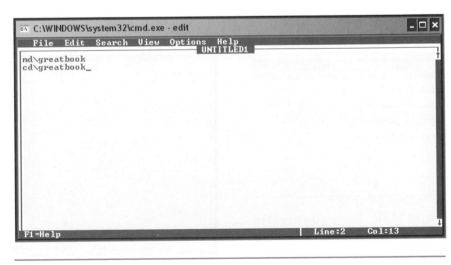

• **Figure 10.19** Edit with two commands

● **Figure 10.20**   Saving the batch file

Most of the keyboard short-cuts used in WordPad, Word, and so on, were first used in the Edit program. If you know keyboard shortcuts for WordPad or Word, many will work in Edit.

Don't try using the TYPE command on anything other than a text file—the results will be unpredictable.

Now that you've saved the file, exit the Edit program by pressing ALT-F and then press X (Exit). You're back at the command prompt. Go ahead and run the program by typing **FIRST** and pressing ENTER. Your results should look something like Figure 10.21.

Super! The batch file created a folder and moved the prompt to focus on that folder. Don't run the first batch file again or you'll create another folder inside the first one!

Now get back to the root directory of C: and edit the FIRST.BAT file again. This time type **EDIT FIRST.BAT** and press ENTER. The batch file will come up, ready to edit. Now change the batch file to look like Figure 10.22. Use the arrow keys to move your cursor and the DELETE key to delete.

The VER command shows the current version of Windows. The ECHO command tells the batch file to put text on the screen. Run the batch file, and it should look like Figure 10.23.

Gee, that's kind of ugly. Try editing the FIRST.BAT file one more time and add the line

```
@echo off
```

as the first line of the batch file. Run FIRST.BAT again. It should look quite a bit nicer! The echo off command tells the system not to show the command, just the result.

Sometimes you just want to look at a batch file. The TYPE command displays the contents of a text file on the screen, as shown in Figure 10.24.

● **Figure 10.21**   Running the batch file

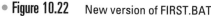

● **Figure 10.22**   New version of FIRST.BAT

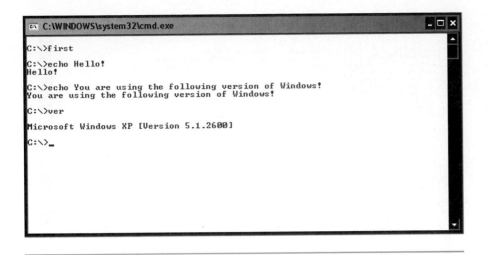

C:\WINDOWS\system32\cmd.exe
C:\>first
C:\>echo Hello!
Hello!
C:\>echo You are using the following version of Windows!
You are using the following version of Windows!
C:\>ver
Microsoft Windows XP [Version 5.1.2600]
C:\>_

• **Figure 10.23** Running VER to show the current version of Windows

One of the more irritating aspects to batch files is that sometimes they don't work unless you run them in the folder in which they are stored. This is due to the path setting. Every time you open a command prompt, Windows loads a number of settings by default. You can see all of these settings by running the SET command. Figure 10.25 shows the results of running the SET command.

Don't worry about understanding everything the SET command shows you, but do notice a line that starts with `Path=`. This line tells

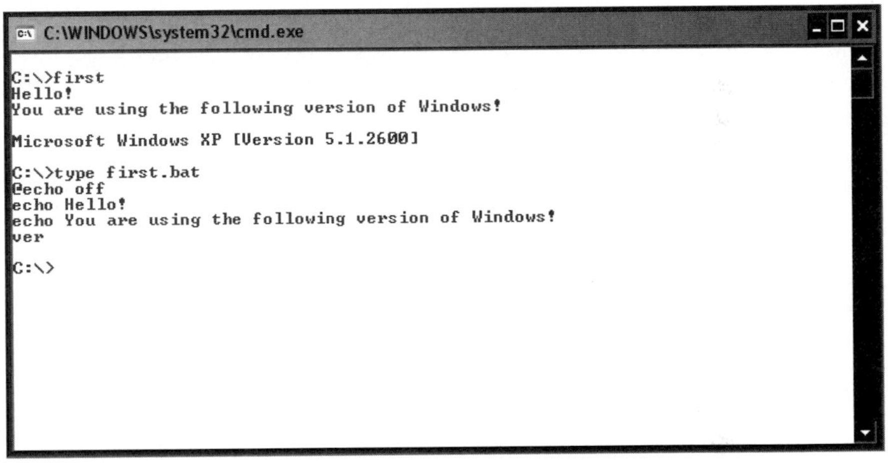

C:\WINDOWS\system32\cmd.exe
C:\>first
Hello!
You are using the following version of Windows!
Microsoft Windows XP [Version 5.1.2600]
C:\>type first.bat
@echo off
echo Hello!
echo You are using the following version of Windows!
ver
C:\>

• **Figure 10.24** Using the TYPE command to see file contents

Cross Check

Command Line versus GUI

Now that you've become familiar with the command-line interface, you should be able to switch between the Windows GUI and the command line with relative ease. Check to make sure you can explain how to do the basic tasks covered in this chapter in both the Windows GUI and the command line.

1. How do you delete a folder in Windows?
2. How do you delete a directory from the command line?
3. Which interface is faster for which tasks?
4. What advantage do wildcards give the command line over the GUI when you're working with files?

You can edit the BOOT.INI file using the Edit program. Just make sure you turn off the System and Hidden attributes using ATTRIB first!

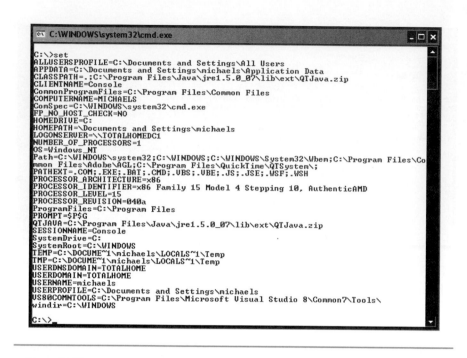

● **Figure 10.25**   Using the SET command to see settings

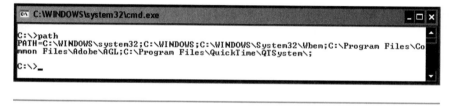

● **Figure 10.26**   Using the PATH command to see the current path

Windows where to look for a program (or batch file) if you run a program that's not in your current folder. For example, say I make a folder called C:\batch to store all my batch files. I can run the PATH command from the command prompt to see my current path (Figure 10.26).

I can then run the PATH command again, this time adding the C:\batch folder (Figure 10.27). I can now place all my batch files in this folder, and they will always work, no matter where I am in the system.

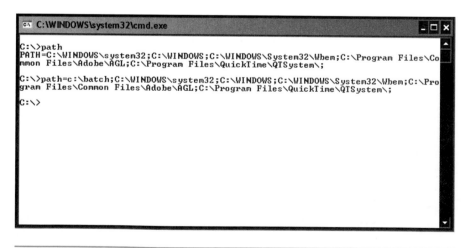

● **Figure 10.27**   Using PATH to add a folder

Beyond A+

Using Special Keys

You might find yourself repeatedly typing the same commands, or at least very similar commands, when working at a prompt. Microsoft has provided a number of ways to access previously typed commands. Type the **DIR** command at a command prompt. When you get back to a prompt, press F1, and the letter *D* will appear. Press F1 again. Now the letter *I* appears after the *D*. Do you see what is happening? The F1 key brings back the previous command one letter at a time. Pressing F3 brings back the entire command at once. Now try running these three commands:

DIR /W

ATTRIB

MD FRED

Now press the up arrow key. Keep pressing it till you see your original DIR command—it's a history of all your old commands. Now use the right arrow key to add /P to the end of your DIR command. Windows command history is very handy.

Compact and Cipher

Windows XP offers two cool commands at the command-line interface: COMPACT and CIPHER. COMPACT displays or alters the compression of files on NTFS partitions. CIPHER displays or alters the encryption of folders and files on NTFS partitions. If you type just the command with no added parameters, COMPACT and CIPHER display the compression state and the encryption state, respectively, of the current directory and any files it contains. You may specify multiple directory names, and you may use wildcards, as you learned earlier in the chapter. You must add parameters to make the commands change things. For example, you add /C to compress and /U to uncompress directories and/or files with the COMPACT command, and you add /E to encrypt and /D to decrypt directories and/or files with the CIPHER command. When you do these operations, you also mark the directories involved so that any files you add to them in the future will take on their encryption or compression characteristics. In other words, if you encrypt a directory and all its files, any files you add later will also be encrypted. Same thing if you compress a directory. I'll run through a quick example of each.

COMPACT

First, try the COMPACT command. Figure 10.28 shows the result of entering the COMPACT command with no switches. It displays the compression status of the contents of a directory called compact on a system's D: drive. Notice that after the file listing, COMPACT helpfully tells you that 0 files are compressed and 6 files (all of them) are not compressed, with a total compression ratio of 1.0 to 1.

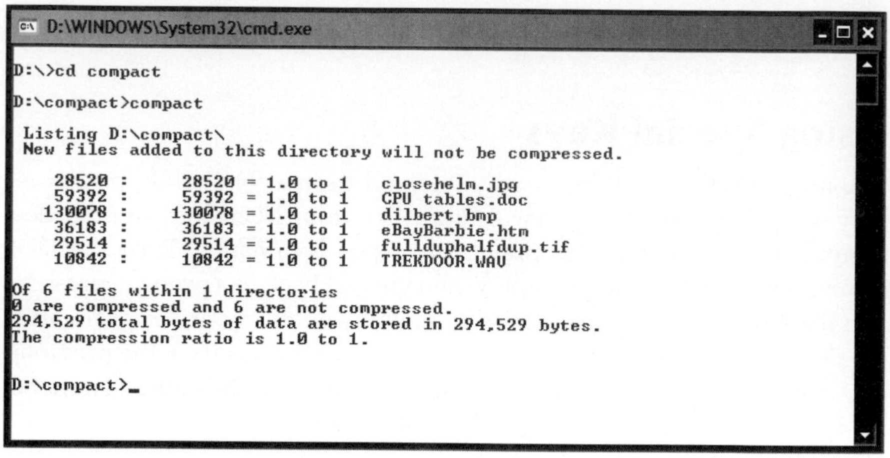

● **Figure 10.28** The COMPACT command with no switches

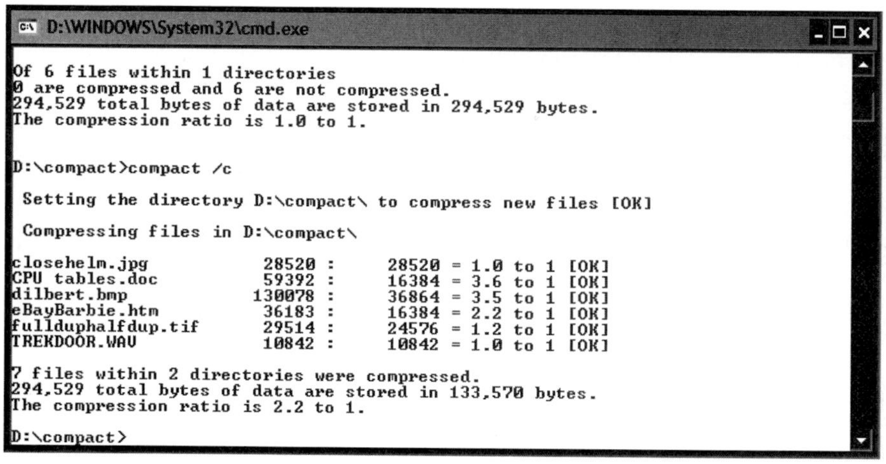

● **Figure 10.29** Typing COMPACT /C compresses the contents of the directory.

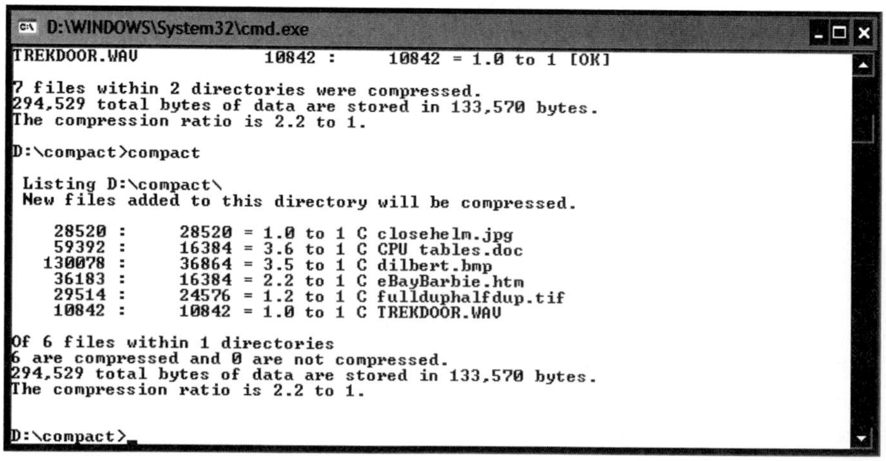

● **Figure 10.30** The contents of D:\COMPACT have been compressed.

If you enter the COMPACT command with the /C switch, it will compress all the files in the directory, as shown in Figure 10.29. Look closely at the listing. Notice that it includes the original and compressed file sizes and calculates the compression ratio for you. Notice also that the JPG (a compressed graphics format) and WAV files didn't compress at all, while the Word file and the BMP file (an uncompressed graphics format) compressed down to less than a third of their original sizes. Also, can you spot what's different in the text at the bottom of the screen? COMPACT claims to have compressed *seven* files in *two* directories! How can this be? The secret is that when it compresses all the files in a directory, it must also compress the directory file itself, which is "in" the D: directory above it. Thus, it correctly reports that it compressed seven files: six in the compact directory and one in the D: directory.

Typing **COMPACT** again shows you the directory listing, and now there's a C next to each filename, indicating that the file is compressed (Figure 10.30).

Okay, now suppose you want to uncompress a file—the Dilbert image, dilbert.bmp. To do this, you must specify the decompression operation, using the /U switch and the name of the file you want decompressed, as shown in Figure 10.31. Note that COMPACT reports the successful decompression of one file only: dilbert.bmp. You could do the same thing in reverse, using the /C switch and a filename to compress an individual file.

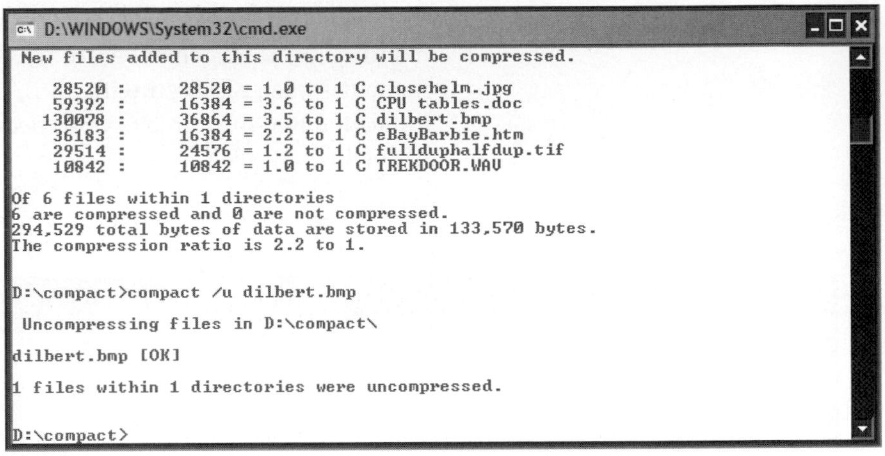

CIPHER

The CIPHER command is a bit complex, but in its most basic implementation, it's pretty straightforward. Figure 10.32 shows two steps in the process. Like the COMPACT command, the CIPHER command simply displays the current state of affairs when entered with no switches. In this case, it displays the encryption state of the files in the D:\Work Files\Armor Pictures directory. Notice the letter *U* to the left of the filenames, which tells you they are unencrypted. The second command you can see on the screen in Figure 10.32 is this:

```
D:\Work Files\Armor Pictures>cipher /E /A
```

This time the CIPHER command carries two switches: /E specifies the encryption operation, and /A says to apply it to the *files* in the directory, not just the directory itself. As you can see, the command-line interface is actually pretty chatty in this case. It reports that it's doing the encryption and then tells you what it's done, and it even warns you that you should clean up any stray unencrypted bits that may have been left in the directory.

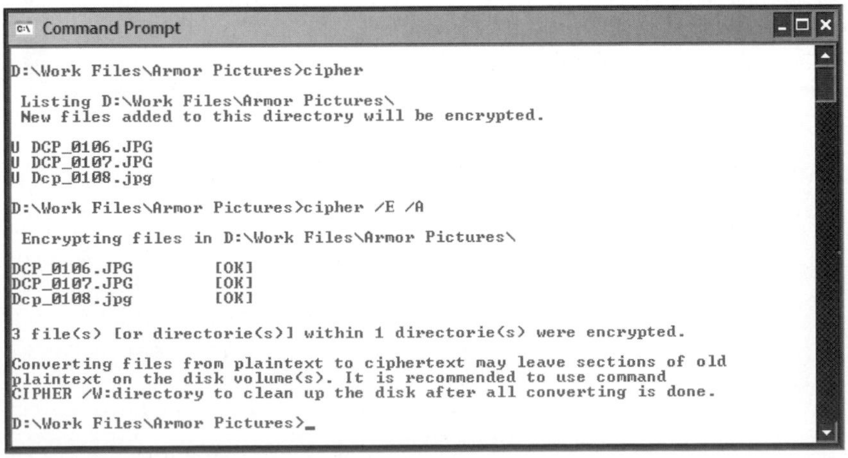

• **Figure 10.31** Typing COMPACT /U DILBERT.BMP decompresses only that file.

• **Figure 10.32** Typing CIPHER /E /A encrypts the contents of the directory.

To confirm the results of the cipher operation, enter the **CIPHER** command again, as shown in Figure 10.33. Note that the *U* to the left of each filename has been replaced with an *E*, indicating an encrypted file. The other indication that this directory has been encrypted is the statement above the file listing:

```
New files added to this directory will be encrypted.
```

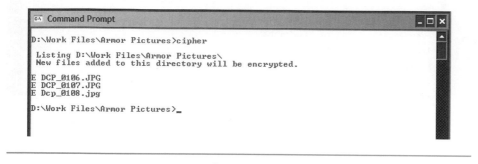

Remember that the CIPHER command works on directories first and foremost, and it works on individual files only when you specifically tell it to do so.

That's great, but suppose you want to decrypt just *one* of the files in the Armor Pictures directory. Can you guess how you need to alter the command? Simply add the filename of the file you want to decrypt after the command and the relevant switches. Figure 10.34 shows the CIPHER command being used to decipher DCP_0106.JPG, a single file.

• **Figure 10.33**   The CIPHER command confirms that the files were encrypted.

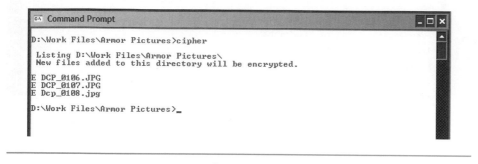

• **Figure 10.34**   Typing CIPHER /D /A DCP_0106.JPG decrypts only that file.

Chapter 10 Review

■ Chapter Summary

After reading this chapter and completing the exercises, you should understand the following about the command line.

Deciphering the Command-Line Interface

■ The text-based DOS-like user interface, now known as the command-line interface, still functions as a basic installation and troubleshooting tool for techs in Windows 2000 and XP. Windows comes with a text editor called EDIT that enables technicians to manipulate text files from within the command prompt.

■ When you use a command-line interface, the computer tells you it's ready to receive commands by displaying a specific set of characters called a prompt. You type a command and press ENTER to send it. The OS goes off and executes the command, and when it's done it displays a new prompt, often along with some information about what it did. Once you get a new prompt, it means the computer is ready for your next instruction.

■ You can access the command-line interface by clicking Start | Run to open the Run dialog box, and then typing **CMD** and pressing ENTER. You can also click Start | Programs | Accessories | Command Prompt in Windows 2000 and XP. To close the command-line–interface window, either click the Close box in the upper-right corner of the window or type **EXIT** at the prompt and press ENTER.

■ The command prompt is always focused on some directory, and any commands you issue are performed *on the files in the directory* on which the prompt is focused. Make sure you focus the prompt's attention on the drive and directory in which you want to work.

■ Windows manifests each program and piece of data as an individual *file.* Each file has a name, which is stored with the file on the drive. Names are broken down into two parts: the filename and the extension. In true DOS, the filename could be no longer than eight characters. The extension, which is optional, could be up to three characters long. No spaces or other illegal

characters (/ \ [ ] | ÷ + = ; , * ?) could be used in the filename or extension. The filename and extension are separated by a period, or "dot." This naming system is known as the "eight-dot-three" (8.3) naming system. All versions of Windows starting with 9*x* allow filenames of up to 255 characters.

■ The filename extension tells the computer the type or function of the file. Program files use the extension .EXE (for executable) or .COM (for command). If the file is data, the extension indicates which program uses that particular data file. Graphics files most often reflect the graphics standard used to render the image, such as .GIF or .JPG. Changing the file extension does not change the data in the file. The Windows GUI doesn't show the file extensions by default.

■ All files are stored on the hard drive in binary format, but every program has its own unique method of binary organization, called a file format. One program cannot read another program's files unless it has the ability to convert the other program's file format into its file format.

■ ASCII (American Standard Code for Information Interchange) was the first universal file format. The ASCII standard defines 256, eight-bit characters, including all the letters of the alphabet (uppercase and lowercase), numbers, punctuation, many foreign characters, box-drawing characters, and a series of special characters for commands such as a carriage return, bell, and end of file. ASCII files, often called text files, store all data in ASCII format. The keyboard sends the characters you press on the keyboard in ASCII code to the PC. Even the monitor outputs in ASCII when you are running a command line.

■ As a rule, the OS treats the first 32 ASCII values as commands. Some of them are both commands and characters. How these first 32 values are treated depends on the program that reads them.

■ Unicode supports thousands of 16-bit characters. The first 256 Unicode characters are the same as the complete 256 ASCII character set, which maintains backward compatibility.

- At boot, the OS assigns a drive letter to each hard drive partition and to each floppy or other disk drive. The first floppy drive is called A:, and the second, if installed, is called B:. Hard drives start with the letter C: and can continue to Z: if necessary. CD-media drives usually get the next available drive letter after the last hard drive.

- Windows uses a hierarchical directory tree to organize the contents of these drives. All files are put into groups called directories. Windows also uses directories, but it calls them folders. Any file not in a directory *within* the tree, which is to say, any file in the directory at the root of the directory tree, is said to be in the root directory. Directories inside directories are called subdirectories. Any directory can have multiple subdirectories. Two or more files or subdirectories with the same name can exist in different directories on a PC, but two files or subdirectories in the same directory cannot have the same name.

- When describing a drive, you use its assigned letter, such as C: for the hard drive. To describe the root directory, add a backslash (\), as in C:\. To describe a particular directory, add the name of the directory after the backslash. To add a subdirectory after the directory, add another backslash and then the subdirectory's name. This naming convention provides for a complete description of the location and name of any file. The exact location of a file is called its path.

Mastering Fundamental Commands

- The command-line interface will do what you *say*, not what you *mean*, so it always pays to double-check that those are the same before you press ENTER. One careless keystroke can result in the loss of crucial data, with no warning and no going back.

- The DIR command shows you the contents of the directory on which the prompt is focused. The DIR command lists the filename, extension, file size in bytes, and creation date/time. The DIR /P command pauses after displaying a screen's worth of the directory contents; press the SPACEBAR to display the next screen. The DIR/W command shows you filenames only, arranged in columns, with directory names in square brackets.

- Extra text typed after a command to modify its operation, such as the /W or /P after DIR, is called a switch. Almost all switches can be used

simultaneously to modify a command. Typing any command followed by a /? brings up a help screen for that particular command.

- The CD command enables you to change the focus of the command prompt to a different directory. Type **CD** followed by the name of the directory on which you want to focus the prompt, and press ENTER. If no such directory exists or if you mistyped the name, Windows will report: "The system cannot find the path specified." To return to the root directory, type **CD** and press ENTER. The CD command also allows you to use a space instead of a backslash. The CD command is not used to move between drives; to point the prompt to another drive, type the drive letter and a colon.

- To make a directory, use the MD (or MKDIR) command. Once you press ENTER, the OS will execute the command, but it won't volunteer any information about what it did. You must use the DIR command to see that you have, in fact, created a new directory. Make sure that the prompt points to the directory in which you want to make the new subdirectory before you execute the MD command.

- To remove a directory, first point the prompt at the directory that contains the subdirectory you want to delete, and then execute the RD (or RMDIR) command. If you get no response, you probably did it right, but use the DIR command to be sure. The RD command will not delete a directory if it contains files or subdirectories; you must first empty that directory using the DEL (for files) or RD (for subdirectories) command. The RD command followed by the /S switch will delete the directory as well as all files and subdirectories.

Working with Files

- All files have four special values, or attributes, that determine how they will act in special situations: hidden, read-only, system, and archive. These attributes can be set through software. If a file is hidden, it will not be displayed when the DIR command is performed. A read-only file cannot be modified or deleted. The system attribute, which is used only for system files such as NTLDR and NTDETECT.COM, provides an easy identifier for these files. The archive attribute is used by backup software to identify files that have been changed since their last backup.

- ATTRIB.EXE is an external program that enables you to inspect and change file attributes. Type the **ATTRIB** command followed by the name of the file and press ENTER. In the resulting list of files, letter codes indicate each file's attributes, if any: *A* stands for archive, *R* means read-only, *H* is hidden, and *S* is system. The ATTRIB command can change a file's attributes. To add an attribute to a file, type the attribute letter preceded by a plus sign (+), and then the filename. To delete an attribute, use a minus sign (–). Multiple attributes can be added or removed in one command.

- Wildcards are two special characters, asterisk (*) and question mark (?), that can be used in place of all or part of a filename to make a command act on more than one file at a time. Wildcards work with all command-line commands that take filenames. The asterisk (*) wildcard replaces any part of a filename, before and/or after the period. The ? wildcard replaces any single character. Virtually every command that deals with files will take wildcards.

- Use the REN (or RENAME) command to rename files and folders. If the new name contains spaces, enclose it in quotation marks.

- To delete files, you use the DEL or ERASE command. DEL and ERASE are identical commands and can be used interchangeably. DEL will not erase directories. To delete a single file, type the **DEL** command followed by the name of the file. No confirmation will appear on the screen. To delete all the files in a directory, you can use the *.* (star-dot-star) wildcard. Upon receiving the DEL *.* command, Windows will respond with "Are you sure? (Y/N)," to which you respond with a *Y* or *N*. Pressing Y will erase every file in the directory. It pays to check twice before you delete, because the command line has no function equivalent to the Windows Recycle Bin that allows you to retrieve an accidentally deleted file; once a file has been erased, it can be recovered only by using a special recovery utility.

- The COPY and MOVE commands are used to copy and move files. The only difference between them is whether the original is left behind (COPY) or not (MOVE). Type **COPY** or **MOVE** and a space. Point the prompt to the directory containing the files to be copied or moved. Type the *name(s)* of the file(s) to be copied/moved (with or without wildcards) and a space. Type the *path* of the new location for the files. Press ENTER. The COPY/MOVE command not only lets you put a file in a new location, but it also lets you change the name of the file at the same time.

- Check for the common typo of substituting a semicolon for a colon, because the semicolon means "end of command" and therefore ignores both the semicolon and anything you type after it.

- XCOPY works similarly to COPY but has extra switches that give XCOPY the power to work with multiple directories. Because XCOPY works on directories, you don't have to use filenames as you would in COPY, although you can use filenames and wildcards. The /S switch tells XCOPY to copy all subdirectories except for empty ones. The /E switch tells it to copy empty subdirectories.

- Batch files are text files that contain a series of commands with one command per line. Batch files must end with the .BAT file extension. You can use the Edit program within the command line to create batch files or a text editor from the Windows GUI such as Notepad.

- The TYPE command displays the contents of a file on the screen. Don't use TYPE on binary files as the results are unpredictable.

- Every time you open a command prompt, Windows loads a number of settings by default. You can see all of these settings by running the SET command.

- When you type a command, Windows will try to run it as an internal command, like CD or DIR. If what you typed is not an internal command, such as EDIT or ATTRIB, Windows will check the folder that currently has the command-prompt focus. If the command is not found there, Windows will check all folders in the path for the command.

- Storing batch files in a folder included in Windows' path will ensure your batch files will run no matter where your command prompt is focused. Use the PATH command to see the current path. To add a folder to the Windows' path, type PATH followed by that folder.

Key Terms

8.3 naming system *(171)*
American Standard Code for
   Information Interchange
   (ASCII) *(172)*
ATTRIB.EXE *(182)*
attributes *(182)*
CD (CHDIR) command *(177)*
COPY command *(186)*

DEL (ERASE) command *(185)*
DIR command *(175)*
MD (MKDIR) command *(178)*
MOVE command *(186)*
path *(174)*
prompt *(168)*
RD (RMDIR) command *(179)*
read-only attribute *(182)*

REN (RENAME) command *(185)*
root directory *(174)*
Run dialog box *(170)*
switch *(175)*
syntax *(175)*
Unicode *(173)*
wildcard *(184)*
XCOPY command *(188)*

Key Term Quiz

Use the Key Terms list to complete the sentences that follow. Not all terms will be used.

1. The command-line interface tells you it's ready to receive commands by displaying a specific set of characters called a(n) _____.

2. Extra text typed after a command to modify its operation is called a(n) _____.

3. _____ was the first universal file format.

4. The _____ shows you the contents of the directory that currently has focus.

5. Each file's _____ determine how programs (like My Computer) treat the file in special situations.

6. The exact location of a file is called its _____.

7. _____ is an external program that enables you to inspect and change file attributes.

8. The asterisk is a special character called a(n) _____ that can be used in place of part of a filename when executing a DOS command.

9. The _____ enables you to rename a file.

10. To move a file from the root directory into a subfolder, use the _____.

Multiple-Choice Quiz

1. Which of the following shows a typical command prompt?
   A. C:\\
   B. C:/>
   C. C:\>
   D. C://

2. Which of the following is an illegal character in a Windows filename?
   A. * (asterisk)
   B. . (dot)
   C. – (dash)
   D. _ (underscore)

3. Which command pauses after displaying a screen's worth of directory contents?

   A. DIR P
   B. PDIR
   C. PD
   D. DIR /P

4. Which of the following commands will delete all the files in a directory?
   A. DEL *.*
   B. DEL ALL
   C. DEL ?.?
   D. DEL *.?

5. Which command enables you to change the focus of the command prompt to a different directory?
   A. DIR /N
   B. CDDIR

C. CD

D. DIR /C

6. Which Windows command will delete a directory as well as all its files and subdirectories?

A. DEL /F /S

B. DEL /ALL

C. KILL

D. RD /S

7. Which attribute keeps a file from being displayed when the DIR command is performed?

A. Hidden

B. Archive

C. Read-only

D. Protected

8. What command enables you to make a new directory in a Windows XP Professional system?

A. MF

B. MKFOL

C. MD

D. MAKEDIR

9. What is the name of the command-line text editor that comes with Windows?

A. Text

B. Edit

C. DOStxt

D. DOSedt

10. What commands can you type at the Run dialog box to access the command-line interface in Windows XP? (Select two.)

A. CMD

B. COMMAND

C. MSDOS

D. PROMPT

11. Joey wants to change the name of a file from START.BAT to HAMMER.BAT. Which of the following commands would accomplish this feat?

A. REN HAMMER.BAT START.BAT

B. REN START.BAT HAMMER.BAT

C. RENAME /S START.BAT HAMMER.BAT

D. RENAME /S HAMMER.BAT START.BAT

12. What are the rules for typing a command correctly called?

A. Protocol

B. Syntax

C. Legacy

D. Instruction set

13. What is the command to make MYFILE.TXT read-only?

A. ATTRIB MYFILE.TXT +R

B. ATTRIB MYFILE.TXT –R

C. READONLY MYFILE.TXT

D. MYFILE.TXT /READONLY

14. What is the maximum number of characters in a Windows 2000/XP filename?

A. 8

B. 255

C. 65,536

D. No limit

15. What is the command to quit the command-line interface?

A. EXIT

B. BYE

C. QUIT

D. STOP

■ Essay Quiz

1. You've been tasked to teach some newbie techs, whose only computer experience involves Windows, about the beauty and power of the command line. For their first lesson, write a short essay explaining how the command-line interface works, including the directory structure, filename limitations, and interaction with the command prompt.

2. You work the help desk at a college computing center. Some applications that the students must use are run from a command line. Write a memo for the help desk personnel explaining how to use the DIR, CD, MD, DEL, and RD commands, including any appropriate cautions.

3. Your coworker needs to remove the hidden attribute from a file called PAYROLL.XLS that is stored in the EMPLOYEE directory on the D: drive. Write an e-mail explaining how to open a command-line window, navigate to the file, verify its presence, and remove the hidden attribute.

4. You've been tasked to teach some newbie techs, whose only computer experience involves Windows, about the beauty and power of the command line. For their second lesson, write a short essay explaining how wildcards work.

5. Write a brief essay explaining in your own words how to use Mike's Five-Step COPY/MOVE process. Give an example.

Lab Projects

• Lab Project 10.1

For each of the following files, translate the location into a path you can type at a command prompt.

① A file named BEACH.JPG in the subdirectory PICTURES in the directory EZIBA on the primary floppy drive:

_____

② A file named BLACKDOG.WAV in the subdirectory LEDZEP in the subdirectory ROCK in the directory MUSIC on the C: drive:

_____

③ A file named WEAPON.PCX in the subdirectory BOBAFETT in the subdirectory

PLAYERS in the subdirectory BASEQ2 in the directory QUAKE2 on the D: drive:

_____

④ A file named AUTOEXEC.BAT in the root directory on a standard PC with a single hard drive:

_____

⑤ A file named MEYERS.DOC in the subdirectory CONTRACTS in the subdirectory LEGAL in the directory ACCOUNTS on a CD-ROM on a system with one hard drive, one CD-ROM drive, and one floppy drive:

_____

• Lab Project 10.2

To practice making/removing directories and copying/moving files, do the following:

① Open a command-line window and point to the root directory C:.

② Use the MD command to create a directory called WHALES. Use the CD command to point to the new directory. Use the MD command again to create a subdirectory of WHALES called MOBYDICK. Use the CD command to point to the new subdirectory.

③ Populate the MOBYDICK subdirectory with files by opening Notepad and creating a "dummy" file called AHAB.TXT. Save it in the MOBYDICK subdirectory.

④ Use the MOVE command to move the file AHAB.TXT to the WHALES directory. Use the DIR command to confirm that the move was successful. Use the COPY command to put a copy of AHAB.TXT back into the MOBYDICK subdirectory while leaving a copy in WHALES. Again use DIR to confirm the operation.

⑤ Use the RD command to delete the MOBYDICK subdirectory. Did it work? Why not? Use the RD command with the /S switch to solve the problem.

Windows Troubleshooting

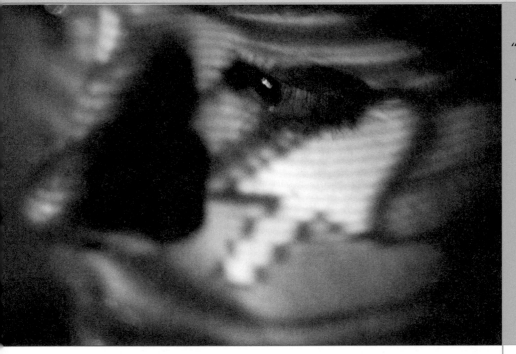

"To err is human, but to really foul things up requires a computer."

—FARMERS' ALMANAC

It's a fine line in the Windows world between installation, maintenance, and troubleshooting. Most troubleshooting is nothing more than a completion of the installation of a new piece of hardware or software that either failed or was not properly maintained. In the Essentials text you saw how to install and maintain Windows—along with a bit of very basic troubleshooting. This chapter picks up where the Essentials text left off, concentrating on the type of troubleshooting you need for a machine that was working properly earlier but suddenly stopped (rather than cases of incomplete installation or configuration, although there are a few exceptions).

In this chapter, you will learn how to

- **Troubleshoot Windows boot failures**
- **Troubleshoot GUI failures**
- **Use troubleshooting utilities**

Essentials Review

You'll find this chapter far more interesting if you are aware of Windows maintenance concepts covered in the A+ Essentials exam. Before beginning this chapter, make sure you can

- Explain service packs and patches and how they are different
- Manually update Windows
- Configure Windows for Automatic Updates and customize Windows Update as needed for individual systems
- Define the different types of user accounts (User, Power User, and Administrator) and briefly explain the differences in these accounts
- Create a new user and edit an existing user account in Windows
- Explain the differences in logon options between Windows 2000 and Windows XP
- Create a password reset disk in Windows XP
- Perform disk defragmentation in Windows
- Maintain the Registry manually
- Add and remove applications from a Windows system
- Add and remove a hardware component from a Windows system
- Perform optimization on a hardware component
- Create a restore point on a Windows XP system
- Explain the difference between Automated System Recovery and the Emergency Rescue Disk and identify situations when each would be used
- Install Recovery Console on a Windows system

IT Technician

■ Troubleshooting Windows

By now you should be familiar with the essential tools for troubleshooting and repairing Windows. You know about Disk Management, Device Manager, Event Viewer, and more. You've spent countless hours preparing systems for disaster with NTBackup and System Restore. While learning about the tools, you also learned how to use them. This section puts it all together and shows you a plan to deal with potential disasters for a Windows computer.

This section looks at Windows problems from the ground up. It starts with catastrophic failure—a PC that won't boot—and then discusses ways to get past that problem. The next section covers the causes and work-arounds when the Windows GUI fails to load. Once you can access the GUI, then the world of Windows diagnostic and troubleshooting tools that you've spent so much time learning about comes to your fingertips. First, however, you have to get there.

Failure to Boot

Windows boot errors take place in those short moments between the time the POST ends and the Loading Windows screen begins. For Windows to start loading the main operating system, the critical system files `NTLDR`, `NTDETECT.COM`, and `BOOT.INI` must reside in the root directory of the C: drive, and BOOT.INI must point to the Windows boot files. If any of these requirements isn't in place, the system won't get past this step. Here are some of the common errors you see at this point:

> No Boot Device Present

> NTLDR Bad or Missing

> Invalid BOOT.INI

Note that these text errors take place very early in the startup process. That's your big clue that you have a boot issue. If you get to the Windows splash screen and then lock up, that's a whole different game, so know the difference.

If you get one of the catastrophic error messages, you have a three-level process to get back up and running. You first should attempt to repair. If that fails, then attempt to restore from a backup copy of Windows. If restore is either not available or fails, then your only recourse is to rebuild. You will lose data at the restore and rebuild phases, so you definitely want to spend a lot of effort on the repair effort first!

Attempt to Repair Using Recovery Console

To begin troubleshooting one of these errors, boot from the installation CD-ROM and have Windows do a repair of an existing installation. Windows will prompt you if you want to use the `Recovery Console` (a text-based startup of Windows that gets you to a command prompt similar to the Windows command prompt) or the emergency repair process (ASR/ERD). Start with the Recovery Console.

If you followed the instructions earlier in the lesson, then you've installed the Recovery Console onto your system and have it as an option when you boot the system. If not, start it as described earlier using the Windows 2000 or XP installation CD-ROM. When you select the Recovery Console, you will see a message about NTDETECT, another one that the Recovery Console is starting up, and then you will be greeted with the following message and command prompt:

```
Microsoft Windows XP<TM> Recovery Console.
The Recovery Console provides system repair and recovery functionality.
Type Exit to quit the Recovery Console and restart the computer.

1: C:\WINDOWS
Which Windows XP installation would you like to log onto
<To cancel, press ENTER>?
```

The cursor is a small, white rectangle sitting to the right of the question mark on the last line. If you are not accustomed to working at the command prompt, this may be disorienting. If there is only one installation of Windows XP on your computer, type the number 1 at the prompt and press the ENTER key. If you press ENTER before typing in a valid selection, the Recovery Console will cancel and the computer will reboot. The only choice you can make in this example is 1. Having made that choice, the only change to the screen above is a new line:

```
Type the Administrator password:
```

This is also followed by the cursor. Enter the Administrator password for that computer and press ENTER. The password will not display on the screen; you will see asterisks in place of the password. The screen still shows everything that has happened so far, unless something has happened to cause an error message. It now looks like this:

```
Microsoft Windows XP<TM> Recovery Console.
The Recovery Console provides system repair and recovery functionality.
Type Exit to quit the Recovery Console and restart the computer.

1: C:\WINDOWS
Which Windows XP installation would you like to log onto
<To cancel, press ENTER>? 1
Type the Administrator password: ********
C:\Windows>
```

By now, you've caught on and know that there is a rectangular prompt immediately after the last line. Now what do you do? Use the Recovery Console commands, of course. Recovery Console uses many of the commands that worked in the Windows command-line interface that you explored in Chapter 10, as well as some uniquely its own. Table 11.1 lists the common Recovery Console commands.

The Recovery Console shines in the business of manually restoring registries, stopping problem services, rebuilding partitions (other than the system partition), and using the **EXPAND** command to extract copies of corrupted files from a CD-ROM or floppy disk.

Using the Recovery Console, you can reconfigure a service so that it starts with different settings, format drives on the hard disk, read and write on local FAT or NTFS volumes, and copy replacement files from a floppy or CD-ROM. The Recovery Console enables you to access the file system, and is still constrained by the file and folder security of NTFS, which makes it a more secure tool to use than some third-party solutions.

The Recovery Console is best at fixing three items: repairing the MBR, reinstalling the boot files, and rebuilding BOOT.INI. Let's look at each of these.

A bad boot sector usually shows up as a No Boot Device error. If it turns out that this isn't the problem, the Recovery Console command to fix it won't hurt anything. At the Recovery Console prompt, just type:

```
fixmbr
```

This fixes the master boot record.

Table 11.1	Common Recovery Console Commands
Command	**Description**
attrib	Changes attributes of selected file or folder
cd (or chdir)	Displays current directory or changes directories
chkdsk	Runs CheckDisk utility
cls	Clears screen
copy	Copies from removable media to system folders on hard disk. No wildcards
del (or delete)	Deletes service or folder
dir	Lists contents of selected directory on system partition only
disable	Disables service or driver
diskpart	Replaces FDISK—creates/deletes partitions
enable	Enables service or driver
expand	Extracts components from .CAB files
fixboot	Writes new partition boot sector on system partition
fixmbr	Writes new Master Boot Record for partition boot sector
format	Formats selected disk
listsvc	Lists all services on system
logon	Lets you choose which W2K installation to log on to if you have more than one
map	Displays current drive letter mappings
md (or mkdir)	Creates a directory
more (or type)	Displays contents of text file
rd (or rmdir)	Removes a directory
ren (or rename)	Renames a single file
systemroot	Makes current directory system root of drive you're logged into
type	Displays a text file

The second problem the Recovery Console is best at fixing is missing system files, usually indicated by the error NTLDR Bad or Missing. Odds are good that if NTDLR is missing, so are the rest of the system files. To fix this, get to the root directory (CD\—remember that from Chapter 10?) and type the following line:

```
copy d:\i386\ntldr
```

Then type this line:

```
copy d:\i386\ntdetect.com
```

This takes care of two of the big three and leads us to the last issue, rebuilding BOOT.INI. If the BOOT.INI file is gone or corrupted, run this command from the recovery console:

```
bootcfg /rebuild
```

The Recovery Console will then try to locate all installed copies of Windows and ask you if you want to add them to the new BOOT.INI file it's about to create. Say yes to the ones you want.

If all goes well with the Recovery Console, then do a thorough backup as soon as possible (just in case something else goes wrong). If the Recovery Console does not do the trick, the next step is to restore Windows XP.

Attempt to Restore

If you've been diligent about backing up, you can attempt to restore to an earlier, working copy of Windows. You have two basic choices, depending on your OS. In Windows 2000, you can try the ERD. Remember the **Emergency Repair Disk** contains critical boot files and partition information and is your main tool for fixing boot problems in Windows 2000, but it is not bootable. Windows XP limits you to the ASR.

If you elected to create an ERD in Windows 2000, you can attempt to restore your system with it. Boot your system to the Windows 2000 installation CD-ROM and select repair installation, but in this case opt for the ERD. Follow the steps outlined earlier in the chapter and you might have some success.

ASR can restore your system to a previously installed state, but you should use it as a last resort. You lose everything on the system that was installed or added after you created the ASR disk.

Rebuild

If faced with a full system rebuild, you have several options, depending on the particular system. You could simply reboot to the Windows CD-ROM and install right on top of the existing system, but that's usually not the optimal solution. To avoid losing anything important, you'd be better off swapping the C: drive for a blank hard drive and installing a clean version of Windows.

Most OEM systems come with a misleadingly-named *Recover CD* or *recovery partition*. The Recover CD is a CD-ROM that you boot to and run. The recovery partition is a hidden partition on the hard drive that you activate at boot by holding down a key combination specific to the manufacturer of that system. (See the motherboard manual or users' guide for the key combination and other details.) Both "recover" options do the same thing—restore your computer to the factory-installed state. If you run one of these tools, you will wipe everything off your system—all personal files, folders, and programs will go away! Before running either tool, make sure all important files and folders are backed up on an optical disc or spare hard drive.

To use the Windows XP System Restore, you need to be able to get into Windows. "Restore" in the context used here means to give you an option to get into Windows.

Failure to Load the GUI

Assuming that Windows gets past the boot part of the startup, it will then begin to load the real Windows OS. You will see the Windows startup image on the screen (Figure 11.1), hiding everything until Windows loads the Desktop.

Several issues can cause Windows to hang during the GUI-loading phase, such as buggy device drivers or Registry problems. Even autoloading programs can cause the GUI to hang on load. The first step in troubleshooting these issues is to use one of the Advanced Startup options (covered later in the chapter) to try to get past the hang spot and into Windows.

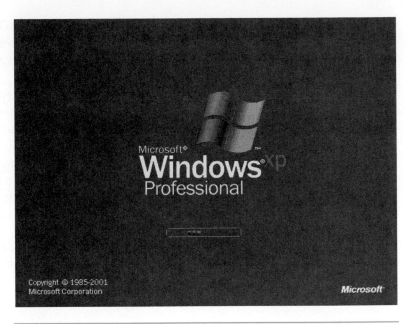

Device Drivers

Device driver problems that stop Windows GUI from loading look pretty scary. Figure 11.2 shows the infamous Windows *Stop error,* better known as the **Blue Screen of Death (BSoD)** . The BSoD only appears when something causes an error from which Windows cannot recover. The BSoD is not limited to device driver problems, but device drivers are one of the reasons you'll see the BSoD.

• **Figure 11.1**   GUI Time!

```
A problem has been detected and windows has been shut down to prevent damage
to your computer.

NO_MORE_IRP_STACK_LOCATIONS

If this is the first time you've seen this Stop error screen,
restart your computer. If this screen appears again, follow
these steps:

Check to make sure that any new hardware or software is properly installed.
If this is a new installation, ask your hardware or software manufacturer
for any windows updates you might need.

If problems continue, disable or remove any newly installed hardware
or software. Disable BIOS memory options such as caching or shadowing.
If you need to use Safe Mode to remove or disable components, restart
your computer, press F8 to select Advanced Startup Options, and then
select Safe Mode.

Technical information:

*** STOP: 0x00000035 (0x00000000,0xF7E562B2,0x00000008,0xC00000000)


***    wdmaud.sys - Address F7E562B2 base at F7E56000, DateStamp 36B047A5
```

• **Figure 11.2**   BSoD

Whenever you get a BSoD, take a moment and read what it says. Windows BSoDs tell you the name of the file that caused the problem and usually suggest a recommended action. Once in a while these are helpful—but not often.

BSoD problems due to device drivers almost always take place immediately after you've installed a new device and rebooted. Take out the device and reboot. If Windows loads properly, head over to the manufacturer's Web site. A new device producing this type of problem is a serious issue that should have been caught before the device was released. In many cases, the manufacturer will have updated drivers available for download or will recommend a replacement device.

The second indication of a device problem that shows up during the GUI part of startup is a freeze-up: the Windows startup screen just stays there and you never get a chance to log on. If this happens, try one of the Advanced Startup Options, covered in the upcoming section.

Registry

Your Registry files load every time the computer boots. Windows does a pretty good job of protecting your Registry files from corruption, but from time to time something may slip by Windows and it will attempt to load a bad Registry. These errors may show up as BSoDs that say "Registry File Failure" or text errors that say "Windows could not start." Whatever the case, you need to restore a good Registry copy. The best way to do this is the Last Known Good Configuration boot option (see the upcoming section). If that fails, then you can restore an earlier version of the Registry through the Recovery Console.

Boot to the Windows installation CD-ROM, select the repair installation to get to the Recovery Console, and type these commands to restore a Registry. Notice I didn't say "your" Registry in the previous sentence. Your Registry is corrupted and gone, so you need to rebuild.

```
delete c:\windows\system32\config\system
delete c:\windows\system32\config\software
delete c:\windows\system32\config\sam
delete c:\windows\system32\config\security
delete c:\windows\system32\config\default

copy c:\windows\repair\system c:\windows\system32\config\system
copy c:\windows\repair\software c:\windows\system32\config\software
copy c:\windows\repair\sam c:\windows\system32\config\sam
copy c:\windows\repair\security c:\windows\system32\config\security
copy c:\windows\repair\default c:\windows\system32\config\default
```

Advanced Startup Options

Windows 9x had an option for Step-by-step confirmation, but that is not a choice in Windows 2000/XP. Look for it as a wrong answer on the exams!

If Windows fails to start up, use the Windows **Advanced Startup Options menu** to discover the cause. To get to this menu, restart the computer and press F8 after the POST messages, but before the Windows logo screen appears. Windows 2000 and Windows XP have similar menus. Central to these advanced options are Safe Mode and Last Known Good Configuration.

There are several differences between the two operating systems in this menu. First, the Windows 2000 option called Boot Normally is called Start Windows Normally in Windows XP. In addition, Windows XP has options not available in Windows 2000: *Disable automatic restart on system failure* and *Reboot*. A Windows system with multiple operating systems might also have the Return to OS Choices menu. Here's a rundown of the menu options.

Safe Mode   `Safe Mode` (Figure 11.3) starts up Windows but loads only very basic, non–vendor-specific drivers for mouse, VGA monitor, keyboard, mass storage, and system services. Some devices, such as your USB mouse, may not work!

Once in Safe Mode, you can use tools like Device Manager to locate and correct the source of the problem. When you use Device Manager in Safe Mode, you can access the properties for all the devices, even those that are not working in Safe Mode. The status displayed for the device is the status for a normal startup. Even the network card will show as enabled. You can disable any suspect device or perform other tasks, such as removing or updating drivers. If a problem with a device driver is preventing the operating system from starting normally, check the Device Manager for yellow question mark warning icons that indicate an unknown device.

● **Figure 11.3**   Safe Mode

Safe Mode with Networking   This mode is identical to plain Safe Mode except that you get network support. I use this mode to test for a problem with network drivers. If Windows won't start up normally, but does start up in Safe Mode, I then reboot into Safe Mode with Networking. If it fails to start up with Networking, then the problem is a network driver. I reboot back to Safe Mode, open Device Manager, and start disabling network components, beginning with the network adapter.

Safe Mode with Command Prompt   When you start Windows in this mode, after you log on, rather than loading the GUI desktop, it loads the command prompt (CMD.EXE) as the shell to the operating system, as shown in Figure 11.4. This is a handy option to remember if the desktop does not display at all, which, after you have eliminated video drivers, can be caused by the corruption of the EXPLORER.EXE program. From the command prompt, you can delete the corrupted version of EXPLORER.EXE and copy in an undamaged version. This requires knowing the command-line commands for navigating the directory structure, as well as knowing the location of the file that you are replacing. Although Explorer is not loaded, you can load other GUI tools that don't depend on Explorer. All you have to do is enter the correct command. For instance, to load Event Viewer, type **eventvwr.msc** at the command line and press ENTER.

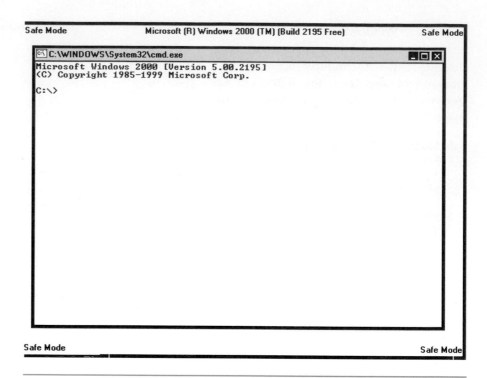

Safe Mode Microsoft (R) Windows 2000 (TM) (Build 2195 Free) Safe Mode

Safe Mode Safe Mode

• **Figure 11.4**   Safe Mode with command prompt

Enable Boot Logging   This option starts Windows normally and creates a log file of the drivers as they load into memory. The file is named Ntbtlog.txt and is saved in the %SystemRoot% folder. If the startup failed because of a bad driver, the last entry in this file may be the driver the OS was initializing when it failed.

Reboot and go into the Recovery Console. Use the Recovery Console tools to read the boot log (**type ntbtlog.txt**) and disable or enable problematic devices or services.

Enable VGA Mode   Enable VGA Mode starts Windows normally but only loads a default VGA driver. If this mode works, it may mean that you have a bad driver, or it may mean that you are using the correct video driver, but it is configured incorrectly (perhaps with the wrong refresh rate and/or resolution). Whereas Safe Mode loads a generic VGA driver, this mode loads the driver Windows is configured to use, but starts it up in standard VGA mode rather than using the settings for which it is configured. After successfully starting in this mode, open the Display Properties and change the settings.

Last Known Good Configuration   When Windows' startup fails immediately after installing a new driver, but before you have logged on again, you may want to try the  option. This can be a rather fickle and limited tool, but it never hurts to try it.

Directory Services Restore Mode (Does Not Apply to Professional)   The title says it all here—this option only applies to Active Directory domain controllers, and Windows 2000 Professional and Windows XP can never be domain controllers. I have no idea why Microsoft includes this option. If you choose it, you simply boot into Safe Mode.

Debugging Mode If you select this choice, Windows 2000/XP starts in kernel debug mode. It's a super-techie thing to do, and I doubt that even über techs do debug mode anymore. To do this, you have to connect the computer you are debugging to another computer via a serial connection, and as Windows starts up, a debug of the kernel is sent to the second computer, which must also be running a debugger program. I remember running debug for an early version of Windows 2000. My coworkers and I did it back then simply because we were studying for the MCSE exams and expected to be tested on it! We all decided that it was an experience that didn't need to be repeated.

Disable Automatic Restart on System Failure

Sometimes a BSoD will appear at startup, causing your computer to spontaneously reboot. That's all well and good, but if it happens too quickly, you might not be able to read the BSoD to see what caused the problem. Selecting *Disable automatic restart on system failure* from the Advanced Startup Options menu stops the computer from rebooting on Stop errors. This gives you the opportunity to write down the error and hopefully find a fix.

Start Windows Normally This choice will simply start Windows normally, without rebooting. You already rebooted to get to this menu. Select this if you changed your mind about using any of the other exotic choices.

Reboot This choice will actually do a soft reboot of the computer.

Return to OS Choices Menu On computers with multiple operating systems, you get an OS Choices menu to select which OS to load. If you load Windows XP and press F8 to get the Advanced Startup Options menu, you'll see this option. This choice will return you to the OS Choices menu, from which you can select the operating system to load.

Troubleshooting Tools in the GUI

Once you're able to load into Windows, whether through Safe Mode or one of the other options, the whole gamut of Windows tools are available for you. If a bad device driver caused the startup problems, for example, you can open Device Manager and begin troubleshooting just as you've learned in previous chapters. If you suspect some service or Registry issue caused the problem, head on over to Event Viewer and see what sort of logon events have happened recently.

Event Viewer might reveal problems with applications failing to load, a big cause of Windows loading problems (Figure 11.5). It might also reveal problems with services failing to start. Finally, Windows might run into problems loading DLLs. You can troubleshoot these issues individually or you can use System Restore in Windows XP to load a restore point that predates the bugginess.

Chapter 18, "Computer Security," goes into a lot more detail on using Event Viewer, especially *auditing*, a way to troubleshoot a buggy system.

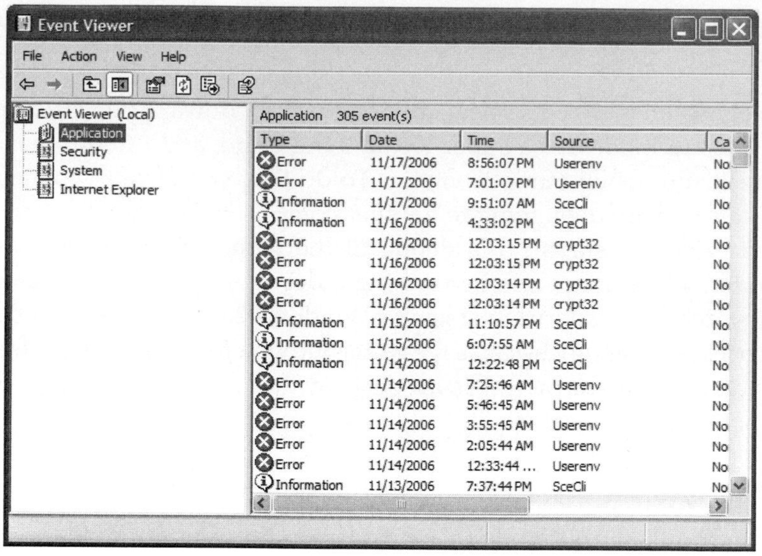

Figure 11.5 Event Viewer showing some serious application errors!

Windows 2000 Professional does *not* have the System Configuration Utility.

Autoloading Programs

Windows loves to autoload programs so they start at boot. Most of the time, this is an incredibly handy option, used by every Windows PC in existence. The problem with Autoloading programs is when one of them starts behaving badly—you need to shut off that program!

There are at least five different locations in folders, files, and the Registry that Windows accesses to autoload programs. To help you, Windows XP includes the handy **System Configuration Utility (MSCONFIG.EXE)**, a one-stop spot to see and maintain every program (and service) that autoloads at startup (Figure 11.6).

The System Configuration Utility enables you to keep individual programs and services from autoloading, but it does not actually remove the programs/services. If you want to completely delete a program, you'll need to find the uninstall or Add/Remove Program option. If the program doesn't have either of these, you'll need a third-party tool like EasyCleaner to delete the program.

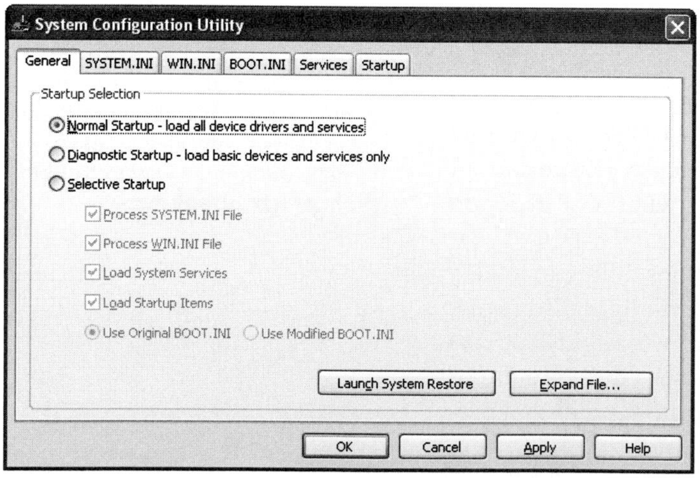

Services

Windows loads a number of services as it starts. If any critical service fails to load, Windows will tell you at this point with an error message. The important word here is *critical*. Windows will not report *all* service failures at this point. If a service that is less than critical in Windows' eyes doesn't start, Windows usually waits until you actually try to use a program that needs that service before it prompts you with an error message (Figure 11.7).

Figure 11.6 MSCONFIG

To work with your system's services, go to the Control Panel | Administrative Tools | Services and verify that the service you need is running. If not, turn it on. Also notice that each service has a Startup Type—Automatic, Manual, or Disabled—that defines when it starts. It's very common to find that a service has been set to Manual when it needs to be set to Automatic so that it starts when Windows boots (Figure 11.8).

System Files

Windows lives on dynamic link library (DLL) files. Almost every program used by Windows—and certainly all of the important ones—call to DLL files to do most of the heavy lifting that makes Windows work. Windows protects all of the critical DLL files very carefully, but once in a while you may get an error saying Windows can't load a particular DLL. Although rare, the core system files that make up Windows itself may become corrupted, preventing Windows from starting properly. You usually see something like "Error loading XXXX.DLL," or sometimes a program you need simply won't start when you double-click on its icon. In these cases, the tool you need is the System File Checker. The System File Checker is a command prompt program (SFC.EXE) that is used to check a number of critical files, including the ever-important DLL cache. SFC takes a number of switches, but by far the most important is /scannow. Go to a command prompt and type the following to start the program:

```
SFC /scannow
```

SFC will automatically check all critical files and replace any it sees as corrupted. During this process, it may ask for the Windows installation CD-ROM, so keep it handy!

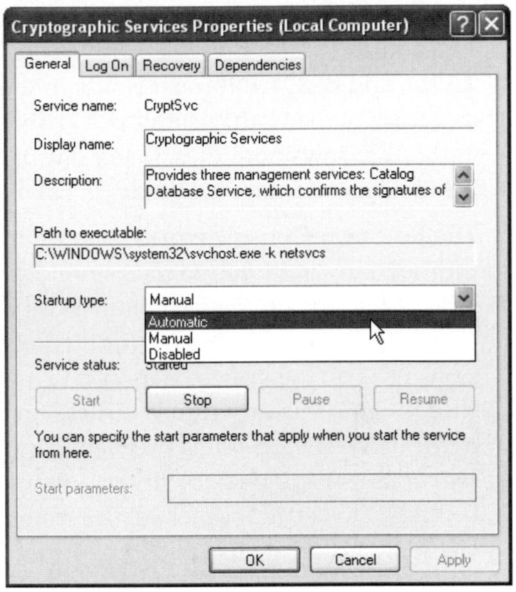

System Restore

Windows XP systems enable you to recover from a bad device or application installation by using System Restore to load a restore point. Follow the process explained earlier in the chapter. System Restore is the final step in recovering from a major Windows meltdown.

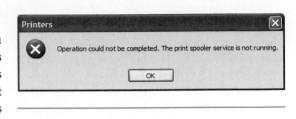

● **Figure 11.7**   Service error

● **Figure 11.8**   Autostarting a service

Chapter 11 Review

■ Chapter Summary

After reading this chapter and completing the exercises, you should understand the following about troubleshooting Windows 2000/XP.

Troubleshooting Windows

■ The critical system files NTLDR, NTDETECT .COM, and BOOT.INI must reside in the root directory of the C: drive, and BOOT.INI must point to the Windows boot files. If any one of these files is missing or damaged, Windows will not start.

■ The Recovery Console works as a command-line utility. Many of its commands should be familiar to DOS users, but some new commands have also been added. Because the file for the Recovery Console is on the system partition in a folder called CMDCONS, this program is useless for system partition crashes, but it is excellent for restoring registries, stopping problem services, or using EXPAND to extract copies of files from the CD-ROM. You can also use it to format hard drives and read and write on local FAT or NTFS volumes.

■ The four items most likely to show up as problems during the GUI portion of startup are device drivers, the Registry, services, and system files. Any one of these can cause a Windows Stop error, more commonly known as the Blue Screen of Death. If a driver is the problem, remove the problem driver and install a new version from the device manufacturer's Web site.

■ You can restore the Registry by choosing the Last Known Good Configuration boot option or use the ASR to return to a restore point you made. You may also boot into Recovery Console, delete the corrupt Registry files, and copy backups from the Repair directory.

■ Use Control Panel | Administrative Tools | Services to manage your system's services. Common problems are caused by a service that needs to start automatically, but is set to start manually.

■ Use the System File Checker to verify important system files and DLLs. At a command prompt,

type **SFC /SCANNOW** to have the System File Checker automatically check all critical files and replace any it sees as corrupt. Be sure to have your Windows CD handy when you do this.

■ If Windows will not start, use the Advanced Startup Options menu that is available when you press F8 after POST and before the Windows logo screen appears. You must log on as Administrator and enter your password. Both OSs offer similar menus, but may use different terminology such as "Boot Normally" with Windows 2000 and "Start Windows Normally" with Windows XP. XP also includes two extra options: *Reboot* and *Return to OS Choices Menu*. The two most commonly used options are Safe Mode and Last Known Good Configuration.

■ Safe Mode starts with only basic, non–vendor-specific drivers. You can then use the Device Manager to locate the source of the problem. Look for warning icons such as a yellow question mark indicating an unknown device or a yellow exclamation mark indicating a conflict with an existing device. If you have a problem with a network driver, use the Safe Mode with Networking option.

■ Another option is Enable Boot Logging, which creates a log file of drivers as they load into memory. If startup fails, the last entry in the file may be a bad driver. If the Enable VGA Mode works, you were using the wrong video driver or had it configured for the wrong refresh rate or resolution.

■ Debugging Mode starts Windows 2000/XP in kernel debug mode and requires a serial connection with another computer that is running a debugger program. This is a high-end procedure that you'll probably never do.

■ The System Configuration Utility is useful in managing programs and services that are set to run at startup. You can disable items you suspect are troublesome, reboot, and see if the problem has gone away.

Key Terms

Advanced Startup Options menu *(210)*

Blue Screen of Death (BSoD) *(209)*

BOOT.INI *(205)*

Emergency Repair Disk (ERD) *(208)*

EXPAND *(206)*

Last Known Good Configuration *(212)*

NTDETECT.COM *(205)*

NTLDR *(205)*

Recovery Console *(205)*

Safe Mode *(211)*

System Configuration Utility (MSCONFIG.EXE) *(214)*

Key Term Quiz

Use the Key Terms list to complete the sentences that follow. Not all terms will be used.

1. If Windows fails but you have *not* logged on, you can select _____ from the Advanced Startup Options to restore the computer to the way it was the last time a user logged on.

2. If Windows won't boot because of a corrupt Registry or a problem service, your best bet is to use the _____ to attempt repairs.

3. The _____ advanced startup option enables you to boot with only basic drivers and services so you can then use Device Manager for troubleshooting.

4. Use the _____ command while in Recovery Console to extract components from .CAB files.

5. If Windows encounters an error from which it cannot recover, it displays the _____.

6. The _____ enables you to display and configure every program and service that autoloads at startup.

7. If Windows fails to boot normally, you can press F8 after the POST message to access the _____.

8. In Windows 2000, you can use the non-bootable _____ in conjunction with the installation CD to repair a damaged system.

9. The critical system files, _____, _____, and _____ must reside at the root of the C: drive.

10. If you are able to boot into Windows, you can use _____ to roll back the system to a previous point in time.

Multiple-Choice Quiz

1. You suspect your system is failing to boot because of a corrupt master boot record. Which utility is the best to fix this?

    A. Automated System Restore

    B. Device Manager

    C. System Restore

    D. Recovery Console

2. What command should you run to check and fix corrupt system files, DLLs, and other critical files?

    A. CMDCONS /FIXBOOT

    B. SFC /SCANNOW

    C. CHKDSK /R

    D. DEFRAG –A

3. You get a tech call from a distraught Windows XP user who can't get into Windows. He says he has a Recover CD from the manufacturer and plans to run it. What would you suggest?

    A. Run the Recover CD to restore the system.

    B. Run the Recover CD to return the system to the factory-installed state.

    C. Try to get the computer to boot into Safe Mode.

    D. Reinstall Windows using a Windows XP disc.

4. What are the main operating system files required for a successful boot of Windows 2000/XP?

    A. NTLDR.COM, NTDETECT, BOOT.INI

    B. NTKERN.OS, COMMAND.COM, IO.SYS

C. NTLDR, NTDETECT.COM, BOOT.INI

D. COMMAND.COM, IO.SYS, MSDOS.SYS

5. Which statement is true about starting the Recovery Console?

A. It can be installed as an advanced startup option, or started from the installation CD.

B. It must be run from the installation CD.

C. It can be run from a floppy.

D. It is automatically started after booting from the Emergency Repair Disk.

6. Which of the following is *not* possible with Recovery Console?

A. Copy files from removable media to system folders to replace corrupt system files

B. Run the CheckDisk utility to repair a corrupt hard drive

C. Enable and disable services for the next normal startup

D. Retrieve a forgotten administrative password

7. What are the proper steps for repairing a Windows XP system with an Emergency Repair Disk?

A. Boot from the ERD and follow the on-screen prompts.

B. Boot from the installation CD, select the repair installation option, select ERD, and follow the on-screen prompts.

C. Boot from the installation CD, press F2 to begin Automated System Recovery, select the ERD option, and follow the on-screen prompts.

D. You cannot use an ERD with Windows XP.

8. Your computer freezes on the Windows startup screen during boot. What is the most likely cause of the problem?

A. Corrupt boot sector

B. Problem with a hardware device

C. Corrupt or missing NTLDR

D. Error in BOOT.INI

9. What is the best way to replace a corrupted Registry with an earlier, good version?

A. Try the Last Known Good Configuration boot option.

B. Start REGEDIT and select Restore from the File menu.

C. Use the Automated System Recovery option.

D. Boot from the installation CD and perform an upgrade install.

10. Which advanced startup option boots the computer with generic drivers and basic services?

A. Last Known Good Configuration

B. Enable VGA Mode

C. Safe Mode

D. Debugging Mode

11. After changing your display settings, the screen becomes unreadable and you are no longer able to navigate the desktop. Which advanced startup option should you use to reset your display options?

A. Last Known Good Configuration

B. Enable VGA Mode

C. Safe Mode

D. Debugging Mode

12. Dianne wants to disable several programs that start automatically when her Windows XP computer boots. What is the best way for her to manage her startup programs?

A. Use Device Manager to disable the unwanted programs

B. Use the Application tab in the Task Manager to disable the unwanted programs

C. Use the System Configuration Utility (MSCONFIG.EXE) to disable the unwanted programs

D. Use the System File Checker (SFC.EXE) to disable the unwanted programs

13. Which utility is useful for inspecting logs that track system events, such as applications failing to load or services failing to start?

A. Event Viewer

B. Logs and Alerts

C. System Monitor

D. Task Manager

14. Kelvin wants to change a service's startup type from Automatic to Manual. Where should he go to do this within the Windows GUI?

A. My Computer | Administrative Tools | Services

B. Control Panel | Administrative Tools | Services

C. Control Panel | Services

D. Start | Programs | Accessories | System Tools | Services

15. Donna's computer is stuck in a reboot loop. It starts, displays a BSoD, and then reboots. To make matters worse, the computer reboots so quickly there is no time to read the BSoD. What should Donna do?

A. Press the PAUSE/BREAK key the instant the BSoD displays to pause the boot process so she can read the BSoD

B. Press F8 and choose the *Disable automatic restart on system failure* option

C. Press CTRL-ALT-DEL to reboot normally

D. Press F2 to begin Automated System Recovery

Essay Quiz

1. A fellow tech sends a message crying for help. He has a Windows 2000 system that has crashed hard, and he's never worked with 2000 before. He's afraid to try to boot the machine up until he hears back from you. He found a copy of the OS disc and a hand-labeled diskette called Emergency Repair Disk. What advice do you give him to try to get the system back up and running quickly?

2. Sonya suspects a corrupt Registry and wishes to restore a good copy. Briefly explain the tools she might use to recover an earlier, good copy of the Registry.

Lab Projects

• Lab Project 11.1

After reading this chapter, you know how critical it is to keep patches, updates, and service packs current to help a computer stay healthy and to protect it from viruses that may exploit flaws in the operating system. Now's a good time to make sure your operating system is current. Run the Windows Update utility and decide which updates to install. (Now, don't you feel better about your system?)

Installing and Troubleshooting Video

*"Traveling in a light beam
laser rays and purple skies.
In a computer fairyland
it is a dream you bring to life."*

—TRANSX, "LIVING ON VIDEO"

In this chapter, you will learn how to

- **Select the right type of video card**
- **Install and configure video cards and monitors**
- **Troubleshoot video problems**

Few devices on your PC are subject to more updating, customizing, and tweaking than your video display. New video cards seem to come out almost weekly, and drivers are updated just as fast. On top of that, you have a thousand opinions as to optimal resolution, correct graphics processor, and even the number of monitors you use for a single system. This chapter helps you apply your knowledge of video cards and monitors gained from the Essentials course into real-world practice.

Essentials Review

You'll find this chapter far more interesting if you are aware of video concepts covered in the A+ Essentials exam. Before beginning this chapter, make sure you can

- Explain the concepts of refresh rate, bandwidth, and pixels
- Differentiate between LCD and CRT technologies and describe the major components of each type of monitor technology
- Define the types of connectors used between your video card and your monitor and identify situations where one might be used over another
- Define the common video modes
- Recognize the different types of motherboard connections used by video cards, including older technologies, and explain the benefit of different connections over others
- Explain the concepts of hyperthreading and multi-core CPUs

IT Technician

■ Choosing a Video Card

Video card discussion, at least among techs, almost always revolves around the graphics processor they use and the amount of RAM onboard. A typical video card might be called an ATI Radeon X1950 XTX 512 MB, so let's break that down. ATI is the manufacturer, Radeon X1950 XTX is the model of the card as well as the graphics processor, and 512 MB is the amount of video RAM.

Graphics Processor

The graphics processor handles the heavy lifting of taking commands from the CPU and translating them into coordinates and color information that the monitor understands and displays.

Many companies make the hundreds of different video cards on the market, but only two companies produce the vast majority of graphics processors found on video cards: NVIDIA and ATI. NVIDIA and ATI make and sell graphics processors to third-party manufacturers who then design, build, and sell video cards under their own branding. ATI also makes and sells its own line of cards. Figure 12.1 shows an NVIDIA GeForce 7900 GT KO on a board made by EVGA.

Your choice of graphics processor is your single most important decision in buying a video card. Low-end graphics processors will usually work fine for the run-of-the-mill user who wants to write letters or run

● **Figure 12.1**　NVIDIA GeForce 7900 GT KO

a Web browser. High-end graphics processors are designed to support the beautiful 3-D games that are so popular today.

NVIDIA and ATI are extremely competitive, and both companies introduce multiple models of graphics processors (and therefore new models of cards) every year. However, unless you're using the Vista Aero glass desktop, all of these extra features you see in video cards are really only for the true driving force in video cards: 3-D gaming. Your PC is capable of providing you with hours of incredible entertainment via a huge number of popular games that immerse you in 3-D environments full of light, shadows, explosions, and other amazing effects that create a fun and beautiful gaming experience.

These 3-D games have special needs to do all this amazing stuff. One need is textures. A *texture* is a small picture that is tiled over and over again on walls, floors, and other surfaces to create the 3-D world. Take a look at the wall in Figure 12.2. It's made up of only three textures that are repeated over and over again on the surface.

Games also use hundreds of lighting effects such as transparency (water), shadows, reflection, and bump mapping—the process of laying multiple textures on the same spot to give a more textured (bumpy) look to the surface. These games are where the higher-quality graphics processors really shine. Learn more about 3-D issues in more depth in the "3-D Graphics" section later in this chapter.

Choosing a graphics processor is a challenge because the video industry is constantly coming out with new models. One of the best guides is price. The best (and newest) graphics cards usually cost around US$400–500. The cheapest cards cost around $50. I usually split the difference and go for a card priced around $180 to $200—such a card will have most of the features you want without breaking your bank account.

If you use your computer only for 2-D programs (most office applications such as word processors, e-mail, and Web browsers are 2-D), then almost all of the features of the more advanced graphics cards will do you little good. If you're not a gamer, a cheap, low-end video card will more than meet your needs.

● **Figure 12.2** Wall of textures

Video Memory

Video memory is crucial to the operation of a PC. It is probably the hardest-working set of electronics on the PC. Video RAM constantly updates to reflect every change that takes place on the screen. Video memory can prove to be a serious bottleneck when working with heavy-duty applications (like games) in three ways: data throughput speed, access speed, and simple capacity.

Manufacturers have overcome these bottlenecks in three ways: upping the width of the bus between the video RAM and video processor; using specialized, super-fast RAM; and adding more and more total RAM.

First, manufacturers reorganized the video display memory on cards from the typical 32-bit-wide structure to 64, 128, or even 256 bits wide. This would not be of much benefit because the system bus is limited to 32 or 64 bits—if it weren't for the fact that video display cards are really coprocessor boards. Most of the graphics rendering and processing is handled on the card by the video processor chip rather than by the CPU. The main system simply provides the input data to the processor on the video card. By making the memory bus on the video card as much as eight times wider than the

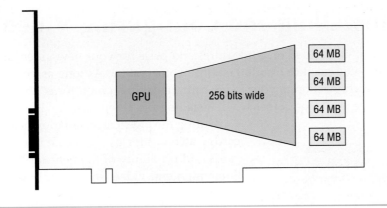

● **Figure 12.3**   Wide path between video processor and video RAM

standard 32-bit pathway (256 bits), data can be manipulated and then sent to the monitor much more quickly (Figure 12.3).

Specialized types of video RAM have been developed for graphics cards, and many offer substantial improvements in video speeds. The single most important feature that separates DRAM from video RAM is that video RAM can read and write data at the same time. Table 12.1 shows a list of common video memory technologies used yesterday and today—make sure you know these for the exams!

Finally, many advanced 3-D video cards come with huge amounts of video RAM. It's very common to see cards with 64, 128, 256, or even 512 MB of RAM! Why so much? Even with PCI Express, accessing data in system RAM always takes a lot longer than accessing data stored in local RAM on the video card. The huge amount of video RAM enables game developers to optimize their games and store more essential data on the local video RAM.

Table 12.1	Video RAM Technologies	
Acronym	**Name**	**Purpose**
VRAM	Video RAM	The original graphics RAM
WRAM	Window RAM	Designed to replace VRAM; never caught on
SGRAM	Synchronous Graphics RAM	A version of SDRAM with features to speed up access for graphics
DDR SDRAM	Double Data Rate Synchronous DRAM	Used on budget graphics cards and very common on laptop video cards
DDR2 SDRAM	Double Data Rate version 2, Synchronous DRAM	Popular on video cards until GDDR3; lower voltage than DDR memory
GDDR3 SDRAM	Graphics Double Data Rate, version 3	Similar to DDR2 but runs at faster speeds; different cooling requirements
GDDR4 SDRAM	Graphics Double Data Rate, version 4	Upgrade of GDDR3; faster clock

■ Installing and Configuring Video

Once you've decided on the features and price for your new video card or monitor, you need to install them into your system. As long as you've got the right connection to your video card, installing a monitor is straightforward. The challenge comes when installing the video card.

During the physical installation of a video card, watch out for two possible issues: long cards and proximity of the nearest PCI card. Some high-end video cards simply won't fit in certain cases or block access to needed motherboard connectors such as the IDE sockets. There's no clean fix for such a problem—you simply have to change at least one of the components (video card, motherboard, or case). Because high-end video cards run very hot, you don't want them sitting right next to another card; make sure the fan on the video card has plenty of ventilation space. A good practice is to leave the slot next to the video card empty to allow better airflow (Figure 12.4).

Once you've properly installed the video card and connected it to the monitor, you've conquered half the territory for making the video process work properly. You're ready to tackle the drivers and tweak the operating system, so let's go!

● **Figure 12.4**   Installing a video card

Try This!

Install a Video Card

You know how to install an expansion card from your reading in earlier chapters. Installing a video card is pretty much the same, so try this!

1. Refer back to Chapter 5, "Installing Internal Devices," for steps on installing a new card.

2. Plug the monitor cable into the video card port on the back of the PC and power up the system. If your PC seems dead after you install a video card, or if the screen is blank but you hear fans whirring and the internal speaker sounding off *long-short-short-short*, your video card likely did not get properly seated. Unplug the PC and try again.

Software

Configuring your video software is usually a two-step process. First you need to load drivers for the video card. Then you need to open the Control Panel and go to the Display applet to make your adjustments. Let's explore how to make the video card and monitor work in Windows.

Drivers

Just like any other piece of hardware, your video card needs a driver to function. Video card drivers install pretty much the same way as all of the other drivers we've discussed thus far: either the driver is already built into Windows or you must use the installation CD that comes with the video card.

Video card makers are constantly updating their drivers. Odds are good that any video card more than a few months old will have at least one driver update. If possible, check the manufacturer's Web site and use the driver located there if there is one. If the Web site doesn't offer a driver, then it's usually best to use the installation CD. Always avoid using the built-in Windows driver as it tends to be the most dated.

We'll explore driver issues in more detail after we discuss the Display applet. Like so many things about video, you can't really fully understand one topic without understanding at least one other!

Using the Display Applet

With the driver installed, you're ready to configure your display settings. The Display applet on the Control Panel is your next stop. The **Display applet** provides a convenient, central location for all of your display settings, including resolution, refresh rate, driver information, and color depth.

The default Display applet window in Windows XP, called the Display Properties dialog box (Figure 12.5), has five tabs: Themes, Desktop, Screen Saver, Appearance, and Settings. Earlier versions of Windows have a subset of these tabs. The first four tabs have options that enable you to change the look and feel of Windows and set up a screen saver; the fifth tab is where you make adjustments that relate directly to your monitor and video card. I'll walk you through each tab.

Making the Screen Pretty

Three tabs in the display applet have the job of adjusting the appearance of the screen: Themes, Desktop, and Appearance. Windows themes are preset configurations of the look and feel of the entire Windows environment. The Desktop tab (Figure 12.6) defines the background color or image. It also includes the handy Customize Desktop button that enables you to define the icons as well as any Web pages you want to appear on the desktop.

The last of the tabs for the look and feel of the desktop is the Appearance tab. Think of the Appearance tab as the way to fine-tune the theme to your liking. The main screen gives only a few options—the real power is when you click the Advanced button (Figure 12.7). Using this dialog box, you may adjust almost everything about the desktop including the types of fonts and colors of every part of a window.

Screen Saver Tab

At first glance the Screen Saver tab seems to do nothing but set the Windows screensaver—no big deal, just about everyone has set a screensaver. But there's another button on the Screen Saver tab that gets you to one of the most important settings of your system—power management. Click on the Power button to get to the Power Options Properties dialog box (Figure 12.8).

These tabs define all of the power management of the system. Power management is a fairly involved process, so we'll save the

● **Figure 12.5**   Display Properties dialog box in Windows XP

● **Figure 12.6**   Desktop tab on Display Properties dialog box

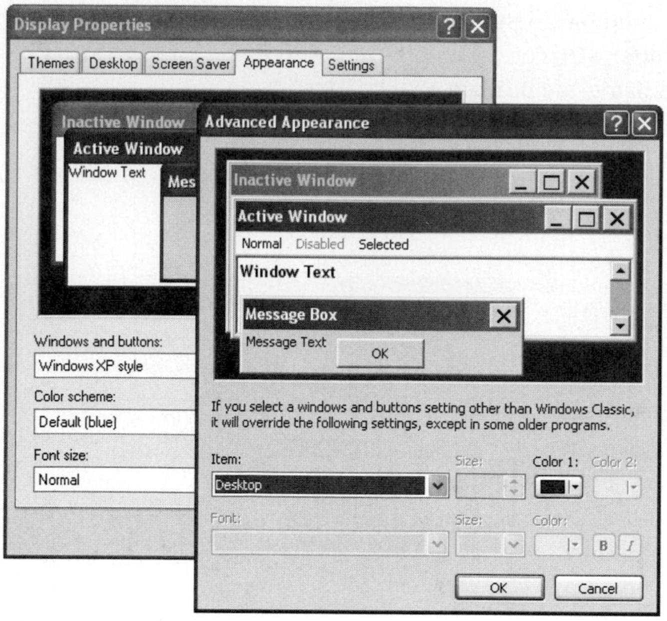

Figure 12.7 Advanced Appearance dialog box

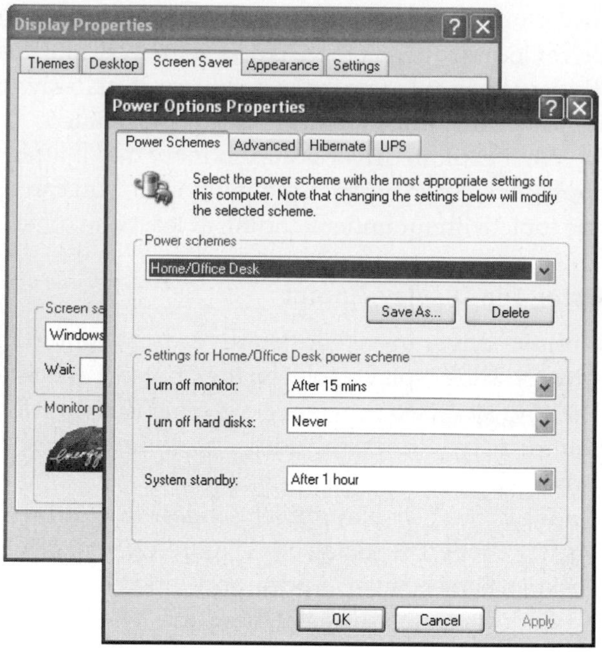

Figure 12.8 Power Options Properties dialog box

big discussion for where we need to save power the most—Chapter 14, "Portable Computing."

Settings Tab

The Settings tab (Figure 12.9) is the centralized location for configuring all of your video settings. From the main screen, you can adjust both the resolution and the color depth. Windows will only display resolutions and color depths your video card/monitor combination can accept and that are suitable for most situations. Everyone has a favorite resolution, and higher isn't always better. Especially for those with trouble seeing small screen elements, higher resolutions can present a difficulty—already small icons are *much* smaller at 1280 × 1024 than at 800 × 600. Try all of the resolutions to see which you like—just remember that LCD monitors look sharpest at their native resolution (usually the highest listed).

The color quality is the number of colors displayed on the screen. You can change the screen resolution with a simple slider, adjusting the color depth from 4-bit all the way up to 32-bit color. Unless you have an older video card or a significant video speed issue, you'll probably set your system for 32-bit color and never touch this setting again.

Another option you may see in the Settings tab is dual monitors. Windows supports the use of two (or more) monitors. These monitors may work together like two halves of one large monitor, or the second monitor might simply show a duplicate of what's happening on the first monitor. Dual monitors are very handy for those who need lots of screen space but don't want to buy a really large, expensive monitor (Figure 12.10).

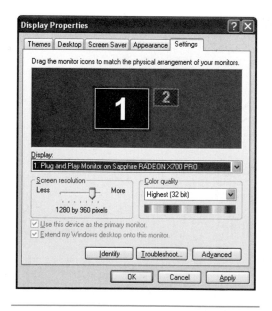

Figure 12.9 Settings tab

There are two ways to set up dual monitors: plug in two video cards or use a single video card that supports two monitors (a "dual-head" video card). Both methods are quite common and work well. Dual monitors are easy to configure—just plug in the monitors and Windows should detect them. Windows will show both monitors in the Settings tab, as shown in Figure 12.11. By default, the second monitor is not enabled. To use the second monitor, just select the *Extend my Windows desktop onto this monitor* checkbox.

If you need to see more advanced settings, click on...that's right, the Advanced button (Figure 12.12). The title of this dialog box reflects the monitor and video card. As you can see in the screen shot, this particular monitor is a ViewSonic A90 running off an NVIDIA GeForce 6800 video card.

The two tabs you're most likely to use are the Adapter and Monitor tabs. The Adapter tab gives detailed information about the video card, including the amount of video memory, the graphics processor, and the BIOS information (yup, your video card has a BIOS, too!). You can also click on the *List all Modes* button to change the current mode of the video card, although there's no mode you may set here that you cannot set in the sliders on the main screen.

If you're still using a CRT, you'll find the Monitor tab a handy place. This is where you can set the refresh rate (Figure 12.13). Windows only shows refresh rates that the monitor says it can handle, but many monitors can take a faster—and therefore easier on the eyes—refresh rate. To see all the modes the video card can support, uncheck the *Hide modes that this monitor cannot display* option.

• **Figure 12.10**   My editor hard at work with dual monitors

All LCD monitors have a fixed refresh rate.

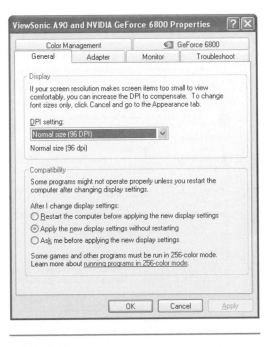

• **Figure 12.11**   Enabling dual monitors

• **Figure 12.12**   Advanced video settings

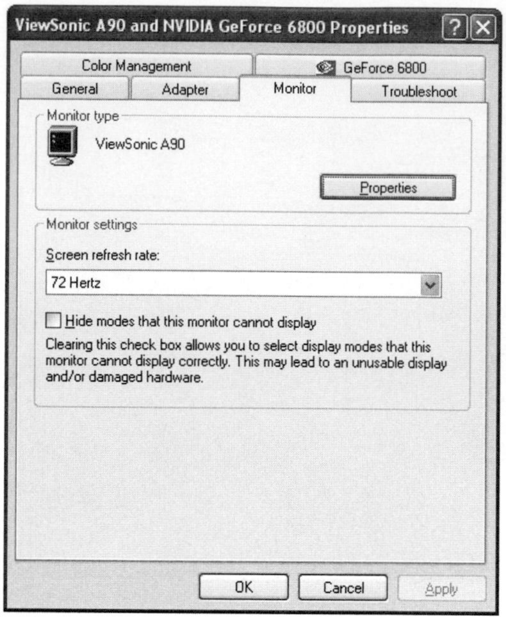

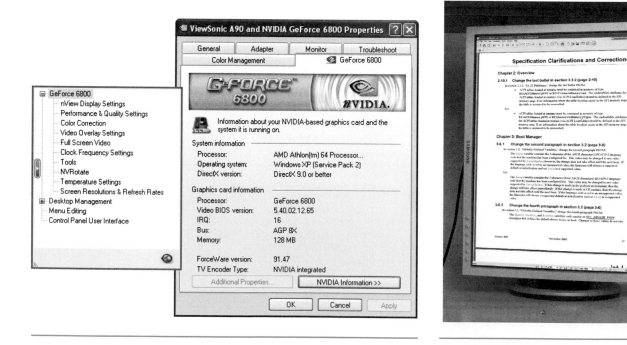

Figure 12.13 Monitor tab

If you try this, always increase the refresh rate in small increments. If the screen looks better, use it. If the screen seems distorted or disappears, wait a moment and Windows will reset back to the original refresh rate. Be careful when using modes that Windows says the monitor cannot display! Pushing a CRT past its fastest refresh rate for more than a minute or two can damage it!

Most video cards add their own tab to the Advanced dialog box like the one shown in Figure 12.14. This tab adjusts all of the specialized settings for that video card. What you see here varies by model of card and version of driver, but here's a list of some of the more interesting settings you might see.

Color Correction Sometimes the colors on your monitor are not close enough for your tastes to the actual color you're trying to create. In this case, you can use color correction to fine-tune the colors on the screen to get the look you want.

Rotation All monitors are by default wider than they are tall. This is called *landscape mode*. Some LCD monitors can be physically rotated to facilitate users who like to see their desktops taller than they are wide (*portrait mode*). Figure 12.15 shows the author's LCD monitor rotated in portrait mode. If you want to rotate your screen, you must tell the system you're rotating it.

Modes Most video cards add very advanced settings to enable you to finely tweak your monitor. These very dangerous settings have names such as "sync polarity" or "front porch" and are outside the scope of both CompTIA A+ certification and the needs of all but the most geeky techs. These settings are mostly used to display a non-standard resolution. Stay out of those settings!

Figure 12.14 Third-party video tab

Figure 12.15 Portrait mode

Working with Drivers

Now that you know the locations of the primary video tools within the operating system, it's time to learn about fine-tuning your video. You need to know how to work with video drivers from within the Display applet, including how to update them, roll back updates, and uninstall them.

Windows is very persnickety when it comes to video card drivers. You can crash Windows and force a reinstall simply by installing a new video card and not uninstalling the old card's drivers. This doesn't happen every time, but certainly can happen. As a basic rule, always uninstall the old card's drivers before you install drivers for a new card.

When you update the drivers for a card, you have a choice of uninstalling the outdated drivers and then installing new drivers— which makes the process the same as for installing a new card—or if you're running Windows XP, you can let it flex some digital muscle and install the new ones right over the older drivers.

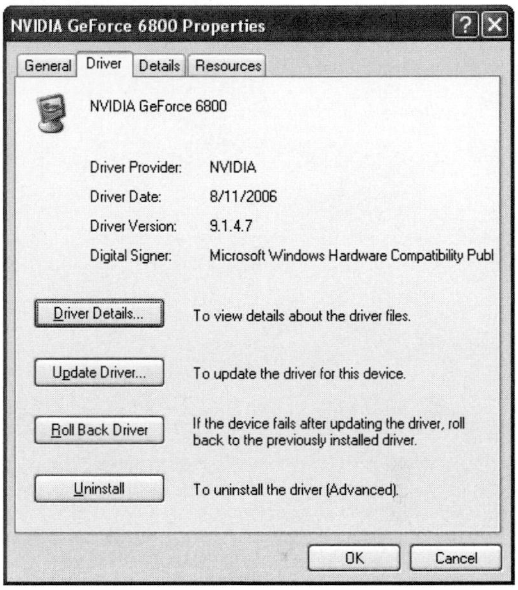

Updating

To update your drivers, go to the Control Panel and double-click the Display applet. In the Display Properties dialog box, select the Settings tab and click the Advanced button. In the Advanced button dialog box, click the Adapter tab and then click the Properties button. In the Properties dialog box for your adapter (Figure 12.16), select the Driver tab and then click the Update Driver button to run the Hardware Update wizard.

• **Figure 12.16**   Adapter Properties dialog box

3-D Graphics

No other area of the PC world reflects the amazing acceleration of technological improvements more than —in particular, 3-D gaming, which attempts to create images that have the same depth and texture as objects seen in the real world. We are spectators to an amazing new world where software and hardware race to produce new levels of realism and complexity displayed on the computer screen. Powered by the wallets of tens of millions of PC gamers always demanding more and better, the video industry constantly introduces new video cards and new software titles that make today's games so incredibly realistic and fun. Although the gaming world certainly leads the PC industry in 3-D technologies, many other PC applications such as *Computer Aided Design (CAD)* programs quickly snatch up these technologies, making 3-D more useful in many ways other than just games. In this section, we'll add to the many bits and pieces of 3-D video encountered over previous chapters in the book and put together an understanding of the function and configuration of 3-D graphics.

Before the early 1990s, PCs did not mix well with 3-D graphics. Certainly, many 3-D applications existed, primarily 3-D design programs such as AutoCAD and Intergraph, but these applications used proprietary methods to generate 3-D graphics and often required the users to purchase

complete systems as opposed to simply dropping an installation disk into their desktop system. Even though these systems worked extremely well, their high cost and steep learning curves kept them hidden inside organizations such as design firms and government entities that needed them. UNIX systems enjoyed 3-D graphics very early on, but even the most powerful UNIX workstations of the early 1980s relegated almost all 3-D functions to CAD applications.

The big change took place in 1992 when a small company called id Software created a new game called Wolfenstein 3D that launched an entirely new genre of games, now called *first-person shooters (FPSs)* (see Figure 12.17). In these games, the player looks out into a 3-D world, interacting with walls, doors, and items, and shoots whatever bad guys the game provides.

Wolfenstein 3D shook the PC gaming world to its foundations. The innovative format turned Wolfenstein 3D and id Software into overnight sensations. The folks at id Software knew that their 3-D game required substantial RAM and CPU strength for the time. They gambled that enough systems existed to handle the massive calculations required to keep track of the position of objects, keyboard inputs, and most importantly, the incredibly complex process of placing the 3-D world on the screen. The gamble paid off, making John Carmack and John Romero, the creators of id Software, the fathers of 3-D gaming.

• **Figure 12.17** Wolfenstein 3D

Early 3-D games used fixed 3-D images called sprites to create the 3-D world. A sprite is nothing more than a bitmapped graphic like a BMP file. These early first-person shooters would calculate the position of an object from the player's perspective and place a sprite to represent the object. Any single object would only have a fixed number of sprites—if you walked around an object, you noticed an obvious jerk as the game replaced the current sprite with a new one to represent the new position. Figure 12.18 shows different sprites for the same bad guy in Wolfenstein 3D. Sprites weren't pretty, but they worked without seriously taxing the 486s and early Pentiums of the time.

The second generation of 3-D began to replace sprites with true 3-D objects, which are drastically more complex than a sprite. A true 3-D object is composed of a group of points called vertices. Each vertex has a defined X, Y, and Z position

• **Figure 12.18** Each figure has a limited number of sprites.

in a 3-D world. Figure 12.19 shows the vertices for an airplane in a 3-D world.

The computer must track all the vertices of all the objects in the 3-D world, including the ones you cannot currently see. Keep in mind that objects may be motionless in the 3-D world (like a wall), may have animation (like a door opening and closing), or may be moving (like bad monsters trying to spray you with evil alien goo). This calculation process is called *transformation* and, as you might imagine, is extremely taxing to most CPUs. Intel's SIMD and AMD's 3DNow! processor extensions were expressly designed to perform transformations.

Once the CPU has determined the positions of all vertices, the system then begins to fill in the 3-D object. The process begins by drawing lines (the 3-D term is *edges*) between vertices to build the 3-D object into many triangles. Why triangles? Well, mainly by consensus of game developers. Any shape works, but triangles make the most sense from a mathematical standpoint. I could go into more depth here, but that would require talking about trigonometry, and I'm gambling you'd rather not read that detailed of a description! All 3-D games use triangles to connect vertices. The 3-D process then groups triangles together into various shapes called **polygons**. Figure 12.20 shows the same model from Figure 12.19, now displaying all the connected vertices to create a large number of polygons.

Originally, the CPU handled these calculations to create triangles, but now special 3-D video cards do the job, greatly speeding up the process.

The last step in second-generation games was texturing. Every 3-D game stores a number of bitmaps called **textures**. The program wraps textures around the object to give it a surface. Textures work well as they provide dramatic detail without the need to use a lot of triangles. A single object may take one texture or many textures applied to single triangles or groups of triangles (polygons). Figure 12.21 shows the finished airplane.

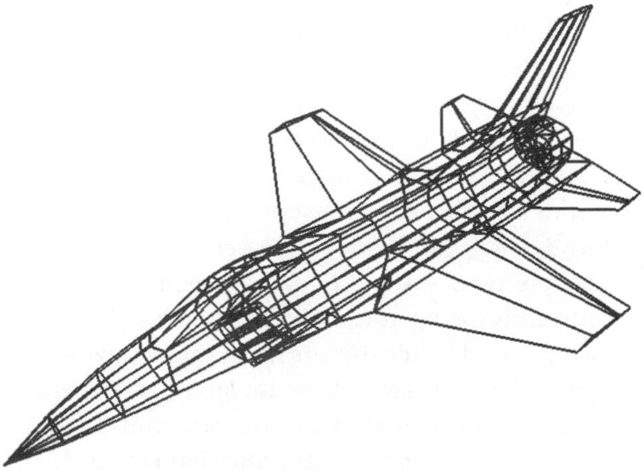

• **Figure 12.19**   Vertices for a 3-D airplane

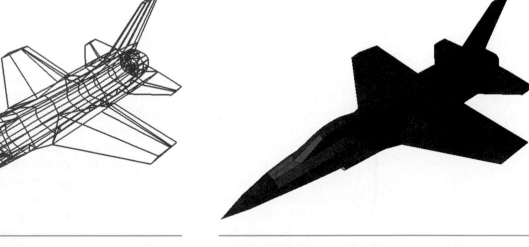

• **Figure 12.20**   Connected vertices forming polygons on a 3-D airplane

• **Figure 12.21**   3-D airplane with textures added

● **Figure 12.22** A mix of 3-D objects and sprites

These second-generation games made a much more realistic environment, but the heavy demands of true 3-D often forced game designers to use both 3-D and sprites in the same game. Figure 12.22 shows the famous game DOOM. Note that the walls, floors, doors, and such were 3-D images, whereas the bad guys continued to manifest as sprites. Notice how pixilated the bad guy looks compared to the rest of the scene.

True 3-D, more often referred to as *rendered* objects, immediately created the need for massively powerful video cards and much wider data buses. Intel's primary motivation for creating AGP was to provide a big enough pipe for massive data pumping between the video card and the CPU. Intel gave AGP the ability to read system RAM to support textures. If it weren't for 3-D games, AGP would almost certainly not exist.

3-D Video Cards

No CPU of the mid-1990s could ever hope to handle the massive processes required to render 3-D worlds. Keep in mind that in order to create realistic movement, the 3-D world must refresh at least 24 times per second. That means that this entire process, from transformation to texturing, must repeat once every 1/24th of a second! Furthermore, while the game re-creates each screen, it must also keep score, track the position of all the objects in the game, provide some type of intelligence to the bad guys, and so on. Something had to happen to take the workload off the CPU. The answer came from video cards.

Video cards were developed with smart onboard **graphics processing units (GPUs)**. The GPU helped the CPU by taking over some, and eventually all, the 3-D rendering duties. These video cards not only have GPUs but also have massive amounts of RAM to store textures.

But a problem exists with this setup: How do we talk to these cards? This is done by means of a device driver, of course, but wouldn't it be great if we could create standard commands to speed up the process? The best thing to do would be to create a standardized set of instructions that any 3-D program could send to a video card to do all the basic work, such as "make a cone" or "lay texture 237 on the cone you just made."

The video card instructions standards manifested themselves into a series of **application programming interfaces (APIs)**. In essence, an API is a library of commands that people who make 3-D games must use in their programs. The program currently using the video card sends API commands directly to the device driver. Device drivers must know how to understand the API commands. If you were to picture the graphics system of your computer as a layer cake, the top layer would be the program making a call to the video card driver that then directs the graphics hardware.

Several different APIs have been developed over the years with two clear winners among all of them: OpenGL and DirectX. The **OpenGL** standard was developed for UNIX systems, but has since been *ported*, or made compatible with, a wide variety of computer systems, including Windows and Apple computers. As the demand for 3-D video became increasingly strong, Microsoft decided to throw its hat into the 3-D graphics ring with its own API, called DirectX. We look at DirectX in-depth in the next section.

Although they might accomplish the same task (for instance, translating instructions and passing them on to the video driver), every API handles things just a little bit differently. In some 3-D games, the OpenGL standard might produce more precise images with less CPU overhead than the DirectX standard. In general, however, you won't notice a large difference between the images produced using OpenGL and DirectX.

DirectX and Video Cards

In the old days, many applications communicated directly with much of the PC hardware and, as a result, could crash your computer if not written well enough. Microsoft tried to fix this problem by placing all hardware under the control of Windows, but programmers balked because Windows added too much work for the video process and slowed down everything. For the most demanding programs, such as games, only direct access of hardware would work.

This need to "get around Windows" motivated Microsoft to unveil a new set of protocols called **DirectX**. Programmers use DirectX to take control of certain pieces of hardware and to talk directly to that hardware; it provides the speed necessary to play the advanced games so popular today. The primary impetus for DirectX was to build a series of products to enable Windows to run 3-D games. That's not to say that you couldn't run 3-D games in Windows *before* DirectX; rather, it's just that Microsoft wasn't involved in the API rat race at the time and wanted to be. Microsoft's goal in developing DirectX was to create a 100-percent stable environment, with direct hardware access, for running 3-D applications and games within Windows.

DirectX is not only for video; it also supports sound, network connections, input devices, and other parts of your PC. Each of these subsets of DirectX has a name like DirectDraw, Direct3D, or DirectSound.

- **DirectDraw** Supports direct access to the hardware for 2-D graphics.

- **Direct3D** Supports direct access to the hardware for 3-D graphics—the most important part of DirectX.

- **DirectInput** Supports direct access to the hardware for joysticks and other game controllers.

- **DirectSound** Supports direct access to the hardware for waveforms.

- **DirectMusic** Supports direct access to the hardware for MIDI devices.

- **DirectPlay** Supports direct access to network devices for multiplayer games.

- **DirectShow** Supports direct access to video and presentation devices.

DirectX Diagnostic Tool

System | DirectX Files | Display 1 | Display 2 | Sound | Music | Input | Network | More Help

This tool reports detailed information about the DirectX components and drivers installed on your system. It lets you test functionality, diagnose problems, and change your system configuration to work best.

If you know what area is causing the problem, click the appropriate tab above. Otherwise, you can use the "Next Page" button below to visit each page in sequence.

The "More Help" page lists some other tools that may help with the problem you are experiencing.

System Information

Current Date/Time:	Tuesday, October 17, 2006, 16:04:21
Computer Name:	MICHAELS
Operating System:	Microsoft Windows XP Professional (5.1, Build 2600)
Language:	English (Regional Setting: English)
System Manufacturer:	NVIDIA
System Model:	AWRDACPI
BIOS:	Award Modular BIOS v6.00PG
Processor:	AMD Athlon(tm) 64 Processor 3200+, MMX, 3DNow, ~2.0GHz
Memory:	2048MB RAM
Page file:	599MB used, 5900MB available
DirectX Version:	DirectX 9.0c (4.09.0000.0904)

☑ Check for WHQL digital signatures

DxDiag 5.03.2600.2180 Unicode Copyright © 1998-2003 Microsoft Corporation. All rights reserved.

Help | Next Page | Save All Information... | Exit

● **Figure 12.23** The DirectX Diagnostic Tool

Microsoft constantly adds and tweaks this list. As almost all games need DirectX and all video cards have drivers to support DirectX, you need to verify that DirectX is installed and working properly on your system. To do this, use the DirectX diagnostic tool in the System Information program. After you open System Information (it usually lives in the Accessories | System Tools area of the Start menu), click the Tools menu and select DirectX Diagnostic Tool (see Figure 12.23).

The System tab gives the version of DirectX. The system pictured in Figure 12.23 runs DirectX 9.0c. You may then test the separate DirectX functions by running through the other tabs and running the tests.

So, what does DirectX do for video cards? Back in the bad old days before DirectX became popular with the game makers, many GPU makers created their own chip-specific APIs. 3dfx had Glide, for example, and S3 had ViRGE. This made buying 3-D games a mess. There would often be multiple versions of the same game for each card. Even worse, many games never used 3-D acceleration because it was just too much work to support all the different cards.

That all changed when Microsoft beefed up DirectX and got more GPU makers to support it. That in turn enabled the game companies to write games using DirectX and have it run on any card out there. The bottom line: When Microsoft comes out with a new version of DirectX, all the GPU companies hurry to support it or they will be left behind.

Try This!

Testing Your Video

Your client needs to know right now whether his system will run the latest game, so turn to the DirectX diagnostic tool and give it a go. Although you can open the tool in System Information, you can also run it directly from the Start menu. Go to Start | Run, type in **DXDIAG**, and click OK.

1. Select the Display tab and then click the Test DirectDraw button.

2. After the DirectDraw test runs, click the Test Direct3D button.

3. How did your system handle the test? If anything failed, you might think about replacing the card!

Trying to decide what video card to buy gives me the shakes—too many options! One good way to narrow down your buying decision is to see what GPU is hot at the moment. I make a point to check out these Web sites whenever I'm getting ready to buy in order to see what everyone says is the best.

- www.arstechnica.com
- www.hardocp.com
- www.tomshardware.com
- www.sharkyextreme.com

■ Troubleshooting Video

People tend to notice when their monitors stop showing the Windows desktop, making video problems a big issue for technicians. A user might temporarily ignore a bad sound card or other device, but they will holler like crazy when the screen doesn't look the way they expect. To fix video problems quickly, the best place to start is to divide your video problems into two groups—video cards/drivers and monitors.

Troubleshooting Video Cards/Drivers

Video cards rarely go bad, so the vast majority of video card/driver problems are bad or incompatible drivers or incorrect settings. Always make sure you have the correct driver installed. If you're using an incompatible driver, Windows defaults to good old 640 × 480, 16-color VGA. A driver that is suddenly corrupted usually doesn't show the problem until the next reboot. If you reboot a system with a corrupted driver, Windows will do one of the following: go into VGA mode, blank the monitor, lock up, or display a garbled screen. Whatever the output, reboot into Safe mode and roll back or delete the driver. Keep in mind that more advanced video cards tend to show their driver as an installed program under Add or Remove Programs, so always check there first before you try deleting a driver using Device Manager. Download the latest driver and reinstall.

Video cards are pretty durable but they do have two components that do go bad: the fan and the RAM. Lucky for you, if either of these goes out, it tends to show the same error—bizarre screen outputs followed shortly by a screen lockup. Usually, Windows keeps running; you may see your mouse pointer moving around and windows refreshing, but the screen turns into a huge mess (Figure 12.24).

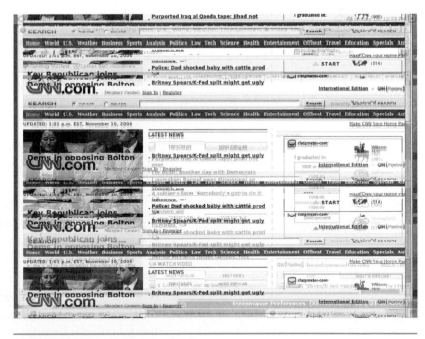

• **Figure 12.24**   Serious video problem

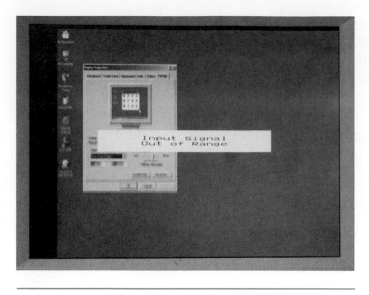

● **Figure 12.25** Pushing a monitor too hard

Bad drivers sometimes also make this error, so always first try going into Safe mode to see if the problem suddenly clears up. If it does, you do not have a problem with the video card!

The last and probably the most common problem is nothing more than improperly configured video settings. Identifying the problem is just common sense—if your monitor is showing everything sideways, someone messed with your rotation settings; if your gorgeous wallpaper of a mountain pass looks like an ugly four-color cartoon, someone lowered the color depth. Go into your Display Properties and reset them to a setting that works! The one serious configuration issue is pushing the resolution too high. If you adjust your resolution and then your monitor displays an error message such as "Input signal out of range" (Figure 12.25), then you need to set your resolution back to something that works for your video card/monitor combination!

Troubleshooting Monitors

Because of the inherent dangers of the high-frequency and high-voltage power required by monitors, and because proper adjustment requires specialized training, this section concentrates on giving a support person the information necessary to decide whether a trouble call is warranted. Virtually no monitor manufacturers make schematics of their monitors available to the public because of liability issues regarding possible electrocution. To simplify troubleshooting, look at the process as three separate parts: common monitor problems, external adjustments, and internal adjustments.

Common Monitor Problems

Although I'm not super comfortable diving into the guts of a monitor, you can fix a substantial percentage of monitor problems yourself. The following list describes the most common monitor problems and tells you what to do—even when that means sending it to someone else.

- Almost all CRT and LCD monitors have replaceable controls. If the Brightness knob or Degauss button stops working or seems loose, check with the manufacturer for replacement controls. They usually come as a complete package.

- For problems with ghosting, streaking, and/or fuzzy vertical edges, check the cable connections and the cable itself. These problems rarely apply to monitors; more commonly, they point to the video card.

- If one color is missing, check cables for breaks or bent pins. Check the front controls for that color. If the color adjustment is already maxed out, the monitor will require internal service.

- As monitors age, they lose brightness. If the brightness control is turned all the way up and the picture seems dim, the monitor will require internal adjustment. This is a good argument for power-management functions. Use the power-management options in Windows to turn off the monitor after a certain amount of time or use the power switch.

Common Problems Specific to CRTs

The complexity of CRTs compared to LCDs requires us to look at a number of monitor problems unique to CRTs. Most of these problems require opening the monitor, so be careful! When in doubt, take it to a repair shop.

- Most out-of-focus monitors can be fixed. Focus adjustments are usually on the inside somewhere close to the flyback transformer. This is the transformer that provides power to the high-voltage anode.

- Hissing or sparking sounds are often indicative of an insulation rupture on the flyback transformer. This sound is usually accompanied by the smell of ozone. If your monitor has these symptoms, it definitely needs a qualified technician. Having replaced a flyback transformer once myself, I can say it is not worth the hassle and potential loss of life and limb.

- Big color blotches on the display are an easy and cheap repair. Find the Degauss button and use it. If your monitor doesn't have a Degauss button, you can purchase a special tool called a degaussing coil at any electronics store.

- Bird-like chirping sounds occurring at regular intervals usually indicate a problem with the monitor power supply.

- Suppose you got a good deal on a used 17-inch monitor, but the display is kind of dark, even though you have the brightness turned up all the way. This points to a dying CRT. So, how about replacing the CRT? Forget it. Even if the monitor was free, it just isn't worth it; a replacement tube runs into the hundreds of dollars. Nobody ever sold a monitor because it was too bright and too sharp. Save your money and buy a new monitor.

- The monitor displaying only a single horizontal or vertical line is probably a problem between the main circuit board and the yoke, or a blown yoke coil. This definitely requires a service call.

- A single white dot on an otherwise black screen means the high-voltage flyback transformer is most likely shot. Take it into the repair shop.

External Adjustments

Monitor adjustments range from the simplest—brightness and contrast—to the more sophisticated—pincushioning and trapezoidal adjustments. The external controls provide users with the opportunity to fine-tune the monitor's image. Many monitors have controls for changing the tint and saturation of color, although plenty of monitors put those controls inside the monitor. Better monitors enable you to square up the visible portion of the screen with the monitor housing.

Finally, most monitors have the ability to **degauss** themselves with the push of a button. Over time, the shadow mask picks up a weak magnetic charge that interferes with the focus of the electron beams. This magnetic field makes the image look slightly fuzzy and streaked. Most monitors have a special built-in circuit called a *degaussing coil* to eliminate this magnetic buildup. When the degaussing circuit is used, an alternating current is sent through a coil of wire surrounding the CRT, and this current generates an alternating magnetic field that demagnetizes the shadow mask. The degaussing coil is activated using the Degauss button or menu selection on the monitor. Degaussing usually makes a rather nasty thunk sound and the screen goes crazy for a moment—don't worry, that's normal. Whenever a user calls me with a fuzzy monitor problem, I always have them degauss first.

Troubleshooting CRTs

As shipped, most monitors do not produce an image out to the limits of the screen because of poor convergence at the outer display edges. **Convergence** defines how closely the three colors can meet at a single point on the display. At the point of convergence, the three colors will combine to form a single white dot. With misconvergence, a noticeable halo of one or more colors will appear around the outside of the white point. The farther away the colors are from the center of the screen, the more likely the chance for misconvergence. Low-end monitors are especially susceptible to this problem. Even though adjusting the convergence of a monitor is not difficult, it does require getting inside the monitor case and having a copy of the schematic, which shows the location of the variable resistors. For this reason, it is a good idea to leave this adjustment to a trained specialist.

I don't like opening a CRT monitor. I avoid doing this for two reasons: (1) I know very little about electronic circuits, and (2) I once almost electrocuted myself. At any rate, the A+ exams expect you to have a passing understanding of adjustments you might need to perform inside a monitor. Before we go any further, let me remind you about a little issue with CRT monitors (see Figure 12.26).

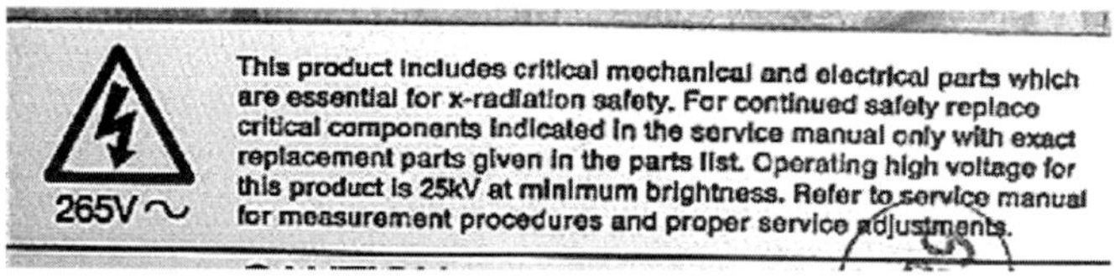

The CRT monitor contains a wire called a **high-voltage anode** covered with a suction cup. If you lift that suction cup, you will almost certainly get seriously electrocuted. The anode wire leads to the flyback transformer and produces up to 25,000 volts. Don't worry about what they do; just worry about what they can do to *you!* That charge is stored in a capacitor, which will hold that charge even if the monitor is turned off. It will hold the charge even if the monitor is unplugged. That capacitor (depending on the system) can hold a charge for days, weeks, months, or even years. Knowing this, you should learn how to discharge a CRT.

This product includes critical mechanical and electrical parts which are essential for x-radiation safety. For continued safety replace critical components indicated in the service manual only with exact replacement parts given in the parts list. Operating high voltage for this product is 25kV at minimum brightness. Refer to service manual for measurement procedures and proper service adjustments.

265V ∿

• **Figure 12.26** Hey! That's 25,000 volts! *Be careful!*

Cross Check

Dangerous Toys

The CRT doesn't have a lock on being the only dangerous piece of high-voltage equipment inside the PC. Check out Chapter 7, "Installing and Troubleshooting Power Supplies," and answer these questions:

1. What other equipment should you avoid when working on a PC?
2. Should you ground yourself at all times?

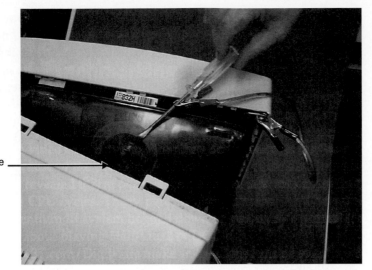

High-voltage
anode

● **Figure 12.27** Discharging a CRT

Discharging a CRT   There are 75,000 opinions on how to discharge a CRT properly. Although my procedure may not follow the steps outlined in someone's official handbook or electrical code, I know this works. Read the rules, and then look at Figure 12.27.

1. Make sure everything is unplugged.
2. If possible, let the monitor sit for a couple of hours. Most good monitors will discharge themselves in two to three hours, and many new monitors discharge in just a few moments.
3. Get a heavy, well-insulated, flat-bladed screwdriver.
4. Get a heavy gauge wire with alligator clips on each end.
5. Do not let yourself be grounded in any way. Wear rubber-soled shoes, and no rings or watches.
6. Wear safety goggles to protect yourself in the very rare case that the CRT implodes.
7. Remove the monitor's case. Remember where the screw went in.
8. Attach one alligator clip to an unpainted part of the metal frame of the monitor.
9. Clip the other end to the metal shaft of the screwdriver.
10. Slide the screwdriver blade under the suction cup. Make triple-sure that neither you nor the screwdriver is in any incidental contact with anything metal.
11. Slide the blade under until you hear a loud pop—you'll also see a nice blue flash.
12. If anyone is in the building, they will hear the pop and come running. Tell them everything's okay.
13. Wait about 15 minutes and repeat.

The main controls that require you to remove the monitor case to make adjustments include those for convergence, gain for each of the color guns, and sometimes the focus control. A technician with either informal or formal training in component-level repair can usually figure out which controls do what. In some cases, you can also readily spot and repair bad solder connections inside the monitor case, and thus fix a dead or dying CRT. Still, balance the cost of repairing the monitor against the cost of death or serious injury—is it worth it? Finally, before making adjustments to the display image, especially with the internal controls, give the monitor at least 15 to 30 minutes of warm-up time. This is necessary for both the components on the printed circuit boards and for the CRT itself.

Troubleshooting LCDs

- If your LCD monitor cracks, it is not repairable and must be replaced.

- If the LCD goes dark but you can still barely see the image under bright lights, you lost either the lamp or the inverter.

- If your LCD makes a distinct hissing noise, an inverter is about to fail.

- You can find companies that sell replacement parts for LCDs, but repairing an LCD is difficult, and there are folks who will do it for you faster and cheaper than you can. Search for a specialty LCD repair company. Hundreds of these companies exist all over the world.

- An LCD monitor may have bad pixels. A bad pixel is any single pixel that does not react the way it should. A pixel that never lights up is a dead pixel. A pixel that is stuck on pure white is a lit pixel, and a pixel on a certain color is a stuck pixel. You cannot repair bad pixels; the panel must be replaced. All LCD panel makers allow a certain number of bad pixels, even on a brand-new LCD monitor! You need to check the warranty for your monitor and see how many they allow before you may return the monitor.

Cleaning Monitors

Cleaning monitors is easy. Always use antistatic monitor wipes or at least a general antistatic cloth. Some LCD monitors may require special cleaning equipment. Never use window cleaners or any liquid because the danger of liquid getting into the monitor may create a shocking experience! Many commercial cleaning solutions will also melt older LCD screens, which is never a good thing.

Beyond A+

Video and CMOS

I'm always impressed by the number of video options provided in CMOS, especially in some of the more advanced CMOS options. I'm equally impressed by the amount of disinformation provided on these settings. In this section, I'll touch on some of the most common CMOS settings that deal with video. You may notice that no power-management video options have been included.

Video

Every standard CMOS setup shows an option for video support. The default setting is invariably EGA/VGA. Many years ago, this setting told the BIOS what type of card was installed on the system, enabling it to know how to talk to that card. Today, this setting has no meaning. No matter what you put there, it will be ignored and the system will boot normally.

Init Display First

This CMOS setting usually resides in an advanced options or BIOS options screen. In multi-monitor systems, Init Display First enables you to decide between PCIe and PCI as to which monitor initializes at boot. This will also determine the initial primary monitor for Windows.

Assign IRQ for VGA

Many video cards do not need an *interrupt request (IRQ)*. This option gives you the ability to choose whether your video card gets an IRQ. In general, lower-end cards that do not provide input to the system do not need an IRQ. Most advanced cards will need one; try it both ways. If you need it, your system will freeze up without an IRQ assigned. If you don't need it, you get an extra IRQ.

VGA Palette Snoop

True-VGA devices only show 16 out of a possible 262,000 colors at a time. The 16 current colors are called the *palette*. VGA Palette Snoop opens a video card's palette to other devices that may need to read or temporarily change the palette. I am unaware of any device made today that still needs this option.

Video Shadowing Enabled

This setting enables you to shadow the Video ROM. In most cases, this option is ignored as today's video cards perform their own automatic shadowing. A few cards require this setting to be off, so I generally leave it off now after years of leaving it on.

SLI and Crossfire

A modern GPU can do some amazing things with video, creating a sense of realism unparalleled in any other technology. Imagine what you could do if you had multiple video cards working together. NVIDIA and ATI did just that; both have come out with competing standards for splitting the graphics processing load between two or more GPUs. NVIDIA calls their standard *Scalable Link Interface (SLI)*, and ATI calls theirs *CrossFire*. In both cases, you install two identical video cards into PCIe slots and connect the two with a tiny bridge card. Applications that understand the technology

Some manufacturers have produced video cards that have two GPUs on a single card, enabling you to do SLI with a single slot or, more importantly, to do four GPUs in SLI using two slots.

draw on both cards to produce a cinematic experience that no single card could produce. Sweet, but expensive!

TV and PCs

It wasn't that long ago that your television and your PC were two totally different devices, but those days are quickly changing. For years, all television signals (at least in the U.S.) used the NTSC standard of 480 interlaced lines and a refresh rate of 59.94 hertz. In the last few years, the high-definition television standards of 480 non-interlaced (480p), 720p, 1080i, and 1080p are bringing the technologies that made PC monitors so attractive into the realm of television sets. Let's talk about some of the new technologies and how you might see them on your PC…err…I mean television.

TV Out

Many modern video cards offer an S-Video port to connect the computer to a standard television set or projector. This is primarily aimed at gaming and presentation software, offering a nice interface between the technologies. The S-Video port is always one way, from the computer to the monitor or projector, so it doesn't offer television on the computer. For that, you need a tuner card.

Tuner Cards

Okay, tuner cards aren't that new, but man are they now getting popular! A *tuner card* is simply a card that accepts television input signals from your cable television box or an antenna. Tuner cards come in regular TV versions (NTSC tuners) and now high-definition versions called ATSC tuners. All of these cards come with the necessary drivers and software so that you can watch television on your PC (Figure 12.28).

Have you ever used the popular TiVo brand *personal video recorder (PVR)*? TiVos are amazing! You plug them in between your cable box and your television and then connect the TiVo to a phone line or network

• **Figure 12.28** Tuner card

connection (Figure 12.29). They enable you to pause live television and record television shows to a built-in hard drive. TiVo is proprietary and you have to pay the TiVo people an ongoing fee to use it.

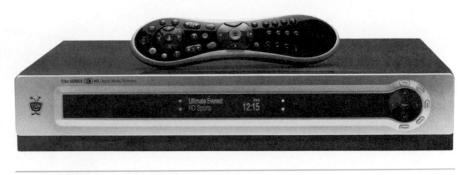

TiVo is so popular that now others have copied the idea. You can turn your PC into a PVR using nothing but a tuner card, an Internet connection, and the right software. Companies such as SnapStream (www.snapstream.com) produce programs like Beyond TV that give

• **Figure 12.29** TiVo *(photo © TiVo Inc. All Rights Reserved.)*

you all the power of PVR for a very small, one-time price for the software. If you like free (and hard to configure), you might want to consider the Linux-based MythTV (www.mythtv.org). Even Microsoft has jumped into the PVR game with its Microsoft Windows XP Media Center edition.

Even if you don't want to turn your PC into a TV, you'll find a number of television technologies that have some overlap into the PC world. Let's look at those technologies and see how they fit into PCs.

HDMI

The newest video connector available today is the *High-Definition Multimedia Interface (HDMI)*. HDMI was developed to replace DVI for televisions by combining both video and sound connections in a single cable (Figure 12.30). HDMI also includes a feature called DDC. DDC is similar to your PC's plug-and-play feature. Imagine plugging a DVD player into your TV using an HDMI cable. When this happens, the two devices talk to each other and the TV tells the DVD player exactly what resolutions it will support, making a perfect setup with no user intervention.

HDMI supports *High-Bandwidth Digital Content Protection (HDCP)*, an anti-copy feature (also called *digital rights management*) designed to prevent unauthorized use of copyrighted material (mainly High Definition DVDs). If you attempt to play an HD DVD without HDCP, you will only get to watch that content in 480p, much lower than the 1080p native resolution of HD DVD.

• **Figure 12.30** HDMI

HDCP is controversial but it is here, even in PCs. You don't need an HDMI cable to support HDCP. Operating system programmers are working furiously to provide some way to support HDCP. If you decide you want to play an HD DVD movie on your Windows Vista systems, go right ahead, as HDCP support is built in!

Plasma

Plasma display panels (PDP) are a very popular technology for displaying movies. Unfortunately, plasma TVs have two issues that make them a bad choice for PC use. First, they have strange native resolutions (such as 1366 × 768) that are hard to get your video card to accept. Second is *burn-in*—the

● **Figure 12.31**   DLP chip *(photo courtesy of Texas Instruments)*

tendency for a screen to "ghost" an image even after the image is off the screen. Plasma TV makers have virtually eliminated burn-in, but even the latest plasma displays are subject to burn-in when used with PC displays.

DLP

The final projector technology to discuss is *Digital Light Processing (DLP)*. DLP is a relatively new technology that uses a chip covered in microscopically small mirrors (Figure 12.31).

These individual mirrors move thousands of times per second toward and away from a light source. The more times per second they move toward a light source, the whiter the image; the fewer times they move, the grayer the image. See Figure 12.32 for a diagram of how the mirrors would appear in a microscopic close-up of the chip.

Figure 12.33 shows a diagram of a typical DLP system. The lamp projects through a color wheel onto the DLP chip. The DLP chip creates the image by moving the tiny mirrors, which in turn reflect onto the screen.

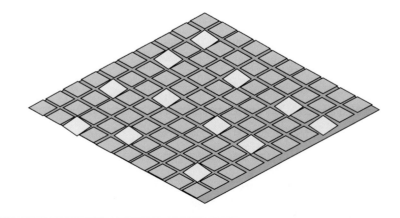

● **Figure 12.32**   Microscopic close-up of DLP showing tiny mirrors—note that some are tilted

DLP is very popular in home theater systems, as it makes an amazingly rich image. DLP has had very little impact on PC monitors, but has had great success as projectors. DLP projectors are much more expensive than LCD projectors, but many customers feel the extra expense is worth the image quality.

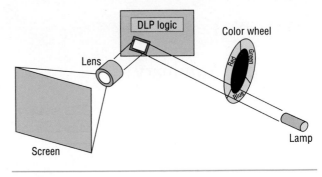

● **Figure 12.33**   DLP in action

Right...SED, FED

Wouldn't it be nice to get a monitor that combined a CRT's excellent contrast ratio, color flexibility, and resolution with an LCD's thin profile and power-sipping trait? Canon, Toshiba, and Sony (among others) have been working on this Holy Grail monitor replacement for some years now, and you might see production displays by the time you read this book. The two technologies are *surface-conduction electron emitter display (SED)* and *field emission display (FED)*. Both put the electronic equivalent of thousands of tiny electron guns into the display, one behind each RGB phosphor, so you get the best of both CRT and LCD monitors. (This is a gross oversimplification of the two technologies, of course, but will suffice for a quick note here.)

At the time of this writing, SED technology seems a lot closer to commercialization. At the Consumer Electronics Show in 2006, for example, Toshiba debuted working prototypes that offered a jaw-dropping 10,000 to 1 contrast ratio. Toshiba claims that production models will hit a 100,000 to 1 contrast ratio (no, that's not a typo!). It won't be long, it seems, before you will be able to replace your aging CRT or LCD with a SED monitor that practically sings, "I'm too sexy for my desk...."

Chapter 12 Review

Chapter Summary

After reading this chapter and completing the exercises, you should understand the following about installing and troubleshooting video.

Choosing a Video Card

- Video cards are identified by their manufacturer, model number, graphic processor, and amount of video RAM. While a number of companies produce video cards, the two major manufacturers of graphics processors are NVIDIA and ATI. The most important decision when buying a video card is the graphics processor, especially if you play 3-D games where texture and layering are important considerations.

- Video RAM has been improved over the years to overcome the bottlenecks of data throughput speed, access speed, and capacity by using specialized fast RAM and adding more and more total video RAM. Video memory technologies include VRAM, WRAM, SGRAM, DDR SDRAM, DDR2 SDRAM, GDDR3 SDRAM, and GDDR4 SDRAM.

Installing and Configuring Video

- During the physical installation of a video card, be conscious of long cards and proximity to other PCI cards. Long cards simply don't fit in some cases, and close proximity to other expansion cards can cause overheating.

- Video card drivers install pretty much the same as all other drivers: either the driver is already built into Windows or you must use the installation CD that comes with the video card.

- As a basic rule, always uninstall an old video card's drivers before you install drivers for a new card.

- The Display applet in the Control Panel provides a convenient, central location for adjusting all of your display settings, including resolution, refresh rate, driver information, and color depth. The Screen Saver tab provides access to the power-management settings. The Settings tab provides access for configuring all of your video settings such as resolution, color depth, and dual monitor configuration. The Settings tab also provides an Advanced button for access to the Monitor and Adapter tabs. The Adapter tab displays information about your video adapter; the Monitor tab enables you to set the refresh rate for your CRT monitor. Most video cards add their own tabs to the Advanced section.

- Dual monitors can be configured by using a video card with two monitor connectors or by using two video cards. Either way, once both monitors are connected, you can enable the second monitor from the Display applet's Settings tab.

- Early 3-D games used sprites to create a 3-D world. Later games replaced sprites with true 3-D objects composed of vertices. Bitmap textures are used to tile a section of the screen to provide a surface in the 3-D world.

- Video cards use a series of APIs to translate instructions for the video device driver. If you were to picture the graphics system of your computer as a layer cake, the top layer would be the program making a call to the graphics hardware. The next layer is the API. The device driver comes next, and way down at the base of the cake is the actual graphics hardware—RAM, graphics processor, and RAMDAC. OpenGL and DirectX are the most popular APIs.

- DirectX includes several subsets, including DirectDraw, Direct3D, DirectInput, DirectSound, DirectMusic, DirectPlay, and DirectShow. You can verify your DirectX installation via the DirectX Diagnostics Tool found under the Tools menu of the System Information utility.

Troubleshooting Video

- Video problems may be divided into two categories: video cards/drivers and monitors.

- If your screen is black or garbled, or if Windows freezes after installing a video card driver, reboot into Safe mode and roll back or delete the driver. Check Add or Remove Programs first, as many video card drivers show up there. If Safe mode doesn't fix the problem, you may have a bad video card that needs to be replaced.

- All monitors have replaceable hardware controls (knobs and buttons). Check with the manufacturer for replacement parts. Ghosting, streaking, or fuzzy images may mean a bad or improperly connected video cable, or the video card may be the cause.

- Monitor troubleshooting falls into two categories: external and internal adjustments. Because monitors have high-voltage power that can harm or kill you, always leave it to trained professionals to work inside the monitor.

- Many CRT monitors have a button to degauss themselves. When the shadow mask picks up a weak magnetic charge, it interferes with the focus of the electron beams, making the monitor appear fuzzy or streaked. A built-in circuit called a degaussing coil generates an alternating magnetic field that eliminates the magnetic buildup on the shadow mask.

- Convergence defines how closely the three colors meet at a single point on the display. With misconvergence, one or more of the colors will appear to have a halo outside the white point, with the problem being more severe toward the outside of the screen.

- Clean CRT monitors with an antistatic monitor wipe. Never use window cleaners or other liquids. LCD monitors need special cleaning equipment or a soft, damp cloth.

- Common monitor problems are often related to cable breaks or bent pins. Monitors also lose brightness over time, especially if you are not using the power-management functions.

- For best performance, keep the screen clean, make sure cables are tightened, use power management, don't block the ventilation slots or place magnetic objects close to the monitor, and don't leave the monitor on all the time, even with a screensaver. If the monitor is dead, use proper disposal methods.

- A cracked LCD monitor must be replaced. If the LCD screen goes dark, starts to hiss, or develops bad pixels, it is best to either replace the monitor or find a company specializing in LCD repair.

■ Key Terms

3-D graphics (229)

application programming interface (API) (232)

convergence (238)

degauss (238)

DirectX (233)

Display applet (225)

graphics processing unit (GPU) (232)

high-voltage anode (238)

OpenGL (232)

polygons (231)

sprite (230)

textures (231)

vertices (230)

■ Key Term Quiz

Use the Key Terms list to complete the sentences that follow. Not all terms will be used.

1. DirectX is a(n) _____, a program that translates instructions for the video device driver.

2. If your monitor displays big color blotches, this indicates that you should _____ the monitor to eliminate the magnetic buildup on the shadow mask.

3. _____ defines how closely the red, green, and blue colors meet at a single point on the display.

4. Use the _____ to configure your resolution, refresh rate, and color depth.

5. Early 3-D games used a fixed 3-D image called a(n) _____ to create the 3-D world.

6. A true 3-D object is composed of a group of points called _____.

7. Every 3-D game stores a number of bitmaps called _____ that wrap around objects to give them surfaces.

8. Two APIs for video include _____ (originally developed for UNIX systems) and _____ (developed by Microsoft).

9. Touching the _____ inside a CRT will almost certainly lead to electrocution.

10. A video card has its own processor, called the _____, similar to the main CPU on the motherboard.

Multiple-Choice Quiz

1. If one of the colors is missing on the monitor and you cannot fix the problem by adjusting the front controls, you should then check for _____.

   A. A refresh rate that is set higher than that recommended by the manufacturer
   B. A corrupted video driver
   C. A broken cable or bent pins
   D. Misconvergence

2. Which of the following problems would make it impossible to repair an LCD monitor?

   A. A blown yoke coil
   B. A broken LCD panel
   C. A bad flyback transformer
   D. Misconvergence

3. If the monitor displays only a single horizontal or vertical line, the problem is likely to be caused by a _____.

   A. Bad flyback transformer
   B. Blown yoke coil
   C. Bad monitor power supply
   D. Bad electron gun

4. Only specially trained technicians should work inside a monitor because the _____ produces over 25,000 V that may harm or kill a person.

   A. Flyback transformer
   B. Yoke
   C. Anode
   D. Electron gun

5. What is the most popular API used by 3-D game developers?

   A. DirectX
   B. OpenGL
   C. DigitalDirector
   D. RAMDAC

6. A user calls in complaining that her monitor is too small. Upon further questioning, you find out that it's not the monitor that's small, but the font and icon size that are too small! What would you do to help the user fix the problem?

   A. In the Control Panel, open the Display applet. Select the Settings tab and increase the screen resolution.
   B. In the Control Panel, open the Display applet. Select the Settings tab and decrease the screen resolution.
   C. In the Control Panel, open the Monitor applet. Select the Settings tab and increase the screen resolution.
   D. In the Control Panel, open the Monitor applet. Select the Settings tab and decrease the screen resolution.

7. Which companies produce the majority of graphics processors? (Choose two.)

   A. ATI
   B. IBM
   C. NVIDIA
   D. GeForce

8. What is true about 2-D and 3-D video cards?

   A. Every computer system will gain substantial benefits by upgrading from a 2-D video card to a 3-D video card.
   B. Every computer system will gain substantial benefits by upgrading from a 3-D video card to a 2-D video card.
   C. Only gaming systems will benefit from a 3-D video card. Users of word processors and Web browsers can stick with the less expensive 2-D video cards.
   D. Only gaming systems will benefit from a 2-D video card. Users of word processors and Web browsers can stick with the less expensive 3-D video cards.

9. What is the most significant feature that differentiates video RAM from DRAM?

   A. Video RAM can read and write data at the same time whereas DRAM cannot.

   B. Video RAM uses transistors whereas DRAM uses capacitors.

   C. Video RAM is static whereas DRAM is dynamic.

   D. Video RAM is easily upgraded whereas DRAM is not.

10. Which of the following are types of video RAM? (Choose all that apply.)

    A. VRAM

    B. XRAM

    C. SGRAM

    D. WRAM

11. How can you connect two monitors to a single PC? (Choose all that apply.)

    A. Install two video cards and connect a monitor to each.

    B. Install a single video card with dual ports and connect a monitor to each port.

    C. Connect one monitor to the video card and then daisy-chain the second monitor to the first monitor's output port.

    D. Connect one monitor to the video card and then connect a USB monitor to any available USB port.

12. Which of the following are components of DirectX? (Choose all that apply.)

    A. Direct2D

    B. DirectOutput

    C. DirectShow

    D. DirectMusic

13. Why were HDMI connections developed?

    A. To accommodate for longer cable lengths

    B. To counteract potentially harmful radiation emitted by CRT monitors

    C. To combine video and audio connections in a single cable

    D. To offer a universal connector compatible with both VGA and DVI ports

14. How can you change the refresh rate of your monitor?

    A. Use the button controls on the front of the monitor

    B. Open My Computer, right-click the monitor, and select the refresh rate from the General tab

    C. Launch the Display applet from the Control Panel, select the Settings tab, click the Advanced button, and then select the Monitor tab

    D. Launch the Video applet from the Control Panel, select the Adapter tab, and then click the Properties button

15. Which statement is true about video card drivers?

    A. The best place to download updates is from the Windows Update Web site.

    B. You should uninstall current drivers before installing updated drivers.

    C. Video card drivers should always be installed via the Add Hardware Wizard.

    D. The safest way to update video card drivers is to boot with a floppy and then run the small command-line program included with the driver to perform the update.

Essay Quiz

1. The editor of your company's newsletter has asked you to prepare a short article for next month's edition that explains how to care for monitors to extend their lifespan. Explain at least four things that the average user can do.

2. Dave and Shannon disagree about whether the monitor should stay on all the time or not. Dave says that it's okay to leave the monitor on as long as you have a screensaver. Shannon disagrees, saying the monitor will become dim and burn out sooner if you leave it on. Dave thinks that leaving it on actually extends its life because turning the monitor on and off is bad for it. They've called you to save their monitor and their marriage. What will you tell them?

3. Brad is very upset because Eli, his four-year-old son, held a magnet up to the screen, and now Brad's new CRT monitor looks terrible. It's got some big spots on the corner and looks fuzzy. Explain to him what happened and what he can do to solve his problem.

4. Your company just hired two new technicians. You've been tapped to teach them what they can and cannot do to troubleshoot and repair a CRT monitor. What will you tell them?

Lab Projects

• Lab Project 12.1

Monitors are not the only output device for the computer. Research one of the following devices and prepare a short essay for the class about how the device works and its features, cost, and connections.

- Rear-view projectors
- Plasma monitors
- Touch screens

Sound and Multimedia

"I can't hear too well. Do you suppose you could turn the music down just a little?"

—PETER SELLERS IN DR. STRANGELOVE OR: HOW I LEARNED TO STOP WORRYING AND LOVE THE BOMB

Racing down the virtual track, pixels flying across the screen, hearing the engine roar as you take another turn and press down the accelerator—or surfing the Web for lovely scenic nature photos with the sweet, mellifluous music of Mozart filling the room—sound has become an integral component of the computing experience. Setting up and optimizing sound for the PC has become an integral skill for all computer techs.

Correctly setting up sound for a PC requires that you know about quite a few things, because the sound process has many components. You need a properly installed sound card with the correct drivers loaded, reasonably high-quality speakers, support software such as the API for a particular game correctly configured in Windows, and a properly set up application that can use the features of the sound card. And every great tech needs to know troubleshooting to handle both routine and uncommon problems with sound.

In this chapter, you will learn how to

- **Describe how sound works in a PC**
- **Select the appropriate sound card for a given scenario**
- **Install a sound card in a Windows system**
- **Troubleshoot problems that might arise with sound cards and speakers**

■ How Sound Works in a PC

Like the ripples that roll across a pond when you drop a rock in the center, sound flows from a source in invisible but measurable waves that cause the membranes in your ears to vibrate and create sound. The sophistication of the human ear enables most people to differentiate the melodious from the raucous, the loud from the soft. Computers aren't nearly as sophisticated as the human ear and brain, so clear standards are a must for converting music into a format that a PC can use to record and play sound. Computer folks use the terms *capture* and *output* instead of record and play.

Sound-Capture Basics

Virtually every PC today comes with four critical components for capturing and outputting sound: a sound card, speakers, microphone, and recording/playback software. Computers capture (record) sound waves in electronic format through a process called **sampling**. In its simplest sense, sampling means capturing the state or quality of a particular sound wave a set number of times each second. The sampling rate is measured in units of thousands of cycles per second, or kilohertz (KHz). The more often a sound is sampled, the better the reproduction of that sound. Most sounds in the PC world are recorded with a sampling rate of from 11 KHz (very low quality, like a telephone) to 192 KHz (ultra-high quality, better than the human ear).

Sounds vary according to their loudness (**amplitude**), how high or low their tone (**frequency**), and the qualities that differentiate the same note played on different instruments (**timbre**). All the characteristics of a particular sound wave—amplitude, frequency, timbre—need to be recorded and translated into ones and zeroes to reproduce that sound accurately within the computer and out to your speakers.

 The most famous of all sound cards is the Creative Labs SoundBlaster series.

The number of characteristics of a particular sound captured during sampling is measured by the **bit depth** of the sample, the number of bits used to describe the characteristics of a sound. The greater the bit depth used to capture a sample, the more characteristics of that sound can be stored and thus re-created. An 8-bit sample of a Jimi Hendrix guitar solo, for example, captures 2^8 (256) characteristics of that sound per sample. It would sound like a cheap recording of a recording, perhaps a little flat and thin. A 16-bit sample, in contrast, captures 2^{16} (65,536) different characteristics of his solo and reproduces all the fuzzy overtones and feedback that gave Hendrix his unique sound.

The last aspect of sound capture is the number of different tracks of sound you capture. Most commonly, you can capture either a single track (**monaural**) or two tracks (**stereo**). More advanced captures record many more sound tracks, but that's a topic for a more advanced sound capture discussion.

The combination of sampling frequency and bit depth determines how faithfully a digital version of a sound captures what your ear would hear. A sound capture is considered **CD quality** when recorded at 44.1 KHz, with

16-bit depth, and in stereo. Most recording programs let you set these values before you begin recording. Figure 13.1 shows the configuration settings for the Windows Sound Recorder.

Hey, wait a minute! Did you notice the Format setting in Figure 13.1? What's that? You can save those sampled sounds in lots of different ways—and that's where the term *format* comes into play.

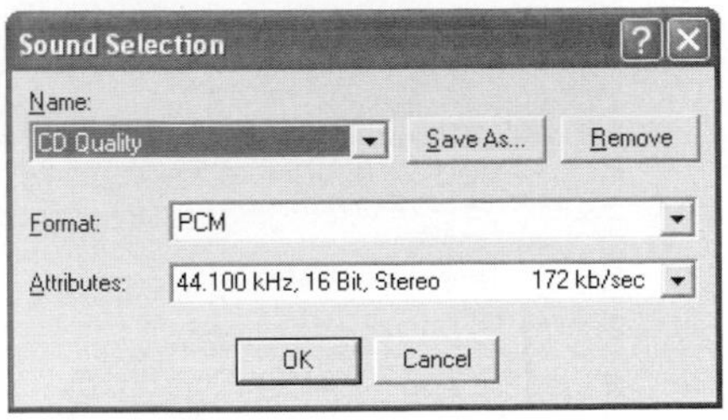

Recorded Sound Formats

The granddaddy of all sound formats is pulse code modulation (PCM). PCM was developed in the 1960s to carry telephone calls over the first digital lines. With just a few minor changes to allow for use in PCs, the PCM format is still alive and well, although it's better known as the *WAV* format so common in the PC world. WAV files are great for storing faithfully recorded sounds and music, but they do so at a price. WAV files can be huge, especially when sampled at high frequency and depth. A 4-minute song at 44.1 KHz and 16-bit stereo, for example, weighs in at a whopping 40-plus MB!

What's interesting about sound quality is that the human ear cannot perceive anywhere near the subtle variations of sound recorded at 44.1 KHz and 16-bit stereo. Clever programmers have written algorithms to store full-quality WAV files as compressed files, discarding unnecessary audio qualities of that file. These algorithms—really nothing more than a series of instructions in code—are called compressor/decompressor programs or, more simply, codecs. The most famous of the codecs is the Fraunhoffer MPEG-1 Layer 3 codec, more often called by its file extension, MP3.

Playing Sounds

A large number of programs can play sounds on a typical Windows computer. First, virtually every Windows computer comes with Windows Media Player, possibly the most popular of all sound players. Figure 13.2 shows the default Media Player for Windows Vista. You can download many other players, of course, including iTunes, Apple's media program for Windows and OS X. This is good, because not all sound players can play all sounds.

MIDI

Every sound card can produce sounds, in addition to playing prerecorded sound files. Every sound card comes with a second processor designed to interpret standardized musical instrument digital interface (MIDI) files. It's important to note that a MIDI file is not an independent music file, unlike a WAV file that will sound more or less the same on many different PCs. A MIDI file is a text file that takes advantage of the sound processing hardware to enable the PC to produce sound. Programmers use these small files to tell the sound card what notes to play, how long, how loud, on which instruments, and so forth. Think of a MIDI file as a piece of electronic sheet music, with the instruments built into your sound card.

The beauty of MIDI files is that they're tiny in comparison to equivalent WAV files. The first movement of Beethoven's Fifth Symphony, for example,

• **Figure 13.1** Sound Recorder settings

WAV and MP3 are only two among a large number of file formats for sound. Not all sound players can play all of these formats; however, many sound formats are nothing more than some type of compressed WAV file, so with the right codec loaded, you can play most sound formats.

Tech Tip

Compressing WAV Files to MP3 Format

Using MP3 compression, it is possible to shrink a WAV file by a factor of 12 without losing much sound quality. When you compress a WAV file into an MP3 file, the key decision is the bit rate. The bit rate is the amount of information (number of bits) transferred from the compressed file to the MP3 decoder in one second. The higher the bit rate of an MP3 file, the higher the sound quality. The bit rate of MP3 audio files is commonly measured in thousands of bits per second, abbreviated Kbps. Most MP3 encoders support a range of bit rates from 24 Kbps up to 320 Kbps (or 320,000 bits per second). A CD-quality MP3 bit rate is 128 Kbps.

MIDI files have the file extension .MID in the PC world.

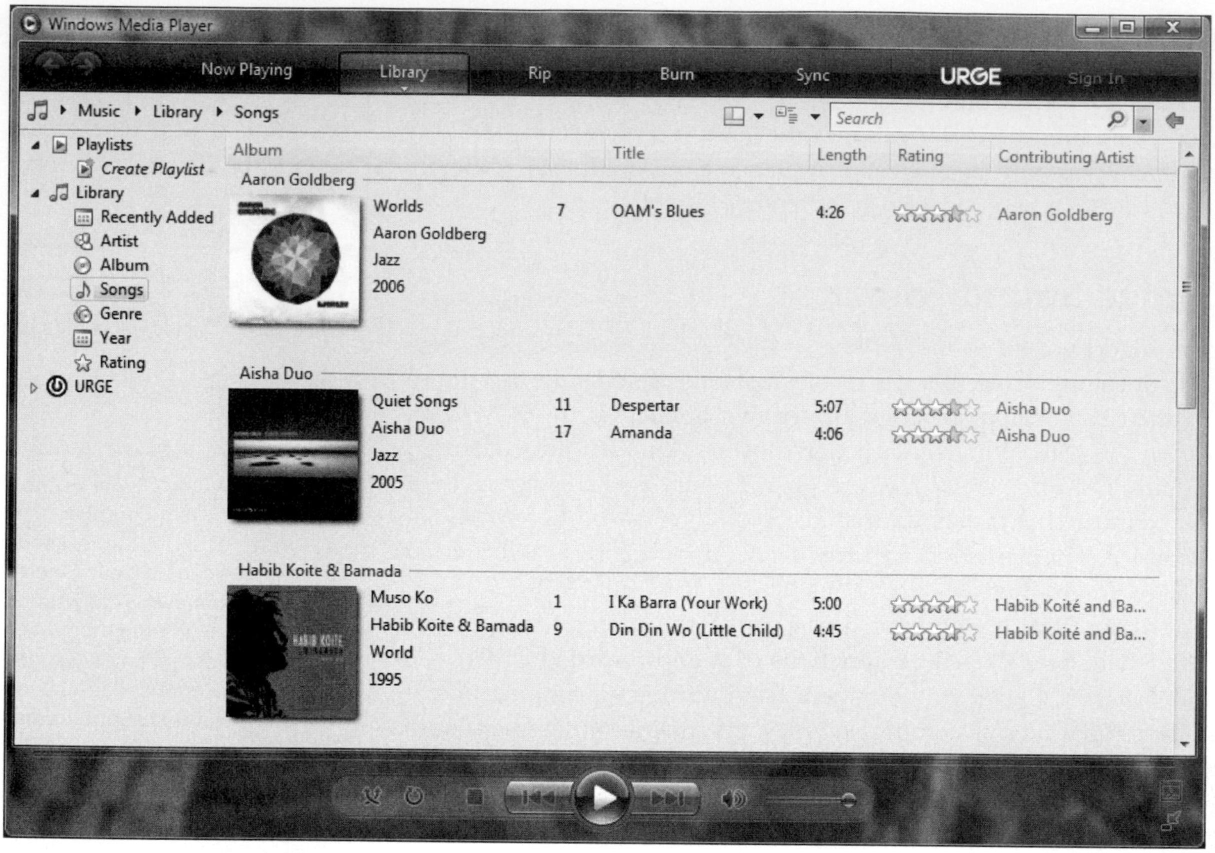

● **Figure 13.2** Windows Media Player

weighs in at a whopping 78 MB as a high-quality WAV file. The same seven-minute composition as a MIDI file, in contrast, slips in at a svelte 60 KB.

MIDI is hardware dependent, meaning the capabilities and quality of the individual sound card make all the difference in the world on the sound produced. Sound cards play MIDI files using one of two technologies: FM synthesis or wave table synthesis.

FM Synthesis

Early processors used electronic emulation of various instruments—a technique often called **FM synthesis**—to produce music and other sound effects. Software developers could tell the sound processor to reproduce a piano playing certain notes, for example, and a sound resembling a piano would pour forth from the speakers. The problem with FM synthesis is that although the modulation sounds okay for a single note, such as middle C, it sounds increasingly electronic the farther up or down the scale you go from that prime note.

Wave Table Synthesis

To address the odd techno-sound of early sound processors, manufacturers began embedding recordings of actual instruments or other sounds in the sound card. Modern sound cards use these recorded sounds to reproduce an instrument much more faithfully than with FM synthesis. When asked to play a C note on a piano or on a viola, for example, the sound processor grabs a prerecorded WAV file from its memory and adjusts it to match the specific sound and timing requested. This technique is called **wave table synthesis**. The number of instruments a sound card can play at once is called the **polyphony** of that card—typically 64 sounds on better cards. Most modern sound cards have samples of 128 instruments—a veritable symphony orchestra on a chip!

MIDI files are much less popular than other recorded formats on computers, but every Windows computer and every sound card still fully supports MIDI.

Other File Formats

The WAV, MP3, and MIDI formats may account for the majority of sound files, but plenty of other less common formats are out there. Here are the extensions of some other sound file formats you may run into in the PC world:

- **AAC**   Advanced Audio Coding is the native format for songs downloaded into the Apple iTunes music library. The AAC format is part of the MPEG-4 standard, offers better compression algorithms than MP3, and is freely distributed. Apple wraps downloaded songs in a Digital Rights Management (DRM) encapsulation called FairPlay that gives them control over distribution of those songs.

- **AIFF**   Audio Interchange File Format files are a popular sound format used on Macintosh computers. These files are often seen at Web sites, and you can use the well-known QuickTime player to play them.

- **ASX**   Microsoft created the ASX format to facilitate streaming audio over the Internet through Windows Media Player. It's more than just a format, though; it acts like a super playlist and enables you to play other sound file types as well. The full name of the format is Microsoft Advanced Streaming Redirector.

- **AU**   This popular format is often seen in the Windows world. Many different players can play these files, including players on non-Windows systems, such as Sun, Next, UNIX, and Macintosh.

- **OGG**   The Vorbis format is an open-source compression codec that competes well with the proprietary AAC and WMA codecs, as well as MP3. Vorbis files are saved with the .OGG filename extension, so you'll hear them (incorrectly) referred to as "Ogg" files.

- **RM**   RealMedia files play either just audio or audio and video. They are proprietary to RealMedia, a popular player often used on the Internet. You must have RealMedia Player installed on your computer to play these files.

- **WMA**   Windows Media Audio is Microsoft's proprietary compression format.

This list scratches the surface of the 100-plus sound file formats available out there, but it represents those you're most likely to encounter.

Video

Recorded audio files and MIDI files aren't the only files that play sounds on your computer. Video files also have sound built into them. However, to play the sound that accompanies the video, the video player program must support the particular video file format. The most common video formats in the PC world are Audio Video Interleave (AVI), Moving Pictures Experts Group (MPEG), QuickTime (MOV), Advanced Streaming Format (ASF), Real Media (RM), Windows Media Video (WMV), DivX, and Flash. The popular video sharing site YouTube was made possible by the amazingly small size of Flash-based video.

Applications

Many applications, especially games, play sounds, too. In the not-too-distant past, a game or an application sometimes had its own sound format, but most applications and games today use standard WAV, MP3, or MIDI files.

Streaming Media

Streaming media is incredibly popular on the Internet. **Streaming** media is a broadcast of data that is played on your computer and immediately discarded. Streaming media has spawned an entire industry of Internet radio stations. The three most popular streaming media players are Windows Media Player, Winamp, and Apple's iTunes. ASF and RM are compressed audio/video file formats that were specially created to stream over the Internet. With the spread of broadband Internet, the quality of streaming radio has improved dramatically. In fact, it is common to see Internet stations streaming 128 Kbps and better MP3 files. Some sites even have surround-sound music for those who have the speakers to appreciate it.

■ Getting the Right Sound Card

Sound cards come with many built-in features, including two separate sound processors (one for all of the recorded formats such as WAV and another for MIDI), support chips for joysticks and other pointing devices that plug into the game port, recording capabilities, support for MIDI instruments, and more. All sound cards, from the cheapest to the most expensive, can play music and drive a pair of speakers, so techs need to delve a little deeper to understand the crucial differences among low-, mid-, and high-end sound cards. Sound cards differ in five basic areas: processor capabilities, speaker support, recording quality, jacks, and extra features.

But the sound card itself is only one part of the equation. You also need good-quality speakers if you have any intention of listening to music or enjoying some of the more advanced features such as surround sound.

> **Tech Tip**
>
> **Sound Cards**
>
> *The hardware portion of sound-processing equipment in the PC comes either as a chip built into the motherboard or on an expansion card. Techs call both forms sound cards, though technically the first type is not a card at all. Still, the generic term has stuck for the time being.*

Processor Capabilities

Sound processor capabilities differ dramatically from the low end to the high end, even though the prices don't reflect the great divide. The sound processor handles the communication among the application, operating system, and CPU and translates commands into sounds coming out of the speakers. Low-end sound processors do little more than translate, which means that the CPU has to do the heavy lifting on the processing front.

Better sound processors, in contrast, shoulder much of the processing burden and bring a series of extra features to the table. By handling a lot of the processing on board, these better sound processors free up the CPU for other duties and, in effect and in name, *accelerate* the sound process. These decent sound processors also provide excellent sound reproduction, so your MP3s sound as awesome on your PC as they do on your stereo.

Most mid-range and all high-end sound processors offer support for various surround sound standards, enabling equally equipped games and other applications to provide positional audio effects and detailed sound modeling—features that make PC gaming take on a whole new dimension. You'll learn about the various standards in detail in the "Speakers" section of this chapter, but for now let an example suffice. With properly implemented positional audio, when you're sneaking down the hall, ready to steal the Pasha's treasure, you will hear behind you the sounds of the guards marching up to capture you. Such added realism has many potential benefits beyond games, but games are currently the primary beneficiary of this technology.

Speaker Support

Every sound card supports two speakers or a pair of headphones, but many better sound cards support five or more speakers in discrete channels. These multiple speakers provide surround sound—popular not only for games

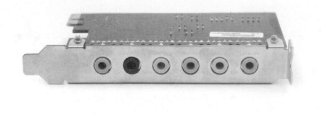

• **Figure 13.3** A sound card with multiple speaker connections

• **Figure 13.4** Surround speakers

• **Figure 13.5** The E-MU 1820 advertises its excellent 112-decibel signal-to-noise ratio for recording.

but also for those who enjoy playing DVDs on their PCs. The card shown in Figure 13.3, for example, supports up to eight speakers.

Another popular speaker addition is a subwoofer. A subwoofer provides the amazing low-frequency sounds that give all of your sounds, from the surround sound of a game to the music of a simple stereo MP3 file, an extra dimension. Almost all modern sound cards support both surround sound and a subwoofer and advertise this with a nomenclature such as Dolby Digital, DTS, or 5.1. The 5 denotes the number of speakers: two in front, two in back, and one in the center. The .1 denotes the subwoofer. Figure 13.4 shows one type of surround speaker system. (You'll learn more about surround sound in the upcoming "Speakers" section.)

Recording Quality

Almost every sound card has an input for a powered microphone, but the high-end cards record with substantially lower amounts of noise or other audible artifacts. The measure that describes the relative quality of an input port is signal-to-noise ratio and is expressed in decibels. The smaller the number, the worse the card is for recording, because you'll more likely get noise. Most sound cards at the low end and in the mid range have a signal-to-noise ratio of 30 to 50 decibels, which makes them unacceptable for recording. High-end cards offer a 96 to 100+ signal-to-noise ratio, a level near what professional musicians use. Check the documentation (see Figure 13.5) before you buy or recommend a sound card for recording purposes.

Jacks

Virtually every sound card comes with at least three connections: one for a stereo speaker system, one for a microphone, and one for a secondary output called line out. If you look at the back of a motherboard with a built-in sound card, you'll invariably see these three connections (Figure 13.6). On most systems, the

Mike Meyers' CompTIA A+ Guide: PC Technician (Exams 220-602, 220-603, & 220-604)

Mini-audio
connectors

● **Figure 13.6** Typical audio connections on a motherboard sound card

main stereo speaker connector is blue, the line-out connector is green, and the microphone connector is pink. You'll often find plenty of other connectors as well (Figure 13.7).

● **Figure 13.7** Lots of connections on a high-end sound card

Take a look at what these connectors do for your sound card:

- **Line out**   The line out is a secondary connector that is often used to connect to an external device such as a cassette or CD player to allow you to output sounds from your computer.

- **Line in**   The line in port connects to an external device such as a cassette or CD player to allow you to import sounds into your computer.

- **Rear out**   The rear out connector connects to the rear speakers for surround sound audio output.

- **Analog/digital out**   The multifunction analog/digital out connection acts as a special digital connection to external digital devices or digital speaker systems, and it also acts as the analog connection to center and subwoofer channels. (See the "Speakers" section later in this chapter for a discussion of surround sound.)

- **Microphone**   The microphone port connects to an external microphone for voice input.

- **Joystick**   The joystick port connects a joystick or a MIDI device to the sound card. The joystick port is a two-row DB15 female connection, but as more and more peripherals go to USB, more motherboard and sound card makers are dropping this venerable port from their models.

Extra Features

With all motherboards including built-in sound these days, expansion sound card makers have responded by adding a host of extra goodies and

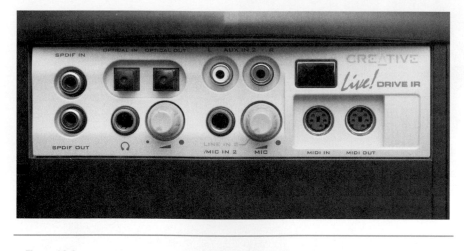

abilities to their cards that, for some folks, prove irresistibly tempting. These include a digital output to integrate the PC with a home entertainment unit, DVD receiver, and surround sound speaker connection abilities; a breakout box that adds recording and output ports in a 5.25-inch bay; and a FireWire connection for direct gaming, file sharing, and immediate MP3 playing from a portable MP3 device. Figure 13.8 shows a version of the Creative Labs SoundBlaster breakout box. These features aren't for everyone, but they are compelling to many consumers.

• **Figure 13.8**   Breakout box for a SoundBlaster Live! Platinum sound card

Audio Cables

In the days of yore, if you wanted to play audio CDs through your sound card, you needed a special cable that ran from your CD-ROM drive to the sound card. These cables have been around for a while, but the connectors were not standardized—for years, you had to use the cable that came with your sound card and hope that it would connect to your CD-ROM drive. Eventually, manufacturers standardized on a connector called *MPC2* (Figure 13.9), and cables usually come with optical drives, not sound cards.

All modern systems run the audio from optical drives to sound cards digitally through the computer, just like any other information, making the MPC2 cable irrelevant. In fact, even if you connect the cable, the computer won't use it without software changes.

If you want to disable digital CD audio and use the old cable, go to the properties of your optical drive. Right-click an optical drive in My Computer and select Properties. Select the Hardware tab, select an optical drive from the list of disk drives, and then click the Properties button. Select the Properties tab (Figure 13.10) and then deselect the checkbox next to *Enable digital CD audio for this CD-ROM device*.

• **Figure 13.9**   MPC2 audio cable

Speakers

It always blows me away when I walk into someone's study and hear tinny music whining from a US$10 pair of speakers connected to a $2000 computer. If you listen to music or play games on your computer, a decent set of speakers can significantly improve the experience. Speakers come in a wide variety of sizes, shapes, technologies, and quality and can stump the uninformed tech who can't easily tell that the $50 set on the right sounds 100 times better than the $25 pair on the left (Figure 13.11).

Speaker Standards

The advent of surround sound in the computing world has created a number of speaker standards. You should know these standards so that you can choose the speakers that work best for you and your clients.

Stereo Stereo is the oldest speaker technology that you'll see in the PC world. Stereo speakers are just what you might imagine: two speakers, a left and a right (Figure 13.12). The two speakers share a single jack that connects to the sound card. Most cheap speakers are stereo speakers.

2.1 Systems A 2.1 speaker system consists of a pair of standard stereo speakers—called satellites —combined with a subwoofer (Figure 13.13). The average 2.1 speaker system has a single jack that connects to the sound card and runs into the subwoofer. Another wire runs from the subwoofer to the two stereo speakers. If you want to enjoy great music and don't need surround sound, this is your speaker standard of choice.

Surround Speaker Standards Going beyond standard two-channel (stereo) sound has been a goal in the sound world since the 1970s. However, it wasn't until the advent of Dolby Laboratory's Dolby Digital sound standard in the early 1990s that surround sound began to take off. The Dolby Digital sound standard is designed to support five channels of sound: front-left, front-right, front-center, rear-left, and rear-right. Dolby Digital also supports a subwoofer—thus, the term 5.1 . Another company, Digital Theatre Systems (DTS) , created a competing standard that also supported a 5.1 speaker system. When DVDs were introduced, they included both Dolby Digital and DTS 5.1 standards, making 5.1 speakers an overnight requirement for home theater. If you want to enjoy your DVDs in full

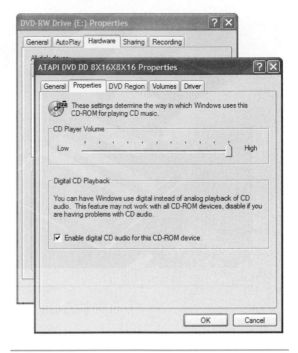

• **Figure 13.10**   Properties for a DVD-RW drive for CD music playback

• **Figure 13.11**   High-quality speaker set (right) versus another manufacturer's low-end speaker set (left)

● **Figure 13.12** Stereo speakers

● **Figure 13.13** Typical 2.1 speakers

Only a few 5.1 PC speaker sets come with S/PDIF. In most cases, you'll have to use the regular audio outputs on the sound card. You'll find the connector more common on 6.1 and 7.1 sets.

● **Figure 13.14** S/PDIF connectors

surround sound on your PC, you must purchase a full 5.1 speaker system. A number of 5.1 speaker systems are available for PCs. The choice you make is usually determined by what sounds best to you.

Many sound cards also come with a special **Sony/Philips digital interface (S/PDIF)** connector that enables you to connect your sound card directly to a 5.1 speaker system or receiver (Figure 13.14). Using a single S/PDIF instead of a tangle of separate wires for each speaker greatly simplifies your sound setup. S/PDIF connections come in two types, optical and coaxial. The optical variety looks like a square with a small door (at right in Figure 13.14). The coaxial is a standard RCA connector (at left), the same type used to connect a CD player to your stereo. It doesn't matter which one you use; just make sure you have an open spot on your receiver or speakers.

Games can also take advantage of 5.1, 6.1, and 7.1 speakers, but they use the DirectX standard. **DirectX** offers numerous commands, also known as APIs, that issue instructions such as "make a sound on the right speaker" or "play music in both the right and left channels." DirectX simplifies the programming needed to create sound and video: rather than having to program sounds in different ways for each sound card option, games can talk DirectX; the hardware manufacturers simply have to ensure that their sound cards are DirectX compatible.

DirectX version 3 introduced **DirectSound3D (DS3D)**, which offered a range of commands to place a sound anywhere in 3-D space. Known as **positional audio**, it fundamentally changed the way most PC games were played. DS3D could not handle all sound information, but it supported extensions to its instructions for more advanced sound features. This challenged the sound card designers to develop more fully the concept of positional audio. Creative Labs responded by rolling out **environmental audio extensions (EAX)**, a set of audio presets that gave developers the capability to create a convincing sense of environment in entertainment titles and a realistic sense of distance between the player and audio events. Figure 13.15 shows an EAX setup screen.

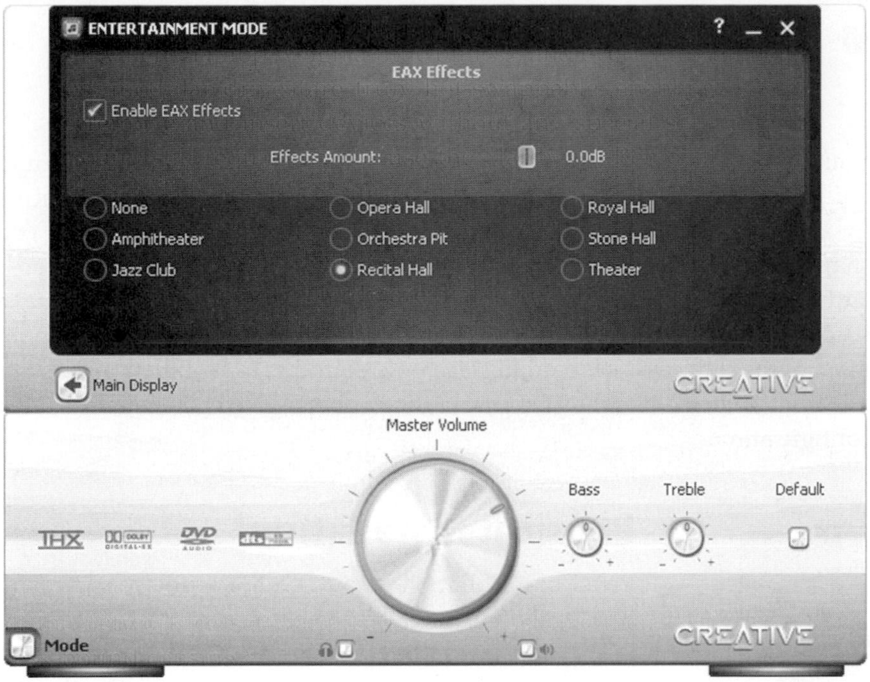

• **Figure 13.15**   EAX setup screen

In late 2000, a number of EAX effects were incorporated into the DirectX audio component of DirectX 8.0. This signaled the acceptance of EAX as the standard for audio effects in gaming. Shortly afterward, Creative Labs started releasing audio cards that were Dolby 5.1 compatible out of the box. This let you plug a 5.1 speaker system directly into your sound card. The sound card automatically decoded the Dolby/DTS sound track when you played a DVD and the EAX effects when you played a game that supports it. All current sound cards support DirectX and EAX.

Not all cards support Dolby Digital/DTS. Most software DVD players and some sound cards support Dolby Digital. DTS support is a little harder to come by. Check the manufacturer's Web site to determine whether your card will work with DTS.

Speaker Features

Speakers also come with a few other features that you should consider when choosing a set for yourself or your clients. Speakers offer a variety of power sources, controls accessibility, and headphone jacks.

Controls   All speakers have volume controls as well as an on/off switch. Get a system that provides easy access to those controls by placing them on an easy-to-reach speaker or on a special control box.

Headphone Jack   The problem with headphones is that you need to plug them into the back of the sound card and then tell Windows to output to them from the Sound applet on the Control Panel. Save yourself a lot of hassle and get a speaker system that has a handy microphone jack on one of the speakers or on a control box.

■ Installing Sound in a Windows System

You've got two choices for sound hardware on today's PCs: onboard sound built into the motherboard or a separate sound card. The installation process for a sound card is basically the same as the process for any other card. You snap the card into a slot, plug some speakers into the card, load a driver—and for the most part, you're done. With onboard sound, you need to make sure the sound is enabled in your CMOS and then load the driver. As with most of the devices discussed in this book, sound card installation consists of three major parts: physical installation, device driver installation, and configuration.

● **Figure 13.16** Typical sound card

Physical Installation

Physical installation is easy. Onboard sound is already physically installed and most sound cards are run-of-the-mill PCI cards (Figure 13.16). The real trick to physical installation is deciding where to plug in the speakers, microphone, and so on. The surround sound devices so common today feature a variety of jacks, so you will probably want to refer to your sound card documentation for details, but here are a few guidelines:

- The typical stereo or 2.1 speaker system will use only a single jack. Look for the jack labeled Speaker or Speaker 1.

- Surround speakers either use a single digital (S/PDIF) connection, which in most cases runs from the sound card to the subwoofer, or they need three separate cables: one for the front two speakers that runs to the Speaker 1 connector, one for the back two speakers that runs to the Speaker 2 connector, and a third cable for the center channel and subwoofer that runs to the digital/audio out or Speaker 3 connector.

Here's a quick look at sound card installation. As with any PCI card, you'll need a Phillips-head screwdriver to install a sound card, as well as your electrostatic discharge (ESD) prevention equipment. Of course, you'll also need the sound card itself, a set of speakers, an audio cable if it's an older system, and a microphone if you want to be able to record sounds.

1. Shut down your computer, unplug it, and open the case.
2. Find an open PCI slot and snap in the sound card. Remember to handle the card with tender loving care—especially if you're installing an expensive, high-end card! Make sure that the card is securely seated, and secure it to the chassis with a hex screw.

3. If you're installing into an older system, connect the CD audio cable to the back of the optical drive, and plug the other end into the CD audio port on your sound card. Be sure to use the correct connector—many sound cards have multiple audio connectors. The one shown in Figure 13.17, for example, has separate connectors to use for an optical drive or modem. This step is irrelevant in modern systems.

• **Figure 13.17** Sound card with multiple audio connectors

Installing Drivers

Once the sound card is installed, start the system and let Windows install the card's drivers. This applies to expansion cards and onboard sound. As you might expect by now, you'll probably have a choice between the built-in Windows drivers and the driver that comes on a CD-ROM with your sound card. Just as with other cards, it's always best to install the driver that comes with the card. All sound devices have easy-to-use autoplay-enabled installation CD-ROMs that step you through the process (Figure 13.18).

You might run into one of the USB sound cards out on the market (Figure 13.19), in which case the installation process is reversed. The only secret to these devices is to follow the important rule of all USB devices: *install the drivers before you plug in the device*. Windows, especially Windows XP and Vista, probably have basic drivers for these USB sound cards, but don't take a chance—always install the drivers first!

After your sound card and driver are installed, make a quick trip to the Device Manager to ensure that the driver was installed correctly, and you're two-thirds of the way there. Installing the driver is never the last step for a

> Sound card drivers are updated occasionally. Take a moment to check the manufacturer's Web site to see whether your sound card has any driver updates.

• **Figure 13.18** Typical autoplay screen for a sound card

• **Figure 13.19** USB sound card *(photo courtesy of Creative)*

sound card. Your final step is to configure the sound card using configuration programs and test it using an application. Most sound cards come with both special configuration programs and a few sound applications on the same CD-ROM that supplies the drivers. Take a look at these extra bits of software that I call *sound programs*.

Installing Sound Programs

You've already seen that you need a program to play sounds on your PC: Windows Media Player, Winamp, or something similar. But two other classes of sound programs also reside on your computer: programs for the configuration of your sound card and special applications that may or may not come with your sound card.

Configuration Applications

Every Windows computer comes with at least one important sound configuration program built right into the operating system: the Control Panel applet called **Sounds and Audio Devices** in Windows XP or Sounds and Multimedia in Windows 2000. Whatever the name, this applet (or applets) performs the same job: it provides a location for performing most or all the configuration you need for your sound card. Consider the Sounds and Audio Devices applet in Windows XP, for example; the Sounds and Multimedia applet in Windows 2000 works roughly the same, although it may have one control or another in a different place.

The Sounds and Audio Devices applet has five tabs: Volume, Sounds, Audio, Voice, and Hardware. The Volume tab is the most interesting. This tab adjusts the volume for the speakers, and it allows you to set up the type of speaker system you have, as shown in Figure 13.20.

The Sounds tab allows you to add customized sounds to Windows events, such as the startup of a program or Windows shutdown. The Audio tab (Figure 13.21) and Voice tab do roughly the same thing: they allow you to specify the device used for input and output of general sounds (Audio tab) and voice (Voice tab). These settings are handy for folks like me who have a regular microphone and speakers but also use a headset with microphone for voice recognition or Internet telephone software. By telling Windows to use the microphone for normal sounds and to use the headset for voice recognition, I don't have to make any manual changes when I switch from listening to an MP3 to listening to my brother when he calls me over the Internet.

The Hardware tab isn't used very often, but it does have one interesting feature: it shows you all of the audio and video codecs installed in your system (Figure 13.22). Not long ago, you had to install codecs manually in your system to play certain compressed file formats. Today, most audio players automatically detect whether a file is using an unrecognized codec and will download the proper codec for you.

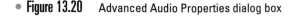
• **Figure 13.20**   Advanced Audio Properties dialog box

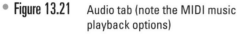

Figure 13.21 Audio tab (note the MIDI music playback options)

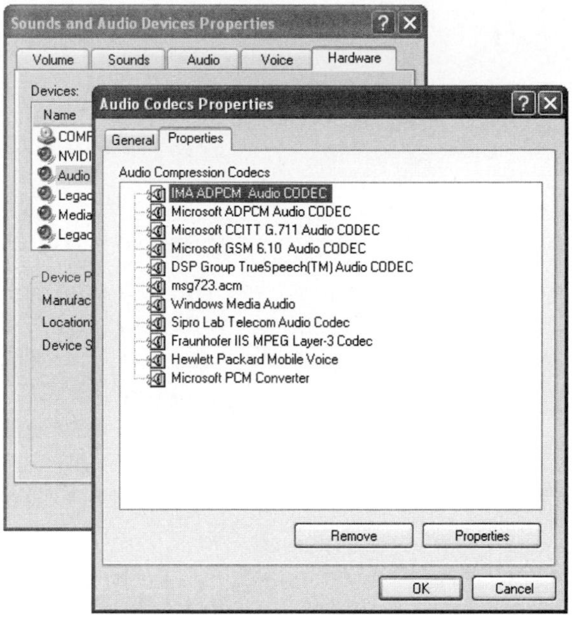

Figure 13.22 Audio codecs

Proprietary Configuration Applications

Many sound cards install proprietary software to support configuration features not provided by Windows. Figure 13.23 shows one such application. This special configuration application comes with Creative Labs sound cards to add a few tweaks to the speaker setup that the Sounds and Audio Devices applet doesn't support.

Figure 13.23 Creative Labs Speakers and Headphone panel

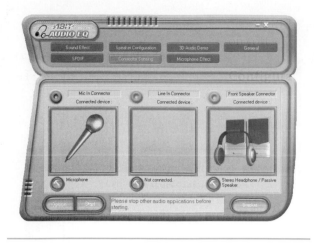

● **Figure 13.24** Autosensing software detecting connected devices

Most sound cards come with some form of configuration program that works with the Control Panel applet to tweak the sound the way you want it. Figure 13.24 shows the applet that came with my motherboard. One of its many interesting features is to detect what types of devices are installed into the sound ports and adjust the system to use them. In other words, I don't even have to look where I'm plugging in anything! If I plug a microphone into the front speakers port, the system just adjusts the outputs—very cool. Software and sound cards that can do this are called **autosensing**.

Take some time to experiment with the program that comes with your sound card—this is a great way to learn about some of the card's features that you might otherwise not even know are there!

Installing Applications

Some sound cards—Creative Labs sound cards are by far the most infamous for this—install one or more applications, ostensibly to improve your sound experience. These are not the configuration programs just described. These programs do anything from organizing your sound files to enabling you to compose music. Personally, I don't have a need for a 3DMIDI Player program (Figure 13.25)—but you might be just the type of person who loves it.

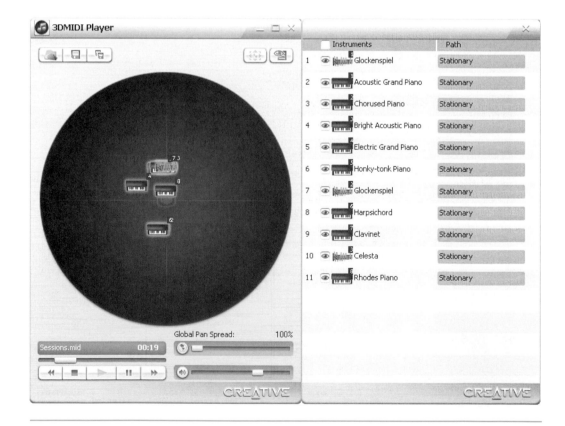

● **Figure 13.25** Creative Labs 3DMIDI Player program

Be sure at least to install the applications that come with your card. If you don't like them, you can easily uninstall them.

■ Troubleshooting Sound

The problems you'll run into with sound seem to fall into one of two camps: those that are embarrassingly simple to repair and those that defy any possible logic and are seemingly impossible to fix. This section divides sound problems into three groups—hardware, configuration, and application problems—and gives you some ideas on how to fix these problems.

Hardware Problems

Hardware problems are by far the most common sound problems, especially if your sound card has worked for some amount of time already. Properly installed and configured sound cards almost never suddenly stop making sounds.

Volume

The absolute first item to check when a sound dies is the volume controls. Remember that you can set the volume in two places: in software and on the speakers. I can't tell you the number of times I've lost sound only to discover that my wife turned down the volume on the speakers. If the speaker volume is okay, open the volume controls in Windows (Figure 13.26) by clicking the little speaker icon on the system tray, and make sure that both the master volume and the volume of the other controls are turned up.

Speakers

The second place to look for sound problems is the speakers. Make sure that the speakers are turned on and are getting good power. Then make sure the speakers are plugged into the proper connection on the back of the

If your system tray (i.e., the *notification area*) is cluttered and the little speaker icon hard to find, you can access the Play Control dialog box by opening the Sounds and Audio Devices applet in the Control Panel. On the Volume tab—the one that's on top by default—click the Advanced button under Device Volume. If you don't have a little speaker in your system tray at all, you can add it. Just check the box next to the *Place volume icon in the taskbar* option in the Volume tab of the Sound and Audio Devices Properties dialog box. Presto!

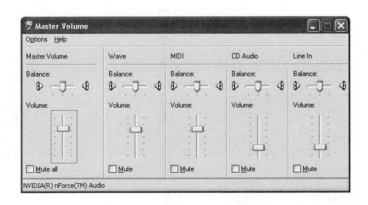

• **Figure 13.26**   Volume controls in Windows

Tech Tip

Sound Quality

Most of the time, speakers come in a matched set—whether it's a 2.1, 4.1, 5.1, or other system— and the manufacturer will include adequate connecting wires for the whole set. On occasion, you might run into a system in which the user has connected pairs of speakers from different sets or rigged a surround-sound system by replacing the stock wires with much longer wires. Either option can create a perfectly functional surround-sound system that works for a specific room, but you should make sure that all the speakers require the same wattage and that high-quality wire is used to connect them.

If you troubleshoot a system in which two are of the speakers are very quiet and two are very loud, the wattages are probably different between the two pairs. A simple check of the labels should suffice to troubleshoot, or you can swap out one pair for a different pair and see if that affects the volume issues. Cheap wire, on the other hand, simply degrades the sound quality. If the speakers sounded good before getting strung on long wires, but they now have a lot of low-grade noise, blame the wires.

Technically speaking, turning down the volume in the volume control program is not a configuration problem; it's just something I always check at the same time that I check the volume on the speakers.

sound card. If this all checks out, try playing a sound using any sound program. If the sound program *looks* like it is playing—maybe the application has an equalizer that is moving or a status marker that shows that the application is playing the sound—you may have blown speakers. Try another pair and see if the sound returns.

Configuration Problems

Configuration errors occur when the sound card is physically good but some setting hasn't been properly configured. I also include drive problems in this category. These errors happen almost exclusively at installation, but they can appear on a working system, too.

The first place to check is the Device Manager. If the driver has a problem, you'll see it right there. Try reinstalling the driver. If the driver doesn't show any problems, again try playing a sound and see if the player acts as though the sound is playing. If that's the case, you need to start touring the Sounds and Audio Devices applet to see if you've made a configuration error—perhaps you have the system configured for 5.1 when you have a stereo setup, or maybe you set the default sound output device to some other device. Take your time and look—configuration errors always show themselves.

Application Problems

Application problems are always the hardest to fix and tend to occur on a system that was previously playing sounds without trouble.

First, look for an error message (Figure 13.27). If an error code appears, write it down *exactly* as you see it and head to the program's support site. Odds are very good that if you have the error text, you'll get the fix right away from the support site. Of course, you can always hope the built-in help has some support, but help systems tend to be a little light in providing real fixes.

Don't always blame the sound application—remember that any sound file might be corrupted. Most sound players will display a clear error message, but not always. Try playing the sound file using another application.

Last, a good approach almost always is to reinstall the application.

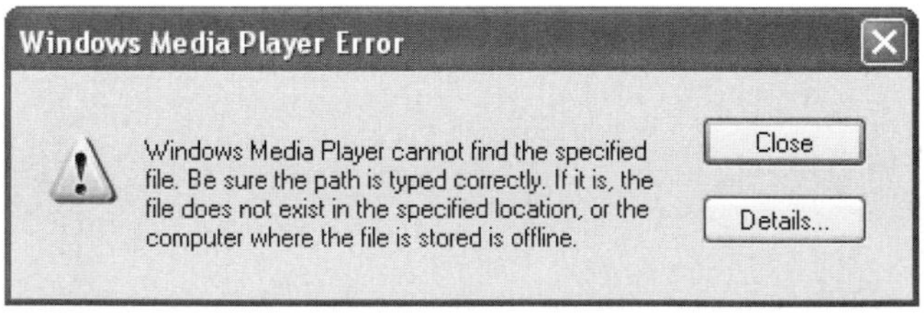

Windows Media Player Error

Windows Media Player cannot find the specified file. Be sure the path is typed correctly. If it is, the file does not exist in the specified location, or the computer where the file is stored is offline.

Close

Details...

• **Figure 13.27**   Sample error message

Beyond A+

Sound Card Benchmarking

Sound cards can demand a huge share of system resources—particularly CPU time—during intense work (like gaming). Most techs who find an otherwise serviceable PC stuttering during games will immediately blame the video card or the video card drivers. What they don't realize is that sound cards can be the cause of the problem. A recent test of a client's built-in audio, for example, revealed that at peak usage the sound card took more than 30 percent of the CPU cycles. Thirty percent? Holy smokes! And he wondered why his Pentium III system bogged down on yesterday's games! He could just forget about playing Half-Life 2 or DOOM 3.

The folks at iXBT.com/Digit-Life make an excellent suite of sound card benchmarking utilities that helps you analyze the particulars of any sound card: RightMark 3DSound (Figure 13.28). It will run a system through fairly serious tests, from regular sound to 3-D positional audio, and will reveal whether or not the sound processor—built-in or expansion card—is causing a problem with resource use. You can find the utility at http://audio.rightmark.org.

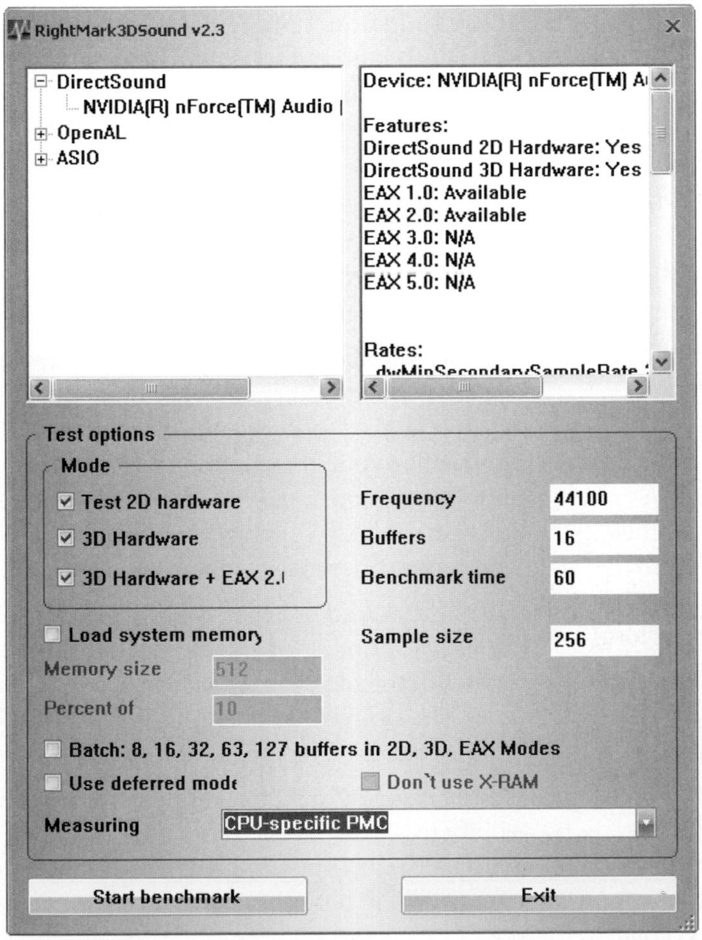

• **Figure 13.28**   RightMark 3DSound

Chapter 13 Review

■ Chapter Summary

After reading this chapter and completing the exercises, you should understand the following aspects of sound.

How Sound Works in a PC

■ The process by which sounds are stored in electronic format on your PC is called sampling. Sampling means capturing the state or quality of a particular sound wave a set number of times each second. All the characteristics of a particular sound wave—amplitude, frequency, and timbre—need to be recorded and translated into ones and zeroes to reproduce that sound accurately within the computer and out to your speakers. Sounds are sampled thousands of times per second. The amount of information stored at each sampling is called the bit depth, and the higher the bit depth, the better the recording.

■ The popular WAV file format (as well as most other recorded sound formats) is based on PCM. WAV files can be huge, especially when sampled at high frequency and depth, so compression is a popular way to reduce the file size of recorded sounds. The most popular compressed file type is MP3.

■ To play sounds, you must have some form of player software, such as Windows Media Player. Not all players can play all types of sound files. Some file formats, such as RealMedia, require their own proprietary players.

■ MIDI files are not recordings like WAV files. A MIDI file is a text file that takes advantage of the sound processing hardware to enable the PC to produce sound. Programmers use these small files to tell the sound card what notes to play, how long, how loud, on which instruments, and so forth.

■ Sound cards use one of two methods to store notes for MIDI: FM synthesis or wave table synthesis. FM synthesis electronically simulates various instruments, whereas wave table synthesis uses pre-recorded instruments.

■ A large number of other sound file formats is available, such as AAC and WMA. Sounds can also be found in video formats, applications, and streaming media, such as the Flash videos on YouTube.

Getting the Right Sound Card

■ Low-end sound processors do little more than translate, which means that the CPU has to do the heavy lifting on the processing front. Better sound processors, in contrast, shoulder much of the processing burden and bring a series of extra features to the table. Most mid-range and all high-end sound processors offer support for various surround sound standards, enabling equally equipped games and other applications to provide positional audio effects and detailed sound modeling.

■ Every sound card supports two speakers or a pair of headphones, but many better sound cards support five or more speakers in discrete channels. These multiple speakers provide surround sound and thumping bass through a subwoofer.

■ Better sound cards have a lower signal-to-noise ratio and support for multiple audio connections, such as a microphone, line in, and S/PDIF. The latter is for high-end audio.

■ Speaker standards include stereo (which uses a left speaker and a right speaker), 2.1 (stereo with an additional subwoofer), and surround sound. Do yourself or your client a favor and spend the extra money for good speakers. They're not that much more than cheap speakers, and they make an enormous difference for the user experience.

■ Surround sound is popular for games and DVD movies. A number of surround sound standards exist, but the most common are Dolby Digital and DTS. The Dolby Digital and DTS standards both require at least five speakers and a subwoofer.

■ DirectSound3D, a feature of DirectX 3, offered the ability to place a sound anywhere in 3-D space. DirectX 8.0 incorporated some EAX effects to add universally accepted support for positional audio.

Installing Sound in a Windows System

■ Sound card installation can be divided into three major steps: physical installation, device driver installation, and configuration.

■ While the physical installation of a sound card is straightforward, knowing where to plug in multiple speakers can be a bit of a challenge.

■ It is preferable to use the driver that comes with the sound card as opposed to the Windows built-in drivers.

■ Look for configuration programs in two places: in the Control Panel Sounds and Audio Devices applet and in any proprietary applications that are installed with the sound card.

Troubleshooting Sound

■ You can divide sound problems into three groups: hardware, configuration, and application problems.

■ The two first places to check when you suspect a hardware problem are the volume controls and speaker connectivity.

■ Configuration errors almost always take place at installation of the sound card.

■ Application problems are often the most challenging of all sound problems. Your best hope is an error message; you can then check the program's Web site for help.

■ Key Terms

2.1 (261)

5.1 (261)

amplitude (252)

autosensing (268)

bit depth (252)

CD quality (252)

codec (253)

decibels (258)

Digital Theatre Systems (DTS) (261)

DirectSound3D (DS3D) (262)

DirectX (262)

Dolby Digital (261)

environmental audio extensions (EAX) (262)

FM synthesis (254)

frequency (252)

monaural (252)

MP3 (253)

musical instrument digital interface (MIDI) (253)

polyphony (255)

positional audio (262)

pulse code modulation (PCM) (253)

sampling (252)

satellites (261)

signal-to-noise ratio (258)

Sony/Philips digital interface (S/PDIF) (262)

Sounds and Audio Devices (266)

stereo (252)

streaming (256)

subwoofer (258)

timbre (252)

wave table synthesis (255)

■ Key Term Quiz

Use the Key Terms list to complete the sentences that follow. Not all terms will be used.

1. _____ allows a sound card to simulate a number of different instruments.

2. Unlike recorded sounds, _____ uses specialized text files that tell the sound card which sounds to play.

3. 44.1 KHz stereo is also known as _____ audio.

4. _____ is the process of capturing the state or quality of a particular sound wave a set number of times each second.

5. The most common compressed audio format is _____.

6. A(n) _____ is a series of instructions telling a computer how to read a compressed file.

7. The Dolby Digital/DTS standards define six speakers using the terminology _____.

8. _____ offered the ability to place a sound anywhere in 3-D space.

9. The loudness of a sound is called its _____.

10. Better sound cards that can detect a device plugged into a port and adapt the features of that port are called _____ sound cards.

■ Multiple-Choice Quiz

1. CD-quality sound samples are recorded at 44 KHz, with 16-bit depth and what else?
   A. Monaural
   B. Stereo
   C. 5.1
   D. 2.1

2. What is the most common compressed sound format?
   A. MP3
   B. WAV
   C. VOC
   D. TXT

3. Almost all sound cards use which expansion bus?
   A. ISA
   B. AGP
   C. Internal
   D. PCI

4. Which audio/video compression format was created specifically to stream over the Internet?
   A. MP3
   B. MIDI
   C. WAV
   D. ASF

5. Which component of DirectX offered only a range of commands to place a sound anywhere in 3-D space?
   A. DirectSound
   B. DirectSound3D
   C. EAX
   D. A3D

6. What is the name of the direct competitor to Dolby Digital?
   A. DirectSound
   B. DirectSound3D
   C. DTS
   D. Surround Sound

7. To what does the *.1* in 5.1 or 2.1 refer?
   A. Volumetric sound positioning
   B. Subwoofer
   C. Subchannels
   D. Reverb positional matrices

8. Which version of DirectX introduced DirectSound3D?
   A. Version 8.0
   B. Version 3
   C. Version 2
   D. Version 1

9. Jane's sound card is suddenly not making any sound. She suspects that the volume is turned down. She checks the speaker volume and sees that it is turned up. What should she check next?
   A. The volume control program
   B. The application
   C. The speaker power
   D. The Device Manager

10. What type of file is a MIDI file?
    A. Audio
    B. Binary
    C. MP3
    D. Text

11. Which company created the SoundBlaster sound card?
    A. Creative Audio
    B. Creative Labs
    C. EAX
    D. Microsoft

12. You want to copy audio from a cassette tape onto your computer. To which jack on the sound card should you connect your cassette deck?
    A. Line in
    B. Microphone
    C. Line out
    D. Digital out

13. Which term refers to recording sound on a PC?

   A. Import

   B. Capture

   C. Encode

   D. Compress/decompress

14. What does PCM stand for?

   A. Pulse code modulation

   B. Pulse code manipulation

   C. Peripheral component management

   D. Packaged codec management

15. If the first movement of Beethoven's 5th Symphony was saved as a computer file, which file type would be the smallest in size?

   A. MP3

   B. WAV

   C. ASF

   D. MIDI

■ Essay Quiz

1. Detail in your own words how you think sound aided the evolution of the computer. What aspects of sound are necessary to computers? Why is sound needed?

2. Outline how you could use the connections provided on a modern sound card to create a multimedia home theater with your computer. Be sure to include hardware discussed in previous chapters, such as DVD-ROM drives.

3. Write an essay on the kind of sound card you would need for your computer. Detail what you personally would like to accomplish with your computer and how a sound card would help you.

4. Your clients have been having trouble with getting sound working on a number of systems recently purchased. Write a memo describing the user-level things that everyone should check before calling for a technician.

5. Your boss has decided that all systems in the office need new speakers, because the company that games together has more cohesion and happiness. Write a few paragraphs describing the speaker choices available and why one is better than the others.

Lab Projects

● Lab Project 13.1

Take a tour of the Web site for Creative Labs: www.creative.com. What sound-related products are currently featured there? Check out the specs for Creative's various SoundBlaster cards. Do you see sound cards that use an interface other than PCI?

Which features are available only on high-end cards? Which model would you choose to upgrade your current system? Which would you choose if you were building a new system?

● Lab Project 13.2

Uninstall and reinstall the audio drivers on your system. Before you do this, check your sound card manufacturer's Web site for an updated driver, and reinstall using the most recent driver that you can

find. Do any problems crop up during the process? After you get the new driver installed and working, do you notice an improvement in performance?

Portable Computing

> *"The great thing about a computer notebook is that no matter how much you stuff into it, it doesn't get bigger or heavier."*
>
> —Bill Gates, *Business @ The Speed of Thought*

In this chapter, you will learn how to

- **Describe the many types of portable computing devices available**
- **Enhance and upgrade portable computers**
- **Manage and maintain portable computers**
- **Troubleshoot portable computers**

There are times when the walls close in, when you need a change of scenery to get that elusive spark that inspires greatness...or sometimes you just need to get away from your coworkers for a few hours because they're driving you nuts! For many occupations, that's difficult to do. You've got to have access to your documents and spreadsheets; you can't function without e-mail or the Internet. In short, you need a computer to get your job done.

Portable computing devices combine mobility with accessibility to bring you the best of both worlds; put more simply, portables let you take some or even all of your computing abilities with you when you go. Some portable computers feature Windows XP systems with all the bells and whistles and all your Microsoft Office apps for a seamless transition from desk to café table. Even the smallest portable devices enable you to check your appointments and address book, or play Solitaire during the endless wait at the doctor's office. This chapter takes an in-depth look at portables, first going through the major variations you'll run into and then hitting the tech-specific topics of enhancing, upgrading, managing, and maintaining portable computers. Let's get started!

IT Technician

■ Portable Computing Devices

All portable devices share certain features. For output, they have LCD screens, although these vary from 20-inch behemoths to microscopic 2-inch screens. Portable computing devices employ sound of varying quality, from simple beeps to fairly nice music reproductions. All of them run on DC electricity stored in batteries, although several different technologies offer a range of battery life, lifespan, and cost. Other than screen, sound, and battery, portable computing devices come in an amazing variety of shapes, sizes, and intended uses.

If you look at the CompTIA A+ exam objectives for the Essentials, IT Technician, and Depot Technician exams, you'll notice that the objectives covered in this chapter are, for all intents and purposes, virtually the same for each exam. CompTIA has not differentiated the questions for each exam covered by this domain, so we have used the same chapter for the Essentials and IT Technician exams.

LCD Screens

Laptops come in a variety of sizes and at varying costs. One major contributor to the overall cost of a laptop is the size of the LCD screen. Most laptops offer a range between 12-inch to 17-inch screens (measured diagonally), while a few offer just over 20-inch screens. Not only are screens getting larger, but also wider screens are becoming the status quo. Many manufacturers are phasing out the standard 4:3 aspect

Cross Check

LCD Monitors

Stretching back to the early days of mobile computing, almost every make and model of portable device has used an LCD monitor of some shape or size. You know all about LCD monitors from the Essentials course and Chapter 12, "Installing and Troubleshooting Video." Everything that applies to desktop LCDs applies to screens designed for portable devices as well, so cross check your knowledge. What are the variations of LCD screen you'll find today? Which technology offers the best picture? What connectors do you find with LCDs? Are there any special rules about cleaning LCD monitors? (Talk about a leading question!)

ratio screen in favor of the widescreen format. **Aspect ratio** is the comparison of the screen width to the screen height. Depending on screen resolution, widescreens can have varying aspect ratios of 10:6, 16:9, 16:9.5, or 16:10. The 16:9 aspect ratio is the standard for widescreen movies while 16:10 is the standard for 17-inch LCD screens.

Laptop LCD screens come in a variety of supported resolutions, described with acronyms such as XGA, WXGA, WSXGA, and more. The *W* in front of the letters indicates widescreen. Table 14.1 lists commonly supported laptop display resolutions.

Table 14.1	Screen Resolutions	
Acronym	**Name**	**Native Resolution**
XGA	eXtended Graphics Array	1024 × 768
SXGA	Super eXtended Graphics Array	1280 × 1024
SXGA+	Super eXtended Graphics Array Plus	1400 × 1050
WSXGA+	Widescreen SXGA Plus	1680 × 1050
UXGA	Ultra eXtended Graphics Array	1600 × 1200
WUXGA	Widescreen UXGA	1920 × 1200

Laptop screens come with two types of finish: matte and high gloss . The matte finish was the industry standard for many years and offers a good trade-off between richness of colors and reflection or glare. The better screens have a wide viewing angle and decent response time. The major drawback for matte-finished laptop screens is that they wash out a lot in bright light. Using such a laptop at an outdoor café, for example, is almost hopeless during daylight.

Manufacturers released high-gloss laptop screens in 2006, and they've rapidly taken over many store shelves. The high-gloss finish offers sharper contrast, richer colors, and wider viewing angles when compared to the matte screens. Each manufacturer has a different name for high-gloss coatings. Dell calls theirs TrueLife; Acer calls theirs CrystalBrite; and HP calls theirs BrightView. The drawback to the high-gloss screens is that, contrary to what the manufacturers' claim, they pick up lots of reflection from nearby objects, including the user! So while they're usable outside during the day, you'll need to contend with increased reflection as well.

Desktop Replacements

When asked about portable computing devices, most folks describe the traditional clamshell laptop computer, such as the one in Figure 14.1, with built-in LCD monitor, keyboard, and input device (a *touchpad*, in this case). A typical laptop computer functions as a fully standalone PC, potentially even replacing the desktop. The one in Figure 14.1, for example, has all of the features you expect the modern PC to have, such as a fast CPU, lots of RAM, a high-capacity hard drive, CD-RW and DVD drives, an excellent sound system, and a functioning copy of Windows XP. Attach it to a

Tech Tip

What's in a Name?

There's no industry standard naming for the vast majority of styles of portable computing devices, so manufacturers let their marketing folks have fun with naming. What's the difference between a portable, a laptop, and a notebook? Nothing. One manufacturer might call its four-pound portable system with 12-inch LCD a notebook, while another manufacturer might call its much larger desktop-replacement portable a notebook as well. A laptop refers in general to the clamshell, keyboard-on-the-bottom and LCD-screen-at-the-top design that is considered the shape of mobile PCs.

• **Figure 14.1**   A notebook PC

Mike Meyers' CompTIA A+ Guide: PC Technician (Exams 220-602, 220-603, & 220-604)

network and you can browse the Internet and send e-mail. Considering it weighs almost as much as a mini-tower PC (or at least it feels like it does when I'm lugging it through the airport!), such a portable can be considered a `desktop replacement`, because it does everything that most people want to do with a desktop PC and doesn't compromise performance just to make the laptop a few pounds lighter or the battery last an extra hour.

For input devices, desktop replacements (and other portables) used trackballs in the early days, often plugged in like a mouse and clipped to the side of the case. Other models with trackballs placed them in front of the keyboard at the edge of the case nearest the user, or behind the keyboard at the edge nearest the screen.

The next wave to hit the laptop market was IBM's `TrackPoint` device, a pencil eraser–sized joystick situated in the center of the keyboard. The TrackPoint enables you to move the pointer around without taking your fingers away from the "home" typing position. You use a forefinger to push the joystick around, and click or right-click using two buttons below the spacebar. This type of pointing device has since been licensed for use by other manufacturers, and it continues to appear on laptops today.

But by far the most common laptop pointing device found today is the `touchpad` (Figure 14.2)—a flat, touch-sensitive pad just in front of the keyboard. To operate a touchpad, you simply glide your finger across its surface to move the pointer, and tap the surface once or twice to single- or double-click. You can also click using buttons just below the pad. Most people get the hang of this technique after just a few minutes of practice. The main advantage of the touchpad over previous laptop pointing devices is that it uses no moving parts—a fact that can really extend the life of a hard-working laptop. Some modern laptops actually provide both a TrackPoint-type device and a touchpad, to give the user a choice.

• **Figure 14.2** Touchpad on a laptop

Desktop Extenders

Manufacturers offer `desktop extender` portable devices that don't replace the desktop, but rather extend it by giving you a subset of features of the typical desktop that you can take away from the desk. Figure 14.3 shows a portable with a good but small 13.3-inch-wide screen. The system has 512 MB of RAM, a 2-GHz processor, a 60-GB hard drive, and a battery that enables you to do work on it for more than five hours while disconnected from the wall socket. Even though it plays music and has a couple of decent, tiny speakers, you can't game on this

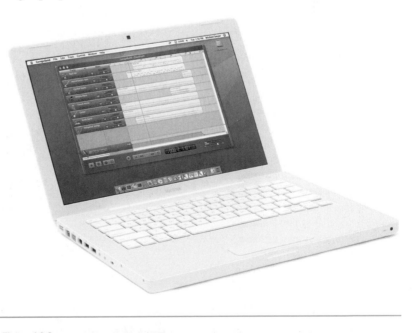

• **Figure 14.3** Excellent mid-sized portable computer

computer (Solitaire, perhaps, but definitely not Half-Life 2!). But it weighs only five pounds, nearly half the weight of the typical desktop replacement portable.

Desktop extenders enable you to go mobile. When I'm on a roll writing, for example, I don't want to stop. But sometimes I do want to take a break from the office and stroll over to my favorite café for a latté or a pint of fine ale. At moments like these, I don't need a fully featured laptop with a monster 15-inch or 17-inch screen, but just a good word processing system—and perhaps the ability to surf the Internet on the café's wireless network so I can research other important topics once I finish my project for the day. A lightweight laptop with a 12-inch or 13-inch screen, a reasonably fast processor, and gobs of RAM does nicely.

PDAs

Having a few computing essentials on hand at all times eases the day and makes planning and scheduling much more likely to succeed. Several companies, such as Palm, Sony, Toshiba, Hewlett-Packard, Dell, and Microsoft, manufacture tiny handheld portable computing devices that hold data such as your address book, personal notes, appointment schedules, and more. Such machines are called **personal digital assistants (PDAs)**. All modern PDAs have many applications, such as word processors for jotting down notes or shopping lists, expense reports, and even image viewers. Figure 14.4 shows a Palm Zire 71 PDA.

PDAs don't run Windows XP or even 98, but rather require specialized OSs such as Windows CE, PocketPC, PalmOS, and Linux. All of these OSs provide a GUI that enables you to interact with the device by touching the screen directly. Many of today's PDAs use handwriting recognition combined with modified mouse functions, usually in the form of a pen-like **stylus** to make a type of input called **pen-based computing**. To make an application load, for example, you would slide the stylus out of its holder in the PDA case and touch the appropriate icon with the stylus tip.

• **Figure 14.4**   Palm Zire 71 displaying a to-do list

HotSync

PDAs make excellent pocket companions because you can quickly add a client's address or telephone number, check the day's schedule before going to your next meeting, and modify your calendar entries when something unexpected arises. Best of all, you can then update all the equivalent features on your desktop PC automatically! PDAs synchronize with your primary PC so you have the same essential data on both machines. Many PDAs come with a cradle, a place to rest your PDA and recharge its battery. The cradle connects to the PC most often through a USB port. You can run special software to synchronize the data between the PDA and the main PC. Setting up the Zire 71 featured previously, for example, requires you to install a portion of the Palm desktop for Windows. This software handles all the synchronization chores. You simply place the PDA in the properly connected cradle and click the button to synchronize. Figure 14.5 shows a PDA in the middle of a **HotSync** operation, PalmOS's term for the process of synchronizing.

• **Figure 14.5**   HotSync in progress

Beaming

Just about every PDA comes with an infrared port that enables you to transfer data from one PDA to another, a process called **beaming**. For example, you can readily exchange business information when at a conference or swap pictures that you carry around in your PDA. The process is usually as simple as clicking a drop-down list and selecting Beam or Beaming from the menu. The PDA searches the nearby area—infrared has a very limited range—to discover any PDA nearby. The receiving PDA flashes a message to its owner asking permission to receive. Once that's granted, you simply stand there and wait for a moment while the PDAs transfer data. Slick!

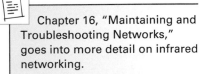

Chapter 16, "Maintaining and Troubleshooting Networks," goes into more detail on infrared networking.

PDA Memory

Almost every PDA has both internal flash ROM memory of 1 MB or more, and some sort of removable and upgradeable storage medium. Secure Digital (SD) technology has the strongest market share among the many competing standards, but you'll find a bunch of different memory card types out there. SD cards come in a variety of physical sizes (SD, Mini SD, and Micro SD) and fit in a special SD slot. Other popular media include CompactFlash (CF) cards and Sony's proprietary Memory Stick. You'll find capacities for all the standards ranging from 128 MB up to 8 GB—on a card the size of a postage stamp! Figure 14.6 shows some typical memory cards.

Tech Tip

Memory Cards

Memory cards of all stripes made the leap in 2003 from the exclusive realm of tiny devices such as PDAs and digital photographic cameras to full-featured portable PCs and even desktop models. Some Panasonic PCs sport SD card slots, for example, and you can expect nearly every Sony PC—portable or otherwise— made in 2003 and later to offer a Memory Stick port.

• **Figure 14.6**   SD, Mini SD, and Micro SD *(photos courtesy of SanDisk)*

Tablet PCs

Tablet PCs combine the handwriting benefits of PDAs with the full-fledged power of a traditional portable PC to create a machine that perfectly meets the needs of many professions. Unlike PDAs, tablet PCs use a full-featured PC operating system such as Microsoft Windows XP Tablet PC Edition 2005. Instead of (or in addition to) a keyboard and mouse, tablet PCs provide a screen that doubles as an input device. With a special pen, called a *stylus*, you can actually write on the screen (Figure 14.7). Just make sure you don't grab your fancy Cross ball-point pen accidentally and start writing on the screen! Unlike many PDA screens, most tablet PC screens are not pressure sensitive—you have to use the stylus to write on the screen. Tablet PCs come in two main form factors: *convertibles*, which include a keyboard that can be folded out of the way, and *slates*, which do away with the keyboard entirely. The convertible tablet PC in Figure 14.7, for example, looks and functions just like the typical clamshell laptop shown back in Figure 14.1. But here it's shown with the screen rotated 180 degrees and snapped flat so it functions as a slate. Pretty slick!

In applications that aren't "tablet-aware," the stylus acts just like a mouse, enabling you to select items, double-click, right-click, and so on. To input text with the stylus, you can either tap keys on a virtual keyboard (shown in Figure 14.8), write in the writing utility (shown in Figure 14.9), or use speech recognition software. With a little practice, most users will find the computer's accuracy in recognizing their handwriting to be sufficient for most text input, although speedy touch-typists will probably still want to use a keyboard when typing longer documents.

Tablet PCs work well when you have limited space or have to walk around and use a laptop. Anyone who has ever tried to type with one hand, while walking around the factory floor holding the laptop with the other hand, will immediately appreciate the beauty of a tablet PC. In this scenario, tablet PCs are most effective when combined with applications designed to

Tech Tip

Power Corrupts, but in This Case, It's Good

Handwriting recognition and speech recognition are two technologies that benefit greatly from increased CPU power. As multicore CPUs become more common, get ready to see more widespread adoption of these technologies!

• **Figure 14.7**   A tablet PC

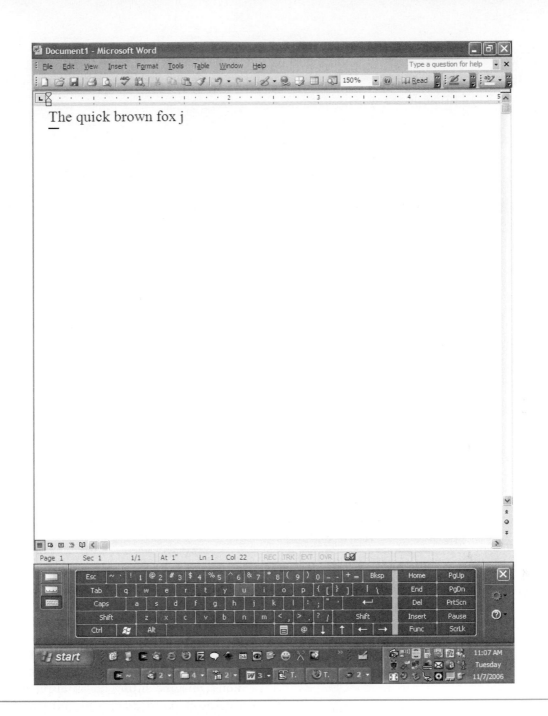

● **Figure 14.8**   The virtual keyboard

be used with a stylus instead of a keyboard. An inventory control program, for example, might present drop-down lists and radio buttons to the user, making a stylus the perfect input tool. With the right custom application, tablet PCs become an indispensable tool.

Microsoft encourages software developers to take advantage of a feature they call *digital ink,* which allows applications to accept pen strokes as input without first converting the pen strokes into text or mouse-clicks. Microsoft Journal (Figure 14.10), which comes with Windows-based tablet PCs, allows you to write on the screen just as though you were writing on a

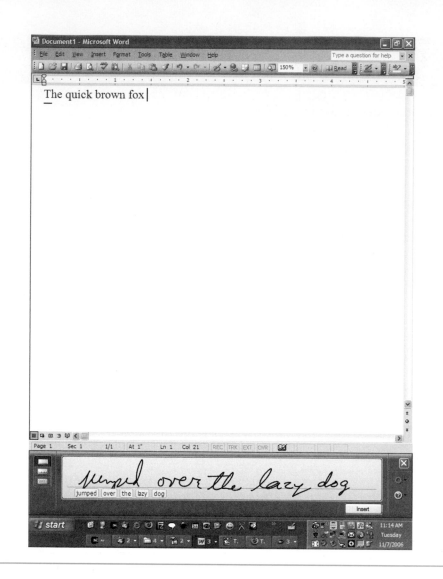

● **Figure 14.9** The writing pad

paper legal pad. Many other applications, including Microsoft Office, allow users to add ink annotations. Imagine sitting on an airplane reviewing a Microsoft Word document and simply scribbling your comments on the screen (Figure 14.11). No more printing out hard copy and breaking out the red pen for me! Imagine running a PowerPoint presentation and being able to annotate your presentation as you go. In the future, look for more applications to support Microsoft's digital ink.

There are many useful third-party applications designed specifically to take advantage of the tablet PC form factor. In fields such as law and medicine where tablet PCs have been especially popular, the choices are endless. One handy free utility that anyone who spends time in front of an audience

● **Figure 14.10** Microsoft Journal preserves pen strokes as digital ink.

(teachers, salespeople, cult leaders, and so on) will appreciate is InkyBoard (http://www.cfcassidy.com/Inkyboard/). Inkyboard provides a virtual dry-erase board, eliminating the need to find a flip chart or dry-erase board when holding meetings. Ever wished you could have a record of everything that was written on the chalkboard in a class (or at a business meeting)? If the professor had used Inkyboard, creating and distributing a copy would be a snap.

Portable Computer Device Types

Sorting through all the variations of portable computing devices out there would take entirely too much ink (and go well beyond CompTIA A+). Table 14.2 lists the seven most common styles of portable computing devices, some of their key features, and the intended use or audience for the product. This table is in no way conclusive, but lists the highlights.

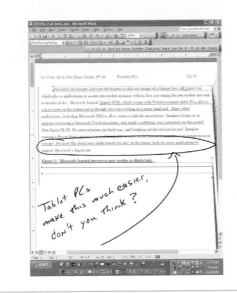

• **Figure 14.11** Microsoft Office supports digital ink.

Table 14.2	Portable Computing Devices			
	Screen Size	**Weight**	**Features**	**Uses**
Desktop replacements	14–20 inch+	8–12+ lbs	Everything on a desktop	Mobile multimedia editing, presentations, mobile gaming
Desktop extenders	10–14 inch	4–7 lbs	Almost everything you'll find on a desktop; better battery life than desktop replacements	Presentations, note-taking in class or meetings, traveling companion for business folks
Ultralights	6–12 inch	2–3 lbs	Ultimate mobility without sacrificing full PC status; excellent battery life; few have internal optical drives	Long-term traveling companion, in the purse or pack for writing or doing e-mail on the road, coolness factor
Tablet PCs	10–12 inch	4 lbs	Pen-based interface enables you to use them like a paper notepad; no optical drives, but integrated wireless networking	Niche market for people who need handwritten notes that have to be transcribed to the PC
Ultra-Mobile PCs	4–7 inch	1–2 lbs	A variation of tablet PCs, UMPCs run Windows XP (Tablet or Home edition); pen-based interface and no optical drives	More of a niche market than tablet PCs, but similar audience; see the "Beyond A+" section for details
PDAs	3–4 inch	1 lbs	Light, multifunction devices that carry address book and scheduler; many offer other features, such as MP3 and video playback	Helps busy people get/stay organized, fun, can carry many electronic books (e-books) so you're never caught waiting in line and being bored
PDA phones	2 inch	< 1 lbs	Tiny PDA built into a cell phone; some offer e-mail and other Internet connectivity	Reduces the number of gadgets some folks carry

Try This!

Variations

Portables come in such a dizzying variety of sizes, styles, features, and shapes that a simple table in a book cannot do justice to the ingenuity and engineering of the manufacturers of these devices. Only a hands-on field trip can bring home the point for you, so try this!

1. Visit your local computer or electronics store and tour the portable computing devices.

2. How many variations of laptops are there? Do any offer funky features, such as a swivel screen or a portrait-to-landscape mode?

3. How many variations of PDA are displayed? What operating systems do they run?

4. What other devices do you find? What about tablet PCs?

5. If you want to wander into the realm of extremes, check out www.dynamism.com. This company specializes in bringing Japanese-only products to the English-speaking market. You'll find the hottest desktop replacement laptops and the sleekest subnotebooks at the site, with all the details beautifully converted from native Japanese to English.

■ Enhance and Upgrade the Portable PC

In the dark ages of mobile computing, you had to shell out top dollar for any device that would unplug, and what you purchased was what you got. Upgrade a laptop? Add functions to your desktop replacement? You had few if any options, so you simply paid for a device that would be way behind the technology curve within a year and functionally obsolete within two.

Portable PCs today offer many ways to enhance their capabilities. Internal and external expansion buses enable you to add completely new functions to portables, such as attaching a scanner or mobile printer or both! You can take advantage of the latest wireless technology breakthrough simply by slipping a card into the appropriate slot on the laptop. Further, modern portables offer a modular interior. You can add or change RAM, for example— the first upgrade that almost every laptop owner wants to make. You can increase the hard drive storage space and, at least with some models, swap out the CPU, video card, sound card, and more. Gone forever are the days of buying guaranteed obsolescence! Let's look at four specific areas of technology that laptops use to enhance functions and upgrade components: PC Cards, single- and multiple-function expansion ports, and modular components.

> With fully one in five questions coving laptops and portables, pay attention to this chapter when studying for the CompTIA A+ certification 220-604 (Depot Technician) exam. You don't have to focus on it nearly as much when studying for the 220-603 (Help Desk) exam, which doesn't have a domain dedicated to portable computing.

PC Cards

The *Personal Computer Memory Card International Association (PCMCIA)* establishes standards involving portable computers, especially when it comes to expansion cards, which are generically called PC Cards. **PC Cards** are roughly credit card–sized devices that enhance and extend the functions of a portable PC. PC Cards are as standard on today's mobile computers as the hard drive. PC Cards are easy to use, inexpensive, and convenient. Figure 14.12 shows a typical PC Card.

Almost every portable PC has one or two PC Card slots, into which you insert a PC Card. Each card will have at least one function, but many have two, three, or more! You can buy a PC Card that offers connections for removable media, for example, such as combination SD and CF card readers. You can also find PC Cards that enable you to plug into multiple types of networks. All PC Cards are hot-swappable, meaning you can plug them in without powering down the PC.

The PCMCIA has established two versions of PC Cards, one using a parallel bus and the other using a serial bus. Each version, in turn, offers two technology variations as well as several physical varieties. This might sound complicated at first, but here's the map to sort it all out.

Parallel PC Cards

Parallel PC Cards come in two flavors, **16-bit** and **CardBus**, and each flavor comes in three different physical sizes, called Type I, Type II, and Type III. The 16-bit PC Cards, as the name suggests, are 16-bit, 5-V cards that can have up to two distinct functions or devices, such as a modem/network card combination. CardBus PC Cards are 32-bit, 3.3-V cards that can have up to eight (!) different functions on a single card. Regular PC Cards will fit into and work in CardBus slots, but the reverse is not true. CardBus totally dominates the current PC Card landscape, but you might still run into older 16-bit PC Cards.

Type I, II, and III cards differ only in the thickness of the card (Type I being the thinnest, and Type III the thickest). All PC Cards share the same 68-pin interface, so any PC Card will work in any slot that's high enough to accept that card type. Type II cards are by far the most common of PC Cards. Therefore, most laptops will have two Type II slots, one above the other, to enable the computer to accept two Type I or II cards or one Type III card (Figure 14.13).

Although PCMCIA doesn't require that certain sizes perform certain functions, most PC Cards follow their recommendations. Table 14.3 lists the sizes and typical uses of each type of PC Card.

ExpressCard

ExpressCard, the high-performance serial version of the PC Card, has begun to replace PC Card slots on

CompTIA uses the older term PCMCIA cards to describe PC Cards. Don't be shocked if you get that as an option on your exams! You'll hear many techs use the phrase as well, though the PCMCIA trade group has not used it for many years.

Many manufacturers use the term *hot-pluggable* rather than hot-swappable to describe the ability to plug in and replace PC Cards on the fly. Look for either term on the exams.

• **Figure 14.12** PC Card

• **Figure 14.13** PC Card slots

Table 14.3	PC Card Types and Their Typical Uses			
Type	**Length**	**Width**	**Thickness**	**Typical Use**
Type I	85.6 mm	54.0 mm	3.3 mm	Flash memory
Type II	85.6 mm	54.0 mm	5.0 mm	I/O (Modem, NIC, and so on)
Type III	85.6 mm	54.0 mm	10.5 mm	Hard drives

newer laptop PCs. While ExpressCard offers significant performance benefits, keep in mind that ExpressCard and PC Cards are incompatible. You cannot use your PC Card in your new laptop's ExpressCard socket. The PC Card has had a remarkably long life in portable PCs, and you can still find it on some new laptops, but get ready to replace all your PC Card devices. ExpressCard comes in two widths: 54 mm and 34 mm. Figure 14.14 shows a 34-mm ExpressCard. Both cards are 75-mm long and 5-mm thick, which makes them shorter than all previous PC Cards and the same thickness as a Type II PC Card.

ExpressCards connect to either the Hi-Speed USB 2.0 bus or a PCI Express bus. These differ phenomenally in speed. The amazingly slow-in-comparison USB version has a maximum throughput of 480 Mbps. The PCIe version, in contrast, roars in at 2.5 Gbps in unidirectional communication. Woot!

Table 14.4 shows the throughput and variations for the parallel and serial PC Cards currently or soon to be on the market.

Software Support for PC Cards

The PCMCIA standard defines two levels of software drivers to support PC Cards. The first, lower level is known as **socket services**. Socket services are device drivers that support the PC Card socket, enabling the system to detect when a PC Card has been inserted or removed, and providing the necessary I/O to the device. The second, higher level is known as **card services**. The card services level recognizes the

© 2003 PCMCIA
www.expresscard.org

● **Figure 14.14** 34-mm ExpressCard *(photo courtesy of PCMCIA)*

Table 14.4	PC Card Speeds
Standard	**Maximum Theoretical Throughput**
PC Card using 16-bit bus	160 Mbps
CardBus PC Card using PCI bus	1056 Mbps
ExpressCard using USB 2.0 bus	480 Mbps
ExpressCard using PCIe bus	2.5 Gbps

function of a particular PC Card and provides the specialized drivers necessary to make the card work.

In today's laptops, the socket services are standardized and are handled by the system BIOS. Windows itself handles all card services and has a large preinstalled base of PC Card device drivers, although most PC Cards come with their own drivers.

Limited-Function Ports

All portable PCs and many PDAs come with one or more single-function ports, such as an analog VGA connection for hooking up an external monitor and a PS/2 port for a keyboard or mouse. Note that contrary to the setup on desktop PCs, the single PS/2 port on most laptops supports both keyboards and pointing devices. Most portable computing devices have a speaker port, and this includes modern PDAs. My Compaq iPAQ doubles as an excellent MP3 player, by the way, a feature now included with most PDAs. Some portables have line-in and microphone jacks as well. Finally, most current portable PCs come with built-in NICs or modems for networking support. (See the section "The Modular Laptop" later in this chapter for more on networking capabilities.)

All limited-function ports work the same way on portable PCs as they do on desktop models. You plug in a device to a particular port and, as long as Windows has the proper drivers, you will have a functioning device when you boot. The only port that requires any extra effort is the video port.

Most laptops support a second monitor via an analog VGA port or a digital DVI port in the back of the box. With a second monitor attached, you can display Windows on only the laptop LCD, only the external monitor, or both simultaneously. Not all portables can do all variations, but they're more common than not. Most portables have a special Function (FN) key on the keyboard that, when pressed, adds an additional option to certain keys on the keyboard. Figure 14.15 shows a close-up of a typical keyboard with the Function key; note the other options that can be accessed with the Function key such as indicated on the F5 key. To engage the second monitor or to cycle through the modes, hold the Function key and press F5.

General-Purpose Ports

Sometimes the laptop doesn't come with all of the hardware you want. Today's laptops usually include several USB ports and a selection of the legacy general-purpose expansion ports (PS/2, RS-232 serial ports, and so on) for installing peripheral hardware. If you're lucky, you might even get a FireWire port so you can plug in your fancy new digital video camera. If you're really lucky, you might even

ExpressCards don't require either socket or card services, at least not in the way PC Cards do. The ExpressCard modules automatically configure the software on your computer, which makes them truly plug and play.

Although many laptops use the Function key method to cycle the monitor selections, that's not always the case. You might have to pop into the Display applet in the Control Panel to click a checkbox. Just be assured that if the laptop has a VGA or DVI port, you can cycle through monitor choices!

• **Figure 14.15** Laptop keyboard with Function (FN) key that enables you to access additional key options, as on the F5 key

have a docking station or port replicator so you don't have to plug in all of your peripheral devices one at a time.

USB and FireWire

Universal serial bus (USB) and FireWire (or more properly, IEEE 1394) are two technologies that have their roots in desktop computer technology, but have also found widespread use in portable PCs. Both types of connections feature an easy-to-use connector and give the user the ability to insert a device into a system while the PC is running—you won't have to reboot a system in order to install a new peripheral. With USB and FireWire, just plug the device in and go! Because portable PCs don't have multiple internal expansion capabilities like desktops, USB and FireWire are two of the more popular methods for attaching peripherals to laptops (see Figure 14.16).

Port Replicators

A **port replicator** plugs into a single port on the portable computer— often a USB port, but sometimes a proprietary port—and offers common PC ports, such as serial, parallel, USB, network, and PS/2. By plugging the port replicator into your notebook computer, you can instantly connect it to non-portable components such as a printer, scanner, monitor, or a full-sized keyboard. Port replicators are typically used at home or in the office with the non-portable equipment already connected. Figure 14.17 shows an Dell Inspiron laptop connected to a port replicator.

Once connected to the port replicator, the computer can access any devices attached to it; there's no need to connect each individual device to the PC. As a side bonus, port replicators enable you to attach legacy devices, such as parallel printers, to a new laptop that only has modern

• **Figure 14.16**   Devices attached to USB or FireWire connector on portable PC

multifunction ports such as USB and FireWire, and not parallel or serial ports.

Docking Stations

Docking stations (see Figure 14.18) resemble port replicators in many ways, offering legacy and modern single-function and multifunction ports. The typical docking station uses a proprietary connection, but has extra features built in, such as a DVD drive or PC Card slot for extra enhancements. You can find docking stations for most laptop models, but you'll find them used most frequently with the desktop extender and ultralight models. Many ultralights have no internal CD or DVD media drive (because the drives weigh too much), and so must rely on external drives for full PC functionality. Docking stations make an excellent companion to such portables.

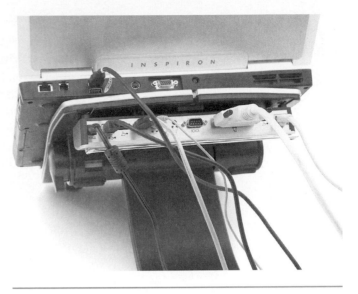

• **Figure 14.17**   Port replicator for a Dell portable computer

The Modular Laptop

For years, portable PC makers required completely proprietary components for each system model they developed. For the most part, this proprietary attitude still prevails, but manufacturers have added some modularity to today's portable PCs, enabling you to make basic replacements and upgrades without going back to the manufacturer for expensive, proprietary components. You need to surf the Web for companies that sell the components, because very few storefronts stock them. The most common modular components are RAM, hard drives, CPUs, video cards, optical drives, and network cards.

RAM

Stock factory portable PCs almost always come with a minimal amount of RAM, so one of the first laptop upgrades you'll be called on to do is to add more RAM. Economy laptops running Windows XP Home routinely sit on

• **Figure 14.18**   Docking station

store shelves and go home to consumers with as little 256 MB of RAM, an amount guaranteed to limit the use and performance of the laptop. The OS alone will consume more than half of the RAM! Luckily, every decent laptop has upgradeable RAM slots. Laptops use one of four types of RAM. Most older laptops use either 72-pin or 144-pin SO-DIMMs with SDRAM technology (Figure 14.19). DDR and DDR2 systems primarily use 200-pin SO-DIMMs although some laptops use micro-DIMMs.

How to Add or Replace RAM   Upgrading the RAM in a portable PC requires a couple of steps. First, you need to get the correct RAM. Many older portable PCs use proprietary RAM solutions, which means you need to order directly from Dell, HP, or Sony and pay exorbitant prices for the precious extra megabytes. Most manufacturers have taken pity on consumers in recent years and use standard SO-DIMMs or micro-DIMMs. Refer to the manufacturer's Web site or to the manual (if any) that came with the portable for the specific RAM needed.

Second, every portable PC offers a unique challenge to the tech who wants to upgrade the RAM because there's no standard for RAM placement in portables. More often than not, you need to unscrew or pop open a panel on the underside of the portable (Figure 14.20). Then you press out on the restraining clips and the RAM stick will pop up (Figure 14.21). Gently remove the old stick of RAM and insert the new one by reversing the steps.

● **Figure 14.19**   72-pin SO-DIMM stick (front and back)

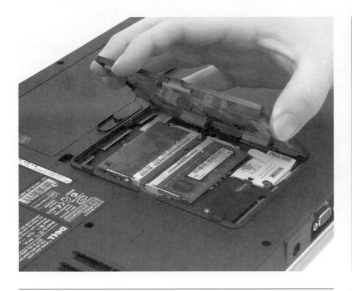

● **Figure 14.20**   Removing a RAM panel

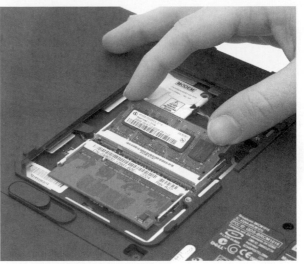

● **Figure 14.21**   Releasing the RAM

Shared Memory   Some laptops (and desktops) support `shared memory`. Shared memory is a means of reducing the cost of video cards by reducing the amount of memory on the video card itself. Instead of a video card with 256 MB of RAM, it might have only 64 MB of RAM but can borrow 192 MB of RAM from the system. This equates to a 256-MB video card. The video card uses regular system RAM to make up for the loss.

The obvious benefit of shared memory is a less expensive video card with performance comparable to its mega-memory alternative. The downside is your overall system performance will suffer because a portion of the system RAM is no longer available to programs. (The term *shared* is a bit misleading because the video card takes control of a portion of RAM. The video portion of system RAM is *not* shared back and forth between the video card processor and the CPU.) Shared memory technologies include TurboCache (developed by NVIDIA) and HyperMemory (developed by ATI).

Some systems give you control over the amount of shared memory while others simply allow you to turn shared memory on or off. The settings are found in CMOS setup and only on systems that support shared memory. Shared memory is not reported to Windows so don't panic if you've got 1 GB of RAM in your laptop, but Windows only sees 924 MB—the missing memory is used for video!

Adding more system RAM to a laptop with shared memory will improve laptop performance. Although it might appear to improve video performance, that doesn't tell the true story. It'll improve overall performance because the OS and CPU get more RAM to work with. On some laptops, you can improve video performance as well, but that depends on the CMOS setup. If the shared memory is not set to maximum by default, increasing the overall memory and upping the portion reserved for video will improve video performance specifically.

Hard Drives

ATA drives in the 2.5-inch drive format now rule in all laptops. Although much smaller than regular ATA drives, they still use all the same features and configurations. These smaller hard drives have suffered, however, from diminished storage capacity compared to their 3.5-inch brothers. Currently, large 2.5-inch hard drives hold up to 120 GB, while the 3.5-inch hard drives can hold more than 750 GB of data! Some manufacturers may require you to set the drive to use a cable select setting as opposed to master or slave, so check with the laptop maker for any special issues. Otherwise, no difference exists between 2.5-inch drives and their larger 3.5-inch brethren (Figure 14.22).

• **Figure 14.22**   The 2.5-inch and 3.5-inch drives are mostly the same.

Tech Tip

Going Inside

To reach most modular components on a laptop, you need to do more than remove an exterior panel. You need to go inside to get access to devices directly connected to the motherboard. Many laptops have an easily removable keyboard that, once removed, gives you access to a metal heat spreader (just a plate that sits over the motherboard) and a half-dozen or more tiny screws. You'll need a special screwdriver to avoid stripping the screws—check a watch or eyeglass shop if your local hardware store doesn't carry anything appropriate.

You need to take major precautions when you remove the keyboard and heat spreader. The keyboard will be attached to a small cable that can easily disconnect if you pull hard. Don't forget to check this connection before you reinsert the keyboard at the end of the procedure! Avoid ESD like you would with any other PC, and definitely unplug the laptop from the wall and remove the battery before you do any work inside!

Modular CPUs

Both AMD and Intel make specialized CPUs for laptops that produce less heat and consume less power, yet only now are folks realizing that they can easily upgrade many systems by removing the old CPU and replacing it with a new one. Be very careful to follow manufacturer's specifications! You should keep in mind, however, that replacing the CPU in a laptop often requires that you disassemble the entire machine. This can be a daunting task, even for professionals. If you want to upgrade the CPU in your laptop, it's often best to let the professionals take care of it.

Video Cards

Some video card makers make modular video cards for laptops. Although no single standard works in all systems, a quick phone call to the tech support department of the laptop maker often reveals upgrade options (if any). Modular video cards are the least standardized of all modular components, but as manufacturers adopt more industry-wide standards, we'll be able to replace video cards in laptops more readily.

Modular Drives

In order to add functionality to laptops, manufacturers include "modular drives" with their machines. CD-ROM, DVD-ROM, CD-R/RW, and CD-RW/DVD-ROM drives are the most common modular drives that are included with portables. The beauty of modular drives is that you can swap easily back and forth between different types of drives. Need more storage space? Pull out the CD-ROM drive and put in another hard drive. Many laptops enable you to replace a drive with a second battery, which obviously can extend the time you can go before you have to plug the laptop into an AC outlet.

I have a laptop that allows me to swap out my CD-ROM drive for a second battery. If I don't need to access any CDs and don't need super-extended battery life, I just take out the component that's currently installed and put a blank faceplate into the empty slot. Traveling with an empty bay makes my hefty laptop weigh a little bit less, and every little bit helps!

Most modular drives are truly hot-swappable, enabling you to remove and insert devices without any special software. Many still require you to use the Hardware Removal Tool (also known as Safely Remove Hardware) located in the system tray or notification area (Figure 14.23). When in doubt, always remove modular devices using this tool. Figure 14.24 shows the Safely Remove Hardware dialog box. To remove a device, highlight it and click the Stop button. Windows will shut down the device and tell you when it's safe to remove the device.

• **Figure 14.23**   Hardware Removal Tool in system tray

Mobile NICs and Mini PCI

Every laptop made in the last few years comes with networking capabilities built in. They have modems for dial-up and Ethernet ports for plugging into a wired network. Because they run Windows, OS X, or some Linux distro, laptops have all the networking software ready to go, just like their desk-bound cousins.

Many laptops now come with integrated wireless networking support by way of a built-in Wi-Fi adapter usually installed in a Mini PCI slot on the laptop motherboard. The **Mini PCI** bus is an adaptation of the standard PCI bus and was developed specifically for integrated communications peripherals such as modems and network adapters. Built-in networking support means you don't need an additional PC Card to provide a network adapter. The Mini PCI bus also provides support for other integrated devices such as Bluetooth, modems, audio, or hard drive controllers. One great aspect of Mini PCI is that if some new technology eclipses the current wireless technology or some other technology that uses the bus, you can upgrade by swapping a card.

Officially released in 1999, Mini PCI is a 32-bit 33-MHz bus and is basically PCI v2.2 with a different form factor. Like PCI, it supports bus mastering and DMA. Mini PCI cards are about a quarter the size of a regular PCI card and can be as small as 2.75 inches by 1.81 inches by .22 inches. They can be found in small products such as laptops, printers, and set-top boxes.

To extend battery life, built-in communication devices such as Wi-Fi and Bluetooth adapters can be toggled on and off without powering down the computer. Many laptops come with a physical switch along the front or side edge allowing you to power on or off the communications adapter. Similarly, you can often use a keyboard shortcut for this, generally by pressing the Function (FN) key along with some other key. The FN key, when pressed, allows other keys to accomplish specific tasks. For example, on my laptop pressing FN-F2 toggles my Wi-Fi adapter on and off; pressing FN-F10 ejects my CD-ROM drive.

• **Figure 14.24**   Safely Remove Hardware dialog box

A typical reason to upgrade a Mini PCI Wi-Fi NIC is to gain access to improved security options such as better encryption.

Chapter 16, "Maintaining and Troubleshooting Networks," covers wireless networking in great detail.

■ Managing and Maintaining Portable Computers

Most portable PCs come from the factory solidly built and configured. Manufacturers know that few techs outside their factories know enough to work on them, so they don't cut corners. From a tech's standpoint, your most common work on managing and maintaining portables involves taking care of the batteries and extending the battery life through proper power management, keeping the machine clean, and avoiding excessive heat.

Everything you normally do to maintain a PC applies to portable PCs. You need to keep current on Windows patches and Service Packs, and use stable, recent drivers. Run Check Disk with some frequency, and definitely defragment the hard drive. Disk Cleanup is a must if the laptop runs Windows XP. That said, let's look at issues specifically involving portables.

Batteries

Manufacturers use three different types of batteries for portable PCs and each battery type has its own special needs and quirks. Once you've got a clear understanding of the quirks, you can *usually* spot and fix battery problems. The three types of batteries commonly used in mobile PCs are Nickel-Cadmium (Ni-Cd), Nickel-Metal Hydride (Ni-MH), and Lithium-Ion (Li-Ion) batteries. Manufacturers have also started working with fuel cell batteries, although most of that work is experimental at this writing.

Nickel-Cadmium

Ni-Cds were the first batteries commonly used in mobile PCs, which means the technology was full of little problems. Probably most irritating was a little thing called battery memory, or the tendency of a Ni-Cd battery to lose a significant amount of its rechargeability if it was charged repeatedly without being totally discharged. A battery that originally kept a laptop running for two hours would eventually only keep that same laptop going for 30 minutes or less. Figure 14.25 shows a typical Ni-Cd battery.

To prevent memory problems, a Ni-Cd battery had to be discharged completely before each recharging. Recharging was tricky as well, because Ni-Cd batteries disliked being overcharged. Unfortunately, there was no way to verify when a battery was fully charged without an expensive charging machine, which none of us had. As a result, most Ni-Cd batteries lasted an extremely short time and had to be replaced. A quick fix was to purchase a conditioning charger. These chargers would first totally discharge the Ni-Cd battery, and then generate a special "reverse" current that, in a way, "cleaned" internal parts of the battery so that it could be recharged more often and would run longer on each recharge. Ni-Cd batteries would, at best, last for 1000 charges, and far fewer with poor treatment. Ni-Cds

● **Figure 14.25**   Ni-Cd battery

were extremely susceptible to heat and would self-discharge over time if not used. Leaving a Ni-Cd in the car in the summer was guaranteed to result in a fully discharged battery in next to no time!

But Ni-Cd batteries didn't stop causing trouble after they died. The highly toxic metals inside the battery made it unacceptable simply to throw them in the trash. Ni-Cd batteries should be disposed of via specialized disposal companies. This is very important! Even though Ni-Cd batteries aren't used in PCs very often anymore, many devices, such as cellular and cordless phones, still use Ni-Cd batteries. Don't trash the environment by tossing Ni-Cds in a landfill. Turn them in at the closest special disposal site; most recycling centers are glad to take them. Also, many battery manufacturers/distributors will take them. The environment you help preserve just might be yours—or your kids'!

Nickel-Metal Hydride

Ni-MH batteries were the next generation of mobile PC batteries and are still quite common today. Basically, Ni-MH batteries are Ni-Cd batteries without most of the headaches. Ni-MH batteries are much less susceptible to memory problems, can better tolerate overcharging, can take more recharging, and last longer between rechargings. Like Ni-Cds, Ni-MH batteries are still susceptible to heat, but at least they are considered less toxic to the environment. It's still a good idea to do a special disposal. Unlike a Ni-Cd, it's usually better to recharge a Ni-MH with shallow recharges as opposed to a complete discharge/recharge. Ni-MH is a popular replacement battery for Ni-Cd systems (Figure 14.26).

Lithium Ion

The most common type battery used today is Li-Ion. Li-Ion batteries are very powerful, completely immune to memory problems, and last at least twice as long as comparable Ni-MH batteries on one charge. Sadly, they can't handle as many charges as Ni-MH types, but today's users are usually more than glad to give up total battery lifespan in return for longer periods between charges. Li-Ion batteries will explode if they are overcharged, so all Li-Ion batteries sold with PCs have built-in circuitry to prevent accidental overcharging. Lithium batteries can only be used on systems designed to use them. They can't be used as replacement batteries (Figure 14.27).

Other Portable Power Sources

In an attempt to provide better maintenance for laptop batteries, manufacturers have developed a new type of battery called the smart battery. Smart batteries tell the computer when they need to be charged, conditioned, or replaced.

Portable computer manufacturers are also looking at other potential power sources, especially ones that don't have the shortcomings of current batteries. The most promising of these new technologies is fuel cells. The technology behind fuel cells is very complex, but to summarize, fuel cells produce electrical power as a result of a chemical reaction between the hydrogen

• **Figure 14.26** Ni-MH battery

• **Figure 14.27** Li-Ion battery

You *must* use disposal companies or battery recycling services to dispose of the highly toxic Ni-Cd batteries.

and oxygen contained in the fuel cell. It is estimated that a small fuel cell could power a laptop for up to 40 hours before it needs to be replaced or refilled. This technology is still a year or two from making it to the consumer market, but it's an exciting trend!

The Care and Feeding of Batteries

In general, keep in mind the following basics. First, always store batteries in a cool place. Although a freezer is in concept an excellent storage place, the moisture, metal racks, and food make it a bad idea. Second, condition your Ni-Cd and Ni-MH batteries by using a charger that also conditions the battery; they'll last longer. Third, keep battery contacts clean with a little alcohol or just a dry cloth. Fourth, *never* handle a battery that has ruptured or broken; battery chemicals are very dangerous. Finally, always recycle old batteries.

Power Management

Many different parts are included in the typical laptop, and each part uses power. The problem with early laptops was that every one of these parts used power continuously, whether or not the system needed that device at that time. For example, the hard drive would continue to spin whether or not it was being accessed, and the LCD panel would continue to display, even when the user walked away from the machine.

The optimal situation would be a system where the user could instruct the PC to shut down unused devices selectively, preferably by defining a maximum period of inactivity that, when reached, would trigger the PC to shut down the inactive device. Longer periods of inactivity would eventually enable the entire system to shut itself down, leaving critical information loaded in RAM, ready to restart if a wake-up event (such as moving the mouse or pressing a key) would tell the system to restart. The system would have to be sensitive to potential hazards, such as shutting down in the middle of writing to a drive, and so on. Also, this feature could not add significantly to the cost of the PC. Clearly, a machine that could perform these functions would need specialized hardware, BIOS, and operating system to operate properly. This process of cooperation among the hardware, the BIOS, and the OS to reduce power use is known generically as *power management*.

System Management Mode (SMM)

Intel began the process of power management with a series of new features built into the 386SX CPU. These new features enabled the CPU to slow down or stop its clock without erasing the register information, as well as enabling power saving in peripherals. These features were collectively called **System Management Mode (SMM)**. All modern CPUs have SMM. Although a power-saving CPU was okay, power management was relegated to special "sleep" or "doze" buttons that would stop the CPU and all of the peripherals on the laptop. To take real advantage of SMM, the system needed a specialized BIOS and OS to go with the SMM CPU. To this end, Intel put forward the **Advanced Power Management (APM)** specification in 1992 and the **Advanced Configuration and Power Interface (ACPI)** standard in 1996.

Requirements for APM/ACPI

APM and ACPI require a number of items in order to function fully. First is an SMM-capable CPU. As virtually all CPUs are SMM-capable, this is easy. Second is an APM-compliant BIOS, which enables the CPU to shut off the peripherals when desired. The third requirement is devices that will accept being shut off. These devices are usually called "Energy Star" devices, which signals their compliance with the EPA's Energy Star standard. To be an Energy Star device, a peripheral must have the ability to shut down without actually turning off and show that they use much less power than the non–Energy Star equivalent. Last, the system's OS must know how to request that a particular device be shut down, and the CPU's clock must be slowed down or stopped.

ACPI goes beyond the APM standard by supplying support for hot-swappable devices—always a huge problem with APM. This feature aside, it is a challenge to tell the difference between an APM system and an ACPI system at first glance.

Don't limit your perception of APM, ACPI, and Energy Star just to laptops! Virtually all desktop systems also use the power management functions.

APM/ACPI Levels

APM defines four different power-usage operating levels for a system. These levels are intentionally fuzzy to give manufacturers considerable leeway in their use; the only real difference among them is the amount of time each takes to return to normal usage. These levels are as follows:

- **Full On**   Everything in the system is running at full power. There is no power management.

- **APM Enabled**   CPU and RAM are running at full power. Power management is enabled. An unused device may or may not be shut down.

- **APM Standby**   CPU is stopped. RAM still stores all programs. All peripherals are shut down, although configuration options are still stored. (In other words, to get back to APM Enabled, you won't have to reinitialize the devices.)

- **APM Suspend**   Everything in the PC is shut down or at its lowest power-consumption setting. Many systems use a special type of Suspend called **hibernation**, where critical configuration information is written to the hard drive. Upon a wake-up event, the system is reinitialized, and the data is read from the drive to return the system to the APM Enabled mode. Clearly, the recovery time between Suspend and Enabled will be much longer than the time between Standby and Enabled.

ACPI handles all these levels plus a few more, such as "soft power on/off," which enables you to define the function of the power button.

Configuration of APM/ACPI

You configure APM/ACPI via CMOS settings or through Windows. Windows settings will override CMOS settings. Although the APM/ACPI standards permit a great deal of flexibility, which can create some confusion among different implementations, certain settings apply generally to CMOS configuration. First is the ability to initialize power management; this enables the system to enter the APM Enabled mode. Often CMOS will then present time frames for entering Standby and Suspend mode, as well as settings to determine which events take place in each of these modes. Also, many CMOS versions will present settings to determine wake-up events, such as directing the system to monitor a modem or a particular IRQ (Figure 14.28). A true ACPI-compliant CMOS provides an ACPI setup option. Figure 14.29 shows a typical modern BIOS that provides this setting.

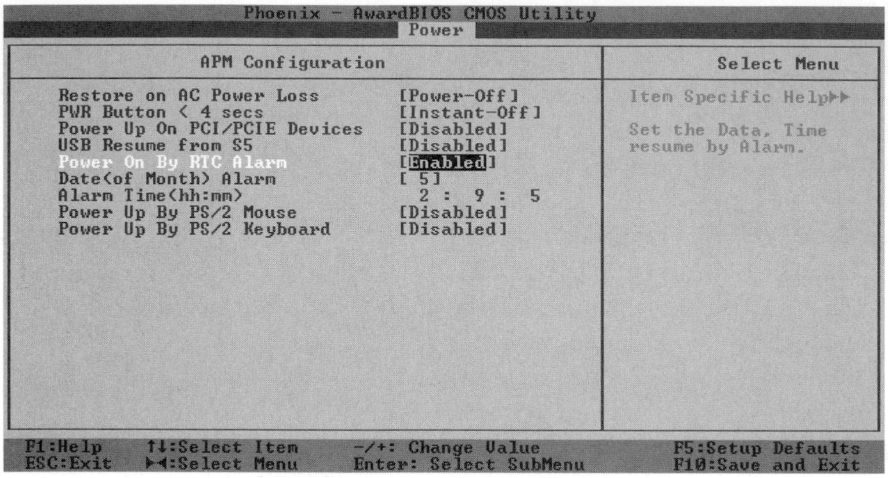

• **Figure 14.28**   Setting a wake-up event in CMOS

You can also access your Power Options by right-clicking on the Desktop, selecting Properties, and then clicking the Power button on the Screen Saver tab.

APM/ACPI settings can be found in the Windows 2000/XP control panel applet Power Options. The Power Options applet has several built-in *power schemes* such as Home/Office and Max Battery that put the system into standby or suspend after a certain interval (Figure 14.30). You can also require the system to go into standby after a set period of time or turn off the monitor or hard drive after a time, thus creating your own custom power scheme.

Another feature, Hibernate mode, takes everything in active memory and stores it on the hard drive just before the system powers down. When the PC comes out of hibernation, Windows reloads all the files and applications into RAM. Figure 14.31 shows the Power Options Properties applet in Windows XP.

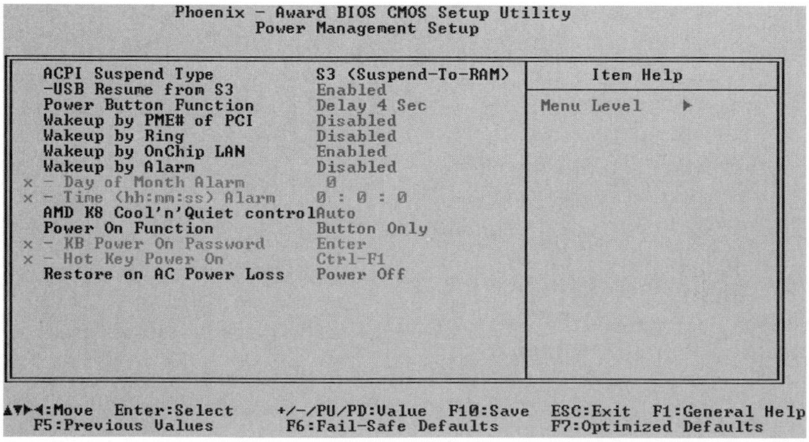

Cleaning

Most portable PCs take substantially more abuse than a corresponding desktop model. Constant handling, travel, airport food on the run, and so on can

• **Figure 14.29**   CMOS with ACPI setup option

Mike Meyers' CompTIA A+ Guide: PC Technician (Exams 220-602, 220-603, & 220-604)

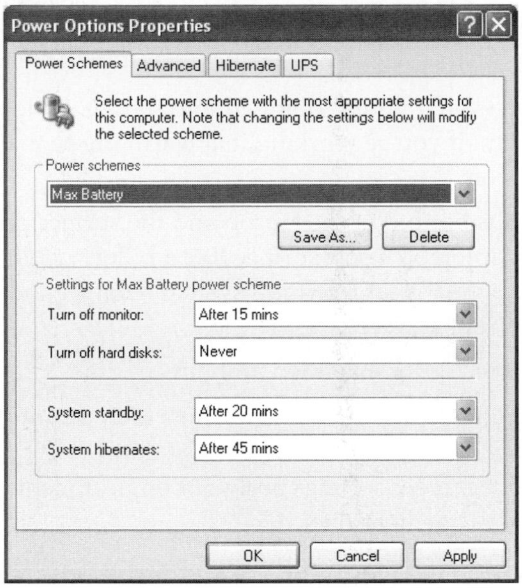

• **Figure 14.30**   The Power Options applet's Power Schemes tab

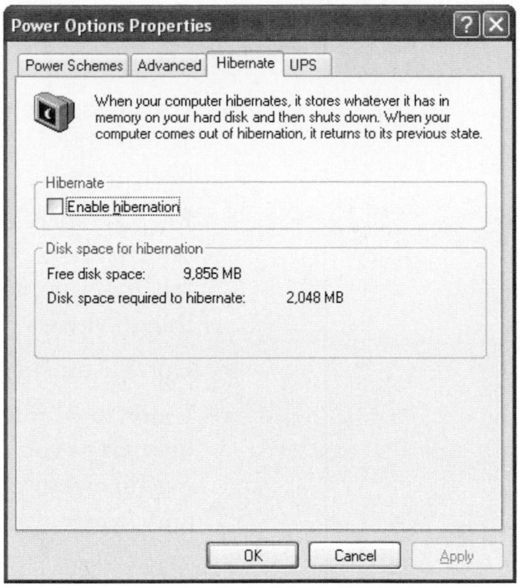

• **Figure 14.31**   Hibernation settings in the Power Options applet

radically shorten the life of a portable if you don't take action. One of the most important things you should do is clean the laptop regularly. Use an appropriate screen cleaner (not a glass cleaner!) to remove fingerprints and dust from the fragile LCD panel. (Refer to Chapter 12 for specifics.)

If you've had the laptop in a smoky or dusty environment where the air quality alone causes problems, try compressed air for cleaning. Compressed air works great for blowing out the dust and crumbs from the keyboard and for keeping PC Card sockets clear. Don't use water on your keyboard! Even a minor amount of moisture inside the portable can toast a component.

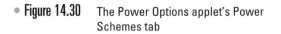

Try This!

Adjusting Your System's Power Management

Go into the Power Options applet and take a look at the various settings. What is the current power scheme for your computer? If you're using a laptop, is your system still using the Home/Office Desktop power scheme? If this is the case, go ahead and change the power scheme to Portable/Laptop.

Try changing the individual settings for each power scheme. For instance, set a new value for the System Standby setting—try making your computer go into standby after five minutes. Don't worry, you aren't going to hurt anything if you fiddle with these settings.

Heat

To manage and maintain a healthy portable PC, you need to deal with issues of heat. Every portable has a stack of electronic components crammed into a very small space. Unlike their desktop brethren, portables don't have lots of freely-moving air space that enables fans to cool everything down. Even with lots of low-power-consumption devices inside, portable PCs still crank out a good deal of heat. Excessive heat can cause system lockups and hardware failures, so you should handle the issue wisely. Try this as a starter guide.

- Use power management, even if you're plugged into the AC outlet. This is especially important if you're working in a warm (more than 80 degrees Fahrenheit) room.

- Keep air space between the bottom of the laptop and the surface on which it rests. Putting a laptop on a soft surface like a pillow on your lap, for example, creates a great heat retention system—not a good thing! Always use a hard, flat surface!

- Don't use a keyboard protector for extended amounts of time.

- Listen to your fan, assuming the laptop has one. If it's often running very fast—you can tell by the high-pitched whirring sound— examine your power management settings and your environment and change whatever is causing heat retention.

- Speaking of fans, be alert to a fan that suddenly goes silent. Fans do fail on laptops, causing overheating and failure. All laptop fans can be replaced easily.

Protect the Machine

While prices continue to drop for basic laptops, a fully loaded system is still pricey. To protect your investment, you'll want to adhere to certain best practices. You've already read tips in this chapter to deal with cleaning and heat, so let's look at the "portable" part of portable computers.

Tripping

Pay attention to where you run the power cord when you plug in a laptop. One of the primary causes of laptop destruction is people tripping over the power cord and knocking the laptop off a desk. This is especially true if you plug in at a public place such as a café or airport. Remember, the life you save could be your portable PC's!

Storage

If your laptop or PDA isn't going to be used for a while, storing it safely will go a long way toward keeping it operable when you do power it up again. It's worth the extra few dollars to invest in a quality case also—preferably one with ample padding. Smaller devices such as PDAs are well protected inside small shock-resistant aluminum cases that clip on to your belt while laptops do fine in well-padded cases or backpacks. Not only will this protect your system on a daily basis when transporting it from home to office, but it will keep dust and pet hair away as well. Lastly, remove the battery if you'll be storing your device for an extended period of time to protect from battery leakage.

Travel

If traveling with a laptop, take care to protect yourself from theft. If possible, use a case that doesn't look like a computer case. A well-padded backpack makes a great travel bag for a laptop and appears less tempting to would-be thieves. Don't forget to pack any accessories you might need, like modular devices, spare batteries, and AC adapters. Make sure to remove any disks, such as CD/DVD or floppies, from their drives. Most importantly—back up any important data before you leave!

Make sure to have at least a little battery power available. Heightened security at airports means you might have to power on your system to prove it's really a computer and not a transport case for questionable materials. And never let your laptop out of your sight. If going through an x-ray machine, request a manual search. The x-ray won't harm your computer like a metal detector will, but if the laptop gets through the line at security before you do, someone else might walk away with it. If flying, keep your laptop out of the overhead bins and under the seat in front of you where you can keep an eye on it.

If you travel to a foreign country, be very careful about the electricity. North America uses ~115-V power outlets, but the most of the rest of the world uses ~230-V outlets. Many portable computers have **auto-switching power supplies**, meaning they detect the voltage at the outlet and adjust accordingly. For these portables, a simple plug converter will do the trick. Other portable computers, however, have *fixed-input power supplies*, which means they run only on ~115-V or ~230-V power. For these portables, you need a full-blown electricity converting device, either a step-down or step-up *transformer*. You can find converters and transformers at electrical parts stores, such as Radio Shack in the U.S.

Shipping

Much of the storage and travel advice can be applied to shipping. Remove batteries and CD/DVD/floppies from their drives. Pack the laptop well and disguise the container as best you can. Back up any data and verify the warranty coverage. Ship with a reputable carrier and always request a tracking number and, if possible, delivery signature. It's also worth the extra couple of bucks to pay for the shipping insurance. And when the clerk asks what's in the box, it's safer to say "electronics" rather than "a new 20-inch laptop computer."

Security

The fact is, if someone really wants to steal your laptop, they'll find a way. There are, however, some things you can do to make yourself, and your equipment, a less desirable target. As you've already learned, disguise is a good idea. While you don't need to camouflage your laptop or carry it in a brown grocery bag on a daily basis, an inconspicuous carrying case will draw less attention.

Another physical deterrent is a laptop lock. Similar to a steel bicycle cable, there is a loop on one end and a lock on the other. The idea is to loop the cable around a solid object, like a bed frame, and secure the lock to the small security hole on the side of the laptop. Again, if someone really wants to steal your computer, they'll find a way. They'll dismantle the bed frame if they're desperate. The best protection is to be vigilant and not let the computer out of your sight.

An alternative to physically securing a laptop with a lock is to use a software tracking system. Software makers, such as Computer Security Products, Inc. at www.computersecurity.com, offer tracking software that transmits a signal to a central office if the laptop is stolen and connected to a phone line or the Internet. The location of the stolen PC can be tracked, and sensitive files can even be deleted automatically with the aid of the stealth signal.

■ Troubleshooting Portable Computers

Many of the troubleshooting techniques you learned about for desktop systems can be applied to laptops. Additionally, there are some laptop-specific procedures to try.

Laptop Won't Power On

- Verify AC power by plugging another electronic device into the wall outlet. If the other device receives power, the outlet is good.

- If the outlet is good, connect the laptop to the wall outlet and try to power on. If no LEDs light up, you may have a bad AC adapter. Swap it out with a known-good power adapter.

- A faulty peripheral device might keep the laptop from powering up. Remove any peripherals such as USB or FireWire devices.

Screen Doesn't Come On Properly

- If the laptop is booting (you hear the beeps and the drives), first make sure the display is on. Press the FN key and the key to activate the screen a number of times until the laptop display comes on.

- If the laptop display is very dim, you may have lost an inverter. The clue here is that inverters never go quietly. They can make a nasty hum as they are about to die and an equally nasty popping noise when they actually fail. Failure often occurs when you plug in the laptop's AC adapter, as the inverters take power directly from the AC adapter.

Wireless Networking Doesn't Work

- Check for a physical switch along the front, rear, or side edges of the laptop that toggles the internal wireless adapter on and off.

- Try the special key combination for your laptop to toggle the wireless adapter. You usually press the FN key in combination with another key.

- You might simply be out of range. Physically walk the laptop over to the wireless router or access point to ensure there are no "out of range" issues.

Handwriting Is Not Recognized

- If your PDA or tablet PC no longer recognizes your handwriting or stylus, you may need to retrain the digitizer. Look for an option in your PDA OS settings to "align the screen." On Windows tablet PCs, you will find a similar option under Start | Settings | Control Panel.

Keypad Doesn't Work

- If none of the keys work on your laptop, there's a good chance you've unseated the keypad connector. These connectors are quite fragile and are prone to unseating from any physical stress on the laptop. Check the manufacturer's disassembly procedures to locate and reseat the keypad.

- If you're getting numbers when you're expecting to get letters, the number lock (NUMLOCK) function key is turned on. Turn it off.

Touchpad Doesn't Work

- A shot of compressed air does wonders for cleaning pet hair out of the touchpad sensors. You'll get a cleaner shot if you remove the keyboard before using the compressed air. Remember to be gentle when lifting off the keyboard and make sure to follow the manufacturer's instructions.

- The touchpad driver might need to be reconfigured. Try the various options in the Control Panel | Mouse applet.

Beyond A+

Centrino Technology

As mentioned previously in this chapter, consumers have always, and will always, demand better performance, more features, and longer battery life from their portable PCs. Intel, for example, promotes a combination of three components—extremely low-power, yet speedy, CPUs; integrated wireless networking technology; and an Intel chipset—that, when combined, produce portable PCs that not only are exceptionally powerful, but also boast an extremely long battery life!

Origami—Ultra-Mobile PCs

Microsoft started pushing the Ultra-Mobile PC (UMPC) standard in 2005 and has started to get some traction in the industry. UMPCs are a small form-factor tablet PC, designed to fill the spot between PDAs and tablet PCs. Most of the versions use a 7-inch widescreen, touch-enabled LCD (although at least one model on the market has a 4.3-inch widescreen LCD) and feature everything you would expect to find in their bigger

> Microsoft initially called the UMPC project "Origami." The name has stuck, even though Microsoft has since shifted over to the more generic UMPC name.

cousins, with the exception of optical drives. They have internal 30–80 GB hard drives, 512 MB to 1 GB of RAM, built-in Wi-Fi and Bluetooth for connectivity, and more. Some even have USB and FireWire ports! All weigh under 2 pounds and come in at under 1 inch thick.

The feature that most distinguishes UMPCs from PDAs is that the former runs a fully featured version of Windows XP, just like your desktop and laptop PCs. Most UMPCs run Windows Tablet PC edition, although a few devices run Windows XP Home or Windows Vista. (A few übergeeks have even installed versions of Linux on UMPCs!) Figure 14.32 shows a Sony VAIO UX UMPC.

• **Figure 14.32**   Sony VAIO UX *(photo courtesy of Sony Electronics)*

Chapter 14 Review

Chapter Summary

After reading this chapter and completing the exercises, you should understand the following about portable computers.

Portable Computing Devices

- All portable devices share certain features: video output using LCD screens, some kind of PC sound, and DC battery power. There's no industry standard naming for the vast majority of styles of portable computing devices.

- A laptop refers in general to the clamshell, keyboard-on-the-bottom, and LCD-screen-at-the-top design that is considered the shape of mobile PCs. The traditional clamshell laptop computer features a built-in LCD monitor, keyboard, and input device, and functions as a fully standalone PC. A portable PC can be considered a desktop replacement if it does everything that most people want to do with a desktop PC.

- Desktop extender portable devices don't replace the desktop, but rather extend it by giving you a subset of features of the typical desktop that you can take away from the desk. They are usually smaller and lighter than desktop replacement portables. Ultralight portables (sometimes called subnotebooks, although the terms aren't necessarily synonymous) normally weigh less than three pounds and are less than an inch in thickness. These machines usually have smaller displays, lower-capacity hard drives, and CPUs that operate at lower speeds than their more full-sized brethren.

- Personal digital assistants (PDAs) are handheld portable computing devices that hold data such as your address book and appointment schedules. PDAs require specialized OSs such as Windows CE, PocketPC, PalmOS, or Linux. All of these OSs provide a GUI that enables you to interact with the device by touching the screen directly. PDAs synchronize with your PC, most often using a cradle and USB port, so you have the same essential data on both machines.

- Over the years, input devices for portables have ranged from trackballs that clipped to the case or were built in near the keyboard to IBM's TrackPoint pencil eraser–sized joystick embedded in the keyboard. The most common laptop pointing device found today, the touchpad, is a flat, touch-sensitive pad that you slide your finger across to move the cursor or pointer around the screen, and tap on to perform "mouse clicks."

Enhance and Upgrade the Portable PC

- PC Cards are roughly credit card–sized devices that enhance and extend the functions of a portable PC. Still commonly known by their older name, PCMCIA cards, PC Cards are as standard on today's mobile computers as the hard drive. Almost every portable PC has one or two PC Card slots. All PC Cards are hot-swappable.

- Parallel PC Cards come in two flavors, 16-bit and CardBus, and each flavor comes in three different physical sizes called Type I, Type II, and Type III. Type I, II, and III cards differ only in the thickness of the card (Type I being the thinnest, and Type III the thickest). Type II cards are by far the most common. All parallel PC Cards share the same 68-pin interface. The 16-bit PC Cards are 16-bit, 5-V cards that can have up to two distinct functions or devices, such as a modem/network card combination. CardBus PC Cards are 32-bit, 3.3-V cards that can have up to eight different functions on a single card. The 16-bit PC Cards will fit into and work in CardBus slots, but the reverse is not true.

- The serial ExpressCard comes in two widths: 54 mm and 34 mm. Both cards are 75 mm long and 5 mm thick, which makes them shorter than all previous PC Cards and the same thickness as a Type II PC Card. ExpressCards connect to either the Hi-Speed USB 2.0 bus (480 Mbps) or a PCI Express bus (2.5 Gbps).

- The PCMCIA standard defines two levels of software drivers to support PC Cards. The first, lower level is known as socket services. Socket services are device drivers that support the PC Card socket, enabling the system to detect when a PC Card has been inserted or removed, and providing the necessary I/O to the device. The second, higher level is known as card services. The card-services level recognizes the function of a particular PC Card and provides the specialized drivers necessary to make the card work. In today's laptops, the socket services are standardized and are handled by the system BIOS. Windows itself handles all card services and has a large preinstalled base of PC Card device drivers, although most PC Cards come with their own drivers.

- Every portable PC and many PDAs come with one or more single-function ports, such as an analog VGA connection for hooking up an external monitor and a PS/2 port for a keyboard or mouse. The single PS/2 port on most laptops supports both keyboards and pointing devices. Most portable computing devices have a speaker port, and some have line-in and microphone jacks as well. Most current portable PCs come with built-in NICs or modems for networking support. Simply plug a device into a particular port and, as long as Windows has the proper drivers, you will have a functioning device when you boot. The only port that requires any extra effort is the video port.

- Most laptops support a second monitor, giving the user the option to display Windows on the laptop only, the external monitor only, or both simultaneously. Usually, a special function key on the keyboard cycles through the different monitor configurations.

- Most portable PCs have one or more general-purpose expansion ports that enable you to plug in many different types of devices. Older portables sport RS-232 serial and IEEE 1284 parallel ports for mice, modems, printers, scanners, external CD-media drives, and more. USB and FireWire are popular and widespread methods for attaching peripherals to laptops. Both have easy-to-use connectors and can be hot-swapped.

- Port replicators are devices that plug into a single port (usually USB, but sometimes proprietary) and offer common PC ports, such as serial, parallel, USB, network, and PS/2. Docking stations resemble port replicators in many ways, offering legacy and modern single-function and multifunction ports, but have extra features built in, such as DVD drives or PC Card slots.

- In the past, manufacturers required proprietary components for portable PCs, but today's portable PCs offer some modularity, making it possible to do basic replacements and upgrades without buying expensive proprietary components from the manufacturer. These replaceable components include RAM, hard drives, video cards, floppy drives, and CD-media devices. Modular video cards are the least standardized of all modular components, but manufacturers are beginning to adopt industry-wide standards. Many manufacturers use modular floppy disk drives and CD-media devices, even allowing users to swap easily between different types of drives.

- Laptops use one of four types of RAM. Most older laptops use either 72-pin or 144-pin SO-DIMMs with SDRAM technology. DDR SDRAM systems primarily use 200-pin SO-DIMMs, although you'll also find 172-pin micro-DIMMs. Every decent laptop has upgradeable RAM slots. Get the correct RAM; many portable PC makers use proprietary RAM solutions. No standard exists for RAM placement in portables. More often than not, you need to unscrew or pop open a panel on the underside of the portable and press out on the restraining clips to make the RAM stick pop up so that you can remove and replace it.

- Laptops that support shared memory benefit from more affordable video cards. The video card has less built-in RAM and uses a portion of the computer's system RAM to make up the difference. This results in a lower cost, but system performance suffers because RAM that is shared with the video card is not available to programs. Shared memory technologies include TurboCache (by NVIDIA) and HyperMemory (by ATI).

- ATA drives in the 2.5-inch drive format now rule in all laptops. Currently, the larger 2.5-inch hard drives holds up to 120 GB while the larger 3.5-inch hard drives hold more than 750 GB.

- Both Intel and AMD have long sold specialized, modular CPUs for laptops; however, replacing the CPU in a laptop often requires disassembling the entire machine.

- To add functionality to laptops, manufacturers include modular drives with their machines. Modular drive bays can accommodate various optical drives, hard drives, or batteries. Most modular drives are truly hot-swappable, enabling you to remove and insert devices without any special software.

- Many laptops now come with integrated wireless networking support by way of a built-in Wi-Fi adapter usually installed in a Mini PCI slot on the laptop motherboard. The Mini PCI bus is an adaptation of the standard PCI bus and was developed specifically for integrated communications peripherals such as modems and network adapters. To extend battery life, built-in communication devices such as Wi-Fi and Bluetooth adapters can be toggled on and off without powering down the computer.

Managing and Maintaining Portable Computers

- Portable computers use three different types of batteries: Nickel-Cadmium (Ni-Cd), Nickel-Metal Hydride (Ni-MH), and Lithium-Ion (Li-Ion).

- The first batteries used in mobile PCs were Nickel-Cadmium (Ni-Cd). If a Ni-Cd battery was not completely discharged before each recharge, it would lose a significant amount of its rechargeability, a condition referred to as battery memory. At best, Ni-Cd batteries would last for 1000 charges, but they were very susceptible to heat. Because of the toxic metals inside these batteries, they had to be disposed of via specialty disposal companies. Although no longer used in PCs, Ni-Cd batteries are still found in cellular and cordless phones.

- The second generation of mobile PC batteries, the Nickel-Metal Hydride (Ni-MH) batteries are less susceptible to memory problems, tolerate overcharging better, take more recharging, and last longer between rechargings, but they are still susceptible to heat.

- Although some portable PCs still use Ni-MH batteries, Lithium-Ion (Li-Ion) is more common today. This third-generation battery takes fewer charges than Ni-MH, but it lasts longer between charges. Li-Ion batteries can explode if they are overcharged, so they have circuitry to prevent overcharging.

- A new type of battery called the smart battery tells the computer when it needs to be charged, conditioned, or replaced.

- Research continues on other power sources, with the most promising technology being fuel cells that produce electrical power as a result of a chemical reaction between hydrogen and oxygen. A small fuel cell may be able to power a laptop for up to 40 hours before it needs to be replaced or refilled.

- Batteries should be stored in a cool place, but not in the freezer because of moisture, metal racks, and food. Condition Ni-Cd and Ni-MH batteries to make them last longer. You can clean battery contacts with alcohol or a dry cloth. Batteries contain dangerous chemicals; never handle one that has ruptured. Always recycle old batteries rather than disposing of them in the trash.

- The process of cooperation among the hardware, the BIOS, and the OS to reduce power use is known generically as power management. Early laptops used power continuously, regardless of whether the system was using the device at the time or not. With power management features, today's laptops can automatically turn off unused devices or can shut down the entire system, leaving the information in RAM ready for a restart.

- Starting with the 386SX, Intel introduced System Management Mode (SMM), a power management system that would make the CPU and all peripherals go to "sleep." In 1992, Intel introduced the improved Advanced Power Management (APM) specification, followed by the Advanced Configuration and Power Interface (ACPI) standard in 1996.

- To use APM or ACPI, the computer must have an SMM-capable CPU, an APM-compliant BIOS, and devices that can be shut off. Referred to as "Energy Star" devices, these peripherals can shut down without actually turning off. The OS must also know how to request that a particular device be shut down. ACPI extends power-saving to include hot-swappable devices.

- Virtually all laptops and desktops use power management functions. APM defines four power-usage levels, including Full On, APM Enabled, APM Standby, and APM Suspend.

- Configure APM/ACPI through CMOS or through the Power Options Control Panel applet in Windows 2000/XP, with Windows settings overriding CMOS settings. Many CMOS versions enable configuration of wake-up events, such as having the system monitor a modem or particular IRQ.

- Hibernation writes information from RAM to the hard drive. Upon waking up, the data is returned to RAM, and programs and files are in the same state as when the computer entered hibernation.

- Use an appropriate screen cleaner (not glass cleaner) to clean the LCD screen. Use compressed air around the keyboard and PC card sockets. Never use water around the keyboard.

- To combat the inevitable heat produced by a portable computer, always use power management, keep an air space between the bottom of the laptop and the surface on which it rests, don't use a keyboard protector for an extended period of time, and be aware of your fan.

- Store your portable computer in a quality case when traveling. Laptops benefit from a cushy carrying case; hard aluminum cases keep your PDA from getting banged up. Well-padded backpacks not only keep your laptop protected, but make your system less appealing to would-be thieves. When traveling, don't forget accessories like AC power cords, additional batteries, or modular devices. Remove all discs from drives and make sure you have enough battery power to boot up for security personnel. If shipping your computer, go with a reputable carrier, keep your tracking number, and request a delivery signature. Use a laptop lock or a software tracking system to protect your laptop when traveling.

Troubleshooting Portable Computers

- If your laptop won't power on, try a different wall outlet. If it still fails to power up, remove all peripheral devices and try again.

- If the screen doesn't come on properly, verify the laptop is configured to use the built-in LCD screen by pressing the appropriate key to cycle through the internal and external monitors. If you hear a popping sound, you may have blown an inverter.

- If wireless networking is not working, check for the physical switch that toggles the internal wireless adapter on and off. If your laptop doesn't have a switch, check for a key combination that toggles the wireless adapter. You also may be out of range. Physically walk the laptop closer to the wireless router or access point.

- If your PDA or tablet PC fails to recognize handwriting, retrain the digitizer. PDAs often have a setting to align the screen; tablet PC users can check the Control Panel for the appropriate applet.

- If the keypad or touchpad doesn't work, try a shot of compressed air, reseat the physical internal connection, or reconfigure the driver settings through the Keyboard or Mouse Control Panel applets.

Key Terms

16-bit (287)

Advanced Configuration and Power Interface (ACPI) (299)

Advanced Power Management (APM) (299)

aspect ratio (277)

auto-switching power supply (303)

battery memory (296)

beaming (281)

card services (288)

CardBus (287)

conditioning charger (296)

desktop extender (279)

desktop replacement (279)

docking station (291)

ExpressCard (287)

fuel cell (297)

hibernation (299)

high gloss (278)

HotSync (281)

laptop (278)

Lithium-Ion (Li-Ion) (296)

matte (278)

Mini PCI (295)

Nickel-Cadmium (Ni-Cd) (296)

Nickel-Metal Hydride (Ni-MH) (296)

PC Card (287)

pen-based computing (280)

personal digital assistant (PDA) (280)

port replicator (290)

shared memory (293)

smart battery (297)

socket services (288)

stylus (280)

System Management Mode (SMM) (299)

tablet PC (282)

touchpad (279)

TrackPoint (279)

Key Term Quiz

Use the Key Terms list to complete the sentences that follow. Not all terms will be used.

1. PC Cards require two levels of software drivers: _____ to allow the laptop to detect when a PC Card has been inserted or removed and _____ to provide drivers to make the card work.

2. Although _____ were the first batteries for mobile PCs, they are limited now to cellular and cordless phones because of their problems with battery memory.

3. The _____ tells the computer when it needs to be charged, conditioned, or replaced.

4. John read an ad recently for a _____ portable PC that had everything he could possibly want on a PC, desktop or portable!

5. Small, reduced-function portable computing devices, called _____, use cut-down operating systems such as Windows CE or Palm OS.

6. Using a chemical reaction between hydrogen and oxygen, _____ may in a few years be able to provide laptops with electrical power for up to 40 hours.

7. With the 386SX, Intel introduced _____, the first power management system with the ability to make the CPU and all peripherals go to sleep.

8. Many newer laptops feature _____ screens offering richer color, higher contrast, and wider viewing angles.

9. Laptops using _____ are less expensive, as the video card has less built-in memory, but the RAM it borrows from the system results in less memory available to programs.

10. A(n) _____ combines the best of PDAs and fully featured laptops.

Multiple-Choice Quiz

1. What infrared process enables you to transfer data from one PDA to another wirelessly?
   A. Beaming
   B. Flashing
   C. Panning
   D. Sending

2. Which of the following statements best describes hard drives typically found in laptops?
   A. They are 2.5-inch ATA drives, but they do not hold as much data as the 3.5-inch hard drives found in desktop PCs.
   B. They are 3.5-inch ATA drives just like those found in desktop PCs, but they usually require "cable select" settings rather than master or slave.
   C. They are 3.5-inch ATA drives that hold more data than the 2.5-inch hard drives found in desktop PCs.
   D. They are 2.5-inch PCMCIA drives while desktops usually have 3.5-inch SCSI drives.

3. Which of the following APM power levels writes information from RAM to the hard drive and then copies the data back to RAM when the computer is activated again?
   A. Full On
   B. APM Enabled
   C. APM Standby
   D. Hibernation

4. Portable PCs typically use which of the following kinds of upgradeable RAM?
   A. 68-pin and 72-pin RIMMs
   B. 30-pin and 72-pin SIMMs
   C. 72-pin and 144-pin SO-DIMMs
   D. 30-pin and 72-pin SO-RIMMs

5. Where do you configure APM/ACPI in Windows XP? (Select all that apply.)
   A. The Power Options applet in the Control Panel
   B. The Display applet in the Control Panel

C. The Power Management applet in the Control Panel

D. The Power and Devices applet in the Control Panel

6. Which of the following kinds of PC Cards is the most commonly used, especially for I/O functions?

   A. Type I

   B. Type II

   C. Type III

   D. Type IV

7. Which of the following input devices will you most likely find on a portable PC?

   A. TrackPoint

   B. Touchpad

   C. Trackball

   D. Mouse

8. When a new USB mouse is plugged in, the laptop does not recognize that a device has been added. What is the most likely cause of this problem?

   A. The device was plugged in while the system was running.

   B. The device was plugged in while the system was off and then booted.

   C. The system is running Windows 98.

   D. The system does not yet have the proper drivers loaded.

9. How should you remove a modular drive?

   A. Use the Hardware Removal Tool in the System Tray.

   B. Shut down, remove the drive, and power back on.

   C. Simply remove the drive with no additional actions.

   D. Use Device Manager to uninstall the device.

10. Which buses do ExpressCards use?

    A. Hi-Speed USB and FireWire

    B. Hi-Speed USB and PCI Express

    C. PCI and PCI Express

    D. Mini PCI and Parallel

11. Convertibles and slates describe what type of device?

    A. Multicore processor

    B. Clamshell laptop computer

    C. PDA

    D. Tablet PC

12. If wireless networking is not working, what should you check?

    A. Check the switch on the side of the laptop that toggles power to the network card.

    B. Make sure the Ethernet cable is plugged into the laptop.

    C. Make sure the digitizer has been trained.

    D. Make sure Power Management is enabled.

13. Which bus was developed specifically for integrated communications peripherals such as modems and network adapters?

    A. FireWire

    B. Mini PCI

    C. PCI

    D. USB

14. Erin has an older laptop with a switch on the back that says 115/230. What does this indicate?

    A. The laptop has an auto-switching power supply.

    B. The laptop has a fixed-input power supply.

    C. The laptop has a step-down transforming power supply.

    D. The laptop has a step-up transforming power supply.

15. John's PDA suddenly stopped recognizing his handwriting. What's a likely fix for this problem?

    A. Replace the stylus.

    B. Retrain the digitizer.

    C. Replace the digitizer.

    D. Retrain the stylus.

■ Essay Quiz

1. At the upcoming training seminar for new techs, your boss wants to make sure they understand and use power management settings. You've been asked to prepare a short presentation showing the range of power management settings available in Windows 2000 and XP and demonstrating how to set them. What will you include in your presentation?

2. You've been tasked to advise your group on current portable computer technology so they can purchase ten new laptops by the end of the quarter. In a short essay, weigh the pros and cons of getting desktop replacements versus smaller laptops that would come with docking stations.

3. Your boss has a new portable computer and is planning to take it with him on a business trip to Paris. He's not all that tech-savvy or much of a traveler, so write a memo that tells him what to do or avoid while traveling, especially overseas.

4. Norm wants to upgrade his laptop's hard drive, CPU, and RAM. He's upgraded all of these components on his desktop, so he doesn't think that he'll run into much trouble. What advice will you give him about selecting the components and upgrading the laptop?

5. Monica just received her aunt's old laptop. It uses a Ni-Cd battery, but no matter how long she charges it, it only runs her PC for about 30 minutes before it dies. She can't understand why the battery runs out so fast, but she figures she needs a new battery. The local computer store has two kinds of batteries, Ni-MH and Li-Ion, both of which will physically fit into her computer. She's not sure which of these to buy or whether either of them will work with her PC. She's asked you whether her old battery is indeed bad and to help her select a new battery. What will you tell her?

Lab Projects

• Lab Project 14.1

This chapter mentioned that, although they are more expensive, portable PCs typically provide less processing power, have smaller hard drives, and in general are not as full-featured as desktop computers. Use the Internet to check sites such as www.ibm.com, www.gateway.com, www.dell.com, and www.hp.com to compare the best equipped, most powerful laptop you can find with the best equipped, most powerful desktop computer you can find. How do their features and prices compare? Now find a less expensive laptop and try to find a desktop computer that is as similar as possible in terms of capabilities, and compare their prices.

• Lab Project 14.2

A local company just donated ten laptops to your school library. They are IBM ThinkPad 600x PIII 500-Mhz laptops with 128 MB of RAM and two Type II PC slots. The school would like to let distance education students check out these computers, but the laptops do not have modems. Your hardware class has been asked to select PC Card modems for these laptops. What features will you look for in selecting the right modem? Either go to the local computer store or search the Internet to find the modem cards you will recommend.

Maintaining and Troubleshooting Printers

chapter 15

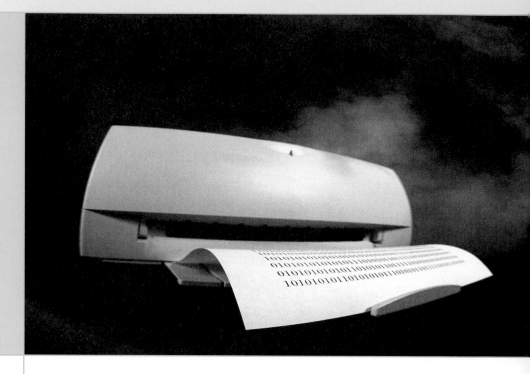

"Words, once they are printed, have a life of their own."

—CAROL BURNETT

In this chapter, you will learn how to

- **Describe current printer technologies**
- **Explain the laser printing process**
- **Install a printer on a Windows PC**
- **Recognize and fix basic printer problems**

Despite all of the talk about the "paperless office," printers continue to be a vital part of the typical office. In many cases, PCs are used exclusively for the purpose of producing paper documents. Many people simply prefer dealing with a hard copy. Programmers cater to this preference by using metaphors such as *page, workbook,* and *binder* in their applications. The CompTIA A+ certification exams strongly stress the area of printing and expect a high degree of technical knowledge of the function, components, maintenance, and repair of all types of printers.

IT Technician

■ Printer Technologies

No other piece of your computer system is available in a wider range of styles, configurations, and feature sets than a printer, or at such a wide price variation. What a printer can and can't do is largely determined by the type of printer technology it uses—that is, how it gets the image onto the paper. Modern printers can be categorized into several broad types: impact, inkjet, dye-sublimation, thermal, laser, and solid ink.

You may notice overlap from the Essentials course, as all of the CompTIA A+ exams expect you to be able to describe printer technologies. You need to know this stuff to pass any of the CompTIA+ exams! The CompTIA A+ certification 220-604 Depot Tech exam asks one in five questions about printer technologies, connectivity, and troubleshooting.

Impact Printers

Printers that create an image on paper by physically striking an ink ribbon against the paper's surface are known as **impact printers**. While *daisy-wheel* printers (essentially an electric typewriter attached to the PC instead of directly to a keyboard) have largely disappeared, their cousins, **dot-matrix printers**, still soldier on in many offices. While dot-matrix printers don't deliver what most home users want—high-quality and flexibility at a low cost—they're still widely found in businesses for two reasons: dot-matrix printers have a large installed base in businesses, and they can be used for multipart forms because they actually strike the paper. Impact printers tend to be relatively slow and noisy, but when speed, flexibility, and print quality are not critical, they provide acceptable results. PCs used for printing multipart forms, such as *point of sale (POS)* machines that need to print receipts in duplicate, triplicate, or more, represent the major market for new impact printers, although many older dot-matrix printers remain in use.

Dot-matrix printers (Figure 15.1) use a grid, or matrix, of tiny pins, also known as **printwires**, to strike an inked printer ribbon and produce images on paper. The case that holds the printwires is called a **printhead**. Using either 9 or 24 pins, dot-matrix printers treat each page as a picture broken up into a dot-based raster image. The 9-pin dot-matrix printers are generically called *draft quality*, while the 24-pin printers are known as *letter quality* or **near-letter quality (NLQ)**. The BIOS for the printer (either built into the printer or a printer driver) interprets the raster image in the same way that a monitor does, "painting" the image as individual dots. Naturally, the more pins, the

• **Figure 15.1**   An Epson FX-880+ dot-matrix printer *(photo courtesy of Epson America, Inc.)*

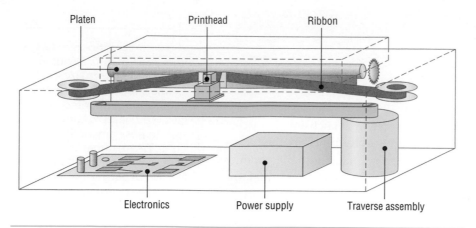

Electronics   Power supply   Traverse assembly

• **Figure 15.2**   Inside a dot-matrix printer

• **Figure 15.3**   Typical inkjet printer

higher the resolution. Figure 15.2 illustrates the components common to dot-matrix printers.

Inkjet Printers

Inkjet printers (also called *ink-dispersion printers*) like the one in Figure 15.3 are relatively simple devices consisting of a printhead mechanism, support electronics, a transfer mechanism to move the printhead back and forth, and a paper feed component to drag, move, and eject paper (Figure 15.4). They work by ejecting ink through tiny tubes. Most inkjet printers use heat to move the ink, while a few use a mechanical method. The heat- method printers use tiny resistors or electroconductive plates at the end of each tube (Figure 15.5), which literally boil the ink; this creates a tiny air bubble that ejects a droplet of ink onto the paper, thus creating portions of the image.

The ink is stored in special small containers called **ink cartridges**. Older inkjet printers had two cartridges: one for black ink and another for colored ink. The color cartridge had separate compartments for cyan (blue), magenta (red), and yellow ink, to print colors using a method known as CMYK (you'll read more about CMYK later in this chapter). If your color cartridge ran out of one of the colors, you had to purchase a whole new color cartridge or deal with a messy refill kit.

Printer manufacturers began to separate the ink colors into three separate cartridges, so that printers

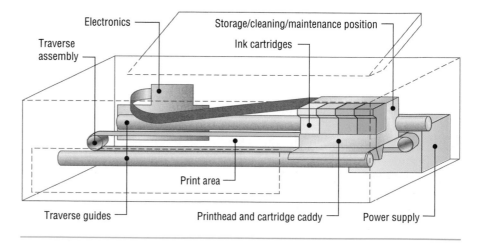

• **Figure 15.4**   Inside an inkjet printer

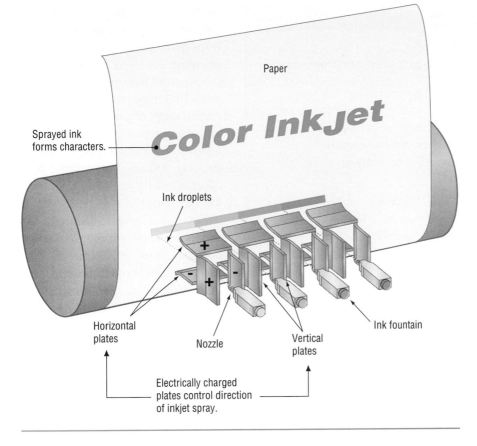

Paper

Color InkJet

Sprayed ink
forms characters.

Ink droplets

Horizontal
plates

Nozzle

Vertical
plates

Ink fountain

Electrically charged
plates control direction
of inkjet spray.

● **Figure 15.5** Detail of the inkjet printhead

came with four cartridges: one for each color and a fourth for black (Figure 15.6). This not only was more cost-effective for the user, but it also resulted in higher quality printouts. Today you can find color inkjet printers with six, eight, or more color cartridges. In addition to the basic CMYK inks, the other cartridges provide for green, blue, gray, light cyan, dark cyan, and more. Typically, the more ink cartridges a printer uses, the higher the quality of the printed image—and the higher the cost of the printer.

The two key features of an inkjet printer are the **print resolution**—that is, the density of ink, which affects print quality—and the print speed. Resolution is measured in **dots per inch (dpi)**; higher numbers mean that the ink dots on the page are closer together, so your printed documents will look better. Resolution is most important when you're printing complex images such as full-color photos, or when you're printing for duplication and you care that your printouts look good. Print speed is measured in **pages per minute (ppm)**, and this specification is normally indicated right on the printer's box. Most printers have one

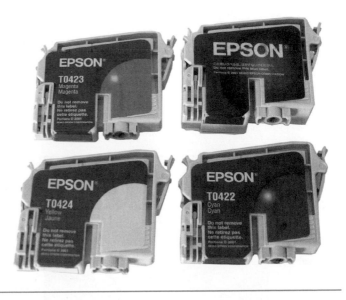

● **Figure 15.6** Inkjet ink cartridges

317

(faster) speed for monochrome printing—that is, using only black ink—and another for full-color printing.

Another feature of inkjet printers is that they can support a staggering array of print media. Using an inkjet printer, you can print on a variety of matte or glossy photo papers, iron-on transfers, and other specialty media; some printers can print directly onto specially coated optical discs, or even fabric. Imagine running a T-shirt through your printer with your own custom slogan (how about "I'm CompTIA A+ Certified!"). The inks have improved over the years, too, now delivering better quality and longevity than ever. Where older inks would smudge if the paper got wet or start to fade after a short time, modern inks are smudge proof and of archival quality—for example, some inks by Epson are projected to last up to 200 years.

Dye-Sublimation Printers

The term *sublimation* means to cause something to change from a solid form into a vapor and then back into a solid. This is exactly the process behind *dye-sublimation printing,* sometimes called *thermal dye transfer* printing. **Dye-sublimation printers** are used mainly for photo printing, high-end desktop publishing, medical and scientific imaging, or other applications for which fine detail and rich color are more important than cost and speed. Smaller, specialized printers called *snapshot* printers use dye-sublimation specifically for printing photos at a reduced cost compared to their full-sized counterparts.

The dye-sublimation printing technique is an example of the so-called CMYK (**c**yan, **m**agenta, **y**ellow, blac**k**) method of color printing. It uses a roll of heat-sensitive plastic film embedded with page-sized sections of cyan (blue), magenta (red), and yellow dye; many also have a section of black dye. A print head containing thousands of heating elements, capable of precise temperature control, moves across the film, vaporizing the dyes and causing them to soak into specially-coated paper underneath before cooling and reverting to a solid form. This process requires one pass per page for each color. Some printers also use a final finishing pass that applies a protective laminate coating to the page. Figure 15.7 shows how a dye-sublimation printer works.

Documents printed through the dye-sublimation process display *continuous tone* images, meaning that the printed image is not constructed of pixel dots, but is a

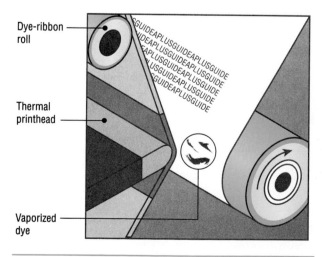

Dye-ribbon roll

Thermal printhead

Vaporized dye

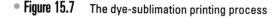

Figure 15.7   The dye-sublimation printing process

continuous blend of overlaid differing dye colors. This is in contrast to other print technologies' *dithered* images, which use closely packed, single-color dots to simulate blended colors. Dye-sublimation printers produce high-quality color output that rivals professional photo lab processing.

Thermal Printers

Thermal printers use a heated printhead to create a high-quality image on special or plain paper. You'll see two kinds of thermal printers in use. The first is the *direct thermal* printer, and the other is the *thermal wax transfer* printer. Direct thermal printers burn dots into the surface of special heat-sensitive paper. If you remember the first generation of fax machines, you're already familiar with this type of printer. It is still used as a receipt printer in many retail businesses. Thermal wax printers work similarly to dye-sublimation printers, except that instead of using rolls of dye-embedded film, the film is coated with colored wax. The thermal print head passes over the film ribbon and melts the wax onto the paper. Thermal wax printers don't require special papers like dye-sublimation printers, so they're more flexible and somewhat cheaper to use, but their output isn't quite as good because they use color dithering.

Laser Printers

Using a process called *electro-photographic imaging*, **laser printers** produce high-quality and high-speed output of both text and graphics. Figure 15.8 shows a typical laser printer. Laser printers rely on the photoconductive properties of certain organic compounds. *Photoconductive* means that particles of these compounds, when exposed to light (that's the "photo" part), will *conduct* electricity. Laser printers usually use lasers as a light source because of their precision. Some lower-cost printers use LED arrays instead.

• **Figure 15.8**   Typical laser printer

The first laser printers created only monochrome images. Today, you can also buy a color laser printer, although the vast majority of laser printers produced today are still monochrome. Although a color laser printer can produce complex full-color images such as photographs, they really shine for printing what's known as *spot color*—for example, eye-catching headings, lines, charts, or other graphical elements that dress up an otherwise plain printed presentation.

Critical Components of the Laser Printer

The CompTIA A+ certification exams take a keen interest in the particulars of the laser printing process, so it pays to know your way around a laser printer. Let's take a look at the many components of a laser printer and their functions (Figure 15.9).

Toner Cartridge   The `toner cartridge` in a laser printer (Figure 15.10) is so named because of its most obvious activity—supplying the toner that creates the image on the page. To reduce maintenance costs, however, many other laser printer parts, especially those that suffer the most wear and tear, have been incorporated into the toner cartridge. Although this makes replacement of individual parts nearly impossible, it greatly reduces the need for replacement; those parts that are most likely to break are replaced every time you replace the toner cartridge.

Photosensitive Drum   The `photosensitive drum` is an aluminum cylinder coated with particles of photosensitive compounds. The drum itself is grounded to the power supply, but the coating is not. When light hits these particles, whatever electrical charge they may have had "drains" out through the grounded cylinder.

Erase Lamp   The `erase lamp` exposes the entire surface of the photosensitive drum to light, making the photosensitive coating conductive. Any electrical charge present in the particles bleeds away into the grounded drum, leaving the surface particles electrically neutral.

Primary Corona   The `primary corona` wire, located close to the photosensitive drum, never touches the drum. When the primary corona is

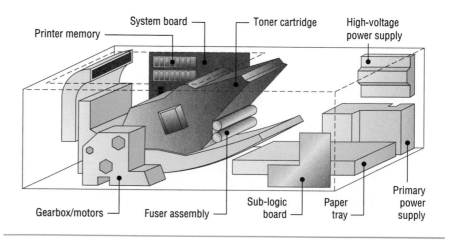

• **Figure 15.9**   Components inside a laser printer

charged with an extremely high voltage, an electric field (or corona) forms, enabling voltage to pass to the drum and charge the photosensitive particles on its surface. The *primary grid* regulates the transfer of voltage, ensuring that the surface of the drum receives a uniform negative voltage of between ~600 and ~1000 volts.

● **Figure 15.10**   Laser printer's toner cartridge

Laser   The laser acts as the writing mechanism of the printer. Any particle on the drum struck by the laser becomes conductive, enabling its charge to be drained away into the grounded core of the drum. The entire surface of the drum has a uniform negative charge of between ~600 and ~1000 volts following its charging by the primary corona wire. When particles are struck by the laser, they are discharged and left with a ~100 volt negative charge. Using the laser, we can "write" an image onto the drum. Note that the laser writes a positive image to the drum.

Toner   The toner in a laser printer is a fine powder made up of plastic particles bonded to iron particles. The *toner cylinder* charges the toner with a negative charge of between ~200 and ~500 volts. Because that charge falls between the original uniform negative charge of the photosensitive drum (~600 to ~1000 volts) and the charge of the particles on the drum's surface hit by the laser (~100 volts), particles of toner are attracted to the areas of the photosensitive drum that have been hit by the laser (that is, areas that have a *relatively* positive charge with reference to the toner particles).

Transfer Corona   To transfer the image from the photosensitive drum to the paper, the paper must be given a charge that will attract the toner particles off of the drum and onto the paper. The transfer corona is a thin wire, usually protected by other thin wires, that applies a positive charge to the paper, drawing the negatively charged toner particles to the paper. The paper, with its positive charge, is also attracted to the negatively charged drum. To prevent the paper from wrapping around the drum, a static charge eliminator removes the charge from the paper.

In most laser printers, the transfer corona is outside the toner cartridge, especially in large commercial grade machines. The transfer corona is prone to a build-up of dirt, toner, and debris through electrostatic attraction, and it must be cleaned. It is also quite fragile—usually finer than a human hair. Most printers with an exposed transfer corona will provide a special tool to clean it, but you can also—very delicately—use a cotton swab soaked in 90 percent denatured alcohol (don't use rubbing alcohol because it contains emollients). As always, never service any printer without first turning it off and unplugging it from its power source.

Fuser Assembly   The fuser assembly is almost always separate from the toner cartridge. It is usually quite easy to locate as it will be close to the bottom of the toner cartridge and will usually have two rollers to fuse the toner. Sometimes the fuser is somewhat enclosed and difficult to recognize, because the rollers are hidden from view. To help you determine the location of the fuser, think about the data path of the paper and the fact that fusing is the final step of printing.

The toner is merely resting on top of the paper after the static charge eliminator has removed the paper's static charge. The toner must be permanently attached to the paper to make the image permanent. Two rollers, a pressure roller and a heated roller, are used to fuse the toner to the paper. The pressure roller presses against the bottom of the page while the heated roller presses down on the top of the page, melting the toner into the paper. The heated roller has a nonstick coating such as Teflon to prevent the toner from sticking to the heated roller.

Power Supplies All laser printers have at least two separate power supplies. The first power supply is called the "primary power supply" or sometimes just the "power supply." This power supply, which may actually be more than one power supply, provides power to the motors that move the paper, the system electronics, the laser, and the transfer corona. The high-voltage power supply usually provides power only to the primary corona. The extremely high voltage of the high-voltage power supply makes it one of the most dangerous devices in the world of PCs! Before opening a printer to insert a new toner cartridge, it is imperative that you *always turn off* a laser printer!

Cross Check

High Voltage—Keep Away!

The power supply inside a laser printer is not the only dangerous high-voltage toy in the world of PC equipment. You've learned about two other potentially hazardous electrical components that you should approach with caution.

1. What are they?
2. Which of these three items is potentially the most deadly?

To refresh your memory, check out Chapter 7, "Installing and Troubleshooting Power Supplies," and Chapter 12, "Installing and Troubleshooting Video."

Turning Gears A laser printer has many mechanical functions. First, the paper must be picked up, printed upon, and kicked out of the printer. Next, the photosensitive roller must be turned and the laser, or a mirror, must be moved from left to right. Finally, the toner must be evenly distributed, and the fuser assembly must squish the toner into the paper. All these functions are served by complex gear systems. In most laser printers, these gear systems are packed together in discrete units generically called *gear packs* or *gearboxes*. Most laser printers will have two or three gearboxes that a tech can remove relatively easily in the rare case when one of them fails. Most gearboxes also have their own motor or solenoid to move the gears.

System Board Every laser printer contains at least one electronic board. On this board is the main processor, the printer's ROM, and RAM used to store the image before it is printed. Many printers divide these functions among two or three boards dispersed around the printer. An older printer may also have an extra ROM chip and/or a special slot where you can install an extra ROM chip, usually for special functions such as PostScript.

On some printer models you can upgrade the contents of these ROM chips (the *firmware*) by performing a process called *flashing* the ROM. Flashing is a lot like upgrading the system BIOS, which you learned about in Chapter 4, "Working with BIOS and CMOS." Upgrading the firmware can help fix bugs, add new features, or update the fonts in the printer.

Of particular importance is the printer's RAM. When the printer doesn't have enough RAM to store the image before it prints, you get a memory overflow problem. Also, some printers will store other information in the RAM, including fonts or special commands. Adding RAM is usually a simple job—just snapping in a SIMM or DIMM stick or two—but getting the *right* RAM is important. Call or check the printer manufacturer's Web site to see what type of RAM you need. Although most printer companies will happily sell you their expensive RAM, most printers can use generic DRAM like the kind you use in a PC.

Ozone Filter   The coronas inside laser printers generate ozone (O_3). Although not harmful to humans in small amounts, even tiny concentrations of ozone will cause damage to printer components. To counter this problem, most laser printers have a special ozone filter that needs to be vacuumed or replaced periodically.

Sensors and Switches   Every laser printer has a large number of sensors and switches spread throughout the machine. The sensors are used to detect a broad range of conditions such as paper jams, empty paper trays, or low toner levels. Many of these sensors are really tiny switches that detect open doors and so on. Most of the time these sensors/switches work reliably. Yet occasionally, they can become dirty or broken, sending a false signal to the printer. Simple inspection is usually sufficient to determine if a problem is real or just the result of a faulty sensor/switch.

Solid Ink

Solid ink printers use just what you'd expect—solid inks. The technology was originally developed by Tektronix, a company that was acquired by Xerox. Solid ink printers use solid sticks of non-toxic "ink" that produce more vibrant color than other print methods. The solid ink is melted and absorbed into the paper fibers; it then solidifies, producing a continuous tone output. Unlike dye-sublimation printers, all colors are applied to the media in a single pass, reducing the chances of misalignment. Solid ink sticks do not rely on containers like ink for inkjet printers and can be "topped off" midway through a print job by inserting additional color sticks without taking the printer offline.

These printers are fast, too! A full-color print job outputs the first page in about six seconds. Of course, all that speed and quality comes at a price. Xerox's base model starts at about twice the cost of a laser printer, with the expensive model selling for about six times the cost! Solid ink printers become a bit more affordable when you factor in the cost of consumables. A single stick of ink costs about as much as an inkjet cartridge, for example, but with a print capacity of 1000 pages, that completely beats the cost of inkjet cartridges over time.

Printer Languages

Now that you've learned about the different types of print devices and techniques, it's time to take a look at how they communicate with the PC. How do you tell a printer to make a letter *A* or to print a picture of your pet iguana? Printers are designed to accept predefined printer languages that handle both characters and graphics. Your software must use the proper language when communicating with your printer so that your printer can output your documents onto a piece of paper. Following are the more common printer languages.

ASCII

You might think of the American Standard Code for Information Interchange (ASCII) language as nothing more than a standard set of characters, the basic alphabet in upper and lowercase with a few strange symbols thrown in. ASCII actually contains a variety of control codes for transferring data, some of which can be used to control printers. For example, ASCII code 10 (or 0A in hex) means "Line Feed," and ASCII code 12 (0C) means "Form Feed." These commands have been standard since before the creation of IBM PCs, and all printers respond to them. If they did not, the PRT SCR (print screen) key would not work with every printer. Being highly standardized has advantages, but the control codes are extremely limited. Printing high-end graphics and a wide variety of fonts requires more advanced languages.

PostScript

Adobe Systems developed the PostScript page description language in the early 1980s as a device-independent printer language capable of high-resolution graphics and scalable fonts. PostScript interpreters are embedded in the printing device. Because PostScript is understood by printers at a hardware level, the majority of the image processing is done by the printer and not the PC's CPU, so PostScript printers print fast. PostScript defines the page as a single raster image; this makes PostScript files extremely portable—they can be created on one machine or platform and reliably printed out on another machine or platform (including, for example, high-end typesetters).

Hewlett Packard Printer Control Language (PCL)

Hewlett Packard developed its printer control language (PCL) as a more advanced printer language to supersede simple ASCII codes. PCL features a set of printer commands greatly expanded from ASCII. Hewlett Packard designed PCL with text-based output in mind; it does not support advanced graphical functions. The most recent version of PCL, PCL6 features scalable fonts and additional line drawing commands. Unlike PostScript, however, PCL is not a true page description language; it uses a series of commands to define the characters on the page. Those commands must be supported by each individual printer model, making PCL files less portable than PostScript files.

Windows GDI

Windows 2000/XP use the `graphical device interface (GDI)` component of the operating system to handle print functions. Although you *can* use an external printer language such as PostScript, most users simply install printer drivers and let Windows do all the work. The GDI uses the CPU rather than the printer to process a print job and then sends the completed job to the printer. When you print a letter with a TrueType font in Windows, for example, the GDI processes the print job and then sends bitmapped images of each page to the printer. Therefore, the printer sees a page of TrueType text as a picture, not as text. As long as the printer has a capable enough raster image processor (explained later in this chapter) and plenty of RAM, you don't need to worry about the printer language in most situations. We'll revisit printing in Windows in more detail later in this chapter.

Printer Connectivity

Most printers connect to one of two ports on the PC: a DB-25 parallel port or a USB port. The parallel connection is the classic way to plug in a printer, but most printers today use USB. You'll need to know how to support the more obscure parallel ports, cables, and connections as well as the plug-and-play USB connections.

Parallel Communication and Ports

The `parallel port` was included in the original IBM PC as a faster alternative to serial communication. The IBM engineers considered serial communication, limited to 1 bit at a time, to be too slow for the "high-speed" devices of the day (for example, dot-matrix printers). The standard parallel port has been kept around for backward compatibility despite several obvious weaknesses.

Parallel ports may be far faster than serial ports, but they are slow by modern standards. The maximum data transfer rate of a standard parallel port is still only approximately 150 kilobytes per second (KBps). Standard parallel communication on the PC also relies heavily on software, eating up a considerable amount of CPU time that could be better used.

Parallel ports are hindered by their lack of true bidirectional capability. One-way communication was acceptable for simple line printers and dot-matrix printers, but parallel communication became popular for a wide range of external devices that required two-way communication. Although it is possible to get two-way communication out of a standard parallel port, the performance is not impressive.

IEEE 1284 Standard

In 1991, a group of printer manufacturers proposed to the *Institute of Electrical and Electronics Engineers (IEEE)* that a committee be formed to propose a standard for a backward-compatible, high-speed, bidirectional parallel port for the PC. The committee was the IEEE 1284 committee (hence the name of the standard).

> Although the phrase "Centronics standard" was commonly used in the heyday of parallel ports, no such animal actually existed. Prior to the development of IEEE 1284, a very loose set of "standards" were adopted by manufacturers in an attempt to reduce incompatibility issues somewhat.

> Many techs confuse the concept of duplex printing—a process that requires special printers capable of printing on both sides of a sheet of paper—with bidirectional printing. They are two different things!

IEEE 1284 Transfer Modes

The five modes of operation for parallel printing specified in the IEEE 1284 standard (compatibility, nibble, byte, EPP, ECP) are inching closer to obsolescence as USB printers take over the market. You can look up these modes by name using various Web search tools, if you find yourself needing to optimize the performance of a legacy parallel printer.

The 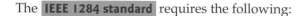 IEEE 1284 standard requires the following:

- Support for five distinct modes of operation: *compatibility mode, nibble mode, byte mode, EPP,* and *ECP*

- A standard method of negotiation for determining which modes are supported both by the host PC and by the peripheral device

- A standard physical interface (that is, the cables and connectors)

- A standard electrical interface (that is, termination, impedance, and so on)

Because only one set of data wires exists, all data transfer modes included in the IEEE 1284 standard are half-duplex: Data is transferred in only one direction at a time.

Parallel Connections, Cabling, and Electricity

Although no true standard exists, "standard parallel cable" usually refers to a printer cable with the previously-mentioned male DB-25 connector on one end and a 36-pin Centronics connector on the other (Figure 15.11). The shielding (or lack thereof) of the internal wiring and other electrical characteristics of a standard parallel printer cable are largely undefined except by custom. In practice, these standard cables are acceptable for transferring data at 150 KBps, and for distances of less than 6 feet, but they would be dangerously unreliable for some transfer modes.

For more reliability at distances up to 32 feet (10 meters), use proper IEEE 1284–compliant cabling. The transfer speed drops with the longer cables, but it does work, and sometimes the trade-off between speed and distance is worth it.

Installing a parallel cable is a snap. Just insert the DB-25 connector into the parallel port on the back of the PC and insert the Centronics connector into the printer's Centronics port, and you're ready to go to press!

• Figure 15.11   Standard parallel cable with 36-pin Centronics connector on one end and DB-25 connector on the other

Some printers come with both USB and parallel connections, but this is becoming increasingly rare. If you need a parallel printer for a system, be sure to confirm that the particular model you want will work with your system!

In almost all cases, you must install drivers before you plug a USB printer into your computer. You'll learn about installing printer drivers later in this chapter.

USB Printers

New printers now use USB connections that can be plugged into any USB port on your computer. USB printers don't usually come with a USB cable, so you need to purchase one at the time you purchase a printer. (It's quite a disappointment to come home with your new printer only to find you can't connect it because it didn't come with a USB cable.) Most printers use the standard USB type A connector on one end and the smaller USB type B connector on the other end, although some use two type A connectors. Whichever configuration your USB printer has, just plug in the USB cable—it's literally that easy!

FireWire Printers

Some printers offer FireWire connections in addition to or instead of USB connections. A FireWire printer is just as easy to connect as a USB printer, as FireWire is also hot-swappable and hot-pluggable. Again, make sure you have the proper cable, as most printers don't come with one. If your printer has both connections, which one should you use? The answer is easy if your PC has only USB and not FireWire. If you have a choice, either connection is just as good as the other, and the speeds are comparable. If you already have many USB devices, you may want to use the FireWire printer connection, to leave a USB port free for another device.

Network Printers

Connecting a printer to a network isn't just for offices anymore. More and more homes and home offices are enjoying the benefits of network printing. It used to be that to share a printer on a network—that is, to make it available to all network users—you would physically connect the printer to a single computer and then share the printer on the network. The downside to this was that the computer to which the printer was connected had to be left on for others to use the printer.

Today, the typical **network printer** comes with its own onboard network adapter that uses a standard RJ-45 Ethernet cable to connect the printer directly to the network by way of a router. The printer can typically be assigned a static IP address, or it can acquire one dynamically from a DHCP server. Once connected to the network, the printer acts independently of any single PC. Some of the more costly network printers come with a built-in Wi-Fi adapter to connect to the network wirelessly. Alternatively, some printers offer Bluetooth interfaces for networking.

Even if a printer does not come with built-in Ethernet, Wi-Fi, or Bluetooth, you can purchase a standalone network device known as a *print server* to connect your printer to the network. These print servers, which can be Ethernet or Wi-Fi, enable one or several printers to attach via parallel port or USB. So take that ancient ImageWriter dot-matrix printer and network it—I dare you!

Other Printers

Plenty of other connection types are available for printers. We've focused mainly on parallel, USB, FireWire, and networked connections. Be aware that you may run into an old serial port printer or a SCSI printer. While this is unlikely, know that it's a possibility.

■ The Laser Printing Process

The laser printing process can be broken down into six steps, and the CompTIA A+ exams expect you to know them all. As a tech, you should be familiar with these phases, as this can help you troubleshoot printing problems. For example, if an odd line is printed down the middle of every page, you know there's a problem with the photosensitive drum or cleaning mechanism and the toner cartridge needs to be replaced.

You'll look into the physical steps that occur each time a laser printer revs up and prints a page; then you'll see what happens electronically to ensure that the data is processed properly into flawless, smooth text and graphics.

The Physical Side of the Process

Most laser printers perform the printing process in a series of six steps. Keep in mind that some brands of laser printers may depart somewhat from this process, although most work in exactly this order:

1. **Clean**
2. **Charge**
3. **Write**
4. **Develop**
5. **Transfer**
6. **Fuse**

Be sure that you know the order of a laser printer's printing process! Here's a mnemonic to help: Clarence Carefully Wrote Down The Facts.

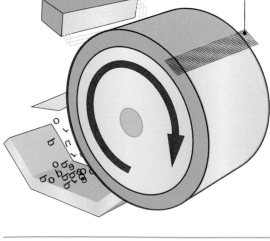

• **Figure 15.12**   Cleaning and erasing the drum

Erase lamp

Cleaning blade

Primary corona

• **Figure 15.13**   Charging the drum with a uniform negative charge

Clean the Drum

The printing process begins with the physical and electrical cleaning of the photosensitive drum (Figure 15.12). Before printing each new page, the drum must be returned to a clean, fresh condition. All residual toner left over from printing the previous page must be removed, usually by scraping the surface of the drum with a rubber cleaning blade. If residual particles remain on the drum, they will appear as random black spots and streaks on the next page. The physical cleaning mechanism either deposits the residual toner in a debris cavity or recycles it by returning it to the toner supply in the toner cartridge. The physical cleaning must be done carefully. Damage to the drum will cause a permanent mark to be printed on every page.

The printer must also be electrically cleaned. One or more erase lamps bombard the surface of the drum with the appropriate wavelengths of light, causing the surface particles to discharge into the grounded drum. After the cleaning process, the drum should be completely free of toner and have a neutral charge.

Charge the Drum

To make the drum receptive to new images, it must be charged (Figure 15.13). Using the primary corona wire, a uniform negative charge is applied to the entire surface of the drum (usually between ~600 and ~1000 volts).

Write and Develop the Image

A laser is used to write a positive image on the surface of the drum. Every particle on the drum hit by the laser will release most of its negative charge into the drum. Those particles with a lesser negative charge will be positively charged relative to the toner particles and will attract them, creating a developed image (Figure 15.14).

Transfer the Image

The printer must transfer the image from the drum onto the paper. The transfer corona is used to give the paper a positive charge. Once the paper has a positive charge, the negatively charged toner

Mike Meyers' CompTIA A+ Guide: PC Technician (Exams 220-602, 220-603, & 220-604)

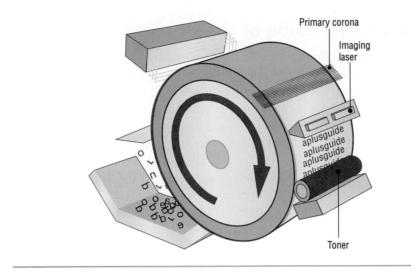

- **Figure 15.14** Writing the image and applying the toner

particles leap from the drum to the paper. At this point, the particles are merely resting on the paper. They must still be permanently fused to the paper.

Fuse the Image

The particles have been attracted to the paper because of the paper's positive charge, but if the process stopped here, the toner particles would fall off the page as soon as the page was lifted. Because the toner particles are mostly composed of plastic, they can be melted to the page. Two rollers—a heated roller coated in a nonstick material and a pressure roller—melt the toner to the paper, permanently affixing it. Finally, a static charge eliminator removes the paper's positive charge (Figure 15.15). Once the page is complete, the printer ejects the printed copy and the process begins again with the physical and electrical cleaning of the printer.

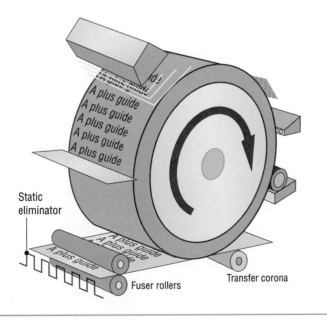

- **Figure 15.15** Transferring the image to the paper and fusing the final image

Tech Tip

Laser Printing in Color

Color laser printers use four different colors of toner (cyan, magenta, yellow, and black) to create their printouts. Most models put each page through four different passes, adding one color at each pass to create the needed results, while others place all the colors onto a special belt and then transfer them to the page in one pass. In some cases, the printer uses four separate toner cartridges and four lasers for the four toner colors, and in others the printer simply lays down one color after the other on the same drum, cleaning after each of four passes per page.

> ⚠ The heated roller produces enough heat to melt some types of plastic media, particularly overhead transparency materials. This could damage your laser printer (and void your warranty), so make sure you're printing on transparencies designed for laser printers!

The Electronic Side of the Process

When you click the Print button in an application, several things happen. First, the CPU processes your request and sends a print job to an area of memory called the print spooler. The **print spooler** enables you to queue up multiple print jobs that the printer will handle sequentially. Next, Windows sends the first print job to the printer. That's your first potential bottleneck—if it's a big job, the OS has to dole out a piece at a time, and you'll see the little printer icon in the notification area at the bottom right of your screen. Once the printer icon goes away, you know the print queue is empty—all jobs have gone to the printer.

Once the printer receives some or all of a print job, the hardware of the printer takes over and processes the image. That's your second potential bottleneck, and it has multiple components.

Raster Images

Impact printers transfer data to the printer one character or one line at a time, whereas laser printers transfer entire pages at a time to the printer. A laser printer generates a **raster image** (a pattern of dots) of the page representing what the final product should look like. It uses a device (the laser) to "paint" a raster image on the photosensitive drum. Because a laser printer has to paint the entire surface of the photosensitive drum before it can begin to transfer the image to paper, it processes the image one page at a time.

A laser printer uses a chip called the **raster image processor (RIP)** to translate the raster image sent to the printer into commands to the laser. The RIP takes the digital information about fonts and graphics and converts it to a rasterized image made up of dots that can then be printed. An inkjet printer also has a RIP, but it's part of the software driver instead of onboard hardware circuitry. The RIP needs memory (RAM) to store the data that it must process. A laser printer must have enough memory to process an entire page. Some images that require high resolutions require more memory. Insufficient memory to process the image will usually be indicated by a memory overflow ("MEM OVERFLOW") error. If you get a memory overflow error, try reducing the resolution, printing smaller graphics, or turning off RET (see the following section for the last option). Of course, the best solution to a memory overflow error is simply to add more RAM to the laser printer.

Do not assume that every error with the word *memory* in it can be fixed simply by adding more RAM to the printer. Just as adding more RAM chips will not solve every conventional PC memory problem, adding more RAM will not solve every laser printer memory problem. The message "21 ERROR" on an HP LaserJet, for example, indicates that "the printer is unable to process very complex data fast enough for the print engine." This means that the data is simply too complex for the RIP to handle. Adding more memory would *not* solve this problem; it would only make your wallet lighter. The only answer in this case is to reduce the complexity of the page image (that is, fewer fonts, less formatting, reduced graphics resolution, and so on).

Tech Tip

Inkjet RIPs

Inkjet printers use RIPs as well, but they're written into the device drivers instead of the onboard programming. You can also buy third-party RIPs that can improve the image quality of your printouts; for an example, see www.colorbytesoftware.com.

Resolution

Laser printers can print at different resolutions, just as monitors can display different resolutions. The maximum resolution that a laser printer can handle is determined by its physical characteristics. Laser printer resolution is expressed in dots per inch (dpi). Common resolutions are 600 × 600 dpi or 1200 × 1200 dpi. The first number, the horizontal resolution, is determined by how fine a focus can be achieved by the laser. The second number is determined by the smallest increment by which the drum can be turned. Higher resolutions produce higher quality output, but keep in mind that higher resolutions also require more memory. In some instances, complex images can be printed only at lower resolutions because of their high-memory demands. Even printing at 300 dpi, laser printers produce far better quality than dot-matrix printers because of **resolution enhancement technology (RET)**.

RET enables the printer to insert smaller dots among the characters, smoothing out the jagged curves that are typical of printers that do not use RET (Figure 15.16). Using RET enables laser printers to output high-quality print jobs, but it also requires a portion of the printer's RAM. If you get a MEM OVERFLOW error, sometimes disabling RET will free up enough memory to complete the print job.

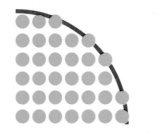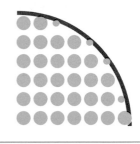

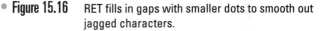

● **Figure 15.16**   RET fills in gaps with smaller dots to smooth out jagged characters.

■ Installing a Printer in Windows

You need to take a moment to understand how Windows 2000 and Windows XP handle printing, and then you'll see how to install, configure, and troubleshoot printers in these operating systems.

To Windows 2000/XP, a "printer" is not a physical device; it is a *program* that controls one or more physical printers. The *physical* printer is called a "print device" to Windows (although I continue to use the term "printer" for most purposes, just like almost every tech on the planet). Printer drivers and a spooler are still present, but in Windows 2000/XP they are integrated into the printer itself (Figure 15.17). This arrangement gives Windows 2000/XP amazing flexibility. For example, one printer can support multiple print devices, enabling a system to act as a print server. If one print device goes down, the printer automatically redirects the output to a working print device.

The general installation, configuration, and troubleshooting issues are basically identical in Windows 2000 and Windows XP. Here's a review of a typical Windows printer installation. I'll mention the trivial differences between Windows 2000 and XP as I go along.

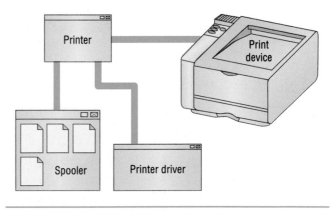

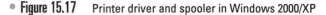

● **Figure 15.17**   Printer driver and spooler in Windows 2000/XP

Setting Up Printers

Setting up a printer is so easy that it's almost scary. Most printers are plug and play, so installing a printer is reduced to simply plugging it in and loading the driver if needed. If the system does not detect the printer or if the printer is not plug and play, click Start | Printers and Faxes in Windows XP to open the Printers applet; in Windows 2000, click Start | Settings | Printers. The icon for this applet can also be found in the Control Panel.

As you might guess, you install a new printer by clicking the Add Printer icon (somehow Microsoft has managed to leave the name of this applet unchanged through all Windows versions since 9*x*). This starts the Add Printer Wizard. After a pleasant intro screen, you must choose to install either a printer plugged directly into your system or a network printer (Figure 15.18). You also have the *Automatically detect and install my Plug and Play printer* option, which you can use in many cases when installing a USB printer.

If you choose a local printer, the applet next asks you to select a port (Figure 15.19); select the one where you installed the new printer. Once you select the port, Windows asks you to specify the type of printer, either by selecting the type from the list or using the Have Disk option, just as you would for any other device (Figure 15.20). Note the handy Windows Update button, which you can use to get the latest printer driver from the Internet. When you click Next on this screen, Windows installs the printer.

Figure 15.21 shows a typical Windows XP Printers and Faxes screen on a system with one printer installed. Note the small check mark in the icon's corner; this shows that the device is the default printer. If you have multiple printers, you can change the default printer by selecting the printer's properties and checking Make Default Printer.

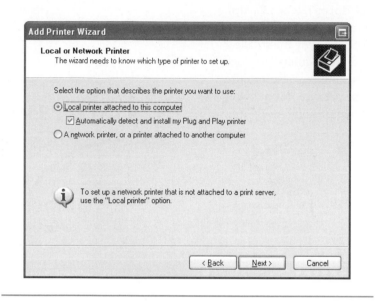

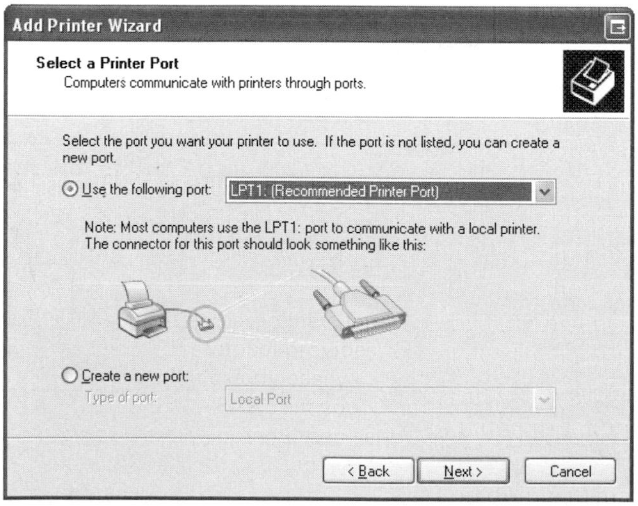

● **Figure 15.18** Choosing local or network printer in Windows XP

● **Figure 15.19** Selecting a port in Windows XP

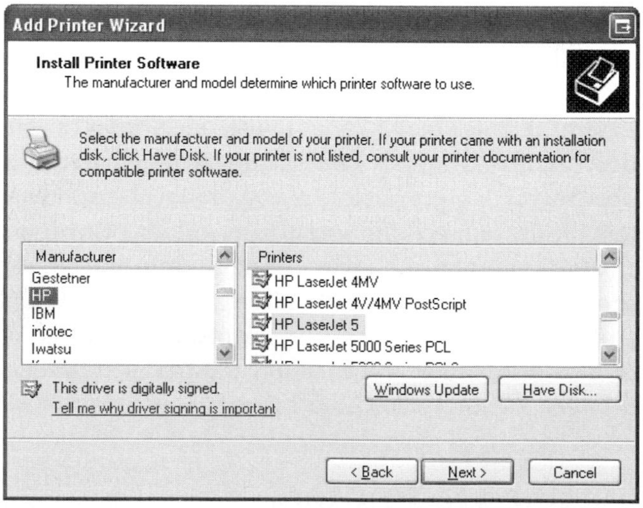

● **Figure 15.20** Selecting a printer model/driver in Windows XP

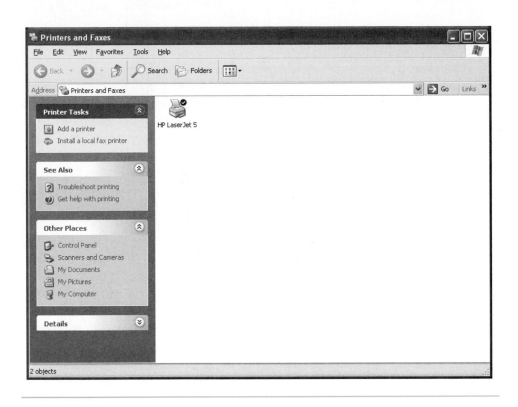

● **Figure 15.21** Installed default printer in the Printers and Faxes applet

In addition to the regular driver installation outlined previously, some installations use printer emulation. *Printer emulation* simply means using a substitute printer driver for a printer, as opposed to using one made exclusively for that printer. You'll run into printer emulation in two circumstances. First, some new printers do not come with their own drivers. They instead emulate a well-known printer (such as an HP LaserJet 4) and run perfectly well on that printer driver. Second, you may see emulation in the "I don't have the right driver!" scenario. I keep about three different HP LaserJet and Epson inkjet printers installed on my PC as I know that with these printer drivers, I can print to almost any printer. Some printers may require you to set them into an *emulation mode* to handle a driver other than their native one.

Optimizing Print Performance

Although a quality printer is the first step toward quality output, your output relies on factors other than the printer itself. What you see on the screen may not match what comes out of the printer, so calibration is important. Using the wrong type of paper can result in less than acceptable printed documents. Configuring the printer driver and spool settings can also affect your print jobs.

Calibration

If you've ever tweaked that digital photograph so it looks perfect on screen, only to discover that the final printout was darker than you had hoped,

Tech Tip

Readme Files

You've seen how to get your system to recognize a printer, but what do you do when you add a brand-new printer? Like most peripherals, the printer will include an installation CD-ROM that contains various useful files. One of the most important, but least used, tools on this CD-ROM is the Readme file. This file, generally in TXT format, contains the absolute latest information on any idiosyncrasies, problems, or incompatibilities related to your printer or printer driver. Usually, you can find it in the root folder of the installation CD-ROM, although many printer drivers install the Readme file on your hard drive, so you can access it from the Start menu. The rule here is read first *to avoid a headache later!*

consider calibrating your monitor. **Calibration** matches the print output of your printer to the visual output on your monitor and governs that through software. All three parts need to be set up properly for you to print what you see consistently.

Computer monitors output in RGB—that is, they compose colors using red, green, and blue pixels—while printers mix their colors differently to arrive at their output. For example, the CMYK method composes colors from cyan (blue), magenta (red), yellow, and black.

The upshot of all this is that the printer tries to output using CMYK (or another technique) what you see on the screen using RGB. Because the two color modes do not create color the same way, you see color shifts and not-so-subtle differences between the onscreen image and the printed image. By calibrating your monitor, you can adjust the setting to match the output of your printer. This can be done manually through "eyeballing" it or automatically using calibration hardware.

To calibrate your monitor manually, obtain a test image from the Web (try sites such as www.DigitalDog.net) and print it out. If you have a good eye, you can compare this printout to what you see on the screen and make the adjustments manually through your monitor's controls or display settings.

Another option is to calibrate your printer through the use of an International Color Consortium (ICC) color profile, a preference file that instructs your printer to print colors a certain way—for example, to match what is on your screen. Loading a different color profile results in a different color output. Color profiles are sometimes included on the installation CD-ROM with a printer, but you can create or purchase custom profiles as well. The use of ICC profiles is not limited to printers; you can also use them to control the output of monitors, scanners, or even digital cameras.

■ Troubleshooting Printers

As easy as printers are to set up, they are equally robust at running, assuming that you install the proper drivers and keep the printer well maintained. But printer errors do occasionally develop. Take a look at the most common print problems with Windows 2000/XP as well as problems that crop up with specific printer types.

General Troubleshooting Issues

Printers of all stripes share some common problems, such as print jobs that don't go, strangely sized prints, and misalignment. Other issues include consumables, sharing multiple printers, and crashing on power-up. Let's take a look at these general troubleshooting issues, but start with a recap of the tools of the trade.

Tools of the Trade

Before you jump in and start to work on a printer that's giving you fits, you'll need some tools. You can use the standard computer tech tools in your toolkit, plus a couple of printer-specific devices. Here are some that will come in handy:

- A multimeter for troubleshooting electrical problems such as faulty wall outlets

- Various cleaning solutions, such as denatured alcohol

- An extension magnet for grabbing loose screws in tight spaces and cleaning up iron-based toner

- An optical disc or USB thumb drive with test patterns for checking print quality

- Your trusty screwdriver—both a Phillips-head and flat-head because if you bring just one kind, it's a sure bet that you'll need the other

Print Job Never Prints

If you click Print but nothing comes out of the printer, first check all the obvious possibilities. Is the printer on? Is it connected? Is it online? Does it have paper? Assuming the printer is in good order, it's time to look at the spooler. You can see the spooler status either by double-clicking the printer's icon in the Printers applet or by double-clicking the tiny printer icon in the notification area if it's present. If you're having a problem, the printer icon will almost always be there. Figure 15.22 shows the print spooler open.

Print spoolers can easily overflow or become corrupt due to a lack of disk space, too many print jobs, or one of a thousand other factors. The status window shows all of the pending print jobs and enables you to delete, start, or pause jobs. I usually just delete the affected print job(s) and try again.

Print spoolers are handy. If the printer goes down, you can just leave the print jobs in the spooler until the printer comes back online. Some versions of Windows require you to select Resume Printing manually, but others will automatically continue the print job(s). If you have a printer that isn't coming on anytime soon, you can simply delete the print job in the spooler window and try another printer.

If you have problems with the print spooler, you can get around it by changing your print spool settings. Go into the Printers and Faxes applet, right-click the icon of the printer in question, and choose Properties. In the resulting Properties window (see Figure 15.23), choose the *Print directly to the printer* radio button and click OK; then try sending your print job again. Note that this window also offers you the choice of printing immediately—that is, starting to print pages as soon as the spooler has enough information to feed to the printer—or holding off on printing until the entire job is spooled.

Another possible cause for a stalled print job is that the printer is simply waiting for the correct paper! Laser printers in particular have settings that tell them what size paper is in

● **Figure 15.22**   Print spooler

● **Figure 15.23**   Print spool settings

their standard paper tray or trays. If the application sending a print job specifies a different paper size—for example, it wants to print a standard No. 10 envelope, or perhaps a legal sheet, but the standard paper tray holds only 8.5 × 11 letter paper—the printer will usually pause and hold up the queue until someone switches out the tray or manually feeds the type of paper that's required for this print job. You can usually override this by pressing the OK or GO button on the printer or by manually feeding any size paper you want just to clear out the print queue, but the printer is doing its best to print the job properly.

The printer's default paper tray and paper size options will differ greatly depending on the printer type and model. To find these settings, go into the printer's Properties window from the Printers and Faxes applet, and then select the Device Settings tab. This list of settings includes Form To Tray Assignment, where you can specify which tray (in the case of a printer with multiple paper trays) holds which size paper.

Strange Sizes

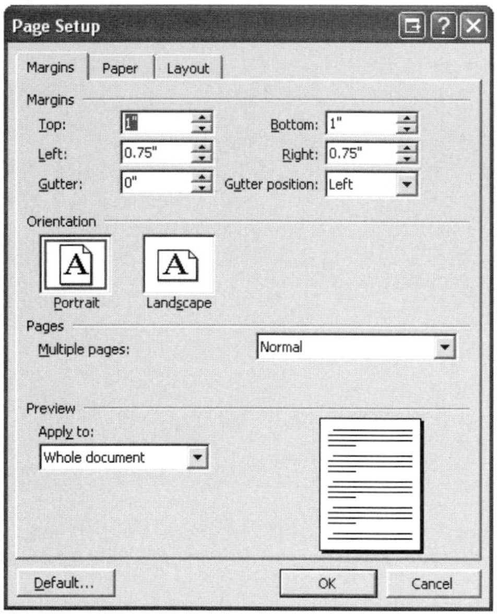

A print job that comes out a strange size usually points to a user mistake in setting up the print job. All applications have a Print command and a Page Setup interface. The Page Setup interface enables you to define a number of print options, which vary from application to application. Figure 15.24 shows the Page Setup options for Microsoft Word. Make sure the page is set up properly before you blame the printer for a problem.

If you know the page is set up correctly, recheck the printer drivers. If necessary, uninstall and reinstall the printer drivers. If the problem persists, you may have a serious problem with the printer's print engine, but that comes up as a likely answer only when you continually get the same strangely sized printouts using a number of different applications.

Misaligned or Garbage Prints

Misaligned or garbage printouts invariably point to a corrupted or incorrect driver. Make sure you're using the right driver (it's hard to mess this up, but not impossible) and then uninstall and reinstall the printer driver. If the problem persists, you may be asking the printer to do something it cannot do. For example, you may be printing to a PostScript printer with a PCL driver. Check the printer type to verify that you haven't installed the wrong type of driver for that printer!

Dealing with Consumables

All printers tend to generate a lot of trash in the form of . Impact printers use paper and ribbons, inkjet printers use paper and ink cartridges, and laser printers use paper and toner cartridges. In today's environmentally sensitive world, many laws regulate the proper disposal of most printer components. Be sure to check with the local sanitation department or disposal services company before throwing away any component. Of course, you should never throw away toner cartridges—certain companies will *pay* for used cartridges!

• **Figure 15.24** Page Setup options for Microsoft Word

Problems Sharing Multiple Printers

If you want to use multiple printers attached to the same parallel port, you have to use a switch box. Laser printers should never be used with mechanical switch boxes. Mechanical switch boxes create power surges that can damage your printer. If you must use a switch box, use a box that switches between printers electronically and has built-in surge protection.

Crashes on Power-up

Both laser printers and PCs require more power during their initial power-up (the POST on a PC and the warm-up on a laser printer) than once they are running. Hewlett Packard recommends a *reverse power-up*. Turn on the laser printer first and allow it to finish its warm-up before turning on the PC. This avoids having two devices drawing their peak loads simultaneously.

Troubleshooting Dot-Matrix Printers

Impact printers require regular maintenance but will run forever as long as you're diligent. Keep the platen (the roller or plate on which the pins impact) clean and the printhead clean with denatured alcohol. Be sure to lubricate gears and pulleys according to the manufacturer's specifications. Never lubricate the printhead, however, because the lubricant will smear and stain the paper.

Bad-Looking Text

White bars going through the text point to a dirty or damaged printhead. Try cleaning the printhead with a little denatured alcohol. If the problem persists, replace the printhead. Printheads for most printers are readily available from the manufacturer or from companies that rebuild them. If the characters look chopped off at the top or bottom, the printhead probably needs to be adjusted. Refer to the manufacturer's instructions for proper adjustment.

Bad-Looking Page

If the page is covered with dots and small smudges—the "pepper look"—the platen is dirty. Clean the platen with denatured alcohol. If the image is faded, and you know the ribbon is good, try adjusting the printhead closer to the platen. If the image is okay on one side of the paper but fades as you move to the other, the platen is out of adjustment. Platens are generally difficult to adjust, so your best plan is to take it to the manufacturer's local warranty/repair center.

Troubleshooting Inkjet Printers

Inkjet printers are reliable devices that require little maintenance as long as they are used within their design parameters (high-use machines will require more intensive maintenance). Because of the low price of these printers, manufacturers know that people don't want to spend a lot of money keeping them running. If you perform even the most basic maintenance tasks, they will soldier on for years without a whimper. Inkjets generally

Tech Tip

Check the MSDS

When in doubt about what to do with a component, check with the manufacturer for a **material safety data sheet (MSDS)** *. These standardized forms provide detailed information about the potential environmental hazards associated with different components and proper disposal methods. For example, surf to www. hp.com/hpinfo/globalcitizenship/ environment/productdata/index .html to find the latest MSDS for all Hewlett-Packard products. This isn't just a printer issue— you can find an MSDS for most PC components.*

have built-in maintenance programs that you should run from time to time to keep your inkjet in good operating order.

Inkjet Printer Maintenance

Inkjet printers don't get nearly as dirty as laser printers, and most manufacturers do not recommend periodic cleaning. Unless your manufacturer explicitly tells you to do so, don't vacuum an inkjet. Inkjets generally do not have maintenance kits, but most inkjet printers come with extensive maintenance software (Figure 15.25). Usually, the hardest part of using this software is finding it in the first place. Look for an option in Printing Preferences, a selection on the Start menu, or an icon on your desktop. Don't worry—it's there!

When you first set up an inkjet printer, it normally instructs you to perform a routine to align the printheads properly, wherein you print out a page and select from sets of numbered lines. If this isn't done, the print quality will show it, but the good news is that you can perform this procedure at any time. If a printer is moved or dropped or it's just been working away untended for a while, it's often worth running the alignment routine.

Inkjet Problems

Did I say that you never should clean an inkjet? Well, that may be true for the printer itself, but there is one part of your printer that will benefit from an occasional cleaning: the inkjet's printer head nozzles. The nozzles are the tiny pipes that squirt the ink onto the paper. A common problem with inkjet printers is the tendency for the ink inside the nozzles to dry out when not used even for a relatively short time, blocking any ink from exiting. If your printer is telling Windows that it's printing and it's feeding paper through, but either nothing is coming out (usually the case if you're just printing black text), or only certain colors are printing, the culprit is almost certainly dried ink clogging the nozzles.

All inkjet inks are water-based, so water works better than alcohol to clean them up.

Every inkjet has a different procedure for cleaning the printhead nozzles. On older inkjets, you usually have to press buttons on the printer to start a maintenance program. On more modern inkjets, you can access the head-cleaning maintenance program from Windows.

Another problem that sometimes arises is the dreaded multi-sheet paper grab. This is often not actually your printer's fault—humidity can cause sheets of paper to cling to each other—but sometimes the culprit is an overheated printer, so if you've been cranking out a lot of documents without stopping, try giving the printer a bit of a coffee break. Also, fan the sheets of the paper stack before inserting it into the paper tray.

Cleaning the heads on an inkjet printer is sometimes necessary, but I don't recommend that you do it on a regular basis as preventive maintenance. The head-cleaning process uses up a lot of that very expensive inkjet ink—so do this only when a printing problem seems to indicate clogged or dirty print heads!

Finally, in the maintenance area where the printheads park is usually a small tank or tray to catch excess ink from the cleaning process. If the printer has one, check to see how full it is. If this tray overflows onto the main board or even the power supply, it will kill your printer. If you discover that it's about to overflow, you can remove excess ink by inserting a twisted paper towel into the tank to soak up some of the ink. It is advisable to wear latex or vinyl gloves while doing this. Clean up any spilled ink with a paper towel dampened with distilled water.

Troubleshooting Laser Printers

Quite a few problems can arise with laser printers, but before getting into those details, you need to review some recommended procedures for *avoiding* those problems.

Laser Printer Maintenance

Unlike PC maintenance, laser printer maintenance follows a fairly well established procedure. Follow these steps to ensure a long, healthy life for your system.

Keep It Clean   Laser printers are quite robust as a rule. A good cleaning every time you replace the toner cartridge will help that printer last for many years. I know of many examples of original HP LaserJet I printers continuing to run perfectly after a dozen or more years of operation. The secret is that they were kept immaculately clean.

Your laser printer gets dirty in two ways: Excess toner, over time, will slowly coat the entire printer. Paper dust, sometimes called *paper dander*, tends to build up where the paper is bent around rollers or where pickup rollers grab paper. Unlike (black) toner, paper dust is easy to see and is usually a good indicator that a printer needs to be cleaned. Usually, a thorough cleaning using a can of pressurized air to blow out the printer is the best cleaning you can do. It's best to do this outdoors, or you may end up looking like one of those chimney sweeps from *Mary Poppins*! If you must clean a printer indoors, use a special low-static vacuum designed especially for electronic components (Figure 15.26).

Every laser printer has its own unique cleaning method, but one little area tends to be skipped in the included cleaning instructions. Every laser printer has a number of rubber guide rollers through which the paper is run during the print process. These little rollers tend to pick up dirt and paper dust over time, making them slip and jam paper. They are easily cleaned with a small amount of 90 percent or better alcohol on a fibrous cleaning towel. The alcohol will remove the debris and any dead rubber. You can also give the rollers and separator pads a textured surface that will restore their feeding properties by rubbing them with a little alcohol on a non-metallic scouring pad.

If you're ready to get specific, get the printer's service manual. Almost every printer manufacturer sells these; they are a key source for information on how to keep a printer clean and running. Sadly, not all printer manufacturers provide these, but most do. While you're at it, see if the manufacturer has a Quick Reference Guide; these can be very handy for most printer problems!

Finally, be aware that Hewlett Packard sells maintenance kits for most of its laser printers. These are sets of replacement parts for the parts most likely to wear out on each particular type of HP LaserJet. Although their use

⚠ Before you service a laser printer, always, *always* turn it off and unplug it! Don't expose yourself to the very dangerous high voltages found inside these machines.

● **Figure 15.26**   Low-static vacuum

⚠ The photosensitive drum, usually contained in the toner cartridge, can be wiped clean if it becomes dirty, but be very careful if you do so! If the drum becomes scratched, the scratch will appear on every page printed from that point on. The only repair in the event of a scratch is to replace the toner cartridge.

is not required to maintain warranty coverage, using these kits when prescribed by HP helps to assure the continuing reliability of your LaserJet.

Periodic Maintenance   Although keeping the printer clean is critical to its health and well being, every laser printer has certain components that will need to be replaced periodically. Your ultimate source for determining the parts that need to be replaced (and when to replace them) is the printer manufacturer. Following the manufacturer's maintenance guidelines will help to ensure years of trouble-free, dependable printing from your laser printer.

Some ozone filters may be cleaned with a vacuum and some can only be replaced—follow the manufacturer's recommendation. The fuser assembly may be cleaned with 90 percent or better denatured alcohol. Check the heat roller (the Teflon coated one with the light bulb inside) for pits and scratches. If you see surface damage on the rollers, replace the fuser unit.

Most printers will give you an error code when the fuser is damaged or overheating and needs to be replaced; others will produce the error code at a preset copy count as a preventive maintenance measure. Again, follow the manufacturer's recommendations.

The transfer corona can be cleaned with a 90 percent denatured alcohol solution on a cotton swab. If the wire is broken, you can replace it; many just snap in or are held in by a couple of screws. Paper guides can also be cleaned with alcohol on a fibrous towel.

Laser Printer Problems

Laser printers usually manifest problems by creating poor output. One of the most important tests you can do on any printer, not just a laser printer, is called a *diagnostic print page* or an *engine test page*. This is done by either holding down the On Line button as the printer is started or using the printer's maintenance software.

Blank Paper   Blank sheets of paper usually mean the printer is out of toner. If the printer does have toner and nothing prints, print a diagnostic print page. If that is also blank, remove the toner cartridge and look at the imaging drum inside. If the image is still there, you know the transfer corona or the high-voltage power supply has failed. Check the printer's maintenance guide to see how to focus on the bad part and replace it.

Dirty Printouts   If the fusing mechanism gets dirty in a laser printer, it will leave a light dusting of toner all over the paper, particularly on the back of the page. When you see toner speckles on your printouts, you should get the printer cleaned.

Ghosting   Ghost images sometimes appear at regular intervals on the printed page. This can be caused either because the imaging drum has not fully discharged (and is picking up toner from a previous image) or because a previous image has used up so much toner that either the supply of charged toner is insufficient or the toner has not been adequately charged. Sometimes it can also be caused by a worn-out cleaning blade that isn't removing the toner from the drum.

Failure of the thermal fuse (used to keep the fuser from overheating) can necessitate replacing the fuser assembly. Some machines contain more than one thermal fuse. As always, follow the manufacturer's recommendations. Many manufacturers have kits that alert you to replace the fuser unit and key rollers and guides at predetermined page counts with an alarm code.

The fuser assembly operates at 200 to 300 degrees Fahrenheit, so always allow time for this component to cool down before you attempt to clean it.

Light Ghosting versus Dark Ghosting   A variety of problems can cause both light and dark ghosting, but the most common source of light ghosting is "developer starvation." If you ask a laser printer to print an extremely dark or complex image, it can use up so much toner that the toner cartridge will not be able to charge enough toner to print the next image. The proper solution is to use less toner. You can fix ghosting problems in the following ways:

- Lower the resolution of the page (print at 300 dpi instead of 600 dpi).
- Use a different pattern.
- Avoid 50 percent grayscale and "dot-on/dot-off patterns."
- Change the layout so that grayscale patterns do not follow black areas.
- Make dark patterns lighter and light patterns darker.
- Print in landscape orientation.
- Adjust print density and RET settings.
- Print a completely blank page immediately prior to the page with the ghosting image, as part of the same print job.

In addition to these possibilities, low temperature and low humidity can aggravate ghosting problems. Check your users' manual for environmental recommendations. Dark ghosting can sometimes be caused by a damaged drum. It may be fixed by replacing the toner cartridge. Light ghosting would *not* be solved in this way. Switching other components will not usually affect ghosting problems because they are a side effect of the entire printing process.

Vertical White Lines   Vertical white lines are usually due to a clogged toner preventing the proper dispersion of toner on the drum. Try shaking the toner cartridge to dislodge the clog. If that doesn't work, replace the toner cartridge.

Blotchy Print   This is most commonly due to uneven dispersion of toner, especially if the toner is low. Try shaking the toner from side to side and then try to print. Also be sure that the printer is sitting level. Finally, make sure the paper is not wet in spots. If the blotches are in a regular order, check the fusing rollers and the photosensitive drum for any foreign objects.

Spotty Print   If the spots appear at regular intervals, the drum may be damaged or some toner may be stuck to the fuser rollers. Try wiping off the fuser rollers. Check the drum for damage. If the drum is damaged, get a new toner cartridge.

Embossed Effect   If your prints are getting an embossed effect (like putting a penny under a piece of paper and rubbing it with a lead pencil), there is almost certainly a foreign object on a roller. Use 90 percent denatured alcohol or regular water with a soft cloth to try to remove it. If the foreign object is on the photosensitive drum, you're going to have to use a new toner cartridge. An embossed effect can also be caused by the contrast control being set too high. The contrast control is actually a knob on the inside of the unit (sometimes accessible from the outside, on older models). Check your manual for the specific location.

Incomplete Characters   Incompletely printed characters on laser-printed transparencies can sometimes be corrected by adjusting the print density. Be extremely careful to use only materials approved for use in laser printers.

Creased Pages   Laser printers have up to four rollers. In addition to the heat and pressure rollers of the fuser assembly, other rollers move the paper from the source tray to the output tray. These rollers crease the paper to avoid curling that would cause paper jams in the printer. If the creases are noticeable, try using a different paper type. Cotton bond paper is usually more susceptible to noticeable creasing than other bonds. You might also try sending the output to the face-up tray, which avoids one roller. There is no hardware solution to this problem; it is simply a side effect of the process.

Paper Jams   Every printer jams now and then. If you get a jam, always refer first to the manufacturer's jam removal procedure. It is simply too easy to damage a printer by pulling on the jammed paper! If the printer reports a jam but there's no paper inside, you've almost certainly got a problem with one of the many jam sensors or paper feed sensors inside the printer, and you'll need to take it to a repair center.

Pulling Multiple Sheets   If the printer grabs multiple sheets at a time, first try opening a new ream of paper and loading that in the printer. If that works, you've got a humidity problem. If the new paper angle doesn't work, check the separation pad on the printer. The separation pad is a small piece of cork or rubber that separates the sheets as they are pulled from the paper feed tray. A worn separation pad will look shiny and, well, *worn!* Most separation pads are easy to replace. Check out www.printerworks .com to see if you can replace yours.

Warped, Overprinted, or Poorly Formed Characters   Poorly formed characters can indicate either a problem with the paper (or other media) or a problem with the hardware.

Incorrect media cause a number of these types of problems. Avoid paper that is too rough or too smooth. Paper that is too rough interferes with the fusing of characters and their initial definition. If the paper is too smooth (like some coated papers, for example), it may feed improperly, causing distorted or overwritten characters. Even though you can purchase laser printer–specific paper, all laser printers will print acceptably on standard photocopy paper. Try to keep the paper from becoming too wet. Don't open a ream of paper until it is loaded into the printer. Always fan the paper before loading it into the printer, especially if the paper has been left out of the package for more than just a few days.

The durability of a well-maintained laser printer makes hardware a much rarer source of character printing problems, but you should be aware of the possibility. Fortunately, it is fairly easy to check the hardware. Most laser printers have a self-test function—often combined with a diagnostic printout but sometimes as a separate process. This self-test shows whether the laser printer can properly develop an image without actually having to send print commands from the PC. The self-test is quite handy to verify the question, "Is it the printer or is it the computer?" Run the self-test to check for connectivity and configuration problems.

Possible solutions include replacing the toner cartridge, especially if you hear popping noises; checking the cabling; and replacing the data cable, especially if it has bends or crimps, or if objects are resting on the cable. If you have a front menu panel, turn off advanced functions and high-speed settings to determine whether the advanced functions are either not working properly or not supported by your current software configuration (check your manuals for configuration information). If these solutions do not work, the problem may not be user serviceable. Contact an authorized service center.

Beyond A+

DOT4

The IEEE 1284.4 standard, commonly known as DOT4, was created for multifunction peripherals (MFPs)—those nifty gadgets that combine the functions of printer, fax, and scanner in one big piece of equipment. The DOT4 protocol enables the individual devices within the MFP to send and receive multiple data packets simultaneously across a single physical channel. All data exchanges are independent of one another, so you can cancel one—for example, a print job—without affecting the others. DOT4 is an enhancement of the IEEE 1284 protocol for parallel printing; look for products that use it the next time you find yourself in a computer superstore.

Chapter 15 Review

■ Chapter Summary

After reading this chapter and completing the exercises, you should understand the following aspects of printers.

Printer Technologies

■ Impact printers create an image on paper by physically striking an ink ribbon against the paper's surface. The most commonly-used impact printer technology is dot matrix. Dot-matrix printers have a large installed base in businesses, and they can be used for multipart forms because they actually strike the paper. Dot-matrix printers use a grid, or matrix, of tiny pins, also known as printwires, to strike an inked printer ribbon and produce images on paper. The case that holds the printwires is called a printhead. Dot-matrix printers come in two varieties: 9-pin (draft quality) and 24-pin (letter quality).

■ Inkjet printers include a printhead mechanism, support electronics, a transfer mechanism to move the printhead back and forth, and a paper feed component to drag, move, and eject paper. They eject ink through tiny tubes. The heat or pressure used to move the ink is created by tiny resistors or electroconductive plates at the end of each tube.

■ Ink is stored in ink cartridges. Older color printers used two cartridges: one for black and one for cyan, magenta, and yellow. Newer printers come with four, six, eight, or more cartridges.

■ The quality of a print image is called the print resolution. The resolution is measured in dots per inch (dpi), which has two values: horizontal and vertical (for example, 600 × 600 dpi). Printing speed is measured in pages per minute (ppm). Modern inkjet printers can print on a variety of media, including glossy photo paper, optical discs, or fabric.

■ Dye-sublimation printers are used to achieve excellent print quality, especially in color, but they're expensive. Documents printed through the dye-sublimation process display continuous tone images, meaning that each pixel dot is a blend of the different dye colors. This is in contrast to other print technologies' dithered images, which use closely packed, single-color dots to simulate blended colors.

■ Two kinds of thermal printers create either quick, one-color printouts (direct thermal), such as faxes or store receipts, or higher-quality (thermal wax transfer) color prints.

■ Using a process called electro-photographic imaging, laser printers produce high-quality and high-speed output. Laser printers usually use lasers as a light source because of their precision, but some lower-cost printers may use LED arrays instead. The toner cartridge in a laser printer supplies the toner that creates the image on the page; many other laser printer parts, especially those that suffer the most wear and tear, have been incorporated into the toner cartridge. Although the majority of laser printers are monochrome, you can find color laser printers capable of printing photographs.

■ Be aware of the cost of consumables when purchasing a printer. Some less expensive printers may seem like a good deal, but ink or toner cartridge replacements can cost as much as the entire printer.

■ The photosensitive drum in a laser printer is an aluminum cylinder coated with particles of photosensitive compounds. The erase lamp exposes the entire surface of the photosensitive drum to light, making the photosensitive coating conductive and leaving the surface particles electrically neutral. When the primary corona is charged with an extremely high voltage, an electric field (or corona) forms, enabling voltage to pass to the drum and charge the photosensitive particles on its surface; the surface of the drum receives a uniform negative voltage of between ~600 and ~1000 volts.

■ The laser acts as the writing mechanism of the printer. When particles are struck by the laser, they are discharged and left with a ~100-volt negative charge. The toner in a laser printer is a fine powder made up of plastic particles bonded to iron particles. The toner cylinder charges the toner with a negative charge of between ~200 and ~500 volts. Because that charge falls between the original uniform negative charge of the photosensitive drum (~600 to ~1000 volts) and the charge of the particles on the drum's surface hit by the laser (~100 volts), particles of toner are attracted to the areas of the photosensitive drum that have been hit by the laser. The transfer corona applies a positive charge to the paper, drawing the negatively charged toner particles on the drum to the paper. A static charge eliminator removes the paper's static charge. Two rollers, a pressure roller and a heated roller, are used to fuse the toner to the paper.

- All laser printers have at least two separate power supplies. The primary power supply, which may actually be more than one power supply, provides power to the motors that move the paper, the system electronics, the laser, and the transfer corona. The high-voltage power supply usually only provides power to the primary corona; it is one of the most dangerous devices in the world of PCs. Always unplug a laser printer before opening it up.

- A laser printer's mechanical functions are served by complex gear systems packed together in discrete units, generically called gear packs or gearboxes. Most laser printers have two or three. Every laser printer has sensors that detect a broad range of conditions such as paper jams, empty paper trays, or low toner levels.

- Every laser printer contains at least one electronic system board (many have two or three) that contains the main processor, the printer's ROM, and RAM used to store the image before it is printed. When the printer doesn't have enough RAM to store the image before it prints, you get a memory overflow problem. Most printers can use generic DRAM like the kind you use in your PC, but check with the manufacturer to be sure.

- Because even tiny concentrations of ozone (O_3) will cause damage to printer components, most laser printers have a special ozone filter that needs to be vacuumed or replaced periodically.

- Solid ink printers use sticks of solid ink to produce extremely vibrant color. The ink is melted and absorbed into the paper fibers, and then it solidifies, producing continuous tone output in a single pass.

- ASCII contains a variety of control codes for transferring data, some of which can be used to control printers; ASCII code 10 (or 0A in hex) means "Line Feed," and ASCII code 12 (0C) means "Form Feed." These commands have been standard since before the creation of IBM PCs, and all printers respond to them; however, the control

codes are extremely limited. Utilizing high-end graphics and a wide variety of fonts requires more advanced languages.

- Adobe Systems' PostScript page description language is a device-independent printer language capable of high-resolution graphics and scalable fonts. PostScript is understood by printers at a hardware level, so the majority of the image processing is done by the printer, not the PC's CPU—so PostScript printers print fast. PostScript defines the page as a single raster image; this makes PostScript files extremely portable.

- Hewlett Packard's printer control language (PCL) features a set of printer commands greatly expanded from ASCII, but it does not support advanced graphical functions. PCL6 features scalable fonts and additional line drawing commands. PCL uses a series of commands to define the characters on the page, rather than defining the page as a single raster image.

- Windows 2000/XP use the graphical device interface (GDI) component of the operating system to handle print functions. The GDI uses the CPU rather than the printer to process a print job and then sends the completed job to the printer. As long as the printer has a capable-enough raster image processor (RIP) and plenty of RAM, you don't need to worry about the printer language at all in most situations.

- Most printers connect to one of two ports on the PC: a DB-25 parallel port or a USB port. The parallel connection is the classic way to plug in a printer, but most new printers use USB. The parallel port was included in the original IBM PC as a faster alternative to serial communication, and has been kept around for backward compatibility. Parallel ports are slow by modern standards, with a maximum data transfer rate of 150 KBps. Parallel ports lack true bidirectional capability. A standard parallel connection usually consists of a female DB-25 connector on the PC and a corresponding male connector on the printer cable. Eight wires are used as grounds, four for control signals, five for status signals, and eight for data signals going from the PC to the device. The parallel connector on the printer side is called a Centronics connector.

- IEEE 1284 was developed as a standard for a backward-compatible, high-speed, bidirectional parallel port for the PC. It requires support for compatibility mode, nibble mode, byte mode, EPP, and ECP; a standard method of negotiating compatible modes between printer and PC; standard cables and connectors; and a standard electrical interface.

- USB is the most popular type of printer connection today. USB printers rarely come with the necessary USB cable, so you may need to purchase one at the same time you purchase the printer. FireWire printers are less prevalent than USB, but offer easy connectivity, high speed, and hot-swapping capability.

- Network printers come with their own network card and connect directly to a network. This can be an RJ-45 port for an actual cable, or a wireless network card. Some printers offer Bluetooth adapters for networking. To connect a printer with a network card directly to a network, use a print server.

The Laser Printing Process

- Laser printing is a six-step process: clean, charge, write, develop, transfer, and fuse.

- The printing process begins with the physical and electrical cleaning of the photosensitive drum. All residual toner left over from printing the previous page must be removed, usually by scraping the surface of the drum with a rubber cleaning blade. One or more erase lamps bombard the surface of the drum with the appropriate wavelengths of light, causing the surface particles to discharge completely into the grounded drum.

- Using the primary corona wire, a uniform negative charge is applied to the entire surface of the drum (usually between ~600 and ~1000 volts) to make the drum receptive to new images. A laser is used to write a positive image relative to the toner particles on the surface of the drum, attracting them and creating a developed image. The transfer corona gives the paper a positive charge, making the negatively charged toner particles leap from the drum to the paper. Two rollers, a heated roller coated in a nonstick material and a pressure roller, melt the toner to the paper, permanently affixing it. Finally, a static charge eliminator removes the paper's positive charge.

- Laser printers generate a pattern of dots, called a raster image, representing what each page should look like. Laser printers use the laser to "paint" the raster image on the photosensitive drum. Laser

printers use a chip called the RIP to translate the raster image sent to the printer into commands to the laser.

- Laser printer resolution is expressed in dpi. Common resolutions are 600 dpi × 600 dpi or 1200 dpi × 1200 dpi. The first number, the horizontal resolution, is determined by how fine a focus can be achieved by the laser. The second number is determined by the smallest increment by which the drum can be turned. Higher resolutions produce higher-quality output, but also require more memory. Even printing at 300 dpi, laser printers produce far better quality than dot-matrix printers because RET enables the printer to insert smaller dots among the characters, smoothing out the jagged curves that are typical of printers that do not use RET.

Installing a Printer in Windows

- In Windows 2000/XP, a "printer" is not a physical device; it is a program that controls one or more physical printers. The physical printer is called a "print device." Print drivers and a spooler are still present, but in 2000 and XP they are integrated into the "printer" itself.

- Select Start | Printers and Faxes in Windows XP to open the Printers applet; in Windows 2000, select Start | Settings | Printers. The icon for this applet can also be found in the Control Panel. Install a new printer by clicking the Add Printer icon to start the Add Printer wizard. You must choose to install a local or a network printer; and you must select a port for a local printer. You must specify the printer type from the wizard's list, or using the Have Disk option. Windows XP's applet features a Windows Update button that gets the latest printer driver from the Internet.

- One printer will always be the default printer. If you have more than one printer installed, you can make any printer the default printer. The icon for the default printer will have a small check mark in the corner. If you have multiple printers, you can change the default printer by selecting the printer's properties and checking Make Default Printer.

- Printer emulation means using a substitute printer driver for a printer, as opposed to one made exclusively for that printer. Some printers are designed to emulate other, more widely supported models. If you don't have the specific driver for a printer, you can often use the driver from a similar model.

- Your monitor creates colors using RGB, whereas a printer outputs in CMYK. This difference can lead to a printed page differing greatly in color and tone from what is seen on the monitor. Calibrating your monitor to your printer is an important step in printing the colors you see on your screen. Manually calibrate your monitor by eyeballing it, use ICC color profiles to instruct the printer to output colors a certain way, or use calibration hardware and software to automate the process.

Troubleshooting Printer Problems

- When troubleshooting a printer, first check all the obvious possibilities. Is the printer on? Is it connected? Is it online? Does it have paper? Then check the spooler status either by double-clicking the printer's icon in the Printers applet, or by double-clicking the tiny printer icon in the notification area, if it's present. You may be able to bypass spooler problems by changing the printer properties setting to print directly to the printer.

- A print job that comes out a strange size usually points to a user mistake in setting up the print job. Use the program's Page Setup feature to fix these problems. If you know the page is set up correctly, recheck the printer drivers. Misaligned or garbage printouts invariably point to a corrupted or incorrect driver.

- Printer manufacturers supply an MSDS for each of their products; these provide detailed information about the potential environmental hazards associated with different components and proper disposal methods.

- Turn on the laser printer first and allow it to finish its warm-up before turning on the PC (a reverse power-up). This avoids having two devices drawing their peak loads simultaneously.

- With regular maintenance, impact printers will run forever. White bars going through the text point to a dirty or damaged printhead. Try cleaning the printhead with 90 percent or better denatured alcohol. If the characters look chopped off at the top or bottom, the printhead probably needs to be adjusted.

- Inkjet printers generally have built-in maintenance programs that you should run from time to time to keep your inkjet in good operating order. A common problem with inkjet printers is the tendency for the ink inside the nozzles to dry out when not used even for a relatively short time, blocking any ink from exiting. To clean the nozzles on older inkjets, you usually have to press buttons on the printer to start a maintenance program. On more modern inkjets, you can access the head-cleaning maintenance program from Windows.

- One of the most important tests you can do on any printer, not just a laser printer, is called a diagnostic print page or an engine test page. There are two types of printer test: the Windows test in which you print a test page, and the printer self-test that runs from the printer itself.

- Over time, excess toner will slowly coat the entire printer. Paper dander will build up where the paper is bent around rollers or where pickup rollers grab paper. Use a small amount of 90 percent or better alcohol on a fibrous cleaning towel to remove the debris and any dead rubber.

- Blank sheets of paper usually mean the printer is out of toner. If the printer has toner and nothing prints, print a diagnostic print page. If that is also blank, remove the toner cartridge and look at the imaging drum inside. If the image is still there, you know the transfer corona or the high-voltage power supply has failed. Blotchy print is most commonly due to uneven dispersion of toner, especially if the toner is low; also check that the printer is level and the paper completely dry.

- Ghost images can be caused either because the imaging drum has not fully discharged (and is picking up toner from a previous image) or because a previous image has used up so much toner that either the supply of charged toner is insufficient or the toner has not been adequately charged. Dark ghosting can sometimes be caused by a damaged drum. It may be fixed by replacing the toner cartridge. Light ghosting would *not* be solved in this way.

- The rollers that move the paper from the source tray to the output tray crease the paper in order to avoid curling that would cause paper jams in the printer. If the creases are noticeable, try using a different paper type. If the printer reports a jam but there's no paper inside, you've almost certainly got a problem with one of the many jam sensors or paper feed sensors. If the printer grabs multiple sheets at a time, the problem may be humidity or a worn separation pad.

- Hardware problems are a much rarer source of character printing problems. Most laser printers have a self-test function that shows whether the laser printer can properly develop an image without having to send print commands from the PC. Run the self-test to check for connectivity and configuration problems.

Key Terms

American Standard Code for Information Interchange (ASCII) *(324)*

calibration *(334)*

Centronics connector *(326)*

charge *(328)*

clean *(328)*

consumables *(336)*

DB-25 connector *(326)*

develop *(328)*

dot-matrix printer *(315)*

dots per inch (dpi) *(317)*

dye-sublimation printer *(318)*

erase lamp *(320)*

fuse *(328)*

fuser assembly *(321)*

graphical device interface (GDI) *(325)*

IEEE 1284 standard *(326)*

impact printer *(315)*

ink cartridge *(316)*

inkjet printer *(316)*

laser *(321)*

laser printer *(319)*

material safety data sheet (MSDS) *(337)*

near-letter quality (NLQ) *(315)*

network printer *(327)*

pages per minute (ppm) *(317)*

parallel port *(325)*

photosensitive drum *(320)*

PostScript *(324)*

primary corona *(320)*

print resolution *(317)*

print spooler *(330)*

printer control language (PCL) *(324)*

printhead *(315)*

printwires *(315)*

raster image *(330)*

raster image processor (RIP) *(330)*

resolution enhancement technology (RET) *(331)*

solid ink printer *(323)*

static charge eliminator *(321)*

thermal printer *(319)*

toner *(321)*

toner cartridge *(320)*

transfer *(328)*

transfer corona *(321)*

write *(328)*

Key Term Quiz

Use the Key Terms list to complete the sentences that follow. Not all terms will be used.

1. A laser printer's _____ translates the raster image of a page into a series of commands for the laser.

2. The transfer corona positively charges the paper in the _____ stage of the laser printing process.

3. Potential environmental hazards associated with a particular printer are outlined in the _____.

4. The _____ process matches the output of your printer to the output of your monitor so that what you see is what you get.

5. Print jobs are queued in the _____.

6. The first step of the laser printing process, the _____ phase, discharges and removes toner particles from the photosensitive drum.

7. Parts that must be replaced periodically, such as paper, ink and toner cartridges, and impact printer ribbons, are called _____.

8. When a page is sent to a laser printer, a representation of that page is created as a dot pattern called a(n) _____.

9. Jagged curves can be smoothed by inserting smaller dots among the other printed characters in a process known as _____.

10. The last step in the laser printing process, the _____ stage, melts the toner and binds it to the paper.

Multiple-Choice Quiz

1. Janet just bought a new Windows XP system. She wants to install her three-year-old inkjet printer on the new system but has lost the driver CD. She can't get on the Internet to download the latest drivers. What should she do?

    A. Install a driver for a similar printer.

    B. She's stuck until she can get on the Internet.

    C. She can use the Windows built-in drivers.

    D. She can install the printer without drivers.

2. Frank's color inkjet printer no longer prints the color yellow, although it prints all the other colors just fine. The printer worked fine last month, the last time he printed in color. Which of the following is the most likely problem?

    A. He turned off the yellow nozzle.

    B. He has run out of yellow ink.

    C. He has a corrupt printer driver.

    D. His printer is set to monochrome mode.

3. Beth's laser printer is printing tiny specks on the paper. What should she do first?

    A. Wipe the paper with bleach.

    B. Run the printer maintenance program.

    C. Clean the nozzles.

    D. Vacuum the printer.

4. Ursula's laser printer has stopped working and is displaying this error message: "Error 81 – Service." What should she do first?

    A. Update the printer's firmware.

    B. Reinstall the printer driver.

    C. Try to find the error in the user's guide, the maintenance program, or online.

    D. Turn off the printer and call the manufacturer's help line.

5. Kevin's inkjet printer isn't printing blue (cyan). He checks the ink levels and sees that there's plenty of ink. What should he consider next?

    A. A printhead is jammed.

    B. A laser is blocked.

    C. A nozzle is clogged.

    D. An ink cartridge is missing.

6. The output from Diane's laser printer is fading evenly. What should she suspect first?

    A. A laser is blocked.

    B. The printer is out of toner.

    C. A nozzle is clogged.

    D. Her printer is dirty.

7. The output from your inkjet printer appears much darker than what you see on your screen. What is the problem?

    A. You are using a paper weight that is not supported in the MSDS.

    B. The printer and monitor need to be calibrated.

    C. The color ink cartridges are almost empty.

    D. The black ink cartridge is almost empty.

8. Your laser printer fails to print your print jobs and instead displays a MEM OVERFLOW error. What can you do to rectify the problem? Choose all that apply.

    A. Install more printer RAM.

    B. Install more PC RAM.

    C. Upgrade the RIP.

    D. Disable RET.

9. What is the proper order of the laser printing process?

    A. Clean, charge, write, develop, transfer, and fuse

    B. Charge, write, transfer, fuse, develop, and clean

    C. Clean, write, develop, transfer, fuse, and charge

    D. Clean, charge, write, develop, fuse, and transfer

10. What is the function of the primary corona?

    A. To apply a negative charge to the photosensitive drum

    B. To apply a positive charge to the photosensitive drum

    C. To apply a negative charge to the paper

    D. To apply a positive charge to the paper

11. What is the function of the transfer corona?

    A. To apply a negative charge to the photosensitive drum

    B. To apply a positive charge to the photosensitive drum

    C. To apply a negative charge to the paper

    D. To apply a positive charge to the paper

12. Which type of printer can have the ink "topped off" in the middle of a print job?

    A. Thermal

    B. Dye-sublimation

    C. Laser

    D. Solid ink

13. To Windows 2000/XP, a "printer" is not the actual physical printer that prints on paper, but the program that controls the physical printer. What is the official Windows term for the physical printer?

  A. Raster image processor

  B. Print unit

  C. Print device

  D. Print spooler

14. What is the purpose of an ICC profile?

  A. To control the energy consumption of printers

  B. To control the output of printers and monitors

  C. To control user preferences such as printing in color versus black, page size, and print quality

  D. To control the resolution of the raster image

15. The output from your impact printer has white lines cutting through the text. What can you do to fix this?

  A. Replace the ribbon

  B. Tighten the paper feed rollers

  C. Clean the printhead with rubbing alcohol

  D. Clean the printhead with denatured alcohol

Essay Quiz

1. Your boss is fascinated by the laser printing process. Write a short memo that outlines how it works in the proper order.

2. While you are visiting family, your mother-in-law asks you to install a printer on the home network that everyone can use. They have one USB inkjet printer connected directly to a desktop PC. They have a second desktop PC and one wireless laptop. All computers are connected to the same router. What can you suggest to your mother-in-law for a solution?

Lab Projects

• Lab Project 15.1

Laser printers often have rather complex maintenance procedures and schedules. Select a laser printer—preferably one that you actually have on hand—and answer the following questions.

① Using the user's guide or online sources, determine the exact cleaning procedures for your laser printer. How often should it be vacuumed? Do any parts need to be removed for cleaning? Does the manufacturer recommend any specialized cleaning steps? Does your printer come with any specialized cleaning tools? Does the manufacturer have any recommended cleaning tools you should purchase?

② Based on the information you gathered, create a cleaning toolkit for your laser printer. Be sure to include a vacuum. Locate sources for these products and determine the cost of the toolkit.

③ Determine the model number of the toner cartridge. Locate an online company that sells brand-name (such as Hewlett-Packard) toner cartridges. Locate an equivalent third-party toner cartridge. Assuming that the printer uses a toner cartridge every three months, what is your annual cost savings per system using third-party toner cartridges?

④ All toner cartridges have a material safety data sheet (MSDS). Locate the MSDS for your model of toner cartridge and read it. Note any potential hazards of the toner cartridges.

⑤ Print out the description of the cleaning kit you created as well as the manufacturer's cleaning instructions.

Maintaining and Troubleshooting Networks

chapter 16

"In all large corporations, there is a pervasive fear that someone, somewhere is having fun with a computer on company time. Networks help alleviate that fear."

—John C. Dvorak

Wireless networking is one of the topics with a blurry line between CompTIA's Essentials and IT Technician exams. Although wireless is most certainly covered in the Essentials exam, CompTIA has placed most of the heavy lifting in the IT Technician exam. If you consider the depth of networking covered in the Essentials exam, this might just be a reflection of CompTIA wanting to spread out the learning a bit more between the two exams. In either case, this chapter really covers two main topics: the installation and configuration of wireless networks and the maintenance and troubleshooting of all types of networks.

In this chapter, you will learn how to

- **Install and configure wireless LANs**
- **Configure security**
- **Recognize and fix basic network problems**

Essentials Review

You'll find this chapter far more interesting if you are aware of networking concepts covered in the A+ Essentials exam. Before beginning this chapter, make sure you can

- Recognize the different types of network topologies
- Discuss the strengths and weaknesses of the different types of network topologies
- Explain packets and frames and how they are used in networking
- Recognize MAC addresses and explain their function
- Define the scope of bus-type Ethernet networks (10Base5 and 10Base2) and recognize the cabling and connections used
- Define the scope of UTP Ethernet networks (10/100/1000BaseT) and recognize the cabling and connections used
- Differentiate between a hub and a switch
- Identify alternatives to Ethernet such as Token Ring, FireWire, and USB
- Explain the use, strengths, and weaknesses of the different types of networking protocols (TCP/IP, IPS/SPX, NetBEUI, and AppleTalk)
- Describe the difference between a client/server and a peer-to-peer network
- Install a NIC into a Windows 2000/XP system, including installing and configuring protocols
- Explain IP addresses, default gateways, and subnet masks
- Recognize Class A, B, and C IP addresses
- Describe what routers do
- Explain DNS and WINS and why they are used
- Explain how and when you would use PING, IPCONFIG, NSLOOKUP, and TRACERT
- Share a folder and a printer in Windows 2000/XP

IT Technician

■ Installing and Configuring a Wireless Network

Wireless networks represent the newest (and to me, one of the coolest) things happening in networking today. The chance to get away from all the cables and mess and just *connect* has a phenomenal appeal. Because I see wireless as one of the most important areas of development in the PC, this section goes a good bit deeper into the technology than the CompTIA A+ exams require. A highly skilled tech today should know this stuff, because that's what your customers will demand. To make it a little easier to study, I've included some exam tips in this section that you can skim before taking the exams.

Instead of a physical set of wires running between network nodes, wireless networks use either radio waves or beams of infrared light to communicate with each other. Different kinds of wireless networking solutions have come and gone in the past. The types of wireless radio wave networks you'll find yourself supporting these days are those based on the IEEE 802.11 wireless Ethernet standard Wireless Fidelity (Wi-Fi)—and those based on Bluetooth technology. Wireless networks using infrared light are limited to those that use the Infrared Data Association (IrDA) protocol. Finally, the cell phone companies have gotten into the mix and offer access to the Internet through cellular networks. (More on each technology later in the chapter.)

Wireless Networking Components

Wireless networking capabilities of one form or another are built into many modern computing devices. Infrared *transceiver* ports have been standard issue on portable computers, PDAs, and high-end printers for years, although they're curiously absent from many of the latest PCs. Figure 16.1 shows the infrared transceiver ports on a laptop computer and a PDA. Wireless Ethernet and Bluetooth capabilities are increasingly popular as integrated components, or they can easily be added using USB, PCI, PCI Express, or PC Card adapters. Figure 16.2 shows a PCI card that accepts a wireless PC Card Ethernet card. You can also add wireless network capabilities using external USB wireless network adapters, as shown in Figure 16.3.

Wireless network adapters aren't limited to PCs. Many handheld computers and PDAs have wireless capabilities built-in or available as add-on options. Figure 16.4 shows a PDA accessing the Internet through a wireless network adapter card.

To extend the capabilities of a wireless Ethernet network, such as connecting to a wired network or sharing a high-speed Internet connection, you need a **wireless access point (WAP)**. A WAP centrally connects wireless

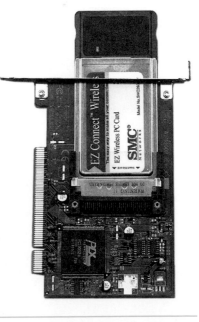

• **Figure 16.2** Wireless PC Card NIC inserted into PCI add-on card

• **Figure 16.1**   Infrared transceiver ports on a PDA and laptop

● **Figure 16.3**   External USB wireless NIC

network nodes in the same way that a hub connects wired Ethernet PCs. Many WAPs also act as switches and Internet routers, such as the Linksys device shown in Figure 16.5.

Wireless communication via Bluetooth comes as a built-in option on newer PCs and peripheral devices, or you can add it to an older PC via an external USB Bluetooth adapter. Figure 16.6 shows a Bluetooth adapter with a Bluetooth-enabled mouse and keyboard.

Wireless Networking Software

Wireless devices use the same networking protocols and client that their wired counterparts use, and they operate using the CSMA/CA networking scheme. The *CA* stands for *collision avoidance,* a slightly different standard

● **Figure 16.4**   PDA with wireless capability

● **Figure 16.5**   Linksys device that acts as wireless access point, switch, and DSL router

● **Figure 16.6**   External USB Bluetooth adapter, keyboard, and mouse than the *collision detection* standard used in wired Ethernet. Here's the difference. Wireless nodes listen in on the wireless medium to see if another node is currently broadcasting data. If so, it waits a random amount of time before retrying. So far, this method is exactly the same as the method used by wired Ethernet networks. Because wireless nodes have a more difficult time detecting data collisions, however, they offer the option of using the *Request to Send/Clear to Send (RTS/CTS)* protocol. When enabled, a transmitting node that determines that the wireless medium is clear to use sends an RTS frame to the receiving node. The receiving node responds with a CTS frame, telling the sending node that it's okay to transmit. Then, once the data is sent, the transmitting node waits for an acknowledgment (ACK) from the receiving node before sending the next data packet. Very elegant, but keep in mind that using RTS/CTS introduces significant overhead to the process and can impede performance.

In terms of configuring wireless networking software, you need to do very little. Wireless network adapters are plug and play, so any modern version of Windows will immediately recognize a wireless network adapter when it is installed into a PCI or PC Card slot, or a USB port, prompting you to load any needed hardware drivers. You will, however, need a utility to set parameters such as the network name.

Windows XP has built-in tools for configuring these settings, but for previous versions of Windows, you need to rely on configuration tools provided by the wireless network adapter vendor. Figure 16.7 shows a typical wireless network adapter configuration utility. Using this utility, you can determine your link state and signal strength, configure your wireless networking *mode* (discussed next), and set security encryption, power saving options, and so on.

Wireless Network Modes

The simplest wireless network consists of two or more PCs communicating directly with each other *sans* cabling or any other intermediary hardware. More complicated wireless networks use a WAP to centralize wireless communication and bridge wireless network segments to wired network segments. These two different methods are called ad-hoc mode and infrastructure mode.

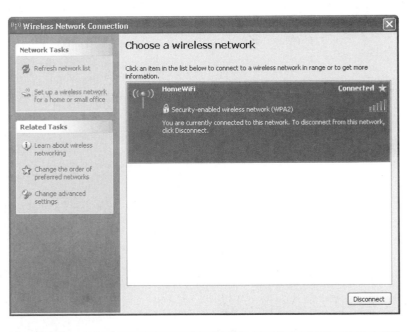

• **Figure 16.7** Wireless configuration utility

Ad-hoc Mode

Ad-hoc mode is sometimes called peer-to-peer mode, with each wireless node in direct contact with each other node in a decentralized free-for-all, as shown in Figure 16.8. Two or more wireless nodes communicating in ad-hoc mode form what's called an *Independent Basic Service Set (IBSS)*. Ad-hoc mode networks are suited for small groups of

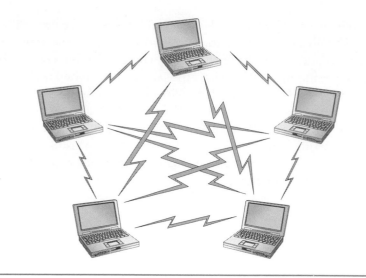

● **Figure 16.8**   Wireless ad-hoc mode network

computers (less than a dozen or so) that need to transfer files or share print-ers. Ad-hoc networks are also good for temporary networks such as study groups or business meetings.

Infrastructure Mode

Wireless networks running in **infrastructure mode** use one or more WAPs to connect the wireless network nodes to a wired network segment, as shown in Figure 16.9. A single WAP servicing a given area is called a *Basic Service Set (BSS)*. This service area can be extended by adding more WAPs. This is called, appropriately, an *Extended Basic Service Set (EBSS)*.

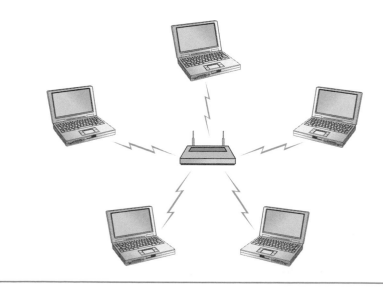

● **Figure 16.9**   Wireless infrastructure mode network

Wireless networks running in infrastructure mode require more planning and are more complicated to configure than ad-hoc mode networks, but they also give you finer control over how the network operates. Infrastructure mode is better suited to business networks or networks that need to share dedicated resources such as Internet connections and centralized databases. If you plan on setting up a wireless network for a large number of PCs or need centralized control over the wireless network, infrastructure mode is what you need.

Wireless Networking Security

One of the major complaints against wireless networking is that it offers weak security. In many cases, the only thing you need to do to access a wireless network is walk into a WAP's coverage area and turn on your wireless device! Furthermore, data packets are floating through the air instead of safely wrapped up inside network cabling. What's to stop an unscrupulous PC tech with the right equipment from grabbing those packets out of the air and reading that data himself?

Wireless networks use three methods to secure access to the network itself and secure the data that's being transferred. The Service Set Identifier (SSID) parameter—also called the *network name*—is used to define the wireless network. This is very handy when you have a number of wireless networks in the same area!

SSID

One of the main security weaknesses with wireless networks is that, out of the box, there's *no* security configured at all. Wireless devices *want* to be heard, and WAPs are usually configured to broadcast their presence to their maximum range and welcome all other wireless devices that respond.

Always change the default SSID to something unique. Configuring a unique SSID name is the very least that you should do to secure a wireless network. The default SSID names are well known and widely available online. This is intended to make setting up a wireless network as easy as possible, but conversely it creates a security hole you could drive a bullet train through. Each wireless network node and access point needs to be configured with the same unique SSID name. This SSID name is then included in the header of every data packet broadcast in the wireless network's coverage area. Data packets that lack the correct SSID name in the header are rejected.

> Changing the default SSID for the WAP is the first step in setting up a new wireless network.

Another trick often seen in wireless networks is to tell the wireless device to not broadcast the SSID. This makes it harder for people not authorized to access the network to know it's there.

MAC Address Filtering

Most WAPs also support MAC address filtering, a method that enables you to limit access to your wireless network based on the physical, hard-wired address of the units' wireless NIC. MAC address filtering is a handy way of creating a type of "accepted users" list to limit access to your wireless

Many techs shorten the term "MAC address filtering" to simply "MAC filtering." Either way works.z

network, but it works best when you have a small number of users. A table stored in the WAP lists the MAC addresses that are permitted to participate in the wireless network. Any data packets that don't contain the MAC address of a node listed in the table are rejected.

WEP

Early on, Wi-Fi developers introduced the Wired Equivalent Privacy (WEP) protocol to attempt to ensure that data is secured while in transit over the airwaves. WEP encryption uses a standard 40-bit encryption to scramble data packets. Many vendors also support 104-bit encryption. Note that some vendors advertise 128-bit encryption, but they actually use a 104-bit encryption key. Unfortunately, WEP encryption includes a flaw that makes it vulnerable to attack. While better than no encryption at all, keep in mind that WEP will not keep out a determined and knowledgeable intruder.

One important note to consider is that WEP doesn't provide complete end-to-end encryption. WEP provides encryption only between the WAP and the wireless device. Encryption is stripped from the data packet as it travels "up" through the subsequent network layers. For true end-to-end encryption, you need to upgrade to WPA or WPA2.

WPA

The Wi-Fi Protected Access (WPA) protocol addresses the weaknesses of WEP and acts as a security protocol upgrade to WEP. WPA offers security enhancements such as an encryption key integrity-checking feature and user authentication through the industry-standard *Extensible Authentication Protocol (EAP)*. EAP provides a huge security improvement over WEP encryption. After all, MAC addresses are fairly easy to "sniff" out, since they're transmitted in unencrypted, clear text format. User names and passwords are encrypted and therefore much more secure. Even with these enhancements, WPA was intended only as an interim security solution until the IEEE 802.11i security standard was finalized and implemented.

WPA2

Recent versions of Mac OS X and Microsoft Windows XP Professional support the full IEEE 802.11i standard, more commonly known as Wi-Fi Protected Access 2 (WPA2), to lock down wireless networks. WPA2 uses the Advanced Encryption Standard (AES), among other improvements, to provide a secure wireless environment. If you haven't upgraded to WPA2, you should.

Speed and Range Issues

Wireless networking data throughput speeds depend on several factors. Foremost is the standard that the wireless devices use. Depending on the standard used, wireless throughput speeds range from a measly 2 Mbps to a respectable 54 Mbps. One of the other factors affecting speed is the distance between wireless nodes (or between wireless nodes and centralized access points). Wireless devices dynamically negotiate the top speed at which they can communicate without dropping too many data packets. Speed decreases as distance increases, so the maximum throughput speed is achieved only at extremely close range (less than 25 feet or so). At the outer reaches of a device's effective range, speed may decrease to around 1 Mbps before it drops out altogether.

Speed is also affected by interference from other wireless devices operating in the same frequency range—such as cordless phones or baby monitors—and by solid objects. So-called *dead spots* occur when something capable of blocking the radio signal comes between the wireless network nodes. Large electrical appliances such as refrigerators are *very* effective at blocking a wireless network signal. Other culprits include electrical fuse boxes, metal plumbing, air conditioning units, and similar objects.

Wireless networking range is difficult to define, and you'll see most descriptions listed with qualifiers, such as "*around* 150 feet" and "*about* 300 feet." This is simply because, like throughput speed, range is greatly affected by outside factors. Interference from other wireless devices affects range, as does interference from solid objects. The maximum ranges listed in the next section are those presented by wireless manufacturers as the theoretical maximum ranges. In the real world, you'll experience these ranges only under the most ideal circumstances. True effective range is probably about half what you see listed.

Wireless Networking Standards

To help you gain a better understanding of wireless network technology, here is a brief look at the standards that they use.

IEEE 802.11-Based Wireless Networking

The IEEE 802.11 wireless Ethernet standard, more commonly known as Wireless Fidelity (Wi-Fi), defines methods by which devices may communicate using *spread-spectrum* radio waves. Spread-spectrum broadcasts data in small, discrete chunks over the different frequencies available within a certain frequency range. All of the 802.11-based wireless technologies broadcast and receive at 2.4 GHz (with the exception of 802.11a, which uses 5 GHz). The original 802.11 standard has been extended to 802.11*a*, 802.11*b*, and 802.11*g* variations used in Wi-Fi wireless networks, and also *hybridized* (combined with another wireless communication technology) to form the *Shared Wireless Access Protocol (SWAP)* used in the now defunct HomeRF networks.

Wireless devices can communicate only with other wireless devices that use the same standard. The exception to this is 802.11g, which is backward compatible with 802.11b devices (although at the lower speed of 802.11b). The following paragraphs describe the important specifications of each of the popular 802.11-based wireless networking standards.

802.11a Despite the "a" designation for this extension to the 802.11 standard, 802.11a was actually developed *after* 802.11b. The 802.11a standard differs from the other 802.11-based standards in significant ways.

You can see the speed and signal strength on your wireless network by looking at the Wireless NIC's properties.

Tech Tip

Increasing Wireless Range

Range can be increased in a couple of ways. You can install multiple WAPs to permit "roaming" between one WAP's coverage area and another's—an EBSS. Or you can install a signal booster that increases a single WAP's signal strength, thus increasing its range.

Look for basic troubleshooting questions on the CompTIA A+ certification exams dealing with factors that affect wireless connectivity, range, and speed.

Tech Tip

Spread-Spectrum Broadcasting

The 802.11 standard defines two different spread-spectrum broadcasting methods: direct-sequence spread-spectrum (DSSS) and frequency-hopping *spread-spectrum (FHSS). DSSS sends data out on different frequencies at the same time, while FHSS sends data on one frequency at a time, constantly shifting (or hopping) frequencies. DSSS uses considerably more bandwidth than FHSS, around 22 MHz as opposed to 1 MHz, respectively. DSSS is capable of greater data throughput, but DSSS is more prone to interference than FHSS. HomeRF wireless networks were the only types that used FHSS; all the other 802.11-based wireless networking standards use DSSS.*

Foremost is that it operates in a different frequency range, 5 GHz. This means that devices that use this standard are less prone to interference from other devices that use the same frequency range. 802.11a also offers considerably greater throughput than 802.11 and 802.11b at speeds up to 54 Mbps, though its actual throughput is no more than 25 Mbps in normal traffic conditions. While its theoretical range tops out at about 150 feet, in a typical office environment, its maximum range will be lower. Despite the superior speed of 802.11a, it isn't widely adopted in the PC world.

802.11b   802.11b is practically ubiquitous in wireless networking. The 802.11b standard supports data throughput of up to 11 Mbps (with actual throughput averaging 4 to 6 Mbps)—on par with older wired 10BaseT networks—and a maximum range of 300 feet under ideal conditions. In a typical office environment, its maximum range will be lower.

802.11b networks can be secured though the use of WEP and WPA encryption. The main downside to using 802.11b is, in fact, that it's the most widely used standard. The 2.4-GHz frequency is already a crowded place, so you're likely to run into interference from other wireless devices.

802.11g   The latest standardized version of 802.11, 802.11g offers data transfer speeds equivalent to 802.11a, up to 54 Mbps, with the wider 300-foot range of 802.11b. More important, 802.11g is backward compatible with 802.11b, meaning that the same 802.11g WAP can service both 802.11b and 802.11g wireless nodes.

Table 16.1 compares the important differences between the versions of 802.11.

Infrared Wireless Networking

Wireless networking using infrared technology is largely overlooked these days, probably due to the explosion of interest in the newer and faster wireless standards. This is a shame, because infrared provides an easy way to transfer data, often without the need to purchase or install any additional hardware or software on your PCs.

Infrared Data Association Standard   Communication through infrared devices is enabled via the **Infrared Data Association (IrDA)** protocol. The IrDA protocol stack is a widely supported industry standard and has been included in all versions of Windows since Windows 95.

Speed- and range-wise, infrared isn't very impressive. Infrared devices are capable of transferring data up to 4 Mbps—not too shabby, but hardly stellar. The maximum distance between infrared devices is 1 meter. Infrared links are direct line-of-sight and are susceptible to interference. An infrared link can be disrupted by anything that breaks the beam of light—a badly placed can of Mountain Dew, a co-worker passing between desks, or even bright sunlight hitting the infrared transceiver can cause interference.

Infrared is designed to make a point-to-point connection between two devices only in ad-hoc mode. No infrastructure mode is available. You can, however, use an infrared access point device to enable Ethernet network communication using IrDA. Infrared devices operate at half-duplex, meaning that while one is talking, the other is listening—they can't talk and listen at the same time. IrDA has a mode that emulates full-duplex communication, but it's

Table 16.1	Comparison of 802.11 Standards		
Standard	**802.11a**	**802.11b**	**802.11g**
Max. throughput	54 Mbps	11 Mbps	54 Mbps
Max. range	150 feet	300 feet	300 feet
Frequency	5 GHz	2.4 GHz	2.4 GHz
Security	SSID, MAC filtering, industry-standard WEP, WPA	SSID, MAC filtering, industry-standard WEP, WPA	SSID, MAC filtering, industry-standard WEP, WPA
Compatibility	802.11a	802.11b	802.11b, 802.11g
Spread-spectrum method	DSSS	DSSS	DSSS
Communication mode	Ad-hoc or infrastructure	Ad-hoc or infrastructure	Ad-hoc or infrastructure
Description	Products that adhere to this standard are considered "Wi-Fi Certified." Eight available channels. Less prone to interference than 802.11b and 802.11g.	Products that adhere to this standard are considered "Wi-Fi Certified." Fourteen channels available in the 2.4-GHz band (only eleven of which can be used in the U.S. due to FCC regulations). Three non-overlapping channels.	Products that adhere to this standard are considered "Wi-Fi Certified." Improved security enhancements. Fourteen channels available in the 2.4-GHz band (only eleven of which can be used in the U.S. due to FCC regulations). Three non-overlapping channels.

really half-duplex. Security-wise, the IrDA protocol offers exactly nothing in the way of encryption or authentication. Infrared's main security feature is the fact that you have to be literally within arm's reach to establish a link. Clearly, infrared is not the best solution for a dedicated network connection, but for a quick file transfer or print job without getting your hands dirty, it'll do in a pinch.

Table 16.2 lists infrared's important specifications.

Bluetooth

Bluetooth wireless technology (named for 9th-century Danish king Harald Bluetooth) is designed to create small wireless **personal area networks (PANs)** that link PCs to peripheral devices such as PDAs and printers, input

Table 16.2	Infrared Specs
Standard	**Infrared (IrDA)**
Max. throughput	Up to 4 Mbps
Max. range	1 meter (39 inches)
Security	None
Compatibility	IrDA
Communication mode	Point-to-point ad-hoc

Know the differences between 802.11a, 802.11b, and 802.11g.

 Tech Tip

Implementing WPA2 on 802.11x Devices

Most Wi-Fi devices you can buy right now support WPA2, but what about the millions of older Wi-Fi devices out there working for a living? You can update many devices to support WP2 with a firmware upgrade or driver update. You'll also need to patch earlier versions of Mac OS X and Windows XP. Windows Vista supports WPA2 out of the box.

Apple computers also support IrDA, as do Linux PCs.

devices such as keyboards and mice, and even consumer electronics such as cell phones, home stereos, televisions, home security systems, and so on. Bluetooth is *not* designed to be a full-function networking solution, nor is it meant to compete with Wi-Fi. If anything, Bluetooth is poised to replace infrared as a means to connect PCs to peripherals.

The IEEE organization has made Bluetooth the basis for its forthcoming 802.15 standard for wireless PANs. Bluetooth uses the FHSS spread-spectrum broadcasting method, switching between any of the 79 frequencies available in the 2.45-GHz range. Bluetooth hops frequencies some 1600 times per second, making it highly resistant to interference. It transfers data from 723 Kbps to 1—count 'em, *1*—Mbps, with a maximum range of 10 meters (just over 30 feet). Some high-powered Bluetooth devices have throughput speed of a whopping 2 Mbps and a maximum range of up to 300 feet, but these are uncommon.

Bluetooth is *not* designed to be a full-fledged wireless networking solution. Bluetooth is made to replace the snake's nest of cables that currently connects most PCs to their various peripheral devices—keyboard, mouse, printer, speakers, scanner, and the like—but you won't be swapping out your 802.11-based networking devices with Bluetooth-based replacements anytime soon.

Having said that, Bluetooth-enabled wireless networking is comparable to other wireless technologies in a few ways:

- Like infrared, Bluetooth is acceptable for quick file transfers where a wired connection (or a faster wireless connection) is unavailable.

- Bluetooth's speed and range make it a good match for wireless print server solutions.

Bluetooth Wireless Networking Hardware   Bluetooth hardware comes either integrated into many newer portable electronic gadgets such as PDAs and cell phones or as an adapter added to an internal or external expansion bus. Bluetooth networking is enabled through ad-hoc styled PC-to-PC (or PDA, handheld computer, or cell phone–to-PC) connections, or in an infrastructure-like mode through Bluetooth access points. Bluetooth access points are very similar to 802.11-based access points, bridging wireless Bluetooth PAN segments to wired LAN segments.

Cellular

Cellular wireless networks enable you to connect to the Internet through a network-aware personal digital assistant (PDA) or cell phone. Figure 16.10 shows a higher-end cell phone with an Internet connection. Using an add-on PC Card, you can connect any laptop to a cellular network as well. Figure 16.11 shows a Sprint Mobile Broadband Card.

In areas with broad cell phone coverage, such as big cities, cellular wireless networks offer high-speed access (400 to 700 Kbps download speeds) anywhere you go. Just fire up your device or portable and start surfing the Web! In remote areas, the speed drops down to something closer to modem connection speeds. (See Chapter 17, "The Internet," for the scoop on modems.)

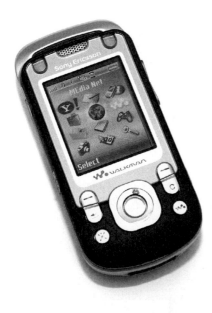

• **Figure 16.10**   Sony Ericsson phone

Cellular networks use various protocols to connect, such as Global System for Mobile Communications (GSM), General Packet Radio Service (GPRS), and Code Division Multiple Access (CDMA). These protocols are handled seamlessly by the software and hardware. What the end user sees is TCP/IP, just as if he or she connected through a wired network.

About the only real downside to cellular wireless networks is the price. The cell phone companies (notably Sprint and Cingular) are quite proud of their network service. As the technology matures, competition among the cellular network providers should bring the price down to something affordable for many people. At this point, though, it's usually much more cost-effective to go to a coffee shop or library and connect via Wi-Fi.

● **Figure 16.11**   Cellular network card

Configuring Wireless Networking

The mechanics of setting up a wireless network don't differ much from a wired network. Physically installing a wireless network adapter is the same as installing a wired NIC, whether it's an internal PCI card, a PC Card, or an external USB device. Simply install the device and let plug and play handle detection and resource allocation. Install the device's supplied driver when prompted, and you're practically done. Unless you're using Windows XP, you also need to install the wireless network configuration utility supplied with your wireless network adapter so that you can set your communication mode, SSID, and so on.

As mentioned earlier, wireless devices want to talk to each other, so communicating with an available wireless network is usually a no-brainer. The trick is in configuring the wireless network so that only specific wireless nodes are able to use it and securing the data that's being sent through the air.

Wi-Fi

Wi-Fi networks support ad-hoc and infrastructure operation modes. Which mode you choose depends on the number of wireless nodes you need to support, the type of data sharing they'll perform, and your management requirements.

Ad-hoc Mode   Ad-hoc wireless networks don't need a WAP. The only requirements in an ad-hoc mode wireless network are that each wireless node be configured with the same network name (SSID), and that no two nodes use the same IP address. Figure 16.12 shows a wireless network configuration utility with ad-hoc mode selected. Clicking the Initiate Ad Hoc button on this particular utility opened the Ad Hoc Setting dialog box

● **Figure 16.12**   Selecting ad-hoc mode in wireless configuration utility

where you can set the speed and the channel (if necessary.) Other utilities have the options in different dialog boxes, but a quick glance should find the same options.

The only other configuration steps to take are to make sure that no two nodes are using the same IP address (this step is usually unnecessary if all PCs are using DHCP) and to ensure that the File and Printer Sharing service is running on all nodes.

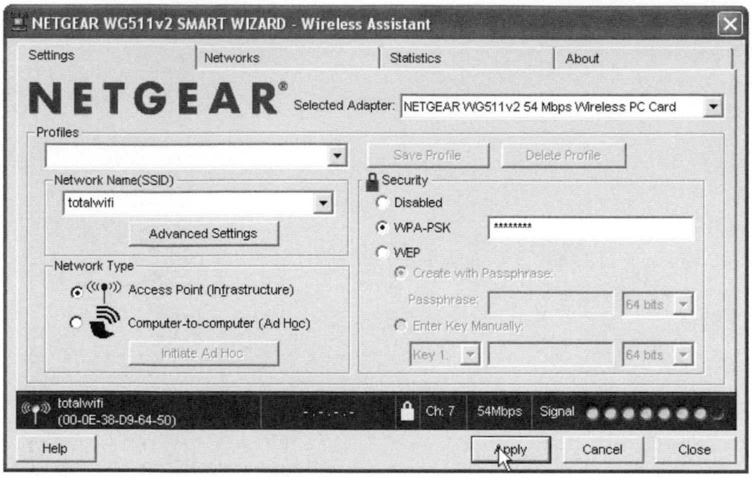

Figure 16.13 Selecting infrastructure mode in wireless configuration utility

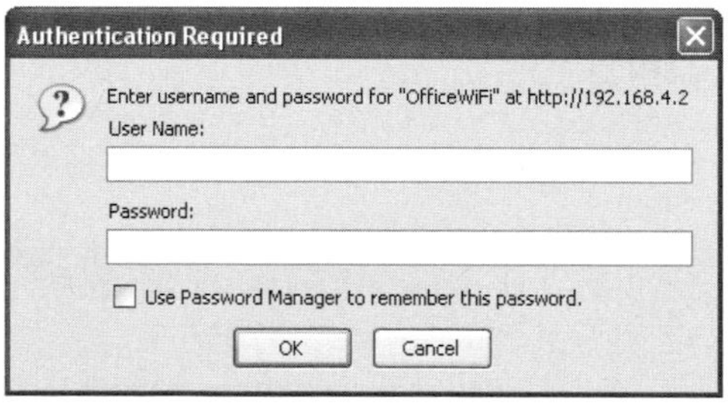

Figure 16.14 Security login for Linksys WAP

As noted earlier in the chapter, the WEP protocol provides security, but it's fairly easily cracked. Use WPA2 or, if you have older equipment, then settle for WPA until you can upgrade.

Infrastructure Mode Typically, infrastructure mode wireless networks employ one or more WAPs connected to a wired network segment, a corporate intranet or the Internet, or both. As with ad-hoc mode wireless networks, infrastructure mode networks require that the same SSID be configured on all nodes and WAPs. Figure 16.13 shows the same NETGEAR Wi-Fi configuration screen, this time set to infrastructure mode and using WPA security.

WAPs have an integrated Web server and are configured through a browser-based setup utility. Typically, you fire up your Web browser on one of your network client workstations and enter the WAP's default IP address, such as 192.168.1.1, to bring up the configuration page. You will need to supply an administrative password, included with your WAP's documentation, to log in (see Figure 16.14). Setup screens vary from vendor to vendor and from model to model. Figure 16.15 shows the initial setup screen for a popular Linksys WAP/router.

Configure the SSID option where indicated. Channel selection is usually automatic, but you can reconfigure this option if you have particular needs in your organization (for example, if you have multiple wireless networks operating in the same area). Remember that it's always more secure to configure a unique SSID than it is to accept the well-known default one. You should also make sure that the option to allow broadcasting of the SSID is disabled. This ensures that only wireless nodes specifically configured with the correct SSID can join the wireless network.

To increase security even more, use MAC filtering. Figure 16.16 shows the MAC filtering configuration screen on a Linksys WAP. Simply enter the MAC address of a wireless node that you wish to allow (or deny) access to your wireless network. Set up encryption by turning encryption on at the WAP and then generating a unique security key. Then configure all connected wireless nodes on the network with the same key information. Figure 16.17 shows the WEP key configuration dialog for a Linksys WAP.

You have the option of automatically generating a set of encryption keys or doing it manually—save yourself a headache and use the automatic method. Select an encryption level—the usual choices are either 64-bit or

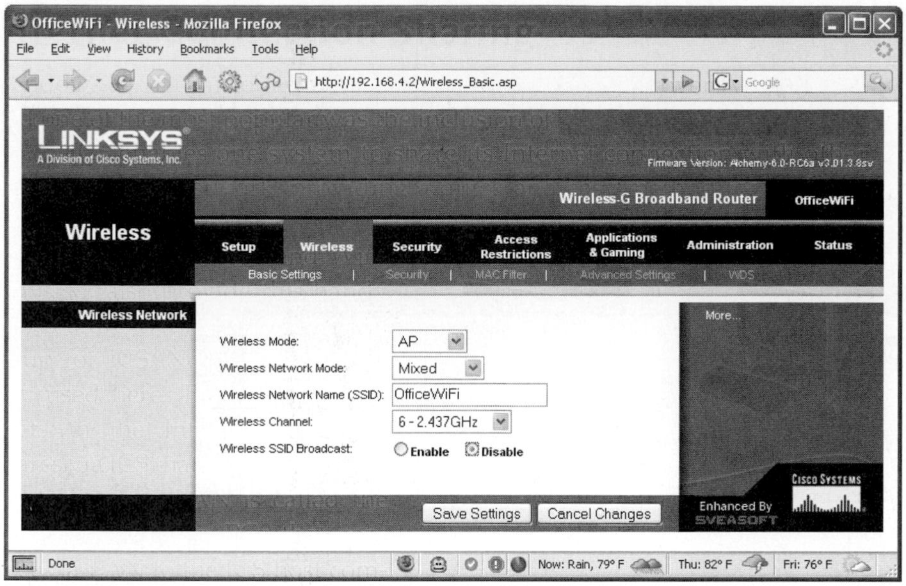

● **Figure 16.15**   Linksys WAP setup screen

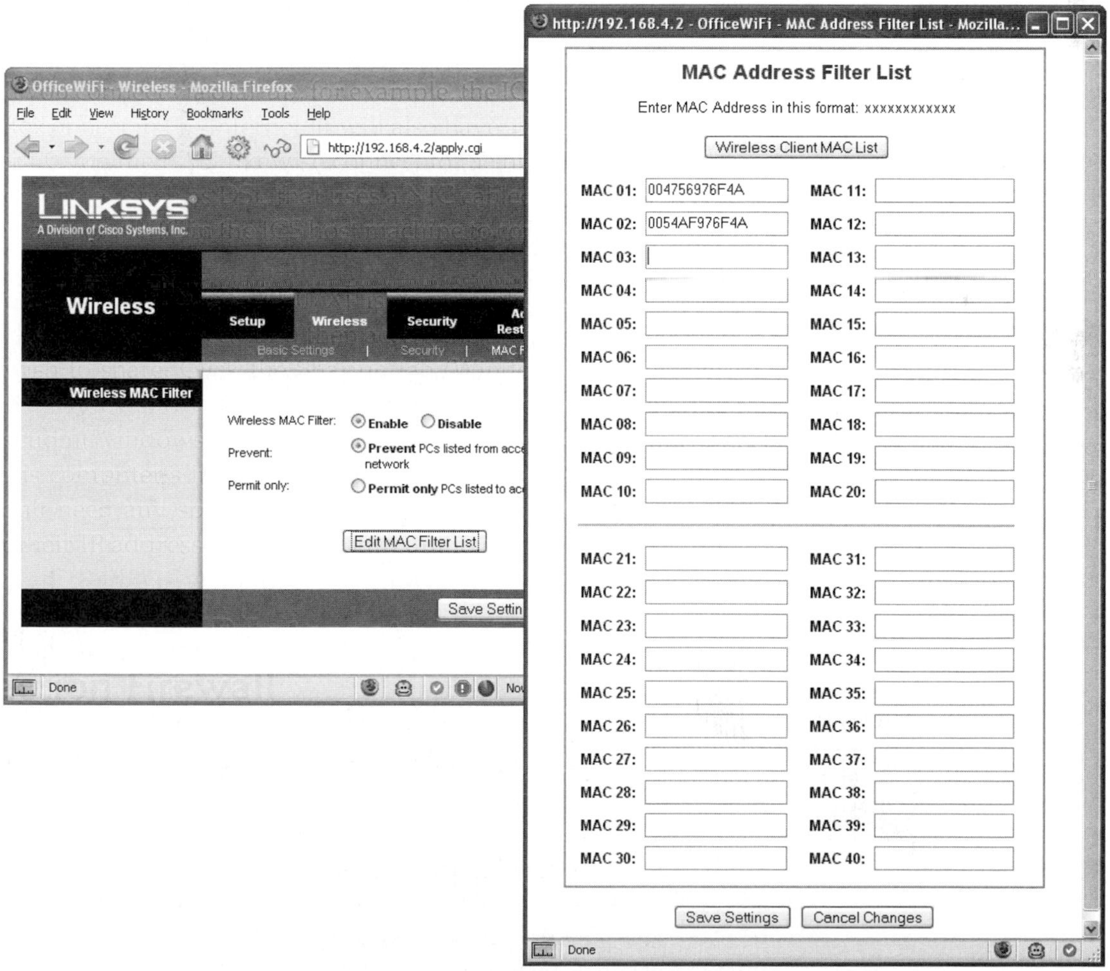

● **Figure 16.16**   MAC filtering configuration screen for a Linksys WAP

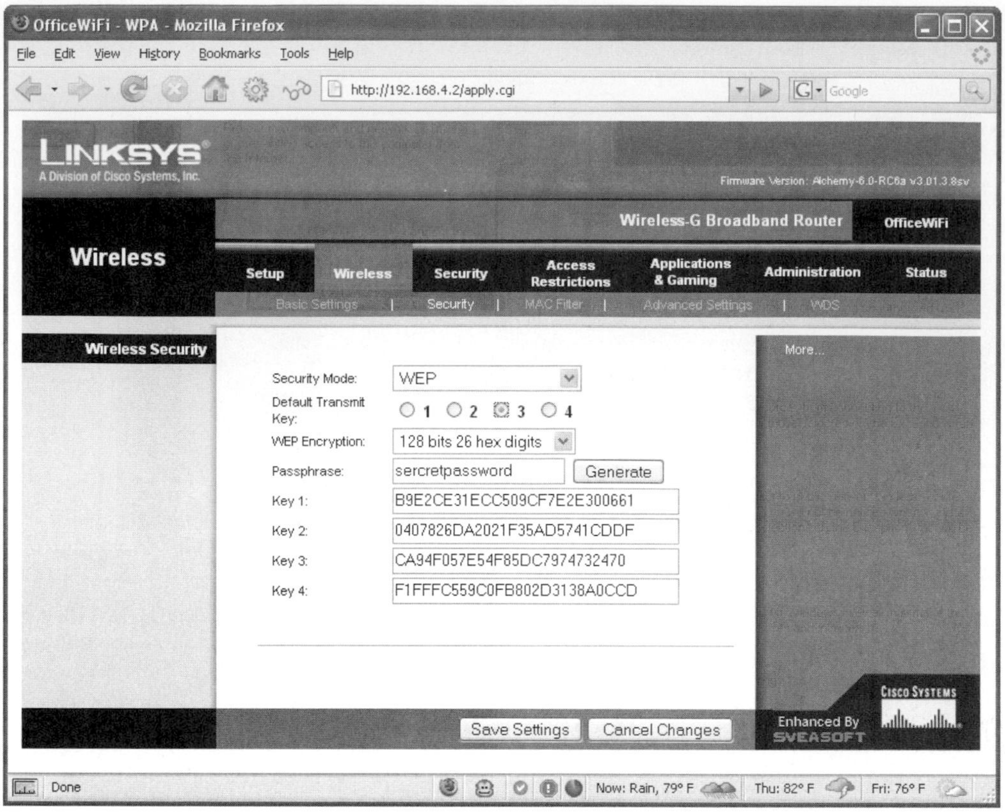

Figure 16.17   Encryption key configuration screen on Linksys WAP

Try This!

Set Up a Wireless Network

Getting a wireless network up and running can be fun, and it's certainly a useful skill to have, so Try This!

1. Install wireless NICs in two or more PCs and then get them chatting in ad-hoc mode. Don't forget to change the SSID!

2. Once you've got them talking in ad-hoc mode, add a WAP and get them chatting in infrastructure mode.

3. If you don't have a lab, but you have access to an Internet café (or coffee shop offering wireless) go there and ask someone to show you how they connect. Don't be shy! People love showing off technology!

128-bit—and then enter a unique passphrase and click the Generate button (or whatever the equivalent button is called on your WAP). Then select a default key and save the settings. The encryption level, key, and passphrase must match on the wireless client node or communication will fail. Many WAPs have the capability to export the encryption key data onto a media storage device for easy importing onto a client workstation, or you can manually configure encryption using the vendor-supplied configuration utility, as shown in Figure 16.18.

Infrared

IrDA device support is very solid in the latest version of Windows—in fact, there's not much for techs to configure. IrDA links are made between devices dynamically, without user interaction. Typically, there's nothing to configure on an infrared-equipped PC. Check your network settings to ensure that you've got the IrDA protocol installed and enabled, and you should be good to go (see Figure 16.19).

As far as infrared networking goes, your choices are somewhat limited. Infrared is designed to connect only two systems in ad-hoc mode. This can be done simply to transfer files, or with a bit more configuration, you can configure the two PCs to use IrDA in *direct-connection* mode. You can also use a special infrared access point to enable Ethernet LAN access via IrDA.

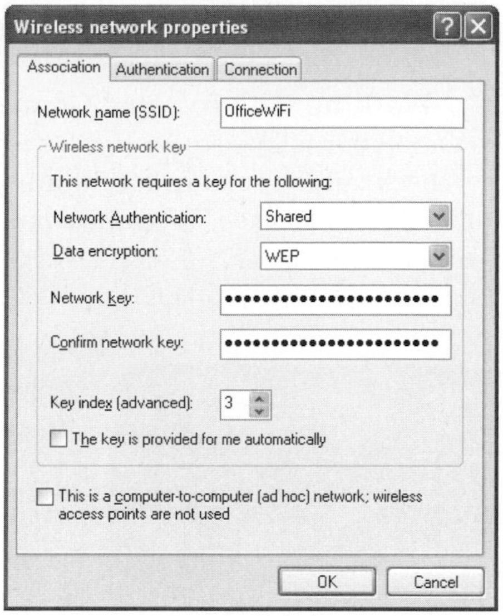

Transferring Files via Infrared   File transfers via IrDA are simple. When two IrDA-enabled devices "see" each other, the sending (primary) device negotiates a connection to the receiving (secondary) device, and *voilà*. It's just "point and shoot"! Figure 16.20 shows Windows 2000's *Wireless Link* applet. Use this to configure file transfer options and the default location for received files. You can send a file over the infrared connection by specifying a location and one or more files using the Wireless Link dialog box; dragging and dropping files onto the Wireless Link icon; right-clicking the file(s) in My Computer and selecting Send To Infrared Recipient; or printing to a printer configured to use an infrared port.

Networking via Infrared   Direct network connections between two PCs using infrared are similar to using a null-modem cable to connect two PCs together via a serial port. Modern versions of Windows make this type of connection extremely easy by employing wizards. Simply select Connect Directly to Another Computer and follow the prompts, choosing your infrared port as the connection device.

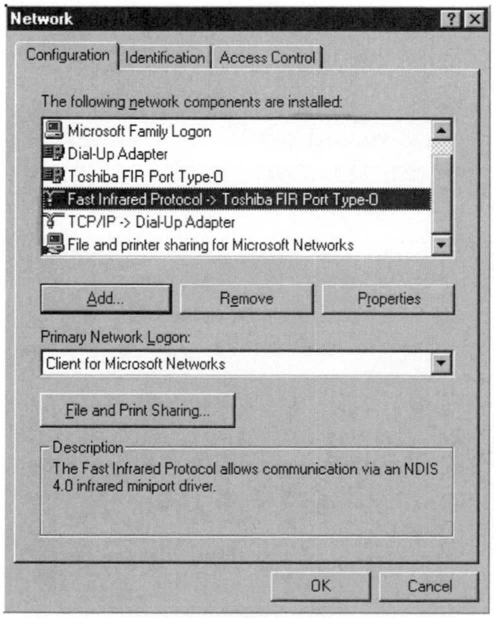

• **Figure 16.18**   Encryption screen on client wireless network adapter configuration utility

• **Figure 16.19**   Confirming the presence of IrDA protocol in Windows Network settings

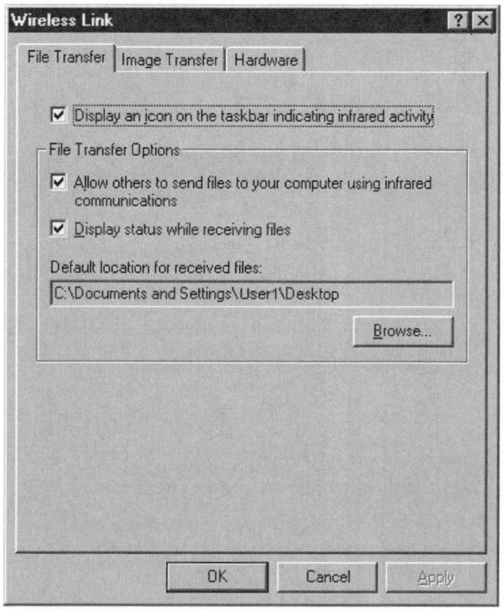

• **Figure 16.20**   Windows 2000 Wireless Link applet

Working with Infrared Connections

If you and your fellow students have a couple of infrared-capable devices, check out the settings for infrared connectivity. With PDAs, the feature is called *beaming*. Try connecting to the other device or devices by sending a file.

An infrared access point combines an infrared transceiver with an Ethernet NIC and translates the IrDA protocol into an Ethernet signal, enabling you to log on to your network and access resources. Figure 16.21 shows a laptop accessing an Ethernet LAN through an infrared access point.

Bluetooth Configuration As with other wireless networking solutions, Bluetooth devices are completely plug and play. Just connect the adapter and follow the prompts to install the appropriate drivers and configuration utilities (these are supplied by your hardware vendor). Once installed, you have little to do: Bluetooth devices seek each other out and establish the master/slave relationship without any intervention on your part.

Connecting to a Bluetooth PAN is handled by specialized utility software provided by your portable device or Bluetooth device vendor. Figure 16.22 shows a Compaq iPAQ handheld computer running the Bluetooth Manager software to connect to a Bluetooth access point. Like their Wi-Fi counterparts, Bluetooth access points use a browser-based configuration utility. Figure 16.23 shows the main setup screen for a Belkin Bluetooth access point. Use this setup screen to check on the status of connected Bluetooth devices; configure encryption, MAC filtering, and other security settings; and use other utilities provided by the access point's vendor.

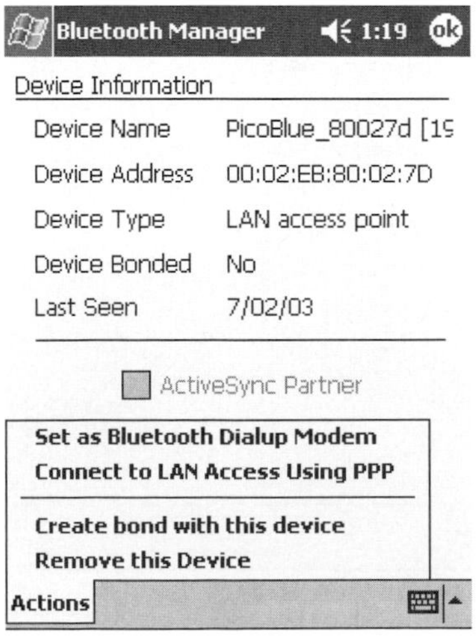

• **Figure 16.21** Laptop using infrared access point

• **Figure 16.22** iPAQ Bluetooth Manager software connected to Bluetooth access point

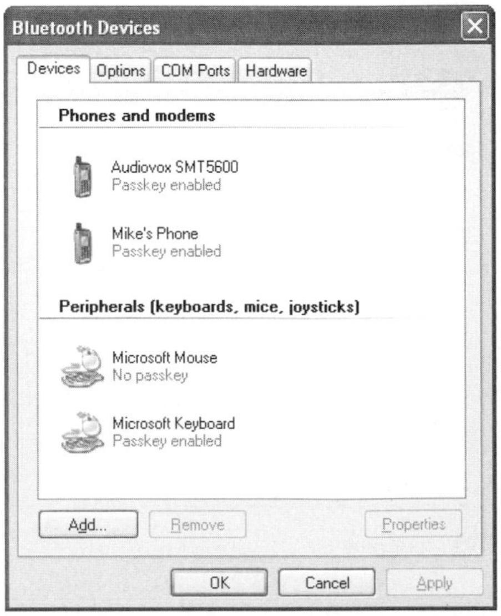

• **Figure 16.23** Windows Bluetooth setup screen

■ Troubleshooting Networks

Once you go beyond a single PC and enter the realm of networked computers, your troubleshooting skills need to take a giant leap up in quality. Think of the complexity added with networks. Suddenly you have multiple PCs with multiple users who could, at the drop of a hat, do all kinds of inadvertent damage to a fully functional PC. Networked PCs have a layer of networked hardware and resource sharing that adds a completely new dimension to a user's cry for help, "I can't print!"

Where can the problem lie in a *non-networked situation* if a person cannot print? Here are the obvious ones:

- Printer is not connected to the PC.
- Printer is out of ink.
- PC doesn't have the proper driver loaded.
- PC points by default to a printer other than the one to which the user thinks should print.

That's about it. Maybe the parallel port configuration is wrong in CMOS or the USB drivers aren't correct, but still.... Now do the same thing with a *networked situation* where a user can't print. Here are the obvious *extra* issues, because all the local machine issues apply as well:

- Print server is down.
- Printer is locked by another user.
- The client PC doesn't have network connectivity.
- The NIC driver is bad or incorrect.
- The client PC doesn't have the proper printer drivers installed for the networked printer.
- The cable between the client PC's NIC and the nearest switch is bad.
- The port to which the cable connects is bad.
- The switch failed.
- Somebody in an office down the hall spilled coffee on the printer inside the mechanism and then didn't fess up to the accident.

That's a lot of variables, and they just scratch the surface of possibilities. You live in a networked world—it's time to elevate your troubleshooting skills and methodologies to the next level. This section offers a series of steps you can use when performing any type of PC or network troubleshooting. You'll look at ways to apply your tech skills and general communication skills to get to the bottom of a problem and get that problem fixed.

Verify the Symptom

The one thing that all PC problems have in common is a symptom. If something odd *wasn't* happening to users as they tried to do whatever they need to do on their computers, you wouldn't have a problem at all, would you? Unfortunately, the vast majority of users out there aren't CompTIA A+

certified technicians. As a tech, you need to overcome a rather nasty communication gap before you can begin to consider a fix. Let's bridge that gap right now.

It usually starts with a phone call:

You: "Tech Support, this is Mike. How can I help you?"
User: "Uh, hi, Mike. This is Tom over in Accounting. I can't get into the network. Can you help me?"

Tom just started over in the Accounting department this week and has been a pain in the rear end so far. Ah, the things you might want to say to this person: "No. I only help non-pain-in-the-rear accountants." Or how about this? "Let me check my appointment schedule … ah, yes. I can check on your problem in two weeks. Monday at 4:00 P.M. okay for you?"

But, of course, you had the audacity to choose the beloved profession of IT tech support, so you don't get to ask the questions you want to ask. Rather, you need to take a position of leadership and get to the bottom of the problem, and that means understanding the symptom. Take a deep breath, smile, and get to work. You have two issues to deal with at this point. First, if you're working with a user, you must try to get the user to describe the symptom. Second, whether you're working on a system alone or you're talking to a user on the telephone, you must verify that the symptom is legitimate.

Getting a user to describe a symptom is often a challenge. Users are not techs and, as a result, their perception of the PC is very different than yours. But by the same token, most users know a bit about PCs—you want to take advantage of a user's skill and experience whenever you can. A personal example of verifying the symptom: Once I got a call from a user telling me that his "screen was blank." I told him to restart his system. To which he responded, "Shouldn't I shut down the PC first?" I said: "I thought you just told me the screen was blank!" He replied: "That's right. There's nothing on the screen but my desktop."

When Did It Happen?

Once you know the symptom, you need to try to inspect the problem yourself. This doesn't mean you need to go to the system, as many real problems are easily fixed by the user, under your supervision. But you must understand when the problem occurs so that you can zero in on where to look for the solution. Does it happen at boot? It might be a CMOS/BIOS issue. Is it taking place as the OS loads? Then you need to start checking initialization files. Does it take place when the system runs untouched for a certain amount of time? Then maybe the power management could come into play.

What Has Changed?

Systems that run properly tend to continue to run properly. Systems that have undergone a hardware or software change have a much higher chance of not running properly than a system that has not been changed. If something has gone wrong, talk to the user to determine whether anything particular has occurred since the system last worked properly. Has new software been installed? Did the user add some new RAM? Change the Windows Domain? Run a Windows Update? Drop the monitor on the floor? Not only do you need to consider those types of changes, you must make sure that any unrelated changes don't send you down the wrong path. The fact that someone installed a new floppy drive yesterday probably doesn't have anything to do with the printer that isn't working today.

Last, consider side effects of changes that don't seem to have anything to do with the problem. For example, I once had a customer whose system kept freezing up in Windows. I knew he had just added a second hard drive, but the system booted up just fine and ran normally—except it would freeze up after a few minutes. The hard drive wasn't the problem. The problem was that he unplugged the CPU fan in the process. When I discover a change has been made, I like to visualize the process of the change to consider how that change may have directly or indirectly contributed to a problem. In other words, if you run into a situation where a person added a NIC to a functioning PC that now won't boot, you need to think about what part of the installation process could be fouled up to cause a PC to stop working.

Check the Environment

I use the term *environment* in two totally different fashions in this book. The first way is the most classic definition: the heat, humidity, dirt, and other outside factors that can affect the operation of the user's system. The other definition is more technical and addresses the computing environment of the system and other surrounding systems: What type of system do they run? What OS? What is their network connection? What are the primary applications they use? What antivirus program do they run? Do other people use the system?

Answering these questions gives you an overview of what is affecting this system both internally and externally. A quick rundown of these issues can reveal possible problems that might not be otherwise recognized. For example, I once got a call from a user complaining they had no network connection. I first checked the NIC to ensure it had link lights (always the first thing to check to ensure a good physical connection!) only to discover that they had no link lights—someone decided to turn on a space heater that destroyed the cable!

Reproducing the Problem

My official rule on problems with a PC is this: "If a problem happens only once, it is not a problem." PCs are notorious for occasionally locking up, popping errors, and displaying all types of little quirks that a quick reboot fixes, and they don't happen again. Why do these things happen? I don't know, although I'm sure if someone wanted me to guess I could come up with a clever explanation. But the majority of PCs simply don't have redundancy built in, and it's okay for them to occasionally "hiccup."

A problem becomes interesting to me if it happens more than once. If it happens twice, there's a much higher chance it will happen a third time. I want to see it happen that third time—under my supervision. I will direct the user to try to reproduce the problem while I am watching to see what triggers the failure. This is a huge clue to helping you localize the real problem. Intermittent failures are the single most frustrating events that take place in a technician's life. But do remember that many seemingly intermittent problems really aren't intermittent—you have simply failed to reproduce the events exactly enough to see the consistency of the problem. Always take the time to match every step that leads to a problem to try to re-create the same error.

Isolating the Symptom

With so many bits and pieces to a PC, you must take the time to try to isolate the symptom to ensure your fix is going to the software or hardware that really needs it. In hardware, that usually means removing suspect parts until only one possible part remains. In software, that usually means removing background programs, booting into Safe mode, or trying to create a situation where only the suspected program is running.

Isolation takes on a whole new meaning with networks. One of the greatest tools in networking is isolation—does this problem happen on other systems, on other workgroups, on other PCs running DHCP? Whenever a problem takes place in networking, isolation is the key to determining the problem.

Separating Hardware from Software

Many problems that occur on a PC are difficult to isolate given that it is difficult to determine whether the problem lies in the software or the hardware. If you find yourself in this situation, you can take a few steps to help you zero in on which side of the PC to suspect.

Known Good Hardware

The absolute best way to know whether a problem is hardware or software related is to replace the suspected piece of hardware with a known good part. If you can't tell whether a Windows page fault comes from bad RAM or a software incompatibility, quickly replacing the RAM with known good RAM should help you determine whether the RAM or the software is to blame.

Uninstall/Reinstall

If you can do so easily, try uninstalling the suspected software and reinstalling. Many hardware/software problems magically disappear with a simple uninstall/reinstall.

Patching/Upgrading

Many hardware or software problems take place due to incompatibilities between the two suspect sides. Try upgrading drivers. Download patches or upgrades to software, especially if the hardware and the software are more than two years apart in age.

Virus Check

Last (maybe I should have put this first), always check for viruses. Today's viruses manifest so many different symptoms that failure to check for them is a study in time wasting. I recently got a new hard drive that started to make a nasty clicking noise—a sure sign of a failing hard drive. However, I ran an extensive virus check and guess what—it was a virus! Who would have thought? I checked with the hard drive maker's Web site, and my fears were confirmed. It just goes to show you—even the best of techs can get caught by the simplest problems.

Research

Once you've got your mind wrapped around the problem, it's time to fix it. Unless the problem is either simple (network cable unplugged) or something you've seen before and know exactly how to fix, you'll almost certainly need to research it. The Internet makes this easy. I use one of my favorite tricks when I get some bizarre error text: I type the error message into my search engine—that would be Google, of course—and most times find a quick fix!

Make the Fix and Test

Once you have a good idea as to the problem and how to fix it, it's time to do the fix. Always make backups—or at least warn the user of the risk to the system. If possible, try to remember how the system was configured before the fix so that you can go back to square one if the fix fails to work. After you perform the fix, do whatever you need to do to make sure the system is again working properly. Make sure the user sees that the system is working properly so that he or she can "sign off" on your work.

OSI Seven-Layer Model

A lot of people think about networks and troubleshoot networking issues using the OSI seven-layer model. Using this model (or my four-layer model, described in the next section of this chapter) helps you isolate problems and then implement solutions. Here are the seven layers of the OSI model:

- **Layer 1**   Physical
- **Layer 2**   Data Link
- **Layer 3**   Network
- **Layer 4**   Transport
- **Layer 5**   Session
- **Layer 6**   Presentation
- **Layer 7**   Application

The *Physical layer* defines the physical form taken by data when it travels across a cable. Devices that work at the Physical layer include NICs, hubs, and switches. Figure 16.24 shows a sending NIC turning a string of ones and

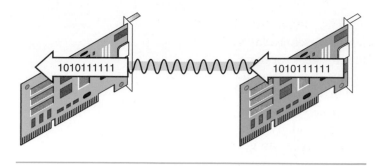

Figure 16.24 The Physical layer turns binary code into a physical signal and back into ones and zeroes.

zeroes into an electrical signal, and a receiving NIC turning it back into the same ones and zeroes.

The *Data Link layer* defines the rules for accessing and using the Physical layer. MAC addresses and Ethernet's CSMA/CD operate at the Data Link layer.

The *Network layer* defines the rules for adding information to the data packet that controls how routers move it from its source on one network to its destination on a different network. The IP protocol that handles IP addressing works on Layer 3.

The *Transport layer*, Layer 4, breaks up data it receives from the upper layers (that is, Layers 5–7) into smaller pieces for transport within the data packets created at the lower layers. In TCP/IP networks, the protocols that typically handle this transition between upper and lower layers are TCP and UDP.

The *Session layer* manages the connections between machines on the network. Protocols such as NetBIOS and sockets enable a computer to connect to a server, for example, and send and receive e-mail or download a file. Each different task you can perform on a server would require a different kind of session.

The *Presentation layer* presents data from the sending system in a form that a receiving system can understand. Most Layer 6 functions are handled by the same software that handles Layer 7 functions.

The *Application layer* is where you (or a user) get to interact with the computers. These are programs that make networking happen, such as Web browsers and e-mail applications. Chapter 17, "The Internet," covers these applications in a lot more detail.

The key to using the OSI seven-layer model is to ask the traditional troubleshooting question: What can the problem be? If Jill can't browse a Web site, for example, could this be a Layer 7 issue? Sure: If her browser software was messed up, this could stop her from browsing. It could also be a lower level problem, though, and you need to run through the questions. Can she do anything over the network? If her NIC doesn't show flashing link lights, that could point all the way down to the Physical layer and a bad NIC, cable, hub, or switch.

If she has good connectivity to the overall network but can't ping the Web server, that could point to a different problem altogether. Figure 16.25 shows the OSI seven-layer model graphically.

The only drawback to the OSI seven-layer model, in my view, is that it's too complex. I like to conceptualize network issues into fewer layers—four to be precise. Let's take a look.

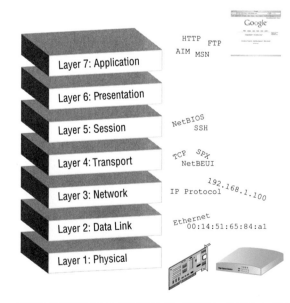

Figure 16.25 OSI

Mike's Four-Layer Model

Network problems, by the very nature of the complexity of a network, usually make for more complex problems. Given that, I have created a four-step process that I modestly call "Mike's

Four-Layer Model." These four things go through my mind every time I have a problem. I think about four distinct "categories" to help me isolate the symptoms and make the right fix.

Hardware

Hardware is probably the most self-explanatory of the four categories. This covers the many different ways data can be moved from one PC to another. Does the system have a good connection—how's the cabling? This also covers network cards—are they installed properly and tested? Plus, the hardware category hits on all of those interesting boxes, such as hubs, switches, and repeaters, among which all of the wires in the network run. If you can see it, it's under this category.

Protocols

This category covers the protocols, such as TCP/IP or NetBEUI. Is the protocol installed? Is it configured properly? Does any particular system's configuration prevent it from working with another system?

Network

The network category has two parts: servers and clients. Network operating systems must differentiate systems that act as servers from those that do not. If a system is a server, some process must take place to tell it to share resources. Additionally, if a system is intended to share, it must be given a name. This category also includes defining and verifying users and groups—does your system need them? Do the right accounts exist, and are they working properly?

Shared Resources

Once all the systems, users, and groups are working properly, you need to identify the resources they will share. If a drive or folder is to be shared, the OS must provide a way to identify that drive or folder as available for sharing. The rules for naming shared resources are called *naming conventions*. A great example would be a system that offers its D:\FRED directory for sharing. This D:\FRED directory needs a network name, such as FRED_FILES. This network name is displayed to all of the devices on the network.

Sharing a resource is only half the battle. Individual systems need to be able to access the shared resources. The network needs a process whereby a PC can look out on the network and see what is available. Having found those available resources, the PC then needs to make them look and act as though they were local resources. A network also needs to control access to resources. A laser printer, for example, might be available for sharing, but only for the accounting department, excluding other departments.

Chapter 16 Review

■ Chapter Summary

After reading this chapter and completing the exercises, you should understand the following about maintaining and troubleshooting networks.

Installing and Configuring a Wireless Network

■ The types of wireless radio wave networks you'll find yourself supporting these days are those based on the IEEE 802.11 wireless Ethernet standard Wi-Fi and those based on the newer Bluetooth technology. Wireless networks using infrared light use the IrDA protocol.

■ Wireless networking capabilities of one form or another are built into many modern computing devices. Infrared *transceiver* ports have been standard issue on portable computers, PDAs, and high-end printers for years. Wireless Ethernet and Bluetooth capabilities are increasingly popular as integrated components, or they can easily be added using USB, PCI, PCI Express, or PC Card adapters. Many handheld computers and PDAs have wireless capabilities built in or available as add-on options.

■ To extend the capabilities of a wireless Ethernet network, such as connecting to a wired network or sharing a high-speed Internet connection, you need a WAP. A WAP centrally connects wireless network nodes in the same way that a hub connects wired Ethernet PCs.

■ Wireless devices use the same networking protocols and client that their wired counterparts use, and they operate using the CSMA/CA networking scheme, where nodes check before broadcasting. Wireless nodes also use the RTS/CTS protocol. When enabled, a transmitting node that determines that the wireless medium is clear to use sends an RTS frame to the receiving node. The receiving node responds with a CTS frame, telling the sending node that it's okay to transmit. Then, once the data is sent, the transmitting node waits for an acknowledgment (ACK) from the receiving node before sending the next data packet.

■ You will need a utility to set parameters such as your SSID. Windows XP has built-in tools for this, but otherwise you must rely on configuration tools provided by the wireless network adapter vendor.

■ The simplest wireless network consists of two or more PCs communicating directly with each other without cabling or any other intermediary hardware (ad-hoc mode). More complicated wireless networks use a WAP to centralize wireless communication and bridge wireless network segments to wired network segments (infrastructure mode). Ad-hoc networks are also good for temporary networks such as study groups or business meetings. Infrastructure mode is better suited to business networks or networks that need to share dedicated resources like Internet connections and centralized databases.

■ Out of the box, wireless networks have no security configured at all. WAPs are usually configured to broadcast their presence to their maximum range and welcome all other wireless devices that respond. Data packets are floating through the air instead of safely wrapped up inside network cabling.

■ Most WAPs support MAC address filtering, a method that enables you to limit access to your wireless network based on the physical, hard-wired address of the unit's wireless network adapter. Enabling WEP encrypts your data to secure it while in transit over the airwaves, but the WEP encryption standard itself is flawed and cannot be relied upon to protect your data against a knowledgeable and motivated attacker.

■ WPA and WPA2 address the weaknesses of WEP and act as a sort of security protocol upgrade to WEP-enabled devices. WPA and WPA2 offer security enhancements such as an encryption key integrity–checking feature and user authentication through the industry-standard EAP.

■ Depending on the standard used, wireless throughput speeds range from 2 Mbps to 54 Mbps. Wireless devices dynamically negotiate the top speed that they can communicate at without dropping too many data packets.

- Wireless networking speed and range are greatly affected by outside factors, such as interference from other wireless devices or solid objects. A wireless device's true effective range is probably about half the theoretical maximum listed by the manufacturer.

- 802.11a differs from the other 802.11-based standards in significant ways. Foremost, it operates in a different frequency range, 5 GHz, so 802.11a devices are less prone to interference. 802.11a also offers considerably greater throughput than 802.11 and 802.11b at speeds up to 54 Mbps, but its range tops out at only about 150 feet. 802.11a isn't widely adopted in the PC world.

- 802.11b is practically ubiquitous in wireless networking. The 802.11b standard supports data throughput of up to 11 Mbps—on par with older wired 10BaseT networks—and a range of up to 300 feet under ideal conditions.

- The 802.11g standard offers data transfer speeds equivalent to 802.11a, up to 54 Mbps, with the wider 300-foot range of 802.11b. Because 802.11g is backward compatible with 802.11b, the same 802.11g WAP can service both 802.11b and 802.11b wireless nodes.

- Wireless networking using infrared (IR) technology is enabled via the Infrared Data Association (IrDA) protocol stack, a widely supported industry standard, and has been included in all versions of Windows since Windows 95. IR is designed to make only a point-to-point connection between two devices in ad-hoc mode of up to 4 Mbps, at a maximum distance of 1 meter.

- Bluetooth wireless technology is designed to create small wireless Personal Area Networks (PANs) that link PCs to peripheral devices such as PDAs and printers, input devices such as keyboards and mice, and even consumer electronics such as cell phones, home stereos, televisions, home security systems, and so on. Bluetooth is not designed to be a full-function networking solution.

- Cellular wireless networks enable you to connect to the Internet through a network-aware PDA or cell phone with download speeds up to 700 Kbps. Cellular networks use various protocols, including GSM, GPRS, and CDMA. While pricey, it is sometimes your only option in remote areas.

- The mechanics of setting up a wireless network don't differ much from a wired network. Physically installing a wireless network adapter is the same as installing a wired NIC, whether it's an internal PCI card, a PC Card, or an external USB device. Simply install the device and let plug and play handle detection and resource allocation. Unless you're using Windows XP, you also need to install the wireless network configuration utility supplied with your wireless network adapter so that you can set your communication mode, SSID, and so on.

- Wi-Fi networks support ad-hoc and infrastructure operation modes. Which mode you choose depends on the number of wireless nodes you need to support, the type of data sharing they'll perform, and your management requirements.

- Ad-hoc wireless networks don't need a WAP. The only requirements in an ad-hoc mode wireless network are that each wireless node be configured with the same network name (SSID) and that no two nodes use the same IP address. You may also have to select a common channel for all ad-hoc nodes.

- Typically, infrastructure mode wireless networks employ one or more WAPs connected to a wired network segment, a corporate intranet or the Internet, or both. As with ad-hoc mode wireless networks, infrastructure mode networks require that the same SSID be configured on all nodes and WAPs.

- WAPs have an integrated Web server and are configured through a browser-based setup utility. Typically, you enter the WAP's default IP address to bring up the configuration page and supply an administrative password, included with your WAP's documentation, to log in.

- Set up WEP encryption—if that's your only option—by turning encryption on at the WAP and then generating a unique security key. Then configure all connected wireless nodes on the network with the same key information. WPA and WPA2 encryption are configured in much the same way. You may be required to input a valid user name and password to configure encryption using WPA/WPA2.

- IrDA links are made between devices dynamically, without user interaction. Typically, there's nothing to configure on an infrared-equipped PC. Just check your network settings to ensure that you've got the IrDA protocol installed and enabled.

- File transfers via IrDA are simple. The sending (primary) device negotiates a connection to the receiving (secondary) device, and transfers the file. To configure file transfer options and the default location for received files, use the Windows Wireless Link applet.

- As with other wireless networking solutions, Bluetooth devices are completely plug and play. Just connect the adapter and follow the prompts to install the appropriate drivers and configuration utilities. Connecting to a Bluetooth PAN is handled by specialized utility software provided by your portable device or Bluetooth device vendor.

Troubleshooting Networks

- The one thing that all PC problems have in common is a symptom. If you're working with a user you must try to get the user to describe the symptom. Then you must verify that the symptom is legitimate. Try to inspect the problem yourself. Find out when it occurs in order to zero in on where to look for the solution.

- Systems are much more likely to have problems after a hardware or software change; check to see if that has happened since the system last worked properly. When you discover a change has been made, try to visualize the process of the change to consider how that change may have directly or indirectly contributed to a problem.

- Check the environment to get an overview of what is affecting this system both internally and externally. The larger environment—heat, humidity, dirt, and other outside factors—may affect the operation of the system, as may the computing environment of this system and other surrounding systems, including the type of system, OS, network connection, primary applications, antivirus program, and other users.

- If a problem happens twice, there's a much higher chance it will happen a third time. Direct the user to try to reproduce the problem while you watch to see what triggers the failure. Many seemingly intermittent problems really aren't intermittent—you just haven't reproduced the events exactly.

- Take the time to try to isolate the symptom to ensure your fix is going to the software or hardware that really needs it. Remove suspect pieces of hardware until only one possible "bad apple" remains. Remove background programs, boot into Safe mode, or try to create a situation in which only the suspected program is running. Isolation is also one of the greatest tools in networking.

- If you aren't sure whether a problem lies in the software or in the hardware, you can take a few steps to help you zero in on which side of the PC to suspect. The best is to replace the suspected piece of hardware with a known good part, and then try uninstalling the suspected software and reinstalling. Try upgrading drivers. Download patches or upgrades to software, especially if the hardware and the software are more than two years apart in age, and always check for viruses.

- Once you've discovered the problem, unless it is either simple (network cable unplugged) or something you've seen before and know exactly how to fix, you'll need to research it. The Internet makes this easy. One of my favorite tricks is to type the error into my search engine and most times I can find a quick fix.

- Make backups—or at least warn the user of the risk—before you try a fix. If possible, try to remember how the system was set up before the fix so that you can go back to square one if the fix fails to work. After you perform the fix, do whatever you need to do to make sure the system is working properly. Have the user experience the system working properly so that he or she can "sign off" on your work.

- You can use the OSI seven-layer model to troubleshoot network problems. The Physical layer defines the physical form taken by data when it travels across a cable. The Data Link layer defines the rules for accessing and using the Physical layer. The Network layer defines the rules for adding information to the data packet that controls how routers move it from its source on one network to its destination on a different network.

- The Transport layer breaks up data it receives from the upper layers into smaller pieces for transport within the data packets created at the lower layers. The Session layer manages the connections between machines on the network. The Presentation layer presents data from the sending system in a form that a receiving system can understand. The Application layer is where you (or a user) get to interact with the computers.

- Mike's Four-Layer Model is an approach to network troubleshooting. First, check the hardware, including connections, NICs, and hubs/switches/routers. Second, check that the protocols, such as TCP/IP or NetBEUI, are installed and properly configured. Third, check the network setup, whether it includes a server or is peer-to-peer. Finally, check the shared resources. Have the appropriate resources been identified and made available for sharing to all relevant users? Are the individual systems set up to access the shared resources?

■ Key Terms

ad-hoc mode *(355)*

Bluetooth *(361)*

cellular wireless networks *(362)*

IEEE 802.11 *(359)*

Infrared Data Association (IrDA) *(360)*

infrastructure mode *(356)*

MAC address filtering *(357)*

personal area network (PAN) *(361)*

Service Set Identifier (SSID) *(357)*

Wi-Fi Protected Access (WPA) *(358)*

Wi-Fi Protected Access 2 (WPA2) *(358)*

wireless access point (WAP) *(353)*

Wired Equivalent Privacy (WEP) *(358)*

Wireless Fidelity (Wi-Fi) *(359)*

■ Key Term Quiz

Use the Key Terms list to complete the sentences that follow. Not all terms will be used.

1. Similar to the way a hub connects wired PCs, a(n) _____ connects wireless network nodes.

2. In a wireless network in _____, nodes have direct connections to each other.

3. In a wireless network in _____, nodes connect to each other through a wireless access point.

4. The _____ parameter, or network name, is used to define a wireless network.

5. You can limit access to your wireless network based on the physical, hard-wired address of a unit's wireless NIC; this is known as _____.

6. The _____ protocol fails to provide complete end-to-end encryption; it encrypts only between the WAP and wireless device.

7. Only intended as an interim security solution until the IEEE 802.11i security standard was finalized and implemented, the _____ protocol offered better security than the previous wireless encryption protocol.

8. Currently, the highest level of encryption available for wireless networks is _____.

9. The _____ wireless Ethernet standard is more commonly known as _____.

10. _____ was developed to create small personal wireless networks.

Multiple-Choice Quiz

1. Everything worked fine on your 100BaseT network yesterday, but today no one can connect to the server. The server seems to be in good running order. Which of the following is the most likely problem?

   A. Someone changed all the passwords for server access.

   B. A malfunctioning switch.

   C. Someone's T connector has come loose on the bus.

   D. The server's cable is wired as TIA/EIA 568A and all the others are wired as TIA/EIA 568B.

2. Two wireless nodes that are communicating directly with each other, without any intermediary systems or hardware, are using what wireless mode?

   A. Ad-hoc

   B. Bluetooth

   C. Infrastructure

   D. 802.11

3. What device centrally connects wireless network nodes in the same way that a hub connects wired Ethernet PCs?

   A. Bluetooth adapter

   B. Wireless NIC

   C. SSID

   D. WAP

4. What wireless security protocol supports user authentication through EAP?

   A. WEP

   B. WPA

   C. MAC filtering

   D. SSID

5. Which encryption method used on wireless networks is the most secure?

   A. WEP

   B. Wi-Fi

   C. WINS

   D. WPA2

6. What can limit wireless connectivity to a list of accepted users based on the hard-wired address of their wireless NIC?

   A. Encryption

   B. MAC Filtering

   C. NWLink

   D. WEP

7. Which wireless standard combines the longest range with the most throughput?

   A. 802.11a

   B. 802.11b

   C. 802.11g

   D. 802.11f

8. Personal area networks are created by what wireless technology?

   A. Bluetooth

   B. IrDA

   C. Wi-Fi

   D. Cellular wireless

9. What is the first step in setting up a new wireless network?

   A. Changing the default SSID

   B. Changing the default WAP

   C. Changing the default WEP

   D. Changing the default MAC address

10. Why is WEP not secure?

    A. It supports only 40-bit encryption.

    B. It encrypts only between the WAP and wireless device.

    C. It uses EAP.

    D. It uses AES.

11. Which statement about wireless ranges and speeds is true?

    A. As distance increases, speed decreases.

    B. As distance increases, speed increases.

    C. As distance increases, there is no effect on speed.

    D. As distance decreases, speed decreases.

12. 802.11a operates in what frequency range?

    A. 2.4 MHz

    B. 5 MHz

    C. 5 GHz

    D. 54 Mbps

13. What protocol supports data transfers up to 4 Mbps?

   A. IrDA

   B. 802.11a

   C. 802.11b

   D. 802.11g

14. What is the maximum throughput and speed of 802.11b?

   A. 11 Mbps, 300 feet

   B. 11 Mbps, 150 feet

   C. 54 Mbps, 300 feet

   D. 54 Mbps, 150 feet

15. Which of the following is *not* a cellular protocol?

   A. GSM

   B. CDMA

   C. GPRS

   D. NPR

■ Essay Quiz

1. Your company has decided to go wireless, but the department heads can't decide on a standard. Write an essay describing the differences between the three common 802.11 standards and any issues with security, and then make a recommendation.

2. A colleague new to networking has a fascination with the OSI model. Briefly explain the various layers of the OSI model and what happens at each layer.

Lab Projects

• Lab Project 16.1

Nearly every wireless hardware manufacturer wants to break the speed limits with wireless, and each has started debuting proprietary devices for running at better than 100 Mbps. Do a search through the bigger companies' product lists and compare the devices—Linksys, Netgear, Microsoft, and D-Link:

www.linksys.com
www.netgear.com
www.microsoft.com
www.dlink.com

• Lab Project 16.2

You have learned about various networking standards such as 802.3, 802.5, and 802.11a/b/g. Using the Internet, research emerging standards such as 802.16 or 802.20. Which standards did you research? What do they define? How far along are these standards in becoming realized and made part of the mainstream?

The Internet

chapter

17

"Let's see what's out there."

—Captain Jean-Luc Picard, *Star Trek: The Next Generation,* "Encounter at Farpoint"

In this chapter, you will learn how to

- **Explain how the Internet works**
- **Connect to the Internet**
- **Use Internet software tools**

Imagine coming home from a long day at work building and fixing PCs, sitting down in front of your shiny new computer, double-clicking the single icon that sits dead center on your monitor...and suddenly you're enveloped in an otherworldly scene, where 200-foot trees slope smoothly into snow-white beaches and rich blue ocean. Overhead, pterodactyls soar through the air while you talk to a small chap with pointy ears and a long robe about heading up the mountain in search of a giant monster...TV show from the SciFi channel? Spielberg's latest film offering? How about an interactive game played by millions of people all over the planet on a daily basis by connecting to the Internet? If you guessed the last one, you're right.

This chapter covers the skills you need as a PC tech to help people connect to the Internet. It starts with a brief section on how the Internet works along with the concepts of connectivity, and then it goes into the specifics on hardware, protocols, and software that you use to make the Internet work for you (or for your client). Let's get started!

■ How the Internet Works

The Internet enables users to communicate with one another over vast distances, often in the blink of an eye. As a PC tech, you need to know how PCs communicate with the larger world for two reasons. First, knowing the process and pieces involved in the communication enables you to troubleshoot effectively when that communication goes away. Second, you need to be able to communicate knowledgeably with a network technician when he or she comes in to solve a more complex issue.

Internet Tiers

You probably know that the Internet is millions and millions of computers all joined together to form the largest network on earth, but not many folks know much about how these computers are organized. In order to keep everything running smoothly, the Internet is broken down into groups called tiers . The main tier, called *Tier 1*, consists of nine companies called *Tier 1 providers.* The Tier 1 providers own long-distance, high-speed fiber-optic networks called *backbones.* These backbones span the major cities of the earth (not all Tier 1 backbones go to all cities) and interconnect at special locations called *network access points (NAPs).* Anyone wishing to connect to any of the Tier 1 providers must pay large sums of money. The Tier 1 providers do not charge each other.

Tier 2 providers own smaller, regional networks and must pay the Tier 1 providers. Most of the famous companies that provide Internet access to the general public are Tier 2 providers. *Tier 3 providers* are even more regional and connect to Tier 2 providers.

The piece of equipment that makes this tiered Internet concept work is called a backbone router. *Backbone routers* connect to more than one other backbone router, creating a big, interwoven framework for communication.

Figure 17.1 illustrates the decentralized and interwoven nature of the Internet. The key reason for interweaving the backbones of the Internet was to provide alternative pathways for data if one or more of the routers went down. If Jane in Houston sends a message to her friend Polly in New York City, for example, the shortest path between Jane and Polly in this hypothetical situation is this: Jane's message originates at Rice University in Houston, bounces to Emory University in Atlanta, flits through Virginia Commonwealth University in Richmond, and then zips into SUNY in

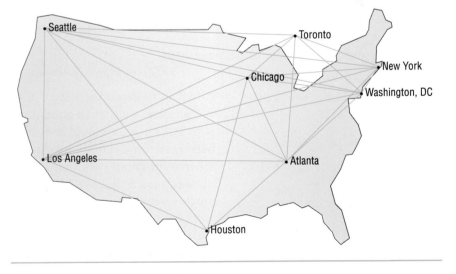

● **Figure 17.1**   Internet Tier 1 connections

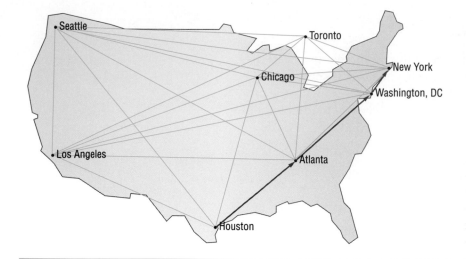

● **Figure 17.2**   Message traveling from Houston to NYC

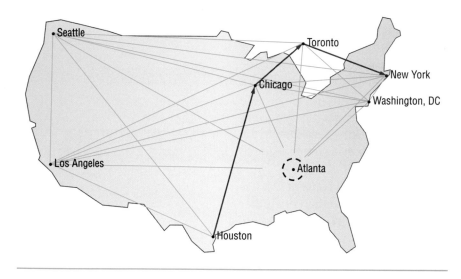

● **Figure 17.3**   Rerouted message from Houston to NYC

New York City (Figure 17.2). Polly happily reads the message and life is great. The Internet functions as planned.

But what happens if the entire southeastern United States experiences a huge power outage and Internet backbones in every state from Virginia to Florida goes down? Jane's message would bounce back to Rice and the Rice computers. Being smart cookies, the routers would reroute the message to nodes that still functioned—say, Rice to University of Chicago, then University of Toronto, and then SUNY (Figure 17.3). It's all in a day's work for the highly redundant and adaptable Internet. At this point in the game (early 2007), the Internet simply cannot go down fully—barring, of course, a catastrophe of Biblical proportions.

TCP/IP—The Common Language of the Internet

As you know from all the earlier chapters in this book, hardware alone doesn't cut it in the world of computing. You need software to make the machines run and create an interface for humans. The Internet is no exception. TCP/IP provides the basic software structure for communication on the Internet.

Because you spent a good deal of time in the Essentials course working with TCP/IP, you should have an appreciation for its adaptability and, perhaps more importantly, its extendibility. TCP/IP provides the addressing scheme for computers that communicate on the Internet through IP addresses, such as 192.168.4.1 or 16.45.123.7. As a protocol, though, TCP/IP is much more than just an addressing system. TCP/IP provides the framework and common language for the Internet. And it offers a phenomenally wide-open structure for creative purposes. Programmers can write applications built to take advantage of the TCP/IP structure and features, creating what are called TCP/IP services. The cool thing about TCP/IP services is that they're limited only by the imagination of the programmers.

You'll learn much more about TCP/IP services in the software and "Beyond A+" sections of this chapter, but I must mention one service that you've most likely worked with yourself, whether you knew them by that term or not. The most famous service is the **Hypertext Transport Protocol (HTTP)**, the service that provides the structure for the **World Wide Web** ("the Web" for short), the graphical face of the Internet. Using your **Web browser**—a program specifically designed to retrieve, interpret, and display Web pages—an almost endless variety of information and entertainment is just a click away. I can't tell you how many times I've started to look up something on the Web, and suddenly it's two hours later and I still haven't looked up what I started out wanting to know, but I don't actually care, because I've learned some amazing stuff! But then when I do go look it up, in just minutes I can find out information it used to take *days* to uncover. The Web can arguably claim the distinction of being both the biggest time-waster and the biggest time-saver since the invention of the book!

At this point, you have an enormous, beautifully functioning network. All the backbone routers connect together with fiber and thick copper cabling backbones, and TCP/IP enables communication and services for building applications for humans to interface across the distances. What's left? Oh, that's right: how do you tap into this great network and partake of its goodness?

Microsoft calls the connections ISPs make to the Internet *access points,* which I think is a very bad name. You'd think we'd be able to come up with new terms for things! Instead, some folks in this industry continue rebranding things with the same phrases or catchwords, only serving to confuse already bewildered consumers.

Internet Service Providers

Every Tier 1 and Tier 2 provider leases connections to the Internet to companies called **Internet service providers (ISPs)**. ISPs essentially sit along the edges of the Tier 1 and Tier 2 Internet and tap into the flow. You can, in turn, lease some of the connections from the ISP and thus get on the Internet.

ISPs come in all sizes. America Online (AOL) has a huge pipe into the Internet, enabling its millions of customers (in the U.S. alone) to connect from their local machines and surf the Web. Contrast AOL with Unisono net, an ISP in San Miguel de Allende, Mexico (Figure 17.4). Billed as the "Best ISP in San Miguel," it services only a small (but delightful) community and the busy tourist crowd. Functionally, though, Unisono net does the same thing AOL does, just without all the bells, whistles, and mountains of free CD-ROMs!

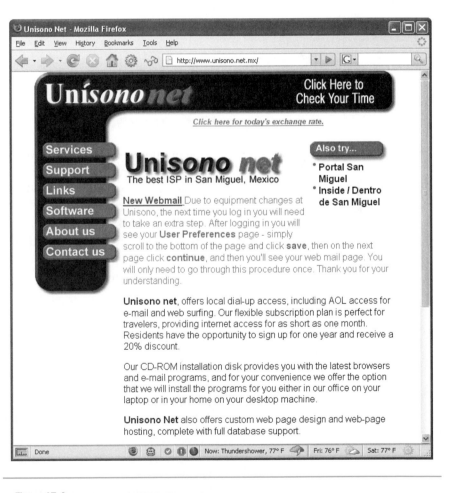

• **Figure 17.4** Unisono net homepage

Connection Concepts

Connecting to an ISP requires two things to work perfectly: hardware for connectivity, such as a modem and a working telephone line; and software, such as protocols to govern the connections and the data flow (all configured in Windows), and applications to take advantage of the various TCP/IP services. Once you have a contract with an ISP to grant you access to the Internet, the ISP gives you TCP/IP configuration numbers and data so you can set up your software to connect directly to a router at the ISP that becomes your gateway to the Internet. The router to which you connect at the ISP, by the way, is often referred to as the **default gateway**. Once you configure your software correctly, you can connect to the ISP and get to the greater Internet. Figure 17.5 shows a standard PC-to-ISP-to-Internet connection. Note that various protocols and other software manage the connectivity between your PC and the default gateway.

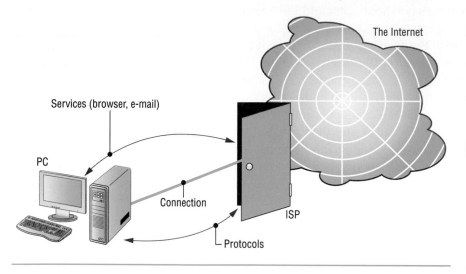

• **Figure 17.5**   Simplified Internet connectivity

■ Connecting to the Internet

PCs commonly connect to an ISP using one of seven technologies: dial-up, both analog and ISDN; dedicated, such as DSL, cable, and LAN; wireless; and satellite. Analog dial-up is the slowest of the bunch and requires a telephone line and a special networking device called a modem. ISDN uses digital dial-up and has much greater speed. All the others use a regular Ethernet NIC. Satellite is the odd man out here; it may use either a modem or a NIC, depending on the particular configuration you have, although most folks will use a modem. Let's take a look at all these various connection options.

Dial-up

A dial-up connection to the Internet requires two pieces to work: hardware to dial the ISP, such as a modem or ISDN terminal adapter; and software to govern the connection, such as Microsoft's **Dial-Up Networking (DUN)**. Let's look at the hardware first, and then we'll explore software configuration.

Modems

At some point in the early days of computing, some bright guy or gal noticed a colleague talking on a telephone, glanced down at a PC, and then put two and two together: why not use telephone lines for data communication? The basic problem with this idea is that traditional telephone lines use analog signals, while computers use digital signals (Figure 17.6). Creating a dial-up network required equipment that could turn digital data into an analog signal to send it over the telephone line, and then turn it back into digital data when it reached the other end of the connection. A device called a modem solved this dilemma.

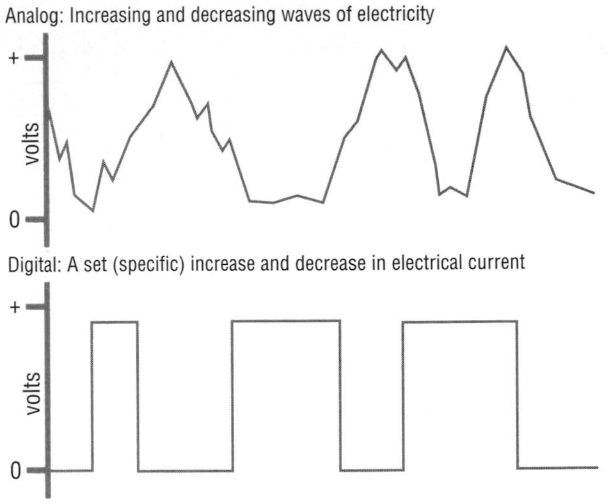

Modems enable computers to talk to each other via standard commercial telephone lines by converting analog signals to digital signals, and vice versa. The term *modem* is short for MOdulator/DEModulator, a description of transforming the signals. Telephone wires transfer data via analog signals that continuously change voltages on a wire. Computers hate analog signals. Instead, they need digital signals, voltages that are either on or off, meaning the wire has voltage present or it does not. Computers, being binary by nature, use only two states of voltage: zero volts and positive volts. Modems take analog signals from telephone lines and turn them into digital signals that the PC can understand (Figure 17.7). Modems also take digital signals from the PC and convert them into analog signals for the outgoing telephone line.

A modem does what's called *serial communication:* It transmits data as a series of individual ones and zeroes. The CPU can't process data this way. It needs parallel communication, transmitting and receiving data in discrete 8-bit chunks (Figure 17.8). The individual serial bits of data are converted into 8-bit parallel data that the PC can understand through the **universal asynchronous receiver/transmitter (UART)** chip (Figure 17.9).

There are many types of UARTs, each with different functions. All serial communication devices are really little more than UARTs. *External* modems

Analog: Increasing and decreasing waves of electricity

Digital: A set (specific) increase and decrease in electrical current

• **Figure 17.6**   Analog signals used by a telephone line versus digital signals used by the computer

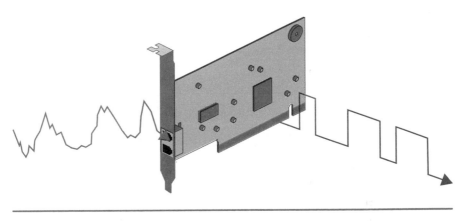

• **Figure 17.7**   Modem converting analog signal to digital signal

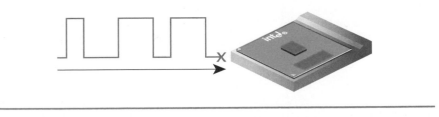

• **Figure 17.8**   CPUs can't read serial data.

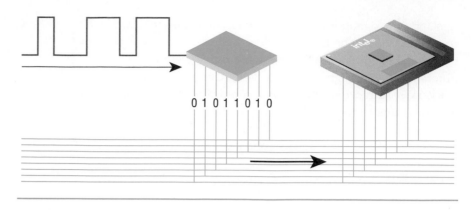

● **Figure 17.9** The UART chip converts serial data to parallel data that the CPU can read.

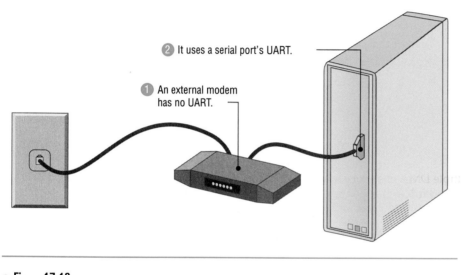

② It uses a serial port's UART.

① An external modem has no UART.

● **Figure 17.10** An external modem uses the PC's serial port.

can convert analog signals to digital ones and vice versa, but they must rely on the serial ports to which they're connected for the job of converting between serial and parallel data (Figure 17.10). Internal modems can handle both jobs because they have their own UART built in (Figure 17.11). Table 17.1 shows the UART chips that have been used in PCs.

Phone lines have a speed based on a unit called a **baud**, which is one cycle per second. The fastest rate that a phone line can achieve is 2400 baud. Modems can pack multiple bits of data into each baud; a 33.6 kilobits per second (Kbps) modem, for example, packs 14 bits into every baud: 2400 × 14 = 33.6 Kbps. Thus, it is technically incorrect to say, "I have a 56 K baud modem."

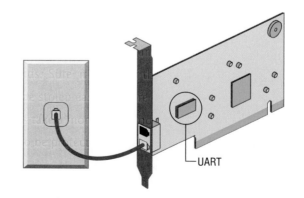

UART

● **Figure 17.11** An internal modem has UART built in.

Table 17.1	UARTs
Chip	**Description**
8250	This is the original chip selected by IBM for use in the PC. It had several bugs, but IBM worked around them with built-in routines written in the PC and XT ROM BIOS.
8250A	This chip was developed to fix the bugs in the 8250, but the fix meant it did not work properly with the PC and XT BIOS, although it does work with the AT BIOS. This chip does not work adequately at speeds at or above 9600 bits per second (bps).
8250B	This chip was developed to fix the bugs in the previous chips, but still came with the interrupt enable bug contained in the 8250 chip. This made it compatible with the PC/XT BIOS, and possibly also with the AT BIOS. It retains the problems with rates above 9600 bps.
16450	This chip was initially picked by IBM for its AT systems. It should be seen as the bare minimum for its OS/2 systems; otherwise, the serial ports will not function properly. This chip has a higher throughput than the previous chips and has an added scratch register to aid in speed. The only drawback is that it cannot be used with the PC/XT BIOS due to the interrupt bug being fixed.
16550	This chip was an improvement over the 16450, but it cannot be used for First In First Out (FIFO) buffering modes. It did enable programmers to use multiple DMA channels, however. This chip is not recommended for standard high-speed communication use and should be replaced by the 16550A, even though it has a higher throughput.
16550A	This chip has 16 built-in FIFO registers for receiving and transmitting. It will increase your throughput without loss of characters at higher rates of speed, due to the added registers. This is the only UART installed on today's systems.

The correct statement is, "I have a 56 Kbps modem." But don't bother; people have used the term "baud" instead of **bits per second (bps)** so often for so long that the terms have become functionally synonymous.

Modern Modem Standards: V.90 vs. V.92 The fastest data transfer speed a modem can handle is based on its implementation of one of the international standards for modem technology: the **V standards**. Set by the International Telecommunication Union (ITU), the current top standards are V.90 and V.92. Both standards offer download speeds of just a hair under 56 Kbps, but they differ in upload speeds: up to 33.6 Kbps for V.90, and up to 48 Kbps for V.92 modems. To get anywhere near the top speeds of a V.90 or V.92 modem requires a comparable modem installed on the other line and connecting telephone lines in excellent condition. In practice, you'll rarely get faster throughput than about 48 Kbps for downloads and 28 Kbps for uploads.

Flow Control (Handshaking)   Flow control, also known as handshaking, is the process by which two serial devices verify a conversation. Imagine people talking on a CB radio. When one finishes speaking, he will say "over." That way, the person listening can be sure that the sender is finished speaking before she starts. Each side of the conversation is verified. During a file transfer, two distinct conversations take place that require flow control: local (between modem and COM port) and end-to-end (between modems).

The modems themselves handle end-to-end flow control. PCs can do local flow control between the modem and COM port in two ways: hardware and software. Hardware flow control employs extra wires in the serial connection between the modem and the COM port to let one device tell the other that it is ready to send or receive data. These extra wires are called *ready to send (RTS)* and *clear to send (CTS)*, so hardware handshaking is often called RTS/CTS. Software flow control uses a special character called XON to signal that data flow is beginning, and another special character called XOFF to signal that data transmission is finished; therefore, software handshaking is often called XON/XOFF. Software handshaking is slower and not as dependable as hardware handshaking, so you rarely see it.

Bells and Whistles   Although the core modem technology has changed little in the past few years, modem manufacturers have continued to innovate on many peripheral fronts—pardon the pun and the bad grammar. You can walk into a computer store nowadays, for example, and buy a V.92 modem that comes bundled with an excellent fax machine and a digital answering machine. You can even buy modems that you can call remotely that will wake up your PC (Figure 17.12). What will they think up next?

Modem Connections: PCI, PCI Express, and USB   Modems connect to the PC in two basic ways: internally or externally. Almost all internal modems connect to a PCI or PCI Express expansion bus slot inside the PC, although cost-conscious manufacturers may use smaller modems that fit in special expansion slots designed to support multiple communications features such as modems, NICs, and sound cards (Figure 17.13). Older AMD motherboards used Audio/Modem Riser (AMR) or Advanced Communication Riser (ACR) slots, while Intel motherboards used Communication and Networking Riser (CNR) slots. Finally, and least expensive of all, many current

> You can test a modem by plugging in a physical device, called a *loopback plug,* and then running diagnostics.

> AMR, ACR, and CNR slots have gone away, although you'll still find them on older systems. Current systems use built-in components or PCIe ×1 slots for modems, sound, and NICs.

• **Figure 17.12**   Some of the many features touted by the manufacturer of the SupraMax modem

motherboards dispense with expansion cards entirely and come with the modem integrated into the motherboard.

External modems connect to the PC through an available serial port (the old way) or USB port (Figure 17.14). Many PCs come with two 9-pin serial ports, whereas most external modems designed to connect to a serial port come with a 25-pin connector. That means you will probably need a 9-to-25-pin converter, available at any computer store. Virtually all computers today have two or more USB ports in addition to serial ports.

If you have the option, choose a USB modem, especially one with a volume control knob. The very low speeds of data communication over a modem make the physical type of the connection unimportant. Even the slowest interface—the aging serial interface—can more than adequately handle 56 Kbps data transfers. USB offers simple plug and play and easy portability between machines, plus such modems require no external electrical source, getting all the power they need from the USB connection.

● **Figure 17.13** A CNR modem

Dial-up Networking

The software side of dial-up networks requires configuration within Windows to include information provided by your ISP. The ISP provides a dial-up telephone number or numbers, as well as your user name and initial password. In addition, the ISP will tell you about any special configuration options you need to specify in the software setup. The full configuration of dial-up networking is beyond the scope of this book, but you should at least know where to go to follow instructions from your ISP. Let's take a look at the Network and Internet Connections applet in Windows XP.

☑ **Cross Check**

Installing a PCI Modem

Installing a PCI modem card involves pretty much the same process as installing any other PCI card. Refer to Chapter 5, "Installing Internal Devices," and cross check your knowledge of the process.

1. What do you need to guard against when installing a PCI card?

2. Any issues involving drivers, plug and play, or other hardware topics?

● **Figure 17.14** A USB modem

Network Connections To start configuring a dial-up connection in Windows XP, open the Control Panel. Select Network and Internet Connections from the Pick a category menu (Figure 17.15), and then choose *Set up or change your Internet connection* from the Pick a task menu (Figure 17.16). The Internet Properties dialog box opens with the Connections tab displayed. All your work will proceed from here (Figure 17.17).

Click the Setup button to run the New Connection Wizard, and then work through the screens (Figure 17.18). At this point, you're going to need information provided by your ISP to configure your connection properly. When you finish the configuration, you'll see a new Connect To option on the Start menu if your system is set up that way. If not, open up Network Connections

● **Figure 17.15**   Opening the Network and Internet Connections applet

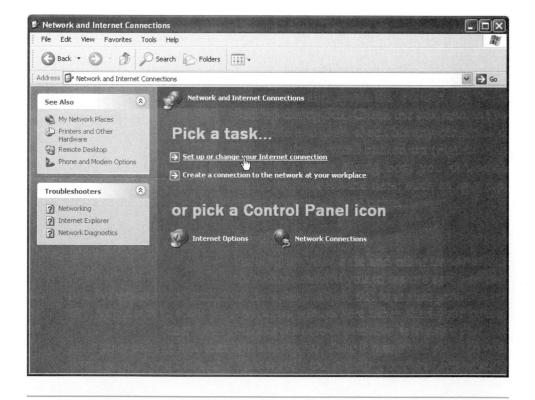

● **Figure 17.16**   Picking a task…set up or change?

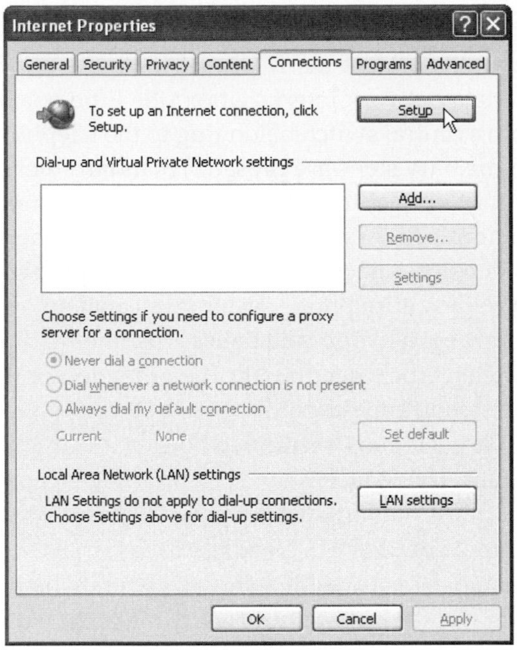

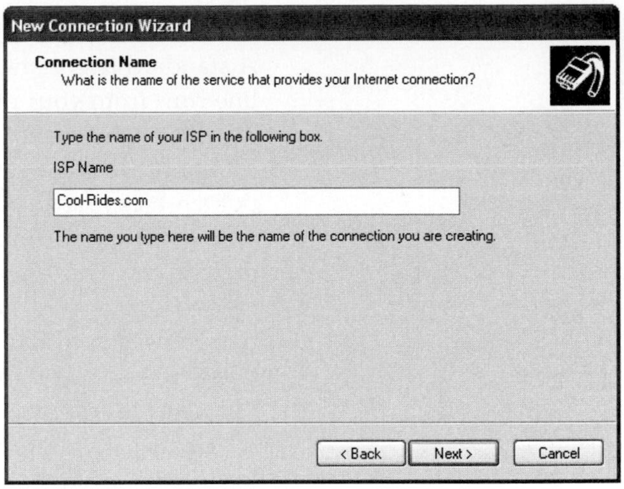

Figure 17.18 The New Connection Wizard

Figure 17.17 The Connections tab in the Internet Properties dialog box

and your new dial-up connection will be available. Figure 17.19 shows the option to connect to a fictitious ISP, Cool-Rides.com.

PPP Dial-up links to the Internet have their own special hardware protocol called **Point-to-Point Protocol (PPP)**. PPP is a streaming protocol developed especially for dial-up Internet access. To Windows, a modem is nothing more than a special type of network adapter. Modems will have their own configuration entry in the Network Connections applet.

Most dial-up "I can't connect to the Internet"–type problems are user errors. Your first area of investigation is the modem itself. Use the modem's properties to make sure the volume is turned up. Have the user listen to the connection. Does she hear a dial tone? If she doesn't, make sure the modem's line is plugged into a good phone jack. Does she hear the modem dial and then hear someone saying, "Hello? Hello?" If so, she probably dialed the wrong number! Wrong password error messages are fairly straightforward— remember that the password may be correct, but the user name may be wrong. If she still fails to connect, it's time to call the network folks to see what is not properly configured in the Dial-up Networking settings.

Figure 17.19 Connection options in Network Connections

ISDN

A standard telephone connection comprises many pieces. First, the phone line runs from your phone out to a network interface box (the little box on the side of your house), and into a central switch belonging to the telephone company. (In some cases, intermediary steps are present.) Standard metropolitan areas have a large number of central offices, each with a central switch. Houston, Texas, for example, has nearly 100 offices in the general metro area. These central switches connect to each other through high-capacity *trunk lines.* Before 1970, the entire phone system was analog; over time, however, phone companies began to upgrade their trunk lines to digital systems. Today, the entire telephone system, with the exception of the line from your phone to the central office, is digital.

During this upgrade period, customers continued to demand higher throughput from their phone lines. The old telephone line was not expected to produce more than 28.8 Kbps. (56 K modems, which were a *big* surprise to the phone companies, didn't appear until 1995.) Needless to say, the phone companies were very motivated to come up with a way to generate higher capacities. Their answer was actually fairly straightforward: make the entire phone system digital. By adding special equipment at the central office and the user's location, phone companies can now achieve a throughput of up to 64 K per line (see the paragraphs following) over the same copper wires already used by telephone lines. This process of sending telephone transmission across fully digital lines end-to-end is called **integrated services digital network (ISDN)** service.

ISDN service consists of two types of channels: Bearer, or B, channels and Delta, or D, channels. B channels carry data and voice information at 64 Kbps. D channels carry setup and configuration information and carry data at 16 Kbps. Most providers of ISDN allow the user to choose either one or two B channels. The more common setup is two B/one D, usually called a *basic rate interface (BRI)* setup. A BRI setup uses only one physical line, but each B channel sends 64 K, doubling the throughput total to 128 K. ISDN also connects much faster than modems, eliminating that long, annoying, mating call you get with phone modems. The monthly cost per B channel is slightly more than a regular phone line, and usually a fairly steep initial fee is levied for the installation and equipment. The big limitation is that you usually need to be within about 18,000 feet of a central office to use ISDN.

The physical connections for ISDN bear some similarity to analog modems. An ISDN wall socket usually looks something like a standard RJ-45 network jack. The most common interface for your computer is a device called a *terminal adapter (TA)*. TAs look much like regular modems, and like modems, they come in external and internal variants. You can even get TAs that are also hubs, enabling your system to support a direct LAN connection.

> Another type of ISDN, called a primary rate interface (PRI), is composed of twenty-three 64-Kbps B channels and one 64-Kbps D channel, giving it a total throughput of 1.5 megabits per second. PRI ISDN lines are rarely used as dial-up connections—they are far more common on dedicated lines.

> The two most common forms of DSL you'll find are *asynchronous (ADSL)* and *synchronous (SDSL)*. ADSL lines differ between slow upload speed (such as 128, 256, or 384 Kbps) and faster download speed (usually 2 Mbps). SDSL has the same upload and download speeds, but telecom companies charge a lot more for the privilege. DSL encompasses many such variations, so you'll often see it referred to as *x*DSL.

DSL

Digital subscriber line (DSL) connections to ISPs use a standard telephone line but special equipment on each end to create always-on Internet connections at blindingly fast speeds, especially when compared with analog dial-up connections. Service levels vary around the U.S., but the typical upload speed is approximately 384 Kbps, while download speed comes in at a very sweet 2+ Mbps!

DSL requires little setup from a user standpoint. A tech comes to the house to install a NIC in the Internet-bound PC and drop off a DSL receiver, often called a DSL modem (Figure 17.20). The receiver connects to the telephone line and the PC (Figure 17.21). The tech (or the user, if knowledgeable) then configures the TCP/IP protocol options for the NIC to match the settings demanded by the DSL provider, and that's about it! Within moments, you're surfing at blazing speeds. You don't need a second telephone line. You don't need to wear a special propeller hat or anything. The only kicker is that your house has to be within a fairly short distance from a main phone service switching center, something like 18,000 feet. This pretty much stops everybody but inner-city dwellers from having access to DSL service.

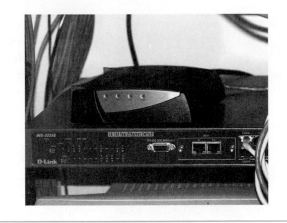

• **Figure 17.20** A DSL receiver

Cable

Cable offers a different approach to high-speed Internet access, using regular cable TV cables to serve up lightning-fast speeds. It offers comparable service to DSL with a 384 Kbps upload and 2+ Mbps download. Cable Internet connections are theoretically available anywhere you can get cable TV.

Cable Internet connections start with an RG-6 or RG-59 cable coming into your house. The cable connects to a cable modem that then connects to a NIC in your PC via UTP Ethernet cable. Figure 17.22 shows a typical cable setup. One nice advantage of cable over DSL is that if you have a TV tuner card in your PC, you can use the same cable connection (with a splitter) to watch TV on your PC. Both DSL and cable modem Internet connections can be used by two or more computers if they are part of a LAN, including those in a home.

> The term *modem* has been warped and changed beyond recognition in modern networking. Both DSL and cable fully digital Internet connections use the term *modem* to describe the box that takes the incoming signal from the Internet and translates it into something the PC can understand.

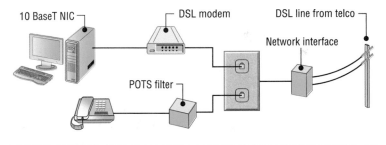

• **Figure 17.21** DSL connections

LAN

Most businesses connect their internal local area network (LAN) to an ISP via some hardware

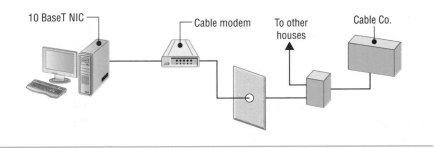

• **Figure 17.22** Cable connections

Figure 17.23 A wiring closet

One form of wireless communication does not require local wires. *Wireless Broadband* relies on the ISP putting up a tower, and then any building within the line of sight (perhaps up to 10 miles) can get a high-speed connection.

solution that Network+ techs deal with. Figure 17.23 shows a typical small-business wiring closet with routers that connect the LAN to the ISP. To complete a LAN connection to the Internet, you need to add a second NIC or a modem to one of the PCs and then configure that PC as the default connection. We'll revisit this idea in a moment with Internet Connection Sharing.

Wireless

Every once in a while a technology comes along that, once the kinks are smoothed out, works flawlessly, creating a magical computing experience. Unfortunately, the various wireless networking technologies out there today don't fulfill that dream yet. When they work, it's like magic. You walk into a coffee shop, sit down, and flip open your laptop computer. After firing up your Internet browser, suddenly you're quaffing lattes and surfing Web sites—with no wires at all.

Connecting to the Internet via wireless means that you must connect to a LAN that's wired to an ISP or connect to a cellular network. The local Internet café purchases high-speed Internet service from the cable or telecom company, for example, and then connects a wireless access point (WAP) to its network. When you walk in with your portable PC with wireless NIC and open a Web browser, the wireless NIC communicates with the *fully wired* DHCP server via the WAP and you're surfing on the Internet. It appears magically wireless, but the LAN to ISP connection still uses wires.

Cellular networking is even more seamless. Anywhere you can connect with your cell phone, you can connect with your cellular network–aware portable or laptop computer.

Satellite

Satellite connections to the Internet get the data beamed to a satellite dish on your house or office; a receiver handles the flow of data, eventually sending it through an Ethernet cable to the NIC in your PC. I can already sense people's eyebrows raising. "Yeah, that's the download connection. But what about the upload connection?" Very astute, me hearties! The early days of satellite required you to connect via a modem. You would upload at the slow 26- to 48-Kbps modem speed, but then get super fast downloads from the dish. It worked, so why complain? Newer technology still requires the initial setup be done via modem, but the download and the upload go through the dish. You really can move to that shack on the side of the Himalayas to write the great Tibetan novel, and still have DSL- or cable-speed Internet connectivity. Sweet!

Satellite might be the most intriguing of all the technologies used to connect to the Internet today. As with satellite television, though, you need to have the satellite dish point at the satellites (toward the south if you live in the U.S.). The only significant issue to satellite is that the distance the signal must travel creates a small delay called the *satellite latency*. This latency is usually unnoticeable unless the signal degrades in foul weather such as rain and snow.

Internet Connection Sharing

Windows 98 SE came out with a number of improvements over Windows 98, and one of the most popular was the inclusion of **Internet Connection Sharing (ICS)**. ICS enables one system to share its Internet connection with other systems on the network, providing a quick and easy method for multiple systems to use one Internet connection. Windows 2000 and Windows XP also provide this handy tool. Figure 17.24 shows a typical setup for ICS. Note the terminology used here. The PC that connects to the Internet and then shares via ICS that connection with machines on a LAN is called the *ICS host* computer. PCs that connect via LAN to the ICS host computer are simply called client computers.

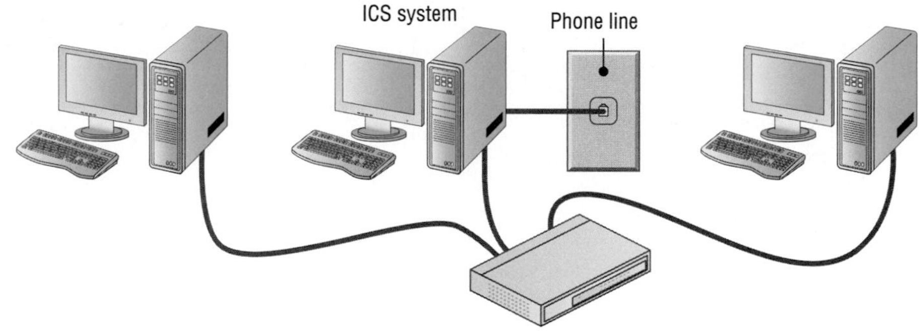

• **Figure 17.24** Typical ICS setup

To connect multiple computers to a single ICS host computer requires several things in place. First, the ICS host computer has to have a NIC dedicated to the internal connections. If you connect via dial-up, for example, the ICS host computer uses a modem to connect to the Internet. It will also have a NIC that plugs into a hub. Other PCs on the LAN likewise connect to the hub. If you connect via some faster service, such as DSL that uses a NIC cabled to the DSL receiver, you'll need a second NIC in the ICS host machine to connect to the LAN and the client computers.

Setting up ICS in Windows 2000/XP is very simple. Open the properties dialog for My Network Places, and then access the properties of the connection you wish to share. Click the Sharing tab (Windows 2000) or the Advanced tab (Windows XP) and select Enable internet connection sharing for this connection (Windows 2000) or Allow other network users to connect through this computer's internet connection (Windows XP, Figure 17.25). Clients don't need any special configuration but should simply be set to DHCP for their IP address and other configurations.

The Windows XP Internet Connection Firewall

Once you've established a connection to the Internet, you should start thinking about security. Windows 2000 requires you to use some third-party tool, such as a hardware firewall, but Windows XP offers the **Internet Connection Firewall (ICF)** built into the system. ICF basically stops all uninvited access from the Internet. ICF keeps track of when you initiate communication with a particular machine over your Internet connection and then allows communication back from that same machine. This works whether your connection is a single machine directly dialed into an ISP or a group of networked PCs connecting through an ICS host computer. ICF tracks the communication and blocks

Tech Tip

Hardware Solutions for Connection Sharing

Several manufacturers offer robust, easy-to-configure hardware solutions that enable multiple computers to connect to a single Internet connection. These boxes require very little configuration and provide a level of firewall protection between the primary computer and the Internet. You'll find these boxes more commonly used with DSL and cable connections rather than any sort of dial-up.

Linksys makes a great little DSL/cable router, for example, that offers four 10/100 Ethernet ports for the LAN computers; plus, you can configure it so that to the outside world the router is the PC. It therefore acts as a firewall, protecting your internal network from probing or malicious users from the outside.

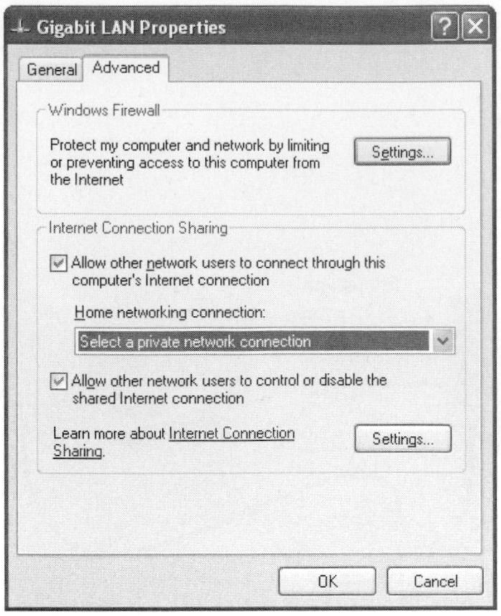

● **Figure 17.25**   Enabling Internet Connection Sharing in Windows XP

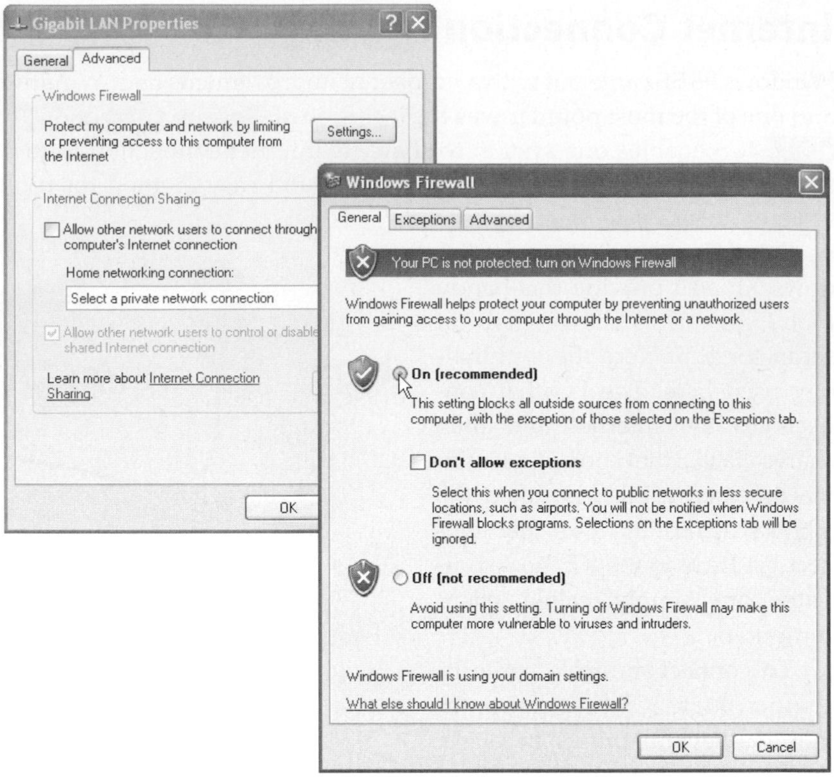

● **Figure 17.26**   Implementing Internet Connection Firewall

---

ICF enables you to open up specific computers inside a LAN for specific tasks, such as running an FTP server.

anything uninvited. You can implement ICF on the same screen as you would ICS (Figure 17.26).

When you're running a LAN, implement ICF only on the machine that directly connects to the Internet. If you enable ICF on other machines on the LAN, you can possibly create problems.

■ Internet Software Tools

Once you've established a connection between the PC and the ISP, you can do nothing on the Internet without applications designed to use one or more TCP/IP services, such as Web browsing and e-mail. TCP/IP has the following commonly used services:

- World Wide Web
- E-mail
- Newsgroups
- FTP
- Telnet
- VoIP

Each of these services (sometimes referred to by the overused term *TCP/IP* protocols) requires a special application, and each of those applications has special settings. You'll look at all five services and learn how to configure them.

The World Wide Web

The Web provides a graphical face for the Internet. Servers running specialized software called *Web servers* provide Web sites and Web pages that you can access and thus get more or less useful information. Using Web-browser software, such as Internet Explorer or Mozilla Firefox, you can click a link on a Web page and be instantly transported, not just to some Web server in your home town, but anywhere in the world. Figure 17.27 shows Internet Explorer at the home page of my company's Web site, www.totalsem.com. Where is the server located? Does it matter? It could be in a closet in my office or on a huge clustered server in Canada. The great part about the Web is that you can get from here to there and access the information you need with a click or two of the mouse.

Although the Web is the most popular part of the Internet, setting up a Web browser takes almost no effort. As long as the Internet connection is working, Web browsers work automatically. This is not to say you can't

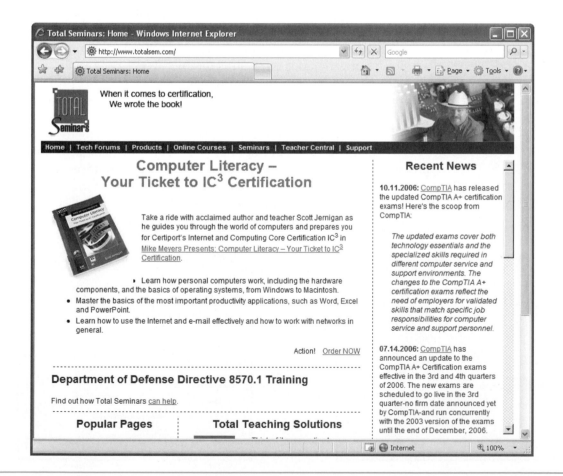

● **Figure 17.27**   Internet Explorer showing a Web page

make plenty of custom settings, but the default browser settings work almost every time. If you type in a Web address, such as the best search engine on the planet—www.google.com—and it doesn't work, check the line and your network settings and you'll figure out where the problem is.

Configuring the Browser

Web browsers are highly configurable. On most Web browsers, you can set the default font size, whether it will display graphics, and several other settings. Although all Web browsers support these settings, where you go to make these changes varies dramatically. If you are using the popular Internet Explorer that comes with Windows, configuration tools are found in the Internet Options Control Panel applet or under the Tools menu.

Proxy Server Many corporations use a **proxy server** to filter employee Internet access, and when you're on their corporate network you will have to set your proxy settings within the Web browser (and any other Internet software you want to use). A *proxy server* is software that enables multiple connections to the Internet to go through one protected PC, much like how ICS works on a home network. Unlike ICS, which operates transparently to the client PCs by manipulating IP packets (we say that it operates at Layer 3—the Network layer in the OSI model—see Chapter 16), proxy servers communicate directly with the browser application (operating at Layer 7, the Application layer). Applications that want to access Internet resources send requests to the proxy server instead of trying to access the Internet directly, both protecting the client PCs and enabling the network administrator to monitor and restrict Internet access. Each application must therefore be configured to use the proxy server. To configure proxy settings in Internet Explorer, choose Tools | Internet Options. Select the Connections tab. Then click the LAN Settings button to open the Local Area Network (LAN) Settings dialog box (Figure 17.28).

Note that you have three options here, with automatic detection of the proxy server being the default. You can specify an IP address for a proxy server by clicking the third checkbox and simply typing it in (Figure 17.29). Your network administrator or a CompTIA Network+ tech will give you information on proxy servers if you need it to configure a machine.

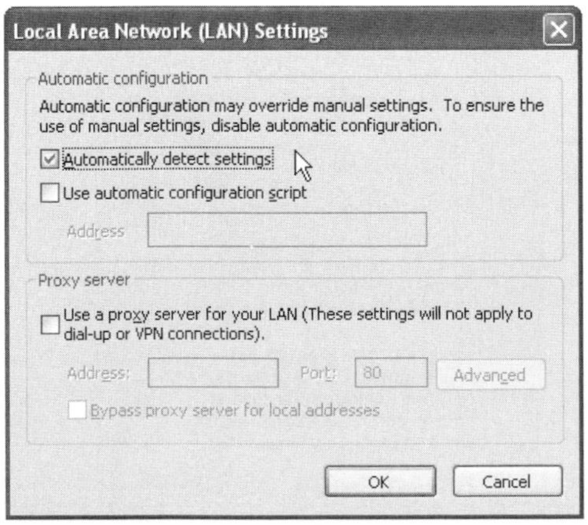

• **Figure 17.28**   The LAN Settings dialog box

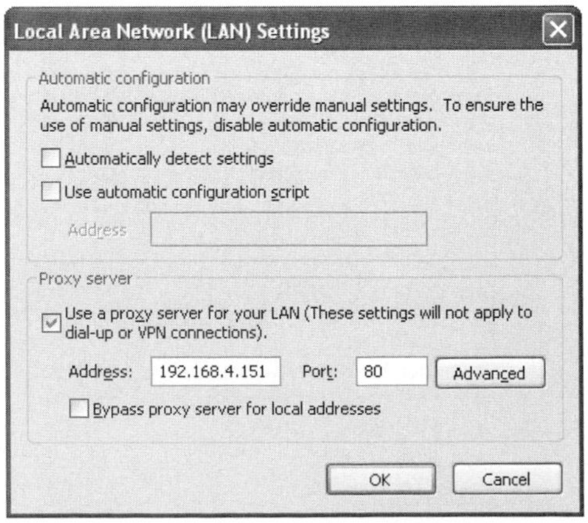

• **Figure 17.29**   Specifying the proxy server address

Mike Meyers' CompTIA A+ Guide: PC Technician (Exams 220-602, 220-603, & 220-604)

Otherwise, you can safely leave the browser configured to search automatically for a proxy server. If proxy servers are not used on your network, the autoconfiguration will fail and your browser will try to connect to the Internet directly, so there is no harm in just leaving Automatically detect settings checked.

Security and Scripts While we're on the subject of configuration, make sure you know how to adjust the security settings in your Web browser. Many Web sites come with programs that download to your system and run automatically. These programs are written in specialized languages and file formats with names like Java and Active Server Pages. These programs make modern Web sites very powerful and dynamic, but they can also act as a portal to evil programs. To help with security, all better Web browsers let you determine whether you want these potentially risky programs to run. What you decide depends on personal factors. If your Web browser refuses to run a Java program (you'll know because you'll get an warning message, like in Figure 17.30), check your security settings, because your browser may simply be following orders! To get to the security configuration screen in Internet Explorer, choose Tools | Internet Options and open the Security tab (Figure 17.31).

• **Figure 17.30**   Warning message about running ActiveX

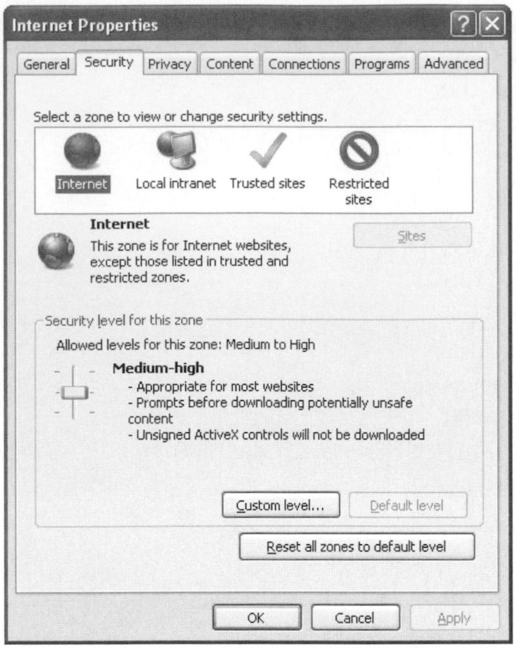

Internet Explorer gives you the option of selecting preset security levels by clicking the Custom level button on the Security tab and then using the pull-down menu (Figure 17.32). Changing from Medium to High security, for example, makes changes across the board, disabling everything from ActiveX to Java. You can also manually select which features to enable or disable in the scrolling menu, also visible in Figure 17.32.

Security doesn't stop with programs. Another big security concern relates to Internet commerce. People don't like to enter credit card information, home phone numbers, or other personal information for fear this information might be intercepted by hackers. Fortunately, there are methods of encrypting this information, the most common being **HTTP over Secure Sockets Layer (HTTPS)** Web sites. It's easy to tell if a Web site is using HTTPS because the Web address starts with *HTTPS*—instead of just *HTTP*, as shown in Figure 17.33. The Web browser also displays a lock symbol in the lower right-hand corner to remind you that you're using an encrypted connection.

There's one security risk that no computer can completely defend against: you. In particular, be very careful when downloading programs from the Internet. The Internet makes it easy to download programs that you can then install and run on your system. There's nothing intrinsically wrong with this unless the program you download has a virus, is corrupted, contains a Trojan horse, or is incompatible with your operating system. The watchword here is *common sense*. Only download programs from reliable sources. Take time to read the online documentation so you're sure you're downloading a version of the program that works on your operating system. Finally, always run a good antivirus program, preferably one that checks incoming programs for viruses before you install them! Failure to do this can lead to lockups, file corruption, and boot problems that you simply should not have to deal with.

● **Figure 17.31** The Security tab in the Internet Properties dialog box

See Chapter 18 for the scoop on Trojans and other viruses.

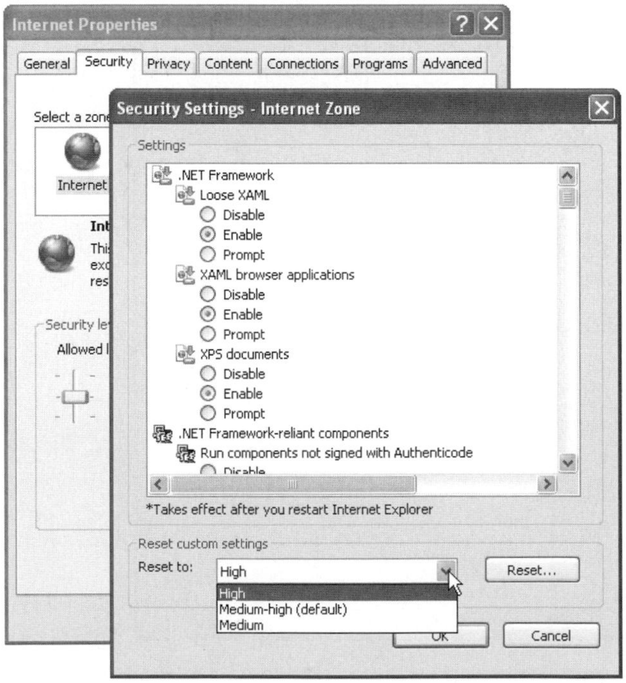

E-Mail

You can use an e-mail program to access e-mail. The two most popular are Microsoft's Outlook Express and Mozilla's Thunderbird. E-mail clients need a little more setup. First, you must provide your e-mail address and password. All e-mail addresses come in the now-famous accountnameInternet domain format. Figure 17.34 shows e-mail information entered into the Outlook Express Internet Connection Wizard.

The second thing you must add are the names of the **Post Office Protocol version 3 (POP3)** or **Internet Message Access Protocol (IMAP)** server and the **Simple Mail Transfer Protocol (SMTP)** server. The POP3 or IMAP server is the computer that handles incoming (to you) e-mail. POP3 is by far the most widely

● **Figure 17.32** Changing security settings

• Figure 17.33 A secure Web page (check out the little lock icon at the right end of the address bar)

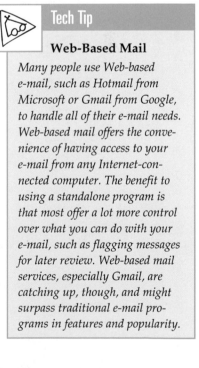

Tech Tip

Web-Based Mail

Many people use Web-based e-mail, such as Hotmail from Microsoft or Gmail from Google, to handle all of their e-mail needs. Web-based mail offers the convenience of having access to your e-mail from any Internet-connected computer. The benefit to using a standalone program is that most offer a lot more control over what you can do with your e-mail, such as flagging messages for later review. Web-based mail services, especially Gmail, are catching up, though, and might surpass traditional e-mail programs in features and popularity.

• Figure 17.34 Adding an e-mail account to Outlook Express

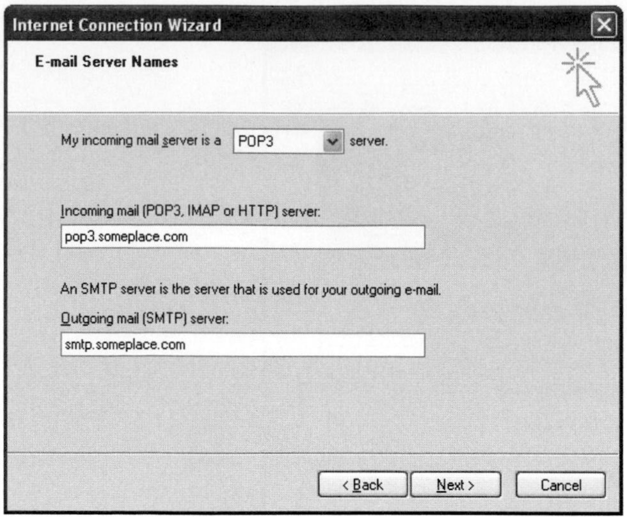

● **Figure 17.35** Adding POP3 and SMTP information in Outlook Express

used standard, although the latest version of IMAP, *IMAP4*, supports some features POP3 doesn't. For example, IMAP4 enables you to search through messages on the mail server to find specific keywords and select the messages you want to download onto your machine. Even with the advantages of IMAP4 over POP3, the vast majority of incoming mail servers use POP3.

The SMTP server handles your outgoing e-mail. These two systems may often have the same name, or close to the same name, as shown in Figure 17.35. All these settings should be provided to you by your ISP. If they are not, you should be comfortable knowing what to ask for. If one of these names is incorrect, you will either not get your e-mail or not be able to send e-mail. If an e-mail setup that has been working well for a while suddenly gives you errors, it is likely that either the POP3 or SMTP server is down, or that the DNS server has quit working.

When I'm given the name of a POP3 or SMTP server, I use ping to determine the IP address for the device, as shown in Figure 17.36. I make a point to write this down. If I ever have a problem getting mail, I'll go into my SMTP or POP3 settings and type in the IP address (Figure 17.37). If my mail starts to work, I know the DNS server is not working.

Newsgroups

Newsgroups are one of the oldest services available on the Internet. To access a newsgroup, you must use a newsreader program. A number of third-party newsreaders exist, such as the popular Forté Free Agent, but Microsoft Outlook Express is the most common of all newsreaders (not surprising since it comes free with most versions of Windows). To access a newsgroup, you must know the name of a news server. *News servers* run the

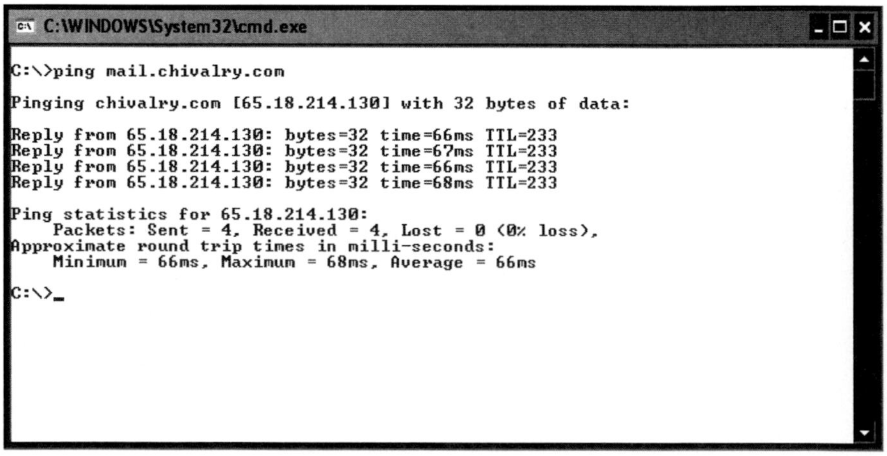

● **Figure 17.36** Using ping to determine the IP address

Figure 17.37 Entering IP addresses into POP3 and SMTP settings

Network News Transfer Protocol (NNTP). You can also use public news servers, but these are extremely slow. Your ISP will tell you the name of the news server and provide you with a user name and password if necessary (Figure 17.38).

File Transfer Protocol (FTP)

File Transfer Protocol (FTP) is also a great way to share files between systems. FTP server software exists for most operating systems, so FTP provides a great way to transfer data between any two systems regardless of the operating system. To access an FTP site, you must use an FTP client such as WS_FTP, although later versions of Internet Explorer and other Web browsers provide support for FTP. Just type in the name of the FTP site. Figure 17.39 shows Internet Explorer accessing ftp.microsoft.com.

Even though you can use a Web browser, all FTP sites require you to log on. Your Web browser will assume that you want to log in as "anonymous." If you want to log on as a specific user, you have to add your user name to the URL. (Instead of typing in **ftp://ftp.example.com**, you would type in **ftp://scottjftp.example.com**.) An anonymous logon works fine for most public FTP sites. Many techs prefer to use third-party programs such as WS_FTP (Figure 17.40) for FTP access because these third-party applications can store user name and password settings. This enables you to access the FTP site more easily later. Keep in mind that FTP was developed during a more trusting time, and that whatever user name and password you send over the network is sent in clear text. Don't use the same password for an FTP site that you use for your domain logon at the office!

Figure 17.38 Configuring Outlook Express for a news server

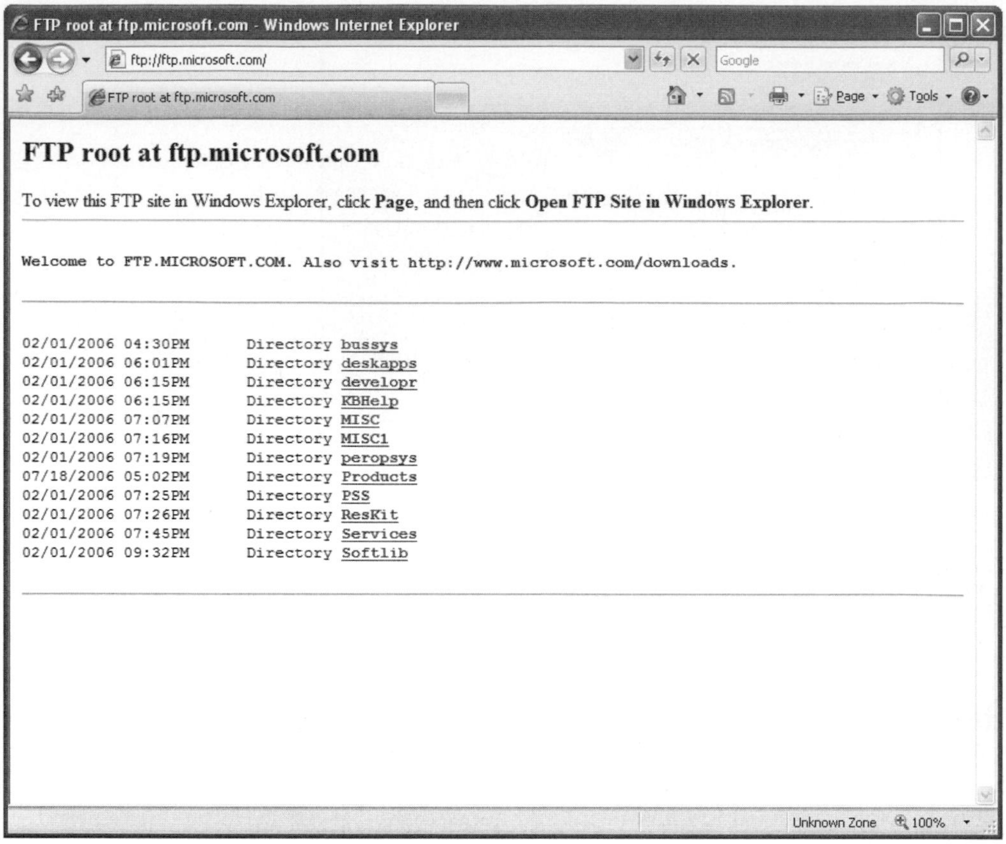

● **Figure 17.39**   Accessing an FTP site in Internet Explorer

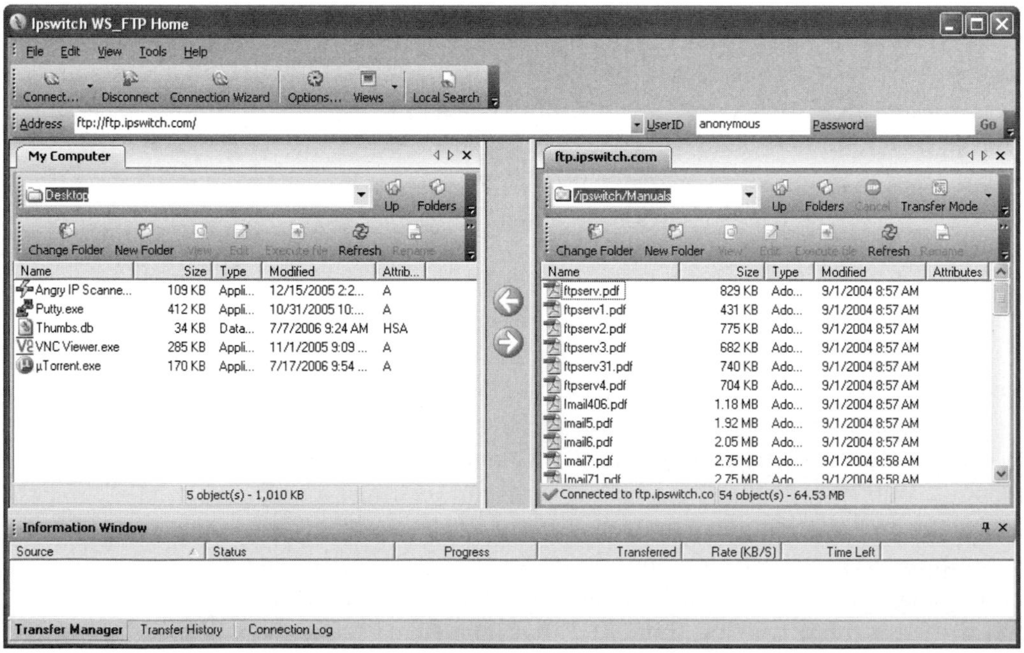

● **Figure 17.40**   The WS_FTP program

Telnet

Telnet is a terminal emulation program for TCP/IP networks that enables you to connect to a server and run commands on that server as if you were sitting in front of it. This way, you can remotely administer a server and communicate with other servers on your network. As you can imagine, this is rather risky. If *you* can remotely control a computer, what's to stop others from doing the same? Of course, Telnet does not allow just *anyone* to log on and wreak havoc with your network. You must enter a special user name and password to run Telnet. Unfortunately, Telnet shares FTP's bad habit of sending passwords and user names as clear text, so you should generally use it only within your own LAN. If you need a remote terminal that works securely across the Internet, investigate more sophisticated tools such as SSH (Secure Shell).

Voice over IP

Voice over IP (VoIP) enables you to make voice calls over your computer network. Why have two sets of wires, one for voice and one for data, going to every desk? Why not just use the extra capacity on the data network for your phone calls? That's exactly what VoIP does for you. VoIP works with every type of high-speed Internet connection, from DSL to cable to satellite.

VoIP doesn't refer to a single protocol, but rather to a collection of protocols that make phone calls over the data network possible. Venders such as Skype and Vonage offer popular VoIP solutions, and many corporations use VoIP for their internal phone networks.

Terminal Emulation

In Microsoft networking, we primarily share folders and printers. At times, it would be convenient to be transported in front of another computer—to feel as if your hands were actually on its keyboard. This is called **terminal emulation**. Terminal emulation is old stuff—Telnet is one of the oldest TCP/IP applications, but the introduction of graphical user interfaces cost it much of its popularity. Today when techs talk about terminal emulation, they are usually referring to graphical terminal emulation programs.

Like so many other types of Windows applications, graphical terminal emulation originally came from third-party companies and was eventually absorbed into the Windows operating system. While many third-party emulators are available, one of the most popular is the University of Cambridge's VNC. VNC is free and totally cross-platform, enabling you to run and control a Windows system remotely from your Macintosh system, for example. Figure 17.41 shows VNC in action.

Windows 2000 Server (not Professional) was the first version of Windows to include a built-in terminal emulator called Windows Terminal Services. Terminal Services has a number of limitations: the server software runs only on Windows Server and the client software runs only on Windows—although the client works on *every* version of Windows and is free. Figure 17.42 shows Windows Terminal Services running on a Windows 2000 computer.

The CompTIA A+ Certification exams test your knowledge of a few networking tools, such as Telnet, but only enough to let you support a Network+ tech or network administrator. If you need to run Telnet (or its more secure cousin, SSH), you will get the details from a network administrator. Implementation of Telnet falls well beyond CompTIA A+.

All terminal emulation programs require separate server and client programs.

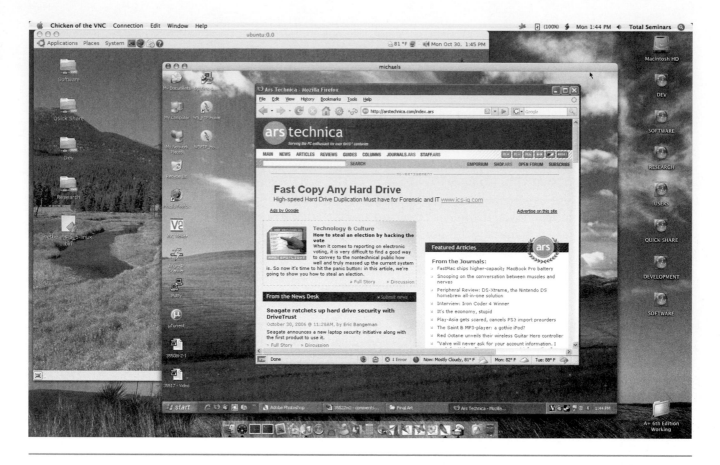

● Figure 17.41   The VNC terminal emulator

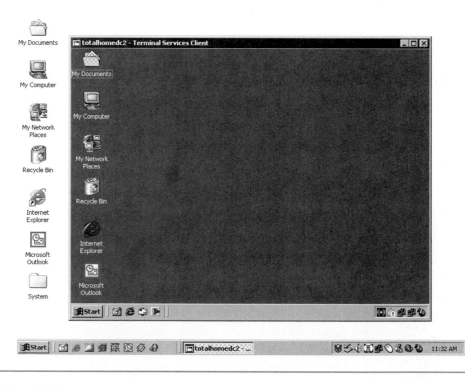

● Figure 17.42   Terminal Services

Windows XP offers an alternative to VNC: Remote Desktop. **Remote Desktop** provides control over a remote server with the fully graphical interface. Your desktop *becomes* the server desktop (Figure 17.43). It's quite incredible—although it's only for Windows XP.

Wouldn't it be cool if, when called about a technical support issue, you could simply see what the client sees? (I'm not talking voyeur cam here.) When the client says that something doesn't work, it would be great if you could transfer yourself from your desk to your client's desk to see precisely what is on the screen. This would dramatically cut down on the miscommunication that can make a tech's life so tedious. Windows XP's Remote Assistance does just that. Based on the Shared Desktop feature that used to come with the popular MSN Messenger program, **Remote Assistance** enables you to give anyone control of your desktop. If a user has a problem, he or she can request support directly from you. Upon receiving the support request e-mail, you can then log in to his or her system and, with permission, take the driver's seat. Figure 17.44 shows Remote Assistance in action.

Remote Assistance enables you to do anything you would do from the actual computer. You can troubleshoot some hardware configuration or driver problem. You can install drivers, roll back drivers, download new ones, and so forth. You're in command of the remote machine as long as the client allows you to be. The client sees everything you do, by the way, and can stop you cold if you get out of line or do something that makes him or her nervous! Remote Assistance can help you teach someone how to use a particular application. You can log on to a user's PC and fire up Outlook, for example, and then walk through the steps to configure it while the user watches. The user can then take over the machine and walk through the steps while you watch, chatting with one another the whole time. Sweet!

The new graphical terminal emulators provide everything you need to access one system from another. They are common, especially now that Microsoft provides free terminal emulators. Whatever type of emulator you use, remember that you will always need both a server and a client program. The server goes on the system to access and the client goes on the system you use to access the server. On many solutions, the server and the client software are integrated into a single product.

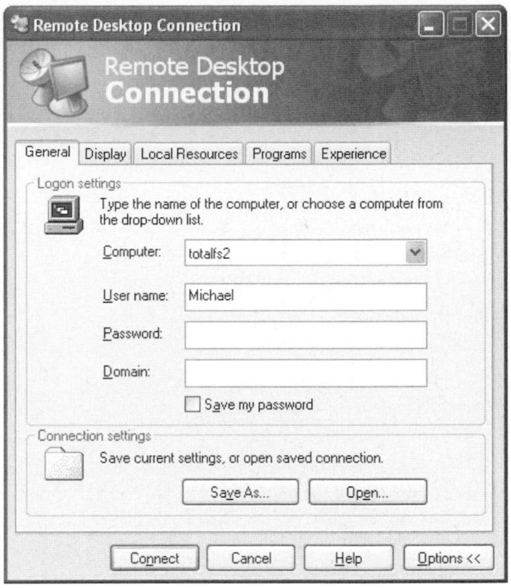

• **Figure 17.43** Windows XP Remote Desktop Connection dialog box

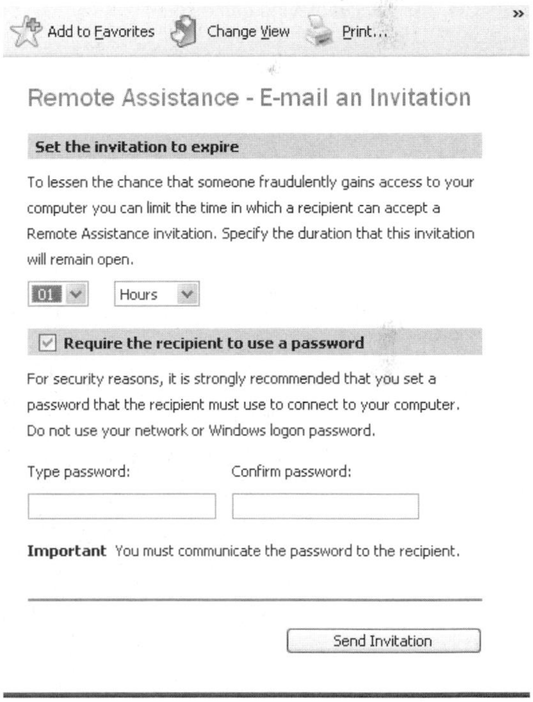

• **Figure 17.44** Remote Assistance in action

Beyond A+

While the areas covered by the CompTIA A+ Certification exams do a great job on the more common issues of dealing with the Internet, a few hot topics, although beyond the scope of the CompTIA A+ exams, are so common and important that you need to know them: online gaming, chatting, and file sharing.

• Ghost Recon	33 players
• Ghost Recon Demo	0 players
• Ghost Recon: Desert Siege	0 players
• Giants: Citizen Kabuto	12 players
• Global Operations	96 players
• Global Operations Public Beta	0 players
• Gore	36 players
• Gore Demo	0 players
• Gruntz	0 players
• Gulf War: Operation Desert Hammer	1 players
• Gunman Chronicles	4 players

H

• Half-Life	58219 players
• Halo (Xbox)	102 players
• Harley Davidson: Race Around the World	0 players

• **Figure 17.45** Folks playing games online

• **Figure 17.46** Counter Strike: Source

Online Gaming

One of the more exciting—and certainly more fun—aspects of the Internet is online gaming. Competing online against a real person or people makes for some amazing games—classics like Hearts and Backgammon. Entire Web sites are devoted to helping you find playing partners and thereby enjoy thousands of different games (Figure 17.45). Another popular genre of online gaming is the "first-person shooters" format. These games place you in a small world with up to 32 other players. A great example is Valve Software's Counter Strike: Source (Figure 17.46).

No discussion of online gaming is complete without talking about the most amazing game type of all—the massively multiplayer online role-playing game (MMORPG). Imagine being an elfin wizard, joined by a band of friends, all going on adventures together in worlds so large that it would take a real 24-hour day to journey across them! Imagine that in this same world, 2000 to 3000 other players, as well as thousands of game-controlled characters, are participating! Plenty of MMORPGs are out there, but the most popular today is World of Warcraft (Figure 17.47).

Each of these games employs good old TCP/IP to send information using special ports either reserved by the game itself or by DirectX. For instance, the Quake series of games uses port 26000, while DirectX uses ports 47624 and 2300–2400.

Chatting

If there's one thing we human beings love to do, it's chat. The Internet provides you with a multitude of ways to do so, whether it be by typing or actual talking. Keep in mind that chatting occurs in real time. As fast as you can type or talk, the other person or persons hear or see what you have to say. In order to chat, however, you need some form of chat software. The oldest family of chat programs is based on the Internet Relay Chat (IRC) protocol, and the single most common IRC chat program is probably mIRC. IRC protocols allow for a number of other little extras as well, such as the ability to share files.

Today, companies such as AOL, Yahoo!, and Microsoft have made their own chat programs that not only provide text chat but also add features such as voice and video, turning your PC into a virtual replacement for your telephone! Figure 17.48 shows the popular Microsoft Windows Live Messenger software.

File Sharing

The last extra Internet function to discuss is also probably the most controversial: file sharing. File sharing basically consists of a whole bunch of computers with one program loaded, such as Napster or Kazaa. The file-sharing program enables each of the computers running that program to offer files to share, such as MP3 music files and MPEG movies. Once all the file-sharing computers

• **Figure 17.47**   World of Warcraft

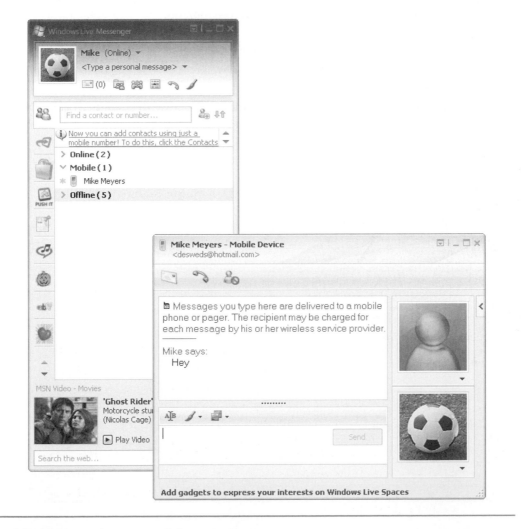

• **Figure 17.48**   Windows Live Messenger in action

Chapter 17: The Internet

Chapter 17: The Internet

log on to the Internet, any of them can download any file offered by any other in the group.

File sharing through such *distributed* sharing software becomes almost anonymous and free—and that's the problem. You can share *anything*, even copyright-protected music, movies, and more. The music industry in particular has come out swinging to try to stop file-sharing practices. As a result, the music industry is working on a way to shut down those persons who share lots of files. But software developers have countered, creating Internet protocols such as BitTorrent to handle the distribution and make the file sharers much more difficult to find and punish. Figure 17.49 shows one of the more popular BitTorrent protocol programs called μTorrent (the μ is the symbol for "micro," so you pronounce it "micro torrent"). BitTorrent has many legitimate uses as well—its protocol is extremely efficient for the distribution of large files and has become the method of choice for distributing Linux distributions and large open-source applications such as Apache and OpenOffice.

These example programs just scratch the surface of the many applications that use the Internet. One of the more amazing aspects of TCP/IP is that its basic design is around 30 years old. We use TCP/IP in ways completely outside the original concept of its designers, yet TCP/IP continues to show its power and flexibility. Pretty amazing!

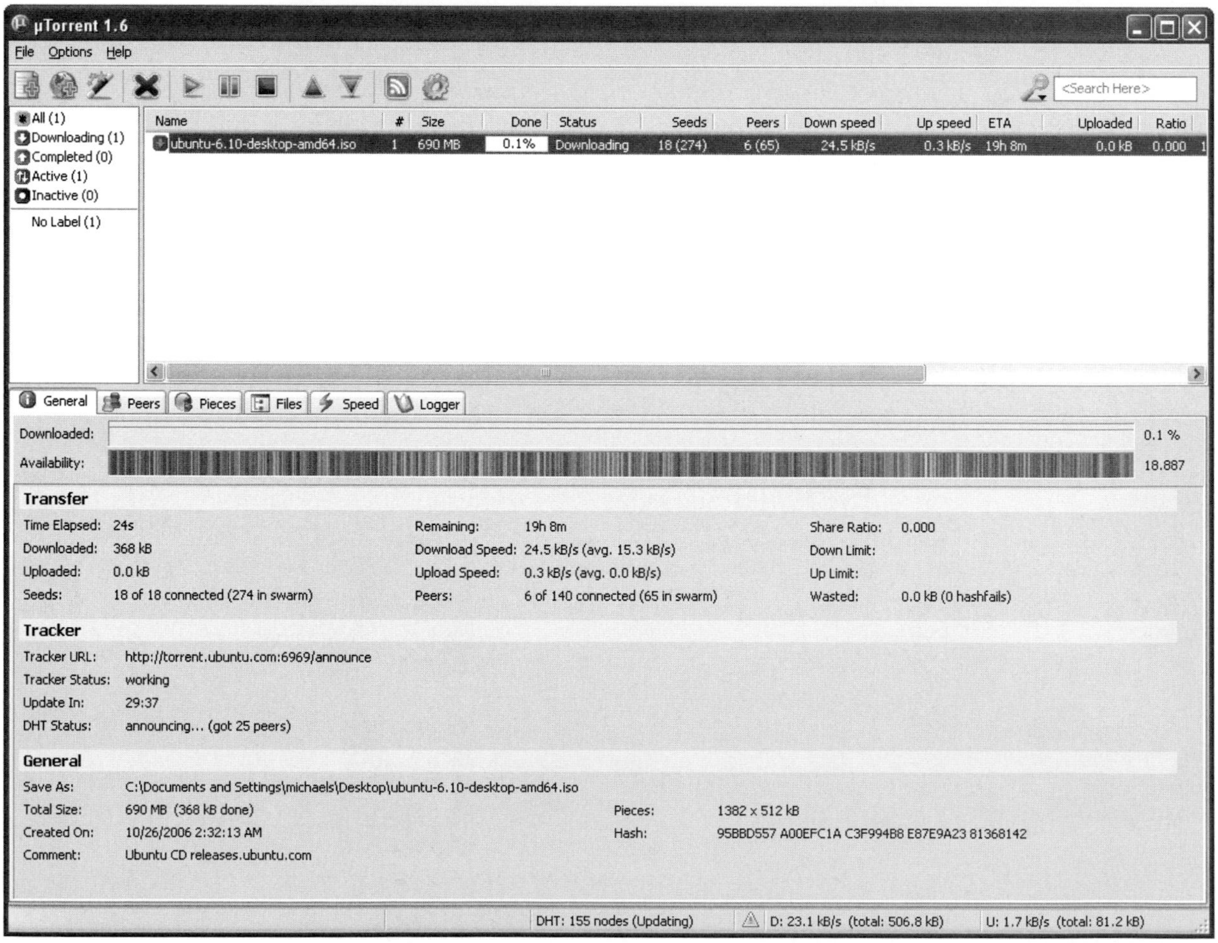

• **Figure 17.49** μTorrent

Chapter 17 Review

■ Chapter Summary

After reading this chapter and completing the exercises, you should understand the following about the Internet:

How the Internet Works

■ A PC tech needs to know how PCs communicate with the world for two reasons: (1) to troubleshoot when a process or piece stops working and (2) to communicate knowledgeably with a network technician when he or she comes in to solve a more complex issue.

■ The Internet is broken down into three tiers. Tier 1 providers own the fiber-optic backbones that interconnect at network access points. Backbone routers create an interwoven framework for redundant communications.

■ TCP/IP provides the basic software structure for Internet communications. It provides IP addresses and the naming scheme for computers on the Internet. This protocol suite also offers a variety of other services, including HTTP that provides structure for the Web.

■ Internet service providers (ISPs) lease connections to the Internet from Tier 1 and Tier 2 providers. In turn, ISPs lease connections to allow individuals and companies to access the Internet. ISPs may serve customers nationwide, such as America Online (AOL), or they may be limited to a small community of users.

■ Connecting to the Internet requires hardware for connectivity and software to govern the connection and data flow. The router that connects you to your ISP is your default gateway.

Connecting to the Internet

■ Seven technologies are commonly used to connect a PC to an ISP. These technologies fit into four categories: (1) dial-up (analog and ISDN), (2) dedicated (DSL, cable, and LAN), (3) wireless, and (4) satellite. An analog dial-up, the slowest connection, uses a telephone line and a modem. ISDN is a much faster digital dial-up method. With the exception of satellite that may use either a modem or a NIC, all the other technologies use an Ethernet NIC.

■ A dial-up connection needs hardware, such as a modem or ISDN terminal adapter, and software such as Microsoft's DUN.

■ A modem converts digital signals from the PC into analog signals that travel on telephone lines, and vice versa. An example of serial communication, the modem transmits data as a series of ones and zeroes. On the other hand, the computer processes data using parallel communication or data in discrete 8-bit chunks. A UART chip converts serial to parallel and parallel to serial. An external modem uses the UART chip in the computer's serial port, while an internal modem has its own built-in UART.

■ Phone lines measure speed in bauds, or cycles per second. However, the fastest baud rate a phone line can achieve is 2400 baud. Today's modems pack multiple bits of data into each baud. Although not technically correct, people use the term *baud* instead of *bps* so often that the terms have become synonymous.

■ The International Telecommunication Union (ITU) sets V standards to define the fastest data transfer speed a modem can handle. Currently V.90 and V.92 are the highest standards, downloading data just a little under 56 Kbps. Upload speeds differ, with 33.6 Kbps being the fastest for V.90 and 48 Kbps proving the fastest for V.92 modems.

■ Modems may be internal or external. The less-expensive internal modems usually connect to a PCI or PCI Express expansion bus slot. Some motherboards include special expansion slots used for multiple communications features such as modems, NICs, and sound cards. AMD calls such slots ACRs; Intel named them CNR slots. Many motherboards come with integrated modems. External modems attach to the PC's serial port or USB port. Most motherboards today include two or more USB ports. It is a good idea to choose a USB modem so that you won't need an external electrical source, and it will likely include a volume control knob.

- Windows includes configuration options to set up dial-up networks. Windows XP uses the Network and Internet Connections applet, while Windows 2000 calls this feature Network and Dial-up Connections. To configure dial-up networking, you'll need information from your ISP. Dial-up links to the Internet use PPP streaming hardware protocol.

- If you can't connect to the Internet, look at the modem's properties to make sure the volume is turned up. Listen, too, for a befuddled voice on the other end that would indicate your modem is dialing the wrong number. Other things to check: Be sure the line is plugged into a good phone jack, and make sure the number and password are correct. If you still can't connect to the Internet, call the network technicians to check that the dial-up networking settings are correct.

- An ISDN consists of two types of channels: Bearer, or B, channels that carry data and voice at 64 Kbps, and Delta, or D, channels that transmit setup and configuration information at 16 Kbps. Users can use one or two B channels, but the most common setup is the BRI consisting of two B channels and one D to provide a throughput total of 128 Kbps. Except for the steep cost of installation and equipment, ISDN lines are only slightly more expensive than regular phone lines, but this service is limited to an area within about 18,000 feet of a central office. ISDN uses a terminal adapter that looks like a regular modem and may be either external or internal.

- DSL modems connect to an ISP using a standard telephone line and special connections on each end. Although service levels vary, typical upload speed is ~384 Kbps with a download speed of ~2+ Mbps. A tech usually comes to the house to install a DSL receiver (often called a DSL modem) as well as a NIC in the PC. DSL is usually limited to about 18,000 feet from a main phone service switching center.

- Cable TV companies offer high-speed Internet access, with an upload speed of about 384+ Kbps and download transmission rates of 2+ Mbps. With a TV tuner card, cable enables you to watch TV on your PC.

- Many businesses connect their local area network (LAN) to an ISP. This configuration requires either a second NIC or a modem.

- Wireless Internet service requires connecting to a LAN that's wired to an ISP. The other wireless option is a satellite connection. Although early satellite technology required uploads through a slow modem (26–48 Kbps) and fast downloads through the dish, newer technology uses the modem only for the initial setup, sending both downloads and uploads through the dish.

- ICS enables multiple systems to use one Internet connection. Included in Windows 2000/XP, ICS uses an ICS host computer connected to the Internet that then shares the connection via a LAN with client computers. The ICS host computer must have a NIC or modem to connect to the Internet and a NIC that plugs into a hub. The other PCs then connect to the hub.

- If you have a connection to the Internet, you should also have some kind of security. Windows 2000 requires you to use a third-party tool such as a hardware firewall. Windows XP, however, has a built-in firewall to stop uninvited access from the Internet. ICF lets you communicate only with machines that are responding to your initial communication.

Internet Software Tools

- Applications provide TCP/IP services, including Web, e-mail, newsgroups, FTP, Telnet, and VoIP. Using Web browser software, such as Internet Explorer or Mozilla Firefox, you can access Web sites and pages from Web servers throughout the world. If you are unsuccessful in connecting to a site, use the command-line tool ping to determine whether the server is up. Simply type **ping** followed by either the DNS name or the IP address. If the device you are trying to ping is not available, you'll see a "Request timed out" message. You can use the loopback address (127.0.0.1) to ping yourself.

- A proxy server is software that enables multiple connections to the Internet to go through one protected PC. Configure proxy settings through the Local Area Network Settings dialog box. Although automatic detection of the proxy server is the default setting, you can also specify an IP address for a proxy server.

- You should also know how to adjust security settings in your Web browser. In IE, choose Tools | Internet Options and open the Security tab. You can set different security levels or manually select the features you want to enable or disable.

- Security also includes encrypting information such as credit card numbers, home phone numbers, or other personal information. The most common method of encrypting this information is HTTPS. You'll identify Web sites using HTTPS by the *HTTPS:* that appears at the beginning of the Web address and the little lock icon.

- You need an e-mail program such as Mozilla Thunderbird to receive e-mail. To set up an e-mail client, provide your e-mail address and password. E-mail addresses use the accountname@Internet domain format. You must also add the names of the POP3 or IMAP server for incoming mail and the SMTP server for outgoing mail.

- You need a newsreader such as Outlook Express to access a newsgroup. News servers run Network News Transfer Protocol (NNTP). Check with your ISP to get the name of the news server, along with a user name and password if necessary.

- FTP enables you to send and receive files. You may use an FTP client such as WS_FTP, although later versions of IE and other Web browsers provide support for FTP. You'll have to log on to an FTP site, although most public FTP sites allow anonymous logon.

- Telnet is a terminal emulation program for TCP/IP networks. It lets you connect to a server and run commands as if you were sitting in front of the server. Telnet requires a special user name and password. The user name and password will be sent over the network in clear text.

- Voice over IP (VoIP) enables you to make voice calls over your computer network and refers to a collection of protocols. Vendors such as Skype and Vonage offer VoIP solutions.

- Today, terminal emulation usually means graphical terminal emulation programs from third-party companies or in the Windows operating system. Terminal emulation programs require separate server and client programs. Windows 2000 Server was the first Windows version to include a built-in terminal emulator called Windows Terminal Services. The client works on every version of Windows and is free. Windows XP uses Remote desktop to provide full functions of Terminal Services. In essence, your desktop seamlessly becomes the server desktop.

- Remote Assistance, available with Windows XP, enables you to give anyone control of your desktop. Useful for giving a tech control of a computer to troubleshoot a hardware configuration or driver problem, Remote Assistance can also be used to install drivers or teach someone how to use a particular application.

■ Key Terms

baud *(388)*

bits per second (bps) *(389)*

default gateway *(386)*

Dial-Up Networking (DUN) *(386)*

digital subscriber line (DSL) *(394)*

File Transfer Protocol (FTP) *(405)*

handshaking *(390)*

HTTP over Secure Sockets Layer (HTTPS) *(402)*

Hypertext Transport Protocol (HTTP) *(385)*

integrated services digital network (ISDN) *(394)*

Internet Connection Firewall (ICF) *(397)*

Internet Connection Sharing (ICS) *(397)*

Internet Message Access Protocol (IMAP) *(402)*

Internet service provider (ISP) *(385)*

modem *(387)*

Network News Transfer Protocol (NNTP) *(405)*

Point-to-Point Protocol (PPP) *(393)*

Post Office Protocol version 3 (POP3) *(402)*

proxy server *(400)*

Remote Assistance *(409)*

Remote Desktop *(409)*

Simple Mail Transfer Protocol (SMTP) *(402)*

Telnet *(407)*

terminal emulation *(407)*

tiers *(383)*

universal asynchronous receiver/ transmitter (UART) *(387)*

V standards *(389)*

Voice over IP (VoIP) *(407)*

Web browser *(385)*

World Wide Web *(385)*

Key Term Quiz

Use the Key Terms list to complete the sentences that follow. Not all terms will be used.

1. Today's computers use the 16550A _____ chip.

2. Internet Explorer is a(n) _____.

3. _____ is the most common method used to encrypt information, such as credit card numbers, on the Internet.

4. A(n) _____ is software that allows multiple connections to access the Internet through one protected PC.

5. Although some people use the term to refer to modem speed, _____ actually means the number of cycles per second, while _____ is a more accurate measurement of actual data throughput.

6. By using an anonymous logon, _____ allows you to send and receive files from a public site.

7. Set by the International Telecommunication Union (ITU), _____ define(s) the fastest transfer speed a modem can handle.

8. _____ is the service that provides the structure for the World Wide Web, allowing documents to be sent across the Web.

9. Dial-up links to the Internet use a streaming hardware protocol called _____.

10. Windows XP has the built-in _____ that stops all uninvited access to your computer from the Internet.

Multiple-Choice Quiz

1. Which statements about Integrated Services Digital Network (ISDN) are true? Choose three.
   A. An ISDN connection uses either an internal or an external terminal adapter (TA).
   B. BRI has two B channels and one D channel for a throughput total of 128 Kbps.
   C. PRI has 23 B channels and 1 D channel for a total throughput of 1.5 Mbps.
   D. ISDN consists of end-to-end high-speed analog lines.

2. Which term refers to the router that your PC uses to connect to your Internet service provider?
   A. Loopback address
   B. Backbone
   C. IP address
   D. Default gateway

3. Which applet should you use to configure dial-up networks with Windows XP?
   A. Network and Internet Connections
   B. Network Neighborhood
   C. Internet Connection Sharing
   D. Remote Assistance

4. Which statements about a UART are true? Choose three.
   A. An external modem uses the UART chip in the computer's serial port.
   B. An internal modem uses the UART chip in the computer's serial port.
   C. An internal modem has a built-in UART chip.
   D. A UART chip converts serial data to parallel data and vice versa.

5. Which command-line utility can you use to see if the Web server you are trying to reach is available?
   A. Ping
   B. ICS
   C. Telnet
   D. NNTP

6. Which of the following Internet connection methods enables you to watch television on your computer if you have a TV tuner card?
   A. DSL
   B. Satellite
   C. Cable
   D. ISDN

7. If your modem cannot connect to the Internet, which of the following can you eliminate as a cause of the problem?

   A. The phone line is dead.

   B. All lines on the Internet are busy.

   C. You dialed the wrong number.

   D. The modem is bad.

8. Which term describes hardware or software that protects your computer or network from probing or malicious users?

   A. Router

   B. Firewall

   C. Protocol

   D. Spyware

9. Liz can receive her e-mail, but she cannot send e-mail. Which of the following is most likely causing her problem?

   A. POP3

   B. SMTP

   C. IMAP

   D. UART

10. What are the extremely fast networking connections through which Internet transmissions take place?

    A. Gateways

    B. Tier 1 providers

    C. Backbones

    D. ISPs

11. Which technology enables you to make voice calls over your computer network?

    A. Internet Voice Protocol

    B. Voice over IP

    C. Digital Telephony Subscriber Service

    D. Universal Asynchronous Receiver Transmitter

12. A user on Windows XP has asked you to teach them how to use a feature of Microsoft Word. What tool should you use?

    A. Remote Assistance

    B. Remote Desktop

    C. Telnet

    D. Secure Shell (SSH)

13. John walked up to a computer that couldn't connect to the Internet and immediately opened a command-line window and typed **ping 127.0.0.1**. Why?

    A. He wanted to test the connection to the default gateway.

    B. He wanted to test the connection to the nearest Tier 2 router.

    C. He wanted to test the NIC on the local machine.

    D. He wanted to test the NIC on the default gateway.

14. Which of the following offers a fast connection for an external modem?

    A. CNR

    B. PCI

    C. Serial port

    D. USB

15. A new client lives in a rural area, outside the connectivity radius of the local cable company and definitely more than 20,000 feet away from the nearest switching center for the phone company. Which Internet option offers him the best performance?

    A. Cable

    B. Dial-up

    C. DSL

    D. Satellite

■ Essay Quiz

1. With the rash of worms and viruses that attack computers connected to the Internet, how can you protect your computer?

2. Andrew's wife, Talena, collects Hull pottery. Andrew found a shop on the Internet that has a piece she's been wanting. He'd love to get it for her birthday next week, but the only way it can arrive by then is if he pays for it with his credit card. He's a bit apprehensive about giving his credit card number over the Internet. He wants you to tell him whether you think the site is safe or not. How can you evaluate the site to determine whether it uses encryption for credit card numbers?

3. Sean is planning to take some distance education courses next term. He currently uses a regular phone line and a modem to connect to the Internet. He's consulted you to figure out what his options are for a faster connection. Review his options, giving him the advantages and disadvantages, along with any restrictions that may prevent his receiving the service.

4. With a child in high school and another at a local college, it's always a struggle in Tom's house about who gets to use the computer to do Internet research. It's not feasible for Tom to install another line, but he does have a second computer. What solution can you offer to solve his problem?

5. By now, you've become a regular columnist for your company's monthly newsletter. Everybody in the company uses e-mail and browses the Web, but you're convinced that the company would benefit if employees knew how to use some of the other Internet services. You've decided that this month's article will highlight three other Internet services. Which three will you discuss and what will you include about each?

Lab Projects

• Lab Project 17.1

Remote Desktop is a great feature of Windows XP Professional. However, making it work when the computer you want to connect to is behind a router or firewall can be difficult. There are many choices to consider and configure, such as the computer's public IP address and port forwarding or network address translation on the router. Using the Internet, find a tutorial or a step-by-step "how-to" article that guides you through configuring a remote computer and router to make a Remote Desktop connection possible.

• Lab Project 17.2

Remote Desktop provides the same functionality as some third-party software and services, such as the open source VNC software, Symantec's commercial pcAnywhere software, and the online service GoToMyPC.com. Each has its own benefits, such as no cost, ease of configuration, or cross-platform use. Research two other solutions that offer similar remote control functionality as Remote Desktop and compare and contrast the three. What are the similarities? What are the unique benefits of each? Which one would you be more likely to use yourself? Why?

• Lab Project 17.3

Have you heard of WebDAV? Web Distributed Authoring and Versioning is a set of extensions added to Hypertext Transfer Protocol to support collaborative authoring on the Web. While HTTP is a reading protocol, WebDAV is a writing protocol created by a working group of the Internet Engineering Task Force (IETF). WebDAV offers a faster, more secure method of file transfer than FTP, and some predict that it may make FTP obsolete. It's already incorporated into most current operating systems and applications. Some authors say that WebDAV will change the way we use the Web. Use the Internet to learn more about WebDAV and its features. Apple calls it "a whole new reason to love the Net." After learning about WebDAV, see if you agree.

• Lab Project 17.4

Are all high-speed Internet connections created equal? Test them to find out! Speakeasy.net hosts one of the best Internet sites for testing the speed of an Internet connection:

http://www.speakeasy.net/speedtest/

Test three to five Internet connections that you can easily access, such as your home, a friend's house, your school, a library, and an Internet café. How do the connections compare? If you can, find out which technology the connections use. Which one seems to offer the best connection in your area?

chapter 18

Computer Security

"First, secure the data."

—Tech version of the Oath attributed to Galen and often associated with physicians: "primum non nocere" ("First, do no harm")

In this chapter, you will learn how to

- **Explain the threats to your computers and data**
- **Describe how to control the local computing environment**
- **Explain how to protect computers from network threats**

Your PC is under siege. Through your PC, a malicious person can gain valuable information about you and your habits. He can steal your files. He can run programs that log your keystrokes and thus gain account names and passwords, credit card information, and more. He can run software that takes over much of your computer processing time and use it to send spam or steal from others. The threat is real and right now. Worse, he's doing one or more of these things to your clients as I write these words. You need to secure your computer and your users from these attacks.

But what does computer security mean? Is it an antivirus program? Is it big, complex passwords? Sure, it's both of these things, but what about the fact that your laptop can be stolen easily? Before you run out in a panic to buy security applications, let's take a moment to understand the threat to your computers, see what needs to be protected, and how to do so.

■ Analyzing the Threat

Threats to your data and PC come from two directions: accidents and malicious people. All sorts of things can go wrong with your computer, from a user getting access to a folder he or she shouldn't see to a virus striking and deleting folders. Files can get deleted, renamed, or simply lost. Hard drives can die, and optical discs get scratched and rendered unreadable. Accidents happen, and even well-meaning people can make mistakes.

Unfortunately, there are a lot of people out there who intend to do you harm. Add that intent together with a talent for computers, and you've got a deadly combination. Let's look at the following issues:

- Unauthorized access
- Data destruction, accidental or deliberate
- Administrative access
- Catastrophic hardware failures
- Viruses/spyware

If you look at the CompTIA A+ exam objectives for the Essentials, IT Technician, and specialization exams, you'll notice that the objectives covered in this chapter are, for all intents and purposes, virtually the same for each exam. CompTIA has not differentiated the questions for each exam covered by this domain, so we have used the same chapter for the Essentials exam and the IT Technician and specialization exams.

Unauthorized Access

Unauthorized access occurs when a user accesses resources in an unauthorized way. Resources in this case mean data, applications, and hardware. A user can alter or delete data; access sensitive information, such as financial data, personnel files, or e-mail messages; or use a computer for purposes the owner did not intend.

Not all unauthorized access is malicious—often this problem arises when users who are randomly poking around in a computer discover that they can access resources in a fashion the primary user did not intend. Unauthorized access can sometimes be very malicious when outsiders knowingly and intentionally take advantage of weaknesses in your security to gain information, use resources, or destroy data!

Data Destruction

Often an extension of unauthorized access, data destruction means more than just intentionally or accidentally erasing or corrupting data. It's easy to imagine some evil hacker accessing your network and deleting all your important files, but consider the case where authorized users access certain data, but what they do to that data goes beyond what they are authorized to do. A good example is the person who legitimately accesses a Microsoft Access product database to modify the product descriptions, only to discover he or she can change the prices of the products, too.

This type of threat is particularly dangerous when users are not clearly informed about the extent to which they are authorized to make changes. A fellow tech once told me about a user who managed to mangle an important database due to someone giving them incorrect access. When confronted, the user said: "If I wasn't allowed to change it, the system wouldn't let me do it!"

Many users believe that systems are configured in a paternalistic way that wouldn't allow them to do anything inappropriate. As a result, users will often assume they're authorized to make any changes they believe are necessary when working on a piece of data they know they're authorized to access.

Administrative Access

Every operating system enables you to create user accounts and grant those accounts a certain level of access to files and folders in that computer. As an administrator, supervisor, or root user, you have full control over just about every aspect of the computer. Windows XP, in particular, makes it entirely too easy to give users administrative access to the computer, especially Windows XP Home because it allows only two kinds of users, administrators and limited users. Because you can't do much as a limited user, most home and small office systems simply use multiple administrator accounts. If you need to control access, you really need to use Windows 2000 or XP Professional.

System Crash/Hardware Failure

Like any technology, computers can and will fail—usually when you can least afford for it to happen. Hard drives crash, the power fails—it's all part of the joy of working in the computing business. You need to create redundancy in areas prone to failure (like installing backup power in case of electrical failure) and perform those all-important data backups. The Essentials course went into detail about using Microsoft Backup and other issues involved in creating a stable and reliable system.

Virus/Spyware

Networks are without a doubt the fastest and most efficient vehicles for transferring computer viruses among systems. News reports focus attention on the many virus attacks from the Internet, but a huge number of viruses still come from users who bring in programs on floppy disks, writable optical discs, and USB drives. This chapter describes the various methods of virus infection, and what you need to do to prevent virus infection of your networked systems in the "Network Security" section.

IT Technician

■ Local Control

To create a secure computing environment, you need to establish control over local resources. You need to back up data and make sure that retired hard drives and optical discs have no sensitive data on them. You should recognize security issues and be able to respond properly. You need to implement good access control policies, such as having all computers in your care locked down with proper passwords or other devices that recognize who should have access. Finally, you need to be able to implement methods for tracking computer usage. If someone is doing something wrong, you and the network or computer administrator should be able to catch him or her!

To mimic the physician's oath, here's the technician's oath: "Technician, first, secure your data." You need to back up data on machines in your care properly. Also, techs need to follow correct practices when retiring or donating old equipment. Let's take a look.

What to Back Up

Systems in your care should have regular backups performed of essential operating system files and, most importantly, data files. The Essentials course covered the process of backing up data, such as running the Backup or Restore Wizard in Windows 2000 and Windows XP, so the mechanics aren't covered here. Instead, this chapter looks more critically at what files to back up and how to protect those files.

Essential Data

By default, the Backup or Restore Wizard in Windows XP offers to back up your Documents and Settings folder (Figure 18.1). You also have options to back up everyone's documents and settings. That takes care of most, but not all, of your critical data. There are other issues to consider.

First, if you use Microsoft Outlook for your e-mail, the saved e-mail messages—both received and sent—will not be backed up. Neither will your address book. If you don't care about such things, then that's fine, but if you share a computer with multiple users, you need to make certain that you or the users back up both their mail and address book manually and then put

Windows 2000 and 2003 open the Backup Wizard with somewhat different settings. You are prompted to back up the entire drive initially, for example, rather than just Documents and Settings. This is also the case when you run the wizard in Windows XP in Advanced Mode.

Backup or Restore Wizard

Welcome to the Backup or Restore Wizard

This wizard helps you back up or restore the files and settings on your computer.

If you prefer, you can switch to Advanced Mode to change the settings used for backup or restore. This option is recommended for advanced users only.

☑ Always start in wizard mode

To continue, click Next.

< Back   Next >   Cancel

• **Figure 18.1**   Backup or Restore Wizard

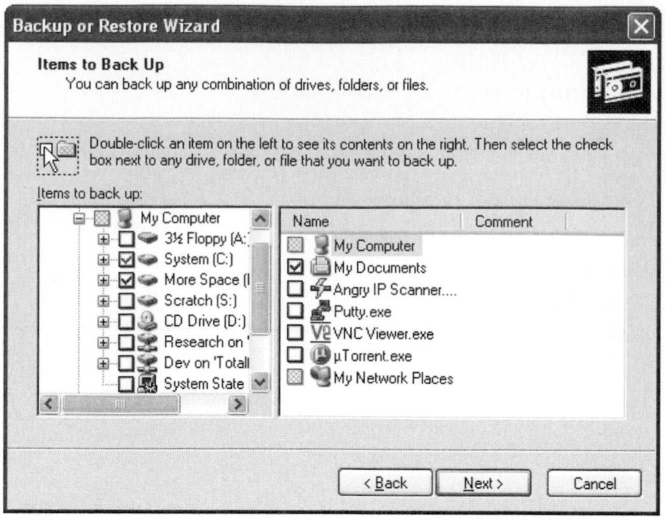

● **Figure 18.2** Selecting items to back up

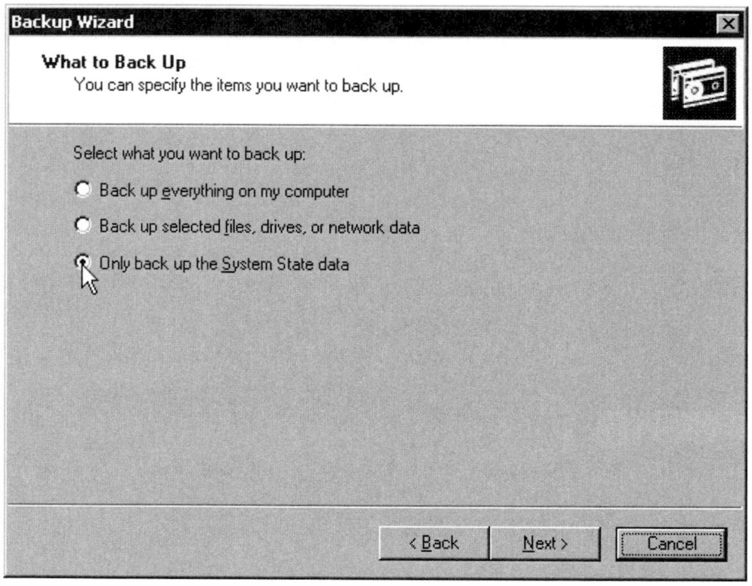

● **Figure 18.3** Backup Wizard

The CompTIA A+ certification exams most likely *won't* ask you about off-site storage, but in today's world, anything less would be illogical.

the backed-up files in the Documents and Settings folder! That way, the Backup or Restore Wizard will grab those files.

Second, if you or others on the computer use any folders outside the Documents and Settings environment, then you need to select the *Let me choose what to back up* option from the Backup or Restore Wizard when prompted. This opens the Items to Back Up dialog where you can select individual files and folders to back up (Figure 18.2).

Server Environments

If you work in an environment that requires you to back up Windows 2000 Server or Windows Server 2003 computers, you need to back up some extra data. This is especially true if you have a Windows network running. Windows networking features **Active Directory**, a system that enables you to share files easily within the network, yet still maintain rock-solid security. A user only has to log in once to an Active Directory server and then they have access to resources throughout the Active Directory network (assuming, of course, that the user has permission to access those resources).

To back up the extra data, you need to run the Backup Wizard and select the radio button that says *Only back up the System State data* (Figure 18.3). The **System State data** takes care of most of the registry, security settings, the desktop files and folders, and the default user.

If you want to back up more than that, close the wizard and select the Backup tab in the Backup dialog box. Check the box next to System State and then check off any other file or folder that you want backed up (Figure 18.4). From this same dialog box, you can select where to back up the data, such as to a tape drive or external hard drive.

Off-Site Storage

Backing up your data and other important information enables you to restore easily in case of a system crash or malicious data destruction, but to ensure proper security, you need to store your backups somewhere other than your office. **Off-site storage** means that you take the tape or portable hard drive that contains your backup and lock it in a briefcase. Take it home and put it in your home safe, if you have one. This way, if the building burns down or some major flood renders your office inaccessible, your company can be up and running very quickly from a secondary location.

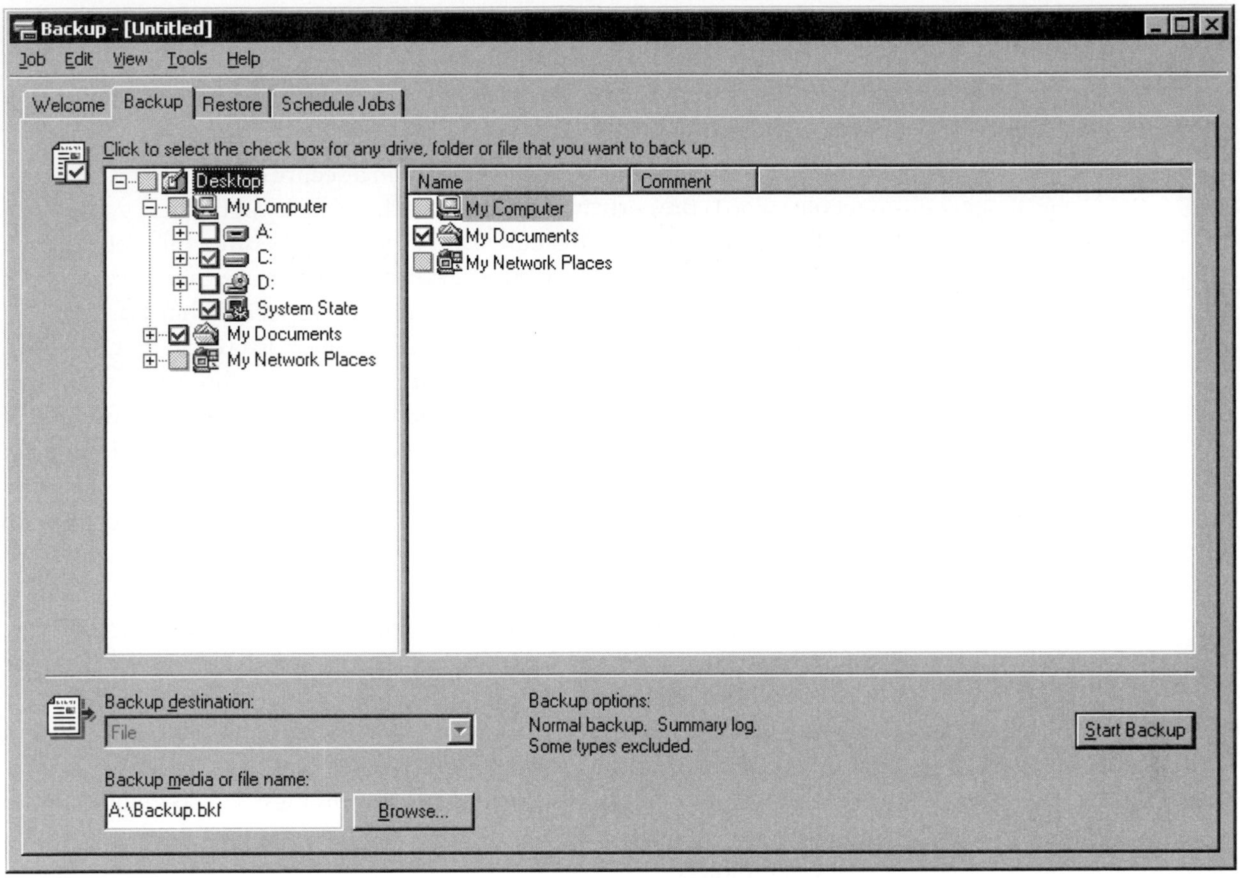

● **Figure 18.4**   Backup tab in the Backup dialog box with System State and My Documents selected

Migrating and Retiring

Seasons change and so does the state of the art in computing. At a certain point in a computer's life, you'll need to retire an old system. This means you must migrate the data and users to a new system or at least a new hard drive—a process called **migration**—and then safely dispose of the old system. When talking about migration or retirement in terms of security, you need to answer one question: what do you do with the old system or drive?

All but the most vanilla new installations have sensitive data on them, even if it's simply e-mail messages or notes-to-self that would cause embarrassment if discovered. Most PCs, especially in a work environment, contain a lot of sensitive data. You can't just format C: and hand over the drive.

Follow three principles when migrating or retiring a computer. First, migrate your users and data information in a secure environment. Until you get passwords properly in place and test the security of the new system, you can't consider that system secure. Second, remove data remnants from hard drives that you store or give to charity. Third, recycle the older equipment; don't throw it in the trash. PC recyclers go through a process of deconstructing hardware, breaking system units, keyboards, printers, and even monitors into their basic plastics, metals, and glass for reuse.

Migration Practices

Migrate your users and data information in a secure environment. Until you get passwords properly in place and test the security of the new system, you can't consider that system secure. Don't set a copy to run while you go out to lunch, but rather be there to supervise and remove any remnant data that might still reside on any mass storage devices, especially hard drives.

You might think that, as easy as it seems to be to lose data, that you could readily get rid of data if you tried. That's not the case, however, with magnetic media such as hard drives and flash memory. It's very difficult to clean a drive completely. Repeated formatting won't do the trick. Partitioning and formatting won't work. Data doesn't necessarily get written over in the same place every time, which means that a solid wipe of a hard drive by writing zeroes to all the clusters still potentially leaves a lot of sensitive and recoverable data, typically called **remnants**, on the drive.

Although you can't make data 100 percent unrecoverable short of physically shredding or pulverizing a drive, you can do well enough for donation purposes by using one of the better drive-wiping utilities, such as Webroot's Window Washer (Figure 18.5). Window Washer gives you the ability to erase your Web browsing history, your recent activity in Windows (such as what programs you ran), and even your e-mail messages permanently. As an added bonus, you can create a bootable disk that enables you to wipe a drive completely.

Recycle

An important and relatively easy way to be an environmentally conscious computer user is to *recycle*. Recycling products such as paper and printer cartridges not only keeps them out of overcrowded landfills, but also ensures that the more toxic products are disposed of in the right way. Safely disposing of hardware containing hazardous materials, such as computer monitors, protects both people and the environment.

Anyone who's ever tried to sell a computer more than three or four years old learns a hard lesson—they're not worth much if anything at all. It's a real temptation to take that old computer and just toss it in the garbage, but never do that!

First of all, many parts of your computer—such as your computer monitor—contain hazardous materials that pollute the environment. Luckily, thousands of companies now specialize in computer recycling and will gladly accept your old computer. If you have enough computers, they might even pick them up. If you can't find a recycler, call your local municipality's waste authority to see where to drop off your system.

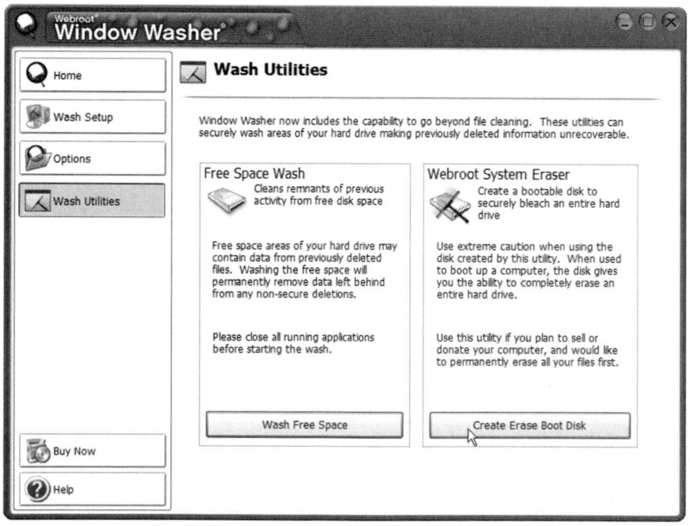

● **Figure 18.5**   Webroot Window Washer security software

An even better alternative for your old computer is donation. Many organizations actively look for old computers to refurbish and to donate to schools and other organizations. Just keep in mind that the computer can be too old—not even a school wants a computer more than five or six years old.

Social Engineering

Although you're more likely to lose data through accident, the acts of malicious users get the vast majority of headlines. Most of these attacks come under the heading of social engineering —the process of using or manipulating people inside the networking environment to gain access to that network from the outside. The term "social engineering" covers the many ways humans can use other humans to gain unauthorized information. This unauthorized information may be a network login, a credit card number, company customer data—almost anything you might imagine that one person or organization may not want a person outside of that organization to access.

Social engineering attacks aren't hacking—at least in the classic sense of the word—although the goals are the same. Social engineering is where people attack an organization through the people in the organization or physically access the organization to get the information they need. Here are a few of the more classic types of social engineering attacks.

Infiltration

Hackers can physically enter your building under the guise of someone who might have a legitimate reason for being there, such as cleaning personnel, repair technicians, or messengers. They then snoop around desks, looking for whatever they can find. They might talk with people inside the organization, gathering names, office numbers, department names   little things in and of themselves, but powerful tools when combined later with other social engineering attacks.

Telephone Scams

Telephone scams are probably the most common social engineering attack. In this case, the attacker makes a phone call to someone in the organization to gain information. The attacker attempts to come across as someone inside the organization and uses this to get the desired information. Probably the most famous of these scams is the "I forgot my user name and password" scam. In this gambit, the attacker first learns the account name of a legitimate person in the organization, usually using the infiltration method. The attacker then calls someone in the organization, usually the help desk, in an attempt to gather information, in this case a password.

> **Hacker:** "Hi, this is John Anderson in accounting. I forgot my password. Can you reset it please?"
> **Help Desk :** "Sure, what's your user name?"
> **Hacker:** "j_w_Anderson"
> **Help Desk:** "OK, I reset it to e34rd3."

It's common for social engineering attacks to be used together, so if you discover one of them being used against your organization, it's a good idea to look for others.

Certainly telephone scams aren't limited to attempts to get network access. There are documented telephone scams against organizations aimed at getting cash, blackmail material, or other valuables.

Dumpster Diving

Dumpster diving is the generic term for anytime a hacker goes through your refuse, looking for information. The amount of sensitive information that makes it into any organization's trash bin boggles the mind! Years ago, I worked with an IT security guru who gave me and a few other IT people a tour of our office's trash. In one 20-minute tour of the personal wastebaskets of one office area, we had enough information to access the network easily, as well as to embarrass seriously more than a few people. When it comes to getting information, the trash is the place to look!

Physical Theft

I once had a fellow network geek challenge me to try to bring down his newly installed network. He had just installed a powerful and expensive firewall router and was convinced that I couldn't get to a test server he added to his network just for me to try to access. After a few attempts to hack in over the Internet, I saw that I wasn't going to get anywhere that way. So I jumped in my car and drove to his office, having first outfitted myself in a techy-looking jumpsuit and an ancient ID badge I just happened to have in my sock drawer. I smiled sweetly at the receptionist and walked right by my friend's office (I noticed he was smugly monitoring incoming IP traffic using some neato packet-sniffing program) to his new server. I quickly pulled the wires out of the back of his precious server, picked it up, and walked out the door. The receptionist was too busy trying to figure out why her e-mail wasn't working to notice me as I whisked by her carrying the 65-pound server box. I stopped in the hall and called him from my cell phone.

> **Me (cheerily):** "Dude, I got all your data!"
> **Him (not cheerily):** "You rebooted my server! How did you do it?"
> **Me (smiling):** "I didn't reboot it—go over and look at it!"
> **Him (really mad now):** "YOU <EXPLETIVE> THIEF! YOU STOLE MY SERVER!"
> **Me (cordially):** "Why, yes. Yes, I did. Give me two days to hack your password in the comfort of my home, and I'll see everything! Bye!"

I immediately walked back in and handed him the test server. It was fun. The moral here is simple—never forget that the best network software security measures can be rendered useless if you fail to protect your systems physically!

Access Control

Access is the key. If you can control access to the data, programs, and other computing resources, you've secured your system. Access control is composed of five interlinked areas that a good, security-minded tech should think about: physical security, authentication, the file system, users and

Tech Tip

Spoofing

Some sophisticated hackers alter the identifying labels or addresses of their computers to appear as if they're someone or something else. This process is called spoofing. An e-mail message that appears to be from a friend but is actually spam is an example of simple spoofing.

groups, and security policies. Much of this you know from previous chapters, but this section should help tie it all together as a security topic.

Secure Physical Area and Lock Down Your System

The first order of security is to block access to the physical hardware from people who shouldn't have access. This isn't rocket science. Lock the door. Don't leave a PC unattended when logged in. In fact, don't ever leave a system logged in, even as a limited user. God help you if you walk away from a server still logged in as an administrator. You're tempting fate.

For that matter, when you see a user's computer logged in and unattended, do the user and your company a huge favor and lock the computer. Just walk up and press CTRL-L on the keyboard to lock the system. It works in Windows 2000 and all versions of Windows XP and Windows Vista.

> Expect questions on controlling access to computers and computer rooms on the CompTIA A+ 220-604 Depot Technician exam.

Authentication

Security starts with properly implemented **authentication**, which means in essence, how the computer determines who can or should access it. And, once accessed, what that user can do. A computer can authenticate users through software or hardware, or a combination of both.

Software Authentication: Proper Passwords It's still rather shocking to me to power up a friend's computer and go straight to his or her desktop; or with my married-with-kids friends, to click one of the parent's user account icons and not get prompted for a password. This is just wrong! I'm always tempted to assign passwords right then and there—and not tell them the passwords, of course—so they'll see the error of their ways when they try to log in next. I don't do it, but always try to explain gently the importance of good passwords.

You know about passwords from the Essentials course so I won't belabor the point here. Suffice it to say that you need to make certain that all your users have proper passwords. Don't let them write passwords down or tape them to the underside of their mouse pads either!

It's not just access to Windows that you need to think about. If you have computers running in a public location, there's always the temptation for people to hack the system and do mean things, like change CMOS settings to render the computer inoperable to the casual user until a tech can undo the damage. All modern CMOS setup utilities come with an access password protection scheme (Figure 18.6).

> ### ✓ Cross Check
>
> #### Proper Passwords
>
> So, what goes into making a good password? Based on what you learned in the Essentials course, see if you can answer these questions. What sorts of characters should make up a password? Should you ask for a user's password when working on his or her PC? Why or why not? If you're in a secure environment and know you'll have to reboot several times, is it okay to ask for a password then? What should you do?

```
[OS Extension v1.0A
ard Software, Inc.

·y Master ... ST10232A
·y Slave  ... None
lary
lary  Enter Password:
```

● **Figure 18.6** CMOS access password request

Hardware Authentication Smart cards and biometric devices enable modern systems to authenticate users with more authority than mere passwords. **Smart cards** are credit card–sized cards with circuitry that can be used to identify the bearer of the card. Smart cards are relatively common for tasks such as authenticating users for mass transit systems, for example, but fairly

● **Figure 18.7**   Keyboard-mounted smart card reader being used for a commercial application (*photo courtesy of Cherry Corp.*)

Full disclosure time. Microsoft does not claim that the keyboard in Figure 18.8 offers any security at all. In fact, the documentation specifically claims that the fingerprint reader is an accessibility tool, not a security device. Because it enables a person to log onto a local machine, though, I think it falls into the category of authentication devices.

uncommon in computers. Figure 18.7 shows a smart card and keyboard combination.

People can guess or discover passwords, but it's a lot harder to forge someone's fingerprints. The keyboard in Figure 18.8 authenticates users on a local machine using fingerprints. Other devices that will do the trick are key fobs, retinal scanners, and PC cards for laptop computers. Devices that require some sort of physical, flesh-and-blood authentication are called **biometric devices**.

Clever manufacturers have developed key fobs and smart cards that use radio frequency identification (RFID) to transmit authentication information, so users don't have to insert something into a computer or card reader. The Prevarius plusID combines, for example, a biometric fingerprint fob with an RFID tag that makes security as easy as opening a garage door remotely! Figure 18.9 shows a plusID device.

NTFS, not FAT32!

The file system on a hard drive matters a lot when it comes to security. On a Windows machine with multiple users, you simply must use NTFS, or you have no security at all. Not just primary drives, but any secondary drives in computers in your care should be formatted as NTFS, with the exception of removable drives, such as the one you use to back up your system.

When you run into a multiple-drive system that has a second or third drive formatted as FAT32, you can use the **CONVERT** command-line utility to go from FAT to NTFS. The syntax is pretty straightforward. To convert a D: drive from FAT or FAT32 to NTFS, for example, you'd type the following:

```
CONVERT D: /FS:NTFS
```

● **Figure 18.8**   Microsoft keyboard with fingerprint accessibility

● **Figure 18.9**   plusID (*photo courtesy of Privaris, Inc.*)

You can substitute a mount name in place of the drive letter in case you have a mounted volume. The command has a few extra switches as well, so at the command prompt, type **a** /? after the CONVERT command to see all your options.

Users and Groups

Windows uses user accounts and groups as the bedrock of access control. A user account gets assigned to a group, such as Users, Power Users, or Administrators, and by association gets certain permissions on the computer. Using NTFS enables the highest level of control over data resources.

Assigning users to groups is a great first step in controlling a local machine, but this feature really shines once you go to a networked environment. Let's go there now.

■ Network Security

The vast majority of protective strategies related to internal threats are based on policies rather than technology. Even the smallest network will have a number of user accounts and groups scattered about with different levels of rights/permissions. Every time you give a user access to a resource, you create potential loopholes that can leave your network vulnerable to unauthorized access, data destruction, and other administrative nightmares. To protect your network from internal threats, you need to implement the correct controls over user accounts, permissions, and policies.

Networks are under threat from the outside as well, so this section looks at issues involving Internet-borne attacks, firewalls, and wireless networking. The section finishes with discussion of the tools you need to track computer and network activity and, if necessary, lock down your systems.

User Account Control Through Groups

Access to user accounts should be restricted to the assigned individuals, and those accounts should have permission to access only the resources they need, no more. Tight control of user accounts is critical to preventing unauthorized access. Disabling unused accounts is an important part of this strategy, but good user account control goes far deeper than that. One of your best tools for user account control is groups. Instead of giving permissions/rights to individual user accounts, give them to groups; this makes keeping track of the permissions assigned to individual user accounts much easier. Figure 18.10 shows me giving permissions to a group for a folder in Windows 2000. Once a group is created and its permissions set, you can then add user accounts to that group as needed. Any user account that becomes a member of a group

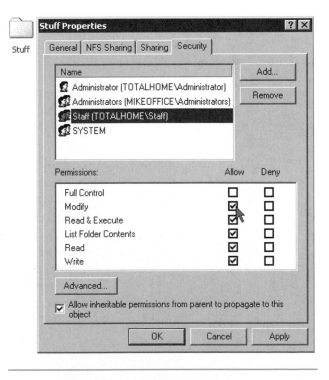

• **Figure 18.10**   Giving a group permissions for a folder in Windows 2000

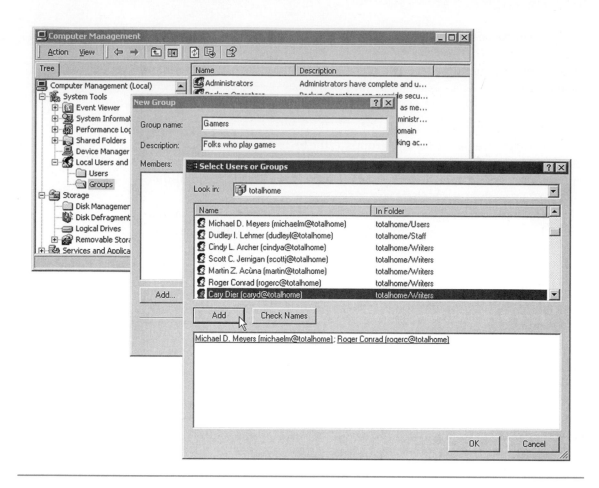

● **Figure 18.11** Adding a user to a newly created group in Windows 2000

automatically gets the permissions assigned to that group. Figure 18.11 shows me adding a user to a newly created group in the same Windows 2000 system.

Groups are a great way to get increased complexity without increasing the administrative burden on network administrators, because all network operating systems combine permissions. When a user is a member of more than one group, which permissions does he or she have with respect to any particular resource? In all network operating systems, the permissions of the groups are *combined,* and the result is what you call the **effective permissions** the user has to access the resource. Let's use an example from Windows 2000. If Rita is a member of the Sales group, which has List Folder Contents permission to a folder, and she is also a member of the Managers group, which has Read and Execute permissions to the same folder, Rita will have both List Folder Contents *and* Read and Execute permissions to that folder.

Watch out for *default* user accounts and groups—they can become secret backdoors to your network! All network operating systems have a default Everyone group, and it can be used to sneak into shared resources easily. This Everyone group, as its name implies, literally includes anyone who connects to that resource. Windows 2000 gives full control to the Everyone group by default, for example, so make sure you know to lock this down!

All of the default groups—Everyone, Guest, Users—define broad groups of users. Never use them unless you intend to permit all those folks to access a resource. If you use one of the default groups, remember to configure them with the proper permissions to prevent users from doing things you don't want them to do with a shared resource!

All of these groups and organizational units only do one thing for you: They let you keep track of your user accounts, so you know they are only available for those who need them, and they only access the resources you want them to use.

Security Policies

While permissions control how users access shared resources, there are other functions you should control that are outside the scope of resources. For example, do you want users to be able to access a command prompt on their Windows system? Do you want users to be able to install software? Would you like to control what systems or what time of day a user can log in? All network operating systems provide you with some capability to control these and literally hundreds of other security parameters, under what Windows calls *policies*. I like to think of policies as permissions for activities as opposed to true permissions, which control access to resources.

A policy is usually applied to a user account, a computer, or a group. Let's use the example of a network composed of Windows XP Professional systems with a Windows 2003 Server system. Every Windows XP system has its own local policies program, which enables policies to be placed on that system only. Figure 18.12 shows the tool you use to set local policies on an individual system, called **Local Security Settings**, being used to deny the user account Danar the capability to log on locally.

Local policies work great for individual systems, but they can be a pain to configure if you want to apply the same settings to more than one PC on your network. If you want to apply policy settings *en masse*, then you need to step up to Windows Active Directory domain-based **Group Policy**. Using Group Policy, you can exercise deity-like—Microsoft prefers to use the term *granular*—control over your network clients.

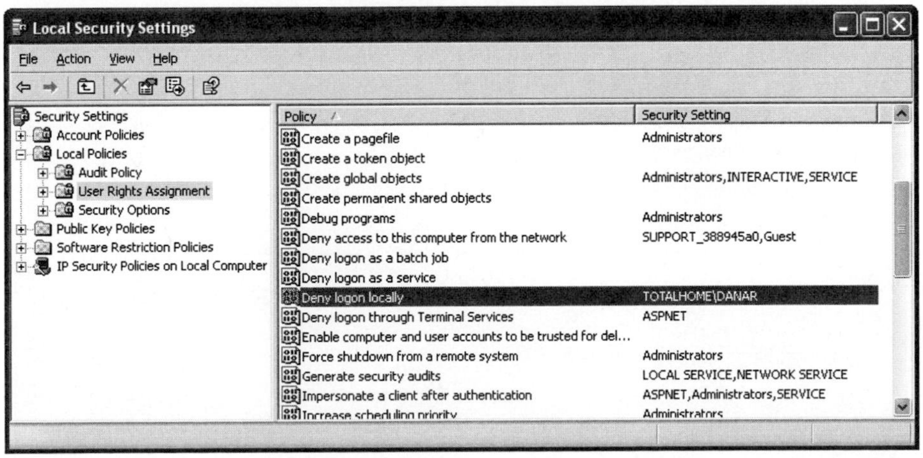

• **Figure 18.12**   Local Security Settings

Want to set default wallpaper for every PC in your domain? Group Policy can do that. Want to make certain tools inaccessible to everyone except authorized users? Group Policy can do that, too. Want to control access to the Internet, redirect home folders, run scripts, deploy software, or just remind folks that unauthorized access to the network will get them nowhere fast? Group Policy is the answer. Figure 18.13 shows Group Policy; I'm about to change the default title on every instance of Internet Explorer on every computer in my domain!

That's just one simple example of the types of settings you can configure using Group Policy. There are literally hundreds of "tweaks" you can apply through Group Policy, from the great to the small, but don't worry too much about familiarizing yourself with each and every one. Group Policy settings are a big topic in the Microsoft Certified Systems Administrator (MCSA) and Microsoft Certified Systems Engineer (MCSE) certification tracks, but for the purposes of the CompTIA A+ exams, you simply have to be comfortable with the concept behind Group Policy.

Although I could never list every possible policy you can enable on a Windows system, here's a list of some of those more commonly used:

- **Prevent Registry Edits**   If you try to edit the Registry, you get a failure message.

- **Prevent Access to the Command Prompt**   This policy keeps users from getting to the command prompt by turning off the Run command and the MS-DOS Prompt shortcut.

Tech Tip

Linux and Policies

Linux doesn't provide a single application that you open to set up policies, like Windows does. In fact, Linux doesn't even use the name "policies." Instead, Linux relies on individual applications to set up policies for whatever they're doing. This is in keeping with the Linux paradigm of having lots of little programs that do one thing well, as opposed to the Windows paradigm of having one program try to be all things for all applications.

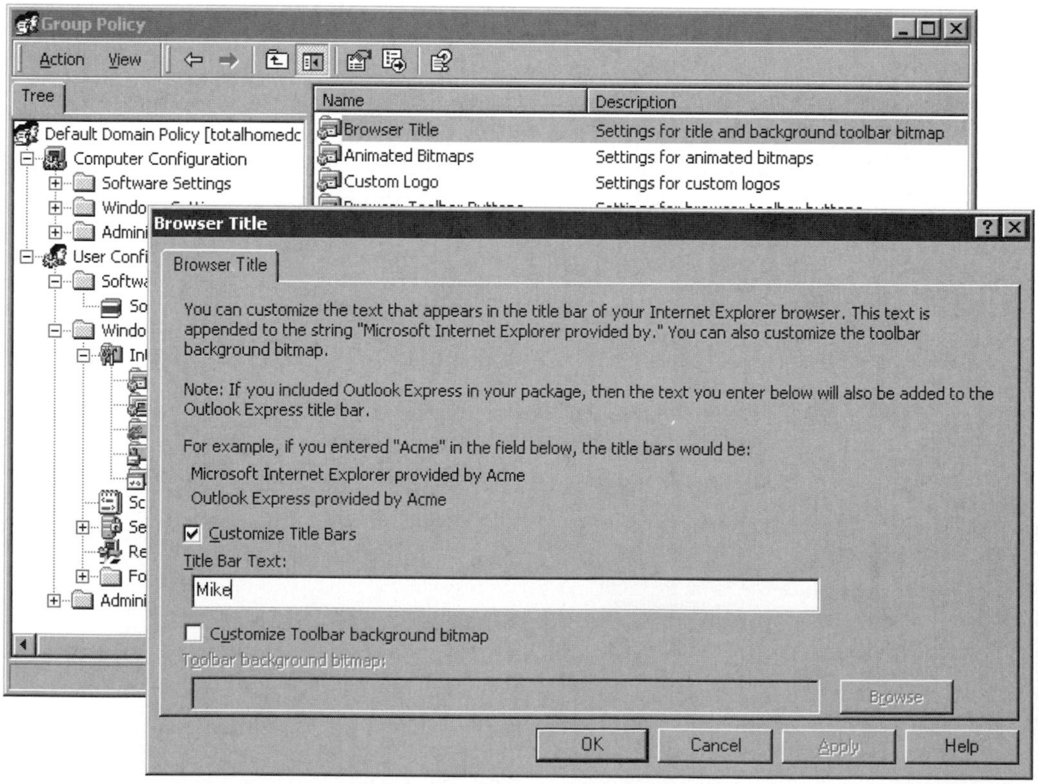

● **Figure 18.13**   Using Group Policy to make IE title say "provided by Mike!"

- **Log on Locally**   This policy defines who may log on to the system locally.

- **Shut Down System**   This policy defines who may shut down the system.

- **Minimum Password Length**   This policy forces a minimum password length.

- **Account Lockout Threshold**   This policy sets the maximum number of logon attempts a person can make before they are locked out of the account.

- **Disable Windows Installer**   This policy prevents users from installing software.

- **Printer Browsing**   This policy enables users to browse for printers on the network, as opposed to using only assigned printers.

While the CompTIA A+ exams don't expect you to know how to implement policies on any type of network, you are expected to understand that policies exist, especially on Windows networks, and that they can do amazing things in terms of controlling what users can do on their systems. If you ever try to get to a command prompt on a Windows system, only to discover the Run command is grayed out, blame it on a policy, not the computer!

Malicious Software

The beauty of the Internet is the ease of accessing resources just about anywhere on the globe, all from the comfort of your favorite chair. This connection, however, runs both ways, and people from all over the world can potentially access your computer from the comfort of their evil lairs. The Internet is awash with malicious software—*malware*—that is even at this moment trying to infect your systems. Malware consists of computer programs designed to break into computers or cause havoc on computers. The most common types of malware are viruses, worms, spyware, Trojan horses, adware, and grayware. You need to understand the different types of malware so you can combat them for you and your users successfully.

Viruses

Just as a biological virus gets passed from person to person, a computer **virus** is a piece of malicious software that gets passed from computer to computer (Figure 18.14). A computer virus is designed to attach itself to a program on your computer. It could be your e-mail program, your word processor, or even a game. Whenever you use the infected program, the virus goes into action and does whatever it was designed to do. It can wipe out your e-mail or even erase your entire hard drive! Viruses are also sometimes used to steal information or send spam e-mails to everyone in your address book.

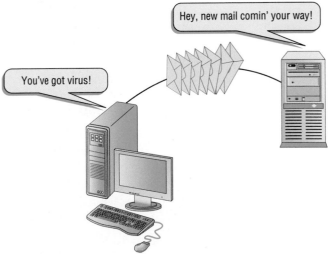

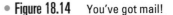
Figure 18.14   You've got mail!

Trojans

Trojans are true, freestanding programs that do something other than what the person who runs the program thinks they will do. An example of a *Trojan virus* is a program that a person thinks is a game but is actually a CMOS eraser. Some Trojans are quite sophisticated. It might be a game that works perfectly well, but when the user quits the game, it causes some type of damage.

Worms

Similar to a Trojan, a worm is a complete program that travels from machine to machine, usually through computer networks. Most worms are designed to take advantage of security problems in operating systems and install themselves on vulnerable machines. They can copy themselves over and over again on infected networks, and can create so much activity that they overload the network, in worst cases even bringing chunks of the entire Internet to a halt.

There are several things you can do to protect yourself and your data against these threats. First, make sure you are running up-to-date virus software—especially if you connect to the Internet via an always-on broadband connection. You should also be protected by a firewall, either as part of your network hardware or by means of a software program. (See the sections on antivirus programs and firewalls later in this chapter.)

Since worms most commonly infect systems because of security flaws in operating systems, the next defense against them is to make sure you have the most current version possible of your operating system and to check regularly for security patches. A *security patch* is an addition to the operating system to patch a hole in the operating system code. You can download security patches from the software vendor's Web site (Figure 18.15).

Microsoft's Windows Update tool is handy for Windows users as it provides a simple method to ensure that your version's security is up to date. The one downside is that not everyone remembers to run Windows Update. Don't wait until something goes wrong on your computer, or you hear on the news that another nasty program is running rampant across the Internet—Run Windows Update weekly (or even better automatically) as a part of your normal system maintenance. Keeping your patches up to date is called *patch management,* and it goes a long way toward keeping your system safe!

Antivirus Programs

The only way to protect your PC permanently from getting a virus is to disconnect from the Internet and never permit any potentially infected software to touch your precious computer. Because neither scenario is likely these days, you need to use a specialized antivirus program to help stave off the inevitable virus assaults.

An antivirus program protects your PC in two ways. It can be both sword and shield, working in an active seek-and-destroy mode and in a passive sentry mode. When ordered to seek and destroy, the program will scan the computer's boot sector and files for viruses, and if it finds any, present you with the available options for removing or disabling them. Antivirus programs can also operate as virus shields that passively monitor your

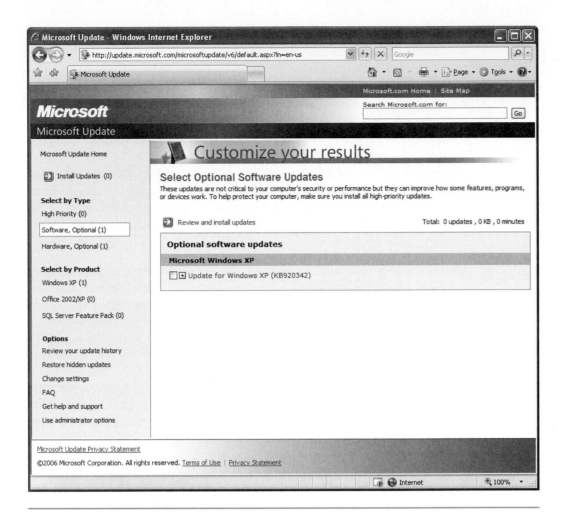

● **Figure 18.15** Microsoft Update

computer's activity, checking for viruses only when certain events occur, such as a program executing or a file being downloaded.

Antivirus programs use different techniques to combat different types of viruses. They detect boot sector viruses simply by comparing the drive's boot sector to a standard boot sector. This works because most boot sectors are basically the same. Some antivirus programs make a backup copy of the boot sector. If they detect a virus, the programs will use that backup copy to replace the infected boot sector. Executable viruses are a little more difficult to find because they can be on any file in the drive. To detect executable viruses, the antivirus program uses a library of signatures. A **signature** is the code pattern of a known virus. The antivirus program compares an executable file to its library of signatures. There have been instances where a perfectly clean program coincidentally held a virus signature. Usually the antivirus program's creator will provide a patch to prevent further alarms. Antivirus programs detect macro viruses through the presence of virus signatures or certain macro commands that indicate a known macro virus. Now that we understand the types of viruses and how antivirus programs try to protect against them, let's review a few terms that are often used when describing certain traits of viruses.

Polymorphics/Polymorphs A `polymorph virus` attempts to change its signature to prevent detection by antivirus programs, usually by continually scrambling a bit of useless code. Fortunately, the scrambling code itself can be identified and used as the signature—once the antivirus makers become aware of the virus. One technique used to combat unknown polymorphs is to have the antivirus program create a checksum on every file in the drive. A *checksum* in this context is a number generated by the software based on the contents of the file rather than the name, date, or size of that file. The algorithms for creating these checksums vary among different antivirus programs (they are also usually kept secret to help prevent virus makers from coming up with ways to beat them). Every time a program is run, the antivirus program calculates a new checksum and compares it with the earlier calculation. If the checksums are different, it is a sure sign of a virus.

Stealth The term "stealth" is more of a concept than an actual virus function. Most `stealth virus` programs are boot sector viruses that use various methods to hide from antivirus software. The AntiEXE stealth virus will hook on to a little-known but often-used software interrupt, for example, running only when that interrupt runs. Others make copies of innocent-looking files.

Virus Prevention Tips The secret to preventing damage from a malicious software attack is to keep from getting a virus in the first place. As discussed earlier, all good antivirus programs include a virus shield that will scan e-mail, downloads, running programs, and so on automatically (see Figure 18.16).

Use your antivirus shield. It is also a good idea to scan PCs daily for possible virus attacks. All antivirus programs include terminate-and-stay resident programs (TSRs) that will run every time the PC is booted. Last but not least, know the source of any software before you load it. While the chance of commercial, shrink-wrapped software having a virus is virtually nil (there have been a couple of well-publicized exceptions), that illegal copy of Unreal Tournament you borrowed from a local hacker should definitely be inspected with care.

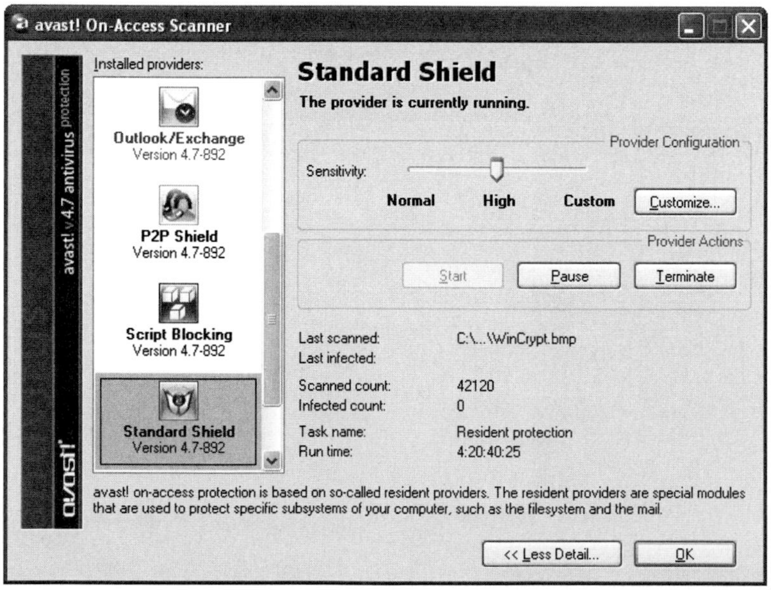

Keep your antivirus program updated. New viruses appear daily, and your program needs to know about them. The list of viruses your antivirus program can recognize is called the `definition file`, and you must keep that definition file up to date. Fortunately, most antivirus programs will update themselves automatically.

Get into the habit of keeping around an antivirus CD-R—a bootable, CD-R disc with a copy of an antivirus program. If you suspect a virus, use the disc, even if your antivirus program claims to have eliminated the virus. Turn off the PC and reboot it from

● **Figure 18.16** A virus shield in action

the antivirus disc. (You might have to change CMOS settings to boot to optical media.) Run your antivirus program's most comprehensive virus scan. Then check all removable media that were exposed to the system, and any other machine that might have received data from it or that is networked to the cleaned machine. A virus or other malicious program can often lie dormant for months before anyone knows of its presence.

E-mail is still a common source of viruses, and opening infected e-mails is a common way to get infected. If you view an e-mail in a preview window, that opens the e-mail message and exposes your computer to some viruses. Download files only from sites you know to be safe, and of course the less reputable corners of the Internet are the most likely places to pick up computer infections.

Viruses are not, however, the only malicious software lurking in e-mail. Sometimes the e-mail itself is the problem.

Spam

E-mail that comes into your Inbox from a source that's not a friend, family member, or colleague, and that you didn't ask for, can create huge problems for your computer and you. This unsolicited e-mail, called **spam**, accounts for a huge percentage of traffic on the Internet. Spam comes in many flavors, from legitimate businesses trying to sell you products to scammers who just want to take your money. Hoaxes, pornography, and get-rich-quick schemes pour into the Inboxes of most e-mail users. They waste your time and can easily offend.

You can use several options to cope with the flood of spam. The first option is defense. Never post your e-mail address on the Internet. One study tested this theory and found that *over 97 percent* of the spam received during the study went to e-mail addresses they had posted on the public Internet.

Filters and filtering software can block spam at your mail server and at your computer. AOL implemented blocking schemes in 2004, for example, that dropped the average spam received by its subscribers by a large percentage, perhaps as much as 50 percent. You can set most e-mail programs to block e-mail from specific people—good to use if someone is harassing you—or to specific people. You can block by subject line or keywords. Most people use a third-party anti-spam program instead of using the filters in their e-mail program.

> The Center for Democracy and Technology conducted the 2003 study entitled "Why Am I Getting All This Spam? Unsolicited Commercial E-mail Research Six Month Report." Here's the Web link if you're curious: www.cdt.org/speech/spam/030319spamreport.shtml.

Pop-Ups, Spyware, and Adware

On most systems, the Internet Web browser client is the most often used piece of software. Over the years, Web sites have come up with more and more ways to try to get you to see what they want you to see: their advertising. When the Web first got underway, we were forced to look at an occasional banner ad. In the last few years, Web site designers have become

Try This!

Fight Spam Right!

Spam filtering software that you purchase and put on your computer can help, but you have to do some research to see which software offers the best performance. You want to avoid software that causes *false positives*—mislabeling acceptable e-mail as spam—because then you miss legitimate e-mail messages from family and friends. So, time to fire up your trusty Web browser and do some searching.

Start by going to Google and searching for **anti-spam software reviews**. One of the first sites that should come up takes you to *PC Magazine*'s review list, which is kept up to date. What's the current Editor's Choice? What other options do you have?

much more sophisticated, creating a number of intrusive and irritating ways to get you to part with your money in one form or another.

There are basically three irritating Web browser problems: pop-ups, spyware, and adware. **Pop-ups** are those surprise browser windows that appear automatically when you visit a Web site, proving themselves irritating and unwanted and nothing else. **Spyware**, meanwhile, defines a family of programs that run in the background on your PC, sending information about your browsing habits to the company that installed it on your system. **Adware** is not generally as malicious as spyware, but it works similarly to display ads on your system. As such, these programs download new ads and generate undesirable network traffic. Of the three, spyware is much less noticeable but far more nefarious. At its worst, spyware can fire up pop-up windows of competing products on the Web site you're currently viewing. For example, you might be perusing a bookseller's Web site only to have a pop-up from a competitor's site appear.

Pop-Ups Getting rid of pop-ups is actually rather tricky. You've probably noticed that most of these pop-up browser windows don't look like browser windows at all. There's no menu bar, button bar, or address window, yet they are each separate browser windows. HTML coding permits Web site and advertising designers to remove the usual navigation aids from a browser window so all you're left with is the content. In fact, as I'll describe in a minute, some pop-up browser windows are deliberately designed to mimic similar pop-up alerts from the Windows OS. They might even have buttons similar to Windows' own exit buttons, but you might find that when you click them, you wind up with more pop-up windows instead! What to do?

The first thing you need to know when dealing with pop-ups is how to close them without actually having to risk clicking them. As I said, most pop-ups have removed all navigation aids, and many are also configured to appear on your monitor screen in a position that places the browser window's exit button—the little *X* button in the upper right-hand corner—outside of your visible screen area. Some even pop up behind the active browser window and wait there in the background. Most annoying! To remedy this, use alternate means to close the pop-up browser window. For instance, you can right-click the browser window's taskbar icon to generate a pop-up menu of your own. Select Close, and the window should go away. You can also bring the browser window in question to the forefront by pressing ALT-TAB until it becomes visible, and then press ALT-F4 to close it.

Most Web browsers have features to prevent pop-up ads in the first place, but I've found that these types of applications are sometimes *too* thorough. That is, they tend to prevent *all* new browser windows from opening, even those you want to view. Still, they're free to try, so have a look to see if they suit your needs. Applications such as AdSubtract control a variety of Internet annoyances, including pop-up windows, cookies, and Java applets, and are more configurable—you can specify what you want to allow on any particular domain address—but the fully functional versions usually cost at least something, and that much control is too confusing for most novice-level users.

Dealing with Spyware Some types of spyware go considerably beyond this level of intrusion. They can use your computer's resources to run *distributed computing* applications, capture your keystrokes to steal passwords, reconfigure your dial-up settings to use a different phone number at a much higher connection charge, or even use your Internet connection and e-mail address list to propagate itself to other computers in a virus-like fashion! Are you concerned yet?

Setting aside the legal and ethical issues, and there are many, you should at least appreciate that spyware can seriously impact your PC's performance and cause problems with your Internet connection. The threat is real, so what practical steps can you take to protect yourself? Let's look at how to prevent spyware installation, and how to detect and remove any installed spyware.

Preventing Spyware Installation How does this spyware get into your system in the first place? Obviously, a sensible person doesn't download and install something that they know is going to compromise their computer. Makers of spyware know this, so they bundle their software with some other program or utility that purports to give you some benefit.

What kind of benefit? How about free access to MP3 music files? A popular program called Kazaa does that. How about a handy *e-wallet* utility that remembers your many screen names, passwords, and even your credit card numbers to make online purchases easier and faster? A program called Gator does that, and many other functions as well. How about browser enhancements, performance boosters, custom cursor effects, search utilities, buddy lists, file savers, or media players? The list goes on and on, yet they all share one thing—they're simply window-dressing for the *real* purpose of the software. So you see, for the most part spyware doesn't need to force its way into your PC. Instead they saunter calmly through the front door. If the graphic in Figure 18.17 looks familiar, you might have installed some of this software yourself.

Some spyware makers use more aggressive means to get you to install their software. Instead of offering you some sort of attractive utility, they instead use fear tactics and deception to try to trick you into installing their software. One popular method is to use pop-up browser windows crudely disguised as Windows' own system warnings (Figure 18.18). When clicked, these may trigger a flood of other browser windows, or may even start a file download.

The lesson here is simple—*don't install these programs!* Careful reading of the software's license agreement before you install a program is a good idea, but realistically, it does little to protect your PC. With that in mind, here are a couple of preventive measures you can take to keep parasitic software off of your system.

If you visit a Web site and are prompted to install a third-party application or plug-in that you've never heard of, *don't install it*. Well-known and reputable plug-ins, such as Adobe's *Shockwave* or *Flash*, are safe, but be suspicious of any others. Don't click

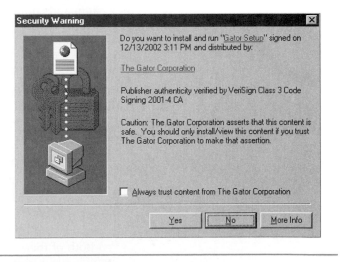

• **Figure 18.17**   Gator Corporation's acknowledgment warning

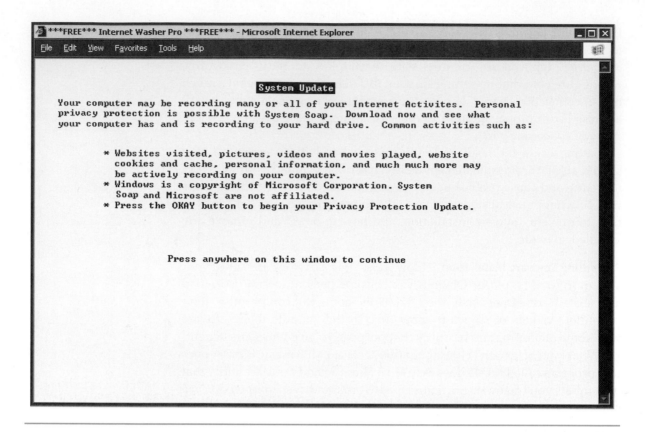

● Figure 18.18   A spyware pop-up browser window, disguised as a Windows alert

anywhere inside of a pop-up browser window, even if it looks just like a Windows alert window or DOS command-line prompt—as I just mentioned, it's probably fake and the Close button is likely a hyperlink. Instead, use other means to close the window, such as pressing ALT-F4 or right-clicking the browser window's icon on the taskbar and selecting Close.

You can also install spyware detection and removal software on your system and run it regularly. Let's look at how to do that.

Removing Spyware   Some spyware makers are reputable enough to include a routine for uninstalling their software. Gator, for instance, makes it fairly easy to get rid of their programs—just use the Windows Add/ Remove Programs applet in the Control Panel. Others, however, aren't quite so cooperative. In fact, because spyware is so—well, *sneaky*—it's entirely possible that your system already has some installed that you don't even know about. How do you find out?

Windows comes with Windows Defender, a fine tool for catching most spyware but it's not perfect. The better solution is to back up Windows Defender with a second spyware removal program. There are several on the market, but two that I highly recommend are Lavasoft's Ad-Aware (Figure 18.19) and PepiMK's Spybot Search & Destroy.

Both of these applications work exactly as advertised. They detect and delete spyware of all sorts—hidden files and folders, cookies, registry keys and values, you name it. Ad-Aware is free for personal use, while Spybot

442

Mike Meyers' CompTIA A+ Guide: PC Technician (Exams 220-602, 220-603, & 220-604)

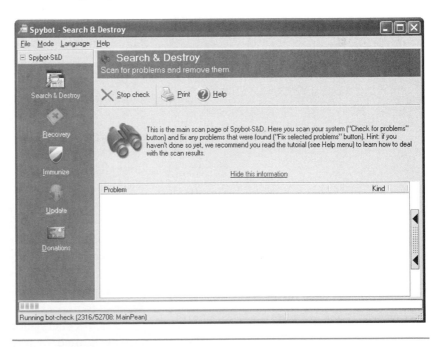

Figure 18.19 Lavasoft's Ad-Aware

Search & Destroy is shareware (Figure 18.20). Many times I've used both programs at the same time because one tends to catch what the other misses.

Grayware

Some programs, called , are not destructive in and of themselves, but they leach bandwidth in networks and can turn a speedy machine into a doddering shell of a modern computer. These programs are called grayware because some people consider them beneficial. They might even be beneficial in the right setting. The primary example of grayware is the highly popular peer-to-peer file-sharing programs, such as Bittorrent. Peer-to-peer file-sharing programs enable a lot of users to upload portions of files on demand so that other users can download them. By splitting the load to many computers, the overall demand on a single computer is light.

The problem is that if you have a tight network with lots of traffic and suddenly you have a bunch of that bandwidth hogged by uploading and downloading files, then your network performance can degrade badly overall. So, is the grayware bad? Only in

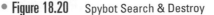

Figure 18.20 Spybot Search & Destroy

Chapter 18: Computer Security

some environments. You need to judge each network or computer according to the situation.

Knowledge is Power

The best way to keep from having to deal with malware and grayware is education. It's your job as the IT person to talk to users, especially the ones whose systems you've just spent the last hour cleaning of nasties, about how to avoid these programs. Show them samples of dangerous e-mails they should not open, Web sites to avoid, and the types of programs they should not install and use on the network. Any user who understands the risks of questionable actions on their computers will usually do the right thing and stay away from malware.

• **Figure 18.21**   Linksys router as a firewall

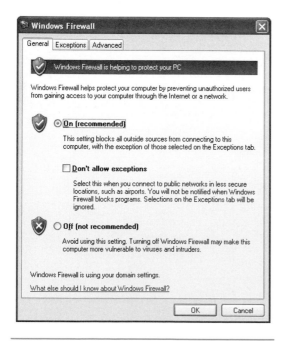

• **Figure 18.22**   Windows Firewall

Firewalls

Firewalls are an essential tool in the fight against malicious programs on the Internet. **Firewalls** are devices or software that protect an internal network from unauthorized access to and from the Internet at large. Hardware firewalls protect networks using a number of methods, such as hiding IP addresses and blocking TCP/IP ports. Most SOHO networks use a hardware firewall, such as the Linksys router in Figure 18.21. These devices do a great job.

Windows XP comes with an excellent software firewall, called the Windows Firewall (Figure 18.22). It can also handle the heavy lifting of port blocking, security logging, and more.

You can access the Windows Firewall by opening the Windows Firewall applet in the Control Panel. If you're running the Control Panel in Category view, click the Security Center icon (Figure 18.23),and then click the Windows Firewall option in the Windows Security Center dialog box. Figure 18.24 illustrates the Exceptions tab on the Windows Firewall, showing the applications allowed to use the TCP/IP ports on my computer.

Encryption

Firewalls do a great job controlling traffic coming into or out of a network from the Internet, but they do nothing to stop interceptor hackers who monitor traffic on the public Internet looking for vulnerabilities. Once a packet is on the Internet itself, anyone with the right equipment can intercept and inspect it. Inspected packets are a cornucopia of passwords, account names, and other tidbits that hackers can use to intrude into your network. Because we can't stop hackers from inspecting these packets, we must turn to **encryption** to make them unreadable.

Network encryption occurs at many different levels and is in no way limited to Internet-based activities. Not only are there many levels of network encryption, but each encryption level provides multiple standards and options, making encryption one of

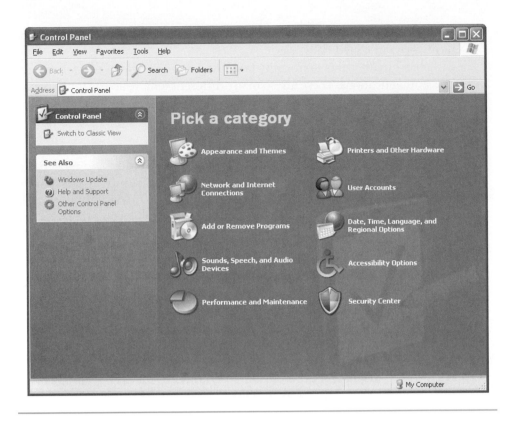

● **Figure 18.23**   Control Panel, Category view

the most complicated of all networking issues. You need to understand where encryption comes into play, what options are available, and what you can use to protect your network.

Network Authentication

Have you ever considered the process that takes place each time a person types in a user name and password to access a network, rather than just a local machine? What happens when this *network* authentication is requested? If you're thinking that when a user types in a user name and password, that information is sent to a server of some sort to be authenticated, you're right—but do you know how the user name and password get to the serving system? That's where encryption becomes important in authentication.

In a local network, encryption is usually handled by the NOS. Because NOS makers usually control software development of both the client and the server, they can create their own proprietary encryptions. However, in today's increasingly interconnected and diverse networking environment, there is a motivation to enable different network operating systems to authenticate any client system from any other NOS. Modern network operating systems such as Windows NT/2000/XP/2003 and NetWare 4.x/5.x/6.x use standard authentication encryptions like MIT's **Kerberos**, enabling multiple brands of servers to authenticate multiple brands

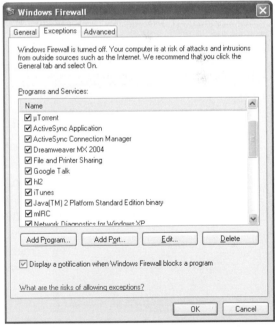

● **Figure 18.24**   Essential programs (doesn't everyone need to run Half-Life 2?)

of clients. These LAN encryptions are usually transparent and work quite nicely even in mixed networks.

Unfortunately, this uniformity falls away as you begin to add remote access authentications. There are so many different remote access tools, based on UNIX/Linux, Novell NetWare, and Windows serving programs, that most remote access systems have to support a variety of different authentication methods.

PAP `Password Authentication Protocol (PAP)` is the oldest and most basic form of authentication. It's also the least safe, because it sends all passwords in clear text. No NOS uses PAP for a client system's login, but almost all network operating systems that provide remote access service will support PAP for backward compatibility with a host of older programs (like Telnet) that only use PAP.

CHAP `Challenge Handshake Authentication Protocol (CHAP)` is the most common remote access protocol. CHAP has the serving system challenge the remote client. A *challenge* is where the host system asks the remote client some secret—usually a password—that the remote client must then respond with for the host to allow the connection.

MS-CHAP `MS-CHAP` is Microsoft's variation of the CHAP protocol. It uses a slightly more advanced encryption protocol.

Configuring Dial-up Encryption

It's the server not the client that controls the choice of dial-up encryption. Microsoft clients can handle a broad selection of authentication encryption methods, including no authentication at all. On the rare occasion when you have to change your client's default encryption settings for a dial-up connection, you'll need to journey deep into the bowels of its properties. Figure 18.25 shows the Windows 2000 dialog box, called Advanced Security Settings, where you configure encryption. The person who controls the server's configuration will tell you which encryption method to select here.

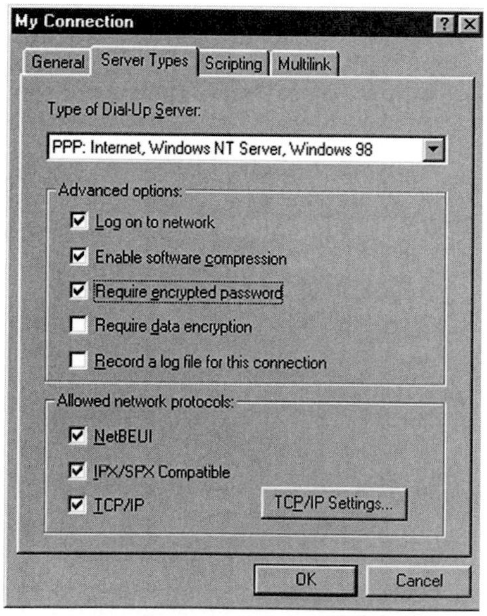

Data Encryption

Encryption methods don't stop at the authentication level. There are a number of ways to encrypt network *data* as well. The choice of encryption method is dictated to a large degree by the method used by the communicating systems to connect. Many networks consist of multiple networks linked together by some sort of private connection, usually some kind of telephone line like ISDN or T1. Microsoft's encryption method of choice for this type of network is called `IPSec` (derived from *IP security*). IPSec provides transparent encryption between the server and the client. IPSec will also work in VPNs, but other encryption methods are more commonly used in those situations.

Application Encryption

When it comes to encryption, even TCP/IP applications can get into the swing of things. The most famous of all application encryptions is Netscape's `Secure Sockets Layer (SSL)` security protocol, which is used

● **Figure 18.25** Setting dial-up encryption in the Windows 2000 Advanced Security Settings dialog box

to create secure Web sites. Microsoft incorporates SSL into its more far-reaching **HTTPS** (HTTP over SSL) protocol. These protocols make it possible to create the secure Web sites used to make purchases over the Internet. HTTPS Web sites can be identified by the *HTTPS://* included in their URL (see Figure 18.26).

To make a secure connection, your Web browser and the Web server must encrypt their data. That means there must be a way for both the Web server and your browser to encrypt and decrypt each other's data. This is done by the server sending a public key to your Web browser so the browser knows how to decrypt the incoming data. These public keys are sent in the form of a **digital certificate**. This certificate not only provides the public key but also is signed by a trusted authority that guarantees the public key you are about to get is actually from the Web server and not from some evil person trying to pretend to be the Web server. There are a number of companies that issue digital certificates to Web sites; probably the most famous is VeriSign, Inc.

Your Web browser has a built-in list of trusted authorities. If a certificate comes in from a Web site that uses one of these highly respected companies, you won't see anything happen in your browser; you'll just go to the secure Web page and a small lock will appear in the corner of your browser. Figure 18.27 shows the list of trusted authorities built into the Firefox Web browser.

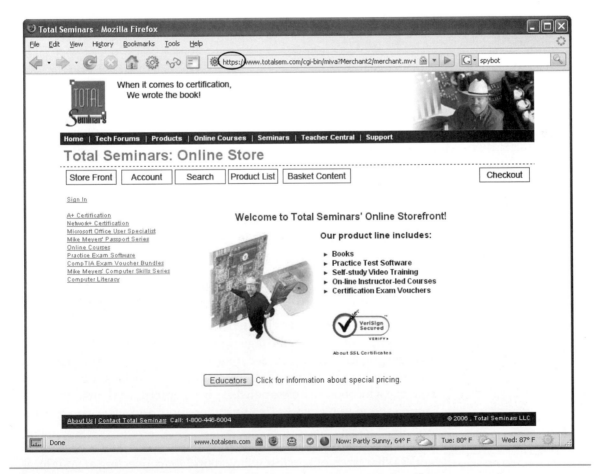

• **Figure 18.26**   A secure Web site

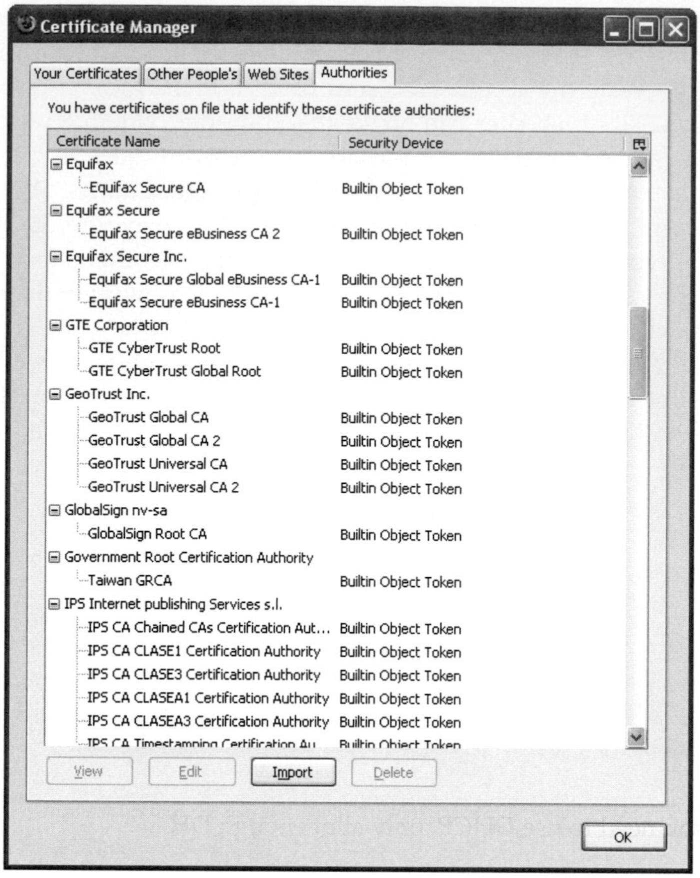

• **Figure 18.27** Trusted authorities

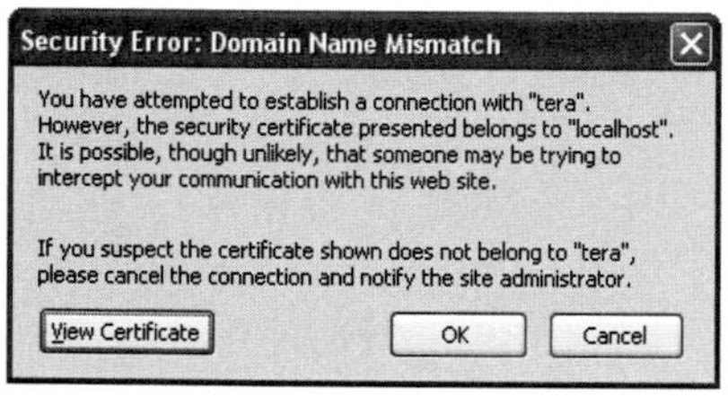

• **Figure 18.28** Incoming certificate

However, if you receive a certificate from someone *not* listed in your browser, the browser will warn you and ask if you wish to accept the certificate, as shown in Figure 18.28.

What you do here is up to you. Do you wish to trust this certificate? In most cases, you simply say yes, and this certificate is added to your SSL cache of certificates. However, there are occasions where an accepted certificate becomes invalid, usually due to something boring, for instance, it goes

---

✓ **Cross Check**

Securing Wireless Networks

Wireless networks are all the rage right now, from your local Starbucks to the neighbors around you. Securing wireless networks has, therefore, become an area that CompTIA A+ certified technicians must master. You read a lot about wireless networks in Chapter 16, "Maintaining and Troubleshooting Networks," so turn there now and see if you can answer these questions.

What is the minimum level of encryption to secure a wireless network? What types of wireless will you find for connecting at your local coffee shop?

out of date or the public key changes. This never happens with the "big name" certificates built into your browser— you'll see this more often when a certificate is used, for example, in-house on a company intranet and the administrator forgets to update their certificates. If a certificate goes bad, your browser issues a warning the next time you visit that site. To clear invalid certificates, you need to clear the SSL cache. The process varies on every browser, but on Internet Explorer, go to the Content tab under Internet Options and click the Clear SSL state button (Figure 18.29).

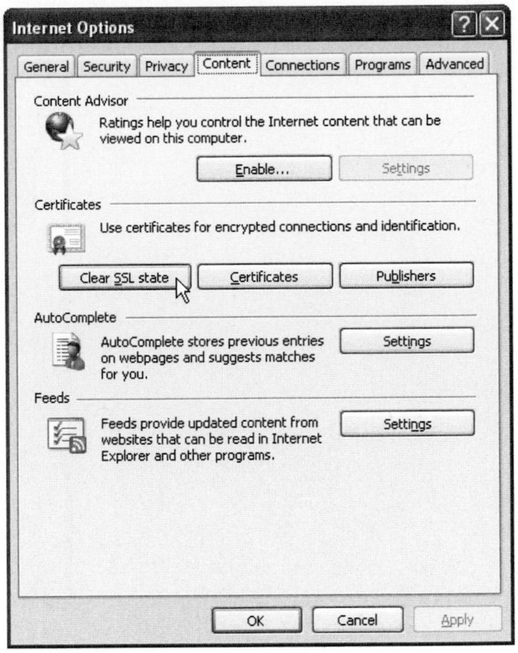

Wireless Issues

Wireless networks add a whole level of additional security headaches for techs to face, as you know from Chapter 16, "Maintaining and Troubleshooting Networks." Some of the points to remember or to go back and look up are as follows:

- Set up wireless encryption—at least WEP, but preferably WPA or the more secure WPA2—and configure clients to use them.

- Disable DHCP and require your wireless clients to use a static IP address.

- If you need to use DHCP, only allot enough DHCP addresses to meet the needs of your network to avoid unused wireless connections.

- Change the WAP's SSID from default and disable SSID broadcast.

- Filter by MAC address to allow only known clients on the network.

- Change the default user name and password. Every hacker has memorized the default user names and passwords.

- Update the firmware as needed.

- If available, make sure the WAP's firewall settings are turned on.

Reporting

As a final weapon in your security arsenal, you need to report any security issues so a network administrator or technician can take steps to make them go away. You can set up two tools within Windows so that the OS reports problems to you: Event Viewer and Auditing. You can then do your work and report those problems. Let's take a look.

Event Viewer

Event Viewer is Window's default tattletale program, spilling the beans about many things that happen on the system. You can find Event Viewer in Administrative Tools in the Control Panel. By default, Event Viewer has three sections, Application, Security, and System, and if you've downloaded Internet Explorer 7, you'll see a fourth option for the browser, Internet Explorer (Figure 18.30). As you'll recall from Chapter 11, the most

• **Figure 18.29**   The Internet Options Content tab

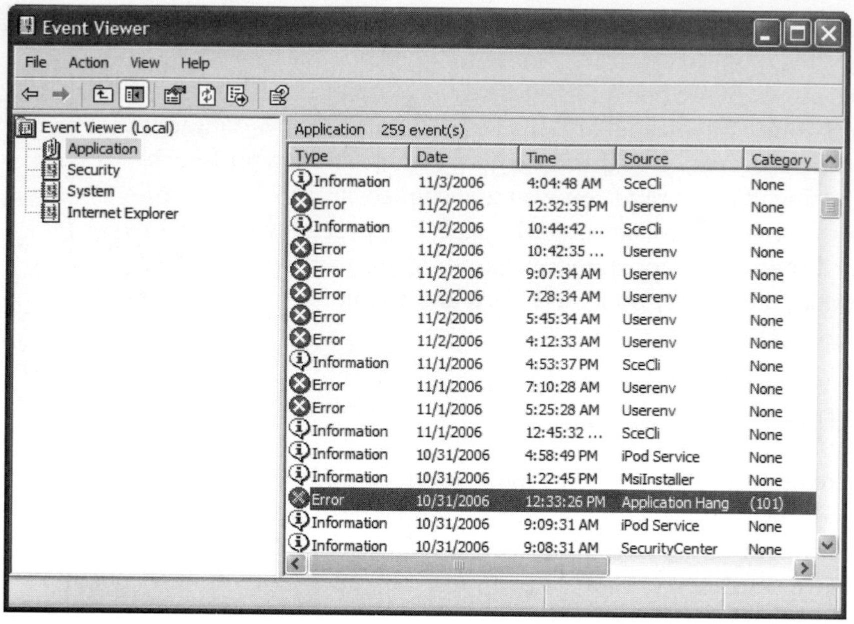

● **Figure 18.30**   Event Viewer

common use for Event Viewer is to view application or system errors for troubleshooting (Figure 18.31).

One very cool feature of Event Viewer is that you can click the link to take you to the online Help and Support Center at Microsoft.com, and the software reports your error (Figure 18.32), checks the online database, and comes back with a more or less useful explanation (Figure 18.33).

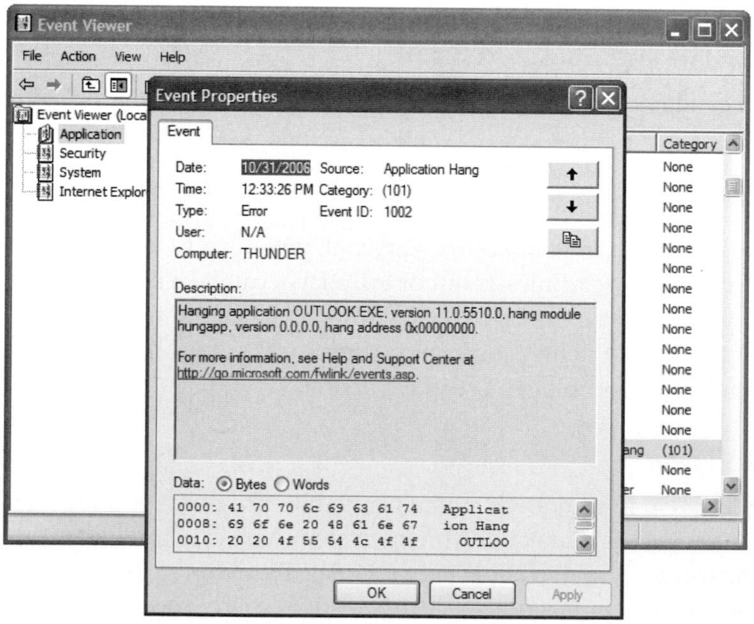

● **Figure 18.31**   Typical application error message

Auditing

The Security section of Event Viewer doesn't show you anything by default. To unlock the full potential of Event Viewer, you need to set up auditing. *Auditing* in the security sense means to tell Windows to create an entry in the Security Log when certain events happen, for example, a user logs on—called **event auditing**—or tries to access a certain file or folder—called **object access auditing**. Figure 18.34 shows Event Viewer tracking logon and logoff events.

The CompTIA A+ certification exams don't test you on creating a brilliant auditing policy for your office—that's what network administrators do. You simply need to know what auditing does and how to turn it on or off so that you can provide support for the network administrators in the field. To turn on auditing at a local level, go to Local Security Settings in Administrative Tools. Select Local Policies and then click Audit Policies. Double-click one of the policy options and select one or both of the

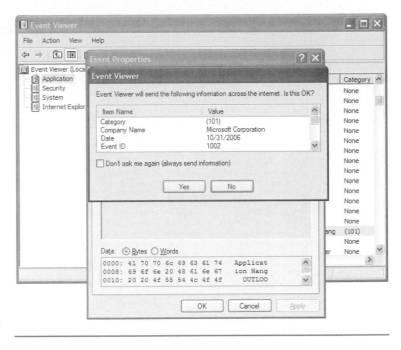

• **Figure 18.32**   Details about to be sent

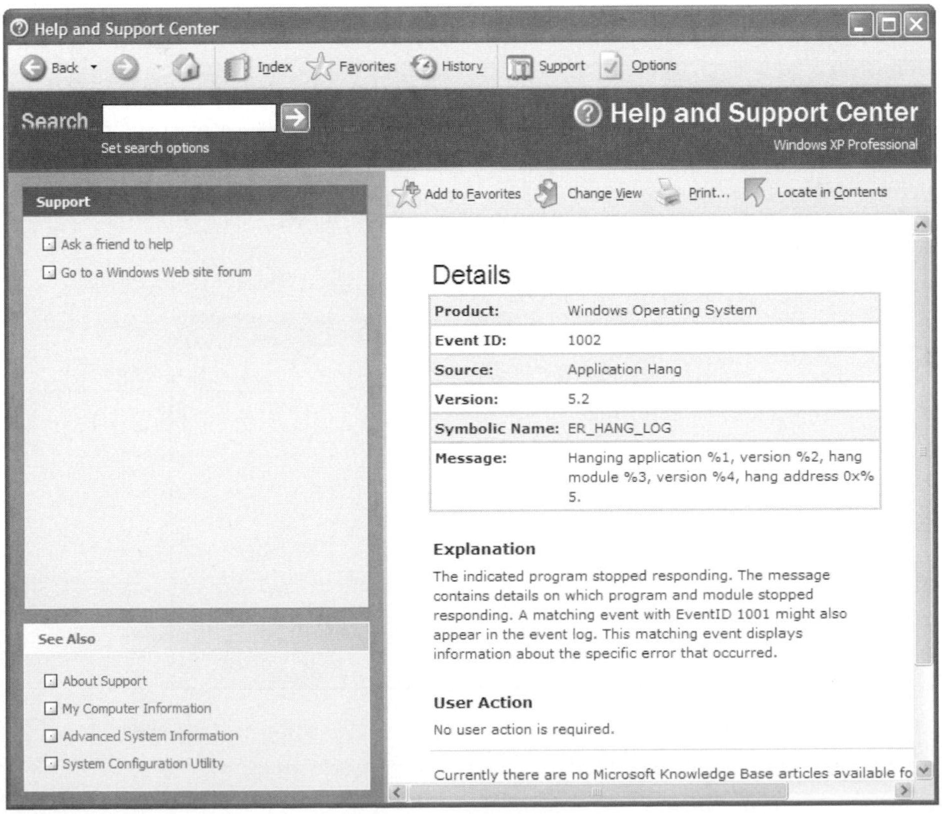

• **Figure 18.33**   Help and Support Center being helpful

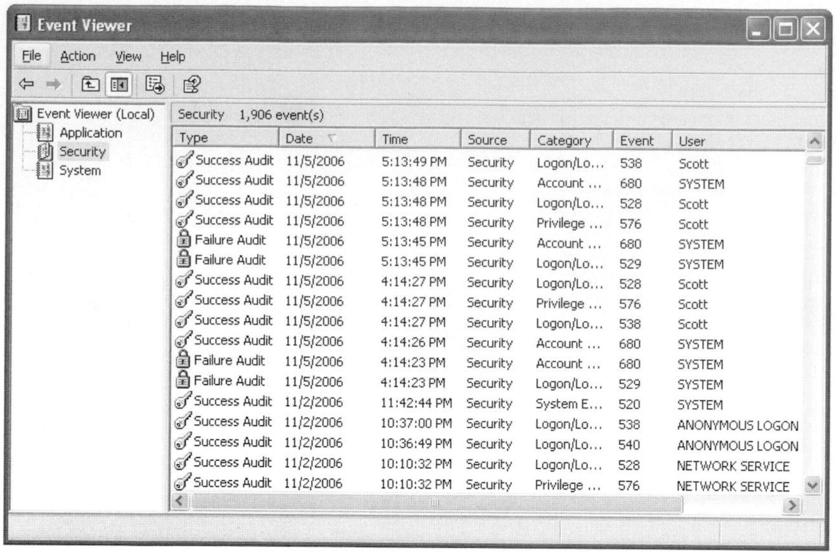

Figure 18.34 shows the Event Viewer displaying security alerts.

Figure 18.34 Event Viewer displaying security alerts

checkboxes. Figure 18.35 shows the Audit object access dialog box.

Incidence Reporting

Once you've gathered data about a particular system or you've dealt with a computer or network problem, you need to complete the mission by telling your supervisor. This is called **incidence reporting**. Many companies have premade forms that you simply fill out and submit. Other places are less formal. Regardless, you need to do this!

Incidence reporting does a couple of things for you. First, it provides a record of work you've done and accomplished. Second, it provides a piece of information that, when combined with other information that you might or might not know, reveals a pattern or bigger problem to someone higher up the chain. A seemingly innocuous security audit report, for example, might match other such events in numerous places in the building at the same time and thus show conscious, coordinated action rather than a glitch was at work.

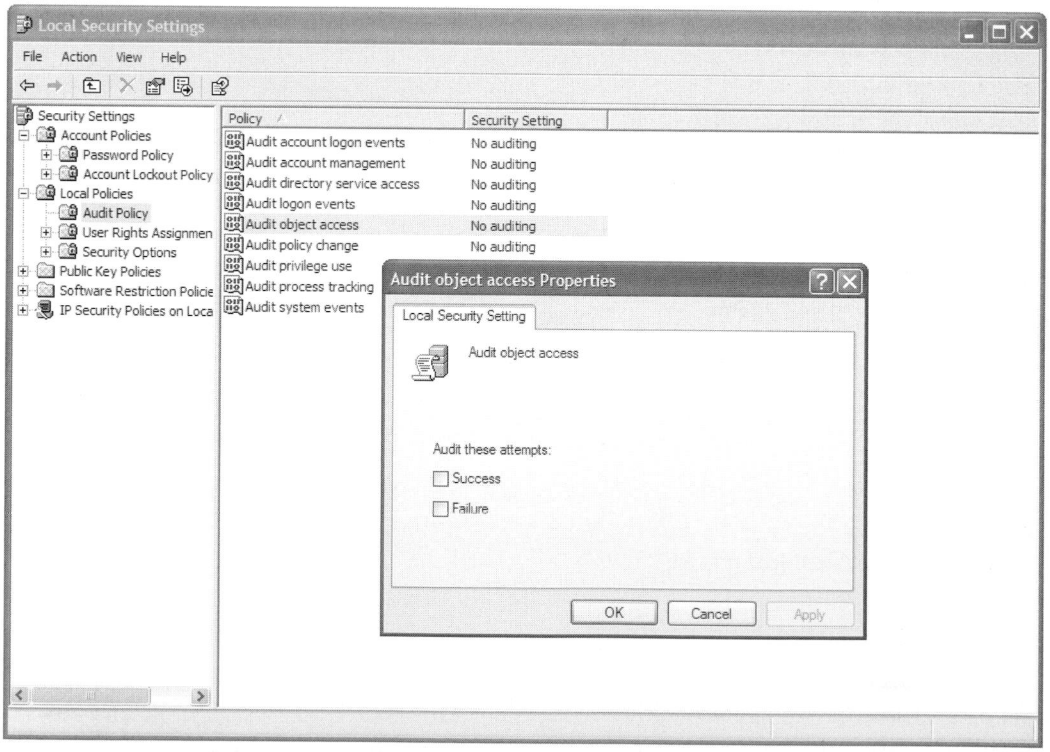

Figure 18.35 Audit object access with the Local Security Settings dialog box open in the background

Mike Meyers' CompTIA A+ Guide: PC Technician (Exams 220-602, 220-603, & 220-604)

Security in Windows Vista

With Windows Vista, Microsoft offers great security features, including tight control over user accounts and actions, a centralized security dialog, and parental controls over content. And these just scratch the surface!

User Account Control

Windows XP made it too easy—and in fact almost necessary—to make your primary account on a computer an Administrator account. Because Limited Users can't do common tasks such as run certain programs, install applications, update applications, update Windows, and so on, most users simply created an Administrator-level account and logged in. Because such accounts have full control over the computer, malware that slipped in with that account could do a lot more harm.

Microsoft addressed this problem with the *User Account Control (UAC)*. This feature enables standard users to do common tasks and provides a permissions dialog (Figure 18.36) when standard users *and* administrators do certain things that could potentially harm the computer (such as attempt to install a program). Vista user accounts now function much more like user accounts in Linux and Mac OS X.

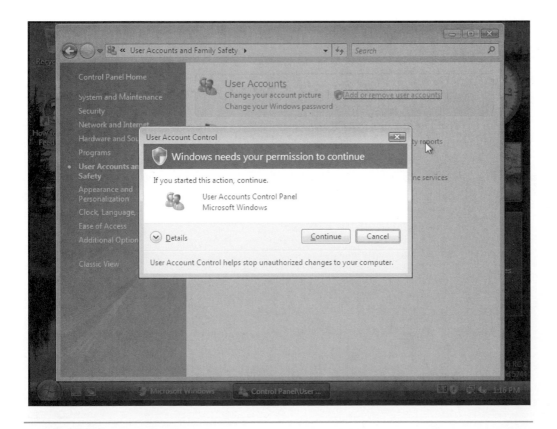

• **Figure 18.36**   Prompting for permission

Security Center

Microsoft has buffed up the *Windows Security Center (WSC)* for Windows Vista to provide a one-stop shop for users to get information about critical security issues (Figure 18.37). First introduced with Windows XP SP2, WSC provides information about whether or not the Windows Firewall, Automatic Updates, and an antivirus program are turned on. That's just a start; the WSC in Vista goes beyond to monitor other malware solutions, such as the spyware- and adware-crushing Windows Defender. The WSC shows Internet security settings and the status of UAC. It even shows third-party security solutions installed, monitors whether they're engaged, and provides an Update Now button so you can download the latest updates to their signatures.

Parental Controls

With Parental Controls, you can monitor and limit the activities of any Standard User in Windows Vista, a feature that gives parents and managers an excellent level of control over the content their children and employees can access (Figure 18.38). Activity Reporting logs applications run or attempted to run, Web sites visited or attempted to visit, any kind of files downloaded, and more. You can block various Web sites by type or specific URL, or you can allow only certain Web sites, a far more powerful option.

Parental Controls enable you to limit the time that Standard Users can spend logged in. You can specify acceptable and unacceptable times of day

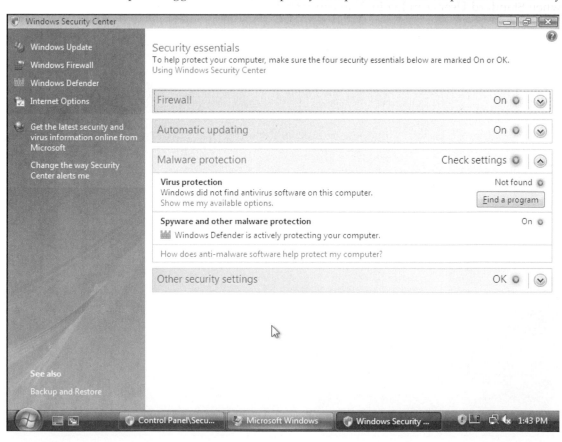

• **Figure 18.37**   Windows Security Center in Vista

Mike Meyers' CompTIA A+ Guide: PC Technician (Exams 220-602, 220-603, & 220-604)

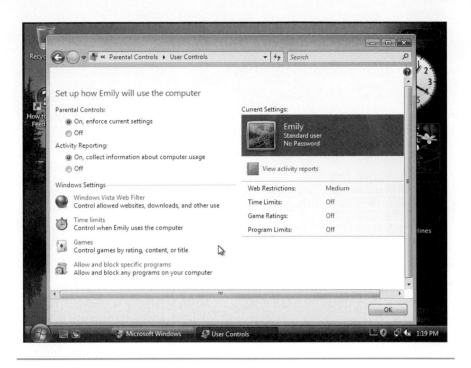

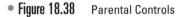
Figure 18.38 Parental Controls

when Standard Users can log in. You can restrict access to types of games and specific applications. For example, if you like playing rather gruesome games filled with monsters and blood that you don't want your kids to play, you can simply block any games with certain ESRB ratings, such as T for teen.

Other Security Features

Vista offers many other security features that you may or may not encounter, such as improved hard drive encryption. In a corporate environment, you might run into Vista machines that completely block USB thumb drives. Underneath all these security features runs an OS that protects essential system files with far greater robustness than Windows XP or Windows 2000.

Chapter 18 Review

■ Chapter Summary

After reading this chapter and completing the exercises, you should understand the following about computer security.

Analyzing the Threat

■ Threats to your data come from two sources: accidents and malicious people.

■ Unauthorized access occurs when a user accesses resources in an unauthorized way. Not all unauthorized access is malicious, and some is even accidental. Authorized access can lead to data destruction by users who do not intend to be malicious. When users have access to a file or database, they typically believe the system won't let them make any changes they are not authorized to make.

■ Windows XP Home has only two types of user accounts: administrative and limited. If you need to control access, you are better off using Windows XP Professional or Windows 2000.

■ Computers, hard drives, and power all fail. As a tech, you need to plan for redundancy in these areas. You also need to protect your computers against viruses distributed through the network and removable media. You should back up data, make sure retired hard drives and optical discs don't have sensitive data, implement good access policies, and implement methods for tracking computer usage.

Local Control

■ In addition to backing up everyone's Document and Settings folders, make sure to back up files users have stored outside their Documents and Settings folder. In server environments, be sure to back up the System State data, which includes portions of the Registry, security settings, desktop files and folders, and the default user. Backups should be stored off-site.

■ When retiring a system and migrating the data to a new machine, three principles should be followed:

migrate user and data information in a secure environment, remove data from hard drives that will be stored or donated, and recycle old equipment rather than throwing it in the trash.

■ To migrate data securely, supervise the file copy rather than setting it to run unattended. Use a disc-wiping utility to remove remnants and make old data virtually impossible to recover. Lastly, your new system is not considered secure until all passwords are in place.

■ Be environmentally responsible: recycle products such as paper and printer cartridges. Some hardware, such as a computer monitor, contains toxic or hazardous materials. Donate these items to an organization that will use them, or contact a company that specializes in the disposal of hazardous materials or computer components.

■ Most computer attacks are accomplished through social engineering rather than hacking. Telephone scams are one of the most common social engineering tactics. Dumpster driving involves physically going through an organization's trash looking for documents that might reveal user names, passwords, or other sensitive information. Be sure to secure your computer equipment in a locked room to prevent physical theft.

■ Controlling access to programs, data, and other computing resources is the key to securing your system. Access control includes five interlinked areas: physical security, authentication, file system, users and groups, and security policies.

■ Store computers with sensitive data in a locked room, and never walk away from your computer while logged in. Log out, or lock the computer by pressing CTRL-L.

■ For software authentication, every user account should have a password to protect against unauthorized access. Additionally, CMOS setup should have a password for any computer in a public place.

- For hardware authentication, try smart cards or biometric devices. Smart cards are the size of credit cards and contain circuitry that can be used to identify the card holder. Biometric devices identify users by physical characteristics such as fingerprints or retinal scans. Some smart cards use radio frequency identification to transmit authentication information, so users don't have to insert something into a computer or card reader.

- All hard drives should be formatted with NTFS, not FAT32. Use the CONVERT command-line utility to convert a drive from FAT to NTFS without losing data.

- Windows controls access with user accounts and groups. Users are assigned user accounts, user accounts are assigned to a group or groups, and groups are granted permission to resources. Using NTFS enables the highest level of control over local data resources.

Network Security

- Accounts should be given permissions to access only what they need, no more. Unused accounts should be disabled.

- When a user account is a member of several groups, and permissions have been granted to groups, the user account will have a set of combined permissions that may conflict. The resulting permissions that ultimately control access are referred to as the effective permissions.

- Make sure to lock down the default Everyone group, as all users are automatically members of this group. Windows 2000 gives full control to the Everyone group by default. Never use the default Everyone or Users groups or the default Guest account unless you intend to permit all those accounts access to resources.

- Policies control permissions for activities, such as installing software, access to a command prompt, or time of day a user can log on. A policy is usually applied to a user account, computer account, or a group. Use the Local Security Settings tool to manage policies for an individual computer.

- Group Policy enables you to control such things as setting each computer in a domain to use the same wallpaper or deploy software. Commonly used policies include Prevent Registry Edits, Prevent Access to the Command Prompt, Log On Locally, and Minimum Password Length.

- Malware includes viruses, worms, Trojan horses, adware, and grayware—all of which can wreak havoc on your system.

- A virus is a piece of malicious software that gets passed from computer to computer and is designed to attach itself to another program on your computer. Trojans are freestanding programs that do something other than what the user expects it to do when run, such as expecting a game to run but erasing CMOS Settings instead. A worm is a freestanding program that takes advantage of security flaws and copies itself over and over again, thereby bogging down a network.

- To help protect a computer from malware, make sure to run up-to-date antivirus software, use a firewall, and apply all security patches for your software and operating system. Run Windows Update automatically, or at least weekly if you choose to configure it for manual updates.

- Antivirus software works in active mode to scan your file system for viruses and in passive mode by monitoring your computer's activity and checking for viruses in response to an action, such as running a program or downloading a file. Antivirus software detects boot-sector viruses by comparing the drive's boot sector to a standard boot sector. To detect executable viruses, a library of virus signatures is used. Macro viruses are detected through virus signatures or the presence of certain macro commands that are known macro viruses.

- Polymorph viruses attempt to change their signature to prevent detection by antivirus software. Fortunately, the scrambled code itself can be used as a signature. A checksum, based on file contents, can be created for every file on the drive. If the checksum changes, it is a sign of a virus infection. Most stealth viruses are boot sector viruses that hide from antivirus software.

- The best way to prevent damage from a virus is to keep from getting a virus in the first place. Use your passive antivirus shield, scan the PC daily, know where software has come from before you load it, and keep your antivirus definitions updated. Don't view e-mail messages in a preview pane, and only download files from sites you know to be safe.

- Unsolicited e-mail is called spam. Never post your e-mail address on the Internet, as over 97 percent of spam comes from e-mail addresses posted online. Spam filters can block spam at the mail server or at your computer. You can set most e-mail programs to block e-mail sent from specific people or to a specific person.

- Irritating Web browser problems include pop-ups, spyware, and adware. Many pop-ups remove the navigation aids from the browser window or mimic Windows dialog boxes. To safely close a pop-up, right-click the pop-up's Taskbar icon and choose Close, or press ALT-TAB until the pop-up window is active, and then press ALT-F4 to close it.

- Spyware can use your computer's resources to run distributed computing applications, capture keystrokes to steal passwords, or worse. Spyware typically disguises itself as useful utilities, so be vigilant about what you install. Some spyware can be removed via Add/Remove Programs, but for stubborn spyware use a third-party tool such as Lavasoft's Ad-Aware or PepiMK's Spybot Search & Destroy.

- Grayware leaches network bandwidth, although some consider the programs beneficial. Peer-to-peer file-sharing programs that enable a lot of users to upload portions of files on demand might seem useful to someone, but these programs can eat up a significant portion of the network bandwidth, causing other users or programs to respond slowly to network or Internet applications.

- Hardware firewalls protect networks by hiding IP addresses and blocking TCP/IP ports. Windows XP comes with a built-in software firewall that is accessible from the Control Panel Security Center applet.

- Encryption makes network packets unreadable by hackers who intercept network traffic. You are especially vulnerable when using the Internet over a public network. Modern operating systems use Kerberos to encrypt authentication credentials over a local network.

- PAP sends passwords in clear text, so it is not very safe. CHAP is the most common remote access protocol, in which the serving system challenges the remote system with a secret, like a password. MS-CHAP is Microsoft's version of CHAP and uses a more advanced encryption protocol.

- Network data can be encrypted similar to authentication credentials. Microsoft's encryption method of choice is called IPSec. Netscape's Secure Sockets Layer (SSL) creates secure Web sites. Microsoft's HTTPS protocol incorporates SSL into HTTP. Web sites whose URL begins with HTTPS:// are used to encrypt credit card purchases.

- To secure a wireless network, use wireless encryption and disable DHCP. Require wireless clients to use a static IP address or allot only enough DHCP addresses to meet the needs of your network. Definitely change the default administrator user name and password on the WAP.

- Use Event Viewer to track activity on your system. Event Viewer offers three sections: Application, Security, and System. The Security section doesn't show you everything by default, so it is good practice to enable event auditing and object auditing. Event auditing creates an entry in the Security Log when certain events happen, like a user logging on. Object Auditing creates entries in response to object access, like someone trying to access a certain file or folder.

- Incidence reporting means telling your supervisor about the data you've gathered regarding a computer or network problem. This provides a record of what you've done and accomplished. It also provides information that, when combined with other information you may or may not know, may reveal a pattern or bigger problem to someone higher up the chain.

■ Key Terms

access control *(428)*
Active Directory *(424)*
adware *(440)*
antivirus program *(436)*
authentication *(429)*
biometric devices *(430)*
Challenge Handshake
   Authentication Protocol
   (CHAP) *(446)*
CONVERT *(430)*
definition file *(438)*
digital certificate *(447)*
dumpster diving *(428)*
effective permissions *(432)*
encryption *(444)*
event auditing *(451)*
Event Viewer *(449)*

firewall *(444)*
grayware *(443)*
Group Policy *(433)*
HTTPS *(447)*
incidence reporting *(452)*
IPSec *(446)*
Kerberos *(445)*
Local Security Settings *(433)*
migration *(425)*
MS-CHAP *(446)*
object access auditing *(451)*
off-site storage *(424)*
Password Authentication Protocol
   (PAP) *(446)*
polymorph virus *(438)*
pop-up *(440)*

remnants *(426)*
Secure Sockets Layer (SSL) *(446)*
signature *(437)*
smart card *(429)*
social engineering *(427)*
spam *(439)*
spyware *(440)*
stealth virus *(438)*
System State data *(424)*
telephone scams *(427)*
Trojan *(436)*
unauthorized access *(421)*
virus *(435)*
virus shield *(436)*
worm *(436)*

■ Key Term Quiz

Use the Key Terms list to complete the sentences that follow. Not all terms will be used.

1. Use the _____ command-line tool to convert a FAT drive to NTFS without losing data.

2. A(n) _____ masquerades as a legitimate program, yet does something different than what is expected when executed.

3. Antivirus software uses an updatable _____ to identify viruses by their _____.

4. Enable _____ to create Event Viewer entries when a specific file is accessed.

5. Not all _____ is malicious, but it can lead to data destruction.

6. Most attacks on computer data are accomplished through _____.

7. A(n) _____ protects against unauthorized access from the Internet.

8. _____ is the most common remote authentication protocol.

9. Before making a credit card purchase on the Internet, be sure the Web site uses the _____ security protocol, which can be verified by checking for the _____ protocol in the address bar.

10. A(n) _____ changes its signature to prevent detection.

■ Multiple-Choice Quiz

1. Which of the following would you select if you need to back up an Active Directory server?

   A. Registry

   B. System State data

   C. My Computer

   D. My Server

2. Johan migrated his server data to a bigger, faster hard drive. At the end of the process, he partitioned and formatted the older hard drive before removing it to donate to charity. How secure is his company's data?

   A. Completely secured. The drive is blank after partitioning and formatting.

   B. Mostly secured. Only super-skilled professionals have the tools to recover data after partitioning and formatting.

   C. Very unsecured. Simple software tools can recover a lot of data, even after partitioning and formatting.

   D. Completely unsecured. The data on the drive will show up in the Recycle Bin as soon as someone installs it into a system.

3. What is the process of using or manipulating people to gain access to network resources?

   A. Cracking

   B. Hacking

   C. Network engineering

   D. Social engineering

4. Which of the following might offer good hardware authentication?

   A. Strong password

   B. Encrypted password

   C. NTFS

   D. Smart card

5. Randall needs to change the file system on his second hard drive (currently the D: drive) from FAT32 to NTFS. Which of the following commands would do the trick?

   A. CONVERT D: /FS:NTFS

   B. CONVERT D: NTFS

   C. NTFS D:

   D. NTFS D: /FAT32

6. Which of the following tools would enable you to stop a user from logging on to a local machine, but still enable him to log on to the domain?

   A. AD Policy

   B. Group Policy

   C. Local Security Settings

   D. User Settings

7. Which type of encryption offers the most security?

   A. MS-CHAP

   B. PAP

   C. POP3

   D. SMTP

8. Zander downloaded a game off the Internet and installed it, but as soon as he started to play, he got a Blue Screen of Death. Upon rebooting, he discovered that his My Documents folder had been erased. What happened?

   A. He installed spyware.

   B. He installed a Trojan.

   C. He broke the Group Policy.

   D. He broke the Local Security Settings.

9. Which of the following should Mary set up on her Wi-Fi router to make it the most secure?

   A. NTFS

   B. WEP

   C. WPA

   D. WPA2

10. A few of your fellow techs are arguing about backup policies for a new network server. Who is right?

    A. Andalyn recommends backing up data to a removable hard drive and then storing the hard drive off-site.

    B. Bart recommends backing up data to a removable hard drive, storing it in the server room so it is easily accessible and restorations can get started quickly.

    C. Carthic recommends backing up files across the network to another computer to save money on additional media.

    D. Dianthus recommends backing up files to another hard drive in the server to keep everything self-contained.

11. What single folder on a standalone PC can be backed up to secure all users' My Documents folders?

    A. All Users folder

    B. Documents and Settings folder

    C. System32 folder

    D. Windows folder

12. A user account is a member of several groups, and the groups have conflicting rights and permissions to several network resources. The culminating permissions that ultimately affect the user's access are referred to as what?

   A. Effective permissions

   B. Culminating rights

   C. Last rights

   D. Persistent permissions

13. What is true about virus shields?

   A. They automatically scan e-mails, downloads, and running programs.

   B. They protect against spyware and adware.

   C. They are effective in stopping pop-ups.

   D. They can reduce the amount of spam by 97 percent.

14. What does Windows use to encrypt the user authentication process over a LAN?

   A. PAP

   B. MS-CHAP

   C. HTTPS

   D. Kerberos

15. Which threats are categorized as social engineering? Choose all that apply.

   A. Telephone scams

   B. Dumpster diving

   C. Trojans

   D. Spyware

▪ Essay Quiz

1. Your boss is considering getting an Internet connection for the office so employees can have access to e-mail, but she is concerned about hackers getting into the company server. What can you tell your boss about safeguards you will implement to keep the server safe?

2. A coworker complains that he is receiving a high amount of spam on his home computer through his personal e-mail account. What advice can you give him to alleviate his junk mail?

3. An intern in your IT department has asked for your help in understanding the differences between a virus, worm, and Trojan horse. What advice can you offer?

4. The boss's assistant has been asked to purchase a new coffee machine for the break room, but is nervous about shopping online with the company credit card. What can you tell her about secure online purchases?

5. You've been tasked to upgrade five computers in your office, replacing hard drives and video cards. Write a short essay describing the steps you'll need to take to migrate the users, secure the company data, and dispose of the excess hardware.

Lab Projects

• Lab Project 18.1

You have learned a little bit about the local security policy in Windows. Fire up your Web browser and do a search for local security policy. Make a list of at least five changes you might consider making to your personal computer using the Local Security Settings tool. Be sure to include what the policy is, what it does, and where in the tool it can be configured.

• Lab Project 18.2

You know you must run antivirus and antispyware software on any computer connected to the Internet, and there are many companies that will sell you good, bad, and indifferent software. Using the Internet, find a free antivirus and free antispyware program. Make sure that these are legitimate and reputable programs, not spyware masquerading as legitimate programs! What free antivirus did you find? What free antispyware did you find? How do you know these are reputable? Would you install these on your own personal computer? Why or why not?

The Complete PC Tech

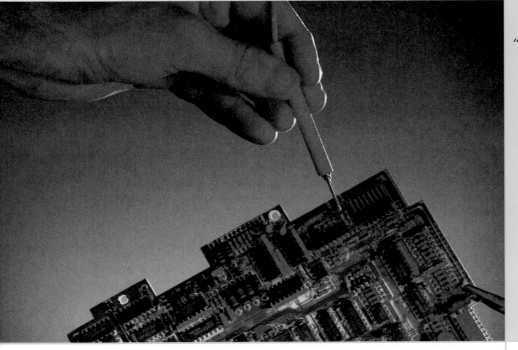

When a mission-critical computer goes down, regardless of the industry, people get upset. Workers can't work, so they feel guilty. Employers can't get product out on time, so they feel anxious. Supervisors blame employees for fouling things up, or at least the employees fear such blame, even if they did not break the machine.

Into this charged atmosphere comes the tech, ready to fix the computer and move on to the next challenge. Accomplishing this task, however, requires three things: First, a good tech must know the broken machine inside and out—how it's *supposed* to work when working properly. Second, the tech has to calm the workers and supervisors, and get answers to questions to gain relevant information about the problem. Third, the tech must troubleshoot the problem and fix the machine.

This chapter starts with an overview of how computers work and then dives into a section on dealing with customers and how to get them to tell you what you need to know and smile about it. The chapter wraps up with a proven troubleshooting methodology to help you figure out the source of problems and point you to the fix quickly.

In this chapter, you will learn how to

- **Describe how computers work**
- **Explain the nuances of dealing with customers**
- **Implement a troubleshooting methodology**

IT Technician

■ How Computers Work

You've spent a lot of time going through this book, reading about technologies and components in great detail. Each chapter contained information and methodologies for the components contained in that chapter. With each chapter, you added more and more information about the pieces that make up the personal computer today.

In this chapter, I want you to distill that knowledge, to think about the computer as a coherent machine. Each of the computer's components works together to enable people to produce some amazing things.

To master the art of troubleshooting as a PC tech, you need to approach a technical problem and answer one question: "What can it be? What can be causing this problem?" (Okay, that was two questions, but you get the idea.) Because every process involves multiple components, you must understand the interconnectedness of those components. If Jane can't print, for example, what could it be? Connectivity? Drivers? Paper jam? Slow network connection? Frozen application? Solar flares? Let's look at the process.

Computing Process

When you run a program, your computer goes through three of the four stages of the **computing process**: input, processing, and output (Figure 19.1). Input requires specific devices, such as the keyboard and mouse, that enable you to tell the computer to do something, such as open a program or type a word. The operating system (OS) provides an interface and tools so that the microprocessor and other chips can process your request. The image on the monitor or sound from the speakers effectively tell you that the computer has interpreted your command and spit out the result. The fourth stage, storage, comes into play when you want to save a document and when you first open programs and other files.

Making this process work, though, requires the complex interaction of many components, including multiple pieces of hardware and layers of software. As a tech, you need to understand all the components and how they work together so when something doesn't work right, you can

● **Figure 19.1** Input, processing, and output

☑ **Cross Check**

Printing Process

You learned all about the printing process in Chapter 15, "Maintaining and Troubleshooting Printers," but now think in terms of the computing process. Does the computing process translate when applied to printers? How? If a user can't print, how does knowledge of the computing process help you troubleshoot the printing process?

track down the source and fix it. A look at a modern program reveals that even a relatively simple-seeming action or change on the screen requires many things to happen within the computer.

Games such as Second Life (Figure 19.2) are huge, taking up multiple gigabytes of space on an Internet server. They simply won't fit into the RAM in most computers, so developers have figured out ways to minimize RAM usage.

In Second Life, for example, you move through the online world in a series of more or less seamlessly connected areas. Crossing a bridge from one island to another triggers the game to update the information you're about to see on the new island quickly, so you won't be out of the action and the illusion of being in the game world remains intact. Here's what happens when you press the W key on your keyboard and your character steps across the invisible zone line.

The keyboard controller reads the grid of your keyboard and, on discovering your input, sends the information to the CPU through the wires of the motherboard (Figure 19.3). The CPU understands the keyboard

Second Life is a massively multiplayer online role-playing game (MMORPG) that offers a unique twist on the genre. You can create just about anything you can imagine, as far as your time and talent can take you. Second Life has a functioning economy that spills out into the real world, meaning you can buy and sell things within the game and turn that into real US dollars, although the more common scenario is to spend real money to get virtual possessions.

• **Figure 19.2** Second Life

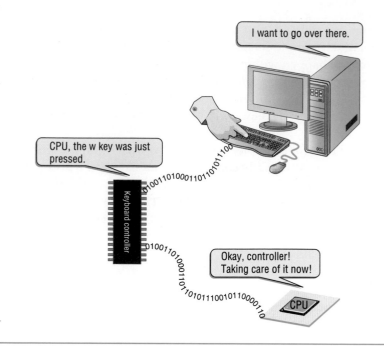

● **Figure 19.3**   Keyboard to CPU

controller because of a small program it loaded into RAM from the system BIOS stored on the system ROM chip on the motherboard when you first booted the computer.

The CPU and the application determine what should happen in the game, and on discovering that your character is about to cross the zone line, they trigger a whole series of actions. The application sends the signal to the OS that it needs a specific area loaded into RAM. The OS sends a signal to the CPU that it needs data stored on the hard drive plus information stored on the Second Life servers. The CPU then sends the commands to the hard drive controller for it to grab the proper stored data and send it to RAM, while at the same time sending a command to the NIC to download the updated information (Figure 19.4).

The hard drive controller tells the hard drive to cough up the data—megabytes worth—and then sends that data through the motherboard to the memory controller, which puts it into RAM and communicates with the CPU when it's finished. The network card and network operating system communicate with the Second Life servers and download the necessary updated information. The CPU then uses the application and OS to process the new data, sending video data to the video card and sound data to the sound card, again through the wires on the motherboard (Figure 19.5).

 Cross Check

Hard Drive Technologies

You learned about several different hard drive technologies way back in Chapter 8, so turn there now and see if you can answer these questions. If an application stumbles or hesitates on the "load from the hard drive" section of the computing process, what could be the problem? Which hard drive technology offers better throughput than other common technologies? What would you recommend to a client who wanted to upgrade?

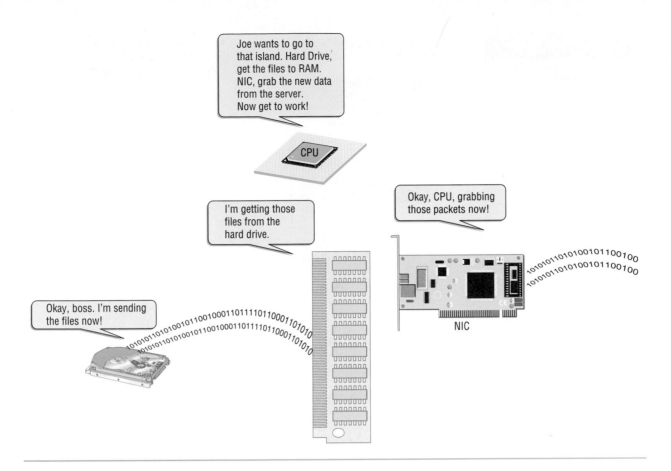

● **Figure 19.4**   CPU to hard drive and NIC

The video card processor puts the incoming data into its RAM, processes the data, and then sends out commands to the monitor to update the screen. The sound card processor likewise processes the data and sends out commands to the speakers to play a new sound (Figure 19.6).

For all of this to work, the PC has to have electricity, so the direct current (DC) provided by the power supply and the alternating current (AC) provided to the power supply must both be the proper voltage and amperage.

Finally, because Second Life is a network application, the OS has to send information through the NIC and onto the Internet to update everyone else's computer. That way, the other characters in the game world see you move forward a step (Figure 19.7).

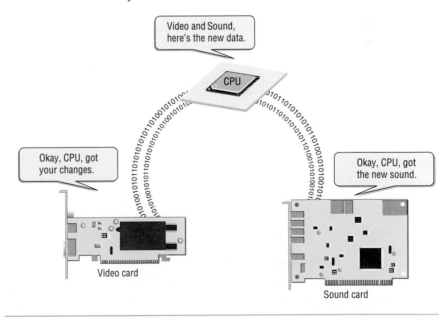

● **Figure 19.5**   CPU to video card and sound card

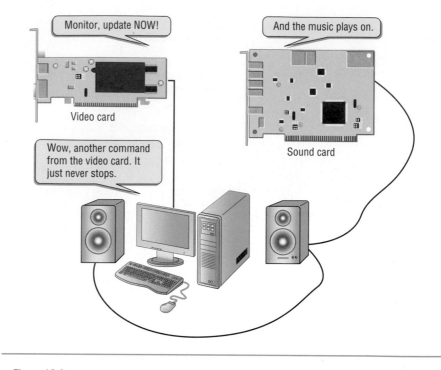

• **Figure 19.6** Updating the screen and speakers

What do you see or hear with all these electrons zipping all over the place? Out of a seemingly blank vista (Figure 19.8), a castle begins to appear, building itself piece by piece as your computer processes the new information and updates the video screen. You hear music begin to play from

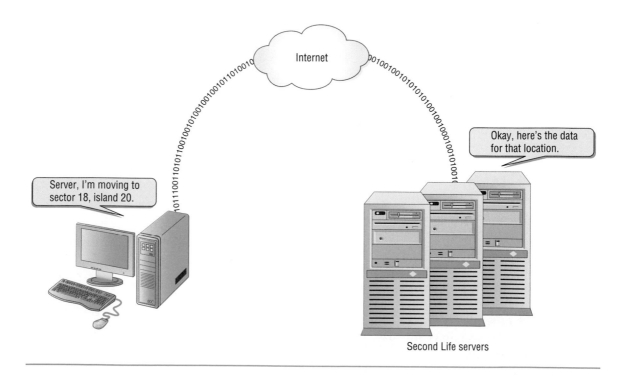

• **Figure 19.7** PC to Second Life servers

Mike Meyers' CompTIA A+ Guide: PC Technician (Exams 220-602, 220-603, & 220-604)

● **Figure 19.8**   New area loading

your speakers. Within a few seconds, with the data describing the new island fully downloaded and processed, the world on your monitor looks very different (Figure 19.9). That's when all goes well. Many megabytes of data have flowed from your hard drive and across the Internet, been processed by multiple processors, and sent to the monitor and the speakers.

To keep the action continuous and unbroken, Second Life, like many current online games, uses a process of continuous or **stream loading**: your computer constantly downloads updated information and data from the Second Life servers, so the world you see changes with every step you take. When done right, stream loading can do some amazing things. In the GameCube game Zelda, for example, the game anticipates where you will go next and loads that new area into RAM before you take the step. You can be in one area and use a telescope to zoom in on another fully developed area (Figure 19.10), making the experience amazingly seamless, just like real life.

● **Figure 19.9** Castle completed

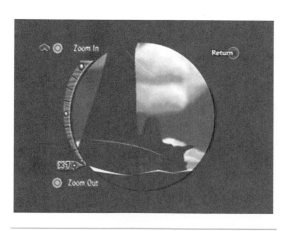

● **Figure 19.10** Zelda zoomed

Troubleshooting

Good techs understand the components involved in inputting, processing, and outputting data, including the devices that store data, such as hard drives. That's because if something doesn't work properly, you can start answering the ultimate trouble-shooting question—what can it be?—accurately. If your screen freezes or the sound goes wonky, where in the process is the problem located?

As you go into any troubleshooting scenario, always keep the computing process in mind. This helps you sort through possibil-ities quickly and accurately. If you know all the stages, you won't miss a simple step, such as figuring out that a user can't print be-cause the cleaning service accidentally turned off the print server the night before, or waste time reinstalling printer drivers when the real issue is a stalled print job in the print queue.

Analyze Your Apps

What applications do you use on your computer? What applications do your clients or potential clients use? Analyzing them in terms of the computing process can help elevate your troubleshooting game by a huge factor. Take for example Microsoft Excel, a program designed to let you take numbers and turn them into charts, among other things. When you sit down to work in Excel, you load it from the hard drive into memory; then you input information via the keyboard and columns with the mouse. Every click requires the CPU to analyze and update RAM and the video card information.

■ Dealing with Customers

When you deal with users, managers, and owners who are frustrated and upset because a computer or network is down and they can't work, your job requires you to take on the roles of detective and psychologist. It takes skill to talk with frazzled and confused people and get answers to questions about how the PC got into the state it's in. It's important to be able to communicate clearly and effectively. Plus, you need to follow the rules of tech-person decorum, acting with personal integrity and respect for the customer. Finally, use assertive communication to empathize with and educate the user. Great techs spend the time needed to develop these essential skills.

This entire chapter applies to Essentials, IT Technician, and Help Desk Technician exams. Expect one out of every five questions on the 220-603 exam to be on communication and professionalism, so you have to know this stuff!

Eliciting Answers

Your job as a tech is to get the computer fixed, and the best way to start that process is to determine what the computer is doing or not doing. You must start by talking to the customer. Allow the customer to explain the problem fully while you record the information. Once the person has described the situation, you must then ask questions. This process is called **eliciting answers**.

Although each person is different, most users with a malfunctioning computer or peripheral will be afraid and often defensive about the problem. To overcome this initial attitude, you need to ask the right questions *and* listen to the customer's answers. Then ask the proper follow-up questions.

Always avoid accusatory questions because they won't help you in the least. "What did you do?" generally gets a confused or defensive "Nothing" in reply, which doesn't get you closer to solving the problem. First, ask questions that help clarify the situation. Repeat what you think is the problem after you've listened all the way through the user's story.

Follow up with fact-seeking questions. "When did it last work?" "Has it ever worked in this way?" "Has any software changed recently?" "Any new hardware?"

By keeping your questions friendly and factual, you show the user that you won't accuse them or judge their actions. You also show them that you're there to help them. After the initial tension drops away, you'll often get more information, for instance, a recitation of something the user might have tried or changed. These clues can help lead to a quick resolution of the problem.

It's important to remember that you may know all about computer technology, but the user probably does not. This means they will often use vague and/or incorrect terms to describe a particular computer component or function. That's just the way it works, so don't bother to correct the user. Wherever possible, avoid using jargon, acronyms, or abbreviations specific to computers. They simply confuse the already upset user. Just ask direct, factual questions in a friendly tone using simple, non-jargon language to zero in on what the user was trying to accomplish and what happened when things went wrong. Point at the machine or go to a working PC to have the user show what went wrong or what he or she did or tried to do.

Although you don't want to overwhelm them, people do usually want to get a handle on what you are doing—although in a simplified way. Don't be afraid to use simple analogies or concepts to give them an idea of what is happening. If you have the time (and the skills), use drawings, equipment, and other visual aids to make technical concepts more clear. If a customer is a "closet tech" and is really digging for answers—to the point that it's affecting your ability to do your job—compliment their initiative and then direct them to outside training opportunities. Better yet, tell them where they can get a copy of this book!

Integrity

A computer tech must bring `integrity` to his or her job, just like any other service professional. Treat anything said to you as a personal confidence, not to be repeated to coworkers or bosses. Respect the privacy and property of the user.

You have a lot of power when you sit in front of someone's computer. You can readily read private e-mail, discover Web sites surfed, and more. With a click of the Start button, you can know the last five programs the user ran, including Word and Solitaire, and the last few documents he or she worked on. Don't do this. You really don't want to know! Plus, if you get caught violating a customer's privacy, you'll not only lose credibility and respect, you could lose your job.

`Passwords` are a big issue for techs. We have to reboot computers and access shares and other jobs that require passwords. The rule here is to *avoid learning other folks' passwords at all costs*. If you know a password to access a mission-critical machine, and that machine ends up compromised or with data missing, who might be blamed? You, that's who, so avoid learning passwords! If you only need a password once, let the user type it in for you. If you anticipate accessing something multiple times (the more usual situation), ask the user to change his or her password temporarily.

It's funny, but people assume ownership of things they use at work. John in accounting doesn't call the computer he uses anything but "my PC." The phone on Susie's desk isn't the company phone, it's "Susie's phone." Regardless of the logic or illogic involved with this sense of ownership, a tech needs to respect that feeling. You'll never go wrong if you follow the

Golden Rule or the `ethic of reciprocity` : "Do unto others as you would have them do unto you." In a tech's life, this can translate as "treat people's things as you would have other people treat yours." Don't use or touch anything—keyboard, printer, laptop, monitor, mouse, phone, pen, paper, or cube toy—without first asking permission. Follow this rule at all times, even when the customer isn't looking!

Beyond basic manners, never assume that just because you are comfortable with friendly or casual behavior, the customer will be, too. Even an apparently casual user will still expect you to behave with professional decorum. On the flip side, don't allow a user to put you in an awkward or even potentially dangerous or illegal situation. Never socialize with customers while on the clock. Never do work outside the scope of your assigned duties without the prior approval of your supervisor (when possible in such cases, try to direct users to someone who *can* help them). You are not a babysitter—never volunteer to "watch the kids" while the customer leaves the job site, or tolerate a potentially unsafe situation if a customer isn't properly supervising a child. Concentrate on doing your job safely and efficiently, and maintain professional integrity.

Respect

The final key in communicating with the user revolves around `respect`. You don't do his or her job, but should respect that job and person as an essential cog in your organization. Communicate with users the way you would like them to communicate with you were the roles reversed. Again, this follows the ethic of reciprocity.

Generally, IT folks are there to support the people doing a company's main business. You are there to serve their needs, and all things being equal, to do so at their convenience, not yours.

Don't assume the world stops the moment you walk in the door and that you may immediately interrupt their work to do yours. Although most customers are thrilled and motivated to help you the moment you arrive, this may not always be the case. Ask the magic question, "May I start working on the problem now?" Give your customer a chance to wrap up, shut down, or do anything else necessary to finish his or her business and make it safe for you to do yours.

Engage the user with the standard rules of civil conversation. Take the time to listen. Don't interrupt a story, but rather let it play out. You might hear something that leads to resolving the problem. Use an even, non-accusatory tone, and although it's okay to try to explain a problem if the user asks, never condescend, and never argue.

Remain positive in the face of adversity. Don't get defensive if you can't figure something out quickly and the user starts hassling you. Remember that an angry customer isn't really angry with you—he's just frustrated—so don't take his anger personally. Take it in stride; smile and assure him that computer troubleshooting sometimes takes awhile!

Avoid letting outside interruptions take your focus away from the user and his or her computer problem. Things that break your concentration slow down the troubleshooting process immensely. Plus, customers will feel insulted if you start chatting on your cell phone with your significant other about a movie date later that night when you're supposed to be fixing their computers! You're not being paid to socialize, so turn those cell phones and pagers to vibrate. That's why the technogods created voicemail. Never take any call except one that is potentially urgent. If a call is potentially urgent, explain the urgency to the customer, step away, and deal with the call as quickly as possible.

If you discover that the user caused the problem, either through ignorance or by accident, don't minimize the importance of the problem, but don't be judgmental or insulting about the cause. We all screw up sometimes, and these kinds of mistakes are your job security! *You get paid because people make mistakes and machines break.* Chances are you'll be back at that workstation six months or a year later, fixing something else. By becoming the user's advocate and go-to person, you create a better work environment. If it's a mistaken action that caused the problem, explain in a positive and supportive way how to do the task correctly and then have the user go through the process while you are there to reinforce what you said.

Assertive Communication

In many cases, a PC problem is due to user error or neglect. As a technician, you must show users the error of their ways without creating anger or conflict. You do this by using assertive communication. **Assertive communication** is a technique that isn't pushy or bossy, but it's also not the language of a pushover. Assertive communication first requires you show the other person that you understand and appreciate the importance of his or her feelings. Use statements such as "I know how frustrating it feels to lose data" or "I understand how infuriating it is when the network goes out and you can't get your job done." Statements like these cool off the situation and let the customer know you are on his or her side.

The second part of assertive communication is making sure the problem is clearly stated—without accusing the user directly: "Not keeping up with defragmenting your hard drive slows it down" or "Help me understand how the network cable keeps getting unplugged during your lunch hour." Lastly, tell the user what you need from them to prevent this error in the future: "Please call me whenever you hear that buzzing sound" or "Please check the company's approved software list before installing anything." Always use "I" and "me," and never make judgments. "I can't promise the keyboard will work well if it's always getting dirty" is much better than "Stop eating cookies over the keyboard, you slob!"

■ Troubleshooting Methodology

Following a sound **troubleshooting methodology** helps you figure out and fix problems quickly. But because troubleshooting is as much art as science, I can't give you a step-by-step list of things to try in a particular order. You've got to be flexible.

First, make sure you have the proper tools for the job. Second, back up everything important before doing repair work. And third, analyze the problem, test your solution, and complete your troubleshooting.

Tech Toolkit

In the Essentials course you learned the basic parts of a **tech toolkit** (Figure 19.11): a Phillips-head screwdriver and a few other useful tools, such as a Torx wrench and a pair of tweezers. You also should carry some computer components.

Always carry several **field replaceable units (FRUs)** —a fancy way to say *spare parts*—when going to a job site or workstation. Having several known good components on hand enables you to swap out a potentially bad piece of hardware to see if that's the problem. Different technicians will have different FRUs. A printer specialist might carry a number of different fusers, for example. Your employer will also have a big effect on what is an FRU and what is not. I generally carry a couple of RAM sticks (DDR and DDR2), a PCI video card, a NIC, and a 300-watt power supply.

Backup

In many troubleshooting situations, it's important to back up critical files before making changes to a system. To some extent, this is a matter of proper ongoing maintenance. If you're in charge of a set of machines for your company, for example, make sure they're set to back up critical files automatically on a regular basis.

If you run into a partially functional system, where you might have to reinstall the OS but can access the hard drive, then you should definitely back up essential data, such as e-mail, browser favorites, important documents, and any data not stored on a regularly backed-up server. Because you can always boot to a copy of Windows and go to the Recovery Console, you should never lose essential data, barring full-blown hard drive death.

Steps

Troubleshooting a computer problem can create a great day for a computer tech—if he or she goes about solving it systematically and logically. Too many techs get into a rut, thinking that when symptom A occurs, the problem must be caused by problem A and require solution A. They might even be right nine times out of ten, but if you think this way, you're in trouble

Tech Tip

Why PCI?

I keep a PCI video card in my kit because every computer made in the past ten years has PCI slots. If you run into a system with video problems, you can almost always simply slap in the PCI video card and discover quickly whether or not the AGP or PCIe video card or card slot is a problem. If the computer boots up with the PCI video card but fails on the AGP card, for example, you know that either the AGP card or slot is causing the problem.

The CompTIA A+ certification exams assume that all techs should back up systems *every time* before working on them, even though that's not how it works in the real world.

Dead hard drives retain their data, so you can recover it—if you're willing to pay a lot of money. Having a good backup in place makes a lot more economic sense!

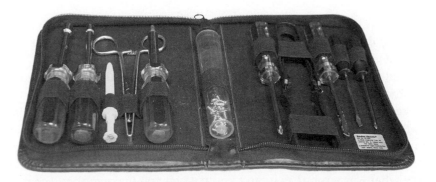

● **Figure 19.11** Typical technician toolkit

when the problem is really Z and requires a completely different solution. What do you do when the fix doesn't work and you're sure it's got to be problem A? Your customer won't be happy, you'll end up frustrated or embarrassed, and you still won't have the problem fixed. Follow the right methodology: analyze, test, and complete your task.

Analyze

Everything starts with analyzing the problem. Because you know how the process should work, when you run into a computer problem, the first question you should ask is, "What can it be?" Don't limit yourself in the initial analysis, but examine all possibilities.

Make sure you understand the nature of the problem first. A big portion of the initial fact-finding involves talking to the user with your newly-honed customer communication skills. Practice asking friendly, factual questions to get the results you want.

When you run into big problems, such as a completely dead PC, or some weird issue that involves networking as well as a local machine, break the problem down into smaller parts. For a dead PC, for example, organize your inquiry into categories, like this:

- **Power**   Check the AC connections and power switches on the power supply and UPS or surge suppressor.

- **Connectivity**   Check inside the box to make sure nothing is unplugged.

- **CMOS**   If you've got power (you see an LED lit up, for example), then check CMOS to see if the hard drive shows up.

- **Operating system**   If you have some life in the PC, but get no boot option, then try booting to the CD and running the recovery console. Check to see if you can access the hard drive. If you have a boot option, then try booting to Safe mode or Last Known Good Configuration.

By breaking the problem into discrete chunks, you make a big problem more manageable. You can determine whether the problem is caused by a hardware failure, connection problem, or perhaps an issue with the operating system or other software.

Test

Once you determine what might have caused the problem, test your theories. The testing procedure follows a simple set of rules:

First, check the easy stuff. Is the failed device plugged in? Is it turned on? Does the printer have paper?

Second, use a process of elimination to home in on the problem. Use a notepad to write down what you've tried and what effect that effort had. Do one thing at a time. If you go into CMOS and make a whole series of changes to various settings, for example, and then the computer works, how do you know what was wrong? You can't know when you make multiple changes. Worse yet, you risk breaking something else while fixing the first problem!

Third, if hardware seems to be the problem, swap out the suspect parts with known good parts from your stash of FRUs. With a dead or dying piece of hardware, you can generally get almost immediate results. A fried stick of RAM, for example, can create a dead PC. Pop in a good stick, and you'll have a functional machine.

Complete

Once you finish the testing phase, you can complete the troubleshooting process with four more steps: evaluate, escalate, clean up, and document.

First, **evaluate** the results of your actions. Run the system through its paces; don't just get it working and walk away. Make certain the user can accomplish his or her primary tasks before you consider a job complete. If you can't get the computer or peripheral working in a fairly short period of time, take the second step and **escalate** the problem—in other words, call for help. Because you've taken notes on the symptoms and each troubleshooting step you've tried, you can very quickly get a more senior tech up to speed on the problem and get suggestions for where you might go next.

Third, **clean up** the work environment. If you installed a drive, for example, do the right thing and tie off the ribbon cables. If you see a mess of cables coming out of the back of the PC or running across the floor, take a moment to tie them off. Good cable management does more than leave your clients with a nice-looking computer and workstation area, it also helps prevent accidents.

Finally, **document** your results. Many companies have specific forms for you to use to describe the problem and its resolution. If not, then make some for yourself and other techs in your workplace. Documenting problems helps you track the troubleshooting history of a machine over time, enabling you to make longer-term determinations about retiring it or changing out more parts. If you and fellow techs fix a specific problem with Mary's machine several times, for example, you might decide to swap out her whole system rather than fix it a fourth time.

Documenting helps fellow techs if they have to follow up on a task you didn't finish or troubleshoot a machine that you've worked on previously. The reverse is also true. If you get a call about Frank's computer, for example, and check the records to find other service calls on his computer, you might find that the fix for a particular problem is already documented. This is especially true for user-generated problems. Having documentation of what you did also means you don't have to rely on your memory when your coworker asks what you did to fix the weird problem with Jane's computer a year ago!

Documenting also comes into play when you or a user has an accident on site. If your colleague Joe drops a monitor on his foot and broke both the monitor and his foot, for example, you need to fill out an *incident report*, just like you would with any kind of accident—electrical, chemical, or physical. An **incident report** should detail what happened and where it happened. This helps your supervisors take the appropriate actions quickly and efficiently.

The power supply provides the only exception to the instant gratification rule of part swapping. If you have a wonky computer that has intermittent problems, swap out the power supply and leave your FRU in the computer for a half day or longer. You need the user to road test the PC and report if he or she has the same problems.

Know the four steps for completing troubleshooting: evaluate, escalate, clean up, and document.

Chapter 19 Review

■ Chapter Summary

After reading this chapter and completing the exercises, you should understand the following about working as a tech.

How Computers Work

■ Good techs must know how their systems are supposed to work when working properly, must be able to calm workers and supervisors and get answers to relevant questions, and must be able to troubleshoot and fix computer problems. A question you must be able to answer is "What can be causing this problem?"

■ When you run a program, computers work through three stages of the four-stage computing process: input, processing, and output. Input requires special input devices such as a keyboard or mouse. The operating system provides the interface and tools so that the CPU and other chips can process requests. The output devices, such as the monitor, speakers, or printer, tell you the computer has interpreted your commands. For all this to work, the PC must have electricity and proper AC/DC voltage and amperage.

■ When a keyboard key is pressed, the keyboard controller reads the grid of your keyboard and discovers your input, and then sends the information to the CPU. The CPU understands the keyboard controller because of a small program that was loaded into RAM from the ROM BIOS on the motherboard when the PC booted up.

■ Good techs understand the components involved in inputting, processing, and outputting, including the devices that store data, such as hard drives.

Dealing with Customers

■ The first step in fixing a computer problem is talking to the client. To determine what the computer is doing or not doing, first allow the client to describe the situation; then ask leading questions to elicit answers.

■ Most people feel defensive when asked to explain computer problems, so it is your job to put them at ease by asking the right kinds of questions. Questions like "What did you do?" generally aren't much help.

A better question might be, "When did it last work?" By taking the user explicitly out of the question, you show that you aren't accusing or judging.

■ Refrain from using computer jargon, acronyms, or abbreviations, as a user is unlikely to be familiar with them and may get confused. Ask simple questions that don't use technical lingo. Have the user physically demonstrate what is happening or what is not happening.

■ Treat every incident with integrity. Respect the confidentiality of what a user said to you and don't repeat it to coworkers. Don't abuse your power as a tech. Although you could read private e-mail, see the last several programs someone used, or see the last few documents someone worked on, don't do it. Your credibility may be damaged beyond repair.

■ Avoid learning other people's passwords. Have the user type in any passwords for you. If you'll need the same password entered many times, have the user temporarily change their password for you to use, and then have them change it back when you are done working.

■ People are protective of their things. Don't touch anything unless necessary—that means the keyboard, printer, monitor, phone, pen, stapler, or anything else.

■ Don't allow yourself to be put in a questionable situation. You're a tech, not a babysitter.

■ Don't assume the customer is ready for you to begin upon your arrival. Ask the customer if it is okay for you to start work, and allow them to close any files and exit any programs. Don't interrupt customers. Let them finish their story. Although you may think it is irrelevant, there may be important information.

■ Stay positive, don't get defensive, and don't take a customer's anger personally. Remind the customer that troubleshooting takes time. Avoid letting outside interruptions take your focus away from the job; set your cell phone and pager to vibrate. While working with a customer, only take phone calls that are urgent. Explain the urgency to your customer and deal with the call as quickly as possible.

- If you determine the problem was caused by the user, don't be judgmental or insulting. Explain to the user how to do the task they wanted to accomplish, and have the user go through the process while you supervise to reinforce what you said.

- Use assertive, but not pushy or bossy, communication. Show the person you understand his or her feelings and appreciate their importance. Make sure the problem is clearly stated without accusing the user directly. Tell the user what you need from them to prevent this error in the future. Use "I" statements rather than accusatory statements.

Troubleshooting Methodology

- Troubleshooting is more art than science, and as such, there is no step-by-step list of actions to follow. You need to be flexible.

- Carry a well-stocked tech toolkit. You should also carry several FRUs. The FRUs you carry will depend on what kind of tech you are, but in general, most techs should carry a few sticks each of DDR and DDR2 RAM, a PCI video card, a NIC, and a 300-watt power supply.

- Be sure to back up critical files before making changes to a system. Back up e-mail, favorites, personal documents, and any data not stored on a regularly backed-up server.

- Begin troubleshooting by analyzing the problem. Make sure you understand the problem. Talk to the client and use your communication skills to gather facts.

- It is helpful to break down large problems into smaller categories. For example, if a PC is completely dead or there is an issue involving both the network and the local machine, organize your inquiry into smaller categories including power, connectivity, CMOS, and operating system.

- Once you determine what might have caused the problem, test your theories. First, check the easy stuff, like is the device plugged in and powered on. Second, use the process of elimination to narrow in on the problem. Third, swap out parts with known good parts from your stash of FRUs. Swapping out bad hardware for good hardware almost immediately yields results. The exception to this rule is the power supply, which should be road tested for half a day or longer.

- Complete the troubleshooting process by testing the results of your actions and running the PC through its paces. If the problem persists, call a senior tech for help. Your notes should get a senior tech up to speed on the problem. Finally, document your results.

■ Key Terms

assertive communication *(474)*
clean up *(477)*
computing process *(464)*
document *(477)*
eliciting answers *(471)*
escalate *(477)*

ethic of reciprocity *(473)*
evaluate *(477)*
field replaceable unit (FRU) *(475)*
incident report *(477)*
integrity *(472)*
passwords *(472)*

respect *(473)*
stream loading *(469)*
tech toolkit *(475)*
troubleshooting
   methodology *(474)*

■ Key Term Quiz

Use the Key Terms list to complete the sentences that follow. Not all terms will be used.

1. _____ are commonly known as spare parts and at a minimum include extra sticks of RAM and a video card.

2. A few screwdrivers and an anti-static wrist strap should be in your _____.

3. Understanding the _____ enables you to troubleshoot problems more efficiently.

4. An effective use of _____ means clearly stating a problem without accusing the user of creating that problem.

5. Better online applications use _____ to download updated information and data constantly.

6. An accomplished computer tech should treat anything said to him or her as a personal confidence, not to be repeated to coworkers or bosses. The tech brings _____ to his or her job.

7. You should avoid learning _____ to other folks' computers so you don't get blamed if something happens to those computers.

8. If you can't solve a troubleshooting problem, the next step is to _____ the problem to a higher-level tech.

9. Treating other people how you want to be treated is an example of the _____.

10. A(n) _____ gives the details about an accident on the job site.

Multiple-Choice Quiz

1. While troubleshooting a fairly routine printing problem, the customer explains in great detail precisely what he was trying to do, what happened when he tried to print, and what he had attempted as a fix for the problem. At what point should you interrupt him?

   A. After he describes the first problem

   B. As soon as you understand the problem

   C. As soon as you have a solution

   D. Never

2. While manning the help desk, you get a call from a distraught user who says she has a blank screen. What would be a useful follow-up question?

   A. Is the monitor turned on?

   B. Did you reboot?

   C. What did you do?

   D. What's your password?

3. While manning the help desk, you get a call from Sharon in accounting. She's lost a file that she knows she saved to her hard drive. Which of the following statements would direct Sharon to open her My Documents folder in the most efficient and professional manner?

   A. Sharon, check My Documents.

   B. Sharon, a lot of programs save files to a default folder, often to a folder called My Documents. Let's look there first. Click on the Start button and move the mouse until the cursor hovers over My Documents. Then click the left mouse button and tell me what you see when My Documents opens.

   C. Probably just defaulted to My Docs. Why don't you open Excel or whatever program you used to make the file, and then open a document, and point it to My Documents.

   D. Look Sharon, I know you're a clueless noob when it comes to computers, but how could somebody lose a file? Just open up My Documents, and look there for the file.

4. What tool should be in every technician's toolkit?

   A. Pliers

   B. Hammer

   C. Straight-slot screwdriver

   D. Phillips-head screwdriver

5. Al in marketing calls in for tech support, complaining that he has a dead PC. What is a good first question to begin troubleshooting the problem?

   A. Did the computer ever work?

   B. When did the computer last work?

   C. When you say "dead," what do you mean? What happens when you press the power button?

   D. What did you do?

6. While manning the help desk, you get a call from Bryce in Sales complaining that he can't print, and every time he clicks on the network shared drive, his computer stops and freezes. He says he thinks it's his hard driver. What would be a good follow-up question or statement?

   A. Bryce, you're an idiot. Don't touch anything. I'll be there in five minutes.

   B. Okay, let's take this one step at a time. You seem to have two problems: one with printing and the second with the network shared drive, right?

C. First, it's not a hard *driver*, but a hard *drive*. It doesn't have anything to do with the network share or printing, so that's just not right.

D. When could you last print?

7. When troubleshooting a software problem on Phoebe's computer and listening to her describe the problem, your beeper goes off. It's your boss. What would be an acceptable action for you to make?

A. Excuse yourself, walk out of the cube, and use a cell phone to call your boss.

B. Pick up Phoebe's phone and dial your boss's number.

C. Wait until Phoebe finishes her description and then ask to use her phone to call your boss.

D. Wait until Phoebe finishes her description and run through any simple fixes; then explain that you need to call your boss on your cell phone.

8. You've just installed new printer drivers into Roland's computer for the big networked laser printer. What should you do to complete the assignment?

A. Document that you installed new printer drivers.

B. Tell Roland to print a test page.

C. Print a test page and go to the printer to verify the results. Assuming everything works, you're done.

D. Print a test page and go to the printer to verify the results. Document that you installed new printer drivers successfully.

9. While fixing a printing problem on Paul's computer, you notice several personal e-mails he has sent sitting in his Sent Items mail folder. Using the company computer for personal e-mail is against regulations. What should you do?

A. Leave the e-mails on the computer and notify your boss.

B. Delete the e-mails from the computer and notify your boss.

C. Delete the e-mails from the computer and remind Paul of the workplace regulations.

D. You shouldn't be looking in his e-mail folders at all, as it compromises your integrity.

10. Upon responding to a coworker's request for help, you find her away from her desk, and Microsoft Excel is on the screen with a spreadsheet open. How do you proceed?

A. Go find the coworker and ask her to exit her applications before touching her computer.

B. Exit Excel, saving changes to the document, and begin troubleshooting the computer.

C. Exit Excel without saving changes to the document and begin troubleshooting the computer.

D. Use the Save As command to save the file with a new name, exit Excel, and begin troubleshooting the computer.

11. You are solving a problem on Kate's computer, which requires you to reboot several times. Upon each reboot, the logon screen appears and prompts you for a user name and password before you can continue working. Kate has gone to another office to continue her work on another computer. How do you proceed?

A. Call Kate, ask her for her password, type it in, and continue working on the problem.

B. Insist that Kate stay with you and have her type the password each time it is needed.

C. Call Kate and have her come in to type the password each time it is needed.

D. Have Kate temporarily change her password for you to use as you work; then have her change it back when you are through.

12. You are working in a customer's home, and his five-year-old child is screaming and kicking the back of your chair. What do you do?

A. Ignore the child and finish your work as quickly as you can.

B. Discipline the child as you see fit.

C. Politely ask your client to please remove the child from your work area.

D. Tell your client you refuse to work under such conditions and leave the premises with the job half done.

13. After replacing a keyboard a user has spilled coffee on for the fifth time, what should you say to the user?

   A. I can't guarantee the new keyboard will work if it gets dirty.

   B. I can't guarantee the new keyboard will work if you continue to spill coffee on it.

   C. These keyboards are expensive. Next time we replace one because you spilled coffee, it's coming out of your paycheck.

   D. You need to be more careful with your coffee.

14. When is it appropriate to yell at a user?

   A. When he screws up the second time

   B. When he interrupts your troubleshooting

   C. When he screws up the fifth time

   D. Never

15. Once you figure out what can be causing a computer to malfunction, what's your next step?

   A. Escalate the problem to a higher-level tech.

   B. Talk to the user about stream loading and other geeky topics because your knowledge will put him or her at ease.

   C. Test your theory by checking for power and connectivity.

   D. Write an incident report to document the problem.

■ Essay Quiz

1. A friend is considering turning his computer hobby into a career and has asked your advice on outfitting himself as a freelance computer technician. What tools can you recommend to your friend?

2. A user phones you at your desk and reports that, after pressing the power button on his computer and hearing the hard drive spin up, his screen remains blank. What questions can you ask to determine the problem?

3. Briefly explain the three steps in a troubleshooting methodology.

Lab Projects

• Lab Project 19.1

Think of items you would like to always have on hand as FRUs. Using the Internet, find prices for these items. Make a list of your items and their individual costs, and then find the total cost for your equipment.

• Lab Project 19.2

Visit your local computer store or hardware store and purchase the items for a hardware tech toolkit. You may want to include a variety of screwdrivers, an anti-static wrist strap, tweezers, or other items.

• Lab Project 19.3

Create a software tech toolkit on CD or a USB flash drive loaded with a variety of drivers for NICs and video cards. Include free/open-source antivirus software, antispyware software, and any other software tools you think might be useful.

About the CD-ROM

Mike Meyers has put together a bunch of resources that will help you prepare for the CompTIA A+ exams and that you will find invaluable in your career as a PC Tech. The CD-ROM included with this book comes complete with a sample version of the Total Tester practice exam software with six full practice exams, an extensive glossary, an electronic copy of the book, a document from CompTIA with a list of acronyms that you should know for the CompTIA A+ exams, a complete list of the objectives for all four of the CompTIA A+ exams, a copy of several freeware and shareware programs that Mike talks about in the book, and a sample of LearnKey's online training featuring Mike Meyers. The practice tests and video software are easy to install on any Windows 98/NT/2000/XP/Vista computer, and must be installed to access the Total Tester practice exams and LearnKey video sample. The glossary, eBook, and CompTIA A+ acronyms list are Adobe Acrobat files. If you don't have Adobe Acrobat Reader, it is available for installation on the CD-ROM.

■ System Requirements

The software on the CD-ROM requires Windows 98 or higher, Internet Explorer 5.0 or above, and 50 MB of hard disk space for full installation. To access the online training from LearnKey, you must have Windows Media Player 9, which will be automatically installed when you launch the online training.

■ Installing and Running Total Tester

If your computer's CD-ROM drive is configured to Autorun, the CD-ROM will automatically start upon inserting the disk. If the Autorun feature does not launch the CD's splash screen, browse to the CD-ROM and double-click the Launch.exe icon.

From the splash screen, install Total Tester by clicking the *Install A+ Practice Exams* button. This will begin the installation process, create a program group named Total Seminars, and put an icon on your desktop. To run Total Tester, go to Start | Programs | Total Seminars or just double-click the icon on your desktop.

To uninstall the Total Tester software, go to Start | Settings | Control Panel | Add/Remove Programs and select the A+ Total Tester program. Select Remove, and Windows will completely uninstall the software.

About Total Tester

The best way to prepare for the CompTIA A+ exams is to read the book and then test your knowledge and review. We have included a sample of Total Seminars' practice exam software to help you test your knowledge as you study. Total Tester provides you with a simulation of the actual exam. There are three suites of exams: 220-602, 220-603, and 220-604. Each suite contains two tests that can be taken in either practice or final mode.

Practice mode provides an assistance window with hints, references to the book, an explanation of the answer, and the ability to check your answer as you take the test. Both practice and final modes provide an overall grade and a grade broken down by certification objective. To launch a test, select Suites from the menu at the top, select an exam, and choose from the list of available practice tests. Additional practice tests are available for all four of the CompTIA A+ exams. Visit our Web site at www.totalsem.com or call 800-446-6004 for more information.

■ Accessing the Glossary, eBook, CompTIA A+ Acronyms List, and CompTIA A+ Exam Objectives

You will find these documents useful in your preparation for the exams. To access these PDF documents, first be sure you have a copy of Adobe Acrobat Reader installed. If you don't have Acrobat Reader installed on your system, you can install it from the CD-ROM by clicking the *Install Adobe Acrobat Reader* button. Once you have installed Acrobat Reader, simply select the document you want to view from the CD-ROM's splash screen to open and view the document.

■ Shareware and Freeware

Mike has put together copies of some of his favorite freeware and shareware programs that are mentioned in this book. The CD-ROM includes a list with short descriptions of the programs. To use these programs, select the Shareware and Freeware option on the CD-ROM splash screen. The next menu lists each program. Select a program and follow the installation instructions to load the utility on your system.

■ LearnKey Online Training

If you like Mike's writing style, you will love listening to him in his LearnKey video training. The CD-ROM includes sample videos of Mike covering several different topics. Check out Mike's video training. If you like it, you can purchase the full 21 hours of interactive video training by contacting Mike's company, Total Seminars, at www.totalsem.com or 800-446-6004. The *Install LearnKey demo* button will launch a wizard to install the software on your computer. Follow the instructions on the wizard to complete the installation. To run the LearnKey demo, use Start | Programs | LearnKey or just double-click the icon on your desktop. Enter a user name and password to begin your video training.

■ Technical Support

For questions regarding the Total Tester software, visit www.totalsem.com or e-mail support@totalsem.com, or e-mail customer.service@mcgraw-hill .com. For customers outside the United States, e-mail international_ cs@mcgraw-hill.com.

LearnKey Technical Support

For technical problems with the software (installation, operation, or uninstalling the software) and for questions regarding LearnKey Video Training, e-mail techsupport@learnkey.com.

%Systemroot% The folder where the Windows boot files are located. This is by default the C:\Windows or C:\WINNT folder.

1.44 MB The storage capacity of a typical 3.5-inch floppy disk.

10BaseT An Ethernet LAN designed to run on UTP cabling. 10BaseT runs at 10 megabits per second. The maximum length for the cabling between the NIC and the hub (or switch, repeater, etc.) is 100 meters. It uses baseband signaling. No industry standard spelling exists, so sometimes written 10BASE-T or 10Base-T.

100BaseFX An Ethernet LAN designed to run on fiber-optic cabling. It runs at 100 megabits per second and uses baseband signaling. No industry standard spelling exists, so sometimes written 100BASE-FX or 100Base-FX.

100BaseT A generic term for an Ethernet cabling system designed to run at 100 megabits per second on UTP cabling. It uses baseband signaling. No industry standard spelling exists, so sometimes written 100BASE-T or 100Base-T.

1000BaseT Gigabit Ethernet on UTP.

16-bit Able to process 16 bits of data at a time.

16-bit ISA bus Also called the **AT bus**. A bus technology introduced with the first AT computers.

2.1 Speaker setup consisting of two stereo speakers combined with a subwoofer.

24-bit color Referred to as 24-bit or true color, using 3 bytes per pixel to represent a color image in a PC display. The 24 bits enable up to 16,777,216 colors to be stored and displayed.

286 Also called **80286**. Intel's second-generation processor. The 286 has a 16-bit external data bus and a 24-bit address bus. It was the first Intel processor to achieve 286 protected mode.

3.5-inch floppy drive format All modern floppy disk drives are of this size; the format was introduced in

1986 and is one of the longest surviving pieces of computer hardware.

30-pin SIMM An obsolete memory package that utilized 30 contacts to connect to the motherboard and required a whole bank to be filled before the memory was recognized.

34-pin ribbon cable This type of cable is used by floppy disk drives.

386 Also called **80386**. Intel's third-generation processor. The 386 has a 32-bit external data bus and 32-bit address bus. It was Intel's first true 32-bit processor.

3-D sound A generic term for making sounds emanate from all directions—i.e., *surround sound*—and for making sounds realistic. Popular in 3-D games and home theaters.

4.1 Four speakers and a subwoofer.

40-pin ribbon cable This type of cable is used to attached EIDE devices (such as hard drives) or ATAPI devices (such as CD-ROMs) to a system.

486 Intel's fourth-generation CPU. Essentially an 80386 with a built-in cache and math coprocessor.

5.1 Four satellite speakers plus a center speaker and a subwoofer.

5.25-inch floppy drive format The predecessor to the modern 3.5-inch floppy drive format; very rarely used currently.

50-pin ribbon cable Also called a **Type A cable**. A type of ribbon cable used for connecting SCSI-1 and SCSI-2 devices.

68-pin ribbon cable Also called a **P type cable**. There are two types of 68-pin ribbon cables: an obsolete Type B used in conjunction with a 50-pin Type A cable to connect early SCSI-2 devices and a P type that can be used singularly.

72-pin SIMM An obsolete memory package that utilized 72 contacts to connect to the motherboard, replacing 30-pin SIMMs and eliminating some of the issues with banking.

8.3 naming system A file naming convention that specified a maximum of eight characters for a filename, followed by a 3-character file extension. Has been replaced by LFN (Long Filename) support.

802.11b A wireless networking standard that operates in the 2.4-GHz band with a theoretical maximum throughput of 11 Mbps.

8086/8088 The first generation of Intel processor used in IBM PCs. The 8086 and 8088 were identical with the exception of the external data bus—the 8086 had a 16-bit bus whereas the 8088 had an 8-bit bus.

80-wire cable Also called a **D type cable**. Special type of cable used with some SCSI-3 devices that allows for devices to be hot-swapped. Alternatively, a ribbon cable used to connect ATA-66/100/133 hard drives to an ATA controller.

AC (alternating current) A type of electricity in which the flow of electrons alternates direction, back and forth, in a circuit.

Access speed The amount of time needed for the DRAM to supply the Northbridge with any requested data.

ACPI (advanced configuration and power interface) A power management specification that far surpasses its predecessor, APM, by providing support for hot-swappable devices and better control of power modes.

Activation The processes of confirming that an installed copy of a Microsoft product (most commonly Windows or a Microsoft Office application) is legitimate. Usually done at the end of software installation.

Active Directory A form of directory service used in networks with Windows 2000 Server and Windows Server 2003 servers.

Active matrix Also called **TFT (thin film transistor)**. A type of liquid crystal display that replaced the passive matrix technology used in most portable computer displays.

Active PFC (power factor correction) Circuitry built into PC power supplies to reduce harmonics.

Active termination A method for terminating fast/wide SCSI that uses voltage regulators in lieu of resistors.

ActiveSync (synchronization) A term used to describe the synchronizing of files between a PDA and a desktop computer. ActiveSync is the name of the synchronization program that is used by Windows OS–based PDAs.

Address bus The wires leading from the CPU to the memory controller chip (usually the Northbridge) that enable the CPU to address RAM. Also used by the CPU for I/O addressing. An internal electronic channel from the microprocessor to random access memory, along which the addresses of memory storage locations are transmitted. Like a post office box, each memory location has a distinct number or address; the address bus provides the means by which the microprocessor can access every location in memory.

Address space The total amount of memory addresses that an address bus can contain.

Administrative Tools A group of Control Panel applets, including Computer Management, Event Viewer, and Performance.

Administrator account A user account, created when the OS is first installed, that is allowed complete, unfettered access to the system without restriction.

ADSL (asymmetric digital subscriber line) A fully digital, dedicated connection to the telephone system that provides download speeds up to 9 Mbps and upload speeds of up to 1 Mbps.

Advanced Startup Options menu A menu that can be reached during the boot process that offers advanced OS startup options, such as boot in Safe mode or boot into Last Known Good Configuration.

AGP (accelerated graphics port) A 32/64-bit expansion slot designed by Intel specifically for video that runs at 66 MHz and yields a throughput of at least 254 Mbps. Later versions (2×, 4×, 8×) give substantially higher throughput.

AIX (Advanced Interactive Executive) IBM's version of UNIX, which runs on 386 or better PCs.

Algorithm A set of rules for solving a problem in a given number of steps.

ALU (arithmetic logic unit)   The CPU logic circuits that perform basic arithmetic (add, subtract, multiply, and divide).

AMD (Advanced Micro Devices)   CPU and chipset manufacturer that competes with Intel. Produces the popular Athlon and Duron processors.

AMI (American Megatrends, Inc)   Major producer of BIOS software for motherboards, as well as many other computer-related components and software.

Amperes (amps or A)   The unit of measure for amperage, or electrical current.

Amplifier   A device that strengthens electrical signals, enabling them to travel further.

AMR (audio/modem riser)   A proprietary slot used on some motherboards to provide a sound inference–free connection for modems, sound cards, and NICs.

Analog   An analog device uses a physical quantity, such as length or voltage, to represent the value of a number. By contrast, digital storage relies on a coding system of numeric units.

Analog video   Picture signals represented by a number of smooth transitions between video levels. Television signals are analog, as opposed to digital video signals, which assign a finite set of levels. Because computer signals are digital, analog video must be converted into a digital form before it can be shown on a computer screen.

ANSI (American National Standards Institute)   Body responsible for standards such as ASCII.

ANSI character set   The ANSI-standard character set, which defines 256 characters. The first 128 are ASCII, and the second group of 128 contain math and language symbols.

Anti-aliasing   In computer imaging, a blending effect that smoothes sharp contrasts between two regions—e.g., jagged lines or different colors. This reduces the jagged edges of text or objects. In voice signal processing, it refers to the process of removing or smoothing out spurious frequencies from waveforms produced by converting digital signals back to analog.

Anti-static bag   A bag made of anti-static plastic into which electronics are placed for temporary or long-term storage. Used to prevent electrostatic discharge.

Anti-static mat   A special surface upon which electronics are laid. These mats come with a grounding connection designed to equalize electrical potential between a workbench and one or more electronic devices. Used to prevent electrostatic discharge.

Anti-static wrist strap   A special device worn around the wrist with a grounding connection designed to equalize electrical potential between a technician and an electronic device. Used to prevent electrostatic discharge.

API (application programming interface)   A software definition that describes operating system calls for application software; conventions defining how a service is invoked.

APM (advanced power management)   The BIOS routines that enable the CPU to turn on and off selected peripherals.

Archive attribute   An attribute of a file that shows whether the file has been backed up since the last change. Each time a file is opened, changed, or saved, the archive bit is turned on. Some types of backups will turn off this archive bit to indicate that a good backup of the file exists on tape.

Archive   To copy programs and data onto a relatively inexpensive storage medium (disk, tape, etc.) for long-term retention.

ARP (Address Resolution Protocol)   A protocol in the TCP/IP suite used with the command-line utility of the same name to determine the MAC address that corresponds to a particular IP address.

ASCII (American Standard Code for Information Interchange)   The industry-standard 8-bit characters used to define text characters, consisting of 96 upper and lowercase letters, plus 32 non-printing control characters, each of which is numbered. These numbers were designed to achieve uniformity among different computer devices for printing and the exchange of simple text documents.

ASD (Automatic Skip Driver)   A utility for preventing "bad" drivers from running the next time that you boot your computer. This utility examines startup log files and removes problematic drivers from the boot process.

Aspect ratio The ratio of width to height of an object. Standard television has a 4:3 aspect ratio.

ASR (Automated System Recovery) A Windows XP tool designed to recover a badly corrupted Windows system; similar to ERD.

Asynchronous Communication whereby the receiving devices must send an acknowledgment, or "ACK," to the sending unit to verify a piece of data has been sent.

AT (advanced technology) The model name of the second-generation, 80286-based IBM computer. Many aspects of the AT, such as the BIOS, CMOS, and expansion bus, have become *de facto* standards in the PC industry. The physical organization of the components on the motherboard is called the AT form factor.

ATA (AT attachment) A type of hard drive and controller. ATA was designed to replace the earlier ST506 and ESDI drives without requiring replacement of the AT BIOS—hence, AT attachment. These drives are more popularly known as IDE drives. (*See* IDE.) The **ATA/33** standard has drive transfer speeds up to 33 MBps; the **ATA/66** up to 66 MBps; the **ATA/100** up to 100 MBps; and the **ATA/133** up to 133 MBps. (*See* Ultra DMA.)

ATAPI (ATA packet interface) A series of standards that enable mass storage devices other than hard drives to use the IDE/ATA controllers. Extremely popular with CD-ROM drives and removable media drives like the Iomega Zip drive. (*See* EIDE.)

Athlon Name used for a popular series of CPUs manufactured by AMD.

ATTRIB.EXE A command used to view the specific properties of a file; can also be used to modify or remove file properties, such as Read-Only, System, or Archive.

ATX (AT eXtended) The popular motherboard form factor, which generally replaced the AT form factor.

ATX12V A series of improvements to the original ATX standard for power supplies, including extra power connections and an increase of the ATX P1 power connector size from 20 pins to 24 pins.

Autodetection The process through which new disks are automatically recognized by the BIOS.

AUTORUN.INF A file included on some CD-ROMs that automatically launches a program or installation routine when the CD-ROM is inserted into a CD-ROM drive.

Award Software Major producer of BIOS software for motherboards.

Back up To save important data in a secondary location as a safety against loss of the primary data.

Backside bus The set of wires that connect the CPU to Level 2 cache. First appearing in the Pentium Pro, most modern CPUs have a special backside bus. Some buses, such as that in the later Celeron processors (300A and beyond), run at the full speed of the CPU, whereas others run at a fraction. Earlier Pentium IIs, for example, had backside buses running at half the speed of the processor. *See also* frontside bus and EDB (external data bus).

Backup or Restore Wizard A utility contained within Windows that allows a user to create system backups and set system restore points.

Bandwidth A piece of the spectrum occupied by some form of signal, such as television, voice, fax data, etc. Signals require a certain size and location of bandwidth in order to be transmitted. The higher the bandwidth, the faster the signal transmission, allowing for a more complex signal such as audio or video. Because bandwidth is a limited space, when one user is occupying it, others must wait their turn. Bandwidth is also the capacity of a network to transmit a given amount of data during a given period.

Bank The total number of SIMMs or DIMMs that can be accessed simultaneously by the chipset. The "width" of the external data bus divided by the "width" of the SIMM or DIMM sticks.

Baseband Digital signaling that has only one signal (a single signal) on the cable at a time. The signals can only be in one of three states at one time: one, zero, and idle.

Baseline Static image of a system's (or network's) performance when all elements are known to be working properly.

Basic disks A hard drive partitioned in the "classic" way with a master boot record (MBR) and partition table. *See also* dynamic disks.

Baud   One analog cycle on a telephone line. In the early days of telephone data transmission, the baud rate was often analogous to bits per second. Due to advanced modulation of baud cycles as well as data compression, this is no longer true.

Beep codes   A series of audible tones produced by a motherboard during the POST. These tones identify whether the POST has completed successfully or whether some piece of system hardware is not working properly. Consult the manual for your particular motherboard for a specific list of beep codes.

Binary numbers   A number system with a base of 2, unlike the number systems most of us use which have bases of 10 (decimal numbers), 12 (measurement in feet and inches), and 60 (time). Binary numbers are preferred for computers for precision and economy. An electronic circuit that can detect the difference between two states (on–off, 0–1) is easier and more inexpensive to build than one that could detect the differences among ten states (0–9).

Biometric device   Hardware device used to support authentication, which works by scanning and remembering unique aspects of a user's various body parts (e.g., retina, iris, face, or fingerprint) using some form of sensing device such as a retinal scanner.

BIOS (basic input/output system)   Classically, the software routines burned onto the system ROM of a PC. More commonly seen as any software that directly controls a particular piece of hardware. A set of programs encoded in Read-Only Memory (ROM) on computers. These programs handle startup operations and low-level control of hardware such as disk drives, the keyboard, and monitor.

Bit   A bit is a single binary digit. Any device that can be in an on or off state.

Bit depth   The number of colors a video card is capable of producing. Common bit depths are 16-bit and 32-bit, representing 65,536 colors and 16.7 million colors, respectively.

Blu-ray Disc   An optical disc format that stores 25 or 50 GB of data, designed to be the replacement media for DVD. Competes with HD DVD.

Boot   To initiate an automatic routine that clears the memory, loads the operating system, and prepares the computer for use. The term is derived from "pull yourself up by your bootstraps." PCs must do that

because RAM doesn't retain program instructions when power is turned off. A *cold boot* occurs when the PC is physically switched on. A *warm boot* loads a fresh OS without turning off the computer, lessening the strain on the electronic circuitry. To do a *warm* boot, press the CTRL-ALT-DELETE keys at the same time twice in rapid succession (the three-fingered salute).

Boot sector   The first sector on a PC hard drive or floppy disk, track 0. The boot-up software in ROM tells the computer to load whatever program is found there. If a system disk is read, the program in the boot record directs the computer to the root directory to load the operating system.

BOOT.INI   A text file used during the boot process that provides a list of all OSs currently installed and available for NTLDR. Also tells where each OS is located on the system.

Bootable disk   A disk that contains a functional operating system; can also be a floppy disk or CD-ROM.

BOOTLOG.TXT   A text file where information concerning the boot process is logged; useful when troubleshooting system boot errors and problems.

Bootstrap loader   A segment of code in a system's BIOS that scans for an operating system, looks specifically for a valid boot sector, and, when one is found, hands control over to the boot sector; then the bootstrap loader removes itself from memory.

bps (bits per second)   Measurement of how fast data is moved from one place to another. A 56K modem can move 56,000 bits per second.

Bridge   A device that connects two networks and passes traffic between them based only on the node address, so that traffic between nodes on one network does not appear on the other network. For example, an Ethernet bridge only looks at the Ethernet address. Bridges filter and forward packets based on MAC addresses and operate at Level 2 (Data Link layer) of the OSI seven-layer model.

Broadband   A type of signaling that sends multiple signals (channels) over the cable at the same time. The best example of broadband signaling is cable television. The zero, one, and idle states (*see* baseband) exist on multiple channels on the same cable. Also, broadband refers to high-speed, always-on communication links such as cable modems and DSL.

Broadcast   A broadcast is a packet addressed to all machines. In TCP/IP, the general broadcast address is 255.255.255.255.

Browser   A program specifically designed to retrieve, interpret, and display Web pages.

BSoD (Blue Screen of Death)   The infamous error screen that appears when Windows encounters an unrecoverable error.

BTX   A motherboard form factor designed as an improvement over ATX.

Buffer   Electronic storage, usually DRAM, that holds data moving between two devices. Buffers are used in situations where one device may send or receive data faster or slower than the other device with which it is in communication.

Buffer underrun   The inability of a source device to provide a CD-burner with a constant stream of data while burning a CD-R or CD-RW.

Bug   A programming error that causes a program or a computer system to perform erratically, produce incorrect results, or crash. The term was coined when a real bug was found in one of the circuits of one of the first ENIAC computers.

Burn   The process of writing data to a writable CD or DVD.

Bus   A series of wires connecting two or more separate electronic devices, enabling those devices to communicate.

Bus topology   A configuration wherein all computers connect to the network via a central bus cable.

Byte   A unit of eight bits, the fundamental data unit of personal computers. Storing the equivalent of one character, the byte is also the basic unit of measurement for computer storage.

CAB files   Short for cabinet files. These files are compressed and most commonly used during OS installation to store many smaller files, such as device drivers.

Cable modem   A network device that enables a PC to connect to the Internet using RG-6 coaxial cabling (i.e., the same coax used for cable television). Capable of download speeds up to 1.5 megabits per second.

Cable tester   Device that tests the continuity of cables. Some testers also test for electrical shorts, crossed wires, or other electrical characteristics.

Cache (disk)   A special area of RAM that stores the data most frequently accessed from the hard drive. Cache memory can optimize the use of your systems.

Cache memory   A special section of fast memory, usually built into the CPU, used by the onboard logic to store information most frequently accessed from RAM.

Caching   The act of holding data in cache memory for faster access and use.

Card   Generic term for anything that you can snap into an expansion slot.

Card services   The uppermost level of PCMCIA services. The card services level recognizes the function of a particular PC Card and provides the specialized drivers necessary to make the card work.

CardBus   32-bit PC Cards that can support up to eight devices on each card. Electrically incompatible with earlier PC Cards (3.3 V versus 5 V).

Case   The metal or plastic enclosure for the system unit.

CAT 3   Category 3 wire; a TIA/EIA standard for UTP wiring that can operate up to 20 megabits per second.

CAT 5   Category 5 wire; a TIA/EIA standard for UTP wiring that can operate up to 100 megabits per second.

CAT 5e   Category 5e wire; a TIA/EIA standard for UTP wiring that can operate up to 1 gigabit per second.

CAT 6   Category 6 wire; a TIA/EIA standard for UTP wiring that can operate up to 10 gigabits per second.

Catastrophic failure   Occurs when a component or whole system will not boot; usually related to a manufacturing defect of a component. Could also be caused by overheating and physical damage to computer components.

CCFL (cold cathode fluorescent lamp)   A light technology used in LCDs and flatbed scanners. CCFLs use relatively little power for the amount of light they provide.

CD quality CD-quality audio has a sample rate of 44.4 KHz and a bit rate of 128 bits.

CD-DA (CD-digital audio) A special format used for early CD-ROMs and all audio CDs; divides data into variable length tracks. A good format to use for audio tracks but terrible for data due to lack of error checking.

CD-I CD Interactive "green disc" format by Philips; designed to play compressed movies.

CD-R (compact disc recordable) A type of CD technology that accepts a single "burn" but cannot be erased after that one burn.

CD-ROM (compact disc/read only memory) A read-only compact storage disc for audio or video data. Recordable devices, such as CD-Rs, are updated versions of the older CD-ROM players. CD-ROMs are read using *CD-ROM drives*.

CD-RW (compact disc rewritable) A type of CD technology that accepts multiple reads/writes like a hard drive.

Celeron A lower-cost CPU based on Intel's Pentium CPUs.

Centronics connector A connector commonly used with printers.

Chipset Electronic chips, specially designed to work together, that handle all of the low-level functions of a PC. In the original PC the chipset consisted of close to 30 different chips; today, chipsets usually consist of one, two, or three separate chips embedded into a motherboard.

CHS (cylinder/heads/sectors per track) The initials for the combination of the three critical geometries used to determine the size of a hard drive—cylinders, heads, and sectors per track.

Clean installation An operating system installed on a fresh drive, following a reformat of that drive. A clean install is often the only way to correct a problem with a system when many of the crucial operating system files have become corrupted.

Cleaning kit A set of tools used to clean a device or piece of media.

Client A computer program that uses the services of another computer program. Software that extracts information from a server; your auto-dial phone is a client, and the phone company is its server. Also a machine that accesses shared resources on a server.

Client/server A relationship in which client software obtains services from a server on behalf of a person.

Client/server application An application that performs some or all of its processing on an application server rather than on the client. The client usually only receives the result of the processing.

Client/server network A network that has dedicated server machines and client machines.

Clock cycle A single charge to the clock wire of a CPU.

Clock multiplying CPU A CPU that takes the incoming clock signal and multiples it inside the CPU to let the internal circuitry of the CPU run faster.

Clock speed The speed at which a CPU executes instructions, measured in MHz or GHz. In modern CPUs, the internal speed is generally a multiple of the external speed. *See also* clock multiplying CPU.

Clock An electronic circuit that uses a quartz crystal to generate evenly-spaced pulses at speeds of millions of cycles per second. These pulses are used to synchronize the flow of information through the computer's internal communication channels.

Cluster The basic unit of storage on a floppy or hard disk. Two or more sectors are contained in a cluster. When Windows stores a file on disk, it writes those files into dozens or even hundreds of contiguous clusters. If there aren't enough contiguous open clusters available, the operating system finds the next open cluster and writes there, continuing this process until the entire file is saved. The FAT tracks how the files are distributed among the clusters on the disk.

CMD.COM In Windows, the file that contains the command processor. Usually located in the C:\WINNT\system32 folder on a Windows PC.

CMOS (complementary metal-oxide semiconductor) Originally, the type of non-volatile RAM that held information about the most basic parts of your PC such as hard drives, floppies, and amount of DRAM. Today, actual CMOS chips have been replaced by Flash-type non-volatile RAM. The information is the same, however, and is still called CMOS—even though it is now almost always stored on Flash RAM.

CNR (Communications and Network Riser) A proprietary slot used on some motherboards to provide a sound inference–free connection for modems, sound cards, and NICs.

Coaxial cable Cabling in which an internal conductor is surrounded by another, outer conductor, thus sharing the same axis.

Code A set of symbols representing characters (e.g., ASCII code) or instructions in a computer program (a programmer writes *source* code, which must be translated into *executable* or *machine* code for the computer to use). Used colloquially as a verb, *to code* is to write computer code; and as a noun, "He writes clean/sloppy/bad code."

Codec (compressor/decompressor) Software that compresses or decompresses media streams.

Collision The result of two nodes transmitting at the same time on a multiple access network such as Ethernet. Both packets may be lost, or partial packets may result.

Collision domain A set of Ethernet segments that receive all traffic generated by any node within those segments. Repeaters, amplifiers, and hubs do not create separate collision domains, but bridges, routers, and switches do.

COM port(s) A system name that refers to the serial communications ports available on your computer. When used as a program extension, .COM indicates an executable program file limited to 64 KB.

Command A request, typed from a terminal or embedded in a file, to perform an operation or to execute a particular program.

Command processor The part of the operating system that accepts input from the user and displays any messages, such as confirmation and error messages.

Command prompt A text prompt for entering commands.

Command-line interface A user interface for an OS devoid of all graphical trappings; interfaces directly with the OS.

Communications program A program that makes a computer act as a terminal to another computer.

Communications programs usually provide for file transfer between microcomputers and mainframes.

Compact Flash (CF) One of the older but still popular flash media formats. Its interface uses a simplified PC Card bus, so it also supports I/O devices.

Component failure Occurs when a system device fails due to manufacturing or some other type of defect.

Compression The process of squeezing data to eliminate redundancies, allowing files to be stored or transmitted using less space.

Conditioning charger A battery charger that contains intelligent circuitry that prevents portable computer batteries from being overcharged and damaged.

Connectionless protocol A protocol that does not establish and verify a connection between the hosts before sending data—it just sends it and hopes for the best. This is faster than connection-oriented protocols. UDP is an example of a connectionless protocol.

Connection-oriented protocol A protocol that establishes a connection between two hosts before transmitting data, and verifies receipt before closing the connection between the hosts. TCP is an example of a connection-oriented protocol.

Connectors Small receptacles that are used to attach cables to a system. Common types of connectors include USB, PS/2, and DB-25.

Control Panel A collection of Windows applets, or small programs, that can be used to configure various pieces of hardware and software in a system.

Controller card A card adapter that connects devices, like a disk drive, to the main computer bus/motherboard.

Convergence A measure of how sharply a single pixel appears on a CRT; a monitor with poor convergence would produce images that are not sharply defined.

Copy backup A type of backup similar to Normal or Full, in that all selected files on a system are backed up. This type of backup *does not* change the archive bit of the files being backed up.

Core Name used for the family of Intel CPUs that succeeded the Pentium 4.

Counter Used to track data about a particular object when using the Performance console.

CPU (central processing unit) The "brain" of the computer. The microprocessor that handles the primary calculations for the computer. CPUs are known by names such as Pentium 4 and Athlon.

CPU fan The cooling unit that sits directly on and cools the CPU.

CPUID Information stored in a CPU that gives very detailed information about every aspect of the CPU including vendor, speed, and model. Many programs access and display this information.

CRC (cyclic redundancy check) A very accurate mathematical method that is used to check for errors in long streams of transmitted data. Before data is sent, the main computer uses the data to calculate a CRC value from the data's contents. If the receiver calculates a different CRC value from the received data, the data was corrupted during transmission and is resent. Ethernet packets have a CRC code.

C-RIMM (continuity RIMM) A passive device added to populate unused banks in a system that uses Rambus RIMMs.

Crossover cable Special UTP cable used to connect hubs or to connect network cards without a hub. Crossover cables reverse the sending and receiving wire pairs from one end to the other.

Crossover port Special port in a hub that crosses the sending and receiving wires, thus removing the need for a crossover cable to connect the hubs.

CRT (cathode ray tube) The tube of a monitor in which rays of electrons are beamed onto a phosphorescent screen to produce images. Also a shorthand way to describe a monitor that uses CRT rather than LCD technology.

CSMA/CD (carrier sense multiple access with collision detection) The access method Ethernet systems use in local area networking technologies enabling packets of data information to flow through the network ultimately to reach address locations.

Cylinder A single track on all the platters in a hard drive. Imagine a hard drive as a series of metal cans, nested one inside another; a single can would represent a cylinder.

Cyrix Company that made CPUs in direct competition with Intel and AMD. Bought by Via Technologies in 2000.

Daily backup Also called **daily copy backup**. A backup of all files that have been changed on that day without changing the archive bits of those files.

Daisy-chaining A method of connecting together several devices along a bus and managing the signals for each device.

DAT (digital audio tape) Higher storage capacity tape recording system that uses digital recording methods. Used for digital audio and video as well as data backups.

Data structure A term that is used interchangeably with the term "file system." *See also* file system.

DB connectors D-shaped connectors used for a variety of connections in the PC and networking world. Can be male (with prongs) or female (with holes) and have a varying number of pins or sockets. Also called D-sub or D-subminiature connectors.

DB-15 A two- or three-row DB connector (female) used for 10Base5 networks, MIDI/joysticks, and analog video.

DB-25 connector DB connector (female), commonly referred to as a parallel port connector.

DC (direct current) A type of electricity in which the flow of electrons is in a complete circle in one direction.

DDR SDRAM (double data rate SDRAM) A type of DRAM that makes two processes for every clock cycle. *See also* DRAM.

DDR2 SDRAM A type of SDRAM that sends four bits of data in every clock cycle. *See* double data rate SDRAM.

Debug To detect, trace, and eliminate errors in computer programs.

Decoder A tool used to decode data that has been encoded; for instance, a DVD decoder breaks down the code used to encrypt the data on a piece of DVD Video media.

Dedicated circuit   Circuit that runs from a breaker box to specific outlets.

Dedicated server   A machine that is not used for any client functions, only server functions.

Dedicated telephone line   A telephone line on a circuit that is always open, or connected. Dedicated telephone lines usually are not assigned numbers.

Default   A software function or operation that occurs automatically unless the user specifies something else.

Default gateway   In a TCP/IP network, the nearest router to a particular host. This router's IP address is part of the necessary TCP/IP configuration for communicating with multiple networks using IP.

Defragmentation (DEFRAG)   A procedure in which all the files on a hard disk are rewritten on disk so that all parts of each file reside in contiguous clusters. The result is an improvement of up to 75 percent of the disk's speed during retrieval operations.

Degauss   The procedure used to break up the electromagnetic fields that can build up on the cathode ray tube of a monitor; involves running a current through a wire loop. Most monitors feature a manual degaussing tool.

Desktop   A user's primary interface to the Windows operating system.

Desktop extenders   A type of portable computer that offers some of the features of a full-fledged desktop computer, but with a much smaller footprint and lower weight.

Desktop replacement   A type of portable computer that offers the same performance of a full-fledged desktop computer; these systems are normally very heavy to carry and often cost much more than the desktop systems they replace.

Detlog.txt   A log file created during the initial operating system installation that tracks the detection, query, and installation of all devices.

Device driver   A program used by the operating system to control communications between the computer and peripherals.

Device Manager   A utility that allows techs to examine and configure all the hardware and drivers in a Windows PC.

DHCP (dynamic host configuration protocol)   A protocol that enables a DHCP server to set TCP/IP settings automatically for a DHCP client.

Differential backup   Similar to an incremental backup. Backs up the files that have been changed since the last backup. This type of backup does not change the state of the archive bit.

Digitally signed driver   All drivers designed specifically for Windows 2000 and Windows XP are digitally signed, meaning they are tested to work stably with these operating systems.

DIMM (dual inline memory module)   A 32- or 64-bit type of DRAM packaging, similar to SIMMs, with the distinction that each side of each tab inserted into the system performs a separate function. DIMMs come in a variety of sizes, with 184- and 240-pin being the most common on desktop computers.

DIPP (dual inline pin package)   An early type of RAM package that featured two rows of exposed connecting pins; very fragile and difficult to install. DIPPs were replaced first with SIPPs and later with SIMMs and DIMMs.

DIR command   A command used in the command-line interface that displays the entire contents of the current working directory.

Directory   Another name for a folder.

DirectX   A set of APIs enabling programs to control multimedia, such as sound, video, and graphics. Used in Windows Vista to draw the Aero desktop.

Disk cache   A piece of DRAM, often integrated into a disk drive, that is used to store frequently accessed data in order to speed up access times.

Disk Cleanup   A series of utilities, built into Windows, that can help users clean up their disks by removing temporary Internet files, deleting unused program files, and more.

Disk drive controller   The circuitry that controls the physical operations of the floppy disks and/or hard disks connected to a computer.

Disk Management   A snap-in available with the Microsoft Management Console that allows a user to configure the various disks installed in a system; available from the Administrative Tools area of the Control Panel.

Disk mirroring   Process by which data is written simultaneously to two or more disk drives. Read and write speed is decreased but redundancy in case of catastrophe is increased.

Disk striping   Process by which data is spread among multiple (at least two) drives. It increases speed for both reads and writes of data. Considered RAID level 0, because it does *not* provide fault tolerance.

Disk striping with parity   A method for providing fault tolerance by writing data across multiple drives and then including an additional drive, called a *parity drive*, that stores information to rebuild the data contained on the other drives. Requires at least three physical disks: two for the data and a third for the parity drive. This provides data redundancy at RAID levels 3–5 with different options.

Disk thrashing   A term used to describe a hard drive that is constantly being accessed due to lack of available system memory. When system memory runs low, a Windows system utilizes hard disk space as "virtual" memory, thus causing an unusual amount of hard drive access.

Distro   Shortened form of "distribution," most commonly used to describe the many different delivered packages for Linux operating systems and applications.

Dithering   A technique for smoothing out digitized images; using alternating colors in a pattern to produce perceived color detail.

DMA (direct memory access)   A technique that some PC hardware devices use to transfer data to and from the memory without using the CPU.

DNS (domain name system)   A TCP/IP name resolution system that translates a host name into an IP address.

DNS domain   A specific branch of the DNS name space. First-level DNS domains include .COM, .GOV, and .EDU.

Documentation   A collection of organized documents or the information recorded in documents. In the computer world, instructional material specifying the inputs, operations, and outputs of a computer program or system; for example, a manual and Getting Started card.

Dolby Digital   A technology for sound reductions and channeling methods.

Domain   Term used to describe groupings of users, computers, or networks. In Microsoft networking, a domain is a group of computers and users that share a common account database, called a SAM, and a common security policy. On the Internet, a domain is a group of computers that share a common element in their hierarchical name. Other types of domains exist—e.g., collision domain, etc.

Domain controller   A Microsoft Windows NT machine that stores the user and server account information for its domain in a database called a SAM (security accounts manager) database.

DOS (Disk Operating System)   The first popular operating system available for PCs. It was a text-based, single-tasking operating system that was not completely replaced until the introduction of Windows 95.

DOS prompt   A symbol, usually a letter representing the disk drive followed by the greater-than sign (>), which tells you that the operating system is ready to receive a command. Windows systems use the term *command prompt* rather than DOS prompt.

DOSKEY   A DOS utility that enables you to type more than one command on a line, store and retrieve previously used command-line commands, create stored macros, and customize all commands. DOSKEY is still supported in Windows XP.

Dot pitch   A value relating to CRTs, showing the diagonal distance between phosphors measured in millimeters.

Dot-matrix printer   A printer that creates each character from an array of dots. Pins striking a ribbon against the paper, one pin for each dot position, form the dots. The printer may be a serial printer (printing one character at a time) or a line printer.

Double word   A unit of 32 binary digits; four bytes.

Double-side high density   A type of floppy disk that is capable of holding 1.2 MB on a 5.25-inch disk and 1.44 MB on a 3.5-inch disk. This format can be read in all modern floppy disk drives.

Double-sided RAM   A RAM stick with RAM chips soldered to both sides of the stick. May only be used with motherboards designed to accept double-sided RAM. Very common.

Downstream   A term used to define the part of a USB connection that plugs into a USB device.

DPI (dots per inch)   A measure of printer resolution that counts the dots the device can produce per linear (horizontal) inch.

DRAM (dynamic random access memory or **dynamic RAM)**   The memory used to store data in most personal computers. DRAM stores each bit in a "cell" composed of a transistor and a capacitor. Because the capacitor in a DRAM cell can only hold a charge for a few milliseconds, DRAM must be continually refreshed, or rewritten, to retain its data.

DS3D (DirectSound3D)   Introduced with DirectX 3.0, DS3D is a command set used to create positional audio, or sounds that appear to come from in front, in back, or to the side of a user. *See also* DirectX.

DSL (digital subscriber line)   A high-speed Internet connection technology that uses a regular telephone line for connectivity. DSL comes in several varieties, including asymmetric (ADSL) and symmetric (SDSL), and many speeds. Typical home-user DSL connections are ADSL with a download speed of up to 1.5 Mbps and an upload speed of 384 Kbps.

DSP (digital signal processor)   A specialized microprocessor-like device that processes digital signals at the expense of other abilities, much as the FPU is optimized for math functions. DSPs are used in such specialized hardware as high-speed modems, multimedia sound cards, MIDI equipment, and real-time video capture and compression.

DTS (Digital Theatre Systems)   A technology for sound reductions and channeling methods, similar to Dolby Digital.

Dual boot   Refers to a computer with two operating systems installed, enabling a user to choose which operating system to load on boot. Can also refer to kicking a device a second time just in case the first time didn't work.

Dual-channel memory   A form of DDR and DDR2 memory access used by many motherboards that requires two identical sticks of DDR or DDR2 RAM.

Duplexing   Also called **disk duplexing** or **drive duplexing**. Similar to mirroring in that data is written to and read from two physical drives, for fault tolerance. Separate controllers are used for each drive, both for additional fault tolerance and additional speed. Considered RAID level 1.

Duron   A lower-cost version of AMD's Athlon series of CPUs.

DVD (digital versatile disc)   An optical media format that provides for 4–17 GB of video or data storage.

DVD Multi   A description given to DVD drives that are capable of reading all six DVD formats.

DVD+RW   A type of rewritable DVD media.

DVD-RAM   A type of rewritable DVD media that uses a cartridge.

DVD-ROM   The DVD-ROM is the DVD equivalent of the standard CD-ROM.

DVD-RW   A type of rewritable DVD media.

DVD-Video   A DVD format used exclusively to store digital video; capable of storing over 2 hours of high-quality video on a single DVD.

DVI (digital video interface)   A special video connector designed for digital-to-digital connections; most commonly seen on PC video cards and LCD monitors. Some versions also support analog signals with a special adapter.

Dynamic disks   A special feature of Windows 2000 and Windows XP that allows a user to span a single volume across two or more drives. Dynamic disks do not have partitions; they have volumes. Dynamic disks can be striped, mirrored, and striped or mirrored with parity.

EAX   3-D sound technology developed by Creative Labs, but now supported by most sound cards.

ECC (error correction code)   Special software, embedded on hard drives, that constantly scans the drives for bad sectors.

ECC DRAM (error correction code DRAM)   A type of RAM that uses special chips to detect and fix memory errors. This type of RAM is commonly used in high-end servers where data integrity is crucial.

EDB (external data bus)   The primary data highway of all computers. Everything in your computer is tied either directly or indirectly to the external data bus. *See also* frontside bus and backside bus.

EDO DRAM (enhanced data out DRAM)   An improvement on FPM DRAM in that more data can be read before the RAM must be refreshed.

EEPROM (electrically erasable programmable read-only memory)   A type of ROM chip that can be erased and reprogrammed electrically. EEPROMs were the most common storage device for BIOS before the advent of Flash ROM.

EFS (encrypting file system)   The encryption tool found in NTFS 5.

EIA/TIA   *See* TIA/EIA.

EIDE (enhanced IDE)   A marketing concept of hard drive–maker Western Digital, encompassing four improvements for IDE drives. These improvements included drives larger than 528 MB, four devices, increase in drive throughput, and non–hard drive devices. (*See* ATAPI, PIO.)

EISA (enhanced ISA)   An improved expansion bus, based on the ISA bus, with a top speed of 8.33 MHz, a 32-bit data path, and a high degree of self-configuration. Backward compatible with legacy ISA cards.

E-mail, email (electronic mail)   Messages, usually text, sent from one person to another via computer. E-mail can also be sent automatically to a group of addresses (mailing list).

EMI (electro-magnetic interference)   EMI is electrical interference from one device to another, resulting in poor performance of the device being interfered with. An example is having static on your TV while running a blow dryer, or placing two monitors too close together and getting a "shaky" screen.

EPROM (erasable programmable read-only memory)   A special form of ROM that can be erased by high-intensity ultraviolet light and then rewritten (reprogrammed).

ERD (emergency repair disk)   This disk saves critical boot files and partition information and is the main tool for fixing boot problems in Windows 2000.

ESD (electrostatic discharge)   The movement of electrons from one body to another. ESD is a real menace to PCs, as it can cause permanent damage to semiconductors.

Ethernet   Name coined by Xerox for the first standard of network cabling and protocols. Ethernet is based on a bus topology.

EULA (end user license agreement)   An agreement that accompanies a piece of software, which the user must agree to in order to use the software. This agreement outlines the terms of use for software and also lists any actions on the part of the user that violate the agreement.

Event Viewer   A utility made available as an MMC snap-in that allows a user to monitor various system events, including network bandwidth usage and CPU utilization.

EXPAND   A CAB file utility program included with Windows 2000. Usage of EXPAND is similar to usage of EXTRACT. *See also* EXTRACT.

Expansion bus crystal   The crystal that controls the speed of the expansion bus.

Expansion bus   Set of wires going to the CPU, governed by the expansion bus crystal, directly connected to expansion slots of varying types (PCI, AGP, PCIe, etc.). Depending on the type of slots, the expansion bus runs at a percentage of the main system speed (8.33–133 MHz).

Expansion slots   Connectors on a motherboard that enable a user to add optional components to a system. *See also* AGP (accelerated graphics port) and PCI (peripheral components interconnect).

ExpressCard   A serial PC Card designed to replace CardBus PC Cards. ExpressCards connect to either a Hi-Speed USB (480 Mbps) or PCI Express (2.5 Gbps) bus.

Extended partition   A type of hard disk partition. Extended partitions are not bootable and you may only have one extended partition per disk. The purpose of an extended partition is to divide a large disk into smaller partitions, each with a separate drive letter.

Extension   The three or four letters that follow a filename; an extension identifies the type of file. Common file extensions are .ZIP, .EXE, and .DOC.

EXTRACT   A program native to Windows 9*x*/Me that can be used to extract data from compressed CAB files. *See also* EXPAND.

Fast Ethernet   Any of several flavors of Ethernet that operate at 100 megabits/second.

FAT (file allocation table)   A hidden table of every cluster on a hard disk. The FAT records how files are stored in distinct clusters. The address of the first cluster of the file is stored in the directory file. In the FAT entry for the first cluster is the address of the second cluster used to store that file. In the entry for the second cluster for that file is the address for the third cluster, and so on until the final cluster, which gets a special "end of file" code. This table is the only way DOS knows where to access files. There are two FATs, mirror images of each other, in case one is destroyed or damaged.

FAT16   File allocation table that uses 16 bits for addressing clusters. Commonly used with DOS and Windows 95 systems.

FAT32   File allocation table that uses 32 bits for addressing clusters. Commonly used with Windows 98 and Windows Me systems. Some Windows 2000 Professional and Windows XP systems also use FAT32, although most use the more robust NTFS.

FDISK   A disk partitioning utility included with Windows.

Fiber optics   A high-speed channel for transmitting data, made of high-purity glass sealed within an opaque tube. Much faster than conventional copper wire such as coaxial cable.

File   A collection of any form of data that is stored beyond the time of execution of a single job. A file may contain program instructions or data, which may be numerical, textual, or graphical information.

File allocation unit   Another term for cluster. *See also* cluster.

File format   The way information is encoded in a file. Two primary types are binary (pictures) and ASCII (text), but within those there are many formats, such as BMP and GIF for pictures. Commonly represented by a suffix at the end of the filename—for example, .txt for a text file or .exe for an executable.

File fragmentation   The allocation of a file in a non-contiguous sector on a disk. Fragmentation occurs because of multiple deletions and write operations.

File server   A computer designated to store software, courseware, administrative tools, and other data on a local- or wide-area network. It "serves" this information to other computers via the network when users enter their personal access codes.

File system   A scheme that directs how an OS stores and retrieves data on and off a drive; FAT32 and NTFS are both file systems.

Filename   A name assigned to a file when the file is first written on a disk. Every file on a disk within the same folder must have a unique name. Filenames can contain any character (including spaces), except the following: \ / : * ? " < > |

Firewall   A device that restricts traffic between a local network and the Internet.

FireWire (IEEE 1394)   An IEEE 1394 interconnection standard to send wide-band signals over a serialized, physically thin connector system. This serial bus developed by Apple and Texas Instruments enables connection of 60 devices at speeds up to 800 megabits per second.

Firmware   Embedded programs or code that is stored on a ROM chip. Firmware is generally OS-independent, thus allowing devices to operate in a wide variety of circumstances without direct OS support. The system BIOS is firmware.

Flash ROM   A type of ROM technology that can be electrically reprogrammed while still in the PC. Flash is the overwhelmingly most common storage medium of BIOS in PCs today, as it can be upgraded without even having to open the computer on most systems.

FlexATX   A motherboard form factor. Motherboards built in accordance with the FlexATX form factor are very small, much smaller than microATX motherboards.

Flexing   Condition that can result when components are installed on a motherboard after it has been installed into a computer case. Excessive flexing can cause damage to the motherboard itself.

Floppy disk   A type of removable storage media that can hold between 720 KB and 1.44 MB of data.

Floppy drive   A piece of system hardware that uses removable 3.5-inch disks as storage media.

Flux reversal   The point at which a read/write head detects a change in magnetic polarity.

FM synthesis   A method for producing sound that used electronic emulation of various instruments to more or less produce music and other sound effects.

Form factor   A standard for the physical organization of motherboard components and motherboard size. The most common form factors are ATX, BTX, and NLX.

Formatting   The process of magnetically mapping a disk to provide a structure for storing data; can be done to any type of disk, including a floppy disk, hard disk, or other type of removable disk.

FPM (fast page mode)   DRAM that uses a "paging" function to increase access speed and to lower production costs. Virtually all DRAMs are FPM DRAM. The name FPM is also used to describe older style, non-EDO DRAM.

FPT (forced perfect termination)   A method for terminating SCSI devices that uses diodes instead of resistors.

FPU (floating point unit)   A formal term for the math coprocessor (also called a *numeric processor*) circuitry inside a CPU. A math coprocessor calculates using floating point math (which allows for decimals). Before the Intel 80486, FPUs were separate chips from the CPU.

Fragmentation   Occurs when files and directories get jumbled on a fixed disk and are no longer contiguous. Fragmentation can significantly slow down hard drive access times and can be repaired by using the DEFRAG utility that is included with each version of Windows. *See also* defragmentation (DEFRAG), file fragmentation.

Freeware   Software that is distributed for free, with no license fee.

Frontside bus   Name for the wires that connect the CPU to the main system RAM. Generally running at speeds of 66–133 MHz. Distinct from the expansion bus and the backside bus, though it shares wires with the former.

FRU (field replaceable unit)   Any part of a PC that is considered to be replaceable "in the field," i.e., a customer location. There is no official list of FRUs—it is usually a matter of policy by the repair center.

FTP (File Transfer Protocol)   A set of rules that enables two computers to talk to one another as a file transfer is carried out. This is the protocol used when you transfer a file from one computer to another across the Internet.

Fuel cells   A type of power source that uses chemical reactions to produce electricity. Lightweight, compact, and stable, these devices are expected to replace batteries as the primary power source for portable PCs.

Full-duplex   Describes any device that can send and receive data simultaneously.

Function key   A keyboard key that gives an instruction to a computer, as opposed to keys that produce letters, numbers, marks of punctuation, etc.

Fuser assembly   A mechanism, found in laser printers, that uses two rollers to fuse toner to paper during the print process.

Gateway   The technical meaning is a hardware or software setup that translates between two dissimilar protocols. For example, Prodigy has a gateway that translates between its internal, proprietary e-mail format and Internet e-mail format. Another, less technical meaning of gateway is any mechanism for providing access to another system, e.g., AOL might be called a gateway to the Internet. *See* default gateway.

General-purpose registers   The registers that handle the most common CPU calculations. *See* register.

Giga-   The prefix for the quantity 1,073,741,824 or for 1 billion. One gigabyte would be 1,073,741,824 bytes, except for with hard drive labeling, where it means 1 billion bytes. One gigahertz is 1 billion hertz.

Gigabyte 1024 megabytes.

Green PC A computer system designed to operate in an energy-efficient manner.

Guest Very limited built-in account type for Windows.

GUI (graphical user interface) An interface is the method by which a computer and a user interact. Early interfaces were text-based; that is, the user "talked" to the computer by typing and the computer responded with text on a CRT. A GUI (pronounced "gooey"), on the other hand, enables the user to interact with the computer graphically, by manipulating icons that represent programs or documents with a mouse or other pointing device.

HAL (hardware abstraction layer) A part of the Windows OS that separates system-specific device drivers from the rest of the NT system.

Half-duplex Any device that at any given moment can either send or receive data, but not both. Most Ethernet transmissions are half-duplex.

Handshaking A procedure performed by modems, terminals, and computers to verify that communication has been correctly established.

Hang When a computer freezes so that it does not respond to keyboard commands, it is said to "hang" or to have "hung."

Hang time The number of seconds a too-often-hung computer is airborne after you have thrown it out a second-story window.

Hard drive A data-recording system using solid disks of magnetic material turning at high speeds to store and retrieve programs and data in a computer.

Hardware Physical computer equipment such as electrical, electronic, magnetic, and mechanical devices. Anything in the computer world that you can hold in your hand. A floppy drive is hardware; Microsoft Word is not.

Hardware profile A list of devices that Windows automatically enables or disables in the Device Manager, depending on what devices the system detects.

Hardware protocol A hardware protocol defines many aspects of a network, from the packet type to the cabling and connectors used.

Hayes command set A standardized set of instructions used to control modems.

HCL (Hardware Compatibility List) Now part of Windows Marketplace, a list that is maintained by Microsoft that lists all the hardware that is supported by an operating system. This list is helpful to use when upgrading a system; with a quick glance, you can make sure that support is available for all the devices in a system before you begin the upgrade.

HD (Hi-Definition) A multimedia transmission standard that defines high-resolution images and 5.1 sound.

HD DVD An optical disc format that stores 15 or 30 GB of data, designed to be the replacement media for DVD. Competes with Blu-ray Disc.

HDMI (hi-definition multimedia interface) A single multimedia connection that includes both high-definition video and audio. HDMI also contains copy protection features.

Hex (hexadecimal) A base-16 numbering system using 10 digits (0 through 9) and six letters (A through F). Used in the computer world as a shorthand way to write binary numbers, by substituting one hex digit for a four-digit binary number (e.g., hex 9 = binary 1001).

Hibernation A power management setting in which all data from RAM is written to the hard drive before going to sleep. Upon waking up, all information is retrieved from the hard drive and returned to RAM.

Hidden attribute A file attribute that, when used, does not allow a file to be seen when using the DIR command.

Hierarchical directory tree The method by which Windows organizes files into a series of folders, called directories, under the root directory. *See also* Root directory.

High-level formatting A type of format that sets up a file system on a drive.

High-voltage anode   A component in a CRT monitor. The high-voltage anode has very high voltages of electricity flowing through it.

Host   A single device (usually a computer) on a TCP/IP network that has an IP address—any device that can be the source or destination of a data packet. Also, in the mainframe world, a computer that is made available for use by multiple people simultaneously.

Host adapter   An expansion card that serves as a host to a particular device; for instance, you can install a SCSI host adapter into a system to allow for SCSI functionality even if SCSI hardware was not originally included with the machine.

Host ID   The portion of an IP address that defines a specific machine.

Hot-swappable   A term used for any type of hardware that may be attached to or removed from a PC without interrupting the PC's normal processing.

HotSync (synchronization)   A term used to describe the synchronizing of files between a PDA and a desktop computer. HotSync is the name of the synchronization program that is used by PalmOS-based PDAs.

HRR (horizontal refresh rate)   The amount of time it takes for a CRT to draw one horizontal line of pixels on a display.

HTML (Hypertext Markup Language)   An ASCII-based, script-like language for creating hypertext documents like those on the World Wide Web.

HTTP (Hypertext Transfer Protocol)   Extremely fast protocol used for network file transfers in the WWW environment.

HTTPS (HTTP over Secure Sockets Layer)   A secure form of HTTP, used commonly for Internet business transactions or any time when a secure connection is required. *See also* HTTP.

Hub   An electronic device that sits at the center of a star topology network, providing a common point for the connection of network devices. Hubs repeat all information out to all ports and have been replaced by switches, although the term is still commonly used.

HVD (high-voltage differential)   A rare type of SCSI device that uses two wires for each bit of information: one wire for data and one for the inverse of this data. The inverse signal takes the place of the ground wire in the single-ended cable. By taking the difference of the two signals, the device can reject the common-mode noise in the data stream.

Hyperthreading   A CPU feature that enables a single pipeline to run more than one thread at once.

I/O (input/output)   A general term for reading and writing data to a computer. The term "input" includes data from a keyboard, pointing device (such as a mouse), or loading a file from a disk. "Output" includes writing information to a disk, viewing it on a CRT, or printing it to a printer.

I/O addressing   The process of using the address bus to talk to system devices.

ICF (Internet Connection Firewall)   A software firewall built into Windows XP that protects your system from unauthorized access from the Internet.

ICH (I/O controller hub)   The official name for the Southbridge chip found in Intel's chipsets.

Icon   A small image or graphic, most commonly found on a system's desktop, that launches a program when selected.

ICS (Internet Connection Sharing)   A method for allowing a single network connection to be shared among several machines. ICS was first introduced with Windows 98.

IDE (intelligent drive electronics)   Also known as **integrated drive electronics**. A PC specification for small- to medium-sized hard drives in which the controlling electronics for the drive are part of the drive itself, speeding up transfer rates and leaving only a simple adapter (or "paddle"). IDE only supported two drives per system of no more than 504 megabytes each, and has been completely supplanted by Enhanced IDE. EIDE supports four drives of over 8 gigabytes each and more than doubles the transfer rate. The more common name for PATA drives. (*See* PATA.)

IEC-320   Type of connector used to connect the cable supplying AC power from a wall outlet into the power supply.

IEEE (Institute of Electronic and Electrical Engineers) IEEE is the leading standards-setting group in the United States.

IEEE 1284 The IEEE standard governing parallel communication.

IEEE 1394 The IEEE standard governing FireWire communication. *See also* FireWire (IEEE 1394).

IFCONFIG A command-line utility for Linux servers and workstations that displays the current TCP/IP configuration of the machine, similar to Windows' IPCONFIG.

Image file A bit-by-bit image of the data to be burned on the CD or DVD—from one file to an entire disc—stored as a single file on a hard drive. Image files are particularly handy when copying from CD to CD or DVD to DVD.

Image installation An operating system installation that uses a complete image of a hard drive as an installation medium. This is a helpful technique to use when installing an operation system on a large number of identical PCs.

Impact printer A type of printer that uses pins and inked ribbons to print text or images on a piece of paper.

Impedance The amount of resistance to an electrical signal on a wire. It is used as a relative measure of the amount of data a cable can handle.

Incremental backup A type of backup that backs up all files that have their archive bits turned on, meaning that they have been changed since the last backup. This type of backup turns the archive bits off after the files have been backed up.

INF file A Windows driver file.

Inkjet printer A type of printer that uses liquid ink, sprayed through a series of tiny jets, to print text or images on a piece of paper.

Instruction set All of the machine-language commands that a particular CPU is designed to understand.

Interlaced TV/video systems in which the electron beam writes every other line; then retraces itself to make a second pass to complete the final framed image. Originally, this reduced magnetic line paring, but took twice as long to paint, which added some flicker in graphic images.

InterNIC Organization run by Network Solutions, Inc. (NSI) and AT&T that provides several services to Internet users, the most prominent being the registration of domain names and assignment of IP addresses.

Interrupt A suspension of a process, such as the execution of a computer program, caused by an event external to the computer and performed in such a way that the process can be resumed. Events of this kind include sensors monitoring laboratory equipment or a user pressing an interrupt key.

Interrupt 13 (INT13) extensions An improved type of BIOS that accepts EIDE drives up to 137 GB.

Intranet A private network inside a company or organization that uses the same kinds of software that you find on the public Internet, but that is only for internal use.

Inverter A device used to convert DC current into AC. Commonly used with CCFLs in laptops and flatbed scanners.

IP (Internet Protocol) The Internet standard protocol that provides a common layer over dissimilar networks used to move packets among host computers and through gateways if necessary. Part of the TCP/IP protocol suite.

IP address Also called **Internet address**. The numeric address of a computer connected to the Internet. The IP address is made up of octets of 8-bit binary numbers that are translated into their shorthand numeric values. The IP address can be broken down into a network ID and a host ID.

IPCONFIG A command-line utility for Windows NT servers and workstations that displays the current TCP/IP configuration of the machine, similar to WINIPCFG and IFCONFIG.

IPX/SPX (Internetwork Packet Exchange/Sequence Packet Exchange) Protocol suite developed by Novell, primarily for supporting Novell NetWare-based networks.

IRC (Internet Relay Chat) The Internet Relay Chat, or just Chat, is an online group discussion.

IRQ (interrupt request) A signal from a hardware device, such as a modem or a mouse, indicating that it needs the CPU's attention. In PCs, IRQs are sent along specific IRQ channels associated with a particular device. IRQ conflicts were a common problem in the past when adding expansion boards, but the plug-and-play specification has removed this headache in most cases.

ISA (industry standard architecture) The Industry Standard Architecture design was found in the original IBM PC for the slots on the motherboard that allowed additional hardware to be connected to the computer's motherboard. An 8-bit, 8.33-MHz expansion bus was designed by IBM for its AT computer and released to the public domain. An improved 16-bit bus was also released to the public domain. Replaced by PCI in the mid-1990s.

ISDN (Integrated Services Digital Network) The CCITT (Comité Consultatif Internationale de Télégraphie et Téléphonie) standard that defines a digital method for communications to replace the current analog telephone system. ISDN is superior to POTS (*see* POTS) telephone lines because it supports up to 128 Kbps transfer rate for sending information from computer to computer. It also allows data and voice to share a common phone line. DSL reduced demand for ISDN substantially.

ISO 9660 CD format to support PC file systems on CD media. Supplanted by the Joliet format.

ISP (Internet service provider) A company that provides access to the Internet, usually for money.

Jack (physical connection) The part of a connector into which a plug is inserted. Jacks are also referred to as ports.

Joliet An extension of the ISO 9660 format. The most popular CD format to support PC file systems on CD media.

Joystick A peripheral often used while playing computer games; originally intended as a multipurpose input device.

Jumper A pair of small pins that can be shorted with a "shunt" to configure many different aspects of PCs. Usually used in configurations that are rarely changed, such as master/slave settings on IDE drives.

K Most commonly used as the suffix for the binary quantity 1024 (2^{10}). Just to add some extra confusion to the IT industry, K is often spoken as "kilo," the metric value for 1000. 10 KB, for example, spoken as "10 kilobytes," actually means 10,240 bytes rather than 10,000 bytes.

Kbps (kilobits per second) Data transfer rate.

Kernel The core portion of the program that resides in memory and performs the most essential operating system tasks.

Keyboard An input device. There are two common types of keyboards—those that use a mini-DIN (PS/2) connection and those that use a USB connection.

KHz (kilohertz) A unit of measure that equals a frequency of one thousand cycles per second.

Knowledge Base A large collection of documents and FAQs that is maintained by Microsoft. Found on Microsoft's Web site, the Knowledge Base is an excellent place to search for assistance on most operating system problems.

LAN (local area network) A group of PCs connected together via cabling, radio, or infrared that use this connectivity to share resources such as printers and mass storage.

Laser A single-wavelength, in-phase light source that is sometimes strapped to the head of sharks by bad guys. Note to henchmen: lasers should never be used with sea bass, no matter how ill-tempered they might be.

Laser printer An electro-photographic printer in which a laser is used as the light source.

Last Known Good Configuration An option on the Advanced Startup Options menu that allows your system to revert to a previous configuration in order to troubleshoot and repair any major system problems.

Latency The amount of delay before a device may respond to a request; most commonly used in reference to RAM.

Layer In the communications field, a grouping of related tasks involving the transfer of information. Also, a level of the OSI reference model used for networking computers. In graphics work, images can be created in layers, which can be manipulated separately and then flattened into a single image.

Layer 2 Switch   Also called a **bridge**. Filters and forwards data packets based on the MAC addresses of the sending and receiving machines.

Layer 3 Switch   Also called a **router**. Filters and forwards data packets based on the network addresses of the sending and receiving machines.

LBA (logical block addressing)   A translation (algorithm) of IDE drives promoted by Western Digital as a standardized method for breaking the 504-MB limit in IDE drives. Subsequently universally adopted by the PC industry and is standard on all EIDE drives.

LCD (liquid crystal display)   A display technology that relies on polarized light passing through a liquid medium rather than on electron beams striking a phosphorescent surface.

LED (light-emitting diode)   Solid-state device that vibrates at luminous frequencies when current is applied.

Legacy device   Any device that is not plug-and-play compatible.

Level 1 (L1) cache   The first RAM cache accessed by the CPU, which stores only the absolute most-accessed programming and data used by currently running threads. This is always the smallest and fastest cache on the CPU.

Level 2 (L2) cache   The second RAM cache accessed by the CPU, which is much larger and often slower than the L1 cache; accessed only if the requested program/data is not in the L1 cache.

Level 3 (L3) cache   The third RAM cache accessed by the CPU, which is much larger and slower than the L1 and L2 cache; accessed only if the requested program/data is not in the L2 cache. Seen only on high-end CPUs.

Li-Ion (lithium ion)   A type of battery commonly used in portable PCs. Li-Ion batteries don't suffer from the memory effects of NiCd batteries and provide much more power for a great length of time.

Limited account   A type of user account in Windows XP that has limited access to a system. Accounts of this type cannot alter system files, cannot install new programs, and cannot edit settings using the Control Panel.

Linux   Open source UNIX-clone operating system.

Local bus   A high-speed data path that directly links the computer's CPU with one or more slots on the expansion bus. This direct link means signals from an adapter do not have to travel through the computer expansion bus, which is significantly slower.

Localhost   An alias for the loopback address of 127.0.0.1, referring to the current machine.

Logical address   An address that describes both a specific network and a specific machine on that network.

Logical drives   Sections of a hard drive that are formatted and assigned a drive letter, each of which is presented to the user as if it were a separate drive.

Loopback address   A reserved IP address for internal testing: 127.0.0.1.

Low-level format   Defining the physical location of magnetic tracks and sectors on a disk.

LPT port   Commonly referred to as a printer port; usually associated with a local parallel port.

Lumens   A unit of measure for the amount of brightness on a projector or other light source.

Luminescence   The part of the video signal that controls the luminance/brightness of the picture. Also known as the "Y" portion of the component signal.

LUNs (logical unit numbers)   A specialized SCSI configuration that allows for multiple devices to share a single SCSI ID. This type of arrangement is found most commonly in high-end servers that have large hard disk arrays.

LVD (low voltage differential)   A type of differential SCSI. LVD SCSI requires less power than HVD and is compatible with existing SE SCSI controllers and devices. LVD devices can sense the type of SCSI and then work accordingly. If you plug an LVD device into an SE chain, it will act as an SE device. If you plug an LVD device into LVD, it will run as LVD. LVD SCSI chains can be up to 12 meters in length.

Mac   Also **Macintosh**. Apple Computer's flagship operating system, currently up to OS X and running on Intel-based hardware.

MAC (Media Access Control) address Unique 48-bit address assigned to each network card. IEEE assigns blocks of possible addresses to various NIC manufacturers to help ensure that the address is always unique. The Data Link layer of the OSI model uses MAC addresses for locating machines.

Machine language The binary instruction code that is understood by the CPU.

Mass storage Hard drives, CD-ROMs, removable media drives, etc.

Math coprocessor Also called **math unit** or **floating point unit (FPU)**. A secondary microprocessor whose function is the handling of floating point arithmetic. Although originally a physically separate chip, math coprocessors are now built into today's CPUs.

MB (megabyte) 1,048,576 bytes.

MBR (master boot record) A tiny bit of code that takes control of the boot process from the system BIOS.

MCA (Micro Channel architecture) Expansion bus architecture developed by IBM as the (unsuccessful) successor to ISA. MCA had a full 32-bit design as well as being self-configuring.

MCC (memory controller chip) The chip that handles memory requests from the CPU. Although once a special chip, it has been integrated into the chipset on all PCs today.

Mega- A prefix that usually stands for the binary quantity 1,048,576 (2^{20}). One megabyte is 1,048,576 bytes. One megahertz, however, is a million hertz. Sometimes shortened to **Meg**, as in "a 286 has an address space of 16 Megs."

Memory A device or medium for temporary storage of programs and data during program execution. The term is synonymous with storage, although it is most frequently used for referring to the internal storage of a computer that can be directly addressed by operating instructions. A computer's temporary storage capacity is measured in kilobytes (KB) or megabytes (MB) of RAM (random-access memory). Long-term data storage on disks is also measured in kilobytes, megabytes, gigabytes, and terabytes.

Memory Stick Sony's flash memory card format; rarely seen outside of Sony devices.

MFT (master file table) An enhanced file allocation table used by NTFS. *See also* FAT (file allocation table).

MHz (megahertz) A unit of measure that equals a frequency of one million cycles per second.

Micro ATX A smaller size of ATX motherboard and case, which uses the ATX power supply.

Micro DIMM A type of memory used in portable PCs because of its small size.

MicroATX A variation of the ATX form factor. MicroATX motherboards are generally smaller than their ATX counterparts, but retain all the same functionality.

Microcomputer A computer system in which the central processing unit is built as a single, tiny semiconductor chip or as a small number of chips.

Microprocessor Also called **CPU**. The "brain" of a computer. The primary computer chip that determines the relative speed and capabilities of the computer.

MIDI (musical instrument digital interface) MIDI is a standard that describes the interface between a computer and a device for simulating musical instruments. Rather than sending large sound samples, a computer can simply send "instructions" to the instrument describing pitch, tone, and duration of a sound. MIDI files are therefore very efficient. Because a MIDI file is made up of a set of instructions rather than a copy of the sound, it is easy to modify each component of the file. Additionally, it is possible to program many channels, or "voices," of music to be played simultaneously, creating symphonic sound.

MIME (Multipurpose Internet Mail Extensions) MIME is a standard for attaching binary files (such as executables and images) to the Internet's text-based mail (24-Kbps packet size). The first packet of information received contains information about the file.

Mini audio connector A very popular, 1/8-inch diameter connector used to transmit two audio signals; perfect for stereo sound.

Mini PCI A specialized form of PCI designed for use in laptops.

Mini power connector   A type of connector used to provide power to floppy disk drives.

Mini-DIN   A very popular small connection most commonly used for keyboards and mice.

MIPS (millions of instructions per second)   Used for processor benchmarks.

Mirrored volume   A volume that is mirrored on another volume. *See also* mirroring.

Mirroring   Also called **drive mirroring**. Reading and writing data at the same time to two drives for fault tolerance purposes. Considered RAID level 1.

MMC (Microsoft Management Console)   A new means of managing a system, introduced by Microsoft with Windows 2000. The MMC allows an Administrator to customize management tools by picking and choosing from a list of snap-ins. Some snap-ins that are available are the Device Manager, Users and Groups, and Computer Management.

MMU (memory management unit)   A chip or circuit that translates virtual memory addresses into physical addresses and may implement memory protection.

MMX (multimedia extensions)   A set of specific CPU instructions that enables a CPU to handle many multimedia functions, such as digital signal processing. Introduced with the Pentium CPU, these instructions are now used on all ×86 CPUs.

Mobile CPU   A CPU designed for use in portable computers that uses much less power than a normal, desktop CPU.

Modem (modulator/demodulator)   A device that converts a digital bit stream into an analog signal (modulation) and converts incoming analog signals back into digital signals (demodulation). The analog communications channel is typically a telephone line, and the analog signals are typically sounds.

Molex connector   A type of computer power connector. CD-ROM drives, hard drives, and case fans all use this type of connector. A Molex connector is keyed to prevent it from being inserted into a power port improperly.

Motherboard   A flat piece of circuit board that resides inside your computer case. The motherboard has a number of connectors on it; you can use these connectors to attach a variety of devices to your system, including hard drives, CD-ROM drives, floppy disk drives, and sound cards.

Motherboard book   A valuable resource when installing a new motherboard. The motherboard book normally lists all the specifications about a motherboard, including the type of memory and type of CPU that should be used with the motherboard.

Mount point   A drive that functions like a folder mounted into another drive.

Mouse   An input device that enables a user to manipulate a cursor on the screen in order to select items.

MP3   Short for MPEG, Layer 3. MP3 is a type of compression used specifically for turning high-quality digital audio files into much smaller, yet similar sounding, files.

MPA (Microsoft Product Activation)   Introduced by Microsoft with the release on Windows XP, Microsoft Product Activation prevents unauthorized use of Microsoft's software by requiring a user to activate the software.

MSCONFIG   The executable file that runs the System Configuration Utility, a utility found in Windows that enables a user to configure a system's boot files and critical system files. Often used for the name of the utility, as in "just run MSCONFIG."

MS-DOS (Microsoft Disk Operating System)   The first operating system released by Microsoft.

Multiboot   A type of OS installation in which multiple operating systems are installed on a single machine. Can also refer to kicking a device several times in frustration.

Multimeter   A device that is used to measure voltage, amperage, and resistance.

Multiplexer   A device that merges information from multiple input channels to a single output channel.

MultiRead   The ability of most modern CD-ROM drives to read a wide variety of discs is called MultiRead. Modern CD-ROMs can read CD-ROM, CD-R, and CD-RW discs.

Multisession drive   A recordable CD drive that is capable of burning multiple sessions onto a single recordable disc. A multisession drive also has the ability to "close" a CD-R so that no further tracks can be written to it.

Multitasking   The process of running multiple programs or tasks on the same computer at the same time.

My Computer   An applet that allows a user to access a complete listing of all fixed and removable drives contained within a system.

My Documents   Introduced with Windows 98, the My Documents folder provides a convenient place for a user to store their documents, log files, and any other type of files.

Native resolution   The resolution on an LCD monitor that matches the physical pixels on the screen. CRTs do not have fixed pixels and therefore do not have a native resolution.

NBTSTAT   A command-line utility used to check the current NetBIOS name cache on a particular machine. The utility compares NetBIOS names to their corresponding IP addresses.

NDS (Novell Directory Services)   The default security and directory system for Novell NetWare 4.*x* and 5.*x*. Organizes users, servers, and groups into a hierarchical tree.

NetBEUI (NetBIOS Extended User Interface)   A protocol supplied with all Microsoft networking products that operates at the Transport layer. Also a protocol suite that includes NetBIOS. NetBEUI does not support routing.

NetBIOS (network basic input/output system)   A protocol that operates at the Session layer of the OSI seven-layer model. This protocol creates and manages connections based on the names of the computers involved.

NetBIOS name   A computer name that identifies both the specific machine and the functions that machine performs. A NetBIOS name consists of 16 characters: 15 characters of a name, with a 16th character that is a special suffix that identifies the role the machine plays.

NETSTAT   A command-line utility used to examine the sockets-based connections open on a given host.

Network   A collection of two or more computers interconnected by telephone lines, coaxial cables, satellite links, radio, and/or some other communication technique. A computer network is a group of computers that are connected together and that communicate with one another for a common purpose.

Network ID   A number that identifies the network on which a device or machine exists. This number exists in both IP and IPX protocol suites.

Newsgroup   The name for discussion groups on Usenet.

Nibble   A unit of four bits.

NIC (network interface card)   An expansion card that enables a PC to physically link to a network.

NiCd (nickel-cadmium)   A type of battery that was used in the first portable PCs. Heavy and inefficient, these batteries also suffered from a memory effect that could drastically shorten the overall life of the battery. *See also* NiMH (nickel metal hydride), Li-Ion (lithium ion).

NiMH (nickel metal hydride)   A type of battery used in portable PCs. NiMH batteries had fewer issues with the "memory" effect than NiCd batteries. NiMH batteries have been replaced by lithium-ion batteries. *See also* NiCd (nickel-cadmium), Li-Ion (lithium ion).

Nit   A value used to measure the brightness of an LCD displays. A typical LCD display has a brightness of between 100 and 400 nits.

Node   A member of a network or a point where one or more functional units interconnect transmission lines.

Noise   Undesirable signals bearing no desired information and frequently capable of introducing errors into the communication process.

Non-system disk or disk error   An error that occurs during the boot process. Common causes for this error are leaving a non-bootable floppy disk in the floppy disk drive while the computer is booting.

Non-volatile   A type of memory that retains data even if power is removed.

Normal backup   A full backup of every selected file on a system. This type of backup turns off the archive bit after the backup.

Northbridge   The chip that connects a CPU to memory, the PCI bus, Level 2 cache, and AGP activities; it communicates with the CPU through the FSB. Newer Athlon 64-bit CPUs feature an integrated Northbridge.

NOS (network operating system)   An NOS is a standalone operating system or part of an operating system that provides basic file and supervisory services over a network. Although each computer attached to the network will have its own OS, the NOS describes which actions are allowed by each user and coordinates distribution of networked files to the user who requests them.

Notification area   Located by default at the right edge of the Windows taskbar, the notification area contains icons representing background processes, and also contains the system clock and volume control. Most users call this area the system tray.

Ns (nanosecond)   A billionth of a second. Light travels 11 inches in one nanosecond.

NTBOOTDD.SYS   A critical Windows system file only for PCs booting to SCSI drives.

NTDETECT.COM   One of the critical Windows startup files.

NTFS (NT File System)   A robust and secure file system that was introduced by Microsoft with Windows NT. NTFS provides an amazing array of configuration options for user access and security. Users can be granted access to data on a file-by-file basis. NTFS enables object-level security, long filename support, compression, and encryption.

NTFS permissions   A set of restrictions that determine the amount of access given to a particular user on a system using NTFS.

NTLDR   A Windows NT/2000/XP boot file. Launched by the MBR or MFT, NTLDR looks at the BOOT.INI configuration file for any installed operating systems.

NVIDIA   A company that is one of the foremost manufacturers of graphics cards and chipsets.

NWLink   Also called **IPX/SPX-Compatible Protocol**. Microsoft's implementation of IPX/SPX. *See also* IPX/SPX.

Object   A system component that is given a set of characteristics and can be managed by the operating system as a single entity.

Ohm(s)   Electronic measurement of a cable's impedance.

OS (operating system)   A series of programs and code that create an interface so that a user can interact with a system's hardware, for example, DOS, Windows, and Linux.

OS X   Pronounced "ten" rather than "ex;" the current operating system on Apple Macintosh computers. Based on a UNIX core, early versions of OS X ran on Motorola-based hardware; current versions run on Intel-based hardware.

OSI (Open Systems Interconnect)   An international standard suite of protocols, defined by the International Organization for Standardization (ISO), that implements the OSI reference model for network communications between computers.

OSI seven-layer model   An architecture model based on the OSI protocol suite that defines and standardizes the flow of data between computers. The seven layers are:

> **Layer 1**   **The Physical layer** defines hardware connections and turns binary into physical pulses (electrical or light). Repeaters and hubs operate at the Physical layer.

> **Layer 2**   **The Data Link layer** identifies devices on the Physical layer. MAC addresses are part of the Data Link layer. Bridges operate at the Data Link layer.

> **Layer 3**   **The Network layer** moves packets between computers on different networks. Routers operate at the Network layer. IP and IPX operate at the Network layer.

> **Layer 4**   **The Transport layer** breaks data down into manageable chunks. TCP, UDP, SPX, and NetBEUI operate at the Transport layer.

> **Layer 5**   **The Session layer** manages connections between machines. NetBIOS and Sockets operate at the Session layer.

> **Layer 6**   **The Presentation layer,** which can also manage data encryption, hides the differences between various types of computer systems.

Layer 7 **The Application layer** provides tools for programs to use to access the network (and the lower layers). HTTP, FTP, SMTP, and POP3 are all examples of protocols that operate at the Application layer.

Overclocking To run a CPU or video processor faster than its rated speed.

P1 connector A type of connector used to provide power to ATX motherboards.

P4 12V connector A type of connector used to provide additional 12-volt power to motherboards that support Pentium 4 and later processors.

P8 and P9 connectors A type of connector used to provide power to AT-style motherboards.

Packet Basic component of communication over a network. A group of bits of fixed maximum size and well-defined format that is switched and transmitted as a single entity through a network. It contains source and destination address, data, and control information.

Paragraph A unit of 64 binary bits; eight bytes. Not a commonly used term.

Parallel port A connection for the synchronous, high-speed flow of data along parallel lines to a device, usually a printer.

Parity A method of error detection where a small group of bits being transferred are compared to a single "parity" bit that is set to make the total bits odd or even. The receiving device reads the parity bit and determines if the data is valid based on the oddness or evenness of the parity bit.

Partition A section of the storage area of a hard disk. A partition is created during initial preparation of the hard disk, before the disk is formatted.

Partition table A table located in the boot sector of a hard drive that lists every partition on the disk that contains a valid operating system.

Password reset disk A special type of floppy disk that can enable a user to recover a lost password without losing access to any encrypted, or password-protected, data.

PATA (parallel ATA) A disk drive implementation that integrates the controller on the disk drive itself. *See also* ATA, IDE, SATA.

Patch A small piece of software released by a software manufacturer that is used to correct a flaw or problem with a particular piece of software.

Patch cables Short (2–5 foot) UTP cables that connect patch panels to hubs.

Patch panel A panel containing a row of female connectors (ports) that terminate the horizontal cabling in the equipment room. Patch panels facilitate cabling organization and provide protection to horizontal cabling.

Path The route the operating system must follow to find an executable program stored in a subdirectory.

PC Card Credit card-sized adapter cards that add functionality in many notebook computers, PDAs, and other computer devices. PC Cards come in 16-bit and CardBus parallel format and ExpressCard serial format. *See also* PCMCIA.

PCI (peripheral component interconnect) A design architecture for the expansion bus on the computer motherboard, which enables system components to be added to the computer. PCI is a "local bus" standard, meaning that devices added to a computer through this port will use the processor at the motherboard's full speed (up to 33 MHz), rather than at the slower 8 MHz speed of the regular bus. In addition to moving data at a faster rate, PCI moves data 32 or 64 bits at a time, rather than the 8 or 16 bits that the older ISA buses supported.

PCIe (PCI Express) The serialized successor to PCI and AGP, which uses the concept of individual data paths called lanes. A PCIe slot may use any number of lanes, although single lanes (×1) and 16 lanes (×16) are the most common on motherboards.

PCL A printer control language created by Hewlett-Packard and used on a broad cross-section of printers.

PCMCIA (Personal Computer Memory Card International Association) A consortium of computer manufacturers who devised the PC Card standard for credit card–sized adapter cards that add functionality in many notebook computers, PDAs, and other computer devices.

PDA (personal digital assistant) A handheld computer that blurs the line between the calculator and computer. Early PDAs were calculators that enabled the user to program in such information as addresses and appointments. Modern PDAs, such as the Palm and PocketPC, are fully programmable computers. Most PDAs use a pen/stylus for input rather than a keyboard. A few of the larger PDAs have a tiny keyboard in addition to the stylus.

Peer-to-peer networks A network in which each machine can act as both a client and a server.

Pentium Name given to the fifth and later generations of Intel microprocessors; has a 32-bit address bus, 64-bit external data bus, and dual pipelining. Also used for subsequent generations of Intel processors—the Pentium Pro, Pentium II, Pentium III, and Pentium 4. The Pentium name was retired after the introduction of the Intel Core CPUs.

Peripheral Any device that connects to the system unit.

PGA (pin grid array) A popular CPU package where a CPU is packaged in a ceramic material and a large number of pins extend from the bottom of the package. There are many variations on PGA.

Phoenix Technologies Major producer of BIOS software for motherboards.

Phosphor An electro-fluorescent material used to coat the inside face of a cathode ray tube (CRT). After being hit with an electron, it glows for a fraction of a second.

Photo CD A compressed image format developed by Kodak that allows for many photos to be stored on a single CD-ROM.

Photosensitive drum An aluminum cylinder coated with particles of photosensitive compounds that is used in a laser printer. The photosensitive drum is usually contained within the toner cartridge.

Physical address Defines a specific machine without any reference to its location or network. A MAC address is an example of a physical address.

Pin I A designator used to ensure proper alignment of floppy disk drive and hard drive connectors.

Ping (packet Internet groper) Slang term for a small network message (ICMP ECHO) sent by a computer to check for the presence and aliveness of another. Used to verify the presence of another system. Also the command used at a prompt to ping a computer.

PIO (programmable input/output) Using the address bus to send communication to a peripheral. The most common way for the CPU to communicate with peripherals.

PIO mode A series of speed standards created by the Small Form Factor committee for the use of PIO by hard drives. The PIO modes range from PIO mode 0 to PIO mode 4.

Pipeline A processing methodology where multiple calculations take place simultaneously by being broken into a series of steps. Often used in CPUs and video processors.

Pixel (picture element) In computer graphics, the smallest element of a display space that can be independently assigned color or intensity.

Platen The cylinder that guides paper through an impact printer and provides a backing surface for the paper when images are impressed onto the page.

Platform Hardware environment that supports the running of a computer system.

Plug A hardware connection with some sort of projection, which connects to a port.

Plug and play (PnP) A combination of smart PCs, smart devices, and smart operating systems that automatically configure all the necessary system resources and ports when you install a new peripheral device.

POP3 (Post Office Protocol) Also called **point of presence**. Refers to the way e-mail software such as Eudora gets mail from a mail server. When you obtain a SLIP, PPP, or shell account you almost always get a POP account with it; and it is this POP account that you tell your e-mail software to use to get your mail.

Port (input/output) A predefined combination of I/O address and IRQ assigned to a physical serial or parallel port. They have names that start with "COM" for serial ports and "LPT" for parallel ports. For example, COM1, one of the preset designations for serial ports, is defined as I/O address 3F8 with IRQ 4.

Port (physical connection) The part of a connector into which a plug is inserted. Physical ports are also referred to as jacks.

Port or port number In networking, the number used to identify the requested service (such as SMTP or FTP) when connecting to a TCP/IP host. Some example port numbers include 80 (HTTP), 20 (FTP), 69 (TFTP), 25 (SMTP), and 110 (POP3).

Port replicator A device that plugs into a USB port or other specialized port that offers common PC ports, such as serial, parallel, USB, network, and PS/2. By plugging your notebook computer into the port replicator, you can instantly connect it to non-portable components such as a printer, scanner, monitor, or a full-sized keyboard. Port replicators are typically used at home or in the office with the non-portable equipment already connected.

POST (power-on self test) A basic diagnostic routine completed by a system at the beginning of the boot process. The POST checks to make sure that a display adapter is installed and that a system's memory is installed; then it searches for an operating system before handing over control of the machine to an operating system, if one is found.

POST cards A diagnostic tool used to identify problems that occur during the POST. These cards usually fit into a PCI slot and have a series of LED indicators to indicate any problems that occur during the POST. *See also* POST (power-on self test).

PostScript A language defined by Adobe Systems, Inc. for describing how to create an image on a page. The description is independent of the resolution of the device that will actually create the image. It includes a technology for defining the shape of a font and creating a raster image at many different resolutions and sizes.

POTS (plain old telephone service) *See* PSTN.

Power conditioning The process of ensuring and adjusting incoming AC wall power to as close to standard as possible. Most UPS devices provide power conditioning.

Power supply A device that provides the electrical power for a PC. A power supply converts standard AC power into various voltages of DC electricity in a PC.

Power supply fan A small fan located in a system power supply that draws warm air from inside the power supply and exhausts it to the outside.

Power User(s) The second most powerful account and group type in Windows after Administrator/ Administrators.

ppm (pages per minute) A measure of the speed of a printer.

PPP (Point-to-Point Protocol) A protocol that enables a computer to connect to the Internet through a dial-in connection and enjoy most of the benefits of a direct connection. PPP is considered to be superior to SLIP because of its error detection and data compression features, which SLIP lacks, and the ability to use dynamic IP addresses.

PPTP (Point-to-Point Tunneling Protocol) Protocol that works with PPP to provide a secure data link between computers using encryption.

Primary corona A wire, located near the photo-sensitive drum in a laser printer, that is charged with extremely high voltage in order to form an electric field, enabling voltage to pass to the photosensitive drum, thus charging the photosensitive particles on the surface of the drum.

Primary partition The partition on a Windows hard drive designated to store the operating system.

Print resolution The quality of a print image.

Printer An output device that can print text or illustrations on paper. Microsoft uses the term to refer to the software that controls the physical print device.

Program, programming A series of binary electronic commands sent to a CPU to get work done.

Promiscuous mode A mode of operation for a network interface card where the NIC processes all packets that it sees on the cable.

Prompt A character or message provided by an operating system or program to indicate that it is ready to accept input.

Proprietary Technology unique to a particular vendor.

Protected mode The operating mode of a CPU allowing more than one program to be run while ensuring that no program can corrupt another program currently running.

Protocol An agreement that governs the procedures used to exchange information between cooperating entities; usually includes how much information is to be sent, how often it is sent, how to recover from transmission errors, and who is to receive the information.

Protocol stack The actual software that implements the protocol suite on a particular operating system.

Protocol suite A set of protocols that are commonly used together and operate at different levels of the OSI seven-layer model.

Proxy server A device that fetches Internet resources for a client without exposing that client directly to the Internet. Most proxy servers accept requests for HTTP, FTP, POP3, and SMTP resources. The proxy server will often cache, or store, a copy of the requested resource for later use. A common security feature in the corporate world.

PSTN (public switched telephone network) Also called **POTS (plain old telephone service)**. Most common type of phone connection that takes your sounds—translated into an analog waveform by the microphone—and transmits them to another phone.

QIC (quarter inch cassette or cartridge) Tape backup cartridges that use quarter-inch tape.

Queue The area where objects wait their turn to be processed. Example: the printer queue, where print jobs wait until it is their turn to be printed.

Quick Launch menu A toolbar that enables you to launch commonly-used programs with a single click.

QVGA Video display mode of 320 × 240.

RAID (redundant array of inexpensive devices) A way of creating a fault-tolerant storage system. There are six levels. Level 0 uses byte-level striping and provides no fault tolerance. Level 1 uses mirroring or duplexing. Level 2 uses bit-level striping. Level 3 stores error-correcting information (such as parity) on a separate disk, and uses data striping on the remaining drives. Level 4 is level 3 with block-level striping. Level 5 uses block level and parity data striping.

RAID-5 volume A striped set with parity. *See also* RAID (redundant array of inexpensive devices).

RAM (random access memory) Memory that can be accessed at random, that is, in which any memory address can be written to or read from without touching the preceding address. This term is often used to mean a computer's main memory.

RAMDAC (random access memory digital-to-analog converter) The circuitry used on video cards that support analog monitors to convert the digital video data to analog.

Raster The horizontal pattern of lines that form an image on the monitor screen.

RDRAM (Rambus DRAM) A patented RAM technology that uses accelerated clocks to provide very high-speed memory.

Read-only attribute A file attribute that does not allow a file to be altered or modified. This is helpful when protecting system files that should not be edited.

Real-time The processing of transactions as they occur rather than batching them. Pertains to an application in which response to input is fast enough to affect subsequent inputs and guide the process, and in which records are updated immediately. The lag from input time to output time must be sufficiently small for acceptable timeliness. Timeliness is a function of the total system: missile guidance requires output within a few milliseconds of input, scheduling of steamships requires response time in days. Real-time systems respond in milliseconds, interactive systems in seconds, and batch systems in hours or days.

Recovery Console A command-line interface boot mode for Windows that is used to repair a Windows 2000 or Windows XP system that is suffering from massive OS corruption or other problems.

Recycle Bin When files are "deleted" from a modern Windows system, they are moved to the Recycle Bin. To permanently remove files from a system, they must be emptied from the Recycle Bin.

Refresh The process of repainting the CRT screen, causing the phosphors to remain lit (or change).

REGEDIT.EXE A program used to edit the Windows registry.

REGEDT32.EXE   A program used to edit the Windows registry. REGEDT32.EXE is available in Windows 2000 and XP only.

Register   A storage area inside the CPU used by the onboard logic to perform calculations. CPUs have many registers to perform different functions.

Registry   A complex binary file used to store configuration data about a particular system. To edit the Registry, a user can use the applets found in the Control Panel or REGEDIT.EXE or REGEDT32.EXE.

Remote access   The ability to access a computer from outside of the building in which it is housed. Remote access requires communications hardware, software, and actual physical links.

Remote Desktop Connection   The Windows XP tool to enable a local system to graphically access the desktop of a remote system.

Repeater   A device that takes all of the data packets it receives on one Ethernet segment and re-creates them on another Ethernet segment. This allows for longer cables or more computers on a segment. Repeaters operate at Level 1 (Physical) of the OSI seven-layer model.

Resistor   Any material or device that impedes the flow of electrons. Electronic resistors measure their resistance (impedance) in Ohms. (*See* Ohm(s).)

Resolution   A measurement for CRTs and printers expressed in horizontal and vertical dots or pixels. Higher resolutions provide sharper details and thus display better-looking images.

Restore point   A system snapshot created by the System Restore utility that is used to restore a malfunctioning system. *See also* system restore.

RG-58   Coaxial cabling used for 10Base2 networks.

RIMM (not an abbreviation)   An individual stick of Rambus RAM.

RIS (Remote Installation Services)   A tool introduced with Windows 2000 that can be used to initiate either a scripted installation or an installation of an image of an operating system onto a PC.

Riser card   A special adapter card, usually inserted into a special slot on a motherboard, that changes the orientation of expansion cards relative to the motherboard. Riser cards are used extensively in slimline computers to keep total depth and height of the system to a minimum.

RJ (registered jack)   UTP cable connectors, used for both telephone and network connections. **RJ-11** is a connector for four-wire UTP; usually found in telephone connections. **RJ-45** is a connector for eight-wire UTP; usually found in network connections.

RJ-11   *See* RJ (registered jack).

RJ-45   *See* RJ (registered jack).

ROM (read-only memory)   The generic term for non-volatile memory that can be read from but not written to. This means that code and data stored in ROM cannot be corrupted by accidental erasure. Additionally, ROM retains its data when power is removed, which makes it the perfect medium for storing BIOS data or information such as scientific constants.

Root directory   The directory that contains all other directories.

Router   A device connecting separate networks that forwards a packet from one network to another based on the network address for the protocol being used. For example, an IP router looks only at the IP network number. Routers operate at Layer 3 (Network) of the OSI seven-layer model.

RS-232C   A standard port recommended by the Electronics Industry Association for serial devices.

Run dialog box   A command box designed to enable users to enter the name of a particular program to run; an alternative to locating the icon in Windows.

S.M.A.R.T. (Self-Monitoring, Analysis, and Reporting Technology)   A monitoring system built into hard drives.

S/PDIF (Sony/Philips Digital Interface Format)   A digital audio connector found on many high-end sound cards. This connector enables a user to connect their computer directly to a 5.1 speaker system or receiver. S/PDIF comes in both a coaxial and an optical version.

Safe mode   An important diagnostic boot mode for Windows that causes Windows to start only running very basic drivers and turning off virtual memory.

Sampling   The process of capturing sound waves in electronic format.

SATA (serial ATA)   A serialized version of the ATA standard that offers many advantages over PATA (parallel ATA) technology, including new, thinner cabling, keyed connectors, and lower power requirements.

ScanDisk   A utility included with Windows designed to detect and repair bad sectors on a hard disk.

SCSI (small computer system interface)   A powerful and flexible peripheral interface popularized on the Macintosh and used to connect hard drives, CD-ROM drives, tape drives, scanners, and other devices to PCs of all kinds. Because SCSI is less efficient at handling small drives than IDE, it did not become popular on IBM-compatible computers until price reductions made these large drives affordable. Normal SCSI enables up to seven devices to be connected through a single bus connection, whereas Wide SCSI can handle 15 devices attached to a single controller.

SCSI chain   A series of SCSI devices working together through a host adapter.

SCSI ID   A unique identifier used by SCSI devices. No two SCSI devices may have the same SCSI ID.

SCSI-1   The first official SCSI standard. SCSI-1 is defined as an 8-bit, 5-MHz bus capable of supporting eight SCSI devices.

SCSI-2   Another SCSI standard that was the first SCSI standard to address all aspects of SCSI in detail. SCSI-2 defined a common command set that allowed all SCSI devices to communicate with one another.

SCSI-3   The latest SCSI standard that offers transfer rates up to 320 MBps.

SD (Secure Digital)   A very popular format for flash media cards; also supports I/O devices.

SDRAM (synchronous DRAM)   A type of DRAM that is synchronous, or tied to the system clock, and thus runs much faster than traditional FPM and EDO RAM. SDRAM is used in all modern systems.

SE (single-ended)   A term used to describe SCSI-1 devices that used only one wire to communicate a single bit of information. Single-ended SCSI devices are vulnerable to common-mode noise when used in conjunction with SCSI cables over 6 meters in length.

SEC (single-edge cartridge)   A radical CPU package where the CPU was contained in a cartridge that snapped into a special slot on the motherboard called *Slot 1*.

Sector   A segment of one of the concentric tracks encoded on the disk during a low-level format. A sector holds 512 bytes of data.

Sector translation   The translation of logical geometry into physical geometry by the onboard circuitry of a hard drive.

Segment   The bus cable to which the computers on an Ethernet network connect.

Serial port   A common connector on a PC used to connect input devices (such as a mouse) or communications devices (such as a modem).

Server   A computer that shares its resources, such as printers and files, with other computers on a network. An example of this is a network file system server that shares its disk space with a workstation that does not have a disk drive of its own.

Service pack   A collection of software patches released at one time by a software manufacturer.

Services   Background programs running in Windows that provide a myriad of different functions such as printer spooling and wireless networking.

Setuplog.txt   A log file that tracks the complete installation process, logging the success or failure of file copying, Registry updates, and reboots.

Share-level security   Security system in which each resource has a password assigned to it; access to the resource is based on knowing the password.

Shareware   A program protected by copyright; holder allows (encourages!) you to make and distribute copies under the condition that those who adopt the software after preview pay a fee to the holder of the copyright. Derivative works are not allowed, although you may make an archival copy.

Shell   A term that generally refers to the user interface of an operating system. A shell is the command processor that is the actual interface between the kernel and the user.

Shunt   A tiny connector of metal enclosed in plastic that creates an electrical connection between two posts of a jumper.

SIMM (single in-line memory module)   A type of DRAM packaging distinguished by having a number of small tabs that install into a special connector. Each side of each tab is the same signal. SIMMs come in two common sizes: 30-pin and 72-pin.

Simple volume   A type of volume created when setting up dynamic disks. A simple volume acts like a primary partition on a dynamic disk.

Single-session drive   An early type of CD-R drive that required a disc to be burned in a single session. This type of drive has been replaced by multisession drives. *See also* multisession drive.

Slimline   A motherboard form factor used to create PCs that were very thin. NLX and LPX were two examples of this form factor.

Slot covers   Metal plates that cover up unused expansion slots on the back of a PC. These items are useful in maintaining proper airflow through a computer case.

Smart battery   A new type of portable PC battery that tells the computer when it needs to be charged, conditioned, or replaced.

SmartMedia   A format for flash media cards; no longer used with new devices.

SMM (System Management Mode)   A special CPU mode that enables the CPU to reduce power consumption via the selective shutdown of peripherals.

SMTP (Simple Mail Transport Protocol)   The main protocol used to send electronic mail on the Internet.

Snap-ins   Small utilities that can be used with the Microsoft Management Console.

SNMP (Simple Network Management Protocol)   A set of standards for communication with devices connected to a TCP/IP network. Examples of these devices include routers, hubs, and switches.

SO DIMM (small outline DIMM)   A type of memory used in portable PCs because of its small size.

Social engineering   The process of using or manipulating people inside the networking environment to gain access to that network from the outside.

Socket   A combination of a port number and an IP address that uniquely identifies a connection. Also a mounting area for an electronic chip.

Soft power   A characteristic of ATX motherboards. They can use software to turn the PC on and off. The physical manifestation of soft power is the power switch. Instead of the thick power cord used in AT systems, an ATX power switch is little more than a pair of small wires leading to the motherboard.

Soft-off by PWRBTN   A value found in the BIOS of most ATX motherboards. This value controls the length of time that the power button must be depressed in order for an ATX computer to turn off. If the on/off switch is set for a four-second delay, you must hold down the switch for four seconds before the computer shuts off.

Software   A single group of programs designed to do a particular job; always stored on mass storage devices.

Sound card   An expansion card that can produce audible tones when connected to a set of speakers.

Sounds and Audio Devices   A Control Panel applet used to configure audio hardware and software in Windows XP.

Southbridge   The Southbridge is part of a motherboard chipset. It handles all the inputs and outputs to the many devices in the PC.

Spanned volume   A volume that uses space on multiple dynamic disks.

SPD (serial presence detect)   Information stored on a RAM chip that describes the speed, capacity, and other aspects of the RAM chip.

Spool   A scheme that enables multiple devices to write output simultaneously to the same device, such as multiple computers printing to the same printer at the same time. The data is actually written to temporary files while a program called a *spooler* sends the files to the device one at a time.

SPS (standby power supply or system) A device that supplies continuous clean power to a computer system immediately following a power failure. *See also* UPS (uninterruptible power supply).

SRAM (static RAM) A type of RAM that uses a flip-flop type circuit rather than the typical transistor/capacitor of DRAM to hold a bit of information. SRAM does not need to be refreshed and is faster than regular DRAM. Used primarily for cache.

Standard account A type of user account in Windows Vista that has limited access to a system. Accounts of this type cannot alter system files, cannot install new programs, and cannot edit some settings using the Control Panel without supplying an administrator password. Replaces the Limited accounts in Windows XP.

Standouts Small connectors that screw into a computer case. A motherboard is then placed on top of the standouts, and small screws are used to secure the motherboard to the standouts.

Start menu A menu that can be accessed by clicking the Start button on the Windows taskbar. This menu enables you to see all programs loaded on the system and to start them.

Startup disk A bootable floppy disk that contains just enough files to perform basic troubleshooting from an A:\ prompt.

Stick The generic name for a single physical SIMM, RIMM, or DIMM.

STP (shielded twisted pair) A popular cabling for networks composed of pairs of wires twisted around each other at specific intervals. The twists serve to reduce interference (also called *crosstalk*). The more twists, the less interference. The cable has metallic shielding to protect the wires from external interference. Token Ring networks are the only common network technology that uses STP, although Token Ring more often now uses UTP.

Stripe set Two or more drives in a group that are used for a striped volume.

Subdirectories A directory that resides inside of another directory.

Subnet In a TCP/IP internetwork, each independent network is referred to as a subnet.

Subnet mask The value used in TCP/IP settings to divide the IP address of a host into its component parts: network ID and host ID.

Subwoofer A powerful speaker capable of producing extremely low-frequency sounds.

Super I/O chip A chip specially designed to control low-speed, legacy devices such as the keyboard, mouse, and serial and parallel ports.

Superuser Default, all-powerful account in UNIX/Linux.

Surge suppressor An inexpensive device that protects your computer from voltage spikes.

SVGA (super video graphics array) Video display mode of 800 × 600.

Swap file A name for the large file used by virtual memory.

Switch A device that filters and forwards traffic based on some criteria. A bridge and a router are both examples of switches.

SXGA Video display mode of 1280 × 1024.

SXGA+ Video display mode of 1400 × 1050.

Synchronous Describes a connection between two electronic devices where neither must acknowledge ("ACK") when receiving data.

System attribute A file attribute used to designate important system files, like CONFIG.SYS or WIN.INI.

System BIOS The primary set of BIOS stored on an EPROM or Flash chip on the motherboard. Defines the BIOS for all the assumed hardware on the motherboard, such as keyboard controller, floppy drive, basic video, RAM, etc.

System bus speed The speed at which the CPU and the rest of the PC operates; set by the system crystal.

System crystal The crystal that provides the speed signals for the CPU and the rest of the system.

System fan The name of any fan controlled by the motherboard but not directly attached to the CPU.

System Monitor A utility that can be used to evaluate and monitor system resources, like CPU usage and memory usage.

System resources   System resources are I/O addresses, IRQs, DMA channels, and memory addresses.

System Restore   A utility in Windows Me that enables you to return your PC to a recent working configuration when something goes wrong. System Restore returns your computer's system settings to the way they were the last time you remember your system working correctly—all without affecting your personal files or e-mail.

System ROM   The ROM chip that stores the system BIOS.

System Tools menu   A menu that can be accessed by selecting Start | Accessories | System Tools. In this menu, you can access tools like System Information and Disk Defragmenter.

System tray   Located by default at the right edge of the Windows taskbar, the system tray contains icons representing background processes, and also contains the system clock. Accurately called the "notification area."

System unit   The main component of the PC in which the CPU, RAM, CD-ROM, and hard drive reside. All other devices like the keyboard, mouse, and monitor connect to the system unit.

Tablet PC   A small portable computer distinguished by the use of a touch screen with stylus and handwriting recognition as the primary mode of input. Also the name of the Windows operating system designed to run on such systems.

Task Manager   The Task Manager shows all running programs, including hidden ones. You access the Task Manager by pressing CTRL-ALT-DEL. You can use it to shut down an unresponsive application that refuses to close normally.

Taskbar   Located by default at the bottom of the desktop, the taskbar contains the Start button, the system tray, the Quick Launch bar, and buttons for running applications.

TCP (Transmission Control Protocol)   Part of the TCP/IP protocol suite, TCP operates at Layer 4 (the Transport layer) of the OSI seven-layer model. TCP is a connection-oriented protocol.

TCP/IP (Transmission Control Protocol/Internet Protocol)   A set of communication protocols developed by the U.S. Department of Defense that enables dissimilar computers to share information over a network.

TCP/IP services   A set of special sharing functions unique to TCP/IP. The most famous is Hypertext Transfer Protocol (HTTP), the language of the World Wide Web. Telnet and Ping are two other widely-used TCP/IP services.

Tera-   A prefix that usually stands for the binary number 1,099,511,627,776 (2^{40}). When used for mass storage, often shorthand usage for a trillion bytes.

Terabyte   1,099,551,627,776 bytes.

Terminal emulation   Software that enables a PC to communicate with another computer or network as if the PC were a specific type of hardware terminal.

Terminal   A "dumb" device connected to a mainframe or computer network that acts as a point for entry or retrieval of information.

Termination   The use of terminating resistors to prevent packet reflection on a network cable.

Terminator   A resistor that is plugged into the end of a bus cable to absorb the excess electrical signal, preventing it from bouncing back when it reaches the end of the wire. Terminators are used with coaxial cable and on the ends of SCSI chains. RG-58 coaxial cable requires resistors with a 50-Ohm impedance.

Text mode   During a Windows installation, the period when the computer displays simple textual information on a plain background, before switching to full graphical screens. During this part of the installation, the system inspects the hardware, displays the EULA for you to accept, enables you to partition the hard drive, and copies files to the hard drive, including a base set of files for running the graphical portion of the OS.

TFT (thin film transistor)   A type of LCD screen. *See also* active matrix.

Thermal compound   Also called **heat dope**. A paste-like material with very high heat transfer properties; applied between the CPU and the cooling device, it ensures the best possible dispersal of heat from the CPU.

Thread   The smallest logical division of a single program.

TIA/EIA (Telecommunications Industry Association, Electronics Industry Association)   The standards body that defines most of the standards for computer network cabling. Most of these standards are defined under the TIA/EIA 568 standard.

Toner cartridge   The object used to store the toner in a laser printer. *See also* laser printer, toner.

Toner   The toner in a laser printer is a fine powder made up of plastic particles bonded to iron particles, used to create the text and images during the printing process.

TRACERT   Also called **TRACEROUTE**. A command-line utility used to follow the path a packet takes between two hosts.

Traces   Small electrical connections embedded in a circuit board.

Trackball   A pointing device distinguished by a ball that is rolled with the fingers.

Transfer corona   A thin wire, usually protected by other thin wires, that applies a positive charge to the paper during the laser printing process, drawing the negatively charged toner particles off of the drum and onto the paper.

Triad   A group of three phosphors—red, green, blue—in a CRT.

TWAIN (technology without an interesting name)   A programming interface that enables a graphics application, such as a desktop publishing program, to activate a scanner, frame grabber, or other image-capturing device.

UAC (User Account Control)   A feature in Windows Vista that enables Standard accounts to do common tasks and provides a permissions dialog when Standard *and* Administrator accounts do certain things that could potentially harm the computer (such as attempt to install a program).

UART (universal asynchronous receiver/transmitter)   A UART is a device that turns serial data into parallel data. The cornerstone of serial ports and modems.

UDP (User Datagram Protocol)   Part of the TCP/IP protocol suite, UDP is an alternative to TCP. UDP is a connectionless protocol.

Ultra DMA   A hard drive technology that enables drives to use direct memory addressing. Ultra DMA mode 3 drives—called ATA/33—have data transfer speeds up to 33 MBps. Mode 4 and 5 drives—called ATA/66 and ATA/100, respectively—transfer data at up to 66 MBps for mode 4 and 100 MBps for mode 5. Both modes 4 and 5 require an 80-wire cable and a compatible controller in order to achieve these data transfer rates.

Unattended install   A method to install Windows without user interaction.

Unintentional install   An installation of a USB device before installing the drivers, creating a nightmare of uninstalling and reinstalling software.

UNIX   A popular computer software operating system developed by and for programmers at Bell Labs in the early 1970s, used on many Internet host systems because of its portability across different platforms.

Upgrade Advisor   The first process that runs on the XP installation CD. It examines your hardware and installed software (in the case of an upgrade) and provides a list of devices and software that are known to have issues with XP. It can also be run separately from the Windows XP installation, from the Windows XP CD.

Upgrade installation   An installation of Windows on top of an earlier installed version, thus inheriting all previous hardware and software settings.

UPS (uninterruptible power supply)   A device that supplies continuous clean power to a computer system the whole time the computer is on. Protects against power outages and sags. The term UPS is often used mistakenly when people mean SPS (stand-by power supply).

Upstream   A term used to define the part of a USB connection that plugs into a USB hub.

URL (uniform resource locator)   An address that defines the location of a resource on the Internet. URLs are used most often in conjunction with HTML and the World Wide Web.

USB (universal serial bus)   A general-purpose serial interconnect for keyboards, printers, joysticks, and many other devices. Enables hot-swapping and daisy-chaining devices.

User account   A container that identifies a user to an application, operating system, or network, including name, password, user name, groups to which the user belongs, and other information based on the user and the OS or NOS being used. Usually defines the rights and roles a user plays on a system.

User interface   A visual representation of the computer on the monitor that makes sense to the people using the computer, through which the user can interact with the computer.

User level security   A security system in which each user has an account and access to resources is based on user identity.

User profiles   A collection of settings that correspond to a specific user account and may follow the user regardless of the computer at which he or she logs on. These settings enable the user to have customized environment and security settings.

UTP (unshielded twisted pair)   A popular type of cabling for telephone and networks, composed of pairs of wires twisted around each other at specific intervals. The twists serve to reduce interference (also called *crosstalk*). The more twists, the less interference. The cable has *no* metallic shielding to protect the wires from external interference, unlike its cousin, STP. 10BaseT uses UTP, as do many other networking technologies. UTP is available in a variety of grades, called *categories*, as follows:

Category 1 UTP   Regular analog phone lines—not used for data communications.

Category 2 UTP   Supports speeds up to 4 megabits per second.

Category 3 UTP   Supports speeds up to 16 megabits per second.

Category 4 UTP   Supports speeds up to 20 megabits per second.

Category 5 UTP   Supports speeds up to 100 megabits per second.

V standards   Standards established by CCITT for modem manufacturers to follow (voluntarily) to ensure compatible speeds, compression, and error correction.

VESA (Video Electronics Standards Association)   A consortium of computer manufacturers that standardized improvements to common IBM PC components. VESA is responsible for the Super VGA video standard and the VLB bus architecture.

VGA (Video Graphics Array)   The standard for the video graphics adapter that was built into IBM's PS/2 computer. It supports 16 colors in a 640 × 480 pixel video display, and quickly replaced the older CGA (Color Graphics Adapter) and EGA (Extended Graphics Adapter) standards.

VIA Technologies   Major manufacturer of chipsets for motherboards. Also produces Socket 370 CPUs through its subsidiary Cyrix that compete directly with Intel.

Video card   An expansion card that works with the CPU to produce the images that are displayed on your computer's display.

Virtual   Pertaining to a device or facility that does not physically exist, yet behaves as if it does. For example, a system with 4 MB of virtual memory may have only 1 MB of physical memory plus additional (slower and cheaper) auxiliary memory. Yet programs written as if 4 MB of physical memory were available will run correctly.

Virtual memory   A section of a system's hard drive that is set aside to be used when physical memory is unavailable or completely in use.

Virus   A program that can make a copy of itself without you necessarily being aware of it; some viruses can destroy or damage files, and generally the best protection is always to maintain backups of your files.

Virus definition or **data file**   These files are also called signature files depending on the virus protection software in use. These files enable the virus protection software to recognize the viruses on your system and clean them. These files should be updated often.

VIS (viewable image size)   A measurement of the viewable image that is displayed by a CRT rather than a measurement of the CRT itself.

Voice coil motor   A type of motor used to spin hard drive platters.

Volatile   Memory that must have constant electricity in order to retain data. Alternatively, any programmer six hours before deadline after a non-stop, 48-hour coding session, running on nothing but caffeine and sugar.

Volts (V)   The pressure of the electrons passing through a wire is called voltage and is measured in units called volts (V).

Volume boot sector   The first sector of the first cylinder of each partition has a boot sector called the volume boot sector, which stores information important to its partition, such as the location of the operating system boot files.

Volume   A physical unit of a storage medium, such as tape reel or disk pack, that is capable of having data recorded on it and subsequently read. Also refers to a contiguous collection of cylinders or blocks on a disk that are treated as a separate unit.

VRAM (video RAM)   A type of memory in a video display adapter that's used to create the image appearing on the CRT screen. VRAM uses dual-ported memory, which enables simultaneous reads and writes, making it much quicker than DRAM.

VRM (voltage regulator module)   A small card supplied with some CPUs to ensure that the CPU gets correct voltage. This type of card, which must be used with a motherboard specially designed to accept it, is not commonly seen today.

VRR (vertical refresh rate)   A measurement of the amount of time it takes for a CRT to completely draw a complete screen. This value is measured in hertz, or cycles per second. Most modern CRTs have a VRR of 60 Hz or better.

VxD (virtual device driver)   A special type of driver file used to support older Windows programs. Windows protection errors take place when VxDs fail to load or unload. This usually occurs when a device somehow gets a device driver in both CONFIG.SYS and SYSTEM.INI or the Registry.

WAN (wide area network)   A geographically dispersed network created by linking various computers and local-area networks over long distances, generally using leased phone lines. There is no firm dividing line between a WAN and a LAN.

Warm boot   A system restart performed after the system has been powered and operating. This clears and resets the memory, but does not stop and start the hard drive.

Wattage (watts or W)   The amount of amps and volts needed by a particular device to function is expressed as how much wattage (watts or W) that device needs.

WAV (Windows Audio Format)   The default sound format for Windows.

Wave table synthesis   A technique that supplanted FM synthesis, wherein recordings of actual instruments or other sounds are embedded in the sound card as WAV files. When a particular note from a particular instrument or voice is requested, the sound processor grabs the appropriate prerecorded WAV file from its memory and adjusts it to match the specific sound and timing requested.

Wildcard   A character used during a search to represent search criteria. For instance, searching for "*.doc" will return a list of all files with a .doc extension, regardless of the filename. "*" is the wildcard in that search.

Windows 2000   The Windows version that succeeded Windows NT; it came in both Professional and Server versions.

Windows 9x   A term used collectively for Windows 95, Windows 98, and Windows Me.

Windows NT   The precursor to Windows 2000, XP, and Vista, which introduced many important features (such as HAL and NTFS) used in all later versions of Windows.

Windows Vista   The latest version of Windows; comes in many different versions for home and office use, but does not have a Server version.

Windows XP   The version of Windows that replaced both the entire Windows 9x line and Windows 2000; does not have a Server version.

WINS (Windows Internet Name Service)   A name resolution service that resolves NetBIOS names to IP addresses.

Word   A unit of 16 binary digits or two bytes.

Worm   A worm is a very special form of virus. Unlike other viruses, a worm does not infect other files on the computer. Instead, it replicates by making copies of itself on other systems on a network by taking advantage of security weaknesses in networking protocols.

WQUXGA   Video display mode of 2560 × 1600.

WS (wait state)   A microprocessor clock cycle in which nothing happens.

WSXGA   Video display mode of 1440 × 900.

WSXGA+   Video display mode of 1680 × 1050.

WUXGA   Video display mode of 1920 × 1200.

WVGA   Video display mode of 800 × 480.

WWW (World Wide Web)   A system of Internet servers that support documents formatted in HTML and related protocols. The Web can be accessed using Gopher, FTP, HTTP, Telnet, and other tools.

WXGA   Video display mode of 1280 × 800.

xD (Extreme Digital)   A very small flash media card format.

Xeon   A line of Intel CPUs designed for servers.

XGA (extended graphics array)   Video display mode of 1024 × 768.

XMS (extended memory services)   The RAM above 1 MB that is installed directly on the motherboard, and is directly accessible to the microprocessor. Usually shortened to simply "extended memory."

ZIF (zero insertion force) socket   A socket for CPUs that enables insertion of a chip without the need to apply pressure. Intel promoted this socket with its overdrive upgrades. The chip drops effortlessly into the socket's holes, and a small lever locks it in.

authentication
 EAP (Extensible Authentication
  Protocol), 358
 hardware authentication, 429–430
 network authentication, 445–446
 software authentication, 429
Auto Insert Notification, optical drives,
 149–150
auto-switching power supplies, 303
autodetection
 hard drives, 133–134
 printers, 332
AutoPlay, Windows XP, 149–150
AUTORUN.INF file, 149
autosensing sound cards, 268
AVI (Audio Video Interleave), 256

■ B

backbone routers, 383
Backup or Restore Wizard, 423–424
backups, 423–425
 essential data, 423–424
 making changes to system and, 475
 off-site storage and, 424–425
 overview of, 423
 in server environments, 424
backward compatibility, 171
barebones systems, 82
basic input/output services. See BIOS
 (basic input/output services)
basic rate interface (BRI), ISDN, 394
Basic Service Set (BSS), 356
batch files, 189–192
 EDIT command, 189–191
 overview of, 189
 PATH command, 192
 SET command, 191–192
batteries
 changing CMOS battery, 52
 Li-Ion, 297
 Ni-Cd, 296–297
 NiMH, 297
 portable computing and, 296–298
battery memory, 296
baud rates, modems, 388–389
beaming, between PDAs, 281
beep codes, POST (power-on self test),
 48–49
benchmarks, sound cards, 271
beta drivers, 65
bidirectional printing, 325
Big Drive, 117
binary system files, 172
biometric devices, 429–430
BIOS (basic input/output services).
 See also CMOS (complementary
 metal-oxide semiconductor)
 beep codes, 48–49
 boot process, 50–51
 BYOB (Bring Your Own BIOS), 62
 device drivers and, 62
 flashing the BIOS, 54
 hard drive support, 132–135
 INT 13 (Interrupt 13)
  extensions, 116

key terms, 56
lab projects, 58
maintaining, 51
overview of, 47
POST cards, 49–50
POST (power-on self test), 48
quizzes, 56–58
review and summary, 55–56
review of topics covered in
 A+ Essentials exam, 48
text errors, 49
upgrades, 80
bit depth, of sound samples, 252–253
bits per second (bps), modems, 389
BitTorrent, 412
Blu-ray Disc, 161
Blue Screen of Death (BSoD)
 GUI fails to load, 209–210
 RAM problems and, 40
Bluetooth
 configuring, 368
 hardware, 362
 overview of, 361–362
 wireless networking in
  laptops, 295
boot devices. See boot disks
boot disks
 BIOS and CMOS maintenance
  and, 51
 ISO images for boot CD, 152
boot files, 206
boot process
 BIOS and, 50–51
 boot failure in Windows
  2000/XP, 205
 boot order of hard drives, 134–135
bootable discs. See boot disks
BOOT.INI
 boot failure and, 205
 Recovery Console for
  repairing, 206
bootstrap loader, 50
bps (bits per second), modems, 389
Brady, Chris, 41
breakout box, sound cards, 260
BRI (basic rate interface), ISDN, 394
brightness, troubleshooting monitors,
 236–237
BSoD (Blue Screen of Death)
 GUI fails to load, 209–210
 RAM problems and, 40
BSS (Basic Service Set), 356
buffer RAM, optical media, 160
burn-in, 243–244
burn-in failure, motherboards, 79
burning issues, optical media, 159–160

■ C

cable select jumper setting, 131
cables. See also connections/connectors
 audio, 260
 Internet, 395
 power supply, 96–97
 printers, 326

cables, drive
 ATA hard drives, 109, 116–117
 floppy drives, 157
 optical drives, 147
 PATA drives, 131–132
 SATA drives, 132
 SCSI drives, 120, 121, 132
CAD (Computer Aided Design), 229
calibration, monitors, 333–334
capture, sound, 252–253
card services, PC Cards, 288
CardBus, 287
carrier sense multiple access/collision
 avoidance (CSMA/CA), 354–355
CAs (certificate authorities), 447–448
cases. See also system unit
 choosing, 75–76
 fans and, 90, 127
 modding, 95–96
 SFF (Small Form Factor), 81
 standouts for mounting
  motherboard to case, 76
catastrophic failure, motherboards, 79
CCIE (Cisco Certified Internetwork
 Engineer), 2
CCNA (Cisco Certified Network
 Associate), 4, 5
CCNP (Cisco Certified Networking
 Professional), 4, 5
CD command, 177
CD drives. See also optical drives
 CD burners, 151
 CD-R/RW modular drives for
  laptops, 294
 installing, 146
CD-media. See also optical media.
 burners, 151
 burning issues, 159–160
 color books, 161
 installation issues, 158–159
 installing CD drives, 146
 ripping MP3s from CD, 153
CD quality, sound capture, 252–253
CD-ROM, accompanying this book
 accessing PDF documents on, 484
 LearnKey online training, 484
 overview of features on, 483
 shareware and freeware on, 484
 system requirements for software
  on, 483
 Total Tester on, 483–484
CD-ROMs, modular drives for
 laptops, 294
CD-Rs (CD-recordable), 294
CD-RWs (CD-rewritable), 294
CDBurnerXP Pro, 151
CDMA (Code Division Multiple Access),
 cellular networks, 363
cell phones, 362–363
cellular wireless networks, 362–363
central processing units. See CPUs
 (central processing units)
Centrino technology, 305
Centronics connectors, printers, 326
certificate authorities (CAs), 447–448
certificates, digital, 447–449

networks (continued)
    OSI model and, 373–374
    overview of, 351, 369
    quizzes, 379–381
    reproducing the problem, 371–372
    researching fixes, 373
    summary/review, 378–379
    symptom isolation, 372
    symptom verification, 369–370
    virus checks, 373
    what changed?, 370–371
    when did the problem occur?, 370
    wireless. *See* wireless networks
news servers, 404
newsgroups, 404–405
newsreaders, 404
Ni-Cd batteries, 296–297
NICs (network interface cards), 289, 295
NiMH batteries, 297
NLQ (near-letter quality), printers, 315
NMI (non-maskable interrupt), Blue
    Screen of Death and, 40
NNTP (Network News Transfer
    Protocol), 405
non-maskable interrupt (NMI), Blue
    Screen of Death and, 40
Norton UNERASE, 185
notification area, 269. *See also* system tray
Novell certification, 2
NTDETECT.COM, 205
NTFS (NT File System), 430–431
NTLDR, 205
NVIDIA video cards, 221–222, 293

■ O

objects, auditing access to, 451
off-site storage, of backups, 424–425
OGG, sound formats, 255
online gaming
    Internet, 410
    stream loading and, 469
OpenGL, 232–233
optical drives. *See also* CD drives
    connections, 146–148
    external, 148
    installing, 146
    troubleshooting printers, 335
optical media. *See also* CD-media
    applications used during
        installation, 150–152
    Auto Insert Notification
        (AutoPlay), 149–150
    CD-media. *See* CD-media
        connections, 146–148
    Device Manager and, 148–149
    DVD-media. *See* DVD-media
    high definition drives, 161
    installing, 146
    ripping MP3s from CD, 153
    troubleshooting, 158–160
orientation markers, CPU installation
    and, 23
Origami UMPC project, 305
OSI seven-layer model, 373–374

OSs (operating systems)
    Apple Macintosh. *See* Mac OSs
    in computing process, 464
    Microsoft Windows.
        See Windows OSs
Outlook Express, Microsoft, 402, 404
Outlook, Microsoft, 423
output, sound output, 252
overclocking CPUs, 26–27
ozone filters, laser printers, 323, 340

■ P

page faults, RAM, 39
page files. *See* swap files
page quality problems
    dot-matrix printers, 337
    laser printers, 340–341
Page Setup, print jobs, 336
palette, VGA colors, 241
PANs (personal area networks), 361–362
PAP (Password Authentication
    Protocol), 446
paper dander, 339
paper feed problems, 342
parallel ATA. *See* PATA (parallel ATA)
parallel connections, 41, 325
parallel PC Cards, 287
Parental Controls, in Vista, 454–455
parity data, 125
parity/ECC errors, 39
Partial Response Maximum Likelihood
    (PRML), 103–104
Password Authentication Protocol
    (PAP), 446
passwords
    authentication and, 429
    CMOS, 52
    PC Tech integrity and, 472
    security policies for, 435
PATA (parallel ATA)
    jumpers and cabling for, 131–132
    types of ATA drives, 108
patches
    security patches, 436
    separating hardware problems
        from software problems, 372
PATH command, batch files, 192
path, file locations, 174
PC Cards, 287–289
    device drivers, 62–65
    ExpressCard, 287–288
    knowledge stage (learning about
        devices before installing), 60
    overview of, 287
    parallel PC Cards, 287
    physical installation, 61–62
    protecting, 288
    software support for, 288–289
    verifying installation, 66
PC techs, 463–482
    backing up before changing
        system, 475
    certification of, 2
    computing process and, 464–469

customer relations, 471–474
how computers work, 464
key terms, 17, 437, 479
lab projects, 440, 482
overview of, 1, 463
quizzes, 17, 437–440, 479–482
review and summary, 478–479
step-based systematic approach to
    problem solving, 475–477
summary/review, 16–17, 436–437
tools of, 475
troubleshooting methodology,
    470, 474
PCBs (printed circuit boards). *See also*
    motherboards
PCI (peripheral component interconnect)
    host adapter for SCSI chains, 120
    modem connections, 390
    PCI card in tech toolkit, 475
PCIe (PCI express), 390
PCL (printer control language), 324
PCM (pulse code modulation), 253
PCMCIA (Personal Computer Memory
    Card International Association),
    287–288. *See also* PC Cards
PCs (personal computers)
    IBM role in developing, 167
    range of people who use, 1
    XPCs, 81
PDAs (personal digital assistants), 285
    cellular wireless networks,
        362–363
    overview of, 280–281
PDF documents, on CD-ROM
    accompanying this book, 484
PDP (Plasma display panels), 243
Pearson/VUE, 9–10
pen-based computing, in PDAs, 280
PepiMK, Spybot Search & Destroy,
    442–443
performance, reasons for replacing
    CPUs, 21
permissions
    assigning to groups, 431–432
    device driver installation, 65
perpendicular recording, hard
    drives, 104
personal area networks (PANs), 361–362
Personal Computer Memory Card
    International Association (PCMCIA),
    287–288. *See also* PC Cards
personal computers. *See* PCs (personal
    computers)
personal digital assistants. *See* PDAs
    (personal digital assistants)
personal RAID, 129–130
personal video recorders (PVRs),
    242–243
PGA (pin-grid array), 23–24
photoconductivity, laser printing
    and, 319
photosensitive drum
    charging, 328
    cleaning, 328

programs, running from command line, 180–181
Prometric, 9–10
prompt. *See* command prompt
Protocols category, in Mike's Four-Layer Model, 375
protocols, e-mail, 402–404
protocols, networking. *See* TCP/IP (Transmission Control Protocol/Internet Protocol)
proxy servers, 400
PS/2 ports, 289
PSU (power supply unit). *See* power supplies
pulse code modulation (PCM), 253
PVRs (personal video recorders), 242–243

■ Q

QDOS (Quick-and-Dirty Operating System), 167
Quick-and-Dirty Operating System (QDOS), 167
QuickTime player
  AIFF format and, 255
  video formats, 256

■ R

radio frequency identification (RFID), 430
radio, streaming media and, 256
Radio Tuner, Windows Media Player, 256
RAID 0 (disk striping), 126
RAID 1 (disk mirroring/duplexing), 126
RAID 2 (disk striping with multiple parity drives), 126
RAID 3 and 4 (disk striping with dedicated parity), 126
RAID 5 (disk striping with distributed parity), 126
RAID 6 (disk striping with extra parity), 126
RAID (redundant array of independent devices), 124–130
  controllers, 129–130
  future of, 130
  hardware vs. software versions, 128–129
  implementing, 127–128
  levels, 126–127
  overview of, 124–126
  personal RAID, 129–130
rail power, 97
RAM (random access memory)
  A+ Essentials exam review, 32
  adding/replacing in portables, 292
  computing process and, 466
  DIMMs/SIMMs, installing, 36–37
  key terms, 43
  lab projects, 46
  laser printing process and, 330
  motherboard installation and, 77
  next generation features, 41–42

portable PCs and, 291–292
printer requirements, 323
purchasing the right RAM, 35
quizzes, 44–45
review and summary, 43
risks of mixing/matching types, 35
risks of mixing speeds, 36
SO-DIMMs, installing in laptops, 37–38
symptoms of need for more, 32–33
system RAM requirements, 33
testing, 40–41
troubleshooting, 38–40
video memory, 222–223
viewing current RAM capacity, 34
working with, 32
RAM sticks
  dangers of mixing/matching, 35
  RAM count, 37
random access memory. *See* RAM (random access memory)
range, wireless networks, 358–359
raster image processor (RIP), 330
raster images, laser printing, 330–331
RD command, 179–180
read-only attribute, files, 182
read-only memory chip. *See* ROM (read-only memory) chips
read/write heads, 102–103
Readme files, printer installation, 333
RealMedia (RM), 255, 256
rear out connector, sound cards, 259
rebuild, Windows 2000/XP, 208
recording quality, sound cards, 258
Recover CD, 208
Recovery Console
  best uses of, 206–208
  common commands, 207
  for repairing boot errors, 205–208
recovery partition, 208
recycling
  consumables, 336
  old computers, 426–427
redundant array of independent devices. *See* RAID (redundant array of independent devices)
Registry
  protecting with security policies, 434
  Registry Editor, 149–150
  repairing corrupted, 210
Registry Editor, 149–150
remnants, drives, 426
Remote Assistance, Windows XP, 409
Remote Desktop, Windows XP, 409
removable face, cases, 75
removable media
  A+ Essentials exam review, 146
  application requirements, 150–152
  AutoPlay/Auto Insert Notification, 149–150
  burning digital music files to CD, 153

connections for optical drives, 146–148
Device manager for viewing information regarding, 148
floppy drives. *See* floppy drives
installing optical drives, 146
key terms, 163
lab projects, 165
optical drives. *See* optical drives
overview of, 145
quizzes, 163–164
review and summary, 162
troubleshooting floppy drives, 154–158
troubleshooting optical drives, 158–160
REN (or RENAME) command, 185
reports, computer security, 449
Request to Send/Clear to Send (RTS/CTS)
  modems and, 390
  wireless protocol, 355
research, troubleshooting networks, 373
resolution enhancement technology (RET), 331
resolution, LCD monitors, 277
resolution, print, 317, 331
restore, Windows 2000/XP, 208
RET (resolution enhancement technology), 331
revolutions per minute (RPM), hard drive spindle speed, 137
RFID (radio frequency identification), 430
RG-59 connectors, 395
RG-6 connectors, 395
RGB color, 334
ribbon cable
  40-pin cable for ATA-1 hard drives, 109
  for internal SCSI devices, 121
  SCSI drives, 120
RightMark 3DSound, from iXBT.com/Digit-Life, 271
RIP (raster image processor), 330
rippers, creating MP3s from CDs, 153
RLL (run length limited), 103–104
RM (RealMedia), 255, 256
RMDIR command, 179–180
ROM (read-only memory) chips, 48
root directory
  CD command and, 177
  files and folders and, 174
rotation options, monitors, 228
routers
  Cisco, 5
  default gateway, 386
  defined, 4
Roxio Easy Media Creator, 151
RPM (revolutions per minute), hard drive spindle speed, 137
RS-232 port, laptops, 289
RTS/CTS (Request to Send/Clear to Send)
  modems and, 390
  wireless protocol, 355

sound cards (*continued*)
　　jacks, 258–259
　　MIDI technologies, 254–255
　　overview of, 257
　　polyphony of, 255
　　recording quality, 258
　　sound processors, 257
　　speaker support, 257–258
　　specialty applications, 268–269
　　summary/review, 272
　　support for Dolby Digital and
　　　　DTS, 263
　　troubleshooting
　　　　configuration, 270
Sound Recorder, Windows OSs, 256
Sounds and Audio Devices, Windows
　　XP, 266
Sounds and Multimedia,
　　Windows 2000, 266
spaces, command syntax and, 175
spam, 439
SPD (serial presence detect), 36–37
speakers, 259–263
　　features, 263
　　laptop ports, 289
　　overview of, 260
　　sound card support for, 257–258
　　sound quality and, 270
　　standards, 261–263
　　troubleshooting, 269–270
special keys, command-line
　　interface, 192
speech recognition, 282
SpeedFan utility, 93
spindles, hard drives
　　fluid bearings for, 105
　　spindle (rotational) speed, 137
sprites, 3-D graphics, 230
Spybot Search & Destroy, from PepiMK,
　　442–443
spyware, 441–443
　　overview of, 441
　　preventing, 441–442
　　removing, 442–443
　　threat analysis and, 422
SSH (Secure Shell), 407
SSID (Service Set Identifier)
　　configuring wireless networks,
　　　　363–364
　　wireless networking and, 357
SSL (Secure Sockets Layer), 446–447
Standard Users, Parental Controls,
　　454–455
standouts, for mounting motherboard
　　to case, 76
startup disks. *See also* boot disks
　　Windows 98, 155
static charge eliminator, laser printers,
　　321, 329
stealth viruses, 437
step-based approach, to problem
　　solving, 475–477
stepper motor, 104
stereo recordings, 252
stereo speakers, 261

sticks, of RAM. *See* RAM sticks
stop errors, GUI fails to load, 209–210
stream loading, online games, 469
streaming media
　　overview of, 256
　　playing streaming audio on
　　　　Windows PCs, 256
study
　　developing study strategy, 11–13
　　setting aside time for, 11
　　techniques, 11–12
stylus
　　for PDAs, 280
　　for tablet PCs, 282
subfolders, 174
subnotebooks, 280
subwoofers, 258
surface-conduction electron emitter
　　display (SED), 245
surround sound
　　sound card support for, 258
　　speaker standards, 261–262
swap files
　　defined, 32
　　RAM requirements and, 32
switch boxes, printers, 337
switches
　　command, 175
　　power supply failures and, 94
switches, laser printers, 323
symptoms
　　motherboard failure, 79
　　networking problems,
　　　　369–370, 372
synchronous DRAM (SDRAM). *See also*
　　DDR-SDRAM (double data rate
　　SDRAM)
synchronous DSL (SDSL), 394
syntax, command, 175
system BIOS, 53–54
system board, laser printers, 322–323
System Configuration Utility
　　(MSCONFIG.EXE), 214
system crashes, threat analysis and, 422
system discs, 51
system files
　　DLL (dynamic link library)
　　　　files, 215
　　Recovery Console for
　　　　repairing, 206
System Management Model (SMM),
　　298–299
system RAM, 33
system requirements, for software on
　　CD-ROM accompanying this
　　book, 483
System Restore, 215
system setup utility. *See* setup program,
　　CMOS
System State data, backing up, 424
system tray
　　Safely Remove Hardware, 295
　　volume control in, 269
system unit. *See also* cases

video cards
        3-D cards, 232–233
        choosing, 221
        CPU's communication with, 467
        graphics processor, 221–222
        installing, 224
        portable computing, 294
        for portables, 294
        shared memory and, 293
        troubleshooting, 235–236
        video memory, 222–223
        Vista and, 468
video memory, 222–223
video shadowing, 241
video training, LearnKey online
    training, 484
virtual memory. *See* swap files
virus prevention, 437–438
virus shields, 436
viruses
        antivirus programs, 436–437
        overview of, 435
        polymorphics/polymorphs, 438
        signatures of, 437
        stealth viruses, 438
        threat analysis and, 422
        tips for preventing, 438–439
        troubleshooting networks, 373
Vista. *See* Windows Vista
VNC, for terminal emulation, 407–408
voice coil, actuator arms and, 104–105
Voice over IP (VoIP), 407
VoIP (Voice over IP), 407
volume controls, troubleshooting, 269
Vonage, 407
Vorbis, sound format, 255

■ W

WANs (wide area networks). *See also*
    networks
WAPs (wireless access points)
        configuring wireless networks,
            364–366
        infrastructure mode and, 356
        MAC address filtering, 357–358
        wireless networking and, 353
WAV format, 253–255
Wave table synthesis, MIDI, 254–255
Web. *See* WWW (World Wide Web)
Web browsers
        accessing Web servers, 399–400
        browsing Web pages with, 385
        configuring, 400
        FTP and, 405–406
        pop-ups, spyware, and adware
            and, 439–440
        security of, 401–402
        trusted authorities and, 447–448
Web servers, 399
Webroot Window Washer, 426
WEP (Wired Equivalent Privacy), 358

WHQL (Windows Hardware Quality
    Labs), 63
Wi-Fi Protected Access 2 (WPA2),
    358, 361
Wi-Fi Protected Access (WPA), 358
Wi-Fi (Wireless Fidelity). *See also*
    wireless networking
        operation modes, 363
        standards. *See* IEEE 802.11
            standards
        wireless networking in
            laptops, 295
wide area networks. *See* WANs (wide
    area networks)
wildcards, working with files from
    command line, 184–185
Winamp sound player, 256
Windows 2000. *See also* Windows
    2000/XP
        formatting floppy disks, 155
        groups, 432–433
        Printers applet, 332
        Sounds and Multimedia
            applet, 266
        Wireless Link applet, 367
Windows 2000 Server, 407–408
Windows 2000/XP. *See also* Windows
    2000; Windows XP
        accessing command-line
            interface, 170
        Advanced Options menu, 171
        APM/ACPI configuration, 300
        Backup or Restore Wizard,
            423–424
        booting directly to prompt, 171
        GDI (graphical device
            interface), 324
        ICS (Internet Connection
            Sharing), 397
        printer installation, 331–333
        software RAID, 128
Windows 3x, 171
Windows 9x
        booting directly to prompt, 171
        ICS (Internet Connection
            Sharing), 397
        startup disk for Windows 98, 155
Windows Defender, 442
Windows Firewall, 444
Windows Hardware Quality Labs
    (WHQL), 63
Windows Installer, 435
Windows Logo Program, 63
Windows Marketplace, 60
Windows Media Audio (WMA), 255, 256
Windows Media Player
        playing sounds, 253, 256
        for watching DVDs, 152
Windows OSs, 203–219
        A+ Essentials exam review, 204
        Add Hardware Wizard, 64, 66
        Advanced Startup Options,
            210–213

APM/ACPI configuration, 300
boot failure, 205
determining current RAM
    capacity, 34
device drivers, 209–210
driver rollback, 65
drivers for USB sound cards, 265
file name extensions and, 172
formatting floppy disks, 155
GUI fails to load, 209
GUI troubleshooting tools, 213
Internet Options, 400–402
key terms, 217
lab projects, 219
laser printing process, 330–331
overview of, 203–205
page faults indicating RAM
    problems, 39
playing sounds in, 256
quizzes, 217–219
RAM requirements and, 33
rebuild, 208
Recovery Console for repairing
    boot errors, 205–208
Registry, 210
restore, 208
services, 214–215
software RAID with Windows
    2000/XP, 128
sound players, 253
summary/review, 216
System Configuration Utility
    (MSCONFIG.EXE) for
    autoloading programs, 214
system files, 215
System Restore, 215
Windows Marketplace for
    compatibility issues, 60
Windows Security Center (WSC), 454
Windows Terminal Services, 407–408
Windows Update, 436
Windows Vista, 453–455
        CompTIA A+ certification and, 14
        other security features, 455
        Parental Controls, 454–455
        support for HHDs, 137
        UAC (User Account Control),
            453–455
        video cards and, 468
        WSC (Windows Security
            Center), 454
Windows XP. *See also* Windows
    2000/XP
        AutoPlay, 149–150
        CD burning capacity, 151–152
        dial-up connections, 392
        driver rollback, 65
        formatting floppy disks, 155
        ICF (Internet Connection
            Firewall) and, 397–398
        Local Security Settings, 433
        Printers and Faxes, 332
        Remote Assistance, 409

Mike Meyers'

CompTIA A+® Guide: PC Technician

(Exams 220-602, 220-603, & 220-604)